People
as
Partners

*individual and family relationships
in today's world*

Jacqueline P. Wiseman
San Francisco State College

CANFIELD PRESS • San Francisco
A Department of Harper & Row Publishers, Inc.
New York • Evanston • London

PEOPLE AS PARTNERS: INDIVIDUAL AND FAMILY
RELATIONSHIPS IN TODAY'S WORLD

Copyright © 1971 by Jacqueline P. Wiseman

For information address Harper & Row, Publishers, Inc.,
49 East 33rd Street, New York, N.Y. 10016

Standard Book Number: 06-389424-6

Library of Congress Catalog Card Number: 76-153133

For Dana and Scott—who will someday
be selecting marriage partners

Contents

Preface

The articles in this preparation for marriage book were selected as a result of many informal discussions with college students about their personal positions and problems on the subjects of dating, selection of marriage partners, and the obligations created by having a family in today's world.

Most striking among these attitudes was the ambivalence of these students toward the institution of marriage and the family as they had experienced and observed it. They seemed simultaneously disenchanted with many aspects of the traditional male-female relationship, while still clinging to the hope that they personally would be able to find a meaningful and lasting love relationship. Many students felt that marriage should not interfere with self-determination, but at the same time closeness and responsibility to other persons were seen as necessary. The high divorce rate was decried, while they insisted that persons should not be forced to continue living with someone whose company was no longer a pleasure and a complement to their own existence.

Some of the students spoke in favor of radical solutions to these dilemmas: no marriage, group marriage, no children. There was talk about the necessity of making major changes in society before the male-female relationship could flourish as it should for both parties. Many wanted to maintain that which seemed good about the family as an institution, but would revitalize it through new approaches both within the family and in the surrounding society.

These readings are an attempt to aid these students in understanding the complex interplay between the changing social structure and culture and their personal decisions and actions as they affect choice of marriage partner and the ultimate family life style. Like all anthologies, this is merely a sampling of possible selections. No volume of readings could possibly cover every problem that people face in their courtship, marriage, or parental spheres, nor could all the studies in these areas that have been conducted by sociologists be included. (Since the results of the 1970 census have not yet been compiled and the 1960 census is outdated, I have omitted a demographic article.) However, an attempt was made to cover those matters that are faced almost universally. In addition, the selections should alert the reader to the general sociological perspective on current marriage and family problems that can be applied to areas not covered in this text. Thus, my hope is that the book will create a sociological bridge between what the family is today and what it might become in the future.

One often reads in acknowledgments about an author-editor-publisher relationship that is a joy to the author because all parties involved are as concerned with content as with production details. Such was the case here and I am grateful for the original encouragement and continuing interest of Canfield Editor Joseph L. Dana and Production Editor Wendy Cunkle. I am especially grateful to Miss Cunkle for her help in maximizing the contemporary aspects of the collection, while maintaining those items that seem basic and timeless to the male-female relationship, regardless of the form it takes. Jean Hoy did her usual competent job of typing despite a short deadline. My husband, Stan, supplied editorial assistance, a critique of the contents, and his usual strong emotional support.

JACQUELINE P. WISEMAN
San Francisco State College

Introduction

MARRIAGE AS AN AREA OF CRUCIAL DECISIONS

Life can be seen as a series of major and minor decisions, made on a day-to-day, hour-by-hour basis. Major decisions, in particular, can and do permanently change life directions. Certainly the decision about whom to marry, for example, is one of the most crucial in adult life. The choice of spouse determines the kind of close companionship one will have during the years of marriage. The decision will also affect the genetic composition and possibly the number of children, and certainly the way they are socialized. The choice of marriage partner influences one's life style in myriad ways, and this style in turn changes the ways in which a spouse's personality and talents can possibly develop. In the literal sense, when one chooses a marriage partner, one is casting lots with fate.

Although choice of mate defines a person's life style to some extent, it does not necessarily determine the many details of married life. Nor does it establish the quality of happiness or unhappiness, satisfaction or dissatisfaction, marriage partners may experience over time. Social forces both within and outside the family unit affect these details, which are so multitudinous as to defy description. These social forces touch on many decisions involving basic relationships—sexual intimacy, use of contraceptives, child rearing, in-laws, and family finances, to name a few. Decisions made in connection with the daily problems of family life create a mini-culture or family climate that affects the enjoyment or disillusionment family members feel about the home and sets the scene for future problems and decisions.

In short, the substance of life—its joys and frustrations, its moments of intimacy and security as well as alienation—are affected by the family a person is born into and the family that he chooses to create. Is it any wonder that there is a booming market for advice to the lovelorn and that "experts" in the fields of courtship and family abound? Every daily newspaper has its columnist who counsels readers on personal problems; women's magazines have page after page of such advice. Marriage counselors (both legitimate and illegitimate) are available in every major city. Psychoanalysts, psychiatrists, psychologists, and knowledgeable family doctors listen to problems of the family and—depending on their theoretical approach—offer sympathy or guidance or both.

One source of information for partners seeking aid in making marital decisions is the research efforts and essays of sociologists, social psychologists, and social philosophers, some of which are presented in this book. Sociologists and social psychologists are in the business of finding out, in a careful and systematic way, what people are doing, why they are doing it, and how various acts affect their lives and future actions. Their goal as scientists is to understand human social life better. They are the more systematic counterparts of the popular writers and friends who offer "common sense" judgments on premarital and marital difficulties.

Sociologists, for instance, are concerned with how a society can affect the behavior of groups and individuals. In pursuit of this goal, they attempt to delineate important elements in the social structure and culture—such as social class, roles, norms, and values that help shape interaction. Sociologists and social psychologists also study specific subgroups—teen-agers, housewives, fathers, aged parents, in-laws. The objective is to understand more of what these types of people do, how they do it, and the effects of their actions on themselves and others.

Finally, sociologists, social psychologists, and philosophers write essays on problems of social interaction primarily for their colleagues, but these can be used by the average person to aid him in clarifying his own thoughts. Philosophers, especially, expand the boundaries of possibilities on a given subject—enriching alike the researcher and those who are seeking practical assistance.

In pursuing their goal of understanding people, family sociologists attempt to keep in simultaneous perspective four levels of social action—the societal, the subcultural, the family, and the individual. To see how each of these affects and is affected by the other is truly the unique contribution of the discipline; this approach has the advantage of offering the "bigger picture" that increases understanding of possible causes and consequences of individual behavior.

Sociological Research and Practical Decisions

What understanding of marriage and the family can one gain from sociological research? Inasmuch as behavior is viewed from four levels of action, as explained above, one comes to understand that although motivations to act or consequences of action are the result of personal decisions, there are societal and cultural pressures to deal with as well. For instance, the fact that young people in America and other Western nations are faced with so many decisions concerning their marriage or family can be traced to the advent of the Industrial Revolution.

In more traditional and industrially undeveloped societies, many family decisions are thought best left to elders who also control the family source of income. They are presumed to have more experience and therefore should have more capability for wise decisions. Thus, mates are chosen for the young family members, often long before they reach the decision-making stage on a personal level. Quite frequently the new family lives with one set of parents, conforms to their pattern of living, and accepts their direction in solving marital problems.

In modern industrial societies, with larger geographically and socially mobile populations, there has been a steady decrease in parental domination, especially in the area of mate selection. This freedom has both advantages and disadvantages. Certainly it gives young men and women more opportunity to determine their own destinies. On the other hand, they must make decisions in areas where they have little experience and where they are likely to be under a great deal of emotional pressure. As a result, young married couples tend to learn "the hard way" from their mistakes. Spouses in families more isolated from other kin must depend on each other for emotional security far more than they would in the extended traditional family. When one partner fails in his role responsibility, the other family members have a much more fragile family unit than their traditional counterparts.

Currently, major social upheavals are having effects on interpersonal relationships as important as those of the Industrial Revolution. The last two decades have witnessed the increase of automation, with the consequent layoff of older workers, difficulty for young untrained men, and shorter hours and more leisure for many of those remaining in the labor force. There has been greater pressure for racial, class, and sexual equality and a heightened awareness of our burgeoning ecological and population problems. Arching over all of this is an increased emphasis on individual development over family welfare. The search for a personally rewarding life style, rather than one that is merely demanding, has drastically changed the parameters of the male-female and parent-child relationships. Consequently, the age-old idea that marriage involves accepting subjugation of personal needs and desires (the degree depending on your sex) for the benefit of the family is under attack.

However, this individualism does not mean that people have less need for meaningful relationships. In fact, without the fortress of security that the traditional family provides, we search for a substitute. But certainly the expectations of marriage and parental relationships are undergoing change. More and more, as men and women fall in love and agree to live together, it is with the hope that their individual destinies (as they see them) will be compatible, and that each will prove an aid and not a hindrance to the other. More and more, parents must earn the respect and easygoing companionship of their children—they cannot demand it.

Thus, we are witnessing a growing doubt among the young that there is a necessity for the formal, legal institution of marriage, for having and caring for children, for the expected roles of men and women in marriage, for the

3

necessity of chastity before marriage, and for faithfulness of both spouses after the vows are spoken. Each of these issues are still in the developmental stage —values undergoing challenge but not yet resolved. This leaves the individual to make decisions about such problems without much guidance. The title of this book, *People as Partners,* acknowledges this trend toward individualism. The contents reflect the ever-increasing decisional demands new freedoms place on people in marriage or about to enter such a partnership.

1

The Partnership
in Social Context

The family is one of the oldest of human social institutions and various aspects of it have been under fire since its earliest recorded appearance. The vital position of the family in any society means that it plays a central role in the lives of individuals and the structuring of major social institutions. From Plato to the present day, individuals have sought to change, improve, or abandon the family altogether, while others have watched aghast and made dire predictions about the consequences of these presumably radical proposals.

Somehow, despite shattering assaults, the family has survived. Although there have been periodic failures of the family, and many attempts to restructure it, family relationships have proved to be more than a private, individually determined matter. Indeed, because of its pivotal position in supplying both individual and societal needs, the family can be changed only very slowly—and even then it often reverts back to a more traditional form. This is because the family is stabilized by social networks that include such intangibles as the general historical role of family members and the major values of society's members. When these roles and values are challenged (for instance in the area of what constitutes proper sexual activity), then both the family and the social structure reflect change through social relationships.

This chapter begins with a discussion of the current problems of marriage and family relationships, followed by a sociological perspective on the personal and societal dilemmas they create. Subsequent readings will elaborate on the complexities of the themes introduced here.

The American Family: Future Uncertain

Time Magazine

The family has lost many of its historical functions—among them the economic, the educational, and the recreational. At the same time, the role of women in society is changing and with it their relationship to men and to their own children. Reflecting the times; the dissatisfied, the imaginative, and the reckless are tampering with the structure of the traditional family form through experimentation with communal living, "arrangements" without benefit of clergy, trio marriages, and one parent families. How widespread are these variations and what do they mean for the future of the family in America? Both individuals and the society as a whole express their growing concern with this question, for the quality of their existence is inexorably bound up with the answer.

America's families are in trouble—trouble so deep and pervasive as to threaten the future of our nation," declared a major report to last week's White House Conference on Children. "Can the family survive?" asks Anthropologist Margaret Mead rhetorically. "Students in rebellion, the young people living in communes, unmarried couples living together call into question the very meaning and structure of the stable family unit as our society has known it." The family, says California Psychologist Richard Farson, "is now often without function. It is no longer necessarily the basic unit in our society."

The data of doom—many familiar, some still startling—consistently seem to support this concern. One in every four U.S. marriages eventually ends in divorce. The rate is rising dramatically for marriages made in the past several years, and in some densely-populated West Coast communities is running as high as 70%. The birth rate has declined from 30.1 births per thousand in 1910 to 17.7 in 1969, and while this is a healthy development in many respects, it implies considerable change in family life and values. Each year, an estimated half-million teen-agers run away from home.

From "The American Family: Future Uncertain," *Time*, December 28, 1970, pp. 34–39. Reprinted by permission of TIME, the Weekly Magazine; © Time Inc. 1970.

The crisis in the family has implications that extend far beyond the walls of the home. "No society has ever survived after its family life deteriorated," warns Dr. Paul Popenoe, founder of the American Institute of Family Relations. Harvard Professor Emeritus Carle Zimmerman has stated the most pessimistic view: "The extinction of faith in the familistic system is identical with the movements in Greece during the century following the Peloponnesian Wars, and in Rome from about A.D. 150. In each case the change in the faith and belief in family systems was associated with rapid adoption of negative reproduction rates and with enormous crises in the very civilizations themselves."

It is not necessary to share this apocalyptic decline-and-fall theory to recognize many interrelated dangers to both society and family. Each of the nation's forces of change and conflict meet within the family. The "counterculture" of the young, the effects of the war, economic stresses and the decay of the cities—all crowd in on the narrow and embattled institution. The question, of course, is not whether the family will "survive," for that is like asking whether man or biology or society will survive. The question is whether it can survive successfully in its present form. All the evidence shows that in order to do so, it needs help.

Precisely that was uppermost in the minds of 4,000 delegates from across the nation who met in Washington last week for the once-in-a-decade Conference on Children. Among the proposals they urged on President Nixon were the establishment of a National Institute for the Family; universal daycare, health and early learning services in which parents would play a major role; the creation of a Cabinet-level Department of Family and Children; and an independent Office of Child Advocacy. There was also a lavish list of demands—though more modest than the one ten years ago—covering everything from prevention of child injuries to reforming the judiciary system.

WEAKENED SUPPORTS

Yet if the demands made on the Government in behalf of the family were too vast, this was in a sense only an understandable reaction against the fact that too many vast demands are made on the family these days. Throughout most of Western history, until the 20th century, society as a whole strongly supported the family institution. It was the family's duty to instruct children in moral values, but it derived those values from church, from philosophers, from social traditions. Now most of these supports are weakened, or gone. Yet politicians and other prophets often blame the family for decline in morals and morale—as if the family could be separated from society. The forces that are weakening the U.S. family structure are at the very heart of the changes that are taking place in American civilization. Some of the most significant:

Mobility

The mass exodus from rural to metropolitan areas, the increasingly common and frequent corporate transfer, the convenience of the automobile and the highway system built to accommodate it—all have contributed to a basic change in the character of the family. In the less complicated, less urbanized days, the average U.S. family was an "extended" or "kinship" family. This meant simply that the parents and their children were surrounded by relatives: in-laws, brothers, sisters, aunts, uncles, grandparents, cousins. If the relatives did not live within the same household, they were next door or down the block or on the next farm. But as Americans became more mobile, the kinfolk have been gradually left behind. As a result, the typical family has evolved into an isolated "nuclear" family. It consists simply of a father, a mother and their children, and is usually located miles away from the home of the nearest relative.

Says Dr. John Platt, associate director of the University of Michigan's Mental Health Research Institute: "All sorts of roles now have to be played by the husband and wife, whereas in the older, extended family they had all sorts of help—psychological support, financial advice, and so on. The pressures of these multiple roles are partially responsible for the high rates of divorce, alcoholism, tranquilizers, etc."

Women's Changing Role

"Put very simply," says Cornell Political Sociologist Andrew Hacker, "the major change in the family in recent years, and the problems of the future, are both summed up in one word: women. In the past and until very recently, wives were simply supplementary to their husbands, and not expected to be full human beings. Today, women are involved in much greater expectations and frustrations. For one thing, 40% of U.S. women are now employed. When a woman is working, she tends to have a new perception of herself. I see this most egregiously in those women who go to liberal arts colleges, because there the professor takes them seriously, and this gives them big ideas. The unhappiest wives are the liberal arts graduates. The trouble comes from the fact that the institution we call marriage can't hold two full human beings —it was only designed for one and a half."

It is not only woman's aspirations that have changed, Hacker adds, but society's support of her as a wife. "In the past, the role of wife and mother was reinforced by the church and the community. The whole complex descended on women and said, 'This is what you are; this is where you will be.' Now marriage has to be on its own, because the reinforcements are no longer there. So women are listening to all the subversive messages."

8

One Women's Lib theoretician, Margaret Benston, has made an economic analysis that places the blame for the "exploitation" of women directly on the family. Since women's work in the home is not paid for, she reasons, it is considered valueless by society. Moreover, at present, equal opportunity of employment simply means that a woman has two jobs: one at work and one at home. All work must therefore be taken out of the home and paid for like any other product; only such innovations as communal kitchens and universal child-care centers will "set women free," she says.

Apotheosis of Childhood

In the Middle Ages, children were considered miniature adults, according to French Sociologist Philippe Aries. At about the age of seven, they were sent to other homes to serve as apprentices and often as servants. Thus they grew up in huge households, with no dependence on their parents. In contrast, the child of today, as the center of the tiny nuclear family, has become its *raison d'être* and is therefore kept psychologically, financially and emotionally bound to it.

Without realizing it, many American mothers, under the aegis of benevolent permissiveness and the pressure of civic obligations, actually neglect their children. Others, imbued by Dr. Spock with the notion that every child has a unique potential and that it is her mission to create a near-perfect being, become the child's shadow, with equally damaging results, according to Brandeis Sociologist Philip Slater. The child soon recognizes that he is the center of an extraordinary effort and that his happiness is a matter of great stakes. He will seldom turn out exactly as planned, and when family dissension ensues, the mother will resent her "sacrifices." Moreover, though she may have brought up her child to be "more cultured, less moneygrubbing, more spontaneous and creative" than she herself was brought up to be, she is nevertheless upset when he then refuses to remain on the same treadmill as his parents.

That refusal takes place in adolescence, which like childhood is a modern development. Thus the family has had no long historical experience in dealing with the new rebelliousness. Unlike youths of the pre-industrial age, who simply entered some form of apprenticeship for the adult world at the age of puberty, millions of teen-agers now remain outside the labor force to go to college. It is this fact that has made possible the existence of today's separate youth culture, by which parents feel surrounded and threatened in their sense of authority. "A stage of life that barely existed a century ago is now universally accepted as an inherent part of the human condition," says Yale Psychiatrist Kenneth Keniston. Keniston, in fact, now postulates still another new stage of life, that between adolescence and adulthood: he calls it "youth." The youth of the technetronic or post-industrial age often remain out of the work force until their late 20s. "They are still questioning family tradition, family destiny, family fate, family culture and family curse." Naturally, their very existence unsettles the families from which they sprang, and delays the development of the new life-styles that they will eventually adopt.

Limited Usefulness

According to Sociologist Reuben Hill, among others, the family has traditionally performed seven functions: reproduction, protection and care of children, economic production of family goods and services, socialization of children, education of children, recreation, and affection giving. But during the past century, he says, the economic, educational, recreational and socializing functions have been lost in varying degrees to industry, schools and government.

In three areas of traditional family life there has been little erosion: reproduction, child care, affection. As a matter of fact, many experts believe that the affectional function is the only one left that justifies the continued support of the family as a social institution. As "community contacts" become more "formal and segmental," says Hill, people turn increasingly to the family "as the source of affectional security that we all crave."

But the insistent demand for affection without the traditional supporting structure has dangers of its own. The pioneering sociologist Edward Westermarck observed that "marriage rests in the family and not the family in marriage." The corollary used to be that the family existed for many practical purposes beyond love. To base it so heavily on love—including the variable pleasures of sexual love—is to weaken its stability.

MOTHER'S KISS

A related danger is to romanticize and sentimentalize the family. From the Greek tragedians to the modern psychoanalysts, men have known that the family, along with being a source of immense comfort, is also a place of savage battles, rivalries, and psychological if not physical mayhem. Psychoanalyst R. D. Laing says that the "initial act of brutality against the average child is the mother's first kiss." He finds it hurtful that a child is completely at the mercy of his parents, even to having to accept affection. Laing's colleague, David Cooper, calls the nuclear family the "ultimately perfected form of non-meeting" and, in a new book called *The Death of the Family,* demands its abolition. These are extreme views, but it may be better to face the fierce aspects of family life than to expect only bliss. There is something of the disillusioned lover in many people who today are trying to live outside the conventional family.

Dissatisfied with the traditional family setup, or simply unable to cope with it, Americans by the thousands are seeking alternatives. One that has most captured the imagination of youth and that has an almost religious appeal to members of the counterculture is a family structure that is as old as antiquity: the commune. Utopians from Plato onward have visualized children as not being raised in traditional families but in various communal organizations; the instinct that pulls man toward a tightly knit "nuclear" family has often been counterbalanced by the dream of escaping from it.

Only five years ago, there were perhaps a hundred "intentional communities" in the U.S., founded mostly by religious fundamentalists, utopian socialists or conscientious objectors. Today, as an outgrowth of the hippie movement, there are about 3,000, a third of which are in rural settings. "There are farms everywhere now, and we might go in any direction on compass to find warm bread and salt," writes Raymond Mungo in *Total Loss Farm*. Although Vermont, Oregon, California and New Mexico are still the favored states, some new commune clusters are cropping up in what Mungo calls "the relatively inferior terrain and vibration of Massachusetts and points south and west, and the huge strain of friendless middle America."

Most of the new communards are fleeing what they regard as the constriction, loneliness, materialism and the hypocrisy in straight society and the family life on which it is based. Yet some of the same old problems reappear— for example, the tug of war between individualism and submission to the group. One contributor to the *Whole Earth Catalog* summed up his own experience. "If the intentional community hopes to survive, it must be authoritarian, and if it is authoritarian, it offers no more freedom than conventional society. Those communes based on freedom inevitably fail, usually within a year."

But when they fail, their members often go on to join other tribes, now that there is a network of communes available to them. Benjamin Zablocki, a Berkeley sociologist who has visited more than 100 communes in the past six years, insists: "The children are incredibly fine. It's natural for children to be raised in extended families, where there are many adults." Yet in spite of the talk of extended families, the extension in the new communes does not reach to a third generation. Indeed, the "families" have a narrow age span, and it is possible that the children have never seen an adult over 30.

DEFORMED MONSTROSITY

Writes Brandeis' Sociologist Philip Slater, in *The Pursuit of Loneliness:* "It is ironic that young people who try to form communes almost always create the same narrow, age-graded, class-homogeneous society in which they were formed. A community that does not have old people and children, white-collar and blue-collar, eccentric and conventional, and so on, is not a community at all, but the same kind of truncated and deformed monstrosity that most people inhabit today."

Some communes actually form compromises with the nuclear family. Nowhere is this point better made than at Lama, a contemporary commune 18 miles north of Taos, N. Mex., which was re-visited last week by Correspondent David DeVoss after an absence of 19 months.

"We work together—we collectively grow and distribute the crops, but we go back to our individual nests at night," explains Satya De La Manitov, 28, who has now moved from a tepee into a still unfinished A-frame house that took him $1,500 and twelve months to build. Most couples are in their upper 20s, are married, have children, own their own homes, have a deep respect for property rights and believe in the value of honest toil. Although the concept of complete sexual freedom retains its followers, it plays only a minor role in Lama society today. Indeed, reports DeVoss, "were it not for their long hair, predilection for grass and rejection of the American political system, Lama residents could pass for solid, middle-class citizens."

Most of today's communes are in the cities, and they indeed do have appeal for many middle-class citizens. To Ethel Herring, 30, married to a Los Angeles lawyer and active in Women's Lib, a city commune seemed the answer to growing frustrations, which culminated when she realized that she was spending $60 to $70 a week for baby sitters; the Herrings had no live-in grandparents or nearby relatives to care for their three children while Ethel was attending her frequent feminist meetings. In effect, she says, "we were suffering from the nuclear family setup."

With six other sympathetic couples in similar circumstances, the Herrings scouted around and finally found a U-shaped, six-unit apartment building in southern Los Angeles. They purchased it last September, and converted it into a successful, middle-class (most of the men are lawyers) city commune. Knocking out walls and doors, they built interjoining apartments and a communal nursery, TV room and library. "The apartments open up so that the kids' rooms can run into each other," Ethel explains, "and yet there is still plenty of privacy for adults."

The families share their services, following a schedule that calls for each couple to do all of the cooking and housework for one week. "That's KP once every six weeks per couple, which keeps everybody happy," says Ethel. Her husband, for instance, has curtailed his practice so that he can spend one day a week at home on child-care and cooking duty. Says Ethel, "The truth is that most men are deprived of a close relationship with their children, and our men are finding out what they've been missing. It's groovy."

Disillusionment with the traditional family has led to other alternative life-styles. In Boston, David, 36, a divorced architect, and Sarah, 29, a researcher for a consulting firm, have an "arrangement"; like an increasing number of other American couples, they live together in David's Cambridge walkup apartment in a "marriage" that has endured solidly for two years without benefit of legal sanction. They sometimes join David's ex-wife and his son, Jonathan, 5, for dinner. Bubbly, attractive Sarah still maintains her own apartment and sometimes spends a few days there.

Both Sarah and David are convinced that their relationship is superior to a conventional marriage. It is the legal tie, they believe, that is the subtle influence in making a marriage go sour. "On the small scale," says David, "there's no difference, except that you know you could call it off when you want to. That makes you more careful and considerate. You don't say subconsciously, 'Oh, she's always going to be there.' So you make that little extra effort." Only under one circumstance would Sarah and David consider a legal marriage: if they decided to have children.

Doubts about conventional family life have also led to the growth of another phenomenon: the "single-parent family." No longer fearful about complete ostracism from society, many single girls who become pregnant now choose to carry rather than abort their babies and to support them after birth without rushing pell-mell into what might be a disastrous marriage.

POPULATION EXPLOSION

Judy Montgomery, 21, is a major in political science at the University of Cincinnati. She lives in the exclusive suburban area of Indian Hill with her parents and her son Nicky, 16 months. She became pregnant at 19 but did not want to get married. "I think having a mother and a father are important for a child, but Nicky can be raised so he isn't scarred. There are now substitutes in society that will allow him to grow up fatherless. I have no feeling of guilt. My only real hassle is with guys I meet who are interested in me, and I say, 'Oh, I have to go home and take care of my kid.' "

Liberalized adoption laws are also making it possible for single and divorced women to have children and to set up housekeeping without the necessity of a father. Ruth Taylor, a secretary at a hospital in suburban Warrensville township, near Cleveland, was divorced shortly after her daughter, Kelley, was born three years ago. Because she did not want the girl to grow up as an only child, she adopted a little boy who was listed as a "slow learner" by the agency (there was a three-year waiting list for normal Caucasian children). But in the year that she has had Corey, 2, the boy's personality and intelligence have blossomed. To Ruth, adopting a child is the answer for both single and married people who have decided to forego children because of their concern about the population explosion. "Form a family with what has already been provided," she suggests. "That way you will be helping to solve the problem."

The re-examination of the traditional family and the desire to try other forms have also produced some bizarre experiments. In La Jolla, Calif., Michael, an oceanographer, and his artist wife, Karen, both 27, had been married for four years when Michael met Janis, who was studying at the Scripps Institute of Oceanography. Janis often came to study at Michael and Karen's apartment, and a strong attachment developed. When Michael took off on a field trip to Antarctica, the two women became good friends and decided that because they both liked Michael, all three ought to live together. Last May the trio formalized it all with an improvised wedding ceremony attended, incidentally, by other trios.

As the three were leaving for a summer session at the University of Oregon, they were delighted to learn that Karen was pregnant. "We'll all take turns caring for it," says Janis, "just as we share all the household chores. That way each of us has time for things we like to do best."

There are other far-out experiments. One group, living at Sandstone, a handsome complex of houses near Los Angeles, has varied in size from three to twelve adults, and currently consists of only five: three men and two women. Says Barbara Williamson, a member of what she calls the "intentional" family: "It's a smorgasbord. It's so much more exciting to have nine different dishes than just one." The group has had no children yet because it wants to stabilize its "marriage" first.

Such eccentric arrangements obviously have no meaning for the vast majority of people, except perhaps as symptoms of an underlying malaise. Thus, while some sociologists and anthropologists make their plans for the reordering of the social structure, most are more immediately concerned with removing—or at least alleviating—the stresses of the nuclear family.

EMANCIPATED WOMEN

Psychologist Richard Farson, for one, believes that the increased emphasis on the role of the family "as an agent for human development and personal growth" will again make the family important in the field of education. "Parents will not necessarily teach the children," he says. "That is probably quite unlikely." But the family itself may become a learning unit, stimulated by new programs and new processes (like cartridge TV) that are even now being introduced into the home by industry. This, he feels, will help strengthen the nuclear family "by involving people in all kinds of interesting mutual experiences of learning."

While some fear that Women's Lib is a threat to the family, many experts believe that its more sensible goals could strengthen it. As women become increasingly emancipated—by child-care centers and equal-employment practices—they could have more time for intellectual and emotional fulfillment. Thus although their housekeeping role may diminish, they could become less frustrated and better wives. Though the idea is still shocking to many, some experts feel that certain women are better mothers if they are not with their children all day.

The Pill and abortion are obviously part of a loosening of morals that undermines the family in some ways; but these developments, too, can have their positive effects by reducing the number of pregnancies that lead to hasty and ill-considered marriages, and by allowing couples to put off having children until they are older and have had time to enjoy themselves, to travel and to grow up themselves. The reduction in unwanted pregnancies will also lessen the number of children who are rejected even before they are born and the financial hardship brought on by unplanned large families.

Adds Psychoanalyst Rollo May: "Even the growing frequency of divorce, no matter how sobering the problems it raises, has the positive psychological effect of making it harder for couples to rationalize a bad marriage by the dogma that they are 'stuck' with each other. The possibility of finding a new lover makes it more necessary for us to accept the responsibility of choosing the one we do have if we stay with him or her."

If the experts have their way, the nuclear family can be further strengthened in the future. Margaret Mead, for example, believes that many bad starts can be avoided if marriages can be postponed. She proposes a kind of universal national service that will take adolescents out of the nuclear home (where they apparently do not fit in), train them and keep them occupied until they are more mature. "We need something to allow those people who don't go to college to grow up without committing themselves to a marriage."

Instead of traditional marriages, Mead would also encourage a "two-step marriage" for young people. During the first phase, which would, in effect, be a trial marriage, the young couple would be required to agree not to have children. If a stable relationship developed and the couple decided to have children, a second license would be obtained and another ceremony performed.

Business, too, has a responsibility to relieve some of the stress on the contemporary family, according to Psychologist Urie Bronfenbrenner. In a report to last week's White House Conference on Children, he urged business to create flexible work schedules, cut back on travel, on transfers and on social obligations that keep parents away from their children. Bronfenbrenner also feels that large corporations should concern themselves with "where and how their families live," and with more part-time positions, better maternity leave, day-care centers and family recreation plans.

Another suggestion of the report, which urges that businesses "adopt" groups of young people to give them the opportunity to see adults at work, has already been tried by a few firms. At the White House conference, delegates saw a film about a highly successful program set up by Bronfenbrenner's colleague, David Goslin, of the Russell Sage Foundation. It showed children from the Detroit public-school system spending three days at the Detroit *Free Press,* learning to relate to the newspapermen and what they were doing, and saying things like "You know, in school you learn a subject, but here you meet people."

In Bronfenbrenner's view, meeting people—especially people of different ages—is all-important to the preservation of the family. Parents now spend their time with other parents, he suggests, children with children, the young with the young and the old with the old. To end this segregation, which is particularly acute in suburban living, Bronfenbrenner and others recommend planning by architects for community clusters where children, their parents and the elderly can intermingle, each group bringing its experience, knowledge and support to the other. University of Michigan's John Platt visualizes clusters he calls "child-care communities" which resemble communes: in addition to enlarged recreational and shopping facilities, they would include centralized schoolrooms, dining rooms (for both adults and children) and kitchens.

GYPSY CARAVAN

For all of the family's ills, the U.S. is still probably the most marriage-and-home oriented nation in the modern world. In the 1960s the number of U.S. families grew at a greater rate than the population; 87% of Americans live in families that include both parents. While the divorce rate is rising, so is the rate of remarriage among divorced people. Thus, the nuclear model will undoubtedly remain the basic family structure in the U.S. But that does not mean that it will function as a healthy institution unless ways are found to strengthen its concept and spirit.

A man's family used to be his fate; he could scarcely change it. In the modern U.S., people think easily of changing their family, like their occupation or their home. The result is psychologically unsettling and yet this changeability has obviously become a part of American life and the family will have to adjust to it. Theologian Sam Keen (*Apology for Wonder*) suggests that one should boldly take the notion of the family as a center for mobility: "It should be thought of like a gypsy caravan. You have that point of stability in the caravan, but it is continually moving and each member of it goes out to forage for food and then catches up with it."

That vision will probably never replace the image—and the dream—of the snug, permanent hearth, even suitably expanded by "clusters." But it may be closer to the reality of American life.

The Family as an Element in the Social Structure

William J. Goode

With the focus of this book on the changing relationships between the sexes as they affect individuals and family members, to understand the possible impact of this phenomenon we must first be aware of the family's history as the most stable and universal of all institutions in society. Society and the family are interconnected, says Goode. He points out how the interplay between the needs and values of society and the needs and values of families and individuals mold and maintain each other. This interrelationship places the family in a significant mediating role that stabilizes the family as an institution.

In all known societies, almost everyone lives his life enmeshed in a network of family rights and obligations called role relations. A person is made aware of his role relations through a long period of socialization during his childhood, a process in which he learns how others in his family expect him to behave, and in which he himself comes to feel this is both the right and the desirable way to act. Some, however, find their obligations a burden, or do not care to take advantage of their rights. This wide range of behavior leads to one of the commonest themes of conversation found in all societies—just what the duties of a given child or parent, husband or wife, cousin or uncle ought to be, and then, whether he *has* done his duty. This type of discussion is especially common in societies undergoing industrialization, where arguments are frequent concerning the duties of women.

Various Views of the Family

The intense emotional meaning of family relations for almost all members of a society has been observable throughout man's history. Philosophers and

From William J. Goode, ed., *The Family* (Englewood Cliffs, N.J.: Prentice-Hall, 1964), pp. 1–3, 4–6. Reprinted by permission of Prentice-Hall, Inc.

social analysts have noted that society is a structure made up of *families,* and that the peculiarities of a given society can be described by outlining its family relations. The earliest moral and ethical writings suggest that a society loses its strength if people fail in their family obligations. Confucius thought, for example, that happiness and prosperity would prevail in the society if only everyone would behave "correctly" as a family member—which primarily meant that no one should fail in his filial obligations. The relationship between a ruler and his subjects, then, was parallel to that of a father and his children. Similarly, much of the early Hebrew writing, in Exodus, Deuteronomy, Ecclesiastes, Psalms, and Proverbs, is devoted to the importance of obeying family rules. In India, too, the earliest codified literature (the *Rig-Veda,* about the last half of the 2nd millenium b.c., and the Law of Manu, about the be-ginning of the Christian Era) devote great attention to the family.

From time to time, imaginative social analysts or philosophers have sketched out plans for societies that *might* be created—utopias—in which new defini-tions of family roles are presented as solutions to traditional social problems. Plato's *Republic* is illustrative of this approach. He was probably the first to urge the creation of a society in which all people, men and women alike, would have an equal opportunity to develop their talents to the utmost, and to achieve a position in society solely through merit. Since family relations in all known societies prevent a selection based solely on individual worth, in Plato's utopia the tie between parents and children would play no part, because no one would know who was his own child or parent. Conception would take place at the same times each year at certain hymeneal festivities. Children born out of season would be eliminated (along with those born defective); all children would be taken from their parents at birth, and reared under chal-lenging conditions by specially designated people. Similarly, experimental or utopian communities, like Oneida, the Shakers, and the Mormons in this country, insisted that changes in family relations were necessary to achieve their goals.

Included among the aims of many revolutions since the French Revolution of 1789 has been a profound alteration in family relations. Since World War II, the leaders of all countries undergoing industrialization have introduced new laws, well ahead of public opinion, intended to create family patterns that would be more in conformity with the demands of urban and industrial life.

All these facts, by demonstrating that philosophers, reformers, and reli-gions, as well as secular leaders, have throughout history been at least im-plicitly aware of the importance of family patterns as a central element in the social structure, also suggest that the social analyst must understand family behavior in order to understand social processes generally.

The strategic significance of the family is to be found in its *mediating* func-tion in the larger society. It links the *individual* to the larger social structure. A society will not survive unless its many needs are met, such as the production and distribution of food, protection of the young and old, the sick and the pregnant, conformity to the law, the socialization of the young, and so on. Only if *individuals* are motivated to serve the needs of the society will it be able to survive. The formal agencies of social control (such as the police) are not enough to do more than force the extreme deviant to conform. Socialization makes most of us wish to conform, but throughout each day we are often tempted to deviate. Thus both the internal controls and the formal authorities are insufficient. What is needed is a set of social forces that responds to the individual whenever he does well or poorly, supporting his internal controls as well as the controls of the formal agencies. The family, by surrounding the individual through much of his social life, can furnish that set of forces.

The family then, is made up of individuals, but it is also part of the larger social network. Thus we are all under the constant supervision of our kin, who feel free to criticize, suggest, order, cajole, praise, or threaten, so that we will carry out our role obligations. Even in the most industrialized and urban of societies, where it is sometimes supposed that people lead rootless and anonymous lives, most people are in frequent interaction with other family members. Men who have achieved high position usually find that even as adults they still respond to their parents' criticisms, are still angered or hurt by a brother's scorn.

Thus it is *through the family* that the society is able to elicit from the *individual* his necessary contribution. The family, in turn, can continue to exist only if it is supported by the larger society. If the society as a larger social system furnishes the family, as a smaller social system, the conditions necessary for its survival, these two types of systems must be interrelated in many important ways.

. . . .

The Family as a Unique Institution

A brief consideration of certain peculiarities of the family as an element of the social structure will suggest how better theory and a fruitful general approach are needed in this area.

The family is the only social institution other than religion which is *formally* developed in all societies. Indeed, the term "social structure" in anthropology is often used to mean the family and kinship structure. By contrast, some have argued that in certain societies legal systems do not exist because there is no formally organized legislative body or judiciary. Of course, it is possible to abstract from concrete behavior the legal *aspects* of action, or the economic aspects, or the political dynamics, even when there are no explicitly labeled agencies formally in control of these areas in the society. However, the kinship statuses and their responsibilities are the object of both formal and informal attention in societies at a high or a low technological level.

Family duties are the *direct* role responsibility of everyone in the society, with rare exceptions. Almost everyone is both born into a family and founds one of his own. Each person is kinsman to many. Many people, on the other

19

hand, may escape the religious duties which others take for granted, or the political burdens of the society. Almost no family role responsibilities can be delegated to others, as more specialized obligations can be in a work situation.

Participation in family activities has a further interesting quality, that though it is not backed by the formal punishments supporting many other kinds of obligations, almost everyone takes part nonetheless. We must, for example, engage in economic or productive acts, or face the alternative of starving. We must enter the army, pay taxes, and appear before courts, or face physical penalties and force. However, no such penalties face the individual who does not wish to marry, or refuses to talk with his father or brother. Nevertheless, so pervasive and recurrent are the social pressures, and so intertwined with indirect or direct rewards and punishments, that almost everyone either conforms, or claims to conform, to family demands.

Next, as suggested earlier, the family is the fundamental *instrumental* foundation of the larger social structure, in that all other institutions depend on its contributions. The role behavior that is learned within the family becomes the model or prototype for role behavior required in other segments of the society. The content of the socialization process is the cultural traditions of the society; by passing them on to the next generation the family acts as a conduit or transmission belt by which the culture is kept alive.

Next, each individual's total range of behavior, how he budgets his time and energies, is more easily visible to the family than to outsiders. Family members can evaluate how the individual is allocating his time and money in various of his role activities. Consequently, the family acts as a source of pressure on him to adjust—to work harder and play less, or go to church less and study his school lessons more. In all these ways, the family is an instrument or agent of the larger society; its failure to perform adequately means that the goals of the larger society may not be attained effectively.

A further striking characteristic of the family is that its major functions are separable from one another, but in fact are not separated in any known family system. The family contributes these services to the society: reproduction of the young, physical maintenance of family members, social placement of the child, socialization, and social control. Clearly, all these activities could be separated. The mother could send her child to be fed in a neighborhood mess hall, and of course some harassed mothers do send their children to buy lunch in a local snack bar. Those who give birth to a child need not socialize the child. They might send the child to specialists, and indeed specialists do take more responsibility for this task as the child grows older. Parents might, as some eugenicists have suggested, be selected for their breeding qualities, but these might not include any great talent for training the young. Status-placement might be accomplished by random drawing of lots, by IQ tests or periodic examinations in physical and intellectual skills, or by polls of popularity, without regard to an individual's parents, those who socialized or fed him, or others who controlled his daily behavior.

Separations of this kind have been suggested from time to time, and a few hesitant attempts have been made here and there in the world to put them into

20

operation. However, three conclusions relevant to this kind of division can be made. (1) In all known societies, the *ideal* (with certain qualifications to be noted) is that the family be entrusted with all these functions. (2) When one or more family tasks are entrusted to another agency by a revolutionary or utopian society, the change can be made only with the support of much ideological fervor, and sometimes political pressure as well. (3) These instances are also characterized by a gradual return to the more traditional type of family. In both the Israeli *kibbutzim* and the Russian experiments in relieving parents of child care, the ideal of completely communal living was urged, in which husband and wife were to have only a personal and emotional tie and not be bound to each other by constraint. The children were to see their parents at regular intervals but to look to their nursery attendants and mother-surrogates for affection and direction during work hours. Each individual was to contribute his best skills to the cooperative unit without regard to family ties or sex status (i.e., there would be few or no "female" or "male" tasks). That ideal was maintained for a while, but behavior has gradually dropped away from the ideal. The only other country in which the pattern has been attempted on a large scale is China. Whether the Chinese commune will retreat from its high ambitions remains to be seen, but chances are good that it will follow the path of the *kibbutz* and the Russian *kolkhoz*.

Various factors contribute to such a deviation from the ideal, but the two most important sets of pressures cannot easily be separated from each other. First is the problem, also noted by Plato, that individuals who develop their own attitudes and behaviors in the usual Western (i.e., European and European-based) family system do not adjust to the problems of the communal "family." The second is the likelihood that when the family is radically changed, the various relations between it and the larger society are changed, so that new strains are created, demanding new kinds of adjustments on the part of the individuals in the society. Perhaps the planners must develop somewhat different agencies, or a different blueprint, to transform the family.

Concretely, some of the factors reported as "causing" a deviation from the ideal of family living are the following. Some successful or ambitious men and women wish to break away from group control, and leave to establish their lives elsewhere. There, of course, they do not attempt to develop a communal pattern of family living. Parents do try to help their own children secure advantages over other children, where this is possible. Parents not only feel unhappy at not being with their children often enough (notice that youngsters need not "be home for meals"!), but perhaps some feel the husband-wife relationship itself is somewhat empty because children do not occupy in it their usually central place. Husband and wife usually desire more intimacy than is granted under communal arrangements. Finally, the financial costs of taking care of children outside the family are rather high.

These comments have nothing to do with "capitalism" in its current political and economic argument with "communism." It merely describes the historical fact that though various experiments in separating the major functions of the family from one another have been conducted, none simply evolved slowly

21

from a previously existing family system; and the two modern important instances represent a retreat from the ideals of a previous generation. It is possible that some functions can be more easily separated than others; or that some family systems might lend themselves to a separation of functions more easily than others. Nevertheless, we have to begin with the data available now. Even cautiously interpreted, they suggest that the family is a rather stable institution.

The Fourth Revolution*

Jessie Bernard

As Goode suggested in the previous article, permanent change in the structure of the family must be accompanied by changes in both individual and societal needs and values. As Bernard discusses, we are now experiencing change in the form of a sexual revolution. She outlines the physiological, cultural, medical, and structural factors that have coalesced to produce a separation between sexual activities for procreation and for pleasure. This article was written before the advent of the Women's Liberation Movement and the tremendous impetus it gave to the "fourth revolution." But even before the current pressures for sexual freedom it was obvious to Bernard that the sexual revolution of today may have an impact on the family equal to that of the Industrial Revolution almost a century earlier.

The Nature of Consensus and Social Issues

The consent given to any specific status quo—the consensus on which it rests—may vary all the way from enthusiastic acceptance to reluctant and grudging tolerance, accompanied even perhaps by nonconformity to it. People sometimes give their implicit consent to a norm but do not feel they must conform to it. During prohibition, many people voted dry but drank wet. People may even give more than grudging consent to norms they violate. They may be active and enthusiastic supporters of norms to which they do not personally conform. Consensus, that is, does not necessarily imply conformity. Institutional nonconformity to community norms is a common sociological phenomenon (Bernard, Chapter 27).

*There are sexual revolutions in process all over the world. The discussion here refers primarily to the West and especially to the United States. This revolution may be viewed as fourth not only in time but also as fourth in the so-called triple revolution of automation, population, and race. Or fourth in the series of revolutions noted by Ira Reiss: urban-industrial, romantic-love, and feminist (Reiss, p. 218).

From Jessie Bernard, "The Fourth Revolution," *Journal of Social Issues*, April, 1966, pp. 76–87. Reprinted by permission of The Society for the Psychological Study of Social Issues.

But when a number of people withdraw their consent—the number is indeterminate, depending on their interest, drive, and insistence—issues arise. Even before issues can be raised, a de-tabooing process must take place with respect to the norms which are to be challenged. For the basic tenets of any status quo—especially those embedded in the mores—tend to have powerful, often mystical, sanctions; they are sacred; not discussable.[1]

Issues are alternative ways for dealing with specific problems. Social issues arise when an old consensus has broken down or when a new one is in process of emerging. There are questions of policy—legislative or attitudinal—on which people have differing positions, none of which is consented to by all. The great fundamental social issues in the area of sex today have to do with the normative control of nonprocreative heterosexuality. Not that nonprocreative sexuality is a new phenomenon, for it is older than man himself, as we shall presently note. But because now it is possible "for the first time [in our history] to separate our reproductivity and our sexuality" (Calderone, p. 501), that is, procreative and nonprocreative heterosexuality.

Four Fundamental Changes in Sexuality[2]

Once bisexual reproduction had evolved, the first great "sexual revolution" or evolutionary change may be said to have come when sex relations became social as well as merely biological in nature. The pollenization of plants was bisexual, but it was not social. The fish who deposited her eggs to be fertilized by a male was not in a social relationship with him. One might cavil about calling the sex life of insects social; but the relations between the sexes among many birds and mammals is undeniably social.[3]

A second major change in the relations between the sexes occurred when mating was no longer restricted to the female estrus. This was the first adumbration of the separation of reproduction and heterosexuality, or between procreative and nonprocreative heterosexuality.[4] Among animals which have a clear-cut mating season, the female's body shows readable signs of her condition when ovulation has taken place, and she either sends out unequivocal signals to the male that she is receptive or takes the initiative in seeking him out, presumably to ensure fertilization of the ready ovum. Ovulation, "the female sex act," is the important thing; the female is in control of sex relations. Coupling does not occur out of season.

Among the primates, however, where there is no such clear-cut mating season—unless one wishes to interpret the annual spring swarming of college youth on Florida or Bermuda beaches as symptomatic of a vestigial "mating season"—the relationships between the sexes become vastly complicated. Ovulation is no longer determinative of sex relations.[5] The female is no longer in control. The male may aggress or the female present herself to him even when she is not in estrus, when procreation is not likely. Reproduction is not, of course, divorced from heterosexuality; but heterosexuality is divorced from

24

reproduction. The female monkey, for example, sometimes uses her sexuality in ways that have been whimsically labelled a form of prostitution; that is, she diverts a male with food by presenting herself to him and thus is able to appropriate the food for herself.

The third great revolution came with culture, which placed both procreative and nonprocreative sexuality under normative controls. These cultural constraints were by no means standardized throughout the world or over time; but, in some form or other, they were universal.

The fourth or current sexual revolution has to do with the confluence of two cultural subrevolutions, one normative and one technological. The normative deals with the resexualization of the female body; the technological, with the increasing feasibility of conception control, which further separates procreative and nonprocreative heterosexuality. Both revolutions began some time ago. The resexualization of the female body began at the turn of the century; it was furthered by a series of so-called marriage manuals in which sexual satisfaction for women was emphasized and the responsibility for producing it made a male concern. The technology of conception control has a long history. What is revolutionary about it in recent years is that it has now become feasible on a mass scale.

Either of the two revolutions alone would have had great impact on the relations of the sexes; in combination the impact was exponentially increased. That is, if the female body had been resexualized at a time when contraception was still uncertain or if feasible contraception on a mass scale had come in Victorian times, the impact of either would have been moderated. Occurring as they did together, they produced revolutionary changes, not so much with respect to procreative as with respect to nonprocreative sexuality.

PROCREATIVE SEXUALITY[6]

It is not possible to make clear-cut distinctions between procreative and nonprocreative heterosexuality. The definition of procreative sexuality would certainly include all sex relations deliberately planned to produce conception and almost certainly all marital sex relations in which, whether conception was actively desired or not, no preventive measures were taken.

So far as procreative sexuality is concerned, the human female simply "deposits" her egg, as does the fish, and waits for the male to fertilize it. This is her contribution to reproduction; this is "the sex act" so far as she is concerned with it. The ejaculation of the sperm into the vagina is the male contribution; it is "the sex act" so far as he is concerned with reproduction. These *are* the processes of sexual reproduction; these *are* the sex acts involved in it. Once they have taken place, sex has no more to do with the matter.

Extrusion of the ovum has so little sensation, let alone pleasure, associated with it that most women never even know when it occurs.[7] Much self-research, in fact, is required to determine precisely when it does. The "male sex act," by way of contrast, is associated with great orgasmic pleasure. Orgasm can occur without ejaculation, even in infancy (Shuttleworth, p. 177), but not ejaculation without orgasm (Shuttleworth, p. 159). But in mature males they probably occur together most of the time. At least often enough that they become psychologically identified with one another (Social Security Administration). "The sex act," therefore, as a strictly reproductive process, has quite different meaning in the two sexes.[8]

Although "the sex act" in females—extrusion of the ovum—is never pleasurable, it is possible, but by no means necessary so far as reproduction is concerned, for "the male sex act" to be pleasurable to women as well as to men. The range of female reaction to "the male sex act" is wide, from painful suffering at one end, through complete indifference,[9] to orgasmic ecstasy at the other. The pleasure may be purely psychosocial, the female experiencing great pleasure as the source of the male's pleasure. At the other extreme, the physiological experience is identical to his. In any case, her suffering, pleasure, or boredom with "the male sex act" has nothing to do with conception, hence with procreation.

Female orgasm, or even pleasure, so far as reproduction is concerned, is extremely expendable. Cultures can "turn it off or on" without affecting their reproductive histories in the least. And, indeed, this is exactly what has been done in the West.

FEMALE SEXUALITY

Procreative sexuality demands nothing of women except ovulation; they can conceive in their sleep. If heterosexual relations—procreative or non-procreative—are to be pleasurable to women, the pleasure must be derived from the "male sex act." Here the impact of cultural constraints has been determinative. They have enormously influenced the responsiveness of the female body to "the male sex act."

Much of the normative structure for the control—often suppression—of sex has had to do with the behavior of women who were, in effect, assigned the task of supporting the existing norms. This was feasible because of the greater sexual plasticity of women. For one difference between the sexes, not often commented upon in the literature of sex differences, is the relatively greater cultural susceptibility of the female than of the male body to sexual constraints. This susceptibility is well documented in the history of the relations between the sexes in Western society. (Hunt). There have, for example, been centuries when the female body was not expected to be sexually responsive to the male sex act. In Victorian times women bragged of their frigidity; they were processed for it from childhood. Contrariwise, there have been centuries when female enjoyment of the male sex act has been permitted, if not necessarily actually cultivated; the female body was even viewed as especially lustful.[10]

26

The current sexual renaissance reflects an era which encourages—compels or coerces, some might say—women to equal if not out-do men in the enjoyment of the male sex act.

NORMATIVE CONTROL OF PROCREATIVE SEXUALITY

With the alleged exception of the Trobriand Islanders, who chose to ignore the relationship between sexual intercourse and conception, there has until recently tended to be practically universal acceptance of reproductive sexuality.[11] When large numbers of births were needed to replenish precarious populations, in the absence of specific knowledge of the processes of ovulation, reproductive sex played a large part in the normative thinking of the relations between the sexes. Because we relied so heavily on parents, or at least families, to take care of children, we did what we could, with varying degrees of success, to restrict even reproductive sex relations to men and women who promised to cleave to one another till death did them part and who would be responsible for the care of all the children resulting from their union. Before or without such commitment, whether it occurred at the betrothal, as in Scandinavia, or at the marriage, sex relations were forbidden.

Since it was clear, even with the limited knowledge available, that the prevention of out-of-wedlock relations would absolutely prevent out-of-wedlock children, powerful sanctions were evolved to prevent such relations.[12] Especially for women there was almost no sin more heinous than non-marital sex relations.

In general, the normative structure with respect to procreative sex outside of marriage remains intact. Since we still rely heavily on parents for the rearing and socialization of children, we will probably continue to frown on out-of-wedlock births, however much we may attempt to mitigate the penalties of their status. But the issue will not necessarily be, as hitherto, the sex relations which produced the children; it may well be the irresponsibility of the partners in not preventing the conception. We will blame them for carelessness or irresponsibility rather than, as in the past, for sinfulness. There will, that is, continue to be consensus with respect to the wrongness of out-of-wedlock births, but the moral basis for the consensus will be disapproval of carelessness and irresponsibility rather than of extra-marital sex relations per se. In this respect, there is no revolution in progress or in sight. Some women may demand the right to have children without marriage; but no large movement in this direction is apparent.

If there is a revolution in the area of norms dealing with procreative sexuality, it will probably have to do with the limitation of family size. If concern about the population explosion grows, there may emerge norms which frown upon even marital procreative sexuality. The suburban matron who produces her sixth child for the community to find recreational and educational facilities for, may provoke negative sanctions from her neighbors struggling under the weight of taxes for schools and other community facilities for children.

Nonprocreative Sexuality

It was early recognized that there was more to sexuality than reproduction, that sexuality had many forms and widespread societal ramifications, that it served psychological and social functions quite unrelated to reproduction. Even the Catholic Church, which struggled with the problem of normative control of nonprocreative sexuality for centuries, insisting that sex relations were justified only for procreative purposes, finally, by permitting the rhythm method of contraception, conceded that sex relations between spouses may have other than only procreative functions within marriage.

If heterosexuality were only for reproduction, it would have the same place in our lives as in the lives of animals with a mating season. There would be incentive to engage in sexual activities only when the female was physiologically ready to conceive and offspring were wanted, or at least welcome. That situation does not even obtain among primates, certainly not among human beings.

But it is by no means easy to specify exactly the nature, let alone the function, of nonprocreative sexuality.[13] It is certainly not simple, unidimensional, or standardized. It is not even easy to define nonprocreative sexuality. Reproductive sexuality is, of necessity and even by definition, genital. The sperm must be deposited in the vagina. But nonprocreative sexuality, though it includes genital sex at one extreme, includes vastly more. Clearly self or manual masturbation, homosexuality, bestialism, fellatio, cunnilingus, biting, petting, kissing, fetishism are sexual but not procreational. How about the pleasure derived from the sight of a beautiful nude body, in the flesh or in marble? Or the reactions to other kinds of stimuli which Kinsey reported? He defined them as sexual; they are not procreational. The pleasure congenial men and women derive from talking to one another—is this sexual? (The original definition of the term "to converse" included "to have sexual intercourse.") Where, in brief, does one draw the line between the sexual and the non-sexual? Where does one leave off and the other begin? The indecisive discussions of Freud's all-encompassing definition of sexuality or libido show how difficult it is to define nonprocreative sexuality. No wonder Mary Calderone states that "society has not yet developed an open and honest answer to the questions 'What is sexuality for?' " and how " 'can it be managed so as to be a constructive and creative force instead of a destructive and distortive one?' " (Calderone, p. 502). One has only to ask what would a society be like if all forms of sexuality were forbidden (except heterosexual relations for the conception of children) to begin to sense the widely ramifying functions of nonprocreative sexuality and the confusing problems of normative control which it raises.

28

Some Current Issues

A variety of current issues exists in the area of sex per se (as distinguished from such *family*-related matters as divorce, abortion, illegitimacy, prostitution, and the like). What, for example, should be our attitudes, or what should be the law, with respect to homosexuality, sexual deviancy, perversions, pornography, obscenity?[14] At least with respect to homosexuality, a consensus appears to be in process of emerging, even among those who consider it wrong, which accepts private homosexual behavior between two consenting adults while at the same time restricting public demonstrations and protecting young men and boys from seduction. There appears to be a growing consensus that any manifestation of sex between adults which is acceptable and pleasurable to them in the privacy of their bedroom should be permitted without guilt or opprobrium. The courts seem to move in the direction of legitimizing fewer and fewer limitations on the written word (Kling).

A few years ago, there was an issue with respect to making contraceptive information freely available to married women at public expense; today that is no longer an issue. Many communities have incorporated the policy of using public funds for this purpose. It was recently an issue whether or not to supply such information to unmarried women; Brown University (Washington Post) and the University of New Hampshire (Washington Post) seem to have settled that one: college women may have such information at the discretion of the college physician. The issue will probably now take the form of whether to supply such information at the high school level and, if so, under what circumstances.

With respect to extra-marital relationships of married women, no revolution as yet appears to have occurred nor an issue to have been raised. There are reports from time to time of "wife-swapping clubs" or of "key clubs" and there is reported to be widespread tolerance of affairs for married women (Buck). But there does not appear to be any movement to establish normative sanctions for, or even reluctant consent to, such standards; and in the case of Negro women, there are still strong normative sanctions against them on the part, at least, of the white population.

The sex relations of mature unmarried women, especially if they are discreet, appear to be accepted in large cities although not, as yet, elsewhere. The private, personal life of mature adults appears less and less to be a matter of public concern.

Beginning in the 1920's, the premarital sex relations of young women was a major social issue. Since most young women are married by their early twenties, the issue had to do essentially with teen-agers. The consensus which broke down and hence gave rise to issues was that premarital sex relations were always and unequivocally wrong under any circumstances. Ira Reiss has traced in detail the dissolution of that consensus and the issues which resulted. He has reported four major standards—abstinence, double standard, permissiveness without

29

affection, and permissiveness with affection—which have successively replaced it (Reiss).

At the other end of the age continuum has been an issue dealing with elderly widowed women who remarry. When it was discovered that some elderly recipients of social security benefits were "living in sin" rather than marrying and thus losing their benefits, provision was made to protect their social security payments even if they remarried.[15]

WHO'S IN CHARGE HERE? THE ISSUE OF FEMALE AUTONOMY

When sex was purely reproductive in nature, ovulation was the central fact. Coupling occurred only when the female was in estrus. She might even make the sexual advances. In any case it was she who determined the relations between the sexes. In animals without a mating season, ovulation ceases to be the determinant in the coupling behavior of the sexes (Carrighar). It becomes incidental. More to the point, coupling ceased to be controlled by the female. She lost her sexual autonomy. She became subjectable to male aggression, even exploitation.

One of the tenets of the fourth revolution is sexual equality for women. It posits, implicitly if not always explicitly, identical sexuality in men and in women. The ideal would be one which eliminated the so-called double standard: "no more sexual exploitation."

The old exploitative pattern—requiring women to "submit" to their husbands—has certainly all but disappeared. Men today are not likely to take advantage of a resisting young woman (Calderwood, p. 89). But this does not mean that exploitation does not still exist. It may take the form of a subtler kind of coercion than a physical kind.

Girls and young women, for example, sometimes complain that if they do not acquiesce in men's urgings they are bludgeoned with the epithet "frigid" (Haworth, Hoffman). When the norms forbade all extramarital sex relations, a girl or woman could easily refuse male requests. When the norms are permissive, she has nothing to hide behind. If she does not wish to engage in sex relations—and most teenage girls probably do not[16]—she is left in an exploitable position. If in the past she had to say no to safeguard her self-respect, she must now say yes for the same reason—to avoid the dreaded epithet "frigid."

The old norms gave men the prerogative of initiating sex relations. This privilege, too, was part of the double standard which the fourth revolution opposes. The rationale for this aspect of the double standard, as Reiss has pointed out (15), has been, in part, that female sex drive and desire in the West was less powerful in women, so they had less need than men actively to seek genital sex relations. It may well be argued, however, that the double standard was a protection for men. It does appear to be true that women can

30

tolerate abstinence better than men. But their orgasmic capacities—because of briefer refractory periods—are greater than men's. It is possible for them to make greater demands on men than men can fulfill. True, a woman cannot aggress against a man sexually; she must incite or excite or stimulate him so that he can "aggress" against her. If she fails, both lose. The reverse is not true. He can "aggress" against her in her sleep.

No Final Answers

The widespread possibility of nonprocreational heterosexuality by no means solves the problem of the relations of the sexes. It is certainly true, as Reiss says, that "for the first time in many millenia, Western society is evolving sexual standards which will tend to make men and women better able to understand and live with each other" (Reiss, p. 264). But there is no final, absolute, and all-purpose pattern for the relations of the sexes equally well suited for all groups, all times, and all places, no solution to the problem of the "best" relations between them. There must, perhaps, always be the seeds of potential hostility between them, intrinsic to the relationship. We tend to hate those we are dependent on; for they have power over us; they can exploit our weaknesses. And no matter what we may say or do, the sexes are dependent on one another; they need one another. But they are different. Some normative patterns of relationships between the sexes favor men, some favor women. A pattern, for example, which puts the initiative in the hands of men means that women will sometimes be approached when they are not ready; a pattern which puts the initiative in the hands of women means that there will be times when men are denied or times when demands are made on them which they are not ready to meet. (Of the two, perhaps the first is the less costly to both sexes.)

It might be argued that different answers are required at different times. It might be argued, for example, that the Victorian consensus was a suitable one for an age that required a vast investment of human energy in the creation of capital. It gave men the prerogative of determining when and how often they would have sex relations; it put them in a dominant sexual position; it freed them from having to concern themselves about pleasing women. They could concentrate on the "really important" masculine things like work, making money, building factories, expanding markets, creating empires, and the like. It was, it could be argued, a good thing that women did not make sex demands on men, that sexuality in women was even viewed with horror. Their demands for attention, payable in sex, may well have been dysfunctional; it was a protection for men to have the sexuality of women soft-pedaled.

The Victorian sexual ethos, however, does not suit the twentieth century. A sex ethos for the twentieth century has to take the resexualization of women into account. It has to be one which reconciles the demands made on men by their work and the demands made on them by women. It has to be one also

31

which reconciles the differences between the sexes in their respective life calendars. It has to be one, finally, which takes into account the separation of heterosexual relations and reproduction. If the achievement of nonprocreative sexuality has solved some issues, it has raised many more. Nor can we anticipate what they will be. For as yet we really do not know what the sexual renaissance ushered in by the fourth revolution implies for the future relations between the sexes.

NOTES

[1] The almost compulsive use of forbidden words and the elaborate preoccupation with coitus in modern writing, usually protected by court decisions, suggest that the detabooing process has not yet run its course. It is part of a vast effort to remove any vestige of taboo from the subject of sex. The professor of creative writing in a woman's college once threatened to go on strike if he received one more story recounting how the heroine lost her virginity. The difficulty many people still have talking about sex illustrates how powerful the taboo has been. Some wonder how much longer the arts will have to concern themselves with the details of sex. When will writers once more take it for granted that the reader can supply the details of sexual intercourse, for example, without having them spelled out for him? When will it no longer be necessary to shout the forbidden words? Some people even question the value of entirely removing the taboo —and along with it the mystery from sex.

[2] The first two changes here delineated should, strictly speaking, be viewed as evolutionary stages rather than as revolutions.

[3] For an evocative and anthropomorphic exposition of this point see (5). The point is also made clear in the work of Harlow, who has shown so unequivocally that young monkeys have to be socialized into adequate adult sexuality; without such socialization they are sexually defective as adults (7).

[4] Frank H. Hankins is credited with the quip that sex was now recreative as well as procreative. The quip is amusing, but the term recreative is not apt. It is too trivial, too superficial in its implications to characterize the phenomena of nonprocreative sexuality in all their variety and complexity. Nonprocreative sexuality may, indeed, be simple recreative—"fun and games"—but it may also be far more.

[5] Actually, among human beings there may even be a reverse rather than a direct relationship between sexual desires and ovulation.

[6] Procreative sexuality is the only kind usually recognized in so-called sex education courses among school children. Until recently it has been the only kind even medical students were exposed to. The fact that there is so much more to sex than procreation has made such limitations very clear. Lester A. Kirkendall (13) has been especially active in helping educators re-think the problem.

[7] William James was once quoted as commenting on the tremendous pleasure a certain insect must experience when she came upon the leaf in a thousand that could stimulate her to release her eggs. This is a purely masculine point of view, seeing the depositing of eggs as analogous to the ejaculation of sperm.

32

[8] It is interesting to speculate on what the reproductive history of mankind would have been if sperm-ejaculation were as lacking in pleasure as ovum extrusion. William Graham Sumner was once quoted as asking who would subject himself to the indignities of parenthood if the sex act were not pleasurable.

[9] "From the most ancient to the most modern erotic art, the female has been portrayed on occasion as reading a book, eating, or engaging in other activities while she is in coitus; but no artist seems to have portrayed males engaged in such extraneous activities while in coitus" (12, p. 669).

[10] Without historical research it is not possible to demonstrate the point, but a superficial glance suggests that the periods in which women were most revered and honored were periods in which their bodies were desexualized and that the periods in which they were least revered were those in which they were lusty and sexually eager. The knight and his lady had a desexualized relationship, or rather a non-genital relationship, and the Victorian lady was in the same kind of relationship, on a pedestal. Conversely, the literary genre known as Satires against Women showed a low opinion of them as highly sexed creatures. Chaucer's *Wife of Bath* is a case in point.

[11] Sometimes the acceptance was grudging, as with Paul, who accepted it only as better than burning. Some off-beat sects, such as the Oneida Community, which practiced Karezza, also rejected procreative sexuality.

[12] The emphasis here on the prevention of out-of-wedlock sex relations to prevent out-of-wedlock births does not mean that other factors were not also involved. The old consensus was also supported by those who invoked the Freudian hypothesis that civilization is, in effect, purchased at the price of sex (6). Bridgse, skyscrapers, atom bombs, and computers are purchased at the expense of libidinous energy. In simple and hence distorted form, if we want libido to be channeled into creative effort, we cannot channel it into sexual expression. The success of married students tended to discount this rationale among college students. The prevention of the spread of venereal diseases was also a rationale for the interdicting of non-marital sex relations. This argument was considerably attenuated with the discovery of antibiotic cures for syphilis. In 1965, it was predicted that syphilis would be eradicated by 1975 (21).

[13] Orgasmic pleasure, to be sure, is one obvious end of nonprocreative sex. But if this were the only goal, the solution of the relations between the sexes would be vastly simplified; not simple, but less baffling than now. But more is usually demanded of nonprocreative sex. Says one male college student, "I think that it is the spiritual aspect of sex that makes it fun. Just plain 'raw' sex—I don't know how much people would be satisfied with that" (4, p. 89). Even after a couple has achieved the summum bonum of complete and synchronized orgasm, they still want more; they can still feel lonely if that is all they have.

[14] Masturbation ceased to be an issue almost a generation ago; a new consensus which is permissive rather than punitive has emerged. A rear-guard action remains, but it is not salient. Bestialism is not an issue either; it is still consensually forbidden.

[15] "If you could have qualified for benefits as a widow and remarried after reaching age 60, you will be eligible for whichever benefit is larger: either one-half the retirement benefit of your former husband, or a wife's benefit based on the earnings of your present husband" (17, p. 13).

[16] Most young women in their teens, although suffused with sexuality, are not driven by strong genital urges. If they had their way, most would not feel compelled

to seek genital sex relations. Since most are married by their early twenties, premarital virginity is no hardship for them. They want caresses, tenderness, sexual appreciation; they want the interested attention of men; the relations they want are playful, meaningful, but biologically superficial. Advice-to-girls columns in newspapers, women columnists, etiquette books, teenage magazines all are approached by girls who want to know how to say no without alienating the boys.

REFERENCES

1. Bernard, Jessie. *American Community Behavior,* revised edition. New York: Holt, Rinehart, and Winston, 1962. Chapter 27.
2. Buck, Pearl. "The Sexual Revolution." *Ladies Home Journal,* 1964, September, 43–45, 102.
3. Calderone, Mary. "Sex and Social Responsibility." *Journal Home Economics,* 1965, 47, 499–505.
4. Calderwood, Deryck. "The Next Generation." *Humanist,* 1965, 25, Special Issue, 88–92.
5. Carrighar, Sally. *Wild Heritage.* Boston: Houghton, Mifflin, 1965.
6. Freud, Sigmund. *Civilization and Its Discontents.* New York: Anchor, Doubleday, 1958.
7. Harlow, H. F., and Harlow, M. K. "Social Deprivation in Monkeys." *Scientific American,* 1962, 207, 34, 136–146.
8. Haworth, Mary. "She'd Rather Be Chaste Than Chased." *Washington Post,* August 12, 1965.
9. Hoffman, Betty Hannah. "How America Lives: Coeds in Rebellion." *Ladies Home Journal,* 1965, October, 82–84, 167–170.
10. Hunt, Morton M. *The Natural History of Love.* New York: Knopf, 1959.
11. Kinsey, Alfred C., Pomeroy, Wardell B., and Martin, Clyde, E. *Sexual Behavior in the Human Male,* Phila.: Saunders, 1948.
12. Kinsey, Alfred C., Pomeroy, Wardell B., Martin, Clyde E., and Gebhard, Paul H. *Sexual Behavior in the Human Female.* Phila.: Saunders, 1953.
13. Kirkendall, Lester A. *Sex Education.* Discussion Guide No. 1, SIECUS, October, 1965.
14. Kling, S. G. *Sexual Behavior and the Law.* New York: Bernard Geis Associates, 1965.
15. Reiss, Ira L. *Premarital Sexual Standards in America.* New York: Free Press, 1960.
16. Schelling, T. C. *The Strategy of Conflict.* Cambridge: Harvard University Press, 1960.
17. Social Security Administration. *Social Security Amendments, 1965, A Brief Explanation.* Washington, D.C.: USDHEW, 1965.
18. Shuttleworth, Frank D. "A Biosocial and Developmental Theory of Male and Female Sexuality." *Marriage and Family Living,* 1959, 21, 163–170.
19. *Washington Post,* September 29, 1965.
20. *Washington Post,* October 13, 1965.
21. *Washington Post,* October 25, 1965.

2

The Partner-
Selection Process

Courtship is traditionally the time when men and women decide with whom they would like to share their adult lives. Although the decision to marry does not imply the permanence it once did, if children are involved divorce is really only a loosening of the legal and social ties. This chapter will discuss ways the courtship process has changed over time, and the many criteria and pressures that enter into partner selection. Included is the influence exercised by the social structure, value changes in the area of sexual liaisons, and in-group pressures, although none of these result in clearcut mandates.

For instance, strictures concerning interreligious affiliations have relaxed for reasons that are a direct reflection of these social variables. Yet the problems resulting from such partnerships remain. Interracial marriages are also increasing, although sanctions against them still can cause great personal strain in participants. Parents continue to attempt to limit their children's selection of marriage partners to social equals or better, but this is becoming more difficult to accomplish. However, some factors do not change in importance over the years. Approximately the same personality traits are sought after in spouses year after year. That important component, love, continues to give the partnership its most essential meaning.

The selection of a partner to a greater or lesser degree, depending on the individual, is always a matter of weighing all these social ingredients. The decision and commitment that follows will have a continuing effect on the kind of family culture the new marital partners will experience.

Courtship as Social Exchange: Some Historical Comparisons

Michael M. McCall

Although we like to think of courtship as an individual matter, it actually takes place within a context of family and societal pressures, and thus changes with the times. McCall attempts to make contemporary courtship understandable by comparing it historically within an exchange or bargaining framework. He suggests that mate selection is the type of process where bargains are struck as to eligibility for courtship, the manner in which it will proceed, and who is ultimately selected as a marriage partner. The criteria for such bargains change through the years and the current mode in sexual values has made bargaining mechanics a whole new game. By today's rules, no person is ever completely out of the marriage market and the relationship between sexual commitment and long-term commitment through marriage has drastically changed.

One signal contribution of Willard Waller's classic treatise on the family[1] was his analysis of courtship conduct as bargaining and/or exploitative behavior. His use of an exchange framework was dictated by the more or less practical reason that ordinary individuals recognized bargaining at work in the courtship process and modified their behavior accordingly.

> When one marries, he makes a number of different bargains. Everyone knows this and this knowledge affects the sentiment of love and the process of falling in love.[2]

Today it is perhaps not so true that "everyone knows this." The courtship bargaining and exploitation that Waller saw and explained theoretically are

From Michael M. McCall, "Courtship as Social Exchange: Some Historical Comparisons," in *Kinship and Family Organization*, ed. Bernard Farber (New York: John Wiley & Sons, 1966), pp. 190–200. Reprinted by permission of John Wiley & Sons. This investigation was supported (in part) by a Public Health Service fellowship from the National Institute of Mental Health.

no longer so widely recognized in the society as being operant. In this sense, Waller's analysis has become a bit dated, and the theory of courtship as exchange and bargaining is therefore in some danger of being discredited. In the hope of averting this possibility, the present paper undertakes an analysis of historical changes in American courtship practices to highlight the changing types of bargaining embodied in these practices.

It should be noted that Waller did recognize that there had been changes in the process of courtship bargaining. However, he failed to account for these changes or to incorporate them into his general model. Furthermore, Waller failed to make consistent use of the exchange framework in his discussion of courtship. That is, he had much more to say about courtship than one would suppose from a look at his rather sketchy discussion of courtship as bargaining. In fact, he was more interested in *exploitation* than in honest bargaining and used the discussion of courtship bargaining almost as a stepping-stone toward that topic.

> ... (T)here is a powerful impulsion toward getting something for nothing, and bargaining tends to go over by imperceptible stages into exploitation.
> ... Within the courtship group, the exploitative attitude spreads like a disease.
> So it is that disillusioned adolescents learn the jungle law: exploit or be exploited.[3]

This interest in exploitation is at least in part a result of Waller's historical setting, as we shall see.

The very sparseness of Waller's discussion of bargaining is itself related to his place in time. Writing as he did in a transitional phase of courtship practices, he could not see clearly what was muddied by transition. Hence, his understanding of courtship and bargaining was restricted, as he himself recognized:

> In modern society, groups are confused, and cultural imperatives are in conflict, and therefore the nature of the bargaining process is more complex and its outlines are confused.[4]

Despite its weaknesses, however, Waller's was an important discussion of courtship bargaining. He pointed out that "two kinds of bargains (are) struck in the courtship process"—those which have to do with the conditions of association in courtship, and those which have to do with marriage. Waller further implied the existence of another and logically prior class of bargains, those which determine the eligibles for a given person, that is, delimit the field within which the bargaining *per se* will take place.[5] By the bargains which determine the conditions for association, Waller meant such decisions as who was to be the dominant (i.e., least interested) member of the pair and whether there would be sexual intimacy (or how much). As for the final bargain,

> The traits which determine whether one will win, place, or show in the marriage competition are such things as family background, economic power, education, and personal qualities such as age, beauty, and sexual attractiveness.[6]

Although it will turn out that even the number of bargains which must be struck in any courtship is to some extent historically relative, Waller's three bargains provide an important organizing principle and, accordingly, can profitably be used to analyze the changing modes of courtship behavior. We will refer to the bargains as: (1) bargains that determine who is eligible to court whom, (2) bargains that determine how courtship will proceed, and (3) bargains that determine who will marry whom. That is, we will discuss them in their chronological order in the courtship process, within each historical period.

Before proceeding to such an analysis, however, it will be necessary to indicate the major outlines of social exchange theory and to examine certain broad changes which have been, and are, taking place in American courtship practices.

Exchange and Bargaining in Social Behavior

The notion of *exchange* as an overarching fact of human behavior is one useful framework in which to view such behavior. Blau defines this sort of "exchange behavior" as

> limited to actions that are contingent on rewarding reactions from others that cease when expected reactions are not forthcoming.[7]

That is, man is seen as choosing those social associations or relationships which are rewarding to him and as continuing in such relationships only so long as these remain rewarding. Likewise, the person is seen as providing rewards to the other party (or parties) to the relationship in exchange for those he has received from them. Rewards of this sort are as varied as are an individual's wants, including money, social approval, power, commitment, prestige, aid, love, and so forth.

To the extent an individual has no viable alternatives to the present relationship as a source of such rewards, the other person is said to possess *power* over him. This other person, being less dependent upon the relationship as a source of rewards, is the person who (in Waller's terms) is "least interested" in the continuation of the relationship.

Bargaining, as distinguished from simple exchange, implies a certain purposive awareness of the exchange of rewards. Individuals bargain about whether they will reward one another, in what ways, under what conditions, and to what degree. In this sense, then, exchange behavior may occur even though bargaining does not. Bargaining entails some knowledge of other sources of reward and an ability to draw on these alternative sources (or to threaten to do so), as well as a sense of how much one can reasonably expect to get in social exchange of a given variety.

38

A View of Contemporary Mate-Selection

Bernard Farber has recently advanced an explanation of changing courtship practices and of marriage in the United States based upon what he calls the "permanent availability model" of marriage;[8] that is, Farber proposes that in some sense all adult persons are permanently available to contract a marriage, even if they happen to be married already. (This model might better have been called the "universal availability model," since Farber means to include complete availability across persons as well as through time.) However, Farber's provocative model fails to provide an explanation of why an individual might remain loyal to his partner in a single marriage relationship or, conversely, might choose to make himself available for other marriages. An exchange theory of courtship, on the other hand, would provide just such an explanation, as will be detailed below. First, we must examine more closely Farber's views of contemporary trends in American marriage and courtship practices.

In this view, these practices are no longer kin-controlled, because of increases in societal complexity and of changes in residence patterns (especially the rural-urban shift). With the consequent losses of power and importance, the kin group no longer delimits the relationships among persons. This means that, as fewer people are "related," more people are eligible as possible mates, including members of religious, ethnic, and social status groups other than one's own. Simultaneously with this broadening of availability, there has been a change toward *permanent* availability through time. Divorce has lost its social stigma in most cases, making both divorce and remarriage more common. Because virginity as a condition for remarriage is obviously impossible, it is less important even for first marriages; that which is impossible for *every* marriage is less important for *any* marriage. Furthermore, the realization that there can be divorce and remarriage has meant that young marriages are more likely than formerly in the middle classes, since one needn't wait to marry until one is most desirable economically and socially and since an unsuccessful first marriage needn't prohibit a remarriage. Finally, the prevalence of divorce and remarriage means that individuals are permanently available, even when already married to someone else; they have only to terminate that relationship to begin another. Since marriages need not last a lifetime, "complementarity of personality" and of needs is no longer at a premium as it was when a couple had to face many crises together, hence needed between them the widest possible range of psychological strengths. Rather, there is today an emphasis upon likeness of personality and of interests, values, and needs, insuring greater compatibility; after all, if a crisis does arise, the couple need not stay together.

Exchange notions are implied here, although Farber does not develop them. If a person has no other choice of relationship than the one he is already in, he must continue in it even though it is no longer rewarding (and may be positively taxing). If, however, he does have other choices, he need not continue in the less rewarding one.[9] He is free to begin again even though the

39

second relationship may turn out to be no more rewarding than was the first one. In that case, the whole process may be repeated, hence, the pattern of multiple divorce and remarriage.

Farber points out that there is also an emerging *courtship* pattern congruent with this model of permanent availability for marriage. This courtship pattern, which he calls the "series of involvements" pattern, is to be differentiated from the older "ever-narrowing field" pattern discussed by Burgess and Locke.[10]

> (These authors) described the stages of courtship in American society as: Dating, keeping company, going steady, a private understanding between the man and the woman to be married, and engagement.[11]

Today all this has changed, even the terms; as Farber points out: "keeping company" is no longer in the courtship vocabulary. As for "going steady," it has come to mean "merely . . . the person with whom the individual is currently involved." In short,

> . . . the system of mate selection of the 1920's and 1930's, in which there was a continual narrowing of the field of prospective spouses, has given way to a series of personal involvements. One of these involvements eventuates in marriage.[12]

Farber might almost have called this model of courtship the "continual series of involvements" model or even the "permanent availability for involvements" model, so well does the courtship arrangement fit the marriage system. Young people are involved with one partner at a time, in various degrees of intimacy. One such involvement "eventuates in marriage." This marriage itself is subject to change, however, and the mates may become involved with other persons. In other words, marriage is merely a more total type of involvement which may end quite as lesser involvements do, leaving the individuals free for new involvements, whether of the marriage type or some other.

The term "involvement" itself points up an apparent contradiction which Farber's analysis of the changed pattern reveals. Along *with* the permanent availability norms and the consequent lack of exclusiveness (which Farber points out in the going-steady phase but which is true as well of all involvements), there is simultaneously an increased emphasis on *total commitment* (including sexual) and deep involvement of both partners. This paradox results from the lack of structural constraints implied by the notion of permanent and universal availability, and the consequent needs for *interpersonal* constraints. In the old days merely breaking an engagement was often grounds for legal action; today one enters and leaves "involvements," including marriage, much more easily, whenever one is "dissatisfied" or "incompatible."

This is related to the dropping of still another of the old terms, not mentioned by Farber. Today no one (except perhaps clandestine lovers) has *private* agreements. Emphasis is rather upon *public* commitments, once again as a means of social control where few such plans exist. Indeed, "dating" has,

40

to a considerable extent, been replaced, both as behavior and term. Today young people are "going with" other people, not merely dating them. The new term (and behavior) implies greater involvement than does mere dating.

This account of Farber's views is less than complete but will serve to delimit one endpoint of the continuum of changing courtship patterns that will be elaborated in the following sections.

THREE HISTORICAL PATTERNS OF COURTSHIP

The courtship patterns under consideration here may be divided into three broad types, each roughly associated with a specific historical period: the traditional, the intermediary, and the contemporary. These patterns are analytic abstractions from concrete courtship behaviors, of course, and therefore cannot be construed as the molds into which all matings in a given period were deliberately cast by the participants. The patterns do seem, however, to have been characteristic of most matings among individuals not located at the extremes of the socioeconomic scale. The feature of these three patterns of primary interest to the present paper is that each pattern (or period) involved highly distinctive types of courtship bargains.

So different have these bargains been, in fact, that to speak of "courtship" rather than the more general phenomenon of "mate-selection" ought actually to limit us to the second of our three historical periods. That we do typically speak of "courtship" is related to the fact that our knowledge of American mate-selection is largely based on a picture that may no longer be valid. This picture, here called the intermediary pattern, has dominated American culture since its beginnings, and it is this mode that Waller described. Thus, it turns out that it is only to this period that Waller's three bargains actually apply directly. They do not apply precisely to the traditional and contemporary patterns.

Exchange and Bargaining in the Traditional Pattern

The traditional pattern of mate selection was characterized by bargaining between kin groups or the parents of two young persons. Eligibility was not *bargained* about; instead, exchange terms were set in much the same way that prices in American stores are set. Goods are marked with a price, and the buyer can either pay the price or he must shop elsewhere. Analogously, the kin group decided[13] in which market they would shop, on the basis of the prices charged there and the quality of the merchandise. That is, they decided who the eligibles were, knowing full well the prices they would have to pay and the kind of mate they would be getting.

Furthermore, because the very act of inclusion in the group of eligibles

41

meant full consideration as a marriage partner, there was only one actual bargain struck—the marriage bargain itself. There was no bargain about the conditions of association in courtship, because *there was no courtship*. Rather, one's kin bargained with the kin of a young member of the opposite sex concerning the terms of marriage. With regard to this third (marriage) bargain, the traditional pattern represented bargaining par excellence.

This bargain, often called the "arranged marriage," is described by Zelditch:

> Arranged marriage is found where the consequences of marriage concern whole groups of kinsmen. Kinsmen usually have three kinds of interest in a marriage. The marriage is often conceived as an alliance between two kinship groups, not simply the relation of the two partners to the marriage, and the group is anxious to select allies carefully. Significant economic interests are usually involved, both in the exchange of goods that accompanies the marriage and in the effect of marriage on the dispersal or concentration of inherited property, wealth, and resources. When the kinship unit as a whole is the unit of the stratification system, so that a "peer marriage" lowers the social rank of the whole group, the kinsmen are concerned to protect the family name.[14]

Thus, in the traditional pattern there is no courtship between individuals, nor is there even any bargaining between kin groups except at the level of the marriage bargain itself, where this bargaining is most explicit indeed.

As mentioned, this pattern has never been characteristic of American mate selection. It is instead an ideal-typical picture of the early European system and of the systems of many primitive societies. It does not apply to the American case because, as Zelditch points out, it occurs only where marriage is a kin affair, and the kindred has never been as powerful or important here as it is elsewhere. An unusually high degree of mobility has always characterized American society. The first settlers came unaccompanied by their entire kin. Unattached males, or in some cases nuclear families, came, but whole clans, tribes, or even complete extended families were unlikely to come at once. Therefore, there was not the rigid control by the kin group which is so characteristic of mate-selection in the traditional mode. Furthermore, the valuables which were bargained about in those more stable societies in which the traditional pattern occurred were fluid in the United States. One could, at that time, have land almost for the asking, so that the protection of family holdings was less important. Social status, too, was won and lost almost daily. Finally, there has been in the United States an important cultural value stressing the freedom of the individual to make his own decisions, a freedom that would be contradicted by the kin-control characteristic of the traditional pattern of mate selection.

Nonetheless, the American mating game did not present a sudden and sharp break with the traditional pattern. Rather, it has throughout its history exemplified the intermediary pattern, which at first tended toward the traditional and has gradually come to resemble the contemporary mode described by Farber.

Exchange and Bargaining in the Intermediary Pattern

This pattern was "intermediary" in the sense that the kin group did not have complete authority in mate selection, but neither was it powerless. The young people themselves were highly involved in the selection process (here properly called "courtship"), but their parents were also. Love was the ideal and was properly encouraged, but restrictions on falling in love remained:

> In Western countries, and especially in America, it is assumed that men and women marry because they are in love. There is a broadly based mythology about the character of love as a violent, irresistible emotion that strikes where it will, a mystery that is the goal of most young people and often of the not-so-young as well. As soon as one investigates, however, which people actually marry each other, one finds that the lightning shaft of cupid seems to be guided rather stringently within very definite channels of class, income, education, racial and religious background. If one investigates a little further into the behavior that is engaged in prior to marriage under the rather misleading euphemism of "courtship," one finds channels of interaction that are often rigid to the point of ritual. . . . In other words, when certain conditions are met or have been constructed, one allows oneself "to fall in love."[15]

It is this intermediary mode, the mode we know the most about, to which we may properly apply the term "courtship" and upon which most theories of mate-selection are based. It was this pattern Waller tried to describe, albeit in its transition to the contemporary pattern, thus producing the "confusion" of which Waller complained. In this intermediary pattern, the three bargains Waller described can indeed be seen.

The first of these, the bargaining over eligibility, was clearly a true bargain in this pattern. Eligibility was decided (but not set) on the basis of one's economic and social position. This meant that the primary bases were still in the positions of the parents, but it was no longer so much a matter of keeping the family lands intact as of marrying one of equal or slightly higher "station" in life. The young person had not only family position and his promise of a portion of his father's wealth or business to bargain with, but also his own level and place of education (where one went to school was socially highly important), his occupation, and his own social position.

All this may sound much like the traditional pattern, but the important thing is that here there was true *bargaining* about eligibility (not mere exchange). That is, one could *raise or lower* one's chances of being considered eligible by those whom one, in turn, considered eligible and desirable; this could be done by increasing one's education, by "hard work," and even by a display of great personal charm.

This becomes clear if we return to Burgess and Locke's depiction of the courtship sequence. Waller's first bargain was a bargain about with whom one would begin the sequence. Not all of one's acquaintances were considered eligible in this sense; not all of one's classmates or neighbors nor even all of

43

one's boyhood or girlhood chums were eligible as suitors. Conversely, a young person whose parents were quite low in the stratification system of status and class might yet be considered eligible, perhaps on the basis of exceptional charm or drive or intelligence. Burgess and Locke's phrase, "to be accepted as a suitor," exemplifies the first bargain in this pattern.

Once accepted as suitor (i.e., once the first bargain has been satisfactorily carried off), Waller's second type of bargain became important in the sequence; suitors began to bargain over the conditions of association in the courtship process. Of primary importance here is that a young woman might begin the sequence with several suitors in the field (and likewise the young man might court several women, although this was not similarly stressed in the folk culture) and that the young people themselves carried on this bargaining.

Individuals did not form exclusive attachments (at least until the latest stages of the courtship process), but rather bargained with several others and narrowed the field of suitors by successively dropping the least favorable bargains. This type of bargaining, where commitment must be allocated among several role relationships in an attempt to maximize reward and minimize loss, has been fruitfully analyzed by Goode.[16] The point was to keep several alters as bargaining partners and to allocate and reallocate commitments among them through bargaining. (This is clearly seen in the picture of behavior at the social dance; a young woman judged the success of her evening by the number of young men who signed her card and danced with her.)

The individuals involved undoubtedly did not perceive this bargaining as being concerned with "commitment." They were interested in finding their "one true love," the "person I was meant for." But one way, perhaps the most important way, of determining which person one was meant for, was on the basis of which person seemed to love one the most (i.e., who was most committed to one, and most willing to admit such commitment). In large part, "being meant for one another" came down to complementarity of personality and of needs, as discussed above. As mentioned there, this complementarity was an important resource for marriage under the societal conditions of this historical period.

As the "ever-narrowing field" model suggests, bargains were attempted and judged favorable or not, and were dropped or continued accordingly. However, at some point in the courtship sequence, two individuals had progressively narrowed the field until only they were left as suitors. Up to this point, the bargaining had been taking place between and among individuals in the field. That is, the young woman, while she bargained with each of her suitors, also played them off against one another, allocating and reallocating her commitment. It was during this process that her sense of what she was worth as a product and her knowledge of what was generally available on the market had been established. Then, when the sole remaining couple turned inward, as it were, and bargained exclusively with one another, they were thus quite aware of market conditions and could drive a vigorous bargain.

This turning inward typically occurred at the stage of engagement, after the couple had already progressed through dating, keeping company, and going steady. The "private understanding" discussed by Burgess and Locke was a sort of intervening, transitional phase during which both persons had fairly clearly decided that the field was narrowed to the other alone, but during which one could still legitimately and without social pressure resume one's bargaining with someone else, too. In any case, the great length of the courtship period was functional in just this fashion. It was intended as a period in which individuals made sure that they were meant for each other, because there could be no turning back (divorce) after marriage.

Thus, we have in a sense already described the third (marriage) bargain as well. The persons bargained until they struck the most favorable bargain, as suggested, and then they made a contract: the marriage contract. The person tried to find the *one* other who was meant for him (who most loved him, whom he most loved, and who was most complementary to him), and then formed a permanent contract of exchange. This contract was a bargain to end any further cross-sex bargaining.

Thus, in the intermediary pattern, there were three true bargains struck in what we can properly call a courtship process. Furthermore, both the young people themselves and the parents of both parties participated in the bargaining. The parents' role was largely implicit, setting the market to a considerable extent by their place in the stratification system. However, they did participate more actively at certain points of the process too. This courtship pattern dictated that the young man ask the girl's father and then, with his consent, propose marriage to the girl. This meant that, although his main bargaining was done with the young lady herself, he was obliged to bargain with her parents as well. Not the least of his selling points was an economic one, as is seen in the famous question, "Young man, are you able to support my daughter in the manner to which she has become accustomed?" The role of the boy's parents was also largely economic; if they disapproved of the young woman of his choice, they might cut him off from a share of an inheritance or, in those days of father-and-son businesses, might even put him out of work. That the young woman bargained with the boy's parents is seen in the practice of "taking her home to meet his mother."

Under the impetus of the two World Wars and all of the social changes they wrought, including the increase in urbanization and residential mobility mentioned above, this intermediary courtship pattern eventually broke down. The change was gradual. Waller recognized its beginnings at the time he wrote, and it has probably not been completed even yet. However, we must deal with a different ideal-typical model of mate-selection when discussing the contemporary period.

Exchange and Bargaining in the Contemporary Pattern

As Farber points out, the kin group has lost much of its power as an agent in mate-selection. The contemporary arrangement includes a joint decision of the two young adults and a subsequent announcement by them to both sets of parents that they will be married and when (or that they *were* married, and when). Thus, from a traditional arrangement in which only the kin groups participated, to an intermediary one in which both sets of parents participated along with the two young people, we have come to an arrangement which does not include the participation of either set of parents as active bargaining agents.[17]

This arrangement does not include all three of Waller's bargains: as in the case of the traditional arrangement, there is only one genuine bargain struck. As Farber's concept of permanent (or universal) availability suggests, there is no bargaining over eligibility, the first of Waller's three bargains. In the contemporary pattern, every person with whom the individual comes in contact is eligible as a possible mate, regardless of marital status, religion, ethnicity, or social class.[18]

The one bargain which *does* take place in this contemporary pattern is the second of Waller's bargains, that dealing with "conditions of association in courtship." However, even this bargain is quite different from its counterpart in the intermediary pattern.

As Farber points out, there is no longer a belief in the inevitability of one's mate. If a person can be married more than once and involved any number of times, it is not possible that there is one and only one person "meant for him." Rather, we may say, there is an emphasis upon the uniqueness of *each* of his successive relationships, in Simmel's sense of "uniqueness."[19] That which the individuals are bargaining about is still commitment to the relationship and to the mate, but an individual is expected to become committed *each* time he becomes involved. The emphasis is upon intimacy or exclusiveness of involvement at any time. Thus, the couple "turns inward" from the beginning in this mode. If this is true, how can there *be* any bargaining, since bargaining requires the presence of an alternative relationship? The nature of the mate-selection process supplies the alternative: each person is free to leave any involvement (including marriage) at any time. The whole pattern is *set up* to give individuals training and experience in "getting along with others" in intimate relationships. Because there is no longer a belief in the "one and only," there is no longer an emphasis upon complementarity; the involvement (including marriage involvements) need not last through crises, and consequently the emphasis is now upon likeness and compatibility and (in the case of differences) upon toleration.

It is obvious that today's mate-selection is no longer a period of determining the best bargain and sealing that bargain in marriage. Rather, today this "courtship" period is one of training in bargaining. In other words, "courtship" teaches the individual how to bargain—how to form, maintain, and leave relationships. The emphasis in modern life is on keeping up one's bargaining skills, for one never entirely leaves the market. This, as Farber points out, helps explain the mania for "youthfulness" and "glamor" in contemporary American culture. Marriage may occur at any time in one's life, so one must make an effort to remain desirable and must polish up his skill in striking a good bargain.

46

In this sense, involvements (including the marriage involvement) are not contracts but restrictive trade agreements. The two individuals agree to exchange only with one another, at least until such time as the balance of trade becomes unfavorable in terms of broader market considerations. They agree to exchange exclusively for so long as the rewards in *this* involvement exceed the costs of continuing it in the face of chances for other rewards elsewhere. The individual, by forming numerous such exclusive and reciprocal trade agreements at various times, gets some idea of his overall worth as a product and of the market conditions, as well as learning bargaining skills, as mentioned above.

Finally, there is no real third (marriage) bargain under this arrangement. Given that marriage is merely one kind (though perhaps a more stable and lasting kind) of involvement, there can be no marriage bargain apart from the second type of bargain. That is, the "conditions for association in *marriage*" are no different in kind from the "conditions for association in courtship."

CHANGES IN SEXUAL BARGAINING AND EXPLOITATION

The sense of change in the American patterns of mate selection may become still stronger if we examine more closely certain aspects of the intermediary pattern, as this pattern grew out of the traditional pattern and then as it approached the shape of the contemporary pattern. The most profitable focus for this examination is the second of Waller's bargains, concerning conditions of association in courtship. With both the intermediary and contemporary patterns, when indeed there was association between the individuals before marriage, these individuals were bargaining over commitment, as we have seen, and the type of commitment has already been shown to have differed characteristically between the intermediary and contemporary patterns. The differences become even sharper, however, if we look at one specific kind of commitment (perhaps the most important kind), namely, sexual intimacies of various degrees.

During the traditional period, and in the first stages of the intermediary, premarital sexual behavior was not involved in the second bargain. Rather, it was involved in the first bargain about eligibility for marriage. In this arrangement, women engaged in "price-fixing" about sexual intimacy. There was a strict dichotomy between "good women" (those who did not engage in sexual behavior) and "bad women" (those who did). Since only the good women were eligible as marriage partners (except in the lowest socioeconomic classes), the young man had either to pay the price in this first bargain (i.e., accept the condition that the girl didn't do such things) or fail to make a purchase at all; there was no haggling about it.

In the later phases of the intermediary pattern, however, this had changed somewhat. Premarital sex was no longer subsumed by the first bargain, and its possibility had become one of the matters which the individuals bargained about in concluding the bargaining about conditions of association in courtship. Women were still engaged in "price-fixing," but the price was now not so rigidly fixed. Some good women could be induced to lower their price, and hence haggling became worthwhile. For a good woman to permit any serious premarital sexual behavior, however, indicated two things: (1) that she was deeply committed to the relationship, and (2) that the young man was being rewarded for his own deep commitment. One only made a *sexual* commitment once—to the "one and only"—and to do so was tantamount to marriage. This is related to the emphasis on virginity at the time of marriage in this pattern. One was a virgin until one met one's true love, and then one married him and submitted. If one submitted *first*, then marriage was a foregone conclusion.

There might, however, be slip-ups in this process. Young women might commit themselves thus to several men, or, more likely, a young man might indicate deep commitment to (and be thus rewarded by) several young women. As a consequence, while a woman might or might not indulge, her popularity depended upon the fact that she did not.

> The interest of girls in protecting the value of sexual favors against depreciation gives rise to social pressures among girls not to grant these favors readily. Coleman's study of high schools shows that these pressures tend to take the form of making a girl's social standing contingent on her reputation in regard to her sexual behavior with boys.[20]

Slip-ups did occur, and it was to slip-ups of the second type mentioned above that Waller referred with his concept of exploitation. As we have seen, exploitation was Waller's chief concern about courtship as bargaining. Having defined exploitation as the withholding of something which is supposed to be given in return for that which one is receiving, he went on to point out that the most common kind of exploitation was sexual exploitation. The gold digger among women and the cad among men, both promised something but failed to meet the terms of exchange; the gold digger offered sexual favors in return for costly attention, and the cad promised marriage in return for sexual favors, but neither delivered.

It is important to realize that exploitation of this kind could occur only in a period during which sexual favors were problematic (i.e., when a person might or might not indulge) and in a time when the granting of them represented deep commitment, with concomitant and legitimate expectations of a permanent relationship. When the young son of a royal house forced sexual attentions upon some slave girl or peasant's daughter, he could not be called a cad; he was not exploiting the girl, since she had no legitimate expectations of anything further. She could not expect that he would marry her, and so his failure to do so in return for her favors was not exploitation. (If, on the other hand, he did promise something else, such as economic recompense or a chance to be his mistress, and failed to keep his promise, he might certainly be considered a cad.) This is true because in the traditional pattern, as mentioned, sexual behavior was not problematic; rather, it was involved in the delimitation of eligibles. Any woman who "did" was automatically ineligible for marriage (although she might be eligible to become a mistress or a paid prostitute).[21]

Likewise, sexual exploitation of this sort is not associated with the contemporary pattern. Today, total commitment is expected in every involvement, whether marriage or otherwise. This total commitment includes sexual commitment. As Farber points out, a young woman is not expected to be a virgin at the time of her first marriage (since she could hardly be expected to be a virgin at the time of any subsequent marriages). The person with whom one enters a marriage involvement is no more the "one and only" than is the person with whom one enters *any* involvement (each involvement partner is the one-and-only for the time being, as indicated by the emphasis upon intimacy and exclusiveness), and it little matters whether the previous involvement of a nonvirgin was a marriage or another kind of involvement.

That which does, however, mark the marriage involvement as different from others is the decision to have children. Farber explains that while this decision does not necessarily imply a permanent commitment (as witnessed by the prevalent belief that divorce is better for children than keeping an unhappy family), it does imply at least a relatively long-term one. Parents expect that they will remain together to rear the offspring and furthermore recognize a permanent link between them in the form of shared parenthood. In addition, insofar as the norm remains one of child rearing under the auspices of "holy matrimony," parenthood sets the marital involvement apart from others.

Thus, exploitation today refers to the impregnation of the woman in an involvement. If a woman becomes pregnant and the man refuses to marry her, he is considered a cad. There is a legitimate expectation that marriage follows impregnation in this pattern, just as the intermediary pattern included a legitimate expectation that marriage followed sexual intimacy. Of course, there were also "shotgun weddings" in the intermediary pattern, but this was because sexual behavior and impregnation were practically coterminous. Today, sexual intimacy need not imply pregnancy, and herein lies the difference between the two patterns. Today sexual behavior is only an involvement; children constitute (marriage) commitment. In fact, an individual may decide not to have children with a specific marital partner, often giving as a reason the fact that the marriage is unstable or that he or she is not fully committed.

Thus Waller's preoccupation with sexual exploitation marks him, once again, as a product of the intermediary period. One gets a definite sense of this (as well as of the breakdown of the "ever-narrowing field" type of courtship in favor of the "series of involvement" type) in the following quotation:

> According to the moral standards which are still formally in force, courtship is a process in which every step is a commitment of the whole person, and the whole process of interaction moves rapidly toward total involvement and total commitment in marriage.... We now face a situation in which these meanings have disappeared and one person seeks to derive thrills from the person or the body of another without any involvement of his own personality.[22]

49

SUMMARY

An historical analysis of American courtship practices has shown three differing types of bargaining embodied in these practices. The traditional pattern has never been characteristic of American mate-selection but is important for an understanding of the other two types.

The intermediary pattern, which is the only one truly meriting the name of "courtship," has been the basis for most sociological theories of mate-selection. However, it is no longer fully characteristic of our society. A shift in mate-selection practices has included a transition to a third, contemporary pattern. Because this third type of bargaining is perhaps dominant today, it has been suggested here that our theories of mate-selection must change to match these changes in actual behavior.

NOTES

[1] Willard Waller, *The Family: A Dynamic Interpretation,* New York: The Cordon Company, 1938, Ch. 10 ("Bargaining and Exploitative Attitudes").

[2] *Ibid.,* p. 239.

[3] *Ibid,* pp. 239, 250.

[4] *Ibid.,* p. 240.

[5] In fact, although Waller merely implied the first type of bargain, concerning the eligibles, in his enumeration of courtship bargain, specifically naming only the second and third types, he discussed in the text only the first and second of these. Such is a further source of confusion and incompleteness in the Waller discussion of courtship as bargaining.

[6] *Ibid.,* p. 240.

[7] Peter M. Blau, *Exchange and Power in Social Life,* New York: Wiley, 1964, p. 6.

[8] Bernard Farber, *Family: Organization and Interaction,* San Francisco: Chandler, 1964, Chs. 4–5.

[9] This may be the sense in which the husband is no longer so powerful in the American family. When neither partner had much choice, a woman, being tied to the home, had even less, both because she met fewer people and because a divorced woman bore greater stigma than did a divorced man. Today, however, women work outside the home and are no longer under any greater onus than are their ex-husbands. In this sense, there is greater equality, and less power, in the marriage; both parties are equally independent of the relationship.

[10] Ernest W. Burgess and Harvey J. Locke, *The Family from Institution to Companionship,* New York: American Book Co., 1953.

[11] Farber, *op. cit.,* p. 160.

[12] *Ibid.,* p. 161.

[13] Of course, this "decision" was never literally a decision. Rather, such things were "decided by" one's place in the social stratification system. A middle-class college girl today knows few construction workers or Boston Brahmins; accordingly, she chooses a mate from among upper-lower to lower-upper-class

men. Similarly, in the traditional pattern, a young prince of France knew precious few commoners, and the ones he did know were of the highest classes.

[14] Morris Zelditch, Jr., "Family, Marriage, and Kinship," Ch. 18 in R. E. L. Faris (ed.), *Handbook of Modern Sociology*, Chicago: Rand McNally, 1964. Quotation from pp. 686–687.

[15] Peter L. Berger, *Invitation to Sociology*, New York: Doubleday Anchor, 1963, pp. 35–36.

[16] William J. Goode, "A Theory of Role Strain," *American Sociological Review*, 1960, 25, pp. 483–496.

[17] Of course, once again, the position of the parents in the stratification system determines to a large extent where the person will stand in that system and, thus, what kinds of people he will meet, as well as his mode of bargaining.

[18] It is important to note that we say "everyone a person comes in contact with," and not merely everyone. This suggests, once again, that one's social position limits the number and variety of individuals considered as possible mates. A college girl is more likely to marry a college boy, because she knows many college boys but very few high school dropouts.

[19] Georg Simmel, *The Sociology of Georg Simmel* (trans. Kurt H. Wolff), New York: Free Press, 1950, pp. 118–144.

[20] Blau, *op. cit.*, pp. 80–81.

[21] If we follow out our analogy about the way in which eligibility was set under the traditional arrangements whereby deciding which market one would shop in was analogous to deciding which persons were eligible and where this choice of markets was based on their price and quality of goods, we might say that while a young man bought his suit at Brooks Brothers (that is, chose his wife in an elite group of eligibles), he might shop for underwear at Sears (that is, have a mistress from a lower class or patronize a prostitute).

[22] Waller, *op. cit.*, p. 244.

Research in Interreligious Dating and Marriage

Larry D. Barnett

An important criterion for courtship and marital eligibility in the past has been religion. Marriages of persons of mixed religious background were negatively sanctioned by both family and churches involved. Yet, increasingly, young people fail to treat religion as an important aspect of partnership-mate selection. Reasons for this apparent decline in the importance of religious compatibility are connected with changes emergent in American society. Some of the problems these mixed religious marriages could bring to participants and some possible solutions are also discussed.

Interfaith dating and marriage appear to have increased during the present century (2, 27), and the consensus of authorities in the marriage and family life field is that the United States will continue to experience an increase in the number of interreligious dates and marriages. This increase and the trend toward earlier dating and marriage—today, the typical female is married about two years, and the typical male about four years, after leaving high school—make it important for family life teachers to be aware of facts pertaining to such intergroup associations, for they will increasingly have to deal with them.

This article, by presenting a summary of recent research on the subject of interreligious dating and marriage, will provide information on the following questions: What has caused the increase in interfaith associations? What conditions are found to accompany it? What special problems are encountered by persons crossing religious lines to find a mate? And how do couples resolve these problems?

Let us first turn to the causes of the increase in cross-faith dating and marriage—causes which may, in fact, apply to all forms of mixed dating and

From Larry D. Barnett, "Research in Interreligious Dating and Marriage," *Marriage and Family Living*, May, 1962, pp. 191–94. Reprinted by permission of the author and The National Council on Family Relations.

marriage. Studies (1, 2, 9, 12, 22, 27) indicate that the following interacting factors foster mixed associations:

1) *Existence of the group as a minority.* In a community in which a group is a minority, its rate of intermarriage will be higher than in a setting in which the group is a majority.

2) *Unbalanced sex ratio.* In a community in which one sex outnumbers the other, traditional barriers are crossed with increased frequency as members of the more numerous sex seek mates.

3) *Development of cultural similarities.* As groups with different backgrounds come into contact, similarities in values and attitudes are developed. This encourages intermarriage, since people tend to marry those who are culturally similar to themselves.

4) *Disturbing psychological factors.* Rebellion against and feelings of rejection toward one's own group lead to an identification with and marriage into an out-group.

5) *Acceptance of certain cultural values.* The democratic ideal, the romantic complex, and the belief in the right of youth to choose their own mates without interference by family and community facilitate the crossing of group lines in dating and in marriage.

6) *Weakening of institutional controls over marriage.* The various religions, for example, are finding their members to be increasingly unwilling to accept church control over the selection of spouses.

The writer suggests that these factors are part and parcel of the broader phenomenon of social and cultural change. As change occurs, these factors obtain, and intermarriages follow. In turn, these factors and intermarriages foster further changes in the social system. Therefore, a society like ours, which is characterized not only by a great deal of change but also by values holding change itself as desirable, will have cross-group dates and marriages to a much greater extent than a cohesive, stable society. Moreover, since change is cumulative, there will be an increasing amount of intermarriage.

In discussing the conditions related to interfaith dating and marrying, we are not saying that the relationship is a cause-and-effect one. Some third factor may produce both the condition and the mixed religious association.

The conditions associated with interreligious dates and marriages are as follows:

1) Apparently more Catholics intermarry than Protestants and more Protestants than Jews (10, 17, 23, 26), although two studies (11, 14) have shown that the Protestants have the highest frequency of mixed marriages and Catholics the next highest.

2) Those who are religiously less devout intermarry to a greater extent than the religiously more devout (3, 8, 13, 17, 23).

An interesting point arises in connection with these first two conditions. According to the first, Jews have the lowest rate of intermarriage; according to the second, the religiously more devout also have a lower frequency of mixed religious marriages. Thus, it would logically follow that Jews are more religious than either Protestants or Catholics. However, this does not seem to be the case, for studies (6, 7, 18) have demonstrated that Jews are the least religious (in terms of religious participation and acceptance of church doctrine) of the three groups.

Can this contradiction be explained? The writer suggests that, in the case of the Jew, it is not adherence to the religion which causes the higher rate of same-group marriage but rather social pressures deriving from the cohesiveness of the Jewish community. That this might be the answer is supported by a study (25) of Jewish-Gentile marriages which found that the family of the Gentile partner is more accepting of the couple than is the family of the Jewish partner.

3) In Jewish-Gentile marriages, it is the Jewish male who marries the Gentile female in the vast majority of cases (14, 17, 19, 24), but research to date is not consistent in its findings of a relationship between sex and mixed Catholic-Protestant marriages: three studies (3, 15, 27) found that it is the Protestant male who marries the Catholic female—that is, Protestant males and Catholic females intermarry more frequently than Protestant females and Catholic males—and one study (2) found just the reverse, while the data from two studies (14, 17) showed no trend.

4) When a Protestant enters an interfaith marriage, the spouse is more likely to be a Catholic than a Jew (2, 4); and when a Catholic enters an interfaith marriage, the mate is more likely to be a Protestant than a Jew. Jews who marry across the lines of religion choose Catholics and Protestants as mates with equal frequency (4).

5) In the case of a cross-religious marriage, Catholics appear to be least inclined to change to their spouse's faith, and Protestants appear most willing to do so, with Jews standing between the two in their willingness to change religions (6, 17, 23).

6) An interreligious marriage is more likely to be a first marriage than a remarriage (2, 5).

7) Persons marrying someone of a different religion are very often partially or completely rejected by parents and in-laws; for example, Slotkin (25) found in his sample of Jewish-Gentile marriages that 43 per cent of the young adults met with at least some rejection by both families. (However, the fact that over half of the couples—57 per cent—were partly or wholly accepted by their families should also be emphasized.)

8) Those who had, as youth, weak ties to their parents, whose parental families have been characterized by disorganization and stress, are more likely to engage in interfaith dates and marriages than those who lived in a cohesive family (8, 9, 13, 15, 20).

9) Apparently, those who engage in mixed religious associations are of a higher socio-economic status as measured by income (20), education (24), and housing (27) than those who do not, although one study (3) reports an inverse correlation between status level and favorable attitudes toward religious intermarriage.

10) Interfaith dating appears to be more characteristic of those who date

54

more frequently than the average (8), and young adults appear to be more willing to cross religious lines when dating than when marrying (23).

11) Interfaith dates and marriages are more frequently found in cities of 5,000 to 100,000 population than in cities having fewer than 5,000 or more than 100,000 persons (27).

12) In terms of divorce, interfaith marriages have a greater failure rate than intrafaith marriages; still, the majority of such marriages are successful (5, 16, 19, 28).

This leads to the third question: What special problems are encountered by those who date and marry persons of another religion? At this point, we must leave research behind. In spite of the significance of the problem, there apparently has been no thorough investigation of it, pointing to a gap in our knowledge which needs attention.

Mace (21), however, out of his long and extensive experience in marriage counseling, believes that there are five problems:

1) *Different religions create attitudes which are basically different.* These attitudinal differences (e.g., on sex) may result in the failure of the marital partners to attain spiritual unity.

2) *Different religions create different action patterns and values.* Religion, as one form of culture, results in patterns of action (e.g., dietary laws) and personal values (e.g., as to the meaning of life) which vary between the different religions, thus providing areas of conflict.

3) *Conflict in ties to church and family is possible.* If both spouses retain their original faith, ties to their church and to the family they have established may often clash.

4) *Tensions with relatives may be serious.*

5) *Religious training of the children may present problems.* If the couple decides to rear their children in one or the other of their original faiths, competition and jealousy may arise over which of the children are to be raised in each religion. Thus the family will be divided.

Notwithstanding the additional problems created by a marriage of persons of different faiths, the fact that the majority of such marriages are successful—if divorce is an adequate criterion of marital success and failure—must be kept in mind. Therefore, the special problems of interfaith marriages are coped with. It appears that there are three major ways in which this is done (2, 19):

1) One or both of the marital partners completely drops his church membership;

2) The two continue in their original faith; or

3) One spouse joins the church of the other.

One study (2) found that the third solution is the one most commonly employed, while another study (19) showed that the first solution is used most often. In any case, Mace (21) suggests the third—where one spouse completely and wholeheartedly changes to the religion of the other—as the best course of action for solving the problems created by a cross-religious marriage.

In summary, we have looked at four aspects of interfaith dates and marriages: (1) their causes, (2) the conditions associated with them, (3) the special problems found in this type of marriage, and (4) the ways in which couples resolve these problems.

REFERENCES

1. Barron, Milton L., "Research on Intermarriage: A Survey of Accomplishments and Prospects," *American Journal of Sociology*, 57 (November, 1951), pp. 249–55.
2. Bossard, James, and Harold C. Letts, "Mixed Marriages Involving Lutherans— A Research Report," *Marriage and Family Living*, 18 (November, 1956), pp. 308–10.
3. Burchinal, Lee G., "Membership Groups and Attitudes Toward Cross-Religious Dating and Marriage," *Marriage and Family Living*, 22 (August, 1960), pp. 248–53.
4. Cantril, Hadley, ed. *Public Opinion, 1935-1946*, Princeton, Princeton University Press, 1951, p. 431.
5. Chancellor, Loren E., and Thomas P. Monahan, "Religious Preference and Inter-religious Mixtures in Marriages and Divorces in Iowa," *American Journal of Sociology*, 61 (November, 1955), pp. 233–39.
6. Christopherson, Victor A., and James Walters, "Responses of Protestants, Catholics, and Jews Concerning Marriage and Family Life," *Sociology and Social Research*, 43 (September-October, 1958), pp. 16-22.
7. Cox, Christine, "A Study of the Religious Practices, Values, and Attitudes in a Selected Group of Families," *Dissertation Abstracts*, 17 (November, 1957), pp. 2703–04.
8. Freeman, Howard E., and Gene G. Kassebaum, "Exogamous Dating in a Southern City," *Jewish Social Studies*, 18 (January, 1956), pp. 55–60.
9. Freeman, Linton, "Homogamy in Interethnic Mate Selection," *Sociology and Social Research*, 39 (July-August, 1955), pp. 369–77.
10. Glick, Paul C., "Intermarriage and Fertility Patterns Among Persons in Major Religious Groups," *Marriage and Family Living*, 22 (August, 1960), pp. 281–82.
11. Golden, Joseph, "Characteristics of the Negro-White Intermarried in Philadelphia," *American Sociological Review*, 18 (April, 1953), pp. 177–83.
12. Golden, Joseph, "Facilitating Factors in Negro-White Intermarriage," *Phylon*, 20 (Fall, 1959), pp. 273–84.
13. Heiss, Jerold S., "Premarital Characteristics of the Religiously Intermarried in an Urban Area," *American Sociological Review*, 25 (February, 1960), pp. 47–55.
14. Hollingshead, August B., "Cultural Factors in the Selection of Marriage Mates," in *Selected Studies in Marriage and the Family*, Robert F. Winch and Robert McGinnis, ed., New York, Henry Holt and Company, 1953, pp. 399–412.
15. Hunt, Chester L., and Richard W. Collier, "Intermarriage and Cultural Change: A Study of Philippine-American Marriages," *Social Forces*, 35 (March, 1957), pp. 223–30.
16. Landis, Judson T., "Marriages of Mixed and Non-Mixed Religious Faiths," *American Sociological Review*, 14 (June, 1949), pp. 401–07.

17. Landis, Judson T., "Religiousness, Family Relationships, and Family Values in Protestant, Catholic, and Jewish Families," *Marriage and Family Living*, 22 (November, 1960), pp. 341–47.
18. Lantz, Herman, "Religious Participation and Social Orientation of 1,000 University Students," *Sociology and Social Research*, 33 (March-April, 1949), pp. 285–90.
19. Leiffer, Murray H., "Mixed Marriages and Church Loyalty," *The Christian Century*, 66 (January 19, 1949), pp. 78–80.
20. Locke, Harvey, George Sabagh and Mary M. Thomes, "Interfaith Marriages," *Social Problems*, 4 (April, 1957), pp. 329–33.
21. Mace, David R., "The Truth About Mixed Marriages," *Woman's Home Companion*, 78 (July, 1951), pp. 36–37, 43–44.
22. Panunzio, Constantine, "Intermarriage in Los Angeles," *American Journal of Sociology*, 47 (March, 1942), pp. 690–701.
23. Prince, Alfred J., "Attitudes of College Students Toward Inter-Faith Marriage," *Coordinator*, 5 (September, 1956), pp. 11–23.
24. Shanks, Hershel, "Jewish-Gentile Intermarriage: Facts and Trends," *Commentary*, 16 (October, 1953), pp. 370–75.
25. Slotkin, J. S., "Adjustment in Jewish-Gentile Intermarriages," *Social Forces*, 21 (December, 1942), pp. 226–30.
26. Sontheimer, Morton, "Would You Approve Your Child's Marrying a Protestant, a Catholic, a Jew?" *Woman's Home Companion*, 80 (March, 1953), pp. 30–31, 100.
27. Thomas, John L., "The Factor of Religion in the Selection of Marriage Mates," *American Sociological Review*, 16 (August, 1951), pp. 487–91.
28. Weeks, H. A., "Differential Divorce Rates by Occupation," *Social Forces*, 21 (March, 1943), pp. 334–37.

Self-Image of the White Member of an Interracial Couple

Rosalind Wolf

Taboos die hard. Interracial marriage (miscegenation) has long been socially —and was in some states, legally—outlawed. Those who selected a partner outside their race did so in the face of possible fury from all levels of society, beginning with family and friends and extending to the community at large. Yet race is another criterion of eligibility, along with religious affiliation, that has been affected by the general change in values, especially among the young. Despite the fact that interracial marriages are on the increase, there is still a lag between attitudes of young people and older adults on marrying outside one's race. Vestiges of racial jealousy and fear are exhibited by members of each race of the couples' own age as well. The affect these attitudes can have on the personal experiences of a racially-mixed couple is poignantly told here.

For the past three years, I have dated a black man. We plan to be married next year—an act which I consider to be the most serious and irrevocable of my life. The decision to marry is, in itself, a momentous one that radically alters anyone's life. But in this society especially, the decision to marry a *black* man changes all mutual interaction to an even greater extent. Ultimately, your self-image cannot help but be affected. I have, therefore, given great thought to my view of myself as reflected in our relationship, in order to be certain that it is a healthy self-image—one which I will be happy to maintain for the remainder of my life.

My self-image is the result of the interaction between my view of myself and the perception others have of me. Thus my self-image is constantly revised as I respond to, and interact with, those around me. Interaction with many is of a temporary nature, in which case the effects on self-image are superficial. However, there is a category of "significant others" with whom one

From Rosalind Wolf, "An Inquiry Into Black-White Interracial Marriage," (unpublished thesis), San Francisco State College, June, 1969, pp. 1--11 (with some revision for this book).

has repeated interactions and on whom one depends for positive reinforcement of self-image. It is these "significant others" who effect important and permanent changes in the way I see myself.

In this paper I will deal with my interaction with three groups of "others" —white society, black society, and my family. The first two groups include friends, business contacts, and "the man on the street." These two groups have had decreasing significance for me as I have matured and become more capable of understanding both their interpretations of me (largely stereotypes) and the underlying motivations for their feelings. Thus, I have become somewhat hardened to their appeals and with a growing personal strength and confidence, I have attained a degree of immunity to them. At the same time, however, my parents have become increasingly significant in their influence on my self-image. In considering marriage, I am approaching their role as parents and consequently more capable of understanding their point of view.

When I was eighteen years of age, I separated myself from my family— emotionally, financially, and physically—by moving to San Francisco. I had dropped out of school for a year in order to be a full-time political activist involved in the civil rights and anti-war movements. I saw myself as a rebel, an idealist. I felt flexible and open to unlimited new ideas, experiences, and people. The "significant others" in my life were members of my peer group (predominately white) who put the greatest value on intelligence, sensitivity, tolerance, and commitment. My self-image was dependent on the successful expression of these qualities and on the social acceptance of my peers.

Among this group, interracial relationships were very natural, common, and valued positively. When Earl and I began to date, our relationship was accepted by my friends, reinforcing to me, and thus provided a positive influence on my self-image. I felt that I was both broadening my experience and expressing my theoretical commitments. Yet even within this group of friends, I found that my relationship with Earl altered their view of me. The white females expressed curiosity and mild jealousy; the white men became rather defensive and competitive. I was mildly surprised and cynically amused to discover this reaction among the supposedly liberated, radical Left. From this experience, I began to see msyelf as unique and slightly superior to my friends who had never experienced an interracial relationship.

Whenever Earl and I were in public together, we were subject to passing remarks. There were little old ladies who shook their heads in dismay and pointed as we passed. There was a truck driver who shouted "nigger-lover" out of his window. There was a carload of young policemen who rolled down their windows and made obscene noises as they turned the corner where we stood. While traveling in Europe last summer, we were stared at in pure curiosity by young children who had never seen a black man before. Though annoying and momentarily painful, I easily dismissed these incidents. Since these people did not know me and were not responding to me as an individual, I could not take them personally. They were responding rather to a stereotype.

59

In general, such incidents had little effect on my self-image, except to reinforce my feeling of difference and uniqueness.

After we had been together for about nine months, we decided to take a
common residence and began looking for an apartment. The ensuing trans-
actions with realtors and landlords were our first interactions as a couple with
the white society outside of our immediate friends and casual encounters on
the street. Because the realtors and landlords were necessary to us in finding
an apartment, their approval was mandatory and their reactions could not be
ignored. During the past three years, we have, for various reasons, moved
three times—and three times we have experienced the same, or similar, reactions from landlords and realtors. I will combine specific instances from
all three occasions in order to represent the variety of attitudes we encountered
and the effect of each one on my self-image. In general, the situation worsened
each successive year as apartments throughout the city became more limited
and as realtors and landlords became more selective in choosing their tenants.

We began our search very innocently, assuming that the problem was to
find an apartment that we liked and that suited our needs. We soon found
that this was the least of our worries. In our naiveté, we went together to see
realtors, landlords, and apartments. We were repeatedly told that the apartment had been rented and there was nothing else available, that an older
couple was wanted, or that exorbitant rents were required. On several occasions I found an apartment and then told them that my husband was black
to avoid later misunderstandings. I was simply and blatantly refused. Finally,
accepting the immorality and unfairness of these people, we began to use an
equally immoral strategy. We each looked separately; the other would not
appear until the apartment had been rented. Using this tactic, I managed to
rent an apartment. A few days after we had moved in, the landlord frantically
tried to get us to move out. His first approach was to protest that I had broken
a rental agreement that the apartment was to be occupied by only one person.

When this failed, he stated that we were not married so living together was
illegal and immoral. Finally, he admitted his real opposition—the fact that Earl
was black and the fear that the other tenants would move out. The man was
so frightened and upset that I really pitied him and was able to see his side
of the situation. He pleaded with us to find another apartment, offering to
allow us to stay rent-free until we did, and to pay for our moving expenses.
We agreed to this arrangement. After looking unsuccessfully for several weeks,
however, we were visited by the landlord again. This time he offered to let
us stay since there had been no complaints from neighbors and we appeared
to be respectable.

It was rather damaging to my pride to stay on under the circumstances.
However, I realized then that we would probably have the same experience
anywhere we moved, and so decided to stay. The necessity of repeatedly
swallowing my pride has been one of the major effects on my self-image
throughout our apartment-hunting. In order to maintain my self-esteem,
I have transformed that weakness into a strength, considering the loss of pride

to be a positive change. Then the ability to assume a humble role before others without damaging my self-image became a source of pride in itself.

Through our apartment hunting, I came to realize that I was automatically seen and classified as being unrespectable, a tramp, because I was living with a black man. My response was to overcompensate. I made certain that I was always well-dressed and groomed; I behaved with the utmost decorum and respectability; I kept my home immaculately clean. In this way I attempted both to support my image of myself as respectable and to force others to respond to me in a like manner.

On another occasion, I went by myself to a realtor who showed me several apartments, one which I decided on at first sight. Earl and I were to return the following day to sign a rental agreement. When we arrived, however, he explained that we had to complete an application to be approved by the owner, instead of the rental agreement he had discussed previously. The owner refused the application—no reason was given. After much dialogue between the three parties, the owner agreed to a year's lease on the condition that the first and last month's rent be paid in advance and that we pay a cleaning deposit of $100—clearly unreasonable, excessive and prohibitive demands. One conversation between myself and the realtor, in which he expressed a complete spectrum of reactions to me and prompted an equally complete set of responses on my part, is particularly significant.

He began by expressing his sympathy for me, claiming that I would have the same problems all of my life. This reaction sparked feelings of self-pity and a mild sense of not-unpleasant martyrdom on my part. He then became very angry that "a nice girl like me" would have anything to do with a nigger. At this, I too became angry and self-righteous, defending both niggers and myself. When this approach failed, he began to fear for the safety and virtue of his daughter, asking me, in all sincerity, how to prevent this horrible fate from befalling her. My response was a mixture of amusement and pain at the similarity to my own parents' feelings. This was followed by an attempt to make passes at me, asking me to work in his office, and offering to rent an apartment as my husband. (I had encountered this attitude numerous times before—men naturally assume that I am fair game because I am going with a black man. I have learned to ignore the passes and the inferences.) Finally, he expressed respect for my determination and my strength. Strangely, even from this man, the remark was strengthening to my self-image. Yet coming at the end of this long and trying conversation, it sent me into tears of fear and anguish as soon as I was out of his sight.

In many ways my interaction with black people has more influence on my self-image than that with whites. I think this is because, until quite recently, I expected other black people to accept me because Earl did. This turned out to be wrong. Furthermore, black men reacted differently to me than black women.

When Earl and I first began to date on a casual basis, a number of his male friends began to visit me as well. They appeared to have the attitude that a white woman who went out with one black man would go out with any black man. It was a long time before I realized that black people had, pitifully, adopted the stereotypes created by white society. They had so fully accepted their imposed role of inferiority, that they believed (like white society) that any white woman who had a black boyfriend had to be a tramp. Again, I over-compensated in order to disprove this stereotype. In addition to the extreme posture of respectability, I severely limited my relationships with other black men, in most cases to casual acquaintances.

After a period of time, however, the problem of interaction with black men assumed a different nature. A number of Earl's good friends began to respond offensively to me, seeing my middle-class respectability as an attempt to separate myself and Earl from them and from black society in general. During one period of apartment-hunting, one of our friends suggested that we look in the Fillmore district, a black district in San Francisco. When I said that we didn't want to live there, he was insulted and became aggressively angry, telling me that if I didn't want to live with black people I shouldn't marry a black man. Though that wasn't our reason (we don't wish to live in a ghetto, black or white), I sensed a great deal of truth in his comment. I feared that I was, in fact, alienating Earl from his people and forcing him to live in a hostile white world. I realized that in spite of all the problems, I was indeed more comfortable in a predominately white neighborhood and world. Most important, I realized that in my self-image, I still saw myself as white—not black or interracial. Further, the incident reemphasized my separateness and alienation from black, as well as white, society.

I have had very little communication with black women. Nonetheless, their influence is strong; they frighten and intimidate me. A large part of this response is purely projective, based on my intellectual knowledge of their historical position and on one very memorable incident. I will not relate the background of the incident, but I had a lengthy and harrowing face-to-face confrontation with the "strong black woman" personified. She began speaking about poor white trash in general. Then she narrowed in on me in particular, accusing me of dressing-down to go into her neighborhood, of lacking respect for her and other black women, and of wanting to sleep with her men. She concluded by warning me to show respect and to stay away from her black men.

I also understand the historical role of black women in this country which led to the matriarchal family structure. This dominant role made black women somewhat unappealing to many black men. I admire their strength and courage and respect their position in regard to white women. Despite, and because of this, I feel fear and guilt in their presence.

The last and most "significant others" I interact with is my family. As with black women, their effect on me is one of fear and guilt. Amazingly and unfortunately, they do not know anything about Earl. I have not told them because I know what their reaction will be—shock, hurt, and total rejection. I am attempting to save myself and them from this as long as possible. My inability to tell them has created a huge burden of guilt. It makes my relationship with Earl often seem illicit and immoral and my relationship with my family dishonest and incomplete. Earl is so much of my life that they can know little about me without knowing of him. I yearn for my family to share my happiness and love for Earl. To satisfy this need, I have attempted to find substitute parents to approve of our marriage. Almost any middle-aged adult will do, but relatives are preferable. This guilt and consequent anxiety are the most negative elements of my self-image. I have learned to live with these elements because there seems to be no solution. I have attempted to convert them into a form of strength as I did with my hurt pride, by separating this guilt from my self-image.

My present self-image is very much a consequence of my involvement in an interracial relationship. Because the people with whom I daily interact have very distinct impressions of, and reactions to me, I necessarily incorporate their impressions into my self-image. As compared to my self-image of three years ago, I am much less idealistic, much more limited, and my rebellion has gained in depth what it has lost in external expression. At the least, I know that I am a distinct and somehow unique person due to my interracial experience. And I believe that I have gained both in strength and compassion as well. In the face of constant assault, I have learned either to fight or to understand. More important, I have learned that my self-image need not be totally dependent on others' reactions, that I can internally and privately maintain my pride and my dignity in spite of seemingly compromising actions and personal affronts. My hope is that the causal relationship can be reversed, and that the strength of my self-image will come to influence others' very perception of, and reaction to me. While this may never be possible with casual encounters, it seems highly probable that the "significant others" in my life may come to form their idea of me on the basis of personal qualities rather than on my marital role. At the same time, it is difficult to think that others can continue to have as great an influence on me in maturity as they have had in my youth. Based on the hope that these less significant groups will eventually cease to be relevant, I look forward to a more secure future.

Sororities and the Husband Game

John F. Scott

Although parents have lost much authority over their "almost-adult" children with the advent of the Industrial Revolution, they have not lost interest in the life styles their children adopt. All parents want their children to "marry well," or not marry "beneath" them, in terms of social class or occupation chances. The means parents use are subtle—usually centering around exposing their sexually vulnerable offspring to worthwhile mates and sheltering them from the "no-goods." Scott suggests that sororities and fraternities on college campuses perform this dual function of exposure and protection plus offering mating rituals that make relationships—once announced—difficult to rescind. But even these tradition-enforcing institutions are tottering on the brink of obscurity, Scott suggests; they cannot adjust to current student values and needs. When and if they go, one more barrier to cross-class dating and marriage will be gone.

Marriages, like births, deaths, or initiations at puberty, are rearrangements of structure that are constantly recurring in any society; they are moments of the continuing social process regulated by custom; there are institutionalized ways of dealing with such events.

> —A. R. Radcliffe-Brown
> *African Systems of Kinship and Marriage*

In many simple societies, the "institutionalized ways" of controlling marriage run to diverse schemes and devices. Often they include special living quarters designed to make it easy for marriageable girls to attract a husband; the Bontok people of the Philippines keep their girls in a special house, called the *olag*, where lovers call, sex play is free, and marriage is supposed to result. The Ekoi of Nigeria, who like their women fat, send them away to be specially fattened for marriage. Other peoples, such as the Yao of central Africa and the aborigines of the Canary Islands, send their daughters away to "convents"

From John F. Scott, "Sororities and the Husband Game," *TRANS-Action*, September-October, 1965, pp. 10–14. Reprinted by permission of TRANS-Action, New Brunswick, N.J.

where old women teach them the special skills and mysteries that a young wife needs to know.

Accounts of such practices have long been a standard topic of anthropology lectures in universities, for their exotic appeal keeps the students, large numbers of whom are sorority girls, interested and alert. The control of marriage in simple societies strikes these girls as quite different from the freedom that they believe prevails in America. This is ironic, for the American college sorority is a pretty good counterpart in complex societies of the fatting houses and convents of the primitives.

Whatever system they use, parents in all societies have more in mind than just getting their daughters married; they want them married to the *right* man. The criteria for defining the right man vary tremendously, but virtually all parents view some potential mates with approval, some with disapproval, and some with downright horror. Many ethnic groups, including many in America, are *endogamous*, that is, they desire marriage of their young only to those within the group. In *shtetl* society, the Jewish villages of eastern Europe, marriages were arranged by a *shatchen*, a matchmaker, who paired off the girls and boys with due regard to the status, family connections, wealth, and personal attractions of the participants. But this society was strictly endogamous—only marriage within the group was allowed. Another rule of endogamy relates to social rank or class, for most parents are anxious that their children marry at least at the same level as themselves. Often they hope the children, and especially the daughters, will marry at a higher level. Parents of the *shtetl*, for example, valued *hypergamy*—the marriage of daughters to a man of higher status—and a father who could afford it would offer substantial sums to acquire a scholarly husband (the most highly prized kind) for his daughter.

The marriage problem, from the point of view of parents and of various ethnic groups and social classes, is always one of making sure that girls are available for marriage with the right man while at the same time guarding against marriage with the wrong man.

THE UNIVERSITY CONVENT

The American middle class has a particular place where it sends its daughters so they will be easily accessible to the boys—the college campus. Even for the families who worry about the bad habits a nice girl can pick up at college, it has become so much a symbol of middle-class status that the risk must be taken, the girl must be sent. American middle-class society has created an institution on the campus that, like the fatting house, makes the girls more attractive; like the Canary Island convent, teaches skills that middle-class wives need to know; like the *shtetl*, provides matchmakers; and without going so far as to buy husbands of high rank, manages to dissuade the girls from making alliances with lower-class boys. That institution is the college sorority.

A sorority is a private association which provides separate dormitory facilities with a distinctive Greek letter name for selected female college students. Membership is by invitation only, and requires recommendation by former members. Sororities are not simply the feminine counterpart of the college fraternity. They differ from fraternities because marriage is a more important determinant of social position for women than for men in American society, and because standards of conduct associated with marriage correspondingly bear stronger sanctions for women than for men. Sororities have much more "alumnae" involvement than fraternities, and fraternities adapt to local conditions and different living arrangements better than sororities. The college-age sorority "actives" decide only the minor details involved in recruitment, membership, and activities; parent-age alumnae control the important choices. The prototypical sorority is not the servant of youthful interests; on the contrary, it is an organized agency for controlling those interests. Through the sorority, the elders of family, class, ethnic, and religious communities can continue to exert remote control over the marital arrangements of their young girls.

The need for remote control arises from the nature of the educational system in an industrial society. In simple societies, where children are taught the culture at home, the family controls the socialization of children almost completely. In more complex societies, education becomes the province of special agents and competes with the family. The conflict between the family and outside agencies increases as children move through the educational system and is sharpest when the children reach college age. College curricula are even more challenging to family value systems than high school courses, and children frequently go away to college, out of reach of direct family influence. Sometimes a family can find a college that does not challenge family values in any way: devout Catholic parents can send their daughters to Catholic colleges; parents who want to be sure that daughter meets only "Ivy League" men can send her to one of the "Seven Sisters"—the women's equivalent of the Ivy League, made up of Radcliffe, Barnard, Smith, Vassar, Wellesley, Mt. Holyoke, and Bryn Mawr, if she can get in.

The solution of controlled admissions is applicable only to a small proportion of college-age girls, however. There are nowhere near the number of separate, sectarian colleges in the country that would be needed to segregate all the college-age girls safely, each with her own kind. Private colleges catering mostly to a specific class can still preserve a girl from meeting her social or economic inferiors, but the fees at such places are steep. It costs more to maintain a girl in the Vassar dormitories than to pay her sorority bills at a land grant school. And even if her family is willing to pay the fees, the academic pace at the elite schools is much too fast for most girls. Most college girls attend large, tax-supported universities where the tuition is relatively low and where admissions policies let in students from many strata and diverse ethnic backgrounds. It is on the campuses of the free, open, and competitive state universities of the country that the sorority system flourishes.

When a family lets its daughter loose on a large campus with a heterogenous population, there are opportunities to be met and dangers to guard against. The great opportunity is to meet a good man to marry, at the age when the girls are most attractive and the men most amenable. For the girls, the pressure of time is urgent; though they are often told otherwise, their attractions are in fact primarily physical, and they fade with time. One need only compare the relative handicaps in the marital sweepstakes of a 38-year-old single male lawyer and a single, female teacher of the same age to realize the urgency of the quest.

The great danger of the public campus is that young girls, however properly reared, are likely to fall in love, and—in our middle-class society at least—love leads to marriage. Love is a potentially random factor, with no regard for class boundaries. There seems to be no good way of preventing young girls from falling in love. The only practical way to control love is to control the type of men the girl is likely to encounter; she cannot fall dangerously in love with a man she has never met. Since kinship groups are unable to keep "undesirable" boys off the public campus entirely, they have to settle for control of counter-institutions within the university. An effective counter-institution will protect a girl from the corroding influences of the university environment.

There are roughly three basic functions which a sorority can perform in the interest of kinship groups:

> It can ward off the wrong kind of men.
> It can facilitate moving-up for middle-status girls.
> It can solve the "Brahmin problem"—the difficulty of proper marriage that afflicts high-status girls.

Kinship groups define the "wrong kind of man" in a variety of ways. Those who use an ethnic definition support sororities that draw an ethnic membership line; the best examples are the Jewish sororities, because among all the ethnic groups with endogamous standards (in America at any rate), only the Jews so far have sent large numbers of daughters away to college. But endogamy along class lines is even more pervasive. It is the most basic mission of the sorority to prevent a girl from marrying out of her group (exogamy) or beneath her class (hypogamy). As one of the founders of a national sorority artlessly put it in an essay titled "The Mission of the Sorority":

> There is a danger, and a very grave danger, that four years' residence in a dormitory will tend to destroy right ideals of home life and substitute in their stead a belief in the freedom that comes from community living . . . culture, broad, liberalizing, humanizing culture, we cannot get too much of, unless while acquiring it we are weaned from home and friends, from ties of blood and kindred.

A sorority discourages this dangerous weaning process by introducing the sisters only to selected boys. Each sorority, for example, has dating relations with one or more fraternities matched rather nicely to the sorority on the basis of ethnicity and/or class. (A particular sorority, for example, will have dating arrangements not with all the fraternities on campus, but only with those whose brothers are a class-match for their sisters. The sorority's frantically busy schedule of parties, teas, meetings, skits, and exchanges keeps the sisters so occupied that they have neither time nor opportunity to meet men outside the channels the sorority provides.

Marrying Up

The second sorority function, that of facilitating hypergamy, is probably even more of an attraction to parents than the simpler preservation of endogamy. American society is not so much oriented to the preservation of the *status quo* as to the pursuit of upward mobility.

In industrial societies, children are taught that if they study hard they can get the kind of job that entitles them to a place in the higher ranks. This incentive actually is appropriate only for boys, but the emphasis on using the most efficient available means to enter the higher levels will not be lost on the girls. And the most efficient means for a girl—marriage—is particularly attractive because it requires so much less effort than the mobility through hard work that is open to boys. To the extent that we do socialize the sexes in different ways, we are more likely to train daughters in the ways of attracting men than to motivate them to do hard, competitive work. The difference in motivation holds even if the girls have the intelligence and talent required for status climbing on their own. For lower-class girls on the make, membership in a sorority can greatly improve the chances of meeting (and subsequently marrying) higher-status boys.

Now we come to the third function of the sorority—solving the Brahmin problem. The fact that hypergamy is encouraged in our society creates difficulties for girls whose parents are already in the upper strata. In a hypergamous system, high-status *men* have a strong advantage; they can offer their status to a prospective bride as part of the marriage bargain and the advantages of high status are often sufficient to offset many personal drawbacks. But a *woman's* high status has very little exchange value because she does not confer it on her husband.

This difficulty of high status women in a hypergamous society we may call the Brahmin problem. Girls of Brahmin caste in India and Southern white women of good family have the problem in common. In order to avoid the horrors of hypogamy, high-status women must compete for high-status men against women from all classes. Furthermore, high-status women are handicapped in their battle by a certain type of vanity engendered by their class. They expect their wooers to court them in the style to which their fathers have accustomed them; this usually involves more formal dating, gift-giving, escorting, taxiing, etc., than many college swains can afford. If upper-stratum men are allowed to find out that the favors of lower-class women are available for a much smaller investment of time, money, and emotion, they may well refuse to court upper-status girls.

In theory, there are all kinds of ways for upper-stratum families to deal with surplus daughters. They can strangle them at birth (female infanticide) ; they can marry several to each available male (polygyny) ; they can offer money to any suitable male willing to take one off their hands (dowries, groom-service fees). All these solutions have in fact been used in one society or another, but for various reasons none is acceptable in our society. Spinsterhood still works, but marriage is so popular and so well rewarded that everybody hopes to avoid staying single.

The industrial solution to the Brahmin problem is to corner the market, or more specifically to shunt the eligible bachelors into a special marriage market where the upper-stratum women are incomplete control of the bride-supply. The best place to set up this protected marriage-market is where many suitable men can be found at the age when they are most willing to marry—in short, the college campus. The kind of male collegians who can be shunted more readily into the specialized marriage-market that sororities run are those who are somewhat uncertain of their own status and who aspire to move into higher strata. These boys are anxious to bolster a shaky self-image by dating obviously high-class sorority girls. The fraternities are full of them.

How does a sorority go about fulfilling its three functions? The first item of business is making sure that the girls join. This is not as simple as it seems, because the values that sororities maintain are more important to the older generation than to college-age girls. Although the sorority image is one of membership denied to the "wrong kind" of girls, it is also true that sororities have quite a problem of recruiting the "right kind." Some are pressured into pledging by their parents. Many are recruited straight out of high school, before they know much about what really goes on at college. High school recruiters present sorority life to potential rushees as one of unending gaiety; life outside the sorority is painted as bleak and dateless.

A membership composed of the "right kind" of girls is produced by the requirement that each pledge must have the recommendation of, in most cases, two or more alumnae of the sorority. Membership is often passed on from mother to daughter—this is the "legacy," whom sorority actives have to invite whether they like her or not. The sort of headstrong, innovative, or "sassy" girl who is likely to organize a campaign inside the sorority against prevailing standards is unlikely to receive alumnae recommendations. This is why sorority girls are so complacent about alumnae dominance, and why professors find them so bland and uninteresting as students. Alumnae dominance extends beyond recruitment, into the daily life of the house. Rules, regulations, and policy explanations come to the house from the national association. National headquarters is given to explaining unpopular policy by any available strategem; a favorite device (not limited to the sorority) is to interpret all nonconformity as sexual, so that the girl who rebels against wearing girdle, high heels, and stockings to dinner two or three times a week stands implicitly

69

accused of promiscuity. This sort of argument, based on the shrewdness of many generations, shames into conformity many a girl who otherwise might rebel against the code imposed by her elders. The actives in positions of control (house manager, pledge trainer or captain) are themselves closely supervised by alumnae. Once the right girls are initiated, the organization has mechanisms that make it very difficult for a girl to withdraw. Withdrawal can mean difficulty in finding alternative living quarters, loss of prepaid room and board fees, and stigmatization.

Sororities keep their members, and particularly their flighty pledges, in line primarily by filling up all their time with house activities. Pledges are required to study at the house, and they build the big paper-mache floats (in collaboration with selected fraternity boys) that are a traditional display of "Greek Row" for the homecoming game. Time is encompassed completely; activities are planned long in advance, and there is almost no energy or time available for meeting inappropriate men.

The girls are taught—if they do not already know—the behavior appropriate to the upper strata. They learn how to dress with expensive restraint, how to make appropriate conversation, how to drink like a lady. There is some variety here among sororities of different rank; members of sororities at the bottom of the social ladder prove their gentility by rigid conformity in dress and manner to the stereotype of the sorority girl, while members of top houses feel socially secure even when casually dressed. If you are born rich you can afford to wear Levi's and sweatshirts.

PRELIMINARY EVENTS

The sorority facilitates dating mainly by exchanging parties, picnics, and other frolics with the fraternities in its set. But to augment this the "fixer-uppers" (the American counterpart of the *shatchen*) arrange dates with selected boys; their efforts raise the sorority dating rate above the independent level by removing most of the inconvenience and anxiety from the contracting of dates.

Dating, in itself, is not sufficient to accomplish the sorority's purposes. Dating must lead to pinning, pinning to engagement, engagement to marriage. In sorority culture, all dating is viewed as a movement toward marriage. Casual, spontaneous dating is frowned upon; formal courtship is still encouraged. Sorority ritual reinforces the progression from dating to marriage. At the vital point in the process, where dating must be turned into engagement, the sorority shores up the structure by the pinning ritual, performed after dinner in the presence of all the sorority sisters (who are required to stay for the ceremony) and attended, in its classic form, by a choir of fraternity boys singing outside. The commitment is so public that it is difficult for either partner to withdraw. Since engagement is already heavily reinforced outside the sorority, pinning ceremonies are more elaborate than engagements.

70

The social columns of college newspapers faithfully record the successes of the sorority system as it stands today. Sorority girls get engaged faster than "independents," and they appear to be marrying more highly ranked men. But what predictions can we make about the system's future?

All social institutions change from time to time, in response to changing conditions. In the mountain villages of the Philippines, the steady attacks of school and mission on the immorality of the *olag* have almost demolished it. Sororities, too, are affected by changes in the surrounding environment. Originally they were places where the few female college students took refuge from the jeers and catcalls of men who thought that nice girls didn't belong on campus. They assumed their present, endogamy-conserving form with the flourishing of the great land-grant universities in the first half of this century.

On the Brink

The question about the future of the sorority system is whether it can adapt to the most recent changes in the forms of higher education. At present, neither fraternities nor sororities are in the pink of health. On some campuses there are chapter houses which have been reduced to taking in non-affiliated boarders to pay the costs of running the property. New sorority chapters are formed, for the most part, on new or low-prestige campuses (where status-anxiety is rife); at schools of high prestige fewer girls rush each year and the weaker houses are disbanding.

University administrations are no longer as hospitable to the Greeks as they once were. Most are building extensive dormitories that compete effectively with the housing offered by sororities; many have adopted regulations intended to minimize the influence of the Greeks on campus activities. The campus environment is changing rapidly; academic standards are rising, admission is increasingly competitive, and both male and female students are more interested in academic achievement; the proportion of graduate students seriously training for a profession is increasing; campus culture is often so obviously pluralist that the Greek claim to monopolize social activity is unconvincing.

The sorority as it currently stands is ill-adapted to cope with the new surroundings. Sorority houses were built to provide a setting for lawn parties, dances, and dress-up occasions, and not to facilitate study; crowding and noise are severe, and most forms of privacy do not exist. The sorority songs that have to be gone through at rushing and chapter meetings today all seem to have been written in 1915 and are mortifying to sing today. The arcane rituals, so fascinating to high school girls, grow tedious and sophomoric to college seniors.

But the worst blow of all to the sorority system comes from the effect of increased academic pressure on the dating habits of college men. A student competing for grades in a professional school, or even in a difficult undergraduate major, simply has not the time (as he might have had in, say, 1925) to get involved in the sorority forms of courtship. Since these days almost all the "right kind" of men *are* involved in demanding training, the traditions of the sorority are becoming actually inimical to hypergamous marriage. Increasingly, then, sororities do not solve the Brahmin problem but make it worse.

One can imagine a sorority designed to facilitate marriage to men who have no time for elaborate courtship. In such a sorority, the girls—to start with small matters—would improve their telephone arrangements, for the fraternity boy in quest of a date today must call several times to get through the busy signals, interminable paging, and lost messages to the girl he wants. They might arrange a private line with prompt answering and faithfully recorded messages, with an unlisted number given only to busy male students with a promising future. They would even accept dates for the same night as the invitation, rather than, as at present, necessarily five to ten days in advance, for the only thing a first-year law student can schedule that far ahead nowadays is his studies. Emphasis on fraternity boys would have to go, for living in a fraternity and pursuing a promising (and therefore competitive) major field of study are rapidly becoming mutually exclusive. The big formal dances would go (the fraternity boys dislike them now); the football floats would go; the pushcart races would go. The girls would reach the hearts of their men not through helping them wash their sports cars but through typing their term papers.

But it is inconceivable that the proud traditions of the sororities that compose the National Panhellenic Council could ever be bent to fit the new design. Their structure is too fixed to fit the changing college and their function is rapidly being lost. The sorority cannot sustain itself on students alone. When parents learn that membership does not benefit their daughters, the sorority as we know it will pass into history.

Campus Values in
Mate Selection: A Replication

John W. Hudson and

Lura Henze

Do some criteria by which people judge possible marriage partners remain constant over time despite major changes in the society at large? Hudson and Henze's research suggests this is indeed the case. When college students were asked to rank various characteristics desirable in a mate, the answers were very close to 1939 and 1956 parallel studies. Major changes were a reduced interest in chastity, which reflects the sexual revolution, and an increased interest (or honesty) among males about preferences for beauty in their female partners.

Past research indicates the influence of social class and family in the mate selection process which, in large part, accounts for the endogamous (restriction of marriage to members of the same tribe, caste, or social group) quality of mate selection.[1]

It has long been recognized that the family is the major agency of socialization. While the process of socialization never ends, it does decelerate with most learning taking place when the person is young.[2] The choice of a mate is limited by the individual's formation of generalized-value systems before maturation.[3] Values learned early in life tend to persist.

In the mass media, college students are often depicted as having departed

From John W. Hudson and Lura F. Henze, "Campus Values in Mate Selection: A Replication," *Journal of Marriage and the Family*, November, 1969, pp. 772–78. Reprinted by permission of the author and The National Council on Family Relations. This is a slightly revised version of a paper prepared for presentation to the annual meetings of the Rocky Mountain Social Science Association, Denver, Colorado, May 3-4, 1968. This research was supported by a grant from Arizona State University. We are indebted to John A. Ballweg, James R. Hudson, George Kupfer, and the registrar at Arizona State University for their part in drawing the random samples at their universities.

from the traditional values of the society.[4] Thus, the youth of today are frequently charged with being less serious in mate selection than were young people a generation ago. Is this mass media image valid?

Since societal values regarding the family tend to change slowly, it is to be expected that values expressed in mate selection would vary little from one generation to the next. Parents play highly significant roles in the courtship of their children in that they have much to do with the kind of person the child will choose as a mate.[5] Whether consciously or unconsciously, the person's value system serves as criteria for mate selection.

The thesis of this paper is that the value system of the current college population regarding mate selection is not as different from the college population of a generation ago as thought by parents and portrayed by the mass media.

To compare values in mate selection held by college students today with those of earlier years, the literature was reviewed for relevant research. This review indicated that among the studies cited most often were the "Campus Values in Mate Selection" done by Hill and McGinnis.[6] These studies were selected for replication as they focused on personal characteristics related to mate selection and because the students who were the respondents in 1939 are the parental generation of today.

The earlier studies of "Campus Values in Mate Selection" were done at the University of Wisconsin in 1939 by Reuben Hill and in 1956 by Robert McGinnis. In the initial study by Hill, participants were enrolled in a non-credit marriage course. In the 1956 study McGinnis drew a one-percent systematic sample from the university student directory.

Procedures

To broaden the base of this study, an investigation was conducted on four campuses located in widely separated geographic regions—three in the United States and one in Canada. The American colleges selected were Arizona State University, the University of Nebraska at Omaha, and the State University of New York at Stony Brook. The Canadian college chosen was the University of Alberta at Edmonton.

A copy of the "Campus Values" questionnaire, together with a cover letter explaining the nature of the study and a postage-paid return envelope, was mailed to each student in the sample. The original questionnaire had been prepared by Reuben Hill and Harold T. Christensen.

Description of the Questionnaire

Included in the questionnaire were the usual background items of age, sex, marital status, education, and family data. The evaluative section included preferences on age at time of marriage, age difference between husband and wife, number of children, and personal characteristics. The personal characteristics were 18 traits to be evaluated according to their degree of importance in choosing a mate. Provision was made for the respondent to add any further personal characteristics which he felt should be included.

Students were asked to assign a numerical weight of "three" to characteristics which they believed were indispensable, "two" to traits important but not indispensable, "one" to those desirable but not important, and "zero" to factors irrelevant in mate selection. Thus, respondents evaluated each trait and assigned an appropriate numerical weight to each; the investigators then ranked the traits on the basis of mean values computed from the numerical weights. For the purposes of this paper, the terms "ranked" and "evaluated" are used synonymously.

Description of the Sample

A one-percent random sample of full-time students at each of the four universities was drawn by the registrars' offices. Questionnaires were mailed to a total of 826 students; 566 (68.5 percent) were returned and usable.

The sample included 337 males and 229 females. The median age was 21.6 years for men and 20.4 years for women. Seventy-six percent of the men and 82 percent of the women were single.

FINDINGS

Age Factors in Mate Selection

College men and women in the 1967 sample indicated a preference for marriage at an earlier age than had been indicated in the previous studies. (See Table 1.) The median preferred age at marriage for men in 1939 was 25.1 years and was 24.9 years for the 1956 sample. The age preference dropped to 24.5 years in 1967. The median age preference for women in 1939 was 24.0 years, and in 1956 and 1967, it declined to 22.9 and 22.5 years, respectively.

TABLE 1.
MEDIAN PREFERENCES (BY SEX AND YEAR) REGARDING AGE AT MARRIAGE, DIFFERENCE IN AGE BETWEEN HUSBAND AND WIFE, AND NUMBER OF CHILDREN

YEAR	PREFERRED AGE AT MARRIAGE		PREFERRED AGE DIFFERENCE BETWEEN HUSBAND AND WIFE		PREFERRED NUMBER OF CHILDREN	
	M	F	M	F	M	F
1939	25.1	24.0	2.3	3.4	3.3	3.5
1956	24.9	22.9	1.2	2.1	3.6	3.9
1967	24.5	22.5	1.5	2.0	2.9	3.3

In all three studies, males and females agreed that the husband should be older than the wife but did not agree on the preferred age difference. Women preferred a greater age gap between spouses than did men.

Number of Children Preferred

In all three time periods investigated, women preferred more children than did men. The trend was toward more children wanted by men and women in 1956 (3.6 and 3.9) than in 1939 (3.3 and 3.5), and fewer children in 1967 (2.9 and 3.3) than in either of the earlier periods.

Personal Factors in Mate Selection

The data indicate that from one time period to the next, three of the 18 items, as evaluated by men, maintained the same rank and 11 did not vary by more than one place. (See Table 2.) Males, in all three studies, evaluated dependable character as the most indispensable personal characteristic in a mate. Sociability and favorable social status consistently held their rank of twelfth and sixteenth place, respectively, in 1939, 1956, and 1967.

TABLE 2.
RANK OF 18 PERSONAL CHARACTERISTICS IN MATE SELECTION
BASED ON MEAN VALUE, BY YEAR AND SEX

	MALE			FEMALE		
	1939	1956	1967	1939	1956	1967
1. Dependable character	1	1	1	2	1	2
2. Emotional stability	2	2	3	1	2	1
3. Pleasing disposition	3	4	4	4	5	4
4. Mutual attraction	4	3	2	5	6	3
5. Good health	5	6	9	6	9	10
6. Desire for home-children	6	5	5	7	3	5
7. Refinement	7	8	7	8	7	8
8. Good cook-housekeeper	8	7	6	16	16	16
9. Ambition-industriousness	9	9	8	3	4	6
10. Chastity	10	13	15	10	15	15
11. Education-intelligence	11	11	10	9	14	7
12. Sociability	12	12	12	11	11	13
13. Similar religious background	13	10	14	14	10	11
14. Good looks	14	15	11	17	18	17
15. Similar educational background	15	14	13	12	8	9
16. Favorable social status	16	16	16	15	13	14
17. Good financial prospect	17	17	18	13	12	12
18. Similar political background	18	18	17	18	17	18

Chastity, as evaluated by men, declined to a greater degree than did any other characteristic. This was indicated by mean scores as well as by rank.

In 1939 the mean score for chastity was 2.06, and in 1967 it was 1.28. In rank, the decline was from tenth place to fifteenth.

Greater emphasis was placed on good looks by males in 1967 than in either of the earlier studies. During the time period under study, health declined in importance from fifth to ninth place. The traits which moved consistently upward from 1939 to 1967 were mutual attraction, good cook-housekeeper, and similar educational background—each moved up two positions. The characteristic which fluctuated the most was similar religious background, which changed from thirteenth place in 1939 to tenth in 1956 and declined to fourteenth in 1967.

In the responses by women, no trait was consistently evaluated as more important in 1956 and 1967 than it had been in 1939. One of the 18 traits— good cook-housekeeper—ranked sixteenth in all three studies; the rank of eight other traits did not vary by more than one place. Emotional stability and dependable character ranked first or second in each time period studied. Women gave the least weight to good looks and similar political background.

For women, the evaluation of chastity declined to a greater extent than for any other characteristic. This was indicated by mean scores and by rank. The mean score for chastity was 2.0 in 1939 and .93 in 1967, while the rank in 1939 was tenth and in 1956 and 1967 it was fifteenth. Ambition, good health, and sociability moved downward with consistency. Fluctuation was greatest for education-intelligence, which ranked ninth in 1939, fourteenth in 1956, and seventh in 1967.

Male and female responses to the additional question asking for further characteristics felt to be important in mate selection were insufficient to warrant analysis.

Preliminary analysis of data from the four colleges indicates no significant differences in student responses from one campus to the others. Analysis of data from each of the campuses will be reported in a subsequent paper.

CONCLUSIONS

Preference in Age Factors

This study has indicated that the preferred age at first marriage has continued to show a decline since the 1939 study. A sidelight of the younger age at first marriage in the United States has been an increase in the proportion of college students who marry and remain in school.[7] It has been noted by other writers that, while student marriage was not unknown during the 1930s, it was not widespread.[8] Prior to World War II married students were rare and frequently prohibited from enrollment. Today they are an accepted fact.

From discussions with college students, the investigators have concluded that there has been increased emphasis on dating at the pre-teen level and that this pattern has been initiated largely by parents and school systems. According to students, a further parental influence in the early stages of dating has been the insistence that dating partners be drawn from the same age and social group. This early requirement of dating a person from the same age group structures the subsequent dating pattern. Since mate selection is a function of whom one dates, the age gap between husband and wife has narrowed in terms of preferences stated by college students and according to Parke and Glick.[9]

The overall decline in preferred age at first marriage is probably a reflection of both economic conditions and the current high value placed on marriage. The convergence in agreement on age differential is probably the result, in part, of changes in dating and mate selection patterns as well as changes in female status.

Preference in Number of Children

The findings do not constitute an adequate basis for predictions of future birth rates. Birth rates and desired number of children are very sensitive to social and cultural conditions. Thus, little significance can be attached to changes in the number of children wanted by students in 1939, 1956, and 1967 since factors which influence preferences are closely linked to cycles and fashions of the time.

Personal Characteristics

When the 18 characteristics were ranked and a comparison was made between the findings of the three studies, it became apparent that over the years there has been a striking consistency in student valuation of desired traits in a mate. For example, college students today assign the same importance to dependable character as did college students a generation ago.

Good health, as evaluated by both men and women, has become less important in mate selection. This is probably a reflection of the general improvement in overall health which has, in part, resulted from the increased availability of comprehensive medical services and health insurance.

The personal characteristic which evidenced the greatest decline in rank was chastity. Although chastity ranked in fifteenth place for both sexes in 1967, this does not indicate that the same importance is placed on this factor by men and by women. When the mean values are examined, it is evident that the double standard is still operating. Men continue to evaluate virginity as a more important characteristic for a wife than women do for a husband, as evidenced by the mean scores. It should be noted that the lowered evaluation of chastity may not indicate that it is less important; the change in rank may simply indicate that other attributes have become more meaningful since the time of the Hill study.

SUMMARY

While this study does not clearly and precisely add to theory construction, it does add substantive material which suggests generational stability in criteria used in mate selection. For although a child may rebel against domination, he cannot escape the ideas conditioned in him from his childhood.[10]

In 1967, compared to 1939, there have been changes in the behavior patterns of the college populations studied in terms of age factors in mate selection and in marrying while in college. However, this change is compatible with the high value placed on marriage by the parental generation—who were the college students of 1939—and the younger generation who are the students today.

The charge that young people have departed from traditional values and are less serious about mate selection is not given support by the present study. Indeed, the findings suggest that youth's values regarding the importance of personal characteristics in mate selection are much the same today as they were a generation ago.

It might be said in conclusion that social change in the area of mate selection has not been as great as indicated by the press, feared by the parent, and perhaps hoped by the youth.

NOTES

[1] Ira L. Reiss, "Social Class and Campus Dating," *Social Problems*, 13:2 (Fall, 1965), p. 195. August B. Hollingshead, "Cultural Factors in the Selection of Marriage Mates," *American Sociological Review*, 15 (October, 1960), p. 627.

[2] Kingsley Davis, "The Sociology of Parent-Youth Conflict," *American Sociological Review*, 5 (August, 1940), p. 524.

[3] Marvin B. Sussman, *Sourcebook in Marriage and the Family*, Boston: Houghton Mifflin Company, 2nd ed., 1963, p. 63.

[4] Stephen Birmingham, "American Youth: A Generation Under the Gun," *Holiday*, 37 (March 1, 1965), p. 44.

[5] Alan Bates, "Parental Roles in Courtship," *Social Forces*, 20 (May, 1942), p. 483.

[6] Reuben Hill, "Campus Values in Mate Selection," *Journal of Home Economics*, 37 (November, 1945). Robert McGinnis, "Campus Values in Mate Selection: A Report Study," *Social Forces*, 36 (May, 1959).

[7] Paul C. Glick, *American Families*, New York: John Wiley and Sons, Inc., 1957, p. 57.

[8] Jessie Bernard, *Dating, Mating and Marriage*, Cleveland: Howard Allen, Inc., 1958, pp. 217–218. Victor A. Christopherson and Joseph S. Vandiver, "The Married College Student, 1959," *Marriage and Family Living*, 22 (May, 1960), p. 122. Ernest Haveman, "To Love, Honor, Obey and Study," *Life*, 38:21 (May 23, 1955), p. 152.

[9] Robert Parke, Jr., and Paul C. Glick, "Prospective Changes in Marriage and the Family," *Journal of Marriage and the Family*, 29:2 (May, 1967), p. 249.

[10] Robert H. Coombs, "Reinforcement of Values in the Parental Home as a Factor in Mate Selection," *Marriage and Family Living*, 24 (May, 1962), p. 155.

The Theory of Love

Erich Fromm

Any discussion of courtship in the United States would be incomplete without a discussion of love. Unlike less industrially developed countries, love is a primary criterion for the selection of a partner in the West. Yet love is a complicated and little understood phenomenon. Sociologists have done very little to fill this void with findings from empirical research. We must turn to Fromm, a social psychologist, for a discussion of the nature of love and its place in human existence. Fromm's analysis starts with man's need for social bonds, without which he would be in unbearable aloneness. Fromm discusses the many ways in which man has attempted to overcome this aloneness, some of which result in drug use, others in creation of community, others in creativity. Loving of another person is giving to oneself as it brings great joy to the giver. The type of personality capable of this mature love and the criteria for its existence are also discussed.

LOVE, THE ANSWER TO THE PROBLEM OF HUMAN EXISTENCE

Any theory of love must begin with a theory of man, of human existence. While we find love, or rather, the equivalent of love, in animals, their attachments are mainly a part of their instinctual equipment; only remnants of this instinctual equipment can be seen operating in man. What is essential in the existence of man is the fact that he has emerged from the animal kingdom, from instinctive adaptation, that he has transcended nature—although he never leaves it; he is a part of it—and yet once torn away from nature, he cannot return to it; once thrown out of paradise—a state of original oneness with nature—cherubim with flaming swords block his way, if he should try to return. Man can only go forward by developing his reason, by finding a new

From Erich Fromm, *The Art of Loving* (New York: Harper & Row, Publishers, 1956), pp. 7–10, 11–14, 16–21, 22–24, 26–33. Reprinted by permission of Harper & Row, Publishers, and Allen & Unwin, London.

harmony, a human one, instead of the prehuman harmony which is irretrievably lost.

When man is born, the human race as well as the individual, he is thrown out of a situation which was definite, as definite as the instincts, into a situation which is indefinite, uncertain and open. There is certainty only about the past—and about the future only as far as that it is death.

Man is gifted with reason; he is *life being aware of itself;* he has awareness of himself, of his fellow man, of his past, and of the possibilities of his future. This awareness of himself as a separate entity, the awareness of his own short life span, of the fact that without his will he is born and against his will he dies, that he will die before those whom he loves, or they before him, the awareness of his aloneness and separateness, of his helplessness before the forces of nature and society, all this makes his separate, disunited existence an unbearable prison. He would become insane could he not liberate himself from this prison and reach out, unite himself in some form or other with men, with the world outside.

The experience of separateness arouses anxiety; it is, indeed, the source of all anxiety. Being separate means being cut off, without any capacity to use my human powers. Hence to be separate means to be helpless, unable to grasp the world—things and people—actively; it means that the world can invade me without my ability to react. Thus, separateness is the source of intense anxiety. Beyond that, it arouses shame and the feeling of guilt. This experience of guilt and shame in separateness is expressed in the Biblical story of Adam and Eve. After Adam and Eve have eaten of the "tree of knowledge of good and evil," after they have disobeyed (there is no good and evil unless there is freedom to disobey), after they have become human by having emancipated themselves from the original animal harmony with nature, i.e., after their birth as human beings—they saw "that they were naked—and they were ashamed." Should we assume that a myth as old and elementary as this has the prudish morals of the nineteenth-century outlook, and that the important point the story wants to convey to us is the embarrassment that their genitals were visible? This can hardly be so, and by understanding the story in a Victorian spirit, we miss the main point, which seems to be the following: after man and woman have become aware of themselves and of each other, they are aware of their separateness, and of their difference, inasmuch as they belong to different sexes. But while recognizing their separateness they remain strangers, because they have not yet learned to love each other (as is also made very clear by the fact that Adam defends himself by blaming Eve, rather than by trying to defend her). *The awareness of human separation, without reunion by love—is the source of shame. It is at the same time the source of guilt and anxiety.*

The deepest need of man, then, is the need to overcome his separateness, to leave the prison of his aloneness. The *absolute* failure to achieve this aim means insanity, because the panic of complete isolation can be overcome only by such a radical withdrawal from the world outside that the feeling of

81

separation disappears—because the world outside, from which one is separated, has disappeared.

Man—of all ages and cultures—is confronted with the solution of one and the same question: the question of how to overcome separateness, how to achieve union, how to transcend one's own individual life and find at-onement. The question is the same for primitive man living in caves, for nomadic man taking care of his flocks, for the peasant in Egypt, the Phoenician trader, the Roman soldier, the medieval monk, the Japanese samurai, the modern clerk and factory hand. The question is the same, for it springs from the same ground: the human situation, the conditions of human existence. The answer varies. The question can be answered by animal worship, by human sacrifice or military conquest, by indulgence in luxury, by ascetic renunciation, by obsessional work, by artistic creation, by the love of God, and by the love of Man. While there are many answers—the record of which is human history— they are nevertheless not innumerable. On the contrary, as soon as one ignores smaller differences which belong more to the periphery than to the center, one discovers that there is only a limited number of answers which have been given, and only could have been given by man in the various cultures in which he has lived. The history of religion and philosophy is the history of these answers, of their diversity, as well as of their limitation in number.

The answers depend, to some extent, on the degree of individuation which an individual has reached. In the infant I-ness has developed but little yet; he still feels one with mother, has no feeling of separateness as long as mother is present. His sense of aloneness is cured by the physical presence of the mother, her breasts, her skin. Only to the degree that the child develops his sense of separateness and individuality is the physical presence of the mother not sufficient any more, and does the need to overcome separateness in other ways arise.

· · · ·

One way of achieving this aim lies in all kinds of *orgiastic states*. These may have the form of an auto-induced trance, sometimes with the help of drugs. Many rituals of primitive tribes offer a vivid picture of this type of solution. In a transitory state of exaltation the world outside disappears, and with it the feeling of separateness from it. Inasmuch as these rituals are practiced in common, an experience of fusion with the group is added which makes this solution all the more effective. Closely related to, and often blended with this orgiastic solution, is the sexual experience. The sexual orgasm can produce a state similar to the one produced by a trance, or to the effects of certain drugs. Rites of communal sexual orgies were a part of many primitive rituals. It seems that after the orgiastic experience, man can go on for a time without suffering too much from his separateness. Slowly the tension of anxiety mounts, and then is reduced again by the repeated performance of the ritual.

As long as these orgiastic states are a matter of common practice in a tribe, they do not produce anxiety or guilt. To act in this way is right, and even virtuous, because it is a way shared by all, approved and demanded by the medicine men or priests; hence there is no reason to feel guilty or ashamed. It is quite different when the same solution is chosen by an individual in a culture which has left behind these common practices. Alcoholism and drug addiction are the forms which the individual chooses in a non-orgiastic culture. In contrast to those participating in the socially patterned solution, such individuals suffer from guilt feelings and remorse. While they try to escape from separateness by taking refuge in alcohol or drugs, they feel all the more separate after the orgiastic experience is over, and thus are driven to take recourse to it with increasing frequency and intensity. Slightly different from this is the recourse to a sexual orgiastic solution. To some extent it is a natural and normal form of overcoming separateness, and a partial answer to the problem of isolation. But in many individuals in whom separateness is not relieved in other ways, the search for the sexual orgasm assumes a function which makes it not very different from alcoholism and drug addiction. It becomes a desperate attempt to escape the anxiety engendered by separateness, and it results in an ever-increasing sense of separateness, since the sexual act without love never bridges the gap between two human beings, except momentarily.

All forms of orgiastic union have three characteristics: they are intense, even violent; they occur in the total personality, mind *and* body; they are transitory and periodical. Exactly the opposite holds true for that form of union which is by far the most frequent solution chosen by man in the past and in the present: the union based on *conformity* with the group, its customs, practices and beliefs. Here again we find a considerable development.

In a primitive society the group is small; it consists of those with whom one shares blood and soil. With the growing development of culture, the group enlarges; it becomes the citizenry of a *polis*, the citizenry of a large state, the members of a church. Even the poor Roman felt pride because he could say *"civis romanus sum"*; Rome and the Empire were his family, his home, his world. Also in contemporary Western society the union with the group is the prevalent way of overcoming separateness. It is a union in which the individual self disappears to a large extent, and where the aim is to belong to the herd. If I am like everybody else, if I have no feelings or thoughts which make me different, if I conform in custom, dress, ideas, to the pattern of the group, I am saved; saved from the frightening experience of aloneness. The dictatorial systems use threats and terror to induce this conformity; the democratic countries, suggestion and propaganda. There is, indeed, one great difference between the two systems. In the democracies non-conformity is possible and, in fact, by no means entirely absent; in the totalitarian systems, only a few unusual heroes and martyrs can be expected to refuse obedience. But in spite of this difference the democratic societies show an overwhelming degree of conformity. The reason lies in the fact that there *has* to be an answer to the quest for union, and if there is no other or better way, then the union of herd conformity becomes the predominant one. One can only understand the power of the fear to be different, the fear to be only a few steps away from the herd, if one understands the depths of the need not to be separated. Sometimes this fear of non-conformity is rationalized as fear of practical dangers which could threaten the non-conformist. But actually, people *want* to conform to a much higher degree than they are *forced* to conform, at least in the Western democracies.

Most people are not even aware of their need to conform. They live under the illusion that they follow their own ideas and inclinations, that they are individualists, that they have arrived at their opinions as the result of their own thinking—and that it just happens that their ideas are the same as those of the majority. The consensus of all serves as a proof for the correctness of "their" ideas. Since there is still a need to feel some individuality, such need is satisfied with regard to minor differences; the initials on the handbag or the sweater, the name plate of the bank teller, the belonging to the Democratic as against the Republican party, to the Elks instead of to the Shriners become the expression of individual differences. The advertising slogan of "it is different" shows up this pathetic need for difference, when in reality there is hardly any left.

• • • •

Union by conformity is not intense and violent; it is calm, dictated by routine, and for this very reason often is insufficient to pacify the anxiety of separateness. The incidence of alcoholism, drug addiction, compulsive sexualism, and suicide in contemporary Western society are symptoms of this relative failure of herd conformity. Furthermore, this solution concerns mainly the mind and not the body, and for this reason too is lacking in comparison with the orgiastic solutions. Herd conformity has only one advantage: it is permanent, and not spasmodic. The individual is introduced into the conformity pattern at the age of three or four, and subsequently never loses his contact with the herd. Even his funeral, which he anticipates as his last great social affair, is in strict conformance with the pattern.

In addition to conformity as a way to relieve the anxiety springing from separateness, another factor of contemporary life must be considered: the role of the work routine and of the pleasure routine. Man becomes a "nine to fiver," he is part of the labor force, or the bureaucratic force of clerks and managers. He has little initiative, his tasks are prescribed by the organization of the work; there is even little difference between those high up on the ladder and those on the bottom. They all perform tasks prescribed by the whole structure of the organization, at a prescribed speed, and in a prescribed manner. Even the feelings are prescribed: cheerfulness, tolerance, reliability, ambition, and an ability to get along with everybody without friction. Fun is routinized in similar, although not quite as drastic ways. Books are selected by the book clubs, movies by the film and theater owners and the advertising slogans paid for by them; the rest is also uniform: the Sunday ride in the car, the television session, the card game, the social parties. From birth to death, from Monday to Monday, from morning to evening—all activities are routinized, and prefabricated. How should a man caught in this net of routine not forget that he is a man, a unique individual, one who is given only this one chance of living, with hopes and disappointments, with sorrow and fear, with the longing for love and the dread of the nothing and separateness?

A third way of attaining union lies in *creative activity*, be it that of the artist, or of the artisan. In any kind of creative work the creating person unites himself with his material, which represents the world outside of himself. Whether a carpenter makes a table, or a goldsmith a piece of jewelry, whether the peasant grows his corn or the painter paints a picture, in all types of creative work the worker and his object become one, man unites himself with the world in the process of creation. This, however, holds true only for productive work, for work in which *I* plan, produce, see the result of my work. In the modern work process of a clerk, the worker on the endless belt, little is left of this uniting quality of work. The worker becomes an appendix to the machine or to the bureaucratic organization. He has ceased to be he—hence no union takes place beyond that of conformity.

The unity achieved in productive work is not interpersonal; the unity achieved in orgiastic fusion is transitory; the unity achieved by conformity is only pseudo-unity. Hence, they are only partial answers to the problem of existence. The full answer lies in the achievement of interpersonal union, of fusion with another person, in *love*.

This desire for interpersonal fusion is the most powerful striving in man. It is the most fundamental passion, it is the force which keeps the human race together, the clan, the family, society. The failure to achieve it means insanity or destruction—self-destruction or destruction of others. Without love, humanity could not exist for a day. Yet, if we call the achievement of interpersonal union "love," we find ourselves in a serious difficulty. Fusion can be achieved in different ways—and the differences are not less significant than what is common to the various forms of love. Should they all be called love? Or should we reserve the word "love" only for a specific kind of union, one which has been the ideal virtue in all great humanistic religions and philosophical systems of the last four thousand years of Western and Eastern history?

As with all semantic difficulties, the answer can only be arbitrary. What matters is that we know what kind of union we are talking about when we speak of love. Do we refer to love as the mature answer to the problem of existence, or do we speak of those immature forms of love which may be called *symbiotic union?* In the following pages I shall call love only the former. I shall begin the discussion of "love" with the latter.

Symbiotic union has its biological pattern in the relationship between the pregnant mother and the foetus. They are two, and yet one. They live "together" (*symbiosis*), they need each other. The foetus is a part of the mother, it receives everything it needs from her; mother is its world, as it were; she feeds it, she protects it, but also her own life is enhanced by it. In the *psychic* symbiotic union, the two bodies are independent, but the same kind of attachment exists psychologically.

The *passive* form of the symbiotic union is that of submission, or if we use a clinical term, of *masochism*. The masochistic person escapes from the unbearable feeling of isolation and separateness by making himself part and parcel of another person who directs him, guides him, protects him; who is his life and his oxygen, as it were. The power of the one to whom one submits is inflated, may he be a person or a god; he is everything, I am nothing, except inasmuch as I am part of him. As a part, I am part of greatness, of power, of certainty. The masochistic person does not have to make decisions, does not have to take any risks; he is never alone—but he is not independent; he has no integrity; he is not yet fully born. In a religious context the object of worship is called an idol; in a secular context of a masochistic love relationship the essential mechanism, that of idolatry, is the same. The masochistic relationship can be blended with physical, sexual desire; in this case it is not only a submission in which one's mind participates, but also one's whole body. There can be masochistic submission to fate, to sickness, to rhythmic music, to the orgiastic state produced by drugs or under hypnotic trance—in all these instances the person renounces his integrity, makes himself the instrument of somebody or something outside of himself; he need not solve the problem of living by productive activity.

The *active* form of symbiotic fusion is domination or, to use the psychological term corresponding to masochism, *sadism*. The sadistic person wants to escape from his aloneness and his sense of imprisonment by making another person part and parcel of himself. He inflates and enhances himself by incorporating another person, who worships him.

The sadistic person is as dependent on the submissive person as the latter is on the former; neither can live without the other. The difference is only that the sadistic person commands, exploits, hurts, humiliates, and that the masochistic person is commanded, exploited, hurt, humiliated. This is a considerable difference in a realistic sense; in a deeper emotional sense, the difference is not so great as that which they both have in common: fusion without integrity. If one understands this, it is also not surprising to find that usually a person reacts in both the sadistic and the masochistic manner, usually toward different objects. Hitler reacted primarily in a sadistic fashion toward people, but masochistically toward fate, history, the "higher power" of nature. His end—suicide among general destruction—is as characteristic as was his dream of success—total domination.

In contrast to symbiotic union, mature *love* is *union under the condition of preserving one's integrity*, one's individuality. *Love is an active power in man;* a power which breaks through the walls which separate man from his fellow men, which unites him with others; love makes him overcome the sense of isolation and separateness, yet it permits him to be himself, to retain his integrity. In love the paradox occurs that two beings become one and yet remain two.

· · · ·

Love is an activity, not a passive affect; it is a "standing in," not a "falling for." In the most general way, the active character of love can be described by stating that love is primarily *giving*, not receiving.

86

What is giving? Simple as the answer to this question seems to be, it is actually full of ambiguities and complexities. The most widespread misunderstanding is that which assumes that giving is "giving up" something, being deprived of, sacrificing. The person whose character has not developed beyond the stage of the receptive, exploitative, or hoarding orientation experiences the act of giving in this way. The marketing character is willing to give, but only in exchange for receiving; giving without receiving for him is being cheated.[1] People whose main orientation is a non-productive one feel giving as an impoverishment. Most individuals of this type therefore refuse to give. Some make a virtue out of giving in the sense of a sacrifice. They feel that just because it is painful to give, one *should* give; the virtue of giving to them lies in the very act of acceptance of the sacrifice. For them, the norm that it is better to give than to receive means that it is better to suffer deprivation than to experience joy.

For the productive character, giving has an entirely different meaning. Giving is the highest expression of potency. In the very act of giving, I experience my strength, my wealth, my power. This experience of heightened vitality and potency fills me with joy. I experience myself as overflowing, spending, alive, hence as joyous.[2] Giving is more joyous than receiving, not because it is a deprivation, but because in the act of giving lies the expression of my aliveness.

It is not difficult to recognize the validity of this principle by applying it to various specific phenomena. The most elementary example lies in the sphere of sex. The culmination of the male sexual function lies in the act of giving; the man gives himself, his sexual organ, to the woman. At the moment of orgasm he gives his semen to her. He cannot help giving it if he is potent. If he cannot give, he is impotent. For the woman the process is not different, although somewhat more complex. She gives herself too; she opens the gates to her feminine center; in the act of receiving, she gives. If she is incapable of this act of giving, if she can only receive, she is frigid. With her the act of giving occurs again, not in her function as a lover, but in that as a mother. She gives of herself to the growing child within her, she gives her milk to the infant, she gives her bodily warmth. Not to give would be painful.

·   ·   ·   ·

What does one person give to another? He gives of himself, of the most precious he has, he gives of his life. This does not necessarily mean that he sacrifices his life for the other—but that he gives him of that which is alive in him; he gives him of his joy, of his interest, of his understanding, of his knowledge, of his humor, of his sadness—of all expressions and manifestations of that which is alive in him. In thus giving of his life, he enriches the other person, he enhances the other's sense of aliveness by enhancing his own sense of aliveness. He does not give in order to receive; giving is in itself exquisite joy. But in giving he cannot help bringing something to life in the other person, and this which is brought to life reflects back to him; in truly giving, he cannot help receiving that which is given back to him. Giving implies to make the other person a giver also and they both share in the joy of what they have brought to life. In the act of giving something is born, and both persons involved are grateful for the life that is born for both of them. Specifically with regard to love this means: love is a power which produces love; impotence is the inability to produce love.

• • • •

It is hardly necessary to stress the fact that the ability to love as an act of giving depends on the character development of the person. It presupposes the attainment of a predominantly productive orientation; in this orientation the person has overcome dependency, narcissistic omnipotence, the wish to exploit others, or to hoard, and has acquired faith in his own human powers, courage to rely on his powers in the attainment of his goals. To the degree that these qualities are lacking, he is afraid of giving himself—hence of loving.

Beyond the element of giving, the active character of love becomes evident in the fact that it always implies certain basic elements, common to all forms of love. These are *care, responsibility, respect* and *knowledge.*

That love implies *care* is most evident in a mother's love for her child. No assurance of her love would strike us as sincere if we saw her lacking in care for the infant, if she neglected to feed it, to bathe it, to give it physical comfort; and we are impressed by her love if we see her caring for the child. It is not different even with the love for animals or flowers. If a woman told us that she loved flowers, and we saw that she forgot to water them, we would not believe in her "love" for flowers. *Love is the active concern for the life and the growth of that which we love.* Where this active concern is lacking, there is no love. This element of love has been beautifully described in the book of Jonah. God has told Jonah to go to Nineveh to warn its inhabitants that they will be punished unless they mend their evil ways. Jonah runs away from his mission because he is afraid that the people of Nineveh will repent and that God will forgive them. He is a man with a strong sense of order and law, but without love. However, in his attempt to escape, he finds himself in the belly of a whale, symbolizing the state of isolation and imprisonment which his lack of love and solidarity has brought upon him. God saves him, and Jonah goes to Nineveh. He preaches to the inhabitants as God had told him, and the very thing he was afraid of happens. The men of Nineveh repent their sins, mend their ways, and God forgives them and decides not to destroy the city. Jonah is intensely angry and disappointed; he wanted "justice" to be done, not mercy. At last he finds some comfort in the shade of a tree which God had made to grow for him to protect him from the sun. But when God makes the tree wilt, Jonah is depressed and angrily complains to God. God answers: "Thou hast had pity on the gourd for the which thou hast not labored neither madest it grow; which came up in a night, and perished in a night. And should I not spare Nineveh, that great city, wherein are more than sixscore thousand people that cannot discern between their right hand and their left hand, and also much cattle?" God's answer to Jonah is to be understood symbolically. God explains to Jonah that the essence of love is to "labor" for something and "to make something grow," that love and labor are inseparable. One loves that for which one labors, and one labors for that which one loves.

Care and concern imply another aspect of love; that of *responsibility*. Today responsibility is often meant to denote duty, something imposed upon one from the outside. But responsibility, in its true sense, is an entirely voluntary act; it is my response to the needs, expressed or unexpressed, of another human being. To be "responsible" means to be able and ready to "respond." Jonah did not feel responsible to the inhabitants of Nineveh. He, like Cain, could ask: "Am I my brother's keeper?" The loving person responds. The life of his brother is not his brother's business alone, but his own. He feels responsible for his fellow men, as he feels responsible for himself. This responsibility, in the case of the mother and her infant, refers mainly to the care for physical needs. In the love between adults it refers mainly to the psychic needs of the other person.

Responsibility could easily deteriorate into domination and possessiveness, were it not for a third component of love, *respect*. Respect is not fear and awe; it denotes, in accordance with the root of the word (*respicere* = to look at), the ability to see a person as he is, to be aware of his unique individuality. Respect means the concern that the other person should grow and unfold as he is. Respect, thus, implies the absence of exploitation. I want the loved person to grow and unfold for his own sake, and in his own ways, and not for the purpose of serving me. If I love the other person, I feel one with him or her, but with him *as he is*, not as I need him to be as an object for my use. It is clear that respect is possible only if *I* have achieved independence; if I can stand and walk without needing crutches, without having to dominate and exploit anyone else. Respect exists only on the basis of freedom: "l'amour est l'enfant de la liberté," as an old French song says; love is the child of freedom, never that of domination.

To respect a person is not possible without *knowing* him; care and responsibility would be blind if they were not guided by knowledge. Knowledge would be empty if it were not motivated by concern. There are many layers of knowledge; the knowledge which is an aspect of love is one which does not stay at the periphery, but penetrates to the core. It is possible only when I can transcend the concern for myself and see the other person in his own terms. I may know, for instance, that a person is angry, even if he does not show it overtly; but I may know him more deeply than that; then I know that he is anxious, and worried; that he feels lonely, that he feels guilty. Then I know that his anger is only the manifestation of something deeper, and I see him as anxious and embarrassed, that is, as the suffering person, rather than as the angry one.

Knowledge has one more, and a more fundamental, relation to the problem of love. The basic need to fuse with another person so as to transcend the prison of one's separateness is closely related to another specifically human desire, that to know the "secret of man." While life in its merely biological aspects is a miracle and a secret, man in his human aspects is an unfathomable secret to himself—and to his fellow man. We know ourselves, and yet even with all the efforts we may make, we do not know ourselves. We know our fellow man, and yet we do not know him, because we are not a thing, and our fellow man is not a thing. The further we reach into the depth of our being, or someone else's being, the more the goal of knowledge eludes us. Yet we cannot help desiring to penetrate into the secret of man's soul, into the innermost nucleus which is "he."

There is one way, a desperate one, to know the secret: it is that of complete power over another person; the power which makes him do what we want, feel what we want, think what we want; which transforms him into a thing, our thing, our possession. The ultimate degree of this attempt to know lies in the extremes of sadism, the desire and ability to make a human being suffer; to torture him, to force him to betray his secret in his suffering. In this craving for penetrating man's secret, his and hence our own, lies an essential motivation for the depth and intensity of cruelty and destructiveness. In a very succinct way this idea has been expressed by Isaac Babel. He quotes a fellow officer in the Russian civil war, who has just stamped his former master to death, as saying: "With shooting—I'll put it this way—with shooting you only get rid of a chap. . . . With shooting you'll never get at the soul, to where it is in a fellow and how it shows itself. But I don't spare myself, and I've more than once trampled an enemy for over an hour. You see, I want to get to know what life really is, what life's like down our way."[3]

In children we often see this path to knowledge quite overtly. The child takes something apart, breaks it up in order to know it; or it takes an animal apart; cruelly tears off the wings off a butterfly in order to know it, to force its secret. The cruelty itself is motivated by something deeper: the wish to know the secret of things and of life.

The other path to knowing "the secret" is love. Love is active penetration of the other person, in which my desire to know is stilled by union. In the act of fusion I know you, I know myself, I know everybody—and I "know" nothing. I know in the only way knowledge of that which is alive is possible for man—by experience of union—not by any knowledge our thought can give. Sadism is motivated by the wish to know the secret, yet I remain as ignorant as I was before. I have torn the other being apart limb from limb, yet all I have done is to destroy him. Love is the only way of knowledge, which in the act of union answers my quest. In the act of loving, of giving myself, in the act of penetrating the other person, I find myself, I discover myself, I discover us both, I discover man.

The longing to know ourselves and to know our fellow man has been expressed in the Delphic motto "Know thyself." It is the mainspring of all psychology. But inasmuch as the desire is to know all of man, his innermost secret, the desire can never be fulfilled in knowledge of the ordinary kind, in knowledge only by thought. Even if we knew a thousand times more of ourselves, we would never reach bottom. We would still remain an enigma to ourselves, as our fellow man would remain an enigma to us. The only way of full knowledge lies in the *act* of love: this act transcends thought, it transcends words. It is the daring plunge into the experience of union. However, knowledge in thought, that is psychological knowledge, is a necessary condition for full knowledge in the act of love. I have to know the other person and myself objectively, in order to be able to see his reality, or rather, to overcome the illusions, the irrationally distorted picture I have of him. Only if I know a human being objectively, can I know him in his ultimate essence, in the act of love.[4]

The problem of knowing man is parallel to the religious problem of knowing God. In conventional Western theology the attempt is made to know God by thought, to make statements *about* God. It is assumed that I can know God in my thought. In mysticism, which is the consequent outcome of monotheism, the attempt is given up to know God by thought, and it is replaced by the experience of union with God in which there is no more room—and no need—for knowledge *about* God.

The experience of union, with man, or religiously speaking, with God, is by no means irrational. On the contrary, it is as Albert Schweitzer has pointed out, the consequence of rationalism, its most daring and radical consequence. It is based on our knowledge of the fundamental, and not accidental, limitations of our knowledge. It is the knowledge that we shall never "grasp" the secret of man and of the universe, but that we can know, nevertheless, in the act of love. Psychology as a science has its limitations, and, as the logical consequence of theology is mysticism, so the ultimate consequence of psychology is love.

Care, responsibility, respect and knowledge are mutually interdependent. They are a syndrome of attitudes which are to be found in the mature person; that is, in the person who develops his own powers productively, who only wants to have that which he has worked for, who has given up narcissistic dreams of omniscience and omnipotence, who has acquired humility based on the inner strength which only genuine productive activity can give.

NOTES

[1] Cf. a detailed discussion of these character orientations in E. Fromm, *Man for Himself*, Rinehart & Company, New York, 1947, Chap. III, pp. 54–117.

[2] Compare the definition of joy given by Spinoza.

[3] I. Babel, *The Collected Stories*, Criterion Books, New York, 1955.

[4] The above statement has an important implication for the role of psychology in contemporary Western culture. While the great popularity of psychology certainly indicates an interest in the knowledge of man, it also betrays the fundamental lack of love in human relations today. Psychological knowledge thus becomes a substitute for full knowledge in the act of love, instead of being a step toward it.

91

3

Sex Partners
and
Sex Problems

The ethic of sex for the purpose of procreation alone has, to many people, been outmoded for some time. Only recently, however, has there been an emerging emphasis in the mass media on sexual openness, sexual satisfaction, and sexual compatibility. The new freedom in sexual expression has opened the eyes of many to the complex nature of this physiological and social drive. In an area so fraught with mystery, tension, fear of failure, guilt, shame, pleasure, and exhilaration, it is hardly surprising that many problems remain to be solved. Yet if men and women are to be equal partners in marriage, this most important relationship must give them equal satisfaction or the family social atmosphere will suffer.

This chapter starts with a discussion of the place of sex in human life. The social effect of "marriage manuals" (actually sex manuals) and sex research is also covered. Orgasm in woman, a baffling problem for years, is receiving increased attention today and two articles provide insights into this phenomenon. These physiological advances, however, sometimes overshadow the crucial social decisions that accompany the sex act. Thus, the importance of the human relationship in regard to sexual intercourse is discussed.

Before the advent of the condom, the diaphragm, and the pill, sex, babies, and parenthood did indeed come all together in one package. The enjoyment of sex without the fear of unwanted pregnancy is, as has been mentioned, one of the vital ingredients of the sexual revolution. In the 1930's, methods of contraception—although denounced by clergy, by lawmakers, and by moralists—received legal sanction from the courts. Currently, a controversy rages over abortion. A new perspective on this problem is discussed.

93

The Place of Sex
Among Human Values

Bertrand Russell

A man ahead of his time, Bertrand Russell shocked his generation with his views on sex. In this article he asks himself the question, "What is the place of sex among human values?," and then answers it in a disarmingly simple fashion. Sex deserves the same attention as any other human need, no more and no less. He then elaborates on this obvious but often ignored solution to a perplexing facet of life and its implications for other areas of human endeavor such as creativity and power.

The writer who deals with a sexual theme is always in danger of being accused, by those who think that such themes should not be mentioned, of an undue obsession with his subject. It is thought that he would not risk the censure of prudish and prurient persons unless his interest in the subject were out of all proportion to its importance. This view, however, is only taken in the case of those who advocate changes in the conventional ethic. Those who stimulate the appeals to harry prostitutes and those who secure legislation, nominally against the White Slave Traffic, but really against voluntary and decent extra-marital relations; those who denounce women for short skirts and lipsticks; and those who spy upon sea beaches in the hope of discovering inadequate bathing costumes, are none of them supposed to be the victims of a sexual obsession. Yet in fact they probably suffer much more in this way than do writers who advocate greater sexual freedom. Fierce morality is generally a reaction against lustful emotions, and the man who gives expression to it is generally filled with indecent thoughts—thoughts which are rendered indecent, not by the mere fact that they have a sexual content, but that morality has incapacitated the thinker from thinking cleanly and wholesomely on this topic. I am quite in agreement with the Church in thinking that obsession with

From Bertrand Russell, *Marriage and Morals* (New York: Liveright Publishing, 1929), pp. 288–302. Copyright 1957 by Bertrand Russell. Reprinted by permission of Liveright Publishing, and George Allen & Unwin, London.

sexual topics is an evil, but I am not in agreement with the Church as to the best methods of avoiding this evil. It is notorious that St. Anthony was more obsessed by sex than the most extreme voluptuary who ever lived; I will not adduce more recent examples for fear of giving offense. Sex is a natural need, like food and drink. We blame the gormandiser and the dipsomaniac because in the case of each an interest which has a certain legitimate place in life has usurped too large a share of his thoughts and emotions. But we do not blame a man for a normal and healthy enjoyment of a reasonable quantity of food. Ascetics, it is true, have done so, and have considered that a man should cut down his nutriment to the lowest point compatible with survival, but this view is not now common, and may be ignored. The Puritans, in their determination to avoid the pleasures of sex, became somewhat more conscious than people had been before of the pleasures of the table. As a seventeenth-century critic of Puritanism says:

"Would you enjoy gay nights and pleasant dinners?
Then must you board with saints and bed with sinners."

It would seem, therefore, that the Puritans did not succeed in subduing the purely corporeal part of our human nature, since what they took away from sex they added to gluttony. Gluttony is regarded by the Catholic Church as one of the seven deadly sins, and those who practice it are placed by Dante in one of the deeper circles of hell, but it is a somewhat vague sin, since it is hard to say where a legitimate interest in food ceases, and guilt begins to be incurred. Is it wicked to eat anything that is not nourishing? If so, with every salted almond we risk damnation. Such views, however, are out of date. We all know a glutton when we see one, and although he may be somewhat despised, he is not severely reprobated. In spite of this fact, undue obsession with food is rare among those who have never suffered want. Most people eat their meals and then think about other things until the next meal. Those, on the other hand, who, having adopted an ascetic philosophy, have deprived themselves of all but the minimum of food, become obsessed by visions of banquets and dreams of demons bearing luscious fruits. And marooned Antarctic explorers, reduced to a diet of whale's blubber, spend their days planning the dinner they will have at the Carlton when they get home.

Such facts suggest that, if sex is not to be an obsession, it should be regarded by the moralists as food has come to be regarded, and not as food was regarded by the hermits of the Thebaid. Sex is a natural human need like food and drink. It is true that men can survive without it, whereas they cannot survive without food and drink, but from a psychological standpoint the desire for sex is precisely analogous to the desire for food and drink. It is enormously enhanced by abstinence, and temporarily allayed by satisfaction. While it is urgent, it shuts out the rest of the world from the mental purview. All other interests fade for the moment, and actions may be performed which will subsequently appear insane to the man who has been guilty of them. Moreover, as in the case of food and drink, the desire is enormously stimulated by prohibition. I have known children refuse apples at breakfast and go straight out into the orchard and steal them, although the breakfast apples were ripe and the stolen apples unripe. I do not think it can be denied that the desire for alcohol among well-to-do Americans is much stronger than it was twenty years ago. In like manner, Christian teaching and Christian authority have immensely stimulated interest in sex. The generation which first ceases to believe in the conventional teaching is bound, therefore, to indulge in sexual freedom to a degree far beyond what is to be expected of those whose views on sex are unaffected by superstitious teaching, whether positively or negatively. Nothing but freedom will prevent undue obsession with sex, but even freedom will not have this effect unless it has become habitual and has been associated with a wise education as regards sexual matters. I wish to repeat, however, as emphatically as I can, that I regard an undue preoccupation with this topic as an evil, and that I think this evil widespread at the present day, especially in America, where I find it particularly pronounced among the sterner moralists, who display it markedly by their readiness to believe falsehoods concerning those whom they regard as their opponents. The glutton, the voluptuary, and the ascetic are all self-absorbed persons whose horizon is limited by their own desires, either by way of satisfaction or by way of renunciation. A man who is healthy in mind and body will not have his interests thus concentrated upon himself. He will look out upon the world and find in it objects that seem to him worthy of his attention. Absorption in self is not, as some have supposed, the natural condition of unregenerate man. It is a disease brought on, almost always, by some thwarting of natural impulses. The voluptuary who gloats over thoughts of sexual gratification is in general the result of some kind of deprivation, just as the man who hoards food is usually a man who has lived through a famine or a period of destitution. Healthy, outward-looking men and women are not to be produced by the thwarting of natural impulse, but by the equal and balanced development of all the impulses essential to a happy life.

I am not suggesting that there should be no morality and no self-restraint in regard to sex, any more than in regard to food. In regard to food we have restraints of three kinds, those of law, those of manners, and those of health. We regard it as wrong to steal food, to take more than our share at a common meal, and to eat in ways that are likely to make us ill. Restraints of a similar kind are essential where sex is concerned, but in this case they are much more complex and involve much more self-control. Moreover, since one human being ought not to have property in another, the analogy of stealing is not adultery but rape, which obviously must be forbidden by law. The questions that arise in regard to health are concerned almost entirely with venereal disease, a subject which we have already touched upon in connection with prostitution. Clearly, the diminution of professional prostitution is the best way, apart from medicine, of dealing with this evil, and diminution of professional prostitution can be best effected by that greater freedom among young people which has been growing up in recent years.

A comprehensive sexual ethic cannot regard sex merely as a natural hunger and a possible source of danger. Both these points of view are important, but it is even more important to remember that sex is connected with some of the greatest goods in human life. The three that seem paramount are lyric love, happiness in marriage, and art. Of lyric love and marriage we have already spoken. Art is thought by some to be independent of sex, but this view has fewer adherents now than it had in former times. It is fairly clear that the impulse to every kind of æsthetic creation is psychologically connected with courtship, not necessarily in any direct or obvious way, but none the less profoundly. In order that the sexual impulse may lead to artistic expression, a number of conditions are necessary. There must be artistic capacity; but artistic capacity, even within a given race, appears as though it were common at one time and uncommon at another, from which it is safe to conclude that environment, as opposed to native capacity, has an important part to play in the development of the artistic impulse. There must be a certain kind of freedom, not the sort that consists in rewarding the artist, but the sort that consists in not compelling him or inducing him to form habits which turn him into a philistine. When Julius II imprisoned Michelangelo, he did not in any way interfere with that kind of freedom which the artist needs. He imprisoned him because he considered him an important man, and would not tolerate the slightest offense to him from anybody whose rank was less than papal. When, however, an artist is compelled to kowtow to rich patrons or town councillors, and to adapt his work to their aesthetic canons, his artistic freedom is lost. And when he is compelled by fear of social and economic persecution to go on living in a marriage which has become intolerable, he is deprived of the energy which artistic creation requires. Societies that have been conventionally virtuous have not produced great art. Those which have, have been composed of men such as Idaho would sterilize. America at present imports most of its artistic talent from Europe, where, as yet, freedom lingers, but already the Americanization of Europe is making it necessary to turn to the Negroes. The last home of art, it seems, is to be somewhere on the Upper Congo, if not in the uplands of Tibet. But its final extinction cannot be long delayed, since the rewards which America is prepared to lavish upon foreign artists are such as must inevitably bring about their artistic death. Art in the past has had a popular basis, and this has depended upon joy of life. Joy of life, in its turn, depends upon a certain spontaneity in regard to sex. Where sex is repressed, only work remains, and a gospel of work for work's sake never produced any work worth doing. Let me not be told that someone has collected statistics of the number of sexual acts *per diem* (or shall we say *per noctem*?) performed in the United States, and that it is at least as great per head as in any other country. I do not know whether this is the case or not, and I am not in any way concerned to deny it. One of the most dangerous fallacies of the conventional moralists is the reduction of sex to the sexual act, in order to be the better able to belabor it. No civilized man, and no savage that I have ever heard of, is satisfied in his instinct by the bare sexual act. If the impulse which leads to the act is to be satisfied, there must be courtship, there must be love, there must be companionship. Without these, while the physical hunger may be appeased for the moment, the mental hunger remains unabated, and no profound satisfaction can be obtained. The sexual freedom that the artist needs is freedom to love, not the gross freedom to relieve the bodily need with some unknown woman; and freedom to love is what, above all, the conventional moralists will not concede. If art is to revive after the world has been Americanized, it will be necessary that America should change, that its moralists should become less moral and its immoralists less immoral, that both, in a word, should recognize the higher values involved in sex, and the possibility that joy may be of more value than a bank-account. Nothing in America is so painful to the traveller as the lack of joy. Pleasure is frantic and bacchanalian, a matter of momentary oblivion, not of delighted self-expression. Men whose grandfathers danced to the music of the pipe in Balkan or Polish villages sit throughout the day glued to their desks, amid typewriters and telephones, serious, important and worthless. Escaping in the evening to drink and a new kind of noise, they imagine that they are finding happiness, whereas they are finding only a frenzied and incomplete oblivion of the hopeless routine of money that breeds money, using for the purpose the bodies of human beings whose souls have been sold into slavery.

It is not my intention to suggest, what I by no means believe, that all that is best in human life is connected with sex. I do not myself regard science, either practical or theoretical, as connected with it, nor yet certain kinds of important social and political activities. The impulses that lead to the complex desires of adult life can be arranged under a few simple heads. Power, sex, and parenthood appear to me to be the source of most of the things that human beings do, apart from what is necessary for self-preservation. Of these three, power begins first and ends last. The child, since he has very little power, is dominated by the desire to have more. Indeed, a large proportion of his activities spring from this desire. His other dominant desire is vanity—the wish to be praised and the fear of being blamed or left out. It is vanity that makes him a social being and gives him the virtues necessary for life in a community. Vanity is a motive closely intertwined with sex, though in theory separable from it. But power has, so far as I can see, very little connection with sex, and it is love of power, at least as much as vanity, that makes a child work at his lessons and develop his muscles. Curiosity and the pursuit of knowledge should, I think, be regarded as a branch of the love of power. If knowledge is power, then the love of knowledge is the love of power. Science, therefore, except for certain branches of biology and physiology, must be regarded as lying outside the province of sexual emotions. As the Emperor Frederick II is no longer alive, this opinion must remain more or less hypothetical. If he were still alive, he would no doubt decide it by castrating an eminent mathematician and an eminent composer and observing the effects upon their respective labors. I should expect the former to be nil and the latter to be considerable. Seeing that the pursuit of knowledge is one of the most valuable elements in human nature, a very important sphere of activity is, if we are right, exempted from the domination of sex.

Power is also the motive to most political activity, understanding this word in its widest sense. I do not mean to suggest that a great statesman is indifferent to the public welfare; on the contrary, I believe him to be a man in whom parental feeling has become widely diffused. But unless he has also a considerable love of power he will fail to sustain the labors necessary for success in a political enterprise. I have known many highminded men in public affairs, but unless they had a considerable dose of personal ambition they seldom had the energy to accomplish the good at which they aimed. On a certain crucial occasion, Abraham Lincoln made a speech to two recalcitrant senators, beginning and ending with the words: "I am the President of the United States, clothed with great power." It can hardly be questioned that he found some pleasure in asserting this fact. Throughout all politics, both for good and for evil, the two chief forces are the economic motive and the love of power; an attempt to interpret politics on Freudian lines is, to my mind, a mistake.

If we are right in what we have been saying, most of the greatest men, other than artists, have been actuated in their important activities by motives unconnected with sex. If such activities are to persist and are, in their humbler forms, to become common, it is necessary that sex should not overshadow the remainder of a man's emotional and passionate nature. The desire to understand the world and the desire to reform it are the two great engines of progress, without which human society would stand still or retrogress. It may be that too complete a happiness would cause the impulses to knowledge and reform to fade. When Cobden wished to enlist John Bright in the free trade campaign, he based a personal appeal upon the sorrow that Bright was experiencing owing to his wife's recent death. It may be that without this sorrow Bright would have had less sympathy with the sorrows of others. And many a man has been driven to abstract pursuits by despair of the actual world. To a man of sufficient energy, pain may be a valuable stimulus, and I do not deny that if we were all perfectly happy we should not exert ourselves to become happier. But I cannot admit that it is any part of the duty of human beings to provide others with pain on the off chance that it may prove fruitful. In ninety-nine cases out of a hundred pain proves merely crushing. In the hundredth case it is better to trust to the natural shocks that flesh is heir to. So long as there is death there will be sorrow, and so long as there is sorrow it can be no part of the duty of human beings to increase its amount, in spite of the fact that a few rare spirits know how to transmute it.

He Taught a Generation How to Copulate – Theodoor Hendrik van de Velde (1873 – 1937)

Edward M. Brecher

It is important for young people verging on partnerships to appreciate van de Velde's contribution to the current sexual revolution. His "marriage manual" was both educational and, even more important, a symbolic break with Victorian ideas concerning sex. Furthermore, his dual emphasis on sex education of novitiates and the maintenance of sex excitement within an established marriage as years go by are twin concerns of professional sexologists and married couples today.

Theodoor Hendrik van de Velde (1873–1937) was a Dutch gynecologist. Raised in the Victorian sexual tradition, he never completely got over it. He gave his most important book, first published in 1926, a title which might equally well have graced a Victorian best seller—*Ideal Marriage*; and he interlarded its pages with platitudes which would surely have earned him the praise of the good Queen herself had he published them a generation earlier:

"A common hobby keeps mutual sympathy warm and active."

"Marriage is sacred to the believing Christian."

"Children are the strongest mental link in normal married life."

Yet it was from this prim and proper Dutchman[1] that an entire generation (my generation) of Europeans and Americans learned that there are more than two ways of performing sexual intercourse—and that such activities as cunnilingus and fellatio are not only enjoyable but permissible preliminaries.

Many hundreds of "how to" sex manuals had been written before *Ideal Marriage,* of course—some of them thousands of years before. Many more have been written since. Van de Velde's was neither the frankest of these coital guides, nor the most comprehensive, nor the most trustworthy. Its limitations and shortcomings were many. Yet it was precisely its limitations, strangely enough, which made *Ideal Marriage* so important to an entire generation. For van de Velde was able to speak to his contemporaries, the post-Victorian victims of Victorian repression, in language which neither alarmed nor repelled them. He intuitively sensed how far they could be led along the path of sexual responsiveness without unduly arousing their qualms and inhibitions—and he very skillfully led them just that far.

"This book will state many things which would otherwise remain unsaid," van de Velde announced in a Personal Introductory Statement to his *magnum opus*. "Therefore it will have many unpleasant results for me. I know this, for I have gradually attained to some knowledge of my fellow human beings and of their habit of condemning what is unusual and unconventional." Yet he felt a duty to "write down what I have learned to be true and right; I could not face the evening of my life with a quiet conscience if I omitted to do so. There is need of this knowledge; there is too much suffering endured which might well be avoided, too much joy untasted which could enhance life's worth. . . .

"My advice and suggestions are offered here in a wholly responsible, *i.e.*, ethical, spirit, and would lose half their moral purpose if proffered anonymously or under an assumed name.

"So I will meet all blame and annoyance arising therefrom with untroubled mind, and in the hope—nay the *certainty*—that many men and women, even if they dare not say so, will breathe their thanks in the privacy of their nuptial chamber."

Van de Velde, however—like many physicians today—misjudged the readiness of his contemporaries to welcome sexual enlightment. Far from suffering for his boldness, he promptly reaped both worldwide renown and financial rewards beyond his fondest imaginings. Written simultaneously in Dutch and German, and promptly translated into most civilized languages, *Ideal Marriage* went through forty-two printings in Germany alone between 1926 and 1932—but was suppressed in 1933, when Hitler came to power. The English translation, published by William Heinemann in 1930, has gone through forty-three printings totaling an estimated 700,000 copies. Figures for the American edition, published by Random House, are not available for the years from 1930 to 1945—but more than half a million hardcover copies have been sold since 1945. A revised edition, published in 1965, is being read today by the grandchildren of van de Velde's original readers.

Van de Velde was a specialist. He aimed his book squarely at legally married husbands and wives embarking on a presumably permanent sexual relationship. He ignored all of the practical problems, emotional stresses, and incompatibilities which provide the fodder for many contemporary marriage manuals. He assumed as a preliminary condition that his readers were mature, loving men and women eager to cherish one another and to give one another joy. He concerned himself solely, moreover, with forms of sexual behavior which he considered physiologically normal, aesthetically acceptable, and ethically justifiable according to his personal standards. And even within these restricting limits, he focused his primary attention on two quite specific aspects of conjugal copulation:

How can a sensitive, considerate, loving bridegroom introduce his eager but inhibited and virginal bride to the delights of sexual responsiveness?

How can a married couple, after years of mutual erotic fulfillment, prevent the coital experience from becoming routine, humdrum, repetitious? How can the freshness, enthusiasm, and excitement ordinarily associated with a change in sexual partners be achieved *within* an enduring marriage?

Much of what van de Velde had to say on these matters has a quaintly old-fashioned flavor. Yet readers today will still find three insights of enduring significance.

First, van de Velde correctly diagnosed the major sexual problem of the generation just emerging from Victorianism—a problem still often met with. His generation no longer believed that sex was inherently evil. It accepted in principle the view that a couple bound in an enduring commitment of love and affection could enjoy sexual fulfillment with a clear conscience. But the delusion still survived that where love and affection reign, sex will take care of itself. Van de Velde's patients illustrated the disastrous consequences of this delusion. He learned from them that no matter how loving a couple may be, sexual response is *not* automatic. He therefore prescribed in detail the specific bodily techniques—the kisses, the caresses, the thrusts—by means of which his patients and his readers could translate their emotional commitments into physiological responses and orgasms—mutual, simultaneous orgasms.

It was a prescription urgently needed by the first post-Victorian generation, and many of them welcomed it wholeheartedly. It remains a useful prescription today.

Van de Velde's second major insight can be paraphrased from a popular saying of his time: "it takes two to tango." He concentrated neither on the male nor on the female role in the sex act, but on the myriad subtle interweavings of sensation and emotion which bind the two together. This theme may seem almost too obvious to be worth noting; yet an amazing amount of writing about sex both before and after van de Velde concentrates so intently on frigidity in the female, or on impotence in the male, or on other familiar problems of the individual, as to obscure altogether the proper focus of concern: the reciprocally functioning human couple. Two generations later, Masters and Johnson were to achieve remarkable therapeutic results by reviving van de Velde's focal concern with the couple as the sexual unit.

. . . .

Van de Velde's prescription that the wife exercise a "conscious intention to enjoy all the stimuli received" plays a significant role in the subsequent history of sex research. During the 1960's, when Dr. William H. Masters and Mrs. Virginia E. Johnson were first reporting at medical meetings on their program for treating sexual inadequacy in married couples, the first question from physicians in the audience was almost always the same: "What do you teach the wife?" Virginia Johnson's answer baffled some of her hearers: "We teach her sensate focus." Yet students of van de Velde understood what she meant quite readily: Forget your worries and cares. Forget your doubts and fears. Concentrate instead on purely sensory awareness; adopt "a conscious intention to enjoy the stimuli received."

. . . .

But orgasm, in van de Velde's view, is not the end of the drama of love. There follows "a sensation of profound gratification, of mental and physical peace, balance, self-confidence, and power which is hardly attainable in such perfection through any other experience." Indeed, "the most profound and exquisite happiness which human beings can taste is tasted by couples who truly *love* one another during this pause of respite and realization, after completed communion. Far, far more closely than even the rapture of mutual orgasm does this bliss and content of the *after-glow* unite true lovers, as they lie embraced, side by side, while nature recuperates, and their thoughts, in a waking dream, once more live through the joys they have experienced, and their souls meet and merge, even though their bodies are no longer linked.

"This is the first stage of Epilogue—the After-play."

To some youthful readers today, all this may sound like an advertising copywriter's plug for a new product called After-play. But for others, today as in the 1920's, van de Velde successfully bridges the gap between romance and physiology in a way no other writer on sex has quite accomplished:

"*After-play* is an essential and most significant act in the love drama, but unfortunately the most neglected of all. Many men are in the habit of going to sleep immediately after coitus; yes, even men who *love* their wives do this sometimes, from ignorance or negligence. They turn round and presently lie torpid and snoring, while their wives feel the slow ebb of sexual longing, and thus they deprive themselves of the most exquisite psychic and emotional experiences, and they also destroy the illusions of the most loving wife, by showing that they have no idea of the woman's nature, of the aesthetic delicacy of her love, of the profound appreciation sexual pleasure arouses in her, of her need for caresses and sweet words, which lasts much longer than the orgasm. This is a closed book to them. In After-play the man proves whether he is (or is not) *an erotically civilized adult*." (The italics, as always, are van de Velde's.)

Nor is After-play a difficult art. "A word of love *will* do it, a kiss, a tender touch, an embrace! It will suffice for a loving wife to know that for him, too, all is not over at once, with the tempest of the orgasm, that his happiness endures and echoes through his whole nature, like hers."

Some husbands and wives, it is true, enjoy and are capable of kindling a new act of intercourse from the embers of the old; but "this means only that *the Epilogue is deferred*." And van de Velde concludes this section, as usual, with a collection of aphorisms:

"Joy is perfection."—Spinoza.

"Here is a perfect poem: to awaken a longing, to nourish it, to develop it, to increase it, to stimulate it—and to gratify it."—Balzac

"The chastest wife can also be the most voluptuous."—Van de Velde.[2]

* * * *

Van de Velde's significance in the *history* of sex research seems to me unchallengeable. He found a way, as noted earlier, to make at least some of the joys of human sexuality aesthetically and ethically acceptable to a severely inhibited generation in many parts of the world. Perhaps the most startling evidence of van de Velde's far-flung influence comes from the state of New South Wales, in Australia, where the state government in 1948 issued a fourteen-page pamphlet entitled *Marriage,* prepared under the direction of the Minister of Justice, to be handed out free by "church and district registrars" to young people about to be married. Surely the Minister of Justice or his subordinates had read and agreed with van de Velde when they officially informed engaged couples, at the state's expense:

> [The man] should realize that a woman is usually slower than a man in arriving at a state of complete sexual satisfaction, that, before every act of sexual union, a preliminary wooing is often necessary, and that he should endeavor to restrain his ardor so that his climax may synchronize with that of his wife.

NOTES

[1] Prim and proper in his published writings; in private life he is described as being warm, witty, affectionate, lighthearted, and very flirtatious.

[2] I am informed that the aphorisms in *Ideal Marriage* were selected by van de Velde's second wife, Martha.

Who Does What, When, and with Whom – Alfred Charles Kinsey (1894 – 1956)

Edward M. Brecher

Kinsey is an important precursor of the sexual revolution. He alerted the average American to the fact that a great deal more sexual activity was occurring than was at that time assumed. His studies were the first attempts to quantify various types of sexual activity in any organized way. Despite some methodological flaws, Sexual Behavior in the Human Male *and* Sexual Behavior in the Human Female *are research landmarks that offer an objective view of a generally hushed-up subject.*

Prior to 1937, much had been learned about human sexuality—but very little had been firmly established. Even the most basic facts were still subject to debate.

Science had progressed centuries earlier in other areas from debate to solid accomplishment by introducing *quantitative* methods—chiefly counting and physical measurements. The achievements of Copernicus, Galileo, Newton, and Einstein all shared this quantitative mathematical foundation. During the nineteenth century, moreover, a special branch of mathematics—statistics —had proved of very great value, especially in the social and biological sciences. It was thus inevitable that, sooner or later, quantitative statistical methods would be harnessed to the scientific study of sex.

Dr. Alfred C. Kinsey (1894–1956) deserves the lion's share of the credit for belatedly placing studies of human sexuality on a firm quantitative foundation.

Three of Kinsey's predecessors—Krafft-Ebing, Freud, and van de Velde—knew nothing of statistics; I can recall not a single point on which any of these three brought statistical evidence to bear. Some of their most serious errors resulted directly from this failure to use even the crudest statistical measures. Krafft-Ebing's belief that masturbation leads to insanity, for example, arose out of his observations, and the observations of many of his predecessors, that insane people masturbated. Those observations remain unchallenged today. But even a primitive statistical approach would have revealed—and later did in fact reveal—that sane people also masturbate, and masturbate just about as often as those Krafft-Ebing labeled "insane." Similarly, Freud's early conclusion that coitus with a condom leads to anxiety neurosis was vitiated by his failure to present statistics showing that anxiety neurosis is more frequent among men who wear condoms, and their wives, than among other couples resembling the condom users in other relevant respects. Statisticians may err on occasion; but those who eschew statistics inevitably err very often.

· · · ·

In 1937, when universities under the prodding of Robert Latou Dickinson and others were beginning to introduce courses in sex education and marriage, Indiana University decided to launch such a course. Dr. Kinsey, as a respected biologist and as a husband and father of irreproachable personal conservatism, was selected to be the teacher.

· · · ·

Knowing a good deal about gall wasps but little about human sexual behavior, Dr. Kinsey went to the library to learn more. He soon discovered that no one else knew very much either. The studies of such pioneers as Ellis, Krafft-Ebing, Freud, and Dickinson, however fruitful and revealing they had been in their time, were from Kinsey's point of view prescientific. They lacked the statistical validity Dr. Kinsey deemed essential. In order to teach the facts, he would first have to gather them himself, much as he had gathered gall wasps.

Making up a preliminary list of questions, Dr. Kinsey secured answers from 62 males and females during the latter half of 1938. Most of his initial respondents were associated with the university in one way or another; but even so, Dr. Kinsey was able to note what most of his predecessors had missed—an amazing variation of sexual behavior and attitudes from one socio-economic class to another. A campus policeman was a member of this early sample whom Dr. Kinsey often recalled in later years. This policeman, who had had no more than an eighth-grade education, complained to Dr. Kinsey that the Indiana students were mostly perverts. "They would lie under the trees in pairs and just pet and pet. Sexual intercourse the policeman could understand; but this interminable petting must be some form of perversion!"

The later Kinsey interviews explained the policeman's attitude. Based on subsequent records of sex histories collected from more than 17,000 men and women, Dr. Kinsey was able to show that petting is primarily an activity of middle-class or upper-level males who have attended high school or college. While some lower-level boys also occasionally pet, their petting "is often incidental, confined to a few minutes of hugging and kissing prior to actual coitus, and quite without the elaborations which are usual among college students. Petting at upper social levels may be indefinitely prolonged, even into hours of intensive erotic play, and usually never arrives at coitus." More precisely, "[male] orgasm as a product of petting occurs among 16 percent of the males of the grade school level, 32 percent of the males of the high school level, and over 61 percent of the college-bred males who are not married by the age of thirty." Among women, curiously enough, there is not a similar relationship of petting to social class.

During 1939, Kinsey added another 671 sex histories to his file, bringing the total to 733. In the course of these 733 interviews, he learned about kinds of sexual behavior he had never imagined existed, and added questions concerning these kinds of behavior to his rapidly growing questionnaire. Fortunately, Kinsey learned fast. More than 400 of the 521 items covered in the later Kinsey interviews were already present in the questionnaire by mid-1939.

The standard Kinsey interviews, unlike any of the earlier surveys, covered all six of the ways in which males and females achieve orgasm in our culture—through nocturnal sex dreams or seminal emissions, masturbation, heterosexual petting, heterosexual intercourse, homosexual intercourse, and contacts with animals of other species. The questions were gathered under nine major rubrics:

1. Social and Economic Data
2. Marital Histories (recorded separately for each marriage)
3. Sex Education
4. Physical and Physiological Data
5. Nocturnal Sex Dreams
6. Masturbation
7. Heterosexual History
8. Homosexual History
9. Animal Contacts

. . . .

Each interview began with nonsexual questions (such as age and education) and continued through sexual but emotionally neutral topics (such as age at puberty and at first orgasm); the more threatening questions came near the end. Since different people feel threatened in different contexts, this meant that the order of questions sometimes had to be varied. "It is often easier to get the professional record from a female prostitute," Kinsey explained, "than it is to get the record of her personal sex life with her boy friend or with her husband. In dealing with an uneducated and timid older woman from a

107

remote farm area or mountain country, the sequence has to become most desultory, including only the simplest questions about each type of sexual experience, with no details on any point until the whole of the history has been covered in a preliminary way. By then the subject should have become more confident, and it will be possible to ask her such details . . . as would have shocked her at the beginning of the interview. A good interviewer becomes very sensitive to the reactions of his subjects, immediately drops any line of inquiry which causes embarrassment, and stays with simpler matters until the subject is ready to talk in more detail. This technique, more than anything else, probably accounts for the fact that among the 12,000 persons who have been interviewed in the present study, all but three or four have completed their histories; and those few would not have been lost if we had known as much at the beginning of this study as we now know about a good sequence of questions in an interview."

Kinsey and his associates phrased their questions in a way which placed the burden of denial on the subject. "We always assume that everyone has engaged in every type of activity," Kinsey explained. "Consequently we always begin by asking *when* they first engaged in such activity. This places a heavier burden on the individual who is inclined to deny his experience; and since it becomes apparent from the form of our question that we would not be surprised if he had had such experience, there seems to be less reason for denying it."

Above all, the Kinsey interviewers asked their questions directly, "without hesitancy and without apology. If the interviewer shows any uncertainty or embarrassment, it is not to be expected that the subject will do better in his answers. Euphemisms should not be used as substitutes for franker terms." Previous studies, Kinsey recalled, used such circumlocutions as "touching yourself" for masturbation, "securing a thrill from touching yourself" for orgasm through masturbation, and "relations with other persons" or even "sex delinquency" for sexual intercourse. "With such questions, the subject cannot help but sense the fact that the interviewer is not sure that sex is an honorable thing, and a thing that can be frankly talked about. Evasive terms invite dishonest answers."

In addition to teaching his interviewers to phrase their questions frankly and directly, Kinsey taught them to tailor their vocabulary to match that of the respondents. Even a neophyte interviewer, of course, would hesitate to ask an Episcopalian dowager in Boston how old she was when she first got laid; Kinsey stressed the equally important lesson that you can't establish rapport with a longshoreman fresh out of a San Francisco brothel by asking him at what age he first had premarital heterosexual intercourse.

These simple examples hardly do justice to the many sensitive ways in which the Kinsey group developed the face-to-face interview into a precision instrument. Readers desiring more details should consult the 27-page chapter entitled "Interviewing" in the 1948 Kinsey report. Many later studies benefited from these interviewing techniques pioneered at the Kinsey Institute.

Much of the popular interest in the Kinsey studies was focused on broad generalizations. It was amazing and fascinating to learn, for example, that two-thirds of all the married women interviewed reported that they had achieved orgasm in one way or another before marriage. Of at least equal importance, however, were Kinsey's findings on the way sexual behavior differed among a wide variety of subgroups—the unmarried, the married, and the formerly married, the devout and the less devout, Protestant, Catholic, and Jewish, grade-school graduates, high-school graduates, and college graduates, unskilled laborers and professional people, young people in their teens and respondents in their seventies, those born before 1900 and those born after 1900.

Dr. Kinsey had planned to present his findings in a series of ten major reports, of which only the first four have to date been published:

Sexual Behavior in the Human Male (1948)
Sexual Behavior in the Human Female (1953) ˙
Pregnancy, Birth, and Abortion (1958)
Sex Offenders (1965)
Sexual Factors in Marital Adjustment
The Heterosexual-Homosexual Balance
Sexual Adjustments in Institutional Populations
Prostitution
Sex Education
Other Special Problems

The first two of these reports are by far the most important. They are based on the histories of more than 5,000 white males and more than 5,000 white females. (Nonwhite respondents were excluded from the data summarized in the first two reports, and women interviewed in prison were excluded from the second report. Kinsey did not trust the size or the typicalness of his nonwhite sample, and deemed it unwise to distort the sample as a whole by averaging in the highly atypical female prison population.)

. . . .

A discussion of some of Kinsey's findings follow.

Female Frigidity

The crucial fact about female frigidity unearthed by the Kinsey study is its rarity. Nine out of ten of the women contributing their sex histories to the Kinsey project reported having experienced orgasm by the age of thirty-five. An additional eight percent reported having experienced sexual arousal, though without orgasm.

This leaves a *maximum* of two percent of women who could be characterized as "frigid" in the strictest sense—that is, incapable throughout their lives of experiencing either erotic arousal or orgasm.

· · · ·

The Kinsey group concluded:

"It is probable that all females are physiologically capable of responding [to sexual stimulation] and of responding to the point of orgasm."

Once that bold central generalization was established, however, the Kinsey study went on to stress the exceedingly wide variations which characterize female sexual behavior in almost all other respects.

Consider, for example, the age at which orgasm is first experienced. One girl baby was observed experiencing orgasm during masturbation at the age of four months. Four cases were observed before the age of one year, and 23 girls aged three or less were observed experiencing orgasm.

Among the women who contributed their histories to the Kinsey project, sixteen out of nearly 5,000 (0.3 percent) recalled having reached orgasm by the age of three. Thereafter the recollection became more common; 2 percent of the women respondents recalled orgasm by the age of five; 4 percent by seven, and 9 percent by eleven years of age. One respondent in seven (14 percent) reported having experienced orgasm before the onset of adolescence.

Thereafter the curve showing age at first orgasm becomes steeper. Nearly a quarter of the women in the sample recalled experiencing orgasm by the age of fifteen, more than half by the age of twenty, and more than three-quarters by the age of twenty-five. More than two-thirds (64 percent) experienced their first orgasm before marriage. At the other extreme, three women in the sample reached their first orgasm between the ages of forty-eight and fifty.

Women also varied enormously in the *frequency* of their orgasmic responses. Some reported only one or two orgasms during their entire lives. "This was true even of some of the females who had been married for long periods of years. There were others who had responded in 1 or 2 percent of their marital coitus, but there were many more who had responded much more often, including some 40 to 50 percent who had responded in nearly all of their coitus." Some women had no orgasm with their first two or three husbands but experienced orgasm thereafter. Some women who never reached orgasm with their husbands experienced it during extramarital affairs—and some who regularly had orgasm with their husbands did not experience it during extramarital affairs.

· · · ·

Havelock Ellis, van de Velde, and many others had reported that women take longer than men to reach orgasm. This observation, of course, was based primarily on marital coitus. The Kinsey group stressed, however, that tardiness is not an inherent limitation on female response.

Actually there are some females who regularly reach orgasm within a matter of fifteen to thirty seconds in their petting and coital activities. Some regularly have multiple orgasms which may come in rapid succession, with lapses of only

110

a minute or two, or in some instances of only a few seconds between orgasms. Such speed is found in only a small percentage of the females. . . . Of the 2,114 females in our sample who supplied data on the time usually taken to reach orgasm in masturbation, some 45 percent had regularly done so in something between one and three minutes, and another 24 percent had averaged four to five minutes. About 19 percent had averaged something between six and ten minutes, and only 12 percent regularly took longer than that to reach orgasm. In all of these groups there were, of course, females who had deliberately taken longer than necessary to reach orgasm in order to prolong the pleasure of the experience.

• • • •

Male inadequacies which more or less parallel female frigidity appear to be far rarer and to pose less of a problem—except, of course, for those individual males who happen to suffer from such a condition and who can draw little comfort from the fact that their problem is relatively rare. Three major types of male inadequacy have been described:

(1) Ejaculatory impotence. Males in this group are unable to ejaculate during coitus despite erotic arousal and durable erection. They generally achieve orgasm and ejaculation by masturbating after coitus. Masters and Johnson have described this rare condition in detail; Kinsey found only six cases among 4,108 respondents.

(2) Erectile impotence, that is, inability to achieve an erection or to maintain one until orgasm. This condition is slightly less rare (66 out of 4,108 respondents). It is exceedingly rare among young men; the Kinsey group found only six cases among 1,627 men aged twenty-five or less (0.4 percent). As men age, however, erectile impotence gradually sets in. Thus 6.7 percent of Kinsey's respondents were impotent by age fifty-five and 25 percent by age sixty-five. Most (but not all) men are impotent in their eighties. Kinsey concluded that the condition is less stressful than female frigidity, for an obvious reason. "In many older persons, erectile impotence is, fortunately, accompanied by a decline in and usually complete cessation of erotic response."

(3) Premature ejaculation, a condition in which the male ejaculates immediately following entry of the penis into the vagina, or even while entry is being attempted. Kinsey cited no statistics, except to report: "For perhaps three-quarters of all males, orgasm is reached within two minutes after the initiation of the sexual relation, and for a not inconsiderable number of males the climax may be reached within less than a minute or even within ten or twenty seconds after coital entrance. Occasionally a male may become so stimulated psychically or through physical petting that he ejaculates before he has affected genital union."

• • • •

How reliable are the Kinsey statistics? Whole books have been written on that subject. At the time the Kinsey reports were first published, the issue was

111

a matter of heated debate. Now that tempers have cooled, four generalizations seem warranted:

(1) Whatever their shortcomings, the Kinsey data remain today the fullest and most reliable sampling of human sexual behavior.

(2) Competent surveys made since 1953 in the U.S. and in other countries tend in most respects to confirm the key Kinsey findings. The better the methodology of the survey, the closer the agreement with Kinsey is likely to be.

(3) The comparative Kinsey findings are even more reliable than the individual figures. When Kinsey reports that 8 percent of his male respondents and 0.4 percent of his female respondents reached orgasms at least once in contacts with animals of other species, for example, the true figures for the American population as a whole may be either somewhat higher or somewhat lower. A larger and better-selected sample might somewhat alter the precise figures. When he reports, however, that such behavior is far more common among males than among females, it seems inconceivable that any improvements in sampling or in data-collecting and data-processing techniques would alter the comparative findings.

(4) To the extent that Kinsey's figures err, they almost certainly understate rather than overstate the facts concerning such taboo kinds of sexual behavior as orgasms with animals of other species.

· · · ·

Computer scientists today measure quality of information in terms of units called "bits." One bit of information is the amount which is secured when a single question is answered "yes" or "no." By the end of 1949, Dr. Kinsey and his associates had secured and recorded many *millions* of bits of information from more than 16,000 respondents.

When the Kinsey reports were published, the most common criticism of them was that they failed to cover certain areas of interest, such as "falling in love," or "the psychic *meaning* of each experience." These criticisms, though literally true, were grossly unfair. They distracted attention from the overwhelming volume of data actually collected and presented. No prior survey of human behavior in history had even approached the Kinsey survey in completeness. As a doggerel poet commented at the time:

When that interview
Was through
What there was to know
Kinsey knew.

Sex Research and Sex Therapy — The Achievement of William H. Masters and Virginia E. Johnson

Edward M. Brecher

Van de Velde offered how-to-do-it sex advice based on clinical experience; Kinsey broke sexual barriers by presenting statistics on sex activity obtained from personal interviews; Masters and Johnson's research was the quintessence of daring—actual observations of intercourse and masturbation. Yet by the time their report was published, the public, conditioned by signs of the sexual revolution found everywhere (especially in the mass media), accepted the findings with nowhere near the hue and cry that first greeted Kinsey and certainly with as much, if not more, eagerness. Masters and Johnson's clinically frank findings offer the possibility of helping men and women to understand their own sexuality and achieve a greater degree of sexual pleasure.

With the publication of their first book, *Human Sexual Response*, in April 1966, Dr. William H. Masters and Mrs. Virginia E. Johnson of the Reproductive Biology Research Foundation in St. Louis became world-renowned almost overnight. Newspapers in many countries carried accounts of their work on the day of publication, plus frequent follow-up stories. More than 250,000 copies of their book, at ten dollars a copy, were sold in the United States. It was translated into nine foreign languages. An additional 500,000 paperback copies of an account of their work by my wife and myself were also sold, and our book was also translated into nine languages. Tens of millions of readers learned of their work through magazine articles; non-readers heard of it through gossip. Not since the Kinsey reports had sex research made such a stir in the world.

The stir was fully warranted. For *Human Sexual Response* described, in scrupulous detail, precisely how the human body responds to erotic stimulation during both masturbation and coitus. Responses of the penis, scrotum, and testes, the breasts, clitoris, labia, vagina, cervix, uterus, and other parts of the body were all presented and explained. The Masters-Johnson study made it possible to follow the entire human sexual cycle from the first stirrings of erotic desire through orgasm to ultimate subsidence as objectively as nineteenth-century physiologists had followed the digestive cycle from mastication to excretion. Their study, moreover, was authoritative; it was not based on speculation or random data but on direct laboratory observation of more than 10,000 male and female orgasms.

Scores of eminent physiologists in many countries contributed through the decades to the gradual exploration of the digestive cycle. Masters and Johnson accomplished their work on the sexual cycle alone, in twelve years of concentrated effort.

The role of Masters and Johnson in the history of science a generation hence, however, will be only partly based on this physiological achievement. Their second book, scheduled for publication in 1970, will almost certainly make a similar stir in the world, and will have an equally profound impact on our sexual insights and our culture. For in their 1970 report, Masters and Johnson will review the *psychological* aspects of sexuality with the same scientific objectivity that they brought to the physiological aspects. They will demonstrate the precise ways in which psychological hang-ups lead to the three major forms of sexual inadequacy in our culture—frigidity in the female, impotence and premature ejaculation in the male. Further, they will demonstrate that these three crippling conditions are readily correctable; and they will describe straightforward, ethically unobjectionable methods by which other therapists can effectively treat them.

Their 1970 report will be as firmly based as their 1966 report; it will draw on their ten years of experience with hundreds of troubled couples who have come to them in St. Louis for treatment of sexual inadequacy and incompatibility. For the first time in the history of the therapy of sexual complaints, they will present follow-up reports evaluating the effects of therapy five years after its conclusion.

· · · ·

It was the predominantly favorable reception accorded the publication of the second Kinsey report in 1953 which gave Dr. Masters the courage to launch his own study the following year. He has often since expressed his indebtedness to Kinsey, whom he never knew personally, for "opening the previously closed doors of our culture to definitive investigation of human sexual response."

114

By 1954, in short, Dr. Masters was ready to launch his lifework. He had made a reputation for himself with his research in other fields. He had the institutional support of a major university medical center.

The 1954 Masters research plan called for a comprehensive study of physiological responses from initial erotic stimulation through orgasm to quiescence, in both masturbation and coitus, in a variety of postures, in both men and women of a wide range of ages, and at various stages in the menstrual cycle, using sophisticated instrumentation as well as direct observation and motion-picture recording on film. As a preliminary to this vast undertaking, Dr. Masters first interviewed at length and in depth 118 female and 27 male prostitutes. Eight of the woman prostitutes and three of the men then participated as experimental subjects in a preliminary series of laboratory observations—a sort of "dry run" for the project.

This use of prostitutes became the subject of snide remarks and leers when the Masters studies first became known. The studies were obviously valueless, it was suggested, because prostitutes were involved in them; besides, what self-respecting scientist would demean himself by contacts with prostitutes?

It seems to me, in contrast, that Dr. Masters was either remarkably perceptive or exceedingly lucky in deciding to turn to prostitutes at this preliminary stage. They, after all, are the best-informed experts in the world on human sexual response—or were, prior to the Masters-Johnson studies. During the routine course of her work, a prostitute is typically visited by a man who has eaten too much and drunk too much to be sexually very effective. It is probably long past his bedtime; fatigue further impairs his sexual responsiveness. In some cases, he is assailed by feelings of guilt at fornication, and of shame that he must resort to a prostitute. The surroundings are hardly inspiring. The client has no affection for his partner of the moment, and usually selects her because she happens to be available rather than because of any particular attraction she might have for him. Despite many such obstacles, the prostitute is expected to and in almost all cases succeeds in arousing her client erotically and triggering his orgasm in as short a time as possible—often within a few minutes. Even a moderately competent and intelligent prostitute, after a few hundreds or thousands of such encounters, is surely a worthwhile informant concerning sexual response patterns. The prostitutes he interviewed, Dr. Masters later affirmed, "described many methods for elevating or controlling sexual tensions and demonstrated innumerable variations in stimulative technique. Ultimately many of these techniques have been found to have direct application in therapy of male and female sexual inadequacy and have been integrated into the clinical research programs." It is hardly to Dr. Masters's discredit, but rather to the discredit of his predecessors,[1] that he tapped and they failed to tap this rich source of clinically valuable data.

For purposes of *physiological* study, however, the St. Louis prostitute population proved to be unsuitable. Many of them were migrants, in St. Louis one month and not to be found the next; an essential feature of the Masters plan was the prolonged observation of responses as they developed through the years in individual subjects. Many of the prostitutes, moreover, exhibited substantial degrees of pelvic pathology—including a condition of chronic congestion of the pelvic region, presumably the result of frequently repeated sexual excitation without orgasmic release. Hence, despite the value of his prostitutional studies in other respects, Dr. Masters was forced to exclude most of his observations of their response patterns from his physiological findings.

The prostitutes themselves, however, provided him with a clue for finding respectable men and women willing to participate in his research project. They cited many examples of sexual activities occurring in the presence of observers. A client might engage two prostitutes, for example, or two clients might engage one or more prostitutes, and other combinations might be arranged. There were both men and women, the prostitutes reported, who enjoyed engaging in sex in the presence of others. Much more important for Dr. Masters's research program, there were respectable men and women who had no strong feeling about privacy either way; they simply lacked, for some reason or other, the strong privacy taboos common in our culture.

Dr. Masters, accordingly, took a gingerly first step toward securing respectable volunteers. He let it be known through the university and medical school community that he was planning a study of human sexual response based on laboratory observations. News such as this spreads quickly along the local grapevine. One medical school professor tells another, who tells his wife, who tells a neighbor. A medical student tells a nurse, who tells her sister-in-law.

The returns from this local gossip were of two kinds. A few of those who heard about the research via the grapevine came to Dr. Masters's office on the medical-school floor of the maternity-hospital building eager to volunteer "for kicks." They were promptly eliminated.

More welcome were visitors who were genuinely concerned with some important human problem which sexual research might solve, and who wanted to help solve it. Some couples were referred by their own physicians; some came because they hoped to learn ways to increase their own satisfaction and enjoyment of sex. Former patients of Dr. Masters came, and brought their husbands, when they heard he needed volunteers.

·   ·   ·   ·

In all, 694 individuals, including 276 married couples, participated in the Masters-Johnson laboratory program. Of the 142 unmarried participants, all but 44 had been previously married; a number of those unmarried on entering the program married during the course of their participation. The men ranged in age from twenty-one to eighty-nine; the women ranged from eighteen to seventy-eight. Of the two participants under the age of twenty-one, one was a girl of eighteen who had been married three years and had a child; she participated with her husband. The other was an unmarried twenty-year-old girl with a special vaginal condition which made her of particular value to the research program;[2] her participation did not include sexual intercourse.

The Masters-Johnson volunteers were on the whole highly educated; more

116

than 200, for example, had attended graduate school following college. But another 200 had not gone to college at all, and some had not finished high school. Most of the volunteers were white, but eleven couples were black. Of special interest was the geriatric group—thirty-four married couples over the age of fifty, including some in their sixties and seventies, plus five men over fifty and their postmenopausal wives in their forties. "Their contribution has been large," Masters and Johnson acknowledged, "for their cooperation has extended over four years of concentrated investigations of geriatric sexual response."

The Masters-Johnson sample, in short, included the young and the old, the fat and the thin, the tall and the short, the rich and the poor, blacks and whites, the single, the married, the divorced, and the widowed, the circumcised and the uncircumcised, women who had never borne a child, women who had one child, and women with two, three, and four children. Indeed, the 694 participants had only one characteristic in common: they were all able to reach orgasm during both masturbation and coitus while under observation in the laboratory setting. Applicants who could not were eliminated.

In all, the participants experienced more than 10,000 orgasms under laboratory conditions. Throughout the twelve years it lasted, this laboratory research program was kept entirely distinct from the therapy program launched in 1959; none of the 694 participants in the laboratory program were therapy patients, and none of the therapy patients participated in the laboratory research.

· · · ·

Among the basic procedures for volunteers during the laboratory research program were the following:
(1) Masturbation with the hand or fingers.
(2) Masturbation (rarely) with the mechanical vibrator.
(3) Sexual intercourse with the woman on her back.
(4) Sexual intercourse with the man on his back.
(5) "Artificial coition" with a transparent probe similar to the one used by Dr. Dickinson but electronically controlled and with improved optical qualities. This was particularly useful in contraceptive studies.
(6) Stimulation of the breasts alone, without genital contact. Several of the women in the Masters-Johnson research group proved capable of reaching orgasm in this way. Observations of genital response were of course very easy in these cases, and hard-to-get data were secured.

The original Masters-Johnson sample did not include any women capable of reaching orgasm through fantasy alone, without direct contact stimulation. Masters and Johnson have since reported, however, that they have now made standard laboratory observations on three such women; the sexual response cycles in these cases proved to be identical with the cycles produced in the more ordinary ways.

It is precisely here that the most important single finding of the Masters-

117

Johnson laboratory research comes into focus. Just as there exists a stereo-typed sequence of events which comprises the normal digestive cycle, and a stereotyped normal cardiovascular cycle, so there exists in ordinary men and women a normal cycle of physiological events in response to erotic stimulation. There are, of course, minor variations from individual to individual—but the basic pattern is the same. The masturbatory cycle very closely resembles the coital cycle; the male and female cycles have many points in common. To illustrate these parallelisms *Human Sexual Response* reviews the entire cycle in terms of four successive levels or phases of arousal: excitement, plateau, orgasm, and resolution.

· · · ·

The orgasm itself is characterized in women primarily by a series of rhythmic contractions of the orgasmic platform—the outer third of the vagina and the tissues surrounding it. These rhythmic contractions are muscular contractions.

The first few contractions occur at intervals of four-fifths of a second. Thereafter the intervals tend to become longer, and the intensity of the contractions tends to taper off. A mild orgasm may be accompanied by only three to five contractions, an intense orgasm by eight to twelve. In an extreme case, actually recorded on an automatic recording drum in the Masters-Johnson laboratory, twenty-five rhythmically recurring contractions of the orgasmic platform followed one another over a period of forty-three seconds.

The onset of female orgasm as experienced subjectively occurs simultane-ously with an initial *spasm* of the orgasmic platform, preceding the rhythmic train of contractions by a few seconds.

Along with this series of contractions of the orgasmic platform, the uterus also contracts rhythmically. Each contraction begins at the upper end of the uterus and moves like a wave through the midzone and down to the lower or cervical end. The more intense the orgasm, the more severe are these con-tractions of the uterus. Labor contractions prior to childbirth move similarly downward along the uterus in a wavelike progression, but are more widely spaced and much stronger.

Other muscles, such as the anal sphincter muscle, may also undergo rhyth-mic contractions at orgasm.

Since the contractions of the uterus progress downward, Masters and Johnson point out, they are more likely to have an expulsive action than a sucking action. Nevertheless, to check the matter further, the investigators prepared a fluid resembling semen but opaque to X-rays, and placed this fluid in a cap covering the cervix—so that if there were a sucking action, the fluid would be aspirated. Six women fitted with such caps masturbated to orgasm, and X-ray films were exposed at intervals. No significant gaping of the cervical opening was noted: thus the research supports Dr. Dickinson's position as against the statements of Beck and Talmey.

The male orgasm is rather similar to the female in several respects. The

118

central occurrence is a series of rhythmic contractions or throbs of the penis, timed, as in the female, at intervals of four-fifths of a second. Following the first few contractions, in the man as in the woman, the intervals between contractions tend to become longer and the intensity of the contractions tapers off. As in the case of women, men may subjectively identify the onset of orgasm a few seconds before the occurrence of the first observable contraction.

The ejaculation of semen, which occurs during the male orgasm, is a complex process. Prior to orgasm, fluid containing millions of sperm cells from the testes has collected in the sacs known as seminal vesicles and in a pair of flask-like containers known as ampullae. At orgasm, these organs contract rhythmically, expelling their contents into the urethra. At the same time the prostrate gland contracts rhythmically and expels prostatic fluid into the urethra. A bulb in the urethra near the base of the penis doubles or triples in size to receive the fluids. These changes constitute the first stage of ejaculation.

During the second stage, a series of rhythmic contractions of the urethral bulb and of the penis itself projects the semen outward under great pressure, so that if it is not contained, the semen may shoot as much as two feet beyond the tip of the penis. In older men, the contractions may be somewhat less vigorous, and the pressure of expulsion somewhat lessened. The urethra may undergo a series of minor throbs for several seconds after the contractions of the penis as a whole are no longer perceptible.

In both men and women, the events occurring in the genital organs during orgasm are accompanied by changes in the rest of the body. Pulse rate, blood pressure, and breathing rate reach a peak. There is often a "sex flush" covering much or most of the body skin. And muscles throughout the body respond in various ways.

The face, for example, may be contorted into a grimace through the tightening of muscle groups. The muscles of the neck and long muscles of the arms and legs usually contract in a spasm. The muscles of the abdomen and buttocks are also often contracted. Of special interest are the reactions of the hands and feet. Often a man or woman grasps his partner firmly during orgasm; the hand muscles then clench vigorously. If the hands are not being used in grasping, a spastic contraction of both hands and feet known as carpo-pedal spasm can be observed. Men and women are usually quite unaware of these extreme muscular exertions during orgasm; but it is not unusual for them to experience muscle aches in the back, thighs, or elsewhere the next day as a result.

· · · ·

Exploring these and other aspects of sexual physiology occupied Masters and Johnson for the twelve years from 1954 to 1966. In addition to being a researcher, however, Dr. Masters is a dedicated clinician. His experience as a practicing gynecologist and as a consultant made him acutely aware of the untold accumulation of misery resulting from sexual inadequacies. The man who ejaculates prematurely, and his wife; the man whose penis will not erect, and his wife; the woman unable to enjoy sexual relations, or whose enjoyment is marred by inability to secure release from tension in orgasm, and her husband—these are seriously crippled human beings whose whole lives may be impoverished by their sexual misfortunes. Beginning in 1959, Dr. Masters and Mrs. Johnson launched a therapy program designed to help couples suffering from these conditions.

In both their physiological research and their therapeutic program, it seems to me, Masters and Johnson represent the high point to date in the grand tradition of sex research stemming from Havelock Ellis. That tradition through the decades has been concerned with the disastrous effects of sexual repression—of sexual Puritanism and Victorianism. It has demonstrated the social roots of sexual frustration. It has not only documented these effects, but has insistently sought remedies. Indeed, sex research itself turns out to be the sovereign remedy; for by determining the facts and making them publicly known, it destroys the ignorance on which the Victorian ethic is founded.

NOTES

[1] Except Robert L. Dickinson and Alfred C. Kinsey, who also recognized the value of data available from prostitutes. See Brecher's discussion of the Kinsey report in the previous article.

[2] This young woman was born without a vagina—an unusual condition, but not as rare as is commonly supposed. In a number of such cases, Dr. Masters and others have operated and constructed vaginas; such a vagina may lubricate normally and may make possible coital orgasm for both the woman and her partner. Instead of surgery in this case, Dr. Masters successfully utilized a technique known as perineal dilation. The patient later cóoperated with the Masters-Johnson research project "to the extent of [supplying] multiple vaginal smears, a vaginal biopsy, cyclic vaginal pH recordings, and a detailed history."

The Myth of the Vaginal Orgasm

Anne Koedt

The Women's Liberation Movement has challenged many so-called "sexist" practices and beliefs in American society today. Perhaps the most threatening attack, so far as men have been concerned, is of alleged male exploitation during intercourse. Koedt's essay charges that female "frigidity" is actually the result of male selfishness and ignorance of female sexuality. She argues that the locus of the orgasm for women is the clitoris, not the vagina, and that the male superior position (male on top of female) gives only the male satisfaction unless he is aware of the female's needs. Findings by Masters and Johnson suggest that Koedt is right.

GENERAL STATEMENT

Whenever female orgasm is discussed, a false distinction is made between the vaginal and the clitoral orgasm. Frigidity has generally been defined by men as the failure of women to have vaginal orgasms. Actually, the vagina is not a highly sensitive area and is not physiologically constructed to achieve orgasm. The clitoris is the sensitive area and is the female equivalent of the penis. I think this explains a great many things. First, the so-called frigidity rate among women is phenomenal. Usually we are told that it is our hang-up if we don't have an orgasm, and most women accept this analysis. But men are hung-up too, and they have orgasms, so I think we must look for the causes elsewhere.

What actually happens is this: there is only one area for sexual climax although there are many areas for sexual arousal—the clitoris. All orgasms are extensions of sensations from this area. Since the clitoris is usually not directly

From Anne Koedt, "The Myth of the Vaginal Orgasm," New England Free Press, 1970. Reprinted by permission of the author.

stimulated in the conventional sexual positions, we are left "frigid." The only other kind of stimulation is purely psychological, the kind of orgasm achieved through fetishes or thinking about someone. But this kind of orgasm is *not* caused by friction with the vagina and therefore cannot be considered a vaginal orgasm. Rather, it is a psychologically caused orgasm which manifests itself physically in the clitoris. Of the orgasms that are caused by physical contact with the clitoris, there may be many degrees of intensity—some more localized and some which are more diffuse and sensitive. The physical organ which causes them, however, is the clitoris.

All this leads to some interesting questions about conventional sex and our role in it. Men have orgasms essentially by friction with the vagina, not the clitoris, which is external and not able to cause friction the way penetration does. Women have thus been defined sexually in terms of what pleases men; our own biology has not been properly analyzed. Instead, we are fed the myth of the liberated woman and her vaginal orgasm, an orgasm which in fact does not exist.

What we must do is redefine our sexuality. We must discard the "normal" concept of sex and create new guidelines which take into account mutual sexual enjoyment. While the ideal of mutual enjoyment is acknowledged in marriage manuals, it is not followed to its logical conclusion. We must begin to demand that if a certain sexual position now defined as "standard" is not mutually conducive to orgasm, then it should no longer be defined as standard. New techniques must be used or devised which transform our current sexual exploitation.

Freud—A Father of the Vaginal Orgasm

Freud contended that the clitoral orgasm was adolescent, and that upon puberty, when women began having intercourse with men, women should transfer the center of orgasm to the vagina. The vagina, it was assumed, was able to produce a parallel, but more mature, orgasm than the clitoris. Much work was done to elaborate on this theory, but not much was done to challenge the basic assumptions.

To fully appreciate this incredible invention, perhaps Freud's general attitude about women must first be realized. Mary Ellman (*Thinking About Women*) said it this way:

> Everything in Freud's patronizing and fearful attitude toward women follows from their lack of a penis, but it is only in his essay "The Psychology of Women" that Freud makes explicit ... the deprecations of women which are implicit in his work. He then describes women as intellectually less able and prescribes for them the abandonment of the life of the mind, which will interfere with their sexual function. When the psychoanalyzed patient is a male, the analyst sets himself the task of developing the man's capacities, but with women patients,

122

the job is to resign them to the limits of their sexuality. As Mr. Rieff puts it: for Freud, "analysis cannot encourage in women new energies for success and achievement, but only teach them the lesson of rational resignation."

Once having laid down the law about our sexuality, Freud, not so strangely, discovered a tremendous problem of frigidity in women. (Frigidity defined as failure to achieve a vaginally caused and experienced orgasm.) His cure was that a woman who was frigid needed psychiatric care. She was suffering from failure to mentally adjust to her 'natural' role as a woman. Frank S. Caprio, a contemporary follower of these ideas:

> ... Whenever a woman is incapable of achieving an orgasm via coitus, provided her husband is an adequate partner, and prefers clitoral stimulation to any other form of sexual activity, she can be regarded as suffering from frigidity and requires psychiatric assistance. (*The Sexually Adequate Female*)

The explanation given was that women were envious of men—"renunciation of womanhood." Thus it was diagnosed as an anti-male phenomenon.

It is important to emphasize that Freud didn't base his theory upon a study of the woman's anatomy, but rather upon his assumptions of woman as an inferior appendage to the man, and her consequent social and psychological role. In their attempts to deal with the ensuing problem of mass frigidity, Freudians created elaborate mental gymnastics. Marie Bonaparte, in *Female Sexuality* (Grove Press, p. 148), goes so far as to suggest surgery to help women back on their rightful path. Having discovered a strange connection between the non-frigid woman and the location of the clitoris near the vagina,

> It then occurred to men that where, in certain women, this gap was excessive, and the clitoridal fixation obdurate, a clitoridal-vaginal reconciliation might be effected by surgical means, which would then benefit the normal erotic function. Professor Halban, of Vienna, as much biologist as surgeon, became interested in the problem and worked out a simple operative technique. In this, the suspensory ligament of the clitoris was severed and the clitoris secured to the underlying structures, thus fixing it in a lower position, with eventual reduction of the labia minora.

But the severest damage was not in the area of surgery, where Freudians absurdly ran around trying to change the anatomy to fit their basic assumptions. The worst damage was done to the mental health of women who either suffered silently with self-blame or flocked to the psychiatrists, looking desperately for the hidden and terrible repression that kept them from their vaginal destiny.

LACK OF EVIDENCE?

One can perhaps at first claim that these areas are unknown and unexplored areas, but upon closer examination this is certainly not true today, but was

123

not even true in the past. For example, men have known that women suffered from frigidity often during intercourse. So the problem was there. Also, there is much specific evidence. Men knew that the clitoris was and is the essential organ for masturbation, whether in children or adult women. So obviously women made it clear where *they* thought their sexuality was located. Men also seem suspiciously aware of the clitoral powers during "foreplay" when they want to arouse women and produce the necessary lubrication for penetration. Foreplay is a concept created for male purposes, but works to the disadvantage of woman since as soon as she is aroused the male changes to vaginal stimulation and leaves her both aroused and unsatisfied.

It has also been known that women need no anesthesia inside the vagina during surgery, thus pointing to the fact that the vagina is in fact not a highly sensitive area.

Today, wtih anatomy and Kinsey and Masters and Johnson, to mention just a few sources, there is *no* ignorance on the subject. There are, however, social reasons why this knowledge has not been accepted. We are living in a male power structure which does not want change in the area of women.

ANATOMICAL EVIDENCE

Rather than starting with what women *ought* to feel, it would seem logical to start out with what the anatomical facts are regarding the clitoris and vagina.

The Clitoris. A small equivalent of the penis, except for the fact that the urethra does not go through it as in the man's penis. Its erection is similar to the male erection, and the head of the clitoris has the same type of structure and function as the head of the penis. G. Lombard Kelly, in *Sexual Feeling in Married Men and Women,* p. 35 (Pocket Books), says:

> The head of the clitoris is also composed of erectile tissue, and it possesses a very sensitive epithelium or surface covering, supplied with special nerve endings called genital corpuscles, which are peculiarly adapted for sensory stimulation that under proper mental conditions terminates in the sexual orgasm. No other part of the female generative tract has such corpuscles.

The clitoris has no other function than that of sexual pleasure.

The Vagina. Its functions are related to the reproductive function. Principally, 1) menstruation, 2) receive penis, 3) hold semen, and 4) birth passage. The interior of the vagina, which according to the defenders of the vaginally caused orgasm is the center and producer of the orgasm, is:

> ... like nearly all other internal body structures, poorly supplied with end organs of touch. The internal entodermal origin of the lining of the vagina makes it similar in this respect to the rectum and other parts of the digestive tract. (Kinsey, *Sexual Behavior in the Human Female,* p. 580)

The degree of insensitivity inside the vagina is so high that "Among the women who were tested in our gynecologic sample, less than 14% were at all conscious that they had been touched. (Kinsey, p. 580.)

Even the importance of the vagina as an *erotic* center (as opposed to center for orgasm) has been found to be minor.

Other Areas. Labia minora and the vestibule of the vagina. These two sensitive areas may trigger off a clitoral orgasm. Because they can be effectively stimulated during 'normal' coitus, though infrequent, this kind of stimulation is incorrectly thought to be vaginal orgasm. However, it is important to distinguish between areas which can stimulate the clitoris, but are incapable of producing the orgasm themselves, and the clitoris:

> Regardless of what means of excitation is used to bring the individual to the state of sexual climax, the sensation is perceived by the genital corpuscles and is localized where they are situated: in the head of the clitoris or penis. (Kelly, p. 49.)

Psychologically Stimulated Orgasm. Aside from the above mentioned direct and indirect stimulations of the clitoris, there is a third way an orgasm may be triggered. This is through mental (cortical) stimulation, where the imagination stimulates the brain, which in turn stimulates the genital corpuscles of the glans to set off an orgasm.

WOMEN WHO SAY THEY HAVE VAGINAL ORGASMS

Confusion. Because of the lack of knowledge of their own anatomy, some women accept the idea that an orgasm felt during 'normal' intercourse was vaginally caused. This confusion is caused by a combination of 2 factors. One, failing to locate the center of the orgasm, and two, by a desire to fit her experience to the male defined idea of sexual normalcy. Considering that women know little about their anatomy, it is easy to be confused.

Deception. The vast majority of women who claim vaginal orgasm to their men are faking it to, as Ti-Grace Atkinson says, "get the job." In a new best-selling Danish book, *I Accuse* (my own transl.), Mette Ejlersen specifically deals with this common problem, which she calls the "sex comedy."

This comedy is caused by many reasons. First of all, the man brings a great deal of pressure to bear on the woman, because he considers his ability as a lover at stake. So as not to offend his ego, the woman will comply with the prescribed role and go through simulated ecstacy. In some of the Danish women mentioned, women who were left frigid were turned off on sex, and pretended vaginal orgasm to hurry up the sex act. Others admitted that they had faked vaginal orgasm to catch a man; in one case, to get him to leave his first wife, who admitted being vaginally frigid. The woman pretended that she was "normal," which greatly pleased the man. Later she was forced to fake orgasm, as she obviously couldn't tell him to stimulate her clitorally.

Many more were simply afraid to establish their right to equal enjoyment, seeing the sexual act as being primarily for the man's benefit, and any pleasure that the woman got as an added extra.

Another woman, with just enough ego to reject the man's idea that she needed psychiatric care, refused to admit her frigidity. She wouldn't accept self-blame, but she didn't know how to solve the problem, not knowing the physiological facts about herself. So she was left in a peculiar limbo.

Perhaps one of the most infuriating and damaging results of this whole charade has been that women who were perfectly healthy sexually were taught that they were not. So aside from being sexually deprived, these women were told to blame themselves when there was none. Looking for a cure to a problem that has none, can lead women on an endless path of self-hatred and insecurity. For she is told by her analyst that not even her one role allowed in a male society—the role of *Women*—is she successful in. She is put on the defensive, with phony data as evidence against her, that she better try to be even more feminine, think more feminine, and reject her envy of men. That is, shuffle even harder, baby.

WHY MEN MAINTAIN THE MYTH

Sexual Penetration Is Preferred. The best stimulant for the penis is the woman's vagina. It supplies the necessary friction and lubrication. From a strictly technical point of view this position offers the best physiological condition, even though the man may try other positions for variation.

"The Invisible Woman." One of the elements of male chauvinism is the refusal or inability to see women as total, separate human beings. Rather than this approach, men have chosen to define women only in terms of how they benefited men's lives. Sexually, a woman was not seen as an individual wanting to share equally in the sexual act, any more than she was seen as a person with independent desires when she did anything else in society. Thus, it was easy to make up what was convenient about women; for on top of that, society was so controlled that women were not organized to even form a vocal opposition to the male experts.

Penis as the Epitome of Masculinity. Men define their lives greatly in terms of masculinity. It is a universal ego builder, whereas racism, for example, is connected with particular areas of racial mixture. Masculinity is defined culturally by what is the most non-female. The essence of chauvinism is not the practical, economic comfortable services women supply. It is the psychological superiority. This negative kind of definition of self, rather than a positive definition based upon one's own achievements and development of one's potentials, has of course chained the victim and the oppressor both. But *by far* the most brutalized of the two is the victim.

The analogy is racism, where the white racist compensates his feeling of unworthiness by creating an image of the black man (this is primarily a male struggle) which is inferior to him. Because of his power in a white male power structure, the white man can socially enforce this mythical division.

To the extent that men try to prove male superiority through physiological differentiation, masculinity depends on being the *most* muscular, the most hairy, the deepest voice, and the biggest penis. Women, on the other hand, are approved of (i.e., called feminine) if they are weak, petite, shave their legs, have high soft voices, and no penis.

Since the clitoris is almost identical to the penis, one finds a great deal of evidence of men in various societies trying to either ignore the clitoris and emphasize the vagina, *or*, as in many places in the Mideast, actually performing clitoridectomy (Bonaparte, p. 151). Freud saw this ancient and still practiced custom as a way of further "feminizing" the female by removing this cardinal vestige of her masculinity (Bonaparte, p. 151). It should be noted also that a big clitoris is considered ugly and "masculine." Some cultures pour chemicals on the clitoris to make it shrivel up into proper size.

It seems clear to me that men in fact fear the clitoris as a threat to their masculinity.

Sexually Expendable Male. Men fear that they will become sexually expendable if the clitoral organ is substituted for the vaginal as the basic pleasure for women. Actually this has a great deal of validity if one considers *only* the anatomy. The position of the penis inside the vagina, while perfect for reproduction, does not usually stimulate an orgasm in women because the clitoris is not usually located there, but rather externally and higher up. Women must thus rely upon indirect stimulations in this "normal" position.

Lesbian sexuality, in rubbing one clitoris against the other, could make an excellent case, based on anatomical data, for the extinction of the male organ. Albert Ellis makes a statement something to the effect that a man without a penis can make a woman an excellent lover.

Considering that the vagina is very desirable from a man's point of view, purely on physical grounds, one begins to see the dilemma for men. And it forces us to discard many "physical" arguments explaining why women go to bed with men. What is left, it seems to me, are psychological reasons why women select men at the exclusion of other women.

Control of Women. One reason given why men cut the clitoris off women in the Mideastern countries is that it will keep the women from straying. Removing the sexual organ capable of orgasm, it must be assumed that her sexual drive will diminish. Considering how much men look upon their women as property, we should begin to consider a great deal more why it is not in the men's interest to have women totally free sexually. The double standard, as practiced for example in Latin America, is set up to keep the women bound as property, while men are free to have affairs as they wish.

Lesbianism. Aside from the strictly anatomical reasons why women might seek women lovers, there is a great fear on men's part that women will seek the company of other women on a full human basis. The establishment of clitoral orgasm as fact would threaten the heterosexual *institution*. The oppressor always fears the unity of the oppressed, and the escape of women from

127

the psychological hold men now maintain. Rather than imagining a future free relationship between individuals, men tend to react with paranoid fears of revenge on the part of women.

REFERENCES

1. Kinsey, Afred C., *Sexual Behavior in the Human Female,* Pocket Books, 1953.
2. Bonaparte, Marie, *Female Sexuality,* Grove Press, 1956.
3. Ellis, Albert, *Sex Without Guilt,* Grove Press, 1965.
4. Kelly, G. Lombard, *Sexual Feelings in Married Men and Women,* Pocket Books, 1961.
5. Ejlersen, Mette, *I Accuse (Jeg Anglager),* Chr. Erichsens Forlag (Danish), 1969.

Factors in Marital Orgasm

Paul H. Gebhard

Satisfaction with sex relations and marital happiness are closely associated for women (and no doubt for men as well, although they are not the focus of this study). Gebhard also discusses the relationship between rates of orgasm in women during coitus, and the length of time of foreplay and/or intromission (penis in the vagina). His careful empirical analysis appears to indirectly reinforce the claims of Koedt in the previous essay, for either lengthy foreplay or lengthy coitus may provide women with the clitoral friction they may need for orgasm.

The Institute for Sex Research has in its standard schedule of questions asked of every interviewee a large number devoted to marriage and marital sexual behavior. The answers to these questions provide us with too large a body of data to be compressed into any journal article; consequently, I have chosen to select one aspect of sexuality in marriage to serve as an illustration of our studies. This aspect is one which has received much attention in marriage manuals but which has never been subjected to any large-scale empirical testing: the matter of the wife's orgasm in marital coitus.

BACKGROUND

From the Victorian middle and upper class unconcern with female orgasm, we have, through the emancipation of women and the emergence of sex as a discussable subject, reached a point of intense concern with orgasm. It has become to no small degree a symbol of woman's being accepted as a human of equal stature and with her own sexual needs. Orgasm in marital coitus has become not only her goal but her due, and inability to achieve it frequently engenders feelings of personal inadequacy and failure in both the husband

From Paul H. Gebhard, "Factors in Marital Orgasm," *Journal of Social Issues,* April, 1966, pp. 88–95. Reprinted by permission of The Society for the Psychological Study of Social Issues.

and wife. The pendulum has swung from unconcern to overconcern in less than a century.

In our culture, enchanted with technology and with a mechanistic conception of the body, the emphasis on female orgasm has produced a veritable flood of marriage manuals and similar publications which say, in essence, that the key to female orgasm is in the length of precoital foreplay and the duration of penile intromission once coitus has begun.

Reacting against this preoccupation with foreplay and intromission Kinsey (1, p. 364) stated, "We are not convinced that the data demonstrate that any limitations or extensions of pre-coital petting are of primary importance in establishing the effectiveness or satisfactoriness of coitus." However, he presented no data supporting this statement. Nevertheless, the decade-of-birth data did clearly show an increase in the orgasm rates of wives and a growing use of more elaborate pre-coital and coital techniques. All of this could be construed to indicate more elaborate and protracted foreplay was, after all, conducive to increased female orgasm. No data were presented on duration of penile intromission.

Considering the emphasis in literature and clinical practice on the importance of female orgasm, the omissions in our prior volumes call for rectification, and this was undertaken in the study now reported in this article.

SAMPLE

The data in this paper derive from some of the interviews conducted in the United States by the Institute for Sex Research between 1939 and 1960. The interview consists of a lengthy series of questions designed to give a comprehensive account of the individual's overt sexual behavior and some of his or her responses and attitudes from childhood to the time of the interview. The respondent's answers are recorded in code at the time and any confusion or ambiguity can be dealt with then. The interview of an adult with one marriage requires on the average about one and one-half hours. The information is, of course, subject to the reservations which accompany any recollected reported data, but by reinterviewing a number of individuals after an interim of years, we have demonstrated that the reliability of such reported data is high.

In order to minimize selective bias the Institute ordinarily chose target groups (e.g., a parent-teacher group, a classroom, a business office) where a complete list of group members could be made so that all could be solicited for interview. Where interviewing all members proved impossible, the group was not abandoned until at least three quarters of the members had been interviewed. A study of reluctant interviewees demonstrated that persons resist being interviewed for a great diversity of reasons and, therefore, they do not constitute a sexually homogeneous unit; hence the refusal rate may have little bias effect. The portion within a group who were not interviewed did not

130

consist wholly of refusals, but included persons not solicited and persons who had agreed to an interview but with whom mutually satisfactory appointments could not be made.

The Institute staff has interviewed roughly 8,000 females and a sample from these case histories was selected for this paper.

Originally the sample was to have consisted of white U.S. females with some college education who had been married for one year or more, and in the case of multiple marriage the data were to derive only from the first marriage. The data obtained from this original sample were confusing, and it became evident that this was due to an uncontrolled variable, which proved to be unhappy marriage terminating in separation or divorce. A series of tabulations revealed that greater marital happiness was associated with a higher percentage of coitus resulting in orgasm for the wife (Table 1). This was not an unexpected finding since our clinical impression has always been that separation or divorce is frequently presaged by a decline in female orgasm rate. It was also found that marriages in our original sample which terminated in separation or divorce tended to be shorter than those marriages which were intact at the time of interview (Table 2). Since we know from our prior studies that female orgasm rates increase with length of marriage (Kinsey *et al*, 1, pp. 383–384), this difference in marriage duration was clearly another analytical problem to be overcome.

Since the number of marriages which terminated in separation or divorce were not equal in the various analytical categories used in this study, one could never be sure whether or not variation was due to this fact rather than to items presumably being tested.

The simple, albeit somewhat painful, solution was to confine the sample to women whose marriages were intact at the time of interview and who expressed no intention of terminating their marriages.[1] This reduced the

TABLE 1
FEMALE ORGASM RATE AND MARITAL HAPPINESS IN INTACT MARRIAGES

	MARITAL HAPPINESS RATING						
PER CENT OF COITUS RESULTING IN ORGASM	1 Very happy	1-2	2 Moderately happy	2-3	3 Moderately unhappy	3-4	4 Very unhappy
	Percent						
0	4.4	3.2	9.0	16.1	15.8		19.0
1-9	3.6	9.5	4.5	12.9	8.8		19.0
10-39	6.5	20.6	11.3	3.2	10.5	Too few to calculate	9.5
40-59	9.5	12.7	17.1	12.9	15.8		4.8
60-89	16.5	17.5	17.1	16.1	14.0		9.5
90-100	59.4	36.5	41.0	38.7	35.1		38.1
Cases	587	63	222	31	57	4	21

TABLE 2
FEMALE ORGASM RATE AND DURATION OF MARRIAGE IN INTACT
MARRIAGES AND MARRIAGES BROKEN BY SEPARATION OR DIVORCE

PER CENT OF COITUS RESULTING IN ORGASM	INTACT MARRIAGES		BROKEN MARRIAGES	
	Median years duration	Cases	Median years duration	Cases
0	7.0	74	4.9	76
1-9	7.0	54	5.0	36
10-39	7.6	87	5.5	46
40-59	8.5	119	6.3	32
60-89	8.3	168	5.3	30
90-100	8.8	524	7.6	94

There were too few widows to merit a category.

sample to 1,026 women. The sample size in some tables totals less than this due to interviewer failure to obtain, or to properly record, usable data.

MARITAL HAPPINESS

Table 1 clearly illustrates that wives who reach orgasm in 90 to 100 per cent of their marital coitus are found more commonly (59 per cent) in very happy marriages than in any other marriages. Curiously, the five other categories of marital happiness do not differ much in terms of female orgasm: the figures for wives who reach orgasm with 90–100 per cent frequency remain within six percentage points of one another (35 to 41 per cent) even when happy marriages are compared to very unhappy marriages, and no trend is visible. If all six of the categories had roughly the same percentages of women experiencing orgasm in all or nearly all their coitus, one could postulate that a sexually responsive female can reach orgasm from sexual activity alone, independent of her customary feeling toward her spouse. However, this is not the case. Rather than abandon the hypothesis, perhaps one should add to it a statement that in the very happy marriages, in addition to the sexually responsive wives who would reach orgasm under most circumstances, there are a number of other women who are less responsive and who would not reach orgasm so often were it not for the happiness of the marriage.

This modified hypothesis fits well with the figures concerning wives who never reach orgasm in marital coitus: here we see a clear negative correlation between the number of such women and happiness. There are but four per cent of the very happy marriages wherein the wives fail to reach orgasm, but this figure gradually increases as marital happiness decreases until in the very unhappy marriages it reaches 19 per cent.

With wives who reach orgasm rarely (1–9%) this correlation is still visible;

in the central categories (orgasm rates of 10–39% and 40–59%) it disappears; and in the 60 to 89 per cent orgasm category the small N in the very unhappy marriages prevents our assuming that the correlation reappears.

One is left with the impression that marital happiness and female orgasm do correlate but only in the extreme categories: at both ends of the orgasm scale (0 and 90–100%) and at both ends of the happiness scale (very happy and very unhappy). Perhaps the correlation is elsewhere simply obscured by other factors, including the physiological.

Duration of Marriage

As Kinsey *et al* (pp. 383–384) demonstrated, the percentage of coitus resulting in the wife's orgasm rises steadily with increased length of marriage. Consequently, it is not surprising to see in Table 2 that there is a distinct tendency for women with higher orgasm rates to have been married longer than women with lower orgasm rates. The differences, however, are not great: the wives without orgasm having been married an average (median) of 7 years while the wives who almost always experienced orgasm had the longest marriages, the average being 8.8 years. This same trend was noted among the marriages which ended in separation or divorce, and which were briefer than the intact marriages.

Duration of Precoital Foreplay

The sample for Table 3 was considerably reduced in size because many wives reported duration of foreplay in terms of ranges rather than averages, and time considerations prevented our converting these ranges into averages. In connection with a later study, we intend to program the computer so as to

Table 3
Female Orgasm Rate and Duration of Pre-coital Foreplay in Intact Marriages

PER CENT OF COITUS RESULTING IN ORGASM	AVERAGE DURATION OF FOREPLAY IN MINUTES			
	0	*1-10*	*15-20*	*21 plus*
		Percent		
0	(2 cases)	3.9	7.6	7.7
1-39	(1 case)	19.5	12.6	7.7
40-89	(1 case)	34.6	28.9	25.6
90-100	(2 cases)	41.9	50.6	58.9
Cases	6	179	79	78

make these conversions. No substantial change in the findings is anticipated since the majority of ranges appear to center about the averages reported here. In order to increase the sample size within categories, several categories were combined. Despite these handicaps it is clear from Table 3 that there is a positive correlation between duration of foreplay and wife's orgasm rate.

Where 1 to 10 minutes of foreplay were involved, two fifths of the wives reached orgasm nearly always; 15 to 20 minutes foreplay raised this percentage to half; and still longer foreplay resulted in nearly three fifths of the women achieving this high orgasm rate. Conversely, wives with lesser orgasm rates received shorter periods of foreplay, the 1–10 minutes category having the most cases.

The women who never experienced orgasm in marital coitus constitute a separate phenomenon. While their number in Table 3 is small, it appears that many of their husbands (most of whom were also college educated) were protracting foreplay with the hope of inducing orgasm. The number of cases in the 15–20 minute and 21-plus minute categories are nearly twice the number in the 1–10 minute category.

One may legitimately raise the possibility that the women were unconsciously giving the interviewers biased data: that the women with lesser orgasm rates were minimizing the amount of foreplay. This possibility seems quite remote in view of the smallness of some of the differences and particularly in view of the fact that the wives without orgasm reported lengthy foreplay.

DURATION OF INTROMISSION

The length of time the penis is in the vagina prior to ejaculation—after which most males soon cease pelvic movements and withdraw—is a matter accorded great importance in our folklore as well as in our marriage manuals. All females with coital experience were questioned as to duration of intromission. Their responses appear to be reasonably accurate since they agree with the time measurements from a small but growing number of cases of observed coitus. Our data here are not easy to interpret: it seems that the effect of duration of intromission is masked by other variables. It is not unlikely that lengthy foreplay with brief intromission may be as effective for female orgasm as brief foreplay and lengthy intromission; this has yet to be tested.[2] Also, the lack of strong distinctions in Table 4 may reflect the fact that most males of this upper and upper-middle socioeconomic level can delay ejaculation for two minutes but seldom can delay for over seven, and hence most cases fall in our 2–3.9 minute and 4–7 minute categories. Yet another complication is the probability of the husband's adjusting himself to the speed of his wife's response: a man with a highly responsive wife being less inclined to delay ejaculation.

TABLE 4
FEMALE ORGASM RATE AND DURATION OF PENILE INTROMISSION IN INTACT MARRIAGES

PER CENT OF COITUS RESULTING IN ORGASM	AVERAGE DURATION OF INTROMISSION IN MINUTES						
	-.9	1-1.9	2-3.9	4-7	8-11	12-15	16 plus
				Percent			
0	12.5	6.9	7.0	4.5	12.4	2.7	5.1
1-9	10.0	5.6	5.1	4.5	5.6	2.7	5.1
10-39	20.0	11.2	9.4	6.5	6.7	6.8	7.7
40-59	12.5	9.4	12.9	13.6	14.6	4.1	7.7
60-89	17.5	15.6	15.2	19.2	12.4	21.9	7.7
90-100	27.5	51.2	50.2	51.6	48.3	61.6	66.7
Cases	40	160	255	308	89	73	39

Nevertheless, one can see a tendency for higher orgasm rates to be associated with lengthier duration of intromission. Note that where intromission is under one minute, only slightly over one quarter of the wives achieved orgasm always or nearly always, while lengthier intromission (1 to 11 minutes) raises this proportion to roughly half, and where intromission is protracted beyond 11 minutes three fifths to two thirds of the wives reach this high orgasm rate. Conversely, the women with low orgasm rates (none, 1–9%, and 10–39%) tend to have experienced brief intromission.

The same correlation was seen, though less clearly, in calculations based on broken marriages. An unexpected fact emerged from these calculations: there was a general tendency for lesser duration of intromission in the marriages which ended in separation or divorce, and considerably fewer wives in any duration-category reached orgasm nine or more times out of ten acts of coitus. In categories 1–1.9, 2–3.9, and 4–7 minutes roughly one third of the women reached orgasm 90 to 100 per cent of the time; in these same categories based on intact marriages (as Table 4 shows) half of the wives had orgasm rates of 90 to 100 per cent.

Examination of Table 4 permits some interesting inferences. Firstly, it is clear that penile intromission of less than one minute is insufficient to cause regular orgasm in most women. Secondly, it appears that about half of the wives are capable of high (90–100%) orgasm rate with intromission ranging from one to eleven minutes. This uniformity regardless of whether intromission is 1–1.9 minutes, 2–3.9, 4–7, or 8–11 minutes is puzzling and one is tempted to hypothesize that, except for extremely brief or extremely prolonged intromission, some physiological or psychological constant is maintaining this plateau. Perhaps about half of the women are capable of this high orgasm rate, although some require but one minute while others require eleven.

Extremely prolonged (i.e., about the upper ten per cent in terms of duration) intromission evidently can raise another ten to fifteen per cent of the wives to the high orgasm rate. We see that intromission of 16 minutes or more results in (the causal implication is intentional) high orgasm rate for two thirds of the wives. The remaining third are scattered so evenly throughout the other orgasm rate categories one gains the impression that these women, too, have reached their physiological ceiling. In brief, 16 or more minutes of intromission suffices to bring essentially all women to the limits of their orgasmic capacities.

CONCLUDING COMMENT

There are certain neurophysiological and unconscious psychological factors which prevent female orgasm in coitus, but the degree of their influence cannot be accurately ascertained by means of the data presently available. However, there are several reasons for believing this influence is of the magnitude of five to ten percentage points:

1. In extremely happy marriages only 4.4 per cent of the wives have not experienced orgasm in marital coitus.
2. In marital coitus preceded by lengthy (21 or more minutes) foreplay only 7.7 per cent of the wives have not experienced orgasm.
3. Where penile intromission lasts 16 minutes or more only 5.1 per cent of the wives had failed to experience orgasm.

Aside from the limitations imposed by physiological and unconscious psychological factors, it is clear that there is a strong correlation between female orgasm and marital happiness (presumably causal in both directions); a definite correlation between female orgasm rate and length of marriage; a moderate correlation between female orgasm rate and duration of pre-coital foreplay; and a moderate (and complex) correlation between female orgasm rate and duration of penile intromission.

NOTES

[1] Tables 1, 3, and 4 in this paper were controlled by duration of marriage (1-3 years; 4-10 years; 11 years) to see if this variable was casually related to the results found. No alteration occurred and thus duration of marriage does not qualify any of the relations reported in these tables.

[2] A check was made on the interrelation of foreplay and intromission with the finding that there generally was little relationship except at the higher orgasm rates (90–100% orgasm) wherein some synergistic effect was found and when duration of intromission was held constant, a greater amount of foreplay was conducive to a higher orgasm rate. Similarly if foreplay was held constant, longer intromission resulted in more orgasm. But in general this control worked only

in a minority of cells in the table, so that tables 3 and 4 may stand by and large as they are.

REFERENCE

Kinsey, Alfred C., Pomeroy, W. B. Martin, C. E., and Gebhard, P. H., *Sexual Behavior in the Human Female*, Philadelphia, W. B. Saunders, 1953.

Interpersonal Relationships –
Crux of the Sexual Renaissance

Lester A. Kirkendall and
Roger W. Libby

In an effort to understand the mechanics of the sex act and sexual satisfaction, it is sometimes easy to forget that sexual intercourse is a highly social act which includes some type of relationship—be it the fleeting one of prostitute-customer or the more permanent one of marriage partners. Unless the act of sexual intercourse is seen in social context, the authors argue, we really cannot begin to understand its meaning to participants. Once the infinite variety of these meanings are realized, we can begin to appreciate the research challenge posed when we attempt to understand the sexual renaissance.

A debate over whether sexual morality is declining, or whether we are experiencing a sexual revolution, has broken into the open. The controversy, which has been brewing for over a decade, has been mulled by news media, magazines, books and professional conferences. Varying views have been expressed, but one thing is clear—the very foundations upon which sexual morality has rested, and which have governed the exercise of sexual behavior, are being challenged (16). This, of course, is characteristic of a renaissance.

Many influential people are moving away from the view that sexual morality is defined by abstinence from nonmarital intercourse toward one in which morality is expressed through responsible sexual behavior and a sincere regard for the rights of others. While these people do not advocate nonmarital sexual relations, this possibility is clearly seen as more acceptable if entered in a responsible manner, and contained within a relationship characterized by integrity and mutual concern. In other words, the shift is from emphasis upon an act to emphasis upon the quality of interpersonal relationships.

From Lester A. Kirkendall and Roger W. Libby, "Interpersonal Relationships—The Crux of the Sexual Renaissance," *Journal of Social Issues,* April, 1966, pp. 45–59. Reprinted by permission of The Society for the Psychological Study of Social Issues.

Liberal religious leaders probably provide the most striking illustration of this change. Selections from their writings and pronouncements could be extended considerably beyond the following quotations, but these three are indicative of the changing emphasis.

Douglas Rhymes, Canon Librarian of Southwark Cathedral, writes:

> We are told that all sexual experience outside marriage is wrong, but we are given no particular rulings about sexual experience within marriage. Yet a person may just as easily be treated as a means to satisfy desire and be exploited for the gratification of another within marriage as outside it. It is strange that we concern ourselves so much with the morality of pre-marital and extra-marital sex, but seldom raise seriously the question of sexual morality within marriage. . . . (21, p. 25)

John A. T. Robinson, Bishop of Woolwich, in his controversial book asserts:

> . . . nothing can of itself always be labelled "wrong." One cannot, for instance, start from the position "sex relations before marriage" or "divorce" are wrong or sinful in themselves. They may be in 99 cases or even 100 cases out of 100, but they are not intrinsically so, for the only intrinsic evil is lack of love (22, p. 118).

Harvey Cox, who is a member of The Divinity School faculty at Harvard University, comments:

> To refuse to deliver a prepared answer whenever the question of premarital intercourse pops up will have a healthy influence on the continuing conversation that is Christian ethics. . . . It gets us off dead-end arguments about virginity and chastity, forces us to think about fidelity to persons. It exposes the . . . subtle exploitation that poisons even the most immaculate Platonic relationships.
>
> By definition premarital refers to people who plan to marry someone some day. Premarital sexual conduct should therefore serve to strengthen the chances of sexual success and fidelity in marriage, and we must face the real question of whether avoidance of intercourse beforehand is always the best preparation (6, p. 215).

What is common to these quotes is readily seen. In each the focus is on what happens to persons within the context of the interpersonal relationship matrix in which they find themselves. Morality does not reside in complete sexual abstinence, nor immorality in having had nonmarital experience. Rather, sex derives its meaning from the extent to which it contributes to or detracts from the quality and meaning of the relationship in which it occurs, and relationships in general.

This changing emphasis is also reflected in marriage manuals—those books purporting to help couples toward an adequate sexual adjustment. One of the earliest to appear in the United States (1926) was *Ideal Marriage* by Theodore van de Velde. The physiological aspect predominates in this 320-page book. Thus 310 pages of the 320 are devoted to detailed descriptions of the genital organs and the reproductive system, their hygiene and care. The last 10 pages (one chapter) are devoted to the psychic, emotional, and mental hygiene of the ideal marriage.

To say that the psychological and emotional aspects are completely ignored except for this chapter is not wholly fair, but the book, written by a physician, carries the vivid imprint of the medical profession with its concentration on physiology. At the time of its publication it was a forward-looking book.

The rising concern for interpersonal relationships, however, can be seen in another book written by a physician, Dr. Mary Calderone, in 1960. Dr. Calderone tries to create for her readers a perception of sexuality which is embedded firmly in the total relationship. At one point she comments:

> Sex responsiveness comes to those who not only view sex as a sacred and cherished factor in living, but who also retain good perspective about it by being sensitive to the needs of their partners and by taking into account the warmth, graciousness and humor inherent in successful marital sex (5, p. 163).

The historical preoccupation with sex as an act has also been reflected in the character of sex research. Until recently it has concentrated on incidences and frequencies of various forms of sexual behavior. Some of the more pretentious studies broke incidences and frequencies of the total research population into smaller groups, e.g., Kinsey (12, 13). He looked for possible differences in sex behavior in sub-groups distinguished by such factors as religious affiliations, socioeconomic levels, rural or urban residence, adequacy of sex education and similar factors. This analysis, of course, took into account situational factors which could and do influence interpersonal relationships. Strictly speaking, however, the research still remained outside the interpersonal relationships framework.

IMPLICATIONS OF THE SHIFT

If an increasing concern for sex as an interpersonal relationship is the trend of the sexual renaissance, and we think it is, then clearly we must know how sex and sexual functioning are affected by relationship and vice versa. An extensive psychological literature has been developed to explain individual functioning; individual differences, individual growth patterns, individual cognitive development have all been explored. But relatively little is known about *relationships as such*—their components, or what precisely causes them to flourish, or to wither and die. A psychology more concerned with interpersonal relationships is now much needed. This also suggests the need to develop a field of research devoted to understanding sex and interpersonal relationships.

Finally, as a psychology and a sociology of relationships is developed, and as research findings provide a tested body of content for teaching, parents and

educators may find a new stance. They can become less concerned with interdicting sexual expression of any kind, and more concerned with building an
understanding of those factors which facilitate or impede the development of
interpersonal relationships.

RESEARCH ASSOCIATING SEX
AND INTERPERSONAL RELATIONSHIPS

It is only within the last few years that some research has come to focus on
interpersonal aspects of sexual adjustment.

That this is a fruitful approach is already evident from the results of some
of the recent studies. Such research is still meager in scope and its methods and
procedures will undoubtedly be much improved with experience. Much still
remains in the realm of speculation and conjecture. But a beginning has been
made, and the findings are enlightening and exciting.

One generalization growing out of the studies can be advanced at this point.
*A sexual relationship is an interpersonal relationship, and as such is subject to
the same principles of interaction as are other relationships.* It too is affected
by social, psychological, physiological and cultural forces. The effort, so
characteristic of our culture, to pull sex out of the context of ordinary living,
obscures this simple but important generalization. Yet research findings constantly remind us of it.

Ehrmann (7) examined the association of premarital sexual behavior and
interpersonal relationships. He studied the progression of individuals through
increasingly intense stages of intimacy as they moved toward or rejected premarital intercourse. He was interested in understanding the various stages
of intimacy behavior in relation to a number of factors. The stages were
related to the attitudes with which acquaintances, friends and lovers regarded
sexual intimacy, the kinds of controls exercised, and other factors which helped
build certain feelings and attitudes in interpersonal relationships.

Two conclusions will illustrate the character of his findings. In discussing
the differences in male-female attitudes which are found as affectional ties
deepen, Ehrmann writes:

> . . . males are more conservative and the females are more liberal in expressed
> personal codes of sex conduct and in actual behavior with lovers than with non-
> lovers. In other words, the degree of physical intimacy actually experienced or
> considered permissible is among males *inversely* related and among females
> *directly* related to the intensity of familiarity and affection in the male-female
> relation. . . .
> Female sexual expression is primarily and profoundly related to being in love
> and going steadily. . . . Male sexuality is more indirectly and less exclusively
> associated with romanticism and intimacy relationships (7, p. 269).

Ehrmann, then, has educed evidence that maleness and femaleness and affection influence the character of those interpersonal relationships expressed in sexual behavior.

Similarly, Schofield (24) in a study of 1,873 London boys and girls between the ages of 15 and 19 found that

> Girls prefer a more permanent type of relationship in their sexual behavior. Boys seem to want the opposite; they prefer diversity and so have more casual partners. . . . There is a direct association between the type of relationship a girl has achieved and the degree of intimacy she will permit . . . (24, p. 92).

Kirkendall (15) conducted a study which centered upon understanding the association which he believed to exist between interpersonal relationships and premarital intercourse. He posited three components of an interpersonal relationship—motivation, communication and attitudes toward the assumption of responsibility—and studied the impact of premarital intercourse on them. Two hundred college-level males reported sexual liaisons with 668 females. These liaisons were arrayed along a continuum of affectional involvement. The continuum was divided into six segments or levels which ranged from the prostitute level, where affection was rejected as a part of the relationship, to fiancées—a level involving deep affection.

The relationship components were then studied to determine their changing character as one moved along the continuum. Thus it was found that communication at the prostitute level had a distinct barter characteristic. At the second (pickup) level there was a testing and teasing type of communication. At the deep affectional and the fiancée level there was much more concern for the development of the kind of communication which would result in understanding and insight.

Similarly, the apparent character of the motivation central to the sexual relationship changed from one end of the continuum to the other. As depth of emotional involvement increased, the motivation changed from a self-centered focus to a relationship-centered one. And, increasing emotional involvement resulted in an increasing readiness to assume the responsibilities involved in the sexual relationship.

The study thus provides clear evidence that considering premarital intercourse in blanket terms—as though intercourse with a prostitute could be equated with intercourse with a fiancée—submerged many nuances and shades of meaning. Until these interpersonal differentiations are taken into account, there is little chance of any realistic or meaningful understanding of the character of premarital intercourse.

Burgess and Wallin (4) explored the possibility that premarital intercourse might strengthen the relationship of fiancées who engaged in it. They asked those subjects (eighty-one men and seventy-four women) who reported experience in premarital intercourse if they felt the experience strengthened or weakened their relationship. Some 92.6% of the men and 90.6% of the women attributed a strengthening effect to intercourse, and only 1.2% of the men and 5.4% of the women considered intercourse to have a weakening effect. The remainder noted no change either way. Burgess and Wallin comment:

> ... This finding could be construed as testimony for the beneficial consequences of premarital relations, but with some reservations. First, couples who refrained from having premarital intercourse were not asked whether not doing so strengthened or weakened their relationship. They might have reported unanimously that their relationship had been strengthened by their restraint.
>
> Such a finding could be interpreted as signifying one of two things: (a) that both groups are rationalizing or (b) that given the characteristics, expectations, and standards of those who have intercourse, the experience strengthens their relationships, and, similarly, that given the standards of the continent couples the cooperative effort of couple members to refrain from sex relations strengthens their union (4, pp. 371–372).

Kirkendall (15), after an analysis of his data, reinterpreted the findings of Burgess and Wallin. He envisioned a more complex interplay than simply a reciprocating association between sexual experience and the strengthening or weakening of a relationship. He suggested this interpretation:

> Some deeply affectionate couples have, through the investment of time and mutual devotion, built a relationship which is significant to them, and in which they have developed a mutual respect. Some of these couples are relatively free from the customary inhibitions about sexual participation. Some couples with this kind of relationship and background can, and do, experience intercourse without damage to their total relationship. The expression "without damage" is used in preference to "strengthening," for it seems that in practically all instances "non-damaging" intercourse occurred in relationships which were already so strong in their own right that intercourse did not have much to offer toward strengthening them (15, pp. 199–200).

Kirkendall's study raised a question which the data from his non-randomly selected population could not answer. What proportion of all premarital intercourse occurs at the various levels of his continuum? Of the 668 sexual associations in his survey, 25 (3.2%) involved fiancées and 95 (14.2%) couples with deep affection. Associations involving prostitutes, pickups or partners dated only for intercourse accounted for 432 (64.6%), and those with dating partners where there was little or no affection numbered 116 (17.4%). But would similar proportions be found if a random sampling were used? A study designed to answer this question is needed.

Several studies have linked sexual behavior at the adolescent or young adult level with presumed casual relationships which existed in childhood, particularly those involving some sort of deprivation, usually affectional. This view, of course, will be nothing new to those familiar with psychiatric literature.

An interesting study which demonstrates this linkage is reported by Harold Greenwald (11). Greenwald studied twenty call girls, prostitutes who minister to a well-to-do clientele. He found that "... many of the tendencies which lead to the choice of the call girl profession appear early in youth..." (11,

p. 182). The childhood backgrounds of the call girls appeared to be lacking in genuine love or tenderness. "The fundamental preventive task, then, becomes strengthening the family as a source of love and growth" (11, p. 182).

Ellis and Sagarin (8), in their study of nymphomania, also suggest that its causation has its roots in inadequate childhood relationships.

In studies made at the San Francisco Psychiatric Clinic, Lion (17) and Safir (23) found that promiscuity was related to personality deficiencies, and that these in turn were related to homes characterized by disorganization, weak or broken emotional ties, and lack of loyalties or identification with any person or group.

If a tie of this kind does exist, it would seem logical that changes in the capacity to experience improved personal relationships (arising, for example, through therapy) should result in some change in the sexual pattern. Support for this view comes from Berelson and Steiner (1). In their inventory of scientific findings concerning human behavior, they say that

> Changes toward a more positive attitude regarding sexual activity and toward freer, more enjoyable sexual activity than the patient was previously capable of having, are reported as correlates of psychotherapy from several camps (1, p. 290).

Graham (10) obtained information on the frequency and degree of satisfaction in coitus from 65 married men and women before they began psychotherapy. The data from these couples was compared with similar information from 142 married men and women who had been in treatment for varying periods of time. The results indicated, with certain reservations, that psychotherapy did free individuals for "more frequent and more satisfactory coitus experience" (10, p. 95).

Let us explore this logic from another side. If disorganized and aberrant sexual patterns are more frequent in adolescents or young adults who have experienced some form of emotional deprivation in childhood, it seems reasonable to hypothesize that those who had experienced normal emotional satisfactions should display more of what is considered conventional in their sexual practices. Since studies are more commonly done with persons who are recognized as problems, this possibility is not so well documented. There is, however, some evidence to support this view.

Loeb (18) in a study involving junior and senior high school youth, attempted to differentiate between boys and girls who do and do not participate in premarital intercourse. He advanced these conclusions:

> First, teenagers who trust themselves and their ability to contribute to others and have learned to rely on others socially and emotionally are least likely to be involved in irresponsible sexual activity.
>
> Second, teen-agers who have learned to be comfortable in their appropriate sex roles (boys who like being boys and wish to be men, and girls who like being girls and wish to be women) are least likely to be involved in activities leading to indiscriminate sexuality (18).

Maslow (19) in his study of self-actualized people makes several comments about the character of sexual functioning and sexual satisfaction in people who are considerably above the average so far as emotional health is concerned. He says:

> ... sex and love can be and most often are very perfectly fused with each other in (emotionally) healthy people ... (19, p. 241).
> ... self-actualizing men and women tend on the whole not to seek sex for its own sake, or to be satisfied with it alone when it comes ... (19, p. 242).
> ... sexual pleasures are found in their most intense and ecstatic perfection in self-actualizing people ... (19, p. 242).
> These people do not *need* sensuality; they simply enjoy it when it occurs (19, p. 243).

Maslow feels that the "we don't need it, but we enjoy it when we have it" attitude can be regarded as mature; though the self-actualized person enjoys sex more intensely than the average person, he considers sex less central in his total frame of reference.

Loeb's and Maslow's findings, then, suggest that responsible sexual behavior and satisfying interpersonal relations and personal development are closely related.

Multifarious Associations Between Sex and Interpersonal Relationships

The data which have emerged from various studies also make it clear that a tremendous range of factors can influence the quality of relationships which contain sexual expression; that these factors can and do change from time to time in the course of the relationship; and that almost an unlimited range of consequences can result.

Thus, one of the very important factors influencing the meaning of sex relationship is the degree of fondness which a couple have for one another. As previously noted, Kirkendall (15) in his study utilized a continuum of affectional involvement. He found that the character of motivation and communication, and the readiness of men to assume responsibility for the consequences of intercourse, changed with the degree of emotional involvement. For example, as the length of elapsed time in a dating relationship prior to intercourse increased, there was an increase in the amount of communication devoted to understanding and a decrease in the amount of argumentative-persuasive communication. This finding parallels the findings of Ehrmann (7).

Maturity and developmental level represent still other factors. Broderick (2, 3) has made some interesting studies on the appearance and progressive development of various sexual manifestations with age. In a study of children in a suburban community he found that for many children interest in the opposite sex begins in kindergarten or before. Kissing "which means something special" is found among boys and girls as early as the third and fourth grades. In some communities dating begins for a substantial number of children in the fifth and sixth grades, while "going steady" is common at the junior high school level.

Schofield (24) also found that "those who start dating, kissing and inceptive behavior at an early age are also more likely to have early sexual intercourse" (24, p. 73). In an analysis of family background he also found that

> ... girls who got on very well with their fathers were far less likely to be sexually experienced....
> ... boys who did not get on well with their mothers were more likely to be sexually experienced....
> ... girls who got on well with their mothers were less likely to be sexually experienced ... (24, p. 144).

Role concepts, which in turn may be influenced by other factors and conditions, influence the interplay between sexual behavior and interpersonal relationships. This association has already been noted in quoting some of Ehrmann's findings.

The interaction becomes extremely complex as role concepts, sexual standards, cultural changes, sheer biology, and still other factors all become involved in a single situation.

Reiss' work (20), especially his discussion of the interplay between role concepts and the double standard, makes this point most vividly. He shows clearly how adherence to the double standard conditions the individual's concept of his own role and the role of his sexual partners. Thus what the individual may conceive of as freely-willed and consciously-chosen behavior is actually controlled by concepts deeply rooted in a long-existing cultural pattern.

The complexity is further emphasized as the origins of the double standard are studied. Reiss sees the roots of the double standard as possibly existing in "man's muscular strength, muscular coordination and bone structure...." These "may have made him a better hunter than woman; it may have made him more adept at the use of weapons. Couple this hunting skill with the fact that women would often be incapacitated due to pregnancy and childrearing, and we have the beginning of male monopoly of power" (20, p. 92).

Reiss feels that "The core of the double standard seems to involve the notion of female inferiority (20, p. 192).

Once the double standard became embedded in the mores, however, cultural concepts reinforced it and helped embed it still more deeply. Now, however, cultural developments have begun to weaken the power of the double standard. The declining importance of the physical strength of the male in the modern economy; the ability to make reproduction a voluntary matter; emphasis on freedom, equality, and rationality—these and other forces have been eroding the power of the double standard, and in the process have been altering the association between sexual behavior and interpersonal relationships.

146

Shuttleworth (25) made an incisive critique of Kinsey's views on masculine-feminine differences in interest in sex as a function and as a physical experience. In the process, he advanced a theoretical position of his own which suggests that much role behavior is inherent in the biological structures of the sexes. He argues that their respective biology disposes male and female to regard their sexual functioning differently. Males, for example, can experience the erotic pleasures of sex more easily and with less likelihood of negative repercussions than can females. This fact, then, has helped to formulate both male and female sex roles, the attitudes of men and women toward sex and themselves, and to condition their sexual behavior. If this theoretical view can be established, it definitely has implications for a better understanding of the kind of interpersonal behavior which can be expected to involve the sexes, and how it may develop.

Vincent's (29) study of unwed mothers helped demonstrate that a wide range of outcomes in interpersonal relationships can arise from the circumstances of premarital pregnancy. The attitudes of unwed mothers ranged from those who found the pregnancy a humiliating and terrifying experience to those who found it maturing and satisfying, from those who rejected their child to those who found great satisfaction in having it, from those who rejected and hated the father to those who accepted him fully. When considering the interpersonal reactions of unwed mothers, no stereotype is possible.

Sexual intercourse in our culture has been invested with so many meanings and such strong emotions have been tied to it that non-participation may have as many consequences for interpersonal relations as participation. Tebor (27) studied 100 virgin college males and found that a large proportion of them felt insecure about their virginity and pressured by their peers to obtain experience. At the same time significant adults—teachers and parents—were quite unaware of what sexual pattern these men were following, and provided them no support in their pattern of chastity.

REQUIREMENTS FOR RESEARCH
ON THE RENAISSANCE

The theme of this article has been that a concern for interpersonal relationships as the central issue in the management of sexuality is displacing the traditional emphasis on the avoidance or renunciation of all non-marital sexual experience. Only as a shift of this sort occurs are we in any way justified in speaking of a sexual renaissance.

Some requirements, however, face social scientists who wish to understand this shift. We have four to suggest.

1. *It will be necessary to commit ourselves fully to the study of relationships rather than simply reflecting on them occasionally.* In the area of sex, concern

has been over-focused on the physical acts of sex. Thus the senior author, while doing the research for his book, *Premarital Intercourse and Interpersonal Relationships,* became aware that he was giving undue attention to the act of premarital intercourse, even while trying to set it in an interpersonal relationship context. As a consequence, crucial data were ignored. For example, in selecting subjects, if one potential subject had engaged in much caressing and petting, but had renounced the opportunity for intercourse many times, while another possible subject had merely gone through the physical act of copulation a single time, the latter one was defined as a subject for the research and the first was by-passed as though he had engaged in no sexual nor any interpersonal behavior.

With this realization came a decision to do research on decisions made by individuals concerning sexual behavior, regardless of whether they had had intercourse. The result is a recently-completed preliminary study in which 131 non-randomly selected males were interviewed (14). Of this group 72 (55%) had not had intercourse, but apparently only 17 (13%) had not been in a situation which required a decision. Eleven of these had made a firm decision against intercourse, quite apart from any decision-requiring situation, thus leaving only six who had never faced the issue of decision-making. In other words, when one thought of sexual decision-making as an aspect of interpersonal relationships, rather than continuing to focus on whether or not an act had occurred, one greatly increased the number who were potential subjects, and vastly increased the range of interpersonal behavior available for study.

We offer one further illustration of the reorientation in thinking necessary as we come to accept a concern for relationships as the central issue. The view which emphasizes the quality of interpersonal relationships as of foremost concern is often labelled as "very permissive" when sex standards and behavior are under discussion. This conclusion is possible when concern is focused solely on whether the commission of a sexual act is or is not acceptable. Certainly the emphasis on interpersonal relationships diverts attention from the act to the consequences. But having moved into this position, one finds himself in a situation which is anything but permissive. Relationships and their outcome seem to be governed by principles which are unvarying and which cannot be repealed. The fiat of parents or the edicts of deans can be softened, but there is no tempering of the consequences of dishonesty, lack of self-discipline, and lack of respect for the rights of others upon interpersonal relationships. If one wishes warm, accepting interpersonal relationships with others he will be defeated by these practices and no one, regardless of his position of authority, can change this fact. Proclamations and injunctions will be of no avail. There is no permissiveness here!

2. *Conceptual definitions of relationships will have to be developed.* Several social scientists have initiated work on this. For example, Foote and Cottrell (9) have identified six components of interpersonal competence—health, intelligence, sympathy, judgment, creativity and autonomy. Schutz (26) has developed his FIRO test to measure interpersonal behavior around three in-

terpersonal needs—the needs for inclusion, control and affection. As has been noted, Kirkendall (15) centered his study around three components—motivation, communication and readiness to assume responsibility. Communication and motivation have both been frequently recognized aspects of interpersonal relationships.

However, the conceptualization of relationships in a manner which will permit effective research is still at an embryonic level. The numerous (for there are undoubtedly many) components of relationships have still to be determined, and methods and instruments for their measurement must be developed and perfected. Interpersonal relationships as a field of psychological study should be developing concurrently, for only in this way can we gain the needed broadening of our horizons.

3. *Methods and procedures will have to be devised which will enable us to study relationships.* The perceptive reader will have noted that while studies have been cited because, in our estimation, they bore on interpersonal relationships, all of them with the exception of that by Burgess and Wallin (4) obtained their information on interpersonal relationships by using individuals rather than pairs or groups as subjects. This is quite limiting. Would we not get a different view of premarital intercourse if we could interview both partners to the experience rather than one?

Methods of dealing with couples and groups, and research procedures which can zero in on that subtle, intangible, yet real tie which binds two or more people in an association are needed. Some work has already been done in this direction, but it has not been applied to sex and interpersonal relationships.

4. *The isolation of the most important problems for research is a requirement for progress.* Opinions would naturally differ in regard to what these problems are. We would suggest, however, that since sex relationships *are* interpersonal relationships, the whole field of interpersonal relationships with sex as an integral part needs to be attacked.

Kirkendall (15) has suggestions for further research scattered throughout his book. He suggests such problems as an exploration of the importance of time spent and emotional involvement in a relationship as a factor in determining whether a relationship can sustain intercourse, the factors which produce "loss of respect" when sexual involvement occurs, the meaning of sexual non-involvement for a relationship, factors which impede or facilitate sexual communication, and the relation of knowledge of various kinds of success or failure in sexual relationships.

His study poses many questions which merit answering. How do the emotional involvements of male and female engaged in a sexual relationship differ, and how do they change as the relationship becomes more (or less) intense? How nearly alike, or how diverse, are the perceptions which male and female hold of the total relationship and of its sexual component at various stages in its development? How does the rejection of a proffered sexual relationship by either partner affect the one who extended the offer? And what are the reactions and what produced them in the person receiving it? If there are no sexual overtures, how does this affect relationships?

Which value systems make it most (and least) possible for a couple to communicate about sex? To adjust to tensions which may accompany intercourse or its cessation? Which enable a couple to cope most effectively to the possible traumas of having their relationship become public knowledge, or of pregnancy?

In what diverse ways do premarital sexual experiences affect marital adjustments? What enables some couples who have been premarital sexual partners to separate as friends? Why do others separate with bitterness and hostility? What relation has maturity in other aspects of life to maturity in assessing the meaning of and coping with sexual manifestations of various kinds in the premarital period?

The questions could go on endlessly, yet the isolation of important areas for research remains one of the important tasks before us.

REFERENCES

1. Berelson, Bernard and Steiner, Gary A. *Human Behavior*. New York: Harcourt, Brace and World, 1964.
2. Broderick, Carlfred B. *Socio-Sexual Development in a Suburban Community*. University Park: Pennsylvania State University. Unpublished manuscript (mimeographed), 1963.
3. Broderick, Carlfred B. and Fowler, S. E. "New Patterns of Relationships between the Sexes among Preadolescents." *Marriage and Family Living,* 1961, 23, 27–30.
4. Burgess, Ernest W. and Wallin, Paul. *Engagement and Marriage*. Philadelphia: J. B. Lippincott, 1953.
5. Calderone, Mary. *Release from Sexual Tensions*. New York: Random House, 1960.
6. Cox, Harvey. *The Secular City,* New York: Macmillan, 1965.
7. Ehrmann, Winston. *Premarital Dating Behavior*. New York: Henry Holt, 1959.
8. Ellis, Albert and Sagarin, Edward. *Nymphomania*. New York: Julian Messner, 1964.
9. Foote, Nelson and Cottrell, Leonard S., Jr. *Identity and Interpersonal Competence*. Chicago: University of Chicago Press, 1955.
10. Graham, Stanley R. "The Effects of Psychoanalytically Oriented Psychotherapy on Levels of Frequency and Satisfaction in Sexual Activity." *Journal of Clinical Psychology,* 1960, 16, 94–98.
11. Greenwald, Harold. *The Call Girl,* New York: Ballantine Books, 1958.
12. Kinsey, Alfred C., et al. *Sexual Behavior in the Human Female*. Philadelphia: W. B. Saunders, 1953.
13. Kinsey, Alfred C., et al. *Sexual Behavior in the Human Male*. Philadelphia: Saunders, 1948.
14. Kirkendall, Lester A. "Characteristics of Sexual Decision-Making." To be published in *The Journal of Sex Research*.
15. Kirkendall, Lester A. *Premarital Intercourse and Interpersonal Relationships*. New York: Julian Press, 1961.

16. Kirkendall, Lester A. and Ogg, Elizabeth. *Sex and Our Society*. New York: Public Affairs Committee, 1964, No. 366.
17. Lion, Ernest G., et al. *An Experiment in the Psychiatric Treatment of Promiscuous Girls*. San Francisco: City and County of San Francisco, Department of Public Health, 1945.
18. Loeb, Martin B. "Social Role and Sexual Identity in Adolescent Males," *Casework Papers*. New York: National Association of Social Workers, 1959.
19. Maslow, Abraham. *Motivation and Personality*. New York: Harpers, 1954.
20. Reiss, Ira L. *Premarital Sexual Standards in America*. Glencoe, Illinois: The Free Press, 1960.
21. Rhymes, Douglas. *No New Morality,* Indianapolis: Bobbs-Merrill, 1964, p. 25.
22. Robinson, John A. T. *Honest to God*. Philadelphia: Westminster Press, 1963; p. 118.
23. Safir, Benno, M.D. *A Psychiatric Approach to the Treatment of Promiscuity*. New York: American Social Hygiene Association, 1949.
24. Schofield, Michael. *The Sexual Behavior of Young People*. London: Longmans, Green, 1965.
25. Shuttleworth, Frank. "A Biosocial and Developmental Theory of Male and Female Sexuality." *Marriage and Family Living*, 1960, 21, 163–170.
26. Schutz, William C. *FIRO: A Three-Dimensional Theory of Interpersonal Behavior*. New York: Rinehart, 1958.
27. Tebor, Irving. "Selected Attributes, Interpersonal Relationships and Aspects of Psychosexual Behavior of One Hundred College Freshmen, Virgin Men." Unpublished Ph.D. thesis, Oregon State College, 1957.
28. van de Velde, Theodore H. *Ideal Marriage*. New York: Random House, 1926.
29. Vincent, Clark E. *Unmarried Mothers*. New York: Free Press of Glencoe, 1961.

Premarital Sexual Experience Among Coeds, 1958 and 1968

Robert R. Bell and
Jay B. Chaskes

There are many who have claimed that the sexual revolution on college campuses is all talk and little additional action when compared with an earlier time. Bell and Chaskes, repeating a 1958 study of premarital intercourse among coeds, found some significant changes over a ten-year period in the pattern of sex activity of the unmarried female college student.

Over the past twenty-five years it has been generally assumed in the mass media that the premarital sexual experiences of American girls have been steadily increasing. Furthermore, it is frequently assumed that the college girl has been at the forefront in attaining greater sexual experience. However, in the past the assumption as to increasing sexual experience among college girls has not been supported by research findings. In general, the studies have shown that the significant increase in premarital coital experience for unmarried girls occurred in the 1920's and since that time there have been no striking changes in their probabilities of having premarital coitus (Bell, 1966). One of the authors, after an extensive look at past studies, came to the conclusion that "there is no evidence to suggest that when women born after 1900 are compared by decades of birth, there are any significant differences in their rates of premarital coitus (Bell, 1966:58).

The writers believed that a change *has* been occurring in the sexual experiences of college girls since the mid 1960's. In recent years, even more so than ever, the group primarily responsible for rebellion among the young has been the college student. While there has always been rebellion by the younger generation toward their elders, it probably never has been as great in the

From Robert R. Bell and Jay B. Chaskes, "Premarital Sexual Experience Among Coeds, 1958 and 1968," *Journal of Marriage and the Family*, February, 1970, pp. 81–84. Reprinted by permission of the authors and The National Council on Family Relations.

United States as it has been since the mid 1960's. In recent years youths have not only rebelled, but have also rejected many aspects of the major institutions in American society. The mid 1960's have produced an action generation and their *modus vivendi* has been to experience, to confront, to participate and sometimes to destroy. Since the mid 1960's a small but highly influential proportion of college students has been deeply involved in the civil rights movement and then in the protest over the Vietnam War. What may be most important about this generation of college students is that many are not just alienated as others have been in the past, but are *actively* alienated.

Many college students now believe that a number of the norms of adult institutions are not only wrong but also immoral. This is the view held by many college students toward the treatment of the Black, toward the war in Vietnam, toward American political procedures, and so forth. It therefore seems logical that if many of the norms of these institutions are viewed as wrong and immoral by large numbers of the younger generation, they are also going to be suspicious and critical about other norms in other adult controlled institutions. Certainly a social institution that one would expect the younger generation to view with skepticism would be that concerned with marriage and sexual behavior. This increasingly negative view of adult institutions plus other factors led to the hypothesis that significant changes have been occurring in the premarital sexual experiences of college students since the mid 1960's. Before examining some research data as to whether or not there have been changes in sexual experience, we may briefly examine some other social factors that might be related to change in premarital sexual experiences.

One important factor of the 1960's has been the development, distribution and general acceptance of the birth control pill. On most large university campuses the pill is available to the coed or it is easy for her to find out where to get it in the local community. While studies have shown that fear of pregnancy has not been a very important deterrent to premarital coitus for a number of years, it now seems to have been largely removed for most college girls.

A second influence since the mid 1960's has been the legitimization of sexual candor. In part the new sexual candor has been legitimized by one of the most venerable of American institutions—the Supreme Court. In recent years the young person has had access to a level of sexual expression far greater than just ten years ago. In the past year, even the most conservative of the mass media, that of television, has begun to show it. This new sexual candor, whatever its original cause, is often seen by the rebelling younger generation as "theirs" in that it, too, critically subverts the traditional institutions. As a result the sexual candor of the late 1960's is often both a manifesto and a guidebook for many in the younger generation.

Finally, it must also be recognized that the rebellion of the younger generation has been given both implicit and explicit approval by many in the older generation. Many adults want to think of themselves as part of the younger generation and its youth culture. For example, this is seen in the music and fashion of the youth culture which has had a tremendous impact on adults. It would seem that if many adults take on the values of the youth culture, this would raise questions as to the significance of many of their adult values for the youth world. In other words, the very identification of many adults with youth culture contributes to adult values having less impact on college youths.

In brief, it was assumed that the social forces developing in the mid 1960's led to a rapid increase in the rejection of many adult values, and the development of increasingly important patterns of behavior common to a general youth culture. For the reasons already suggested, one change would be an increased rate of premarital coitus among college girls along with less feelings of guilt about these experiences.

METHOD

In 1958, the senior author did a study of premarital sexual behavior and attitudes among a sample of coeds in a large urban university (Bell and Blumberg, 1959, 1960). In 1968 it was decided to use the same questionnaire with a sample of coeds in the same university. A careful effort was made to match the 1968 population with that of 1958 according to a number of variables. It was possible to match the two samples by age and by the class standings of the coeds. The two time groups were alike in social class background as measured by the education and occupations of their fathers. The distribution of the two samples by religious backgrounds was also the same. The 1958 sample included 250 coeds and that of 1968 included 205 coeds.

There had been no change in the ten-year period as to the mean age of first date for the two samples; in 1958 it was 13.3 and in 1968 it was 13.2 years of age. There was a significant difference in the number of different individuals ever dated by the coeds in the two time samples. In 1958 the mean number of different individuals dated was 53, while in 1968 it was only 25. In 1968 the coeds went out on dates just as often but went out more often with the same individuals in a dating relationship than did the coeds in 1958.

There was no significant difference in the two time samples as to whether the coeds had ever gone steady. In 1958, 68 percent of the coeds had gone steady at least once, while in 1968 this had been the experience for 77 percent. Furthermore, there was no significant difference as to age at first going steady. In 1958 the mean age was 17.0 years and in 1968 it was 16.7 years of age. There were some slight differences as to engagement experience. Somewhat more girls in 1968 had ever been engaged; 37 percent as compared to 22 percent in 1958. However, coeds in 1968 were somewhat older when they first became engaged (20.5 years) than were the coeds in 1958 (19.1 years).

In the discussion that follows there will first be a presentation of some comparative data about the two coed populations of 1958 and 1968. Secondly there will be a discussion with further analysis of the 1968 population of coeds.

154

COMPARISONS OF 1958 AND 1968
COED POPULATIONS

The data to be discussed refers to the highest level of intimacy ever reached by the coed in a specific relationship of dating, going steady, and engagement. Table 1 shows the number and percent of girls in 1958 and 1968, by religion, who had intercourse while dating, going steady, or engaged. An examination of the totals indicate some significant changes from 1958 to 1968. The number of girls having premarital coitus while in a dating relationship went from 10 percent in 1958 to 23 percent in 1968, and the coitus rates while going steady went from 15 percent in 1958 to 28 percent in 1968. While there was some increase in the rates of premarital coitus during engagement, from 31 percent in 1958 to 39 percent in 1968, the change was not as striking as for the dating and going steady stages. Further examination of the data suggests that in 1958, the relationship of engagement was very often the prerequisite to a girl having premarital sexual intercourse. Engagement often provided her with a high level of emotional and future commitment which she often felt justified having coitus. However, in 1968 it appeared that the need to be engaged and all it implied was much less a condition the coed thought necessary before sexual intercourse. Therefore, the data suggests that the decision to have intercourse in 1968 was much less dependent on the commitment of engagement and more a question of individual decision regardless of the level of the relationship. To put it another way, if, in 1958, the coed had premarital coitus, it most often occurred while she was engaged. But in 1968, girls were more apt to have their first sexual experience while dating or going steady.

TABLE 1.
FEMALES, NUMBER AND PERCENT HAVING INTERCOURSE, BY DATING RELATIONSHIP AND RELIGION, 1958 AND 1968

	JEWISH		PROTESTANT		CATHOLIC		TOTALS	
	1958	*1968*	*1958*	*1968*	*1958*	*1968*	*1958*	*1968*
	% No.	*% No.*	*% No.*	*% No.*	*% No.*	*% No.*	*% No.*	*% No.*
Engaged	11 (15)	20 (25)	10 (6)	35 (17)	8 (4)	15 (6)	10 (25)	23 (48)
Dating	14 (13)	26 (26)	20 (8)	41 (16)	14 (4)	17 (4)	15 (25)	28 (46)
Going Steady	20 (7)	40 (19)	38 (6)	67 (8)	56 (7)	18 (3)	31 (20)	39 (30)

Table 1 also shows the changes that have occurred in rates of premarital coitus at the three stages of dating involvement by religious background. Both the Protestant and Jewish girls show a consistent increase in rates of premarital coitus at dating, going steady, and engaged levels from 1958 to 1968. (The number of Catholic coeds is too small for analysis.) In general, the pattern by religious background in 1968 was the same as 1958. Protestant girls had the highest rates of premarital coitus, next came the Jewish coeds, and the lowest rates were for Catholic girls. It would appear that both the Protestant and Jewish girls have been susceptible to the patterns of change, although the rates are greater for Protestant coeds.

The respondents were also asked at each stage of the dating relationship if they had ever felt they had gone "too far" in their level of intimacy. Table 2 shows the percentage of coeds, by dating relationship, who said they had at some time felt they had gone "too far." Table 2 reveals that the percentage of coeds feeling guilty about coitus was reduced by approximately half at all three dating levels from 1958 to 1968. It may also be seen that there were significantly less feelings of guilt about coitus during engagement, while in 1968 variations in feelings of guilt were less differentiated at the three stages of dating involvement. In general, when the data of 1958 is compared with 1968, the indication is that in 1968 the coeds were more apt to have had intercourse at all levels of the dating relationship and at the same time felt less guilty than did their counterparts in 1958.

TABLE 2.
FEMALES, PERCENT HAVING INTERCOURSE,
BY DATING RELATIONSHIP WHO FELT THEY "WENT TOO FAR,"
IN 1958 AND 1968

	1958 PERCENT (N = 250)	1968 PERCENT (N = 205)
While dating	65	36
While going steady	61	30
While engaged	41	20

SOME FURTHER ANALYSIS OF THE
1968 SAMPLE

Given the indication of change in the sexual behavior and attitudes of coeds from 1958 to 1968, it is useful to look a little more in detail at the 1968 sample. The sample was analyzed by a number of variables to see if there were any significant differences. No significant differences were found by father's occupation, father's education, marital status of parents, mother working, or number of siblings. One variable that did show statistically significant differences was that of religious attendance. Those coeds, regardless of religious background, who had the highest rates of religious attendance had the lowest rates of premarital coitus and the greatest feelings of guilt when they did have coitus.

In the 1968 population of coeds it was found that there was a relationship

156

between age of first date and the probability of having premarital coitus. Coeds who had their first date at 14 years of age and younger (as compared to 15 years of age and older) had overall higher rates of coitus (31 percent vs. 12 percent). However, there were no significant differences as related to age at first going steady or first engagement. One explanation for the higher frequency of coitus among those who start dating younger is that they have been dating relatively longer and therefore have had more opportunity. It may also be that girls who start dating younger are more sexually mature, both physically and socially.

It was found that girls who dated more different boys (21 or more vs. 20 or less) had higher rates of premarital coitus (36 percent vs. 14 percent). This difference is in part a reflection of the fact that some girls who have few dates are extremely conservative in their sexual behavior. On the other hand the coeds who dated a large number of different boys often had a wide variety of experiences and a greater probability of sexual intimacy. There was also some indication of a relationship between the number of times a girl went steady and her probability of having premarital coitus. When coeds who had gone steady three or more times were compared with those who had gone steady one or two times, the intercourse rates were 46 percent vs. 22 percent. It may be that some girls who have intercourse are inclined to define that relationship as going steady whether in actual fact it may or may not have been.

As pointed out, studies in the past have consistently shown that for the coed who has premarital coitus, it has usually been limited to one partner and then during engagement. "The studies indicate that being nonvirgin at the time of marriage is not an indication of extensive premarital experiences with a variety of partners" (Bell, 1966:58). If the assumption earlier suggested is true, it would be expected that a number of the coeds in the 1968 sample would have had their first premarital sexual experiences while dating and going steady, rather than waiting until engagement.

When all girls in the 1968 sample who were ever engaged and who had ever had premarital coitus were analyzed, it was found that only 19 percent had limited their coital experience just to the period of engagement. Expressing it another way, of all girls who were ever engaged and ever had premarital coital experience, 75 percent had their first experience while dating, 6 percent while going steady and 19 percent during engagement. For all coeds with premarital coital experience at each stage, 60 percent had coitus while dating, going steady, and engagement.

These data suggest important changes in the premarital coital experience of coeds. No longer is the girl so apt to have her degree of sexual intimacy influenced by the level of the dating relationship. There is also some evidence that girls having premarital coitus are having this experience with more different individuals. For example, of all those girls who had premarital coitus while in a dating relationship 56 percent had more than one partner—in fact, 22 percent had coitus in a dating relationship with five or more partners.

SUMMARY

If one were to construct a continuum of sexual experience and attitudes by which coeds in various colleges and universities in the United States might be measured, it seems that the sample studied would fall somewhere in the middle. In fact, there is some reason to argue that the sample may be somewhat conservative in that most of the coeds lived at home and a disproportionate number of them were Jewish. Yet, in dealing with the same general population over a ten-year period the factor of change can be noted. The most important finding of this study appears to be that the commitment of engagement has become a less important condition for many coeds engaging in premarital coitus as well as whether or not they will have guilt feelings about that experience. If these findings are reasonably accurate, they could indicate the first significant change in premarital sexual behavior patterns since the 1920's. The findings indicate, furthermore, a widening slit between the conventional morality of the adult world and the real behavior common to many groups of young people. However, it should be kept in mind that this study was with small samples at one university and must be seen only as an indication of sexual behavior change and not as an argument that a national change has occurred. Further research with larger and better samples is needed before any broad generalizations may be made.

REFERENCES

1. Bell, Robert R., *Premarital Sex in a Changing Society*. Englewood Cliffs, N.J.: Prentice-Hall, Inc., 1966.
2. Bell, Robert R. and Leonard Blumberg, "Courtship intimacy and religious background," *Marriage and Family Living*, XXXI (4) (November 1959): 356–360.
3. Bell, Robert R. and Leonard Blumberg, "Courtship stages and intimacy attitudes," *The Family Life Coordinator*, VIII (3) (March 1960): 61–63.

Abortion — or Compulsory Pregnancy?

Garrett Hardin

Controversy surrounding legal control of abortion has become more heated in the past few years. One of the mottos of the Women's Liberation Movement is "abortion on demand," and three states—Hawaii, Alaska, and New York— have enacted such legislation. Other states have liberalized their abortion laws to some extent. Hardin suggests that if people stop considering the abortion side of the problem and look instead at the injustice and suffering caused by "compulsory pregnancy," they will be more sympathetic to this approach to birth control.

The year 1967 produced the first fissures in the dam that had prevented all change in the abortion-prohibition laws of the United States for three-quarters of a century. Two states adopted laws that allowed abortion in the "hardship cases" of rape, incest, and probability of a deformed child. A third approved the first two "indications," but not the last. All three took some note of the mental health of the pregnant woman, in varying language; how this language will be translated into practice remains to be seen. In almost two dozen other states, attempts to modify the laws were made but foundered at various stages in the legislative process. It is quite evident that the issue will continue to be a live one for many years to come.

The legislative turmoil was preceded and accompanied by a fast-growing popular literature. The word "abortion" has ceased to be a dirty word—which is a cultural advance. However, the *word* was so long under taboo that the ability to think about the *fact* seems to have suffered a sort of logical atrophy from disuse. Popular articles, regardless of their conclusions, tend to be over-emotional and to take a moralistic rather than an operational view of the

From Garrett Hardin, "Abortion—or Compulsory Pregnancy?" *Journal of Marriage and the Family,* May, 1968, pp. 246–51. Reprinted by permission of the author and The National Council on Family Relations.

matter. Nits are picked, hairs split. It is quite clear that many of the authors are not at all clear what question they are attacking.

It is axiomatic in science that progress hinges on asking the right question. Surprisingly, once the right question is asked the answer seems almost to tumble forth. That is a retrospective view; in prospect, it takes genuine (and mysterious) insight to see correctly into the brambles created by previous, ill-chosen verbalizations.

The abortion problem is, I think, a particularly neat example of a problem in which more of the difficulties are actually created by asking the wrong question. I submit further that once the right question is asked the whole untidy mess miraculously dissolves, leaving in its place a very simple public policy recommendation.

Rape as a Justification

The wrong question, the one almost invariably asked, is this: "How can we justify an abortion?" This assumes that there are weighty public reasons for encouraging pregnancies, or that abortions, per se, somehow threaten public peace. A direct examination of the legitimacy of these assumptions will be made later. For the present, let us pursue the question as asked and see what a morass it leads to.

Almost all the present legislative attempts take as their model a bill proposed by the American Law Institute which emphasizes three justifications for legal abortion: rape, incest, and the probability of a defective child. Whatever else may be said about this bill, it is clear that it affects only the periphery of the social problem. The Arden House Conference Committee[1] estimated the number of illegal abortions in the United States to be between 200,000 and 1,200,000 per year. A California legislator, Anthony C. Beilenson,[2] has estimated that the American Law Institute bill (which he favors) would legalize not more than four percent of the presently illegal abortions. Obviously, the "problem" of illegal abortion will be scarcely affected by the passage of the laws so far proposed in the United States.

I have calculated[3] that the number of rape-induced pregnancies in the United States is about 800 per year. The number is not large, but for the woman raped the total number is irrelevant. What matters to her is that she be relieved of her unwanted burden. But a law which puts the burden of proof on her compels her to risk a second harrowing experience. How can she *prove* to the district attorney that she was raped? He could really know whether or not she gave consent only if he could get inside her mind; this he cannot do. Here is the philosopher's "egocentric predicament" that none of us can escape. In an effort to help the district attorney sustain the illusion that he can escape this predicament, a talented woman may put on a dramatic performance, with copious tears and other signs of anguish. But what if the raped woman is not an actress? What if her temperament is stoic? In its operation, the law will act against the interests of calm, undramatic women. Is that what we want? It is safe to say also that district attorneys will hear less favorably the pleas of poor women, the general assumption of middle-class agents being that the poor are less responsible in sex anyway.[4] Is it to the interest of society that the poor bear more children, whether rape-engendered or not?

A wryly amusing difficulty has been raised with respect to rape. Suppose the woman is married and having regular intercourse with her husband. Suppose that following a rape by an unknown intruder she finds herself pregnant. Is she legally entitled to an abortion? How does she know whose child she is carrying anyway? If it is her husband's child, abortion is illegal. If she carries it to term, and if blood tests then exclude the husband as the father, as they would in a fraction of the cases, is the woman then entitled to a *delayed* abortion? But this is ridiculous: this is infanticide, which no one is proposing. Such is the bramble bush into which we are led by a *reluctant* consent for abortion in cases of rape.

HOW PROBABLE MUST DEFORMITY BE?

The majority of the public support abortion in cases of a suspected deformity of the child[5] just as they do in cases of rape. Again, however, if the burden of proof rests on the one who requests the operation, we encounter difficulties in administration. Between 80,000 and 160,000 defective children are born every year in the United States. The number stated depends on two important issues: (a) how severe a defect must be before it is counted as such and (b) whether or not one counts as birth defects those defects that are not *detected* until later. (Deafness and various other defects produced by fetal rubella may not be detected until a year or so after birth.) However many defective infants there may be, what is the prospect of detecting them before birth?

The sad answer is: the prospects are poor. A small percentage can be picked up by microscopic examination of tissues of the fetus. But "amniocentesis"—the form of biopsy required to procure such tissues—is itself somewhat dangerous to both mother and fetus; most abnormalities will not be detectable by a microscopic examination of the fetal cells; and 96 to 98 percent of all fetuses are normal anyway. All these considerations are a contra-indication of routine amniocentesis.

When experience indicates that the probability of a deformed fetus is above the "background level" of 2 to 4 percent, is abortion justified? At what level? 10 percent? 50? 80? Or only at 100 percent? Suppose a particular medical history indicates a probability of 20 percent that the baby will be defective. If we routinely abort such cases, it is undeniable that four normal fetuses will be destroyed for every one abnormal. Those who assume that a fetus is an object of high value are appalled at this "wastage." Not uncommonly they ask, "Why not wait until the baby is born and then suffocate those that are deformed?" Such a question is unquestionably rhetoric and sardonic; if serious, it implies that infanticide has no more emotional meaning to a woman than abortion, an assumption that is surely contrary to fact.

Should the Father Have Rights?

Men who are willing to see abortion-prohibition laws relaxed somewhat, but not completely, frequently raise a question about the "rights" of the father. Should we allow a woman to make a unilateral decision for an abortion? Should not her husband have a say in the matter? (After all, he contributed just as many chromosomes to the fetus as she.)

I do not know what weight to give this objection. I have encountered it repeatedly in the discussion section following a public meeting. It is clear that some men are disturbed at finding themselves powerless in such a situation and want the law to give them some power of decision.

Yet powerless men are—and it is nature that has made them so. If we give the father a right of veto in abortion decisions, the wife has a very simple reply to her husband: "I'm sorry, dear, I wasn't going to tell you this, but you've forced my hand. This is not your child." With such a statement she could always deny her husband's right to decide.

Why husbands should demand power in such matters is a fit subject for depth analysis. In the absence of such, perhaps the best thing we can say to men who are "hung up" on this issue is this: "Do you really want to live for another eight months with a woman whom you are compelling to be pregnant against her will?"

Or, in terms of public policy, do we want to pass laws which give men the right to compel their wives to be pregnant? Psychologically, such compulsion is akin to rape. Is it in the public interest to encourage rape?

"Socio-Economic"—an Anemic Phrase

The question "How can we justify an abortion?" proves least efficient in solving the real problems of this world when we try to evaluate what are usually called "socio-economic indications." The hardship cases—rape, incest, probability of a deformed child—have been amply publicized, and as a result the majority of the public accepts them as valid indicators; but hardship cases constitute only a few percent of the need. By contrast, if a woman has more children than she feels she can handle, or if her children are coming too close together, there is little public sympathy for her plight. A poll conducted by the National Opinion Research Center in December, 1965, showed that only 15 percent of the respondents replied "Yes" to this question: "Please tell me whether or not you think it should be possible for a pregnant woman to obtain a legal abortion if she is married and does not want any more children." Yet this indication, which received the lowest rate of approval, accounts for the vast majority of instances in which women want—and illegally get—relief from unwanted pregnancy.

There is a marked discrepancy between the magnitude of the need and the degree of public sympathy. Part of the reason for this discrepancy is attributable to the emotional impact of the words used to describe the need. "Rape," "incest," "deformed child"—these words are rich in emotional connotations. "Socio-economic indications" is a pale bit of jargon, suggesting at best that the abortion is wanted because the woman lives by culpably materialistic standards. "Socio-economic indications" tugs at no one's heartstrings; the hyphenated abomination hides the human reality to which it obliquely refers. To show the sort of human problem to which this label may be attached, let me quote a letter I received from one woman. (The story is unique, but it is one of a large class of similar true stories.)

> I had an illegal abortion 2½ years ago. I left my church because of the guilt I felt. I had six children when my husband left me to live with another woman. We weren't divorced and I went to work to help support them. When he would come to visit the children he would sometimes stay after they were asleep. I became pregnant. When I told my husband, and asked him to please come back, he informed me that the woman he was living with was five months pregnant and ill, and that he couldn't leave her—not at that time anyway.
>
> I got the name of a doctor in San Francisco from a Dr. friend who was visiting here from there. This Dr. (Ob. and Gyn.) had a good legitimate practice in the main part of the city and was a kindly, compassionate man who believes as you do, that it is better for everyone not to bring an unwanted child into the world.
>
> It was over before I knew it. I thought I was having an examination at the time. He even tried to make me feel not guilty by telling me that the long automobile trip had already started a spontaneous abortion. He charged me $25. That was on Friday and on Monday I was back at work. I never suffered any ill from it.
>
> The other woman's child died shortly after birth and six months later my husband asked if he could come back. We don't have a perfect marriage but my children have a father. My being able to work has helped us out of a deep financial debt. I shall always remember the sympathy I received from that Dr. and wish there were more like him with the courage to do what they believe is right.

Her operation was illegal, and would be illegal under most of the "reform" legislation now being proposed, if interpreted strictly. Fortunately some physicians are willing to indulge in more liberal interpretations, but they make these interpretations not on medical grounds, in the strict sense, but on social and economic grounds. Understandably, many physicians are unwilling to venture so far from the secure base of pure physical medicine. As one Catholic physician put it:

> Can the patient afford to have another child? Will the older children have sufficient educational opportunities if their parents have another child? Aren't two, three or four children enough? I am afraid such statements are frequently

163

made in the discussion of a proposed therapeutic abortion. [But] we should be doctors of medicine, not socio-economic prophets.[6]

To this a non-Catholic physician added: "I sometimes wish I were an obstetrician in a Catholic hospital so that I would not have to make any of these decisions. The only position to take in which I would have no misgivings is to do no interruptions at all."[7]

Who Wants Compulsory Pregnancy?

The question "How can we justify an abortion?" plainly leads to great difficulties. It is operationally unmanageable: it leads to inconsistencies in practice and inequities by any moral standard. All these can be completely avoided if we ask the right question, namely: *"How can we justify compulsory pregnancy?"*

By casting the problem in this form, we call attention to its relationship to the slavery issue. Somewhat more than a century ago men in the Western world asked the question: "How can we justify compulsory servitude?" and came up with the answer: *"By no means whatever."* Is the answer any different to the related question: "How can we justify compulsory pregnancy?" Certainly pregnancy is a form of servitude; if continued to term it results in parenthood, which is also a kind of servitude, to be continued for the best years of a woman's life. It is difficult to see how it can be argued that this kind of servitude will be more productive of social good if it is compulsory rather than voluntary. A study[8] made of Swedish children born when their mothers were refused the abortions they had requested showed that unwanted children, as compared with their controls, as they grew up were more often picked up for drunkenness, or antisocial or criminal behavior; they received less education; they received more psychiatric care; and they were more often exempted from military service by reason of defect. Moreover, the females in the group married earlier and had children earlier, thus no doubt tending to create a vicious circle of poorly tended children who in their turn would produce more poorly tended children. How then does society gain by increasing the number of unwanted children? No one has volunteered an answer to this question.

Of course if there were a shortage of children, then society might say that it needs all the children it can get—unwanted or not. But I am unaware of any recent rumors of a shortage of children.

Alternatives: True and False

The end result of an abortion—the elimination of an unwanted fetus—is surely good. But is the act itself somehow damaging? For several generations it was widely believed that abortion was intrinsically dangerous, either phy-

164

sically or psychologically. It is now very clear that the widespread belief is quite unjustified. The evidence for this statement is found in a bulky literature which has been summarized in Lawrence Lader's *Abortion*[9] and the collection of essays brought together by Alan Guttmacher.[10]

In tackling questions of this sort, it is imperative that we identify correctly the alternatives facing us. (All moral and practical problems involve a comparison of alternative actions.) Many of the arguments of the prohibitionists implicitly assume that the alternatives facing the woman are these:

abortion————no abortion

This is false. A person can never do nothing. The pregnant woman is going to do something, whether she wishes to or not. (She cannot roll time backward and live her life over.)

People often ask: "Isn't contraception better than abortion?" Implied by this question are these alternatives:

abortion————contraception

But these are not the alternatives that face the woman who asks to be aborted. She *is* pregnant. She cannot roll time backward and use contraception more successfully than she did before. Contraceptives are never foolproof anyway. It is commonly accepted that the failure rate of our best contraceptive, the "pill," is around one percent, i.e., one failure per hundred woman-years of use. I have earlier shown[11] that this failure rate produces about a quarter of a million unwanted pregnancies a year in the United States. Abortion is not so much an alternative to contraception as it is a subsidiary method of birth control, to be used when the primary method fails—as it often does.

The woman *is* pregnant: this is the base level at which the moral decision begins. If she is pregnant against her will, does it matter to society whether or not she was careless or unskillful in her use of contraception? In any case, she is threatening society with an unwanted child, for which society will pay dearly. The real alternatives facing the woman (and society) are clearly these:

abortion————compulsory pregnancy

When we recognize that these are the real, operational alternatives, the false problems created by pseudo-alternatives vanish.

Is Potential Value Valuable?

Only one weighty objection to abortion remains to be discussed, and this is the question of "loss." When a fetus is destroyed, has something valuable been destroyed? The fetus has the potentiality of becoming a human being. A human being is valuable. Therefore is not the fetus of equal value? This question must be answered.

It can be answered, but not briefly. What does the embryo receive from its parents that might be of value? There are only three possibilities: substance, energy, and information. As for the substance in the fertilized egg, it is not remarkable: merely the sort of thing one might find in any piece of meat, human or animal, and there is very little of it—only one and a half micrograms, which is about a half of a billionth of an ounce. The energy content of this tiny amount of material is likewise negligible. As the zygote develops into an embryo, both its substance and its energy content increase (at the expense of the mother) ; but this is not a very important matter—even an adult, viewed from this standpoint, is only a hundred and fifty pounds of meat!

Clearly, the humanly significant thing that is contributed to the zygote by the parents is the information that "tells" the fertilized egg how to develop into a human being. This information is in the form of a chemical tape called "DNA," a double set of two chemical supermolecules each of which has about three billion "spots" that can be coded with any one of four different possibilities, symbolized by *A, T, G,* and *C.* (For comparison, the Morse code offers three possibilities in coding: dot, dash, and space.) It is the particular sequence of these four chemical possibilities in the DNA that directs the zygote in its development into a human being. The DNA constitutes the information needed to produce a valuable human being. The question is: is this information precious? I have argued elsewhere[12] that it is not:

> Consider the case of a man who is about to begin to build a $50,000 house. As he stands on the site looking at the blueprints a practical joker comes along and sets fire to the blueprints. The question is: can the owner go to the law and collect $50,000 for his lost blueprints? The answer is obvious: since another set of blueprints can be produced for the cost of only a few dollars, that is all they are worth. (A court might award a bit more for the loss of the owner's time, but that is a minor matter.) The moral: *a non-unique copy of information that specifies a valuable structure is itself almost valueless.*
>
> This principal is precisely applicable to the moral problem of abortion. The zygote, which contains the complete specification of a valuable human being, is not a human being, and is almost valueless. . . . The early stages of an individual fetus have had very little human effort invested in them; they are of very little worth. The loss occasioned by an abortion is independent of whether the abortion is spontaneous or induced. (Just as the loss incurred by the burning of a set of blueprints is independent of whether the casual agent was lightning or an arsonist.)
>
> A set of blueprints is not a house; the DNA of a zygote is not a human being. The analogy is singularly exact, though there are two respects in which it is deficient. These respects are interesting rather than important. First, we have the remarkable fact that the blueprints of the zygote are constantly replicated and incorporated in every cell of the human body. This is interesting, but it has no moral significance. There is no moral obligation to conserve DNA—if there were, no man would be allowed to brush his teeth and gums, for in this brutal operation hundreds of sets of DNA are destroyed daily.
>
> The other anomaly of the human information problem is connected with the fact that the information that is destroyed in an aborted embryo *is* unique (unlike the house blueprints). But it is unique in a way that is without moral significance. A favorite argument of abortion-prohibitionists is this: "What if Beethoven's mother had had an abortion?" The question moves us; but when we think it over we realize we can just as relevantly ask: "What if Hitler's mother had had an abortion?" Each conceptus is unique, but not in any way

that has a moral consequence. The *expected* potential value of each aborted child is exactly that of the average child born. It is meaningless to say that humanity loses when a *particular* child is not born, or is not conceived. A human female, at birth, has about 30,000 eggs in her ovaries. If she bears only 3 children in her lifetime, is there any meaningful sense in which we can say that mankind has suffered a loss in those other 29,997 fruitless eggs? (Yet one of them might have been a super-Beethoven!)

People who worry about the moral danger of abortion do so because they think of the fetus as a human being, hence equate feticide with murder. Whether the fetus is or is not a human being is a matter of definition, not fact; and we can define any way we wish. In terms of the human problem involved, it would be unwise to define the fetus as human (hence tactically unwise ever to refer to the fetus as an "unborn child"). Analysis based on the deepest insights of molecular biology indicates the wisdom of sharply distinguishing the information for a valuable structure from the completed structure itself. It is interesting, and gratifying, to note that this modern insight is completely congruent with common law governing the disposal of dead fetuses. Abortion-prohibitionists generally insist that abortion is murder, and that an embryo is a person; but no state or nation, so far as I know, requires the dead fetus to be treated like a dead person. Although all of the states in the United States severely limit what can be done with a dead human body, no cognizance is taken of dead fetuses up to about five months' prenatal life. The early fetus may, with impunity, be flushed down the toilet or thrown out with the garbage —which shows that we never have regarded it as a human being. Scientific analysis confirms what we have always known.

The Management of Compulsory Pregnancy

What is the future of compulsory pregnancy? The immediate future is not hopeful. Far too many medical people misconceive the real problem. One physician has written:

> Might not a practical, workable solution to this most difficult problem be found by setting up, in every hospital, an abortion committee comprising a specialist in obstetrics and gynecology, a psychiatrist, and a clergyman or priest? The patient and her husband—if any—would meet with these men who would do all in their power to persuade the woman not to undergo the abortion. (I have found that the promise of a postpartum sterilization will frequently enable even married women with all the children they can care for to accept this one more, final pregnancy.) If, however, the committee members fail to change the woman's mind, they can make it very clear that they disapprove of the abortion, but prefer that it be safely done in a hospital rather than bungled in a basement somewhere.[13]

What this author has in mind is plainly not a system of legalizing abortion but a system of managing compulsory pregnancy. It is this philosophy which governs pregnancies in the Scandinavian countries,[14] where the experience of a full generation of women has shown that women do not want their pregnancies to be managed by the state. Illegal abortions have remained at a high level in these countries, and recent years have seen the development of a considerable female tourist trade to Poland, where abortions are easy to obtain. Unfortunately, American legislatures are now proposing to follow the provably unworkable system of Scandinavia.

The drift down this erroneous path is not wholly innocent. Abortion-prohibitionists are showing signs of recognizing "legalization" along Scandinavian lines as one more roadblock that can be thrown in the way of the abolition of compulsory pregnancy. To cite an example: on February 9, 1916, the *Courier,* a publication of the Winona, Minnesota, Diocese, urged that Catholics support a reform law based on the American Law Institute model, because the passage of such a law would "take a lot of steam out of the abortion advocate's argument" and would "defeat a creeping abortionism of disastrous importance."[15]

Wherever a Scandinavian or American Law Institute type of bill is passed, it is probable that cautious legislators will then urge a moratorium for several years while the results of the new law are being assessed (though they are easily predictable from the Scandinavian experience). As Lord Morley once said: "Small reforms are the worst enemies of great reforms." Because of the backwardness of education in these matters, caused by the long taboo under which the subject of abortion labored, it seems highly likely that our present system of compulsory pregnancy will continue substantially without change until the true nature of the alternatives facing us is more widely recognized.

NOTES

[1] Mary Steichen Calderone (ed.), *Abortion in the United States,* New York: Hoeber-Harper, 1958, p. 178.

[2] Anthony C. Beilenson, "Abortion and Common Sense," *Per/Se,* 1 (1966), p. 24.

[3] Garrett Hardin, "Semantic Aspects of Abortion," *ETC.,* 24 (1967), p. 263.

[4] Lee Rainwater, *And the Poor Get Children,* Chicago: Quadrangle Books, 1960, p. *ix* and chap. 1.

[5] Alice S. Rossi, "Abortion Laws and Their Victims," *Trans-action,* 3 (September-October, 1966), p. 7.

[6] Calderone (ed.), *op. cit.,* p. 103.

[7] *Ibid.,* p. 123.

[8] Hans Forssman and Inga Thuwe, "One Hundred and Twenty Children Born after Application for Therapeutic Abortion Refused," *Acta Psychiatrica Scandinavica,* 42 (1966), p. 71.

[9] Lawrence Lader, *Abortion,* Indianapolis: Bobbs-Merrill, 1966.

[10] Alan F. Guttmacher (ed.), *The Case for Legalized Abortion,* Berkeley, California: Diablo Press, 1967.

[11] Garrett Hardin, "A Scientist's Case for Abortion," *Redbook* (May 1967), p. 62.

[12] Garrett Hardin, "Blueprints, DNA, and Abortion: A Scientific and Ethical Analysis," *Medical Opinion and Review*, 3:2 (1967), p. 74.

[13] H. Curtis Wood, Jr., "Letter to the Editor," *Medical Opinion and Review*, 3:11 (1967), p. 19.

[14] David T. Smith (ed.), *Abortion and the Law*, Cleveland: Western Reserve University, 1967, p. 179.

[15] Anonymous, *Association for the Study of Abortion Newsletter*, 2:3 (1967), p. 6.

4

Partnerships and Role Relationship Adjustments

Once any kind of partnership is formed, the problems of its existence as a unit begin. In the case of the marriage partnership these adjustment problems are myriad and only a selected few can be presented. Perhaps the two problems confronted first are the division of labor, and relationships with in-laws. Yet when probing into the *details* of working out and maintaining role relationships, it is seen they are anything but simple. Men and women must expect to deal with the failure, as well as the success, of their spouses in fulfilling role expectations.

Currently, other important aspects of role allocation in marriage are undergoing change. Many women are rebelling against accepting the traditional tasks of housewife and mother as their sole responsibilities. Men, too, feel that some role demands on husbands require great sacrifice of freedom.

One role responsibility that merits more attention from researchers is the maintenance of excitement in marital companionship, an element presumably present when the couple were first attracted to each other. Much discontent in marriage results when this ingredient is missing. Yet the talents peculiar to this very crucial area are not well known. An attempt is made in the final article of the chapter to suggest some of these abilities, because of their importance to the partnership in an era when personal relationships overshadow marital commitments.

The Components of Marital Roles

Nathan Hurvitz

Lists of the roles or duties of spouses to one another are often presented in discussions of marriage, and it is assumed that the content of these roles is standard and self-explanatory. Actually, role content is quite complicated, as Hurvitz's research shows. It is also interesting that the current role responsibilities of husband and wives are simultaneously quite similar by title while having many subtle differences by sex. The components of these role-responsibilities also include many emotional qualities. It is suggested that merely "doing one's duty" by one's spouse is not sufficient role enactment for today's demanding male-female partnerships.

The concept of role, which plays a central part in the study of the family, is gaining increasing importance in efforts to apply sociological concepts and knowledge in the clinical setting.[1] However, investigators from varied but related fields are using this concept in widely different ways. In general, three different kinds of family roles are described: (1) functional, which link the individual as an actor to his family and the social structure; (2) control, which identify the source and kind of authority exercised within the family; and (3) symbolic, which are related to the developmental needs that the husband and wife satisfy for each other.[2]

The functional roles have two general characteristics: (1) they have two valences and (2) they subsume different components as a result of individual experiences. The two valences of these roles are their performance and the expectation of how they will be performed. The compatibility of role performances and role expectations of the spouses can be measured and interpreted as an index of strain between them.[3]

Each role also subsumes a number of concrete and specific actions which are defined by the normative expectations of the members of the group as defined by its social traditions. These roles, which are organized into a role-

From Nathan Hurvitz, "Components of Marital Roles," *Sociology and Social Research,* April, 1961, pp. 301–09. Reprinted by permission of the University of Southern California.

set, become part of the individual's personality. As Parsons points out, in the course of the process of socialization the individual absorbs—to a greater or lesser degree—the standards and ideals of his group so that they become effective motivating forces in his own conduct, independently of external sanctions.[4] Roles thus serve as norms that guide the individual in his relationships with others;[5] however, because each individual's experiences are unique, he may define his roles' components differently and may have idiosyncratic norms of performed and expected behavior, thus creating a strain upon his role partner.[6]

In the counseling situation it is often apparent that the spouses have a different order of role performances and role expectations and that they define their own and their spouse's roles' components differently. Thus the role of "companion," which both spouses share, may have different meanings for each of them although both spouses may consider "companion" to be their primary role and expect it as the primary role from the other spouse. The husband may interpret "companion" to mean that his wife may not have any interests outside their home, that she must participate in a planned activity with him even in an emergency situation, or that she must be deeply interested in each one of his activities. If his wife does not define the components of the "companion" role in the same way, this can be a source of strain between them. Since the roles' components are defined on the basis of one's own growing-up experiences, the kind of family group in which he was raised, his social class position, educational level, rural or urban origin, exposure to mass communication media, or ethnic group identification, each individual may be expected to define the roles' components differently. Marriage counseling, which often involves the discussion of the different pattern of role performances and role expectations between the spouses, can therefore utilize empirically developed role-sets for husbands and wives. The components of the role-sets should be regarded as sociological ideal or constructed types and not as actual specific and concrete actions which each spouse performs or expects; and as ideal types the components can serve as norms of performance and expectation of the marital partners.[7]

SAMPLE AND PROCEDURE

The Marital Roles Inventory,[8] which was devised by the writer and utilized in a recent study of marriage,[9] lists the role-sets of the spouses and is an instrument that the writer utilized to secure responses regarding the roles' components. The data for this study were secured during the summer of 1957 from a random sample of 104 married couples living in the Baldwin Hills area, a middle-class neighborhood in southwestern Los Angeles. The data were collected by the writer through interviews with the subjects in their homes. Couples who agreed to participate were interviewed together, and the husband and wife completed separate questionnaires simultaneously but independently in the presence of the writer.

Significant social characteristics of the subjects indicate their middle-class status. The mean age of the husbands in the sample is approximately 40; the mean age of the wives is approximately 35; and the mean length of marriage to the present spouse is approximately 12.5 years. The modal family group is composed of a couple married 8 to 14 years with two children. Half the sample is Jewish, Protestants constitute more than a third, Catholics about 10 percent, and 5 percent indicated no religious affiliation or preference. Forty percent of the husbands and almost 30 percent of the wives are college graduates; one third of the husbands are professionals and another third are business owners or managers; and the mean income is $9,615.00 a year.

After the spouses had completed the Marital Roles Inventory, which was the last part of the schedule, they were asked to report what they believed were the most important role components, the usual functions or actions subsumed or implied by each role. The responses of the subjects were recorded at the time of the interview; later each role component was typed on a slip of paper, and the similar statements from all the subjects were grouped together. The most common or the most expressive statement about a particular component was taken to stand for all those similar to it. Following, presented in the same random order as they appear on the Marital Roles Inventory, are the roles of the husband-and-father and wife-and-mother and their components as defined by this middle-class sample.[10]

THE HUSBAND'S ROLES

He does his jobs around the house. He performs the man's household chores, yard work, and various repairs related to his skill and ability. He shows an interest in his home to make it more pleasant and livable.

He is a companion to his wife. He shares his activities, leisure time, and thoughts with his wife. He is related to his wife more than to any other interests such as his occupation or business, his parents, children, friends, various organizations of which he is a member and in which he holds office, hobbies, etc. He shows interest in his wife's concerns such as their children, relatives, neighbors, etc. He is aware that he needs his wife for the fulfillment of himself as a person, and he seeks to help his wife fulfill herself as a person also. He regards his wife as a friend and confidante and refrains from abuse or ridicule of her.

He helps the children grow by being their friend, teacher, and guide. He is involved with the children as a friendly and concerned adult. He helps the children make choices and orients them to effective participation in their growing world. He interacts with the children about their experiences and feelings. He participates in leisure-time activities with the children and assists them with their school work, youth organization activities, etc. He helps them in their relationships with other children and adults. He is aware of what is desirable, preferred, or "proper" behavior for the children in particular situations and helps them to perform in this way. He uses punishment under-

174

standingly, he disciplines in relation to the realities of the situation, and he refrains from abuse and ridicule of the children.

He earns the living and supports the family. He is the breadwinner. He recognizes and accepts the responsibility for the financial support of his family.

He does his wife's work around the house if his help is needed. He performs part of his wife's roles if she or the children are ill or this is required by a particular circumstance; or he carries all of his wife's roles on a temporary basis if this is necessary. He accepts carrying out his wife's roles in emergencies as part of the marital relationship.

He practices the family religion or philosophy. He expresses and/or identifies with a religious belief and/or philosophical attitude toward life and the world. He gives the children an understanding of the family's religious identification, minority group and/or ethnic group values, or the family's nonreligious philosophy such as secular humanism, etc.

He is a sexual partner to his wife. He gains and gives sexual gratification with his wife. He shows his wife special tender attention and interest. He understands that his wife's sexual needs are part of her total feeling for him. He wants to have children with his wife. He does not show sexual interest in other women. He does not abuse his wife sexually.

He serves as the model of men for his children. He serves as the "ideal-model" of men, husbands, and fathers for his children; and he expresses this in the manner in which he performs his other roles. He is organized as a person and does not show deviant behavior as alcoholism, criminality, etc. He can understand and respond properly to the behavior and feeling of others. He is interested in his own physical health and psychological well-being. He accepts his roles as husband-and-father and stays with his family while attempting to work through problems that may arise through the performance of his other roles.

He decides when the family is still divided after discussing something. He is recognized, acknowledged, and referred to by his wife and children as the decision-maker about family affairs. He casts the "tie-breaking vote" when decisions are made. He makes decisions which are fair and in the interests of the entire family.

He represents and advances his family in the community. He is the legal head of the family and household. He is concerned with his own and his family's educational and vocational future. He participates in community affairs and accepts civic responsibilities. He joins groups of various kinds for his own recreational or other interests and to further his occupational, business, or family interests. He wants his wife to reflect the status to which he is aspiring. He wants to "get ahead," and he wants to keep his family from dependence upon "outsiders." He holds attitudes and values that do not challenge the community in which he functions.

He helps manage the family income and finances. He manages his earnings and/or other income for the benefit of the entire family. He brings home his earnings. He helps plan the use of the family income for all the members of the family. He subordinates his immediate needs to the long-range goals of the family. He plans for the future security of his family through such programs as savings and insurance.

The Wife's Roles

She helps earn the living when her husband needs her help or when the family needs more money. She accepts the responsibility to assist in the financial support of her family if her help is needed. She accepts her husband's role as breadwinner temporarily in an acute crisis such as illness or incapacity, or she assists her husband in this role permanently in a chronic situation which has diminished his earning power. She does not regard herself, nor does she aspire to be, the primary breadwinner in the family.

She practices the family religion or philosophy. She expresses and/or identifies with a religious belief and/or philosophical attitude toward life and the world. She gives the children an understanding of the family's religious identification, minority group and/or ethnic values, or the family's nonreligious philosophy such as secular humanism, etc.

She cares for the children's everyday needs. She is responsible for the immediate, daily needs of her children from infancy through adolescence: feeding, clothing, cleaning, getting off to school, transporting, etc. She supervises the children's interaction with playmates and neighbor children. She is the liaison between her family and the children's and youth clubs and activities in which her children participate. Her involvement with the children changes as they grow and experience new privileges and responsibilities. She rewards and punishes the children in relation to the immediate situation.

She is a companion to her husband. She shares her activities, leisure time, and thoughts with her husband. She is related to her husband more than to any other interests such as her occupation or business, her parents, friends, various organizations of which she is a member and in which she holds office, hobbies, etc. She is related to her husband and his needs more than to her children except in emergencies such as illness, etc. She shows interest in her husband's concerns such as his occupation or business, their children, relatives, neighbors, etc. She is aware that she needs her husband for the fulfillment of herself as a person, and she seeks to help her husband fulfill himself as a person also. She regards her husband as a friend and confidant and refrains from abuse or ridicule of him.

She is the homemaker. She performs the everyday tasks of running the home: planning and preparing meals, cleaning the house, laundering, supplying clean and repaired clothes, etc. She budgets the household expenses and manages the everyday household affairs.

She is a sexual partner to her husband. She gains and gives sexual gratification with her husband. She shows her husband special tender attention and interest. She understands that her husband's sexual needs are part of his total feeling for her. She wants to have children with her husband. She does not show sexual interest in other men. She does not use the sexual relationship to manipulate her husband and wants to satisfy him sexually. She expects sexual attention and loyalty from her husband and continues to hold her husband's sexual interest.

She serves as the model of women for her children. She serves as the "ideal-model" of women, wives, and mothers for her children; and she expresses this in the manner in which she performs her other roles. She is organized as a person and does not show such deviant behavior as alcoholism, criminality, etc. She can understand and respond properly to the behavior and feelings of others. She is interested in her own physical health and psychological well-being. She subordinates her own interests to the economic role of the husband. She gains fulfillment of herself as a woman in relation to her family responsibilities; she accepts a limited range of activities and interests outside her home; and she believes that it is more desirable to be married and rear a family than not. She accepts her roles as wife-and-mother and stays with her family while attempting to work through problems that may arise through the performance of her other roles.

She represents and advances her family socially and in the community. She is the "social" head of the family and plans the family's social activities at home and away from home. She is concerned with her own and her family's educational and vocational future. She participates in community affairs and accepts civic responsibilities. She joins groups of various kinds for her own recreational or other interests and to further the interest of the family as a whole. She plays the social role her husband's status aspirations require and she cultivates associations which may help her husband to succeed in his primary role obligations. She wants her husband to "get ahead," and she wants to keep her family from dependence upon "outsiders." She is the correspondent in social and family matters for her family. She holds attitudes and values that do not challenge the community in which she functions.

She helps the children grow by being their friend, teacher, and guide. She is involved with the children as a friendly and concerned adult. She helps the children make choices and orients them to effective participation in their growing world. She interacts with the children about their experiences and feelings. She participates in leisure-time activities with the children and assists them with their school work, youth organization activities, etc. She helps them in their relationships with other children and adults. She is aware of what is desirable, preferred, or "proper" behavior for the children in particular situations and helps them to perform in this way. She uses punishment understandingly, she disciplines in relation to the realities of the situation, and she refrains from abuse and ridicule of her children.

She helps manage the family income and finances. She manages her husband's earnings and/or other income for the benefit of the entire family. She helps plan the use of the family income for all the members of the family so that each can have the most benefit from the available income.

She decides when the family is still divided after discussing something. She is recognized, acknowledged, and deferred to by her husband and children as the decision-maker about family affairs. She casts the "tie-breaking vote" when decisions are made. She makes decisions that are fair and in the interests of the entire family.

Summary and Discussion

The developing use of the concept of role in the behavioral sciences, in marriage and family research, and in marriage counseling, requires that all persons concerned with the relationship between the spouses develop a clear understanding of marital roles and their components. This paper indicated that in general there are three kinds of roles described in the studies about the family: (1) functional, (2) control, and (3) symbolic.

This paper outlined the components of the functional roles and indicated that their exposition can be utilized in marriage and family counseling. Since these roles embody and reflect norms, they guide our relatedness to other people. Thus, presenting the roles of the husband-and-father and wife-and-mother to a young married couple may give them reciprocal norms of conduct which may have considerable significance for them in helping them to accept the socially defined responsibilities of marriage. Also, exploring the differential pattern of role performances and role expectations of the individual, definitions of the roles' components of a pair of spouses in marital conflict may reveal areas where counseling or reeducation is indicated.

The roles and their components which have been outlined and described in this paper have certain limitations: (1) they were prepared by middle-class husbands and wives and reflect middle-class attitudes and values; (2) there is overlapping in some of the roles and roles' components as in "companion" and "sexual partner," and "care for the children's everyday needs" and "help the children grow"; and (3) these roles and their components may be defined differently and have different significance at various stages of family growth. Although these limitations are present, it should also be pointed out that (1) even those persons who may not be in the middle class by objective criteria identify themselves as members of the middle class and accept the middle-class attitudes and values which pervade our society; (2) although there is overlapping and there are common elements in some roles, they are different in their function and in their place in the social structure of the family; and (3) since the roles and their components may be defined differently, this may serve to indicate how the definition of these roles changes during various stages in the natural history of the family in our society.

Other investigators may utilize this material in both research and counseling and modify the components to make them more useful for themselves and the field of marriage and family counseling as a whole.

178

NOTES

[1] Otto Pollak, *Integrating Sociological and Psychoanalytic Concepts* (New York: Russell Sage Foundation, 1956).

[2] Nathan Hurvitz, "Marital Roles and Adjustment in Marriage in a Middle-Class Group" (unpublished Ph.D. dissertation, University of Southern California, 1958).

[3] Hurvitz, "The Measurement of Marital Strain," *American Journal of Sociology,* 65:610–15 (May, 1960).

For a theoretical approach to role strain, "the felt difficulty in fulfilling role obligations," which places the present research in the larger context of role theory and the social structure, see William J. Goode, "A Theory of Role Strain," *American Sociological Review,* 25:483–96 (August, 1960).

[4] Talcott Parsons, *Essays in Sociological Theory* (rev. ed.) (Glencoe, Ill.: The Free Press, 1954), pp. 230–31.

[5] George C. Homans, *The Human Group* (New York: Harcourt, Brace, 1950), pp. 123–24.

[6] Parsons, *The Social System* (Glencoe, Ill.: The Free Press, 1951), p. 252.

[7] The importance of the "ideal type" in family research is indicated by Burgess and Locke, who state that the ideal type may be distinguished by four general characteristics: 1. "the prefix 'ideal' denotes merely logical perfection and not evaluation or approval"; 2. "the ideal type represents the extremes and not the average"; 3. "the ideal type is a logical construction, an abstraction, and, therefore, by its very nature cannot be found in reality"; and 4. "the ideal-type procedure is not merely a method for formulating concepts but for the analysis and measurement of social reality." Ernest W. Burgess and Harvey J. Locke, *The Family, from Institution to Companionship* (New York: American Book Company, 1950), Appendix A, pp. 754–57.

[8] Published by Western Psychological Services, Box 775, Beverly Hills, California.

[9] Nathan Hurvitz, "Marital Roles and Adjustment in Marriage in a Middle-Class Group," *op. cit.*

[10] As a result of this study, the Marital Roles Inventory was modified to include the role "He [She] helps manage the family income or finances," for both spouses; and "She decides when the family is still divided after discussing something," for the wife.

Roles of Family Members

Theodore B. Johannis, Jr.

In the second article of this book Goode said that people living in families have reciprocal role obligations. He did not, however, elaborate as to the content of these responsibilities or how they are divided among family members. Johannis investigated family participation in three spheres of family life—economic activity, household tasks, and child care. From his results, shown in table form, we see that a great deal of family living is composed of mundane activities that are divided in certain patterned ways among family members. The grounds for this division of labor appear to be based in part on what has been traditionally considered to be man's or woman's work.

Participation in Family Economic Activity

One of the topics seldom discussed in the texts used in functional courses on marriage and the family is the division of responsibility within the family, especially in the area of economic activity. Data describing the participation by fathers and mothers and their teen-age offspring in such activity are presented below.

The data were supplied by 1,027 high school sophomores living in non-broken white families in Tampa, Florida in the spring of 1953. The median age of the fathers was 43.7 years, of the mothers 39.6 years and of respondents 15.1 years. The fathers and mothers had been married a median of 19.0 years and had a median of 2.2 children of whom a median of 1.9 were still living at home. The median education of fathers was 9.1 years, of mothers 8.9 years. One-half of the fathers and one-half of the mothers who worked were in

From Theodore B. Johannis, "Roles of Family Members," in *Family Mobility in Our Dynamic Society*, ed., Iowa State University Center for Agricultural Economic Development (Ames, Iowa: Iowa State University Press, 1965), pp. 69–79. Reprinted by permission of Iowa State University Press. Appreciation is due the E. C. Brown Trust and the Graduate School of the University of Oregon for financial assistance in the data analysis phase of this study.

"blue-collar" and service occupations. Seven out of ten fathers and mothers had been reared in the southeastern section of the United States.

TABLE 1

PERCENT OF FATHERS, MOTHERS, AND TEEN-AGE SONS AND
DAUGHTERS PARTICIPATING IN SELECTED FAMILY
ECONOMIC ACTIVITY*

(A Study of 1,027 Nonbroken White Families)

| | Family Member | | | | |
Activity	A Shared Activity (Percent)	Father (Percent)	Mother (Percent)	Teen-age Son (Percent)	Teen-age Daughter (Percent)
Selects large household equipment	61.9	68.7	90.2	5.0	6.8
Shops for furniture and furnishings	61.3	62.3	93.5	4.6	13.7
Shops for groceries	55.1	42.5	84.1	32.0	37.4
Plans family's savings	47.2	68.8	73.2	3.0	2.1
Shops for family's clothes	46.4	29.3	95.6	30.1	44.3
Provides for family's new car	46.4	91.3	46.5	10.8	15.0
Provides children's spending money	45.7	77.3	56.1	21.4	4.6
Pays bills	39.7	76.8	58.2	7.4	7.6
Earns money for family	38.3	97.9	32.8	15.7	2.2
Range High	61.9	97.9	95.6	32.0	44.3
Low	38.3	29.3	32.8	3.0	2.1

*These items are listed in rank order according to the percentage of the families in which the activity was shared, i.e., usually participated in by two or more members of the family.

181

TABLE 2
PERCENT OF FATHERS, MOTHERS, AND TEEN-AGE SONS AND DAUGHTERS PARTICIPATING IN SELECTED HOUSEHOLD TASKS*
(A study of 1,027 Nonbroken White Families)

Activity	A Shared Activity (Percent)	Father (Percent)	Mother (Percent)	Teen-age Son (Percent)	Teen-age Daughter (Percent)
Picks up and puts away clothes	60.2	18.1	82.0	38.5	78.0
Makes beds	50.0	3.5	75.3	28.8	72.9
Takes care of yard	49.4	49.5	24.4	79.8	31.9
Cleans and dusts	48.6	5.3	71.7	12.8	74.3
Does main meal's dishes	46.4	5.8	51.6	27.0	76.9
Does ironing	44.7	1.9	69.3	6.5	67.0
Locks up at night	36.7	63.4	40.7	45.7	28.2
Clears table for main meal	36.1	4.7	49.2	28.6	72.2
Sets table for main meal	32.5	3.5	50.1	23.3	75.5
Fixes broken things	29.1	77.5	9.2	51.6	4.1
Sets breakfast table	29.1	9.4	74.2	13.4	39.8
Takes care of garbage and trash	28.8	27.5	25.1	66.0	33.3
Does family wash	28.4	4.9	75.8	5.5	30.8
Gets main meal	27.3	7.8	86.6	9.4	33.1
Does breakfast dishes	22.7	4.1	70.8	10.1	34.4
Clears breakfast table	23.1	6.0	70.0	16.4	38.8
Gets breakfast	22.4	13.4	87.7	12.6	26.6
Mends family's clothes	20.4	3.2	88.8	2.8	27.5
Range High	60.2	77.5	88.8	79.8	78.0
Low	20.4	1.9	9.2	2.8	4.1

*These items are listed in rank order according to the percentage of the families in which the activity was shared, i.e., usually participated in by two or more members of the family.

TABLE 3
PERCENT OF FATHERS, MOTHERS, AND TEEN-AGE SONS AND DAUGHTERS PARTICIPATING IN SELECTED CHILD CARE AND CONTROL ACTIVITY
(A study of 1,027 Nonbroken White Families)

Activity	A Shared Activity (Percent)	Father (Percent)	Mother (Percent)	Teen-age Son (Percent)	Teen-age Daughter (Percent)
Teaches children right from wrong and correct behavior	75.5	77.4	92.2	7.8	8.0
Sees children have fun	68.2	66.0	80.7	23.4	22.6
Teaches children facts and skills	65.4	75.5	76.9	13.7	11.4
Punishes children for doing wrong	60.7	76.0	77.4	2.1	3.2
Helps children choose what they will do after finishing school	56.1	61.6	65.5	18.7	19.5
Sees children come in on time at night	53.5	69.0	73.8	7.0	3.0
Sees children have good table manners	51.2	47.8	86.0	11.2	18.3
Helps children with schoolwork	45.3	42.9	56.6	25.1	30.9
Sees children do homework	40.8	43.1	69.5	13.4	18.5
Sees children go to bed on time	40.6	45.7	71.9	11.3	13.5
Cares for children when sick	39.3	34.7	95.6	3.2	8.2
Sees children get to school or work on time	28.9	26.8	75.6	19.1	21.7
Sees children eat right foods	24.9	19.7	84.9	12.3	14.7
Sees children get up in morning on time	22.5	23.8	72.5	14.2	20.2
Sees children wear right clothes	19.8	5.6	66.4	25.1	35.4
Sees children get dressed	19.7	5.6	60.8	25.6	39.2
Range High	75.5	77.4	95.6	25.6	39.2
Low	19.7	5.6	56.6	2.1	3.0

*These items are listed in rank order according to the percentage of the families in which the activity was shared, i.e., usually participated in by two or more members of the family.

Initial Adjustment Processes in Young Married Couples

Beverly R. Cutler and
William G. Dyer

How do husbands and wives cope with the failure of a spouse to "do what he should" (so far as they are concerned) in areas of affection, companionship, taking care of the house, family finances, and so on? What are the possible outcomes of their attempts to adjust role expectations and realities of performance? How do husbands and wives differ in the action they take? Which is better—to talk the matter through openly or to adopt a "wait and see" attitude?

The matter of "adjustment" in marriage is an area of discussion in almost every marriage textbook and class. A number of years ago, Kirkpatrick stated, "The investigation of marital adjustment is still almost a virgin field for sociological research. There is a need for checking of previous research, for contributing additional fragments of evidence, and for a piecing together of the results of isolated studies into a meaningful whole."[1] This condition still appears to exist.

ADJUSTMENT AS PROCESS OR GOAL

In the literature on marital adjustment, two different approaches are often taken and sometimes intermingled indiscriminately. Some writers refer to adjustment as a state of marriage to be achieved,[2] while other writers refer to adjustment primarily as a process of interaction.[3]

Bowerman feels that both conditions are important. He says:

From Beverly R. Cutler and William G. Dyer, "Initial Adjustment Processes in Young Married Couples," *Social Forces,* December, 1965, pp. 195–201. Reprinted by permission of University of North Carolina Press.

In addition to measures of overall evaluation of the marriage, there would seem to be considerable use, in both research and counseling, for measures of the *degree of adjustment* in the various aspects of the relationship, such as adjustment about financial matters, recreation, homemaking duties, etc. In studying the *processes of adjustment* in marriage, it is necessary to take into account the relationship between different kinds of adjustment which must be made, how these types of adjustment are differentially affected by the various forces affecting the marriage, and how each contributes to the evaluation of the marriage as a whole.[4]

When seen as a goal, marital adjustment is commonly equated with such conditions as marital success, marital satisfaction, and marital happiness. It would seem that these terms are all referring to the same end condition which is arrived at through some interactive process. Research-wise it is much easier to develop a measure of marital adjustment or success and then relate a series of independent variables to this dependent condition and discover which variables are most highly related to the condition of adjustment, than it is to investigate the processes couples go through to arrive at the end condition. This paper is an attempt to add "an additional fragment of evidence" to the matter of adjustment as a process. Very little research actually shows the process married couples go through to achieve adjustment.

The focus of this research report is centered on the question, "When a young married person finds that his spouse engages in behavior that violates his expectations, what kinds of actions does he engage in to deal with this disturbance in the relationship?" Adjustment, generally speaking, is the process used in successfully reducing disturbance in a relationship.

Adjustment Possibilities Using Role Theory

In a previous paper, a theoretical analysis of marital adjustment using role theory was presented.[5] This formulation is the basis for the following analysis.

Adjustment is defined as the bringing into agreement the behavior of one person with the expectation of another accompanied by a feeling of acceptance of the modified behavior by the one making the adjustment.

From the point of view of role behavior, when conflict in marriage occurs because one person has violated the expectations of his spouse the possible adjustments are:

1. The husband (or wife) can change his role performance completely to meet the role expectations of his partner.
2. The husband (or wife) can change his role expectations, completely, to coincide with the role performance of the partner.
3. There can be a mutual adjustment, each partner altering some. The husband (or wife) can alter his role to a degree and the partner alters his role expectations to a similar degree so that role performance and role expectations are com-

patible. In each of the above cases the end result is an agreement between role performance and role expectations.

4. There is also another type of adjustment possible. In some cases the couple might recognize a disparity between role performance and role expectations or between norms and also acknowledge that change is difficult or impossible and could "agree to disagree." In such cases the one partner recognizes and respects the position of the other without accepting or adjusting to it. This pattern of "agreeing to disagree" is not adjustment in the same sense as the others listed above. The "adjustment" comes from both partners agreeing that a certain area is "out of bounds" as far as the application of sanctions are concerned. There is no change in behavior but some change in expectations in that each now expects certain areas not to be raised as issues and that no sanctions will be applied over these "out of bound" issues.[6]

This study focuses on the following problems:

1. Are the initial reactions of young married partners to violations of role expectations (in the sense described above) adjustive or non-adjustive?
2. Do husbands and wives differ in their adjustment processes?
3. Do couples use different adjustments in different areas of marriage?

METHODOLOGY

Following an initial pilot study of depth interviews with ten couples, an extensive questionnaire on marital adjustment was administered to a random sample of young married couples at Brigham Young University during the fall and winter of the 1962–63 school year. Couples were selected on the basis of the husband's enrollment in the University. Since the study was aimed at the adjustment in young married couples, only those couples were selected where the husband was under 23 years of age. There were 75 couples in the sample. Fifteen couples were eliminated for various reasons leaving 60 couples in the study. Participants were asked to fill out the questionnaire separately and privately and not consult the marital partner.

DESCRIPTION OF THE SAMPLE

Eighty-five percent of the couples had been married less than three years. Fifty-five percent had no children while 35 percent had one child. All of the couples were members of the L.D.S. (Mormon) church. Seventy-four percent of the couples had known each other for more than one year prior to marriage. Only 13 percent of the husbands and 18 percent of the wives were reared in communities over 100,000. While all of the husbands were in college, 30 percent of the wives had not attended college.

The following areas of marriage were examined in the questionnaire:

1. Verbal expressions of affection.
2. Frequency of sexual intimacy.
3. Spending time at home.
4. Sharing ideas.
5. Care of the home.
6. Personal neatness and appearance.
7. Spending family income.

From the pilot study, it was indicated that the above represented the primary areas within which couples were making adjustments to each other. The questionnaire was constructed to determine the following:

1. The expectations of husbands and wives towards each other in the areas listed above.
2. The ways these expectations are violated by husbands and wives.
3. The responses by the marriage partner when the spouse has violated one's expectations.
4. The reaction of the spouse to the initial responses of the marriage partner.
5. The current feelings of the couple about the area of marriage following the initial adjustment responses and reactions.

For each of the seven areas of marriage examined in the study, the following questions were asked concerning responses to the violation of expectations: (1) In what ways has your spouse failed to live up to your expectations? What has he (she) done to violate your expectations you held for him (her) concerning this aspect of your marriage relationship? (2) If your spouse did not meet your expectations, what did you do? (3) When you responded as indicated in the previous question, what did your spouse do in return?

Initial responses and subsequent reactions were judged either adjustive, non-adjustive, or non-action. An adjustive response is one that brings behavior and expectations closer together and reduces the degree of negative sanction. A non-adjustive response is one that either does not reduce the disparity or sanction or may actually intensify the difference. A third type of response was noted in the pilot study, namely non-action. The problem is recognized but no action is taken in hopes that the problem will resolve itself through the passing of time. One might conclude that non-action is a non-adjustive response, but the non-adjustive response actually represents a behavioral strategy that was being attempted in some types of behavior. There was no behavior strategy being attempted in non-action, only the hopes were that it would be adjustive in the long run, hence, the decision to make this a special category.

In addition to being adjustive or non-adjustive, responses and reactions to responses were categorized in terms of two dimensions: sharing and valence [either positive or negative]. This gave the following possible responses in the coding guide:

1. *Adjustive Response*
A. shared positive response—This is a response that is shared with the marriage partner and positive in the sense that it appears to be directed toward achieving adjustment.

B. non-shared positive—This is a non-shared response but also adjustively centered.

2. *Non-Adjustive Response*

A. shared negative—This is a shared response but apparently not given with the idea of facilitating adjustment, hence, a negative valence.

B. non-shared negative—A non-shared response not geared toward facilitating adjustment.

3. *Non-Action*—A non-shared response with suspended valence.

Following are examples of the various possible responses: Respondents would check these categories in response to the question "If your spouse did not meet your expectations, what did you do?"

A. Shared positive response: "Talked it over rather openly and calmly."

B. Non-shared positive: "Didn't say anything at all; just accepted the situation as it was—didn't let it bother me."

C. Shared negative: "Got upset and argued, quarreled, pouted or sulked with spouse."

D. Non-shared negative: "Got upset, worried about it, cried, or felt sorry for myself; but didn't say anything to my spouse."

E. Non-action: "Didn't say anything at first; just waited to see if things would work out."

DISCUSSION OF FINDINGS

Initial Reactions to Expectation Violations

Husbands: From Table 1, the totals indicate that the generally most prevalent strategy adopted by husbands when they felt their wives had violated their expectations was a non-action response. The husbands indicated they initially took a "wait and see" stance but these data do not tell us how the wives perceived these same responses.

The next most prevalent response of the husbands, as perceived by themselves, was an open talking about the problem in a calm manner. These shared, adjustive type responses were followed numerically by non-shared adjustive responses. These two adjustive type responses account for 51 percent of all responses made by husbands. Husbands felt that only five percent of their initial responses were of a non-adjustive type.

For each of the areas taken separately, some differences appear. The non-action strategy is most apparent in *Area 2* which is frequency of sexual intimacy. There were more violations of expectations in this area than any of the others, yet this is the one area where no husband checked a non-shared adjustive response—that is, "didn't say anything at all; just accepted the situation as it was—didn't let it bother me." While non-adjustive responses were rarely indicated at all, this area, more than any other, was one where some husbands admitted making some non-adjustive responses.

188

TABLE 1
INITIAL RESPONSES OF HUSBANDS AND WIVES TO VIOLATIONS OF EXPECTATIONS

TYPE OF RESPONSE	VERBAL EXPRESSION OF AFFECTION	FREQUENCY OF SEXUAL INTIMACY	SPENDING TIME AT HOME	SHARING IDEAS	CARE OF HOME	PERSONAL NEATNESS, APPEARANCE	SPENDING FAMILY INCOME	TOTAL
	I	II	III	IV	V	VI	VII	
Husband								
S+	3	5	2	6	6	4	7	33
NS+	8	0	1	3	1	1	1	15
Non-Action	8	14	0	5	9	3	2	41
S−	0	1	0	1	0	0	1	3
NS−	0	2	0	0	0	0	0	2
Total	19	22	3	15	16	8	11	94
Wife	I	II	III	IV	V	VI	VII	
S+	8	12	6	6	10	9	6	57
NS+	5	0	2	2	4	0	1	14
Non-Action	9	6	6	8	5	2	5	41
S−	1	0	4	2	5	0	2	14
NS−	2	2	1	1	1	0	1	8
Total	25	20	19	19	25	11	15	134

Area 1—(Verbal Expressions of Affection) appears to be the area most easily accepted by the husband without talking it over with his wife. Eight out of 19 husbands with non-met expectations in this area indicated that they accepted this situation as it was—didn't let it bother them.

Area 7—(Spending Family Income) appears to be the area most easily talked about openly and calmly. Seven of 11 violations were met in this manner. *Area 3*—(Spending Time at Home) was the area of least violations. Apparently most of these new husbands were satisfied with the amount of time the wife was spending in the home. Such is not the case, however, with the wives.

Wives. While 44 percent of the husbands' initial reactions were of the non-action variety, only 31 percent of the responses of the wives were in this category. Wives indicated they responded initially with more shared, adjustive type responses than their husbands and also with more non-adjustive type responses than were admitted by their spouses. Again it should be remembered, this is how the wives perceived their initial responses—not how the spouse experienced it.

Rather consistently, the pattern for the wives in most areas was one of more open sharing in contrast to the non-action strategy which characterized many areas for the husbands. This is especially true in the area of frequency of sexual intimacy. Husbands indicated they generally took a "wait and see" approach, while the wives' initial response was to talk about the problem. Interestingly enough this sensitive area resulted in only two admitted non-adjustive type initial responses. Like the husband, this was one area where no wife adopted a non-shared adjustive response.

As with the husbands, *Area 1*—(Verbal Expressions of Affection) was the area where more wives adjusted internally without talking about this with their spouses.

Areas 1 and *5* had the highest number of violations marked. These are Verbal Expressions of Affection and Care of the Home, respectively. *Area 5* is also the area with more non-adjustive reactions than any other. It should be remembered that this does not indicate which of the areas was the most important to the couple, only which areas showed the most number of violations of expectations. Care of the Home had the most non-adjustive type reactions on the part of the wife. This may indicate not that she felt strongest about this, but that she felt freer to express her negative feelings about this than any other area.

The area with the fewest expressed violations of expectations was *Area 6*—(Personal Neatness and Appearance). This was followed by *Area 7*—(Spending the Family Income).

As indicated above, the biggest area of disparity in terms of numbers of violations in the areas was in *Area 3*—(Spending Time at Home). Wives checked violations in this area six times as often as did the husbands. The other areas were relatively similar with some noticeable difference occurring in *Area 5*—(Care of the Home), where the wives had more non-met expectations than did the husbands at a ratio of 25 to 16.

Subsequent Reactions to Initial Responses

Table 2 shows the subsequent reactions to the initial responses as perceived by the spouse making the initial response. Both husbands and wives felt that the majority of their spouses' reactions to them were of an adjustive nature. In the questionnaire subjects were asked, "When you responded as indicated in the previous question, what did your spouse do in return?" Adjustive responses were the following:

1. "Made a real attempt to change and meet my expectations."
2. "We agreed that we differed, but we have tried to accept this difference."
3. "Said he (she) was sorry and would try to do better, but didn't really change."

This last response was considered to be an adjustive type response even though the spouse with the non-met expectations felt the other had not "really changed." The initial part of adjustment had begun—the spouse knew of the violation, had expressed regret for this and indicated a willingness to "do better." Final adjustment does not come until expectation and behavior are in agreement, but this response indicates that perhaps adjustment has started.

Subjects were also asked to list other responses. Considered as adjustive were such responses as: "He is patient with me and tries to be understanding." "Made a genuine effort to change every now and then." "Got professional doctor's help and counseling."

It is interesting to note that while 44 percent of the husbands' responses and 31 percent of the wives' initial responses were of the non-action type, there were very few subsequent non-action responses. One would normally think that a non-action response would be followed by non-action. This may indicate that when one's expectations are violated, one really does give off certain cues about his feelings to which the spouse subsequently responds. A non-action response to the initial reaction was: "(Spouse did) nothing, since he (she) didn't know how I felt."

Thirty-three percent of the wives' subsequent reactions were felt by the husbands to be non-adjustive, while 26 percent of the husbands' reactions to the wife were seen by the wife as non-adjustive. Non-adjustive responses were as follows:

1. "Got upset and argued, complained, or grumbled back."
2. "Suggested that I accept him (her) as he (she) was."
3. "I told him (her) but nothing happened—we just dropped it."

Considered as non-adjustive were written-in comments such as: "We quarrel occasionally about it." "He thought it was funny and persisted more strongly."

Some interesting patterns are indicated when we examine the non-adjustive responses and the behavior that elicits a non-adjustive pattern. Nearly half of the non-adjustive responses for both husbands and wives came as a result of

TABLE 2
SUBSEQUENT REACTION TO INITIAL RESPONSES

| | VERBAL EXPRESSIONS OF AFFECTION | FREQUENCY OF SEXUAL INTIMACY | SPENDING TIME AT HOME | SHARING IDEAS | CARE OF HOME | PERSONAL NEATNESS, APPEARANCE | SPENDING INCOME OF FAMILY | |
	I	II	III*	IV	V	VI*	VII	TOTAL
Wives Reaction to Husband (as perceived by husband)								
Adj.	14	10		6	9		5	44
No Action	2	5		2	1		2	12
Non Adj.	5	7		7	6		3	28
Total	21	22		15	16		10	84
Husbands Reaction to Wife (as perceived by wife)								
	I	II	III	IV	V	VI	VII	
Adj.	14	13	10	12	19	6	7	81
No Action	2	2	4	4	0	0	0	12
Non Adj.	5	5	4	2	5	5	6	32
Total	21	20	18	18	24	11	13	125

*Too few responses to be tabulated.

an initial shared adjustive reaction. This immediately raises the question—why should a shared adjustive initial reaction result in non-adjustive responses? There are at least these possibilities:

1. While the one reacting initially thinks he is reacting in an open, adjustive way, the marriage partner may not experience this in the way the first intended. The partner may see the initial reaction as critical and punitive while the reacting party thinks he is just talking it over "openly and calmly."

2. The initial reaction may be an open, calm sharing of one's feelings about a problem situation but an adjustive response from the mate presumes such conditions as an adequate level of maturity of the mate, proper timing and suitable circumstances for sharing sensitive information, and a non-threatening method of presenting the information.

3. The shared information may be presented calmly and openly but the information may be a hard blow to the self-image of the partner and the response may be immediately defensive and not adjustive.

4. Sharing sensitive information may be a violation of the expectations of the other partner. He or she may not expect such things to be talked about and when this is done, non-adjustive type responses result.

Seven non-adjustive responses for both husbands and wives came as a result of initial "non-action." This is another apparent contradiction. How can a non-response result in any type of reaction? The problem here may be in the weakness of the questionnaire in carefully sorting out the sequence of reactions. (Or it may be, as indicated above, that cues as to how the person feels are given off even though he feels there was no response made). There are indications in examining the data that a person filling out the questionnaire coming to the question, "What was your initial response?" marked a non-action category. The next question asked, "What did your spouse do in return?" It appears that a number of subjects jumped the time sequence and checked what may have been a response later in time. Thus, it appears that a non-adjustive reaction followed a non-action response. This same condition may account for non-shared reactions eliciting non-adjustive responses.

Percentage-wise, the biggest number of non-adjustive responses came as a result of initial negative type reactions for both husbands and wives. There were five negative reactions listed by husbands and these resulted in three non-adjustive reactions. In fact, all three shared negative initial reactions resulted in non-adjustive responses.

Wives indicated 22 negative type reactions initially and these resulted in 11 non-adjustive type subsequent responses from the spouse.

One would tend to predict that a negative reaction would result in further negative type reactions. The data from the husbands in this study are too limited in this area to allow for any support of this generalization. For the wives, it shows from a limited number of responses, that about 50 percent of the time negative responses on their part resulted in non-adjustment on the part of the other. The data here do not tell us how the other partner feels about making an adjustment to a negative reaction by his spouse. It would seem that adjustments that came from shared positive type responses would be made out of a more positive feeling than adjustments that resulted from negative reactions.

SUMMARY

This study was designed to investigate the initial adjustment processes in young, married couples attending college. Adjustment was conceptualized in terms of role expectations, response to expectation violations and the subsequent reaction to the initial response. The data indicate the following trends in these couples:

1. Husbands, more than wives, appear to adopt a "wait and see" strategy when their wives violate their expectations, according to their self-perceptions. Wives say they more often meet a violation of expectation with an open sharing or talking about the situation or reacting negatively.

2. When difficulties occur, the several areas of marriage appear to be handled differently by married couples. Husbands say they talk openly about violations of expectations in the area of finance but not in the area of frequency of sexual intimacy.

3. Wives and husbands differ in the number of expectation violations in certain areas of marriage. In the area of spending time at home, wives checked a violation of expectations in this area six times more frequently than did husbands. Wives also had more non-met expectations in the area of care of the home.

4. While a considerable number of both husbands and wives reacted to an initial violation of expectations with a non-action response—a "wait and see" strategy—subsequent reactions to the spouse's initial response were very infrequently found in this category. Husbands more than wives felt their spouses' reactions to them were non-adjustive in nature.

5. The data of this study indicate that nearly half of the non-adjustive reponses for both husbands and wives came as a result of an open sharing of the feelings about the violation of expectations. Contrary to what might be expected, an open talking about the violation of expectations does not always lead to an adjustment.

6. The data, especially for wives, also show that in a large percentage of times, a negative reaction on the part of one partner does result in an adjustive response by the other. Negative reactions are apparently not always followed by reciprocal negative reactions.

NOTES

[1] Clifford Kirkpatrick, "Factors in Marital Adjustment," *American Journal of Sociology,* 43 (November 1957), p. 270.
[2] Judson T. Landis, "Length of Time Required to Achieve Adjustment in Marriage," *American Sociological Review,* 11 (December 1946), pp. 666–677.

[3] Clifford Kirkpatrick, "Marriage as a Process," *The Family* (New York: Ronald Press, 1955), pp. 443–448.

[4] Clark Bowerman, "Adjustment in Marriage, Overall and in Specific Areas," *Sociology and Social Research,* 41 (March-April 1957), pp. 257–263.

[5] William G. Dyer, "Analyzing Marital Adjustment Using Role Theory," *Marriage and Family Living,* 24 (November 1962).

[6] *Ibid.,* p. 374.

In-Laws, Pro and Con

Evelyn M. Duvall

One of the major adjustments the married pair must make is that of arriving at workable role relationships with in-laws (with the possible exception of those couples who live great distances from them). This may pose some aggravating problems, for the family of procreation is usually loath to forsake all control over its children even though they are grown and married. In addition, each married partner runs the danger of becoming a relative by marriage to someone of whom he cannot approve or for whom he has no feelings of warmth. The saying, "You cannot choose your relatives, but thank God, you can choose your friends," no doubt stems from these sentiments. Yet the married pair themselves will someday be in-laws. Perhaps a better adjustment can be achieved if they perceive the universal problems of in-law relationships as developed by Duvall's timeless study.

MOTHER-IN-LAW IS THE MOST DIFFICULT

Mother-in-law heads the list of difficult in-laws by a wide margin. Of the 992 having in-law difficulties of any kind (the total of 1,337 minus 345 having "no problems"), one out of every two (49.5%; 491) mentions mother-in-law as most difficult.

More than one-third of the total 1,337 men and women, 491 (36.8%) named mother-in-law their most difficult in-law. These mother-in-law mentions were not evenly distributed among the groups. Individual groups mentioning mother-in-law as most troublesome ranged from 11.9% to 76.5%.

Nine out of ten complaints about mothers-in-law came from women (1,227 specific complaints; 89.6%); while men list only 142 (10.4%) specific complaints against their mothers-in-law out of a total of 1,369 from the entire group. (Table 1) These data do not support the popular notion that it is the man who professes the greater difficulty with his mother-in-law. These data

From Evelyn M. Duvall, *In-laws, Pro and Con* (New York: Association Press, 1954), pp. 117, 221, 244–45, 260–61, 286–90, 328–30. Reprinted by permission of Association Press.

show that it is the woman who feels the mother-in-law problem more often. In this respect our findings corroborate Paul Wallin's[1] report that among those couples in the Burgess-Wallin sample, more wives (17.1%) than husbands (8.3%) dislike their mothers-in-law.

In general, younger women mentioned mother-in-law most difficult significantly more frequently than did older women.

. . . .

TABLE 1
MOTHER-IN-LAW DIFFICULTIES REPORTED BY 491 PERSONS

WHAT MOTHER-IN-LAW DOES THAT MAKES HER MOST DIFFICULT IN-LAW	SPECIFIC CRITICISM NAMED	
	NUMBER	PER CENT
1. Meddles, interferes, dominates, intrudes on our privacy, etc.	383	28.0
2. Is possessive, demanding, overprotective, forces attention, etc.	193	14.1
3. Nags, criticizes, complains, finds fault, ridicules, etc.	150	10.9
4. Ignores us, is indifferent, uninterested, not helpful, aloof, does not accept me/us, not close, unsociable, etc.	99	7.2
5. Clings, is irresponsible, immature, childish, dependent, has no life of her own, no interests beyond us, undependable, etc.	93	6.8
6. Disagrees on traditions, has different standards, is old-fashioned, resists change, is intolerant of our ways, has nothing in common with us	84	6.2
7. Is thoughtless, inconsiderate, selfish, unappreciative, etc.	76	5.6
8. Takes sides, plays favorites, shows partiality, spoils and pampers my husband, plays one family against the other, etc.	72	5.3
9. Abuses hospitality, comes without invitation, overstays visits, lives with us more than necessary, does not reciprocate, etc.	58	4.2
10. Is self-righteous, superior, always right, egotistical, smug, boastful, lords it over me/us, brags, knows all the answers	41	3.0
11. Talks too much, asks useless questions, doesn't listen, is full of idle chatter, gushes, doesn't try to understand	39	2.8
12. Tattles, gossips, misrepresents facts, exaggerates, lies, is dishonest, insincere, deceitful, etc.	34	2.5
13. Is jealous, rivalrous, envious, covets what we have, etc.	33	2.4
14. Does not do own job well, is not a good mother, neglects her family, is extravagant, doesn't take care of her home, etc.	12	0.9
15. Drinks, gambles	2	0.1
Total	1,369	100.0

SISTER-IN-LAW IS A REAL PROBLEM

Sister-in-law is the Number Two hazard among in-laws. She comes second to mother-in-law in number of complaints and in the experience of most people. In several respects sister-in-law out distances mother-in-law in troublesomeness.

Sister-in-law is a center of strain in other cultures too. Margaret Mead[2] reports that in the Admiralty Islands the sister-in-law relationship is one of strain and opposition. The wife enters the husband's family as a stranger and hostility ensues between her and his sisters, who until then have given him female companionship. Among the Manus, Mead reports that the wife is obligated to care for her sister-in-law during pregnancy and childbirth; and that this is a troublesome, annoying, and nonreciprocal discharge of duty. Generally, among these peoples, sisters-in-law are institutionally opposed to each other.

Here in the United States it is generally expected that mother-in-law is most troublesome. The stereotyped hostility-humor and avoidance are directed exclusively toward her. Sister-in-law, however, is *not* the butt of in-law jokes. Nor is she generally assumed to be particularly troublesome. Yet, she is mentioned as being difficult significantly more frequently than any other in-law except the mother-in-law.

Out of 2,611 criticisms directed at in-laws, 701 (26.8%) are those attributed to sisters-in-law.

• • • •

The roster of things sister-in-law does that make life difficult for her relatives by marriage is found in Table 2. These are the things reported by the 272 men and women who in their experience have found sister-in-law most

TABLE 2
SISTER-IN-LAW DIFFICULTIES REPORTED BY 272 PERSONS

WHAT SISTER-IN-LAW DOES THAT MAKES HER MOST DIFFICULT	SPECIFIC CRITICISM NAMED	
	NUMBER	PER CENT
1. Meddles, interferes, dominates, intrudes on privacy, etc.	130	18.5
2. Ignores us, is indifferent, uninterested, unsociable, aloof, etc.	72	10.3
3. Is thoughtless, inconsiderate, selfish, unappreciative, etc.	72	10.3
4. Nags, criticizes, complains, finds fault, ridicules, etc.	69	9.8
5. Clings, is immature, irresponsible, childish, dependent, etc.	49	7.0
6. Is jealous, rivalrous, envious, covets what we have, etc.	48	6.9
7. Tattles, gossips, exaggerates, lies, is deceitful, insincere, etc.	47	6.7
8. Is self-righteous, always right, egotistical, smug, bragging, etc.	39	5.6
9. Is not a good mother, neglects her family, is extravagant, etc.	37	5.2
10. Disagrees on traditions, has different standards, uncongenial	36	5.1
11. Is possessive, demanding, overprotective, forces attention, etc.	33	4.7
12. Talks too much, asks useless questions, doesn't listen, etc.	28	4.0
13. Takes sides, plays favorites, shows partiality, pampers, spoils	18	2.6
14. Abuses hospitality, comes without invitation, overstays visits	18	2.6
15. Drinks, gambles, is unconventional, unfaithful, etc.	5	0.7
Total	701	100.0

difficult of in-laws. These 272 persons represent 27.4% of the 992 men and women who report that they have trouble with their in-laws (1,337 minus 345 persons with no in-law problems.

BROTHER-IN-LAW IS NOT SO BAD

People do not often find brothers-in-law difficult to get along with. Out of the 1,337 men and women who participated in the group interview phase of this study, 72 (5.4%) report brother-in-law as their most difficult in-law. Of the 2,611 things that in-laws do that makes life difficult, 186 (7.2%) are attributed to brothers-in-law. In both the number of times he is named the most difficult in-law and in the number of criticisms made of him, brother-in-law ranks third of all relatives by marriage, being significantly less difficult than either sister-in-law or mother-in-law. He outranks father-in-law by but a fraction of one per cent (0.4%) in both criticisms and persons reporting. Men and women both mention brother-in-law as most difficult in proportions equivalent to their numbers in the sample.

The problems people report having with their brothers-in-law appear in rank order in Table 3.

TABLE 3
BROTHER-IN-LAW DIFFICULTIES REPORTED BY 72 PERSONS

WHAT BROTHER-IN-LAW DOES THAT MAKES HIM MOST DIFFICULT IN-LAW	SPECIFIC CRITICISM NAMED	
	NUMBER	PER CENT
1. Incompetency—does not do own job well	27	14.5
2. Immaturity—is childish, irresponsible, dependent, etc.	24	12.9
3. Thoughtlessness—is selfish, unappreciative, etc.	23	12.4
4. Indifference—is uninterested, not close, non-accepting, etc.	18	9.7
5. Self-righteousness—is superior, egotistical, boastful, etc.	17	9.1
6. Interference—is meddling, dominating, etc.	16	8.6
7. Criticalness—nags, complains, finds fault, etc.	14	7.5
8. Uncongeniality—different standards, intolerant, old-fashioned	12	6.5
9. Misrepresentation—gossips, tattles, exaggerates, etc.	8	4.3
10. Unconventionality—drinks, gambles, etc.	8	4.3
11. Possessiveness—is demanding, overprotective, forces attention	5	2.7
12. Rivalrousness—is jealous, envious, covetous, etc.	5	2.7
13. Partiality—takes sides, plays favorites, spoils, pampers, etc.	3	1.6
14. Intrusion—comes without invitation, abuses hospitality, etc.	3	1.6
15. Talkativeness—asks useless questions, chatters, etc.	3	1.6
Total	186	100.0

In several ways difficulties with brothers-in-law are different from those that people report they have with their mothers-in-law, fathers-in-law, and sisters-in-law.

Some Fathers-in-Law Are Troublesome

When 1,337 men and women name their most difficult in-law relationship, only 52 mention father-in-law (1.5%). Of the 2,611 things that are specifically mentioned as making in-law relationships difficult, 179 (6.8%) are attributed to fathers-in-law. This is significantly fewer than criticisms of mothers-in-law. Specific criticisms of father-in-law rank as shown in Table 4.

Table 4
Father-in-Law Difficulties Reported by 52 Persons

WHAT FATHER-IN-LAW DOES THAT MAKES HIM THE MOST DIFFICULT IN-LAW	SPECIFIC CRITICISM NAMED	
	NUMBER	PER CENT
1. Meddles, interferes, dominates, intrudes on our privacy, etc.	31	17.3
2. Nags, criticizes, complains, finds fault, ridicules, etc.	26	14.5
3. Resists change, disagrees on traditions, uncongenial, etc.	21	11.7
4. Ignores us, is indifferent, uninterested, aloof, not close, etc.	17	9.5
5. Is possessive, demanding, overprotective, forces attention, etc.	13	7.3
6. Is self-righteous, superior, always right, smug, bragging, etc.	13	7.3
7. Talks too much, asks useless questions, doesn't listen, etc.	13	7.3
8. Is thoughtless, inconsiderate, selfish, unappreciative, etc.	11	6.1
9. Is irresponsible, immature, childish, dependent, no life of own	8	4.5
10. Drinks, gambles, is unconventional, etc.	8	4.5
11. Does not do his own job well, incompetent, lazy, etc.	7	3.9
12. Takes sides, plays favorites, shows partiality, pampers the children, plays one of us against the other, etc.	5	2.8
13. Abuses hospitality, comes without invitation, overstays visits	4	2.2
14. Tattles, gossips, exaggerates, lies, is insincere	2	1.1
15. Is jealous, rivalrous, envious, covets what we have, etc.	0	0.0
Total	179	100.0

Some interesting differences are apparent in the rank order of criticisms of father-in-law as compared with that of mother-in-law (Tables 4 and 1 respectively). Possessiveness, which ranks second for mother-in-law, ranks fifth for father-in-law. Immaturity, which ranks fifth for mother-in-law, ranks ninth for father-in-law. Pampering, which ranks eighth for mother-in-law, ranks twelfth for father-in-law. Intrusion, ranking ninth for mother-in-law, ranks thirteenth for father-in-law. Thus, in four characteristics mother-in-law offends perceptibly more frequently than does father-in-law: possessiveness, immaturity, pampering, and intrusion.

On the other hand, where uncongeniality ranks sixth for mother-in-law, it appears in third place for father-in-law. Where self-righteousness ranks tenth for mother-in-law, it ranks sixth for father-in-law. Where talkativeness ranks eleventh for mother-in-law, it comes in seventh place for father-in-law. Where unconventionality as seen in drinking, gambling, etc., ranks last at fifteenth place for mother-in-law, it ranks tenth for father-in-law. Incompetence in terms of not doing one's own job well ranks fourteenth for mother-in-law and eleventh for father-in-law. So, five criticisms rank considerably higher for father-in-law than mother-in-law; uncongeniality, self-righteousness, talkativeness, unconventionality, and incompetence.

. . . .

WHY SOME PEOPLE HAVE NO PROBLEMS WITH THEIR IN-LAWS

Some people have no trouble getting along with their in-laws. They tell us in no uncertain terms that they have no problems with their relatives by marriage. How they do it and what the factors are that lead to family harmony give us many leads on how to be better in-laws.

"They accept me," is the primary reason for accord among in-laws given nearly one out of five times (18.6%). When this top-ranking category is merged with other responses of similar attitude, the factor of acceptance looms imposingly large, as we see in Table 5.

TABLE 5
REASON FOR NO PROBLEMS WITH IN-LAWS
REPORTED BY 345 PERSONS

WHY IN-LAWS ARE "NO PROBLEM"	SPECIFIC CRITICISM REPORTED	
	NUMBER	PER CENT
1. They accept me; they are friendly, helpful, close	139	18.6
2. They do not meddle, interfere, or butt into my life	112	14.9
3. They are thoughtful, kind, considerate, generous	88	11.8
4. They are too far away; we rarely see them; haven't met	88	11.8
5. No reason given for "No problem" report	54	7.2
6. No in-laws: I married an orphan, etc.	43	5.8
7. Determination to adjust: we respect each other's rights; we work things out as they come up; etc.	38	5.1
8. They are mature, have outside interests, are independent	36	4.8
9. They love me; we have mutual affection and trust; they back me when I need it; etc.	33	4.4
10. We are congenial, have similar interests and standards; they fit in, are tolerant of our differences; etc.	33	4.4
11. They come only when invited, do not overstay visits, are always welcome, do not abuse hospitality, etc.	29	3.9
12. They understand me, listen to me, are understanding people	25	3.3
13. They are not critical, do not get impatient with me, etc.	18	2.4
14. They are not demanding or possessive; let us be free; etc.	9	1.2
15. They do not act superior, nor make me feel inferior, etc.	3	0.4
Total	748	100.0

LET THE REST OF THE WORLD GO BY (SUMMARY)

"With someone like you," so the popular song goes, "a pal good and true, I'd like to leave it all behind, and go and find, some place that's known to God alone—just a spot to call our own. We'll find perfect peace, where joys never cease—out there beneath the kindly sky. We'll build a sweet little nest, somewhere in the West—and let the rest of the world go by."

This might well be the theme song of those who would escape the intrusion of the world. It is close to the heart of the in-law situation; for what these young lovers are saying is, "Let's give ourselves a chance to settle down and make our own home, far from the possibilities of intruding in-laws, meddling relatives, and the family responsibilities, loyalties, and conditionings that both of us have."

Everybody is "in-laws" when you are married. The big task of marriage is to develop the mutual loyalty that makes *Our* family come before either *Yours* or *Mine*.

Some in-law problems have their bases in the family history or the early development of the man or the woman, which, carrying over into marriage, may make that person vulnerable to certain types of in-law problems, or "allergic" to in-laws.

Any member of either family who threatens the autonomy of the couple or delays the independence of the pair is in danger of being a difficult in-law. So we find aunts-in-law, grandparents-in-law, nieces-in-law, cousins-in-law, as well as closer relatives by marriage being reported as troublesome. Criticisms of these other in-laws follow the same general pattern as those for all in-laws.

Apparent in the constellations of complaints about in-laws is the mother-in-law syndrome of meddlesomeness, possessiveness, and nagging; the complaint of distance, including mentions of thoughtlessness and indifference; the sibling syndrome of self-righteousness, incompetency, playing favorites, gossiping, and jealousy; and the father-in-law syndrome of ineffectuality, unconventionality, talkativeness, and incompetence.

Women more than men are involved in in-law problems, possibly because of the role assignment to the women of the family of close interpersonal and intrafamily relationships. Older family members are criticized more frequently than are younger for two apparent reasons: (1) the emancipatory thrust of youth that makes them more critical of older family members than vice versa; and (2) the traditional taboo on discussing family matters outside the family that restrains more older than younger persons.

NOTES

[1] Paul Wallin, "Sex Differences in Attitudes to In-Laws," *American Journal of Sociology*, March, 1954, pp. 466–69.
[2] Margaret Mead, *Kinship in the Admiralty Islands*. New York: Anthropological Papers of the American Museum of Natural History, 1934, p. 305.

Housewife and Woman?
The Best of Both Worlds?

Hilda Sidney Krech

How can the modern, educated woman who falls in love and marries keep a husband happy, raise her children, and yet maintain an intellectually stimulating and creative existence for herself? Krech discusses the many facets of this problem: the prejudice against career women, the time problem encountered in handling jobs inside and outside the home, the strong demands of the husband's career, the empty feeling of the woman who has no preparation for work when her children leave home. The solution posed by the author would not be totally acceptable to the Women's Liberation Movement, for it is a compromise. Because it is just that, however, it will be of interest to the average young housewife concerned for her lifestyle 20 years from now.

Scoldings, dissections, and revolutionary proposals—all about modern woman—have been filling the air for ten or fifteen years. They've also been filling newspaper columns, books, TV programs, learned journals, not-so-learned journals, and symposia from the Vassar campus to the University of California Medical School. Surprisingly, words about modern woman have been flowing and symposia have been gathering at an increasing rather than a decreasing rate. More surprising still, a lot of people seem to be willing (sometimes even eager) to hear about her once again. I find myself challenged to say something new about her before the subject (and the discussers of the subject) are exhausted.

When I considered the concern—the serious, frivolous, scientific, sympathetic, and sometimes furious concern—that's been lavished on modern woman, and most especially modern American woman, I started wondering why she remains bewildered and bewildering, why her dilemma remains un-

From Hilda S. Krech, "Housewife and Woman? The Best of Both Worlds?" in *The Family's Search for Survival,* eds., Seymour M. Farber, Piero Mustacchi, and Roger H. Wilson (New York: McGraw-Hill, 1964), pp. 136–52. Reprinted by permission of McGraw-Hill Book Company.

solved. And I was struck by the fact that we haven't all been talking about the same American woman.

Most of the talk and most of the criticism has been lavished on the more or less privileged, more or less educated, presumably intelligent woman. She is the one who has encouraged the word "discontented" to be linked with the words "American woman." She has been forced to add the feeling of guilt to her feelings of frustration because so many people for so many years have been telling her how lucky she is. And she is. And she knows it. But still—but still what? Her dissatisfaction is about equally divided between what she *does* do and what she *does not* do.

Speaking with women who are quite happily married, one often gets the feeling that housework and child care are both too much and too little for each one of them; too much because they take all her time, energy, and thought during the period when her children need constantly to be fed, clothed in clean clothes, fetched and carried, and tended to in one way or another; too little in that she'd somehow been led to believe that she would be using her time and her talents and her energy quite differently—at least for a portion of each day. All through school and, for many, through college as well, these talents—whether artistic, intellectual, practical, or human—have been respected and encouraged.

Though, deep inside, there is nothing she would rather do than be a mother, she often feels, while her children are young, like a drudge. When they are grown, she is a has-been—sometimes feeling that she's a *has*-been without ever really having *been*. She is no longer needed as a full-time mother, yet no longer able to be whatever it was she set out to be all those long years ago. For, contrary to polite and gallant statements which suggest that simply "being a woman" is a vocation, this is not the case.

To make such a woman's discontent stronger still, the truly lucky woman is married to a man who does interesting, challenging, perhaps useful, and sometimes lucrative work which often gets more challenging and useful as the years go by, while her work gets less challenging, less useful. Growing up, she didn't wish she were a boy. She doesn't wish now that she were a man. Yet something is wrong with this picture of the luckiest woman in the world.

In answer to the countless articles, speeches, and books which have painted just such a picture, *The Saturday Evening Post* recently ran an article defending the American woman, refuting the countless statements which accuse her of being "lonely, bored, lazy, sexually inept, frigid, superficial, harried, militant, overworked." The adjectives are those of the authors, Dr. George Gallup and Evan Hill, who made a survey and then described what they call the "typical" American woman.

(Though one-third of the married women in America are employed outside the home, and though nearly 15 per cent of women over forty-five are widowed or divorced, the authors specifically state that these women are not "typical," and therefore, they are neither discussed nor included in the composite picture. Getting ahead of my story for a moment, I'd like to point out, also, that Gallup and Hill's typical American woman is forever young, forever surrounded by young children.)

The charges against the American woman are untrue, say Dr. Gallup and Mr. Hill. She is happy; she is content; she wants only "the simple pleasures"; her family is "her whole life." Their typical wife sums up her situation by saying: "If I don't want to do the dishes or laundry right now, I can do them later. My only deadline is when my husband comes home. I'm much more free than when I was single and working. A married woman has it made."

Her house may be cluttered, but her mind is not. Only half of the women interviewed read books at all; only 13 per cent consider "intelligence as a pre-requisite in husbands." The only reference to the life of the mind in this article quotes the typical wife as saying: "I spend my spare time broadening my interests so I won't bore Jim." So I won't bore Jim! Apparently she doesn't mind boring herself. She may be free, she may be content, but if she is indeed typical, I can't help considering the possibility that modern woman, for all her modern appliances, isn't modern any more.

The Saturday Evening Post's typical woman, at any rate, knows neither the nagging worry of poverty nor the nagging pull to be part of the activity and thought of a world that extends beyond her eventually made bed, her even-tually cleaned house. But, of course, *she* is not the woman that commentators have in mind when they talk about "frustration" or when they describe the Radcliffe diploma mildewing over the kitchen sink.

And when we read the *Report of the President's Commission on the Status of Women*, the emphasis is on a still different woman, a woman who works because she has to or because she wants to give her children a better life. She cannot be called a career women, for she is likely to do clerical work or sales-work, service work, factory work or agricultural work, and only a small per-centage of the women working in our country today are in professional or managerial jobs.

Clearly, it is impossible to speak in the same breath about all these kinds of women, at least in any meaningful way. Even within these groups, of course, there are enormous differences between individual women—differences in ability, in intellect, in preferences, in temperament, in values. But about these differences remarkably little is ever said. This tendency to speak of women as though they were interchangeable units like the parts of a Ford is one reason why (for all the talk) woman's dilemma remains unsolved.

A second reason is that while we've been talking, the picture has been changing. For women have not turned a deaf ear to this talk. If anything fascinates them, it's the topic of themselves—a fact which suggests a close relation to the rest of the human race—and they have tried to follow the suggestions, heed the warnings. While reflecting the feminine condition, there-fore, some of the commentators have, at the same time, helped to shape that condition.

"Womanpower"—the word and the commodity—was discovered during World War II. When the war was over and womanpower was no longer needed in factories and hospitals and schools (or so they thought), many voices started urging women to go home, stay home, and like it. In 1947 Marnya Farnham and Ferdinand Lundberg wrote *Modern Woman: The Lost Sex,* in which they predicted: "Close down the commercial bakeries and canning factories today and women will start being happier tomorrow."

They were talking to the young women of my generation who had started out to do great things—not only the privileged and the educated; all kinds of girls were going to have "careers" in those days. Then, as each girl married (always to her great surprise, for she never dreamed she was going to meet George or Bill or Frederick, or if she did, she kept her dreams to herself), she would "throw over her career," as she liked to put it. Sometimes she did so cheerfully, for she knew there really was no career in the making, sometimes reluctantly because it was nearly impossible to keep on after her first or second child arrived. She became a housewife or, as she tended to put it, "just a housewife."

Dorothy Thompson created a new cliché or, at the very least, gave new life to an old one, when she pointed out in 1949 that a wife and mother should never feel apologetic for being "just a housewife" because that homely word means that she is a professional "business manager, cook, nurse, chauffeur, dressmaker, interior decorator, accountant, caterer, teacher, private secretary" all rolled into one. "I simply refuse to share your self-pity," Miss Thompson told the American housewife in the *Ladies' Home Journal.* "You are one of the most successful women I know."

The following year, in *The Atlantic Monthly,* another woman journalist wrote an even angrier article. Agnes E. Meyer not only tried to reassure those women who spent their entire time being mothers; she fiercely denounced those who made some effort to be something in addition to being mothers. She wrote:

> Women must boldly announce "that no job is more exacting, more necessary, or more rewarding than that of housewife and mother. . . . There have never been so many women who are unnecessarily torn between marriage and a career. There have never been so many mothers who neglect their children because they find some trivial job more interesting. . . . The poor child whose mother has to work has some inner security because he knows in his little heart that his mother is sacrificing herself for his well-being. But the neglected child from a well-to-do home, who realizes instinctively that his mother prefers her job to him, often hates her with a passionate intensity."[1]

Each time such a statement was made, and they were made often, it was a shot in the arm for those who had felt aimless and demoralized, who had, to quote one of them, "begun to feel stupid with nothing to contribute to an evening's discussion after a solitary morning of housecleaning and an afternoon of keeping peace between the children." Now they were able to face themselves with more self-respect, for they were doing the most important job of all. What's more, they were able to look with *less* respect at their friends who had outside work or interests.

As for these women, the ones involved outside the home as well as within, many of them were intimidated by the strong voices. It was confusing to them, even frightening, to be told they weren't good mothers, to be accused of preferring their outside activities to their children. Increasingly, therefore, many turned their full attention, their full energies upon their little families and shut the door on the world.

And so, while the canneries and bakeries did not literally close down, the spirit of this advice was taken; and many highly educated or trained women have been making their own bread, putting up endless little jellies. But according to the latest attack on the subject, *The Feminine Mystique* by Betty Friedan, these women aren't happy at all but are slowly going mad and battering their children's heads!

Nobody's happy about them either. The consensus at the Vassar symposium held in the spring of 1962 was that: "If the performance of college women from 1920 through World War II has been somewhat disappointing, the mental attitudes of young women since World War II are alarming."

This kind of criticism came from looking inside woman's head and heart. Looking at her from the outside came another kind of criticism—first, the accusation that having no other interest in her life, she latched fiercely onto her children, ruining them, being a "Mom." More recently, still another kind of criticism has been coming: that she hasn't been pulling her weight. "A Huge Waste: Educated Womanpower" is the title of a typical *New York Times* article, this one published in May, 1961. Two years later, under the heading "Tapping a U.S. National Resource," came another *Times* article concerning itself with "the educated woman."

This past summer Max Lerner wrote an article called "Let's Draft Our Girls," and he meant all kinds of girls. Four years earlier *Harper's* had published an article in which Marion Sanders discussed the possibility of drafting not only girls before they become mothers, but also strong, able women after they have finished their full-time mothering, unless they are already engaged in work that has some value. Though her style is gay, almost frivolous, and I don't think Mrs. Sanders seriously wants a draft for women, she does want us to pull our socks up and is quite serious both about the need for teachers, nurses, and social welfare workers and about her scorn for what she calls Non-Work or Sub-Work or Redundant Housewifery—the pointless tasks with which so many middle-aged women fill their lives.

As an example of women she would *not* exempt, she tells about a hospital ladies' auxiliary in Long Island which "boasted that its 900 Pink Pinafore Volunteers last year spent 51,280 hours reading to sick children, giving patients alcohol rubs, and running a gift shop. This averages out to a little more than an hour a week per volunteer—scarcely time to don and doff the pinafores."

In addition, then, to the great differences between different women (about which too little is said), and in addition to the changes constantly taking place in our attitudes and in our ways of living, there is a third reason we've been progressing so slowly in gaining insight into modern woman—her role,

207

her function, her old dilemma. Many true things have been said, but since they aren't all said at the same time, we get part of the picture in one strong statement, another part in another (seemingly contradictory) statement. We never get a full, accurate picture in one glance, but a blurred and confused impression. And while I can't say everything all at once either (not even the things I do know, let alone the things I don't), I'd like to give an example of what I mean.

One often hears that too much is expected of the American woman. "How can she be wife, lover, confidante, companion, hostess, cook, seamstress, floor scrubber, purchasing agent, teacher, chauffeur, child analyst?" ask her defenders.

But in Mrs. Sanders's "Proposition for Women" she speaks of middle-aged and older women with "time for leisurely jaunts to the lonely housewife's dream world of 'shopping'—so different from 'marketing.' " And she describes clubs with many meetings which "did not contribute to anyone's enlightenment since their programs revealed no coherent purpose. (January: Flower Arrangement. February: The Bright Side of Menopause. March: Whither the UN?)" Women caught up in such activities spend an enormous amount of time telephoning to arrange similar meetings which, in Mrs. Sanders's terms, is "Circular (or self-perpetuating) Puttering, a form of Sub-Work."

Both kinds of descriptions are valid, although it's obvious that both apply more accurately to middle-class and upper-class women. What people *don't* always recognize, however, is that the demanding description applies only to a woman's early years when her children are young and she is in constant demand, that the idleness comes later and, worse, it comes gradually, imperceptibly. Most of us have heard a great deal about this bonus of twenty, thirty, or even forty years women now have because they stop bearing children at an earlier age and they live—with health and vigor—much longer than people have ever lived before. And though we're still floundering, are not yet sure exactly what we want to do with this bonus and how to plan for it, many girls and young women are completely unaware of it. This may be hard to believe; but the one sour note in the otherwise sweet *Saturday Evening Post* article is that Dr. Gallup and Mr. Hill report the women they interviewed could not imagine having their children grown and out of the house, leaving them jobless. They had simply never given a thought to this eventuality.

And so women were scolded for going out of the home and then, more recently, they've been scolded for staying in. The next logical step is to urge women out of the house and into high-powered careers on a par with men's, thus bringing us full circle, back to the feminist days. I'm afraid this step is coming. Whether advertisements follow public opinion or make it I don't quite know, but I've noticed a small straw blowing in the wind which may be significant, the beginning of a trend. After years of picturing lovely ladies who beam with joy while cleaning their toilet bowls or waltzing around the living room with a roll of Alcoa Wrap, some advertisers are taking a new tack. One blouse manufacturer has announced a new advertising campaign addressed to the 24,584,000 "Wonderful Women Who Work." Going even further, a different shirt company recently ran an ad picturing a girl as a naval architect and running a caption which said: "Man's world? Bah! Women are in everything."

The girl is extremely pretty and looks about eighteen and is totally unconvincing as an architect, naval or otherwise. But when I think of the other kind of ad, I realize it's not the unconvincingness that's new, and I wonder if, after pushing housewifery to the limits, they're now going to push for "a career for every girl." Look out for that swinging pendulum; here we go again.

What really alarms me is the strident voice, the strong note of resentment in Betty Friedan's *The Feminine Mystique* when she asks why women are always supposed to be satisfied with second-string careers and second-level positions. Having said that, I suppose I've put myself on the spot and had better explain why *I'm* satisfied. Am I being wishy-washy? Or have I boldly taken the position of defending "the radical middle"? I'll say what I believe and you can decide.

I believe that only the rare, truly exceptional woman with way-above-average ability, energy, and drive can—while maintaining a home and being a real mother to several children—achieve a full-fledged career. It takes enormous flexibility and ingenuity, for the children *do* come first, and women *do* move when the husbands are transferred on their jobs, and they don't have their mothers living nearby or maiden aunts or maids to lend a hand when the unpredictable but inevitable complications arise. In our society, husbands carry the main financial burden of supporting the family, whether or not their wives have salaries. And in the same spirit, whether it's a matter of tradition or instinct, wives are usually the ones who carry the main responsibility for keeping things running smoothly at home, for being emotionally supportive to their husbands as well as to their children.

We have to face the fact that for all these same reasons, it is extremely difficult to work out even a half-time job or profession or avocation. Why, then, should anyone bother? And why should I believe this to be a sound and satisfying course for a great many women in our time? If someone has strong, specific interests, proven ability, or a shining talent, it may be worthwhile; but why should other young women go out of their way to seek goals, to seek spheres of interest and activity? Aren't they just looking for trouble? In a sense, yes; it may seem that they're deliberately choosing the hard way and that I'm egging them on.

By not making a deliberate choice, however, by drifting along as so many have been doing, being buffeted by the changing winds of social pressure, present-day women who are in a position to choose haven't found their lives hard, exactly, but too many have found them empty, purposeless. Deliberately making their lives hard by adding all sorts of do-it-yourself chores—from paper hanging and upholstery to weaving and preserving—has been tried by many but has turned out to be the answer for relatively few. Not only is it artificial, but it puts something of a strain on the marriage relationship to ask a woman to live in a homespun, horse-and-buggy age while her husband continues to forge ahead in a Dacron, Acrilan, jet age.

209

However, since so many traditional functions have gradually been taken away from mothers—not only the weaving, canning, and baking which many of us would cheerfully forego, but even teaching children about sex and sewing and social problems (whatever happened to mother's knee, by the way, and all the things a child used to learn there?)—it's obvious that unless she and her life are to become empty, something must be substituted.

As long ago as 1950, Lynn White, Jr., former president of Mills College, recognized this problem clearly. In his book *Educating Our Daughters*, he said:

> If the housewife no longer pumps water from the well, she must be sure that the city water supply is pure. She no longer wrings the necks of barnyard hens for dinner, but an honest meat inspection in the interests of public health affects the health of her family. Her children learn their letters at school rather than at her knee, but in return she must work for the P.T.A.

Mr. White saw the question and he gave us one answer. But I believe that in considering it the *only* answer, we may have lost as much as we gained. By calling "homemaking plus volunteer community work" *the* ideal pattern for modern woman, we are threatened with a new kind of standardization. During the years that girls have been educated much as their brothers and their future husbands, they have come to be appreciated as individuals. Parents and teachers, too, have recognized and have even emphasized individual differences, drumming home the idea that there are all kinds of ways of being a valuable person, that "different" doesn't necessarily mean "better or worse." When a girl marries, is she supposed to forget all this and learn, just as girls learned in the past: *this* is the kind of life a good wife and mother leads; this and no other?

There is a second fallacy in the "homemaking-plus volunteer-community-work" formula—at least when it is recommended as a suitable formula for most women. In the old days each mother had (using Lynn White's own example) to haul each pail of water into the house and had to wring the neck of each chicken. But the way things are now, we don't need *all* mothers working for pure food and drug laws, for fluoridation or antifluoridation, or even for the P.T.A. Women going into these volunteer efforts soon find out that not all of them are needed. It soon becomes clear that the purpose of much of their work is occupational therapy—not for others but for themselves. Wanting to be useful, many flit from one volunteer or creative activity to another—one year marching for diseases, the next year making mosaics out of broken bottles, the next year being crazy about mental health.

Since the family itself has shrunk, it's true that certain community concerns have taken the place of certain family concerns. We might say that today's extended family has, reasonably and legitimately, been extended to include the community. But different women can make different contributions to the community—both because different women are different *and* because all sorts of things are needed and duplication of effort is tremendously wasteful. Nor are all contributions measurable by the same standards. Some, such as pure research or pure art, cannot be evaluated at all by most of us. And I wish we could just accept that, as we do with much of man's work, not making a woman feel guilty about or accountable for any work she does which is not clearly contributing to her family—or her extended family, the community.

Now that I'm nearing the end of my paper, I'll make three more wishes. I would like to see less distinction made between the woman who must work for financial reasons and the one who has decided to work. The borderline is so hazy, so vague that only in cases of extreme poverty or where no husband is present and employed can one say that this woman simply must work in order for her family to survive. Beyond that who can say whether women are working for necessities or luxuries? Is a washing machine a necessity or a luxury? Is a college education for her children a necessity or a luxury? I maintain that this is for each couple to decide.

Making a sharp distinction between women who must work and those who have decided to work leaves out of account the powerful but often ignored phenomenon of "mixed motivation." Certainly, in most cases, the second income is needed or at least warmly welcomed; but there are other satisfactions, too, whether it's a feeling of usefulness, of accomplishment, or simply the human contact to be found in any store or office.

In the eyes of many people, saying that a woman *must* work for financial gain casts a reflection on her husband. The question is raised: "Can't he support her?" Ironically, reflections are also cast on the woman who has chosen to work. The question is raised: "Does she really love her children? Is she a good mother?" For all these reasons, then, I think the question of whether a woman is working through choice or necessity is often meaningless and destructive.

My second wish for women is that a less sharp distinction be made between the paid and the volunteer worker. I would like to see a climate of opinion in which the paid woman worker is neither apologetic about needing the money nor arrogant about being "a professional." Were it taken for granted that everyone works to capacity, the professional would become less defensive and the volunteer would become more professional—that is, she would feel a strong and continuing sense of responsibility toward her work and her colleagues, a sense of commitment which would keep her from quitting whenever the going got rough (or boring).

My third wish, then, is just that: a climate of opinion in which it's taken for granted that women will do something with their training, their abilities, their energy once their children are half-grown and they have free time at their disposal. First of all, there is the obvious waste of "womanpower" which was first noticed during the war, but was then forgotten until relatively recently— perhaps because of the Sputnik and our "educational lag," as the shortage of first-rate teachers was called. People can understand that, just as they understand a shortage of nurses. But, again, we have to appreciate that there are all sorts of less obvious needs, and women can make contributions in various and quite varied ways.

I latch onto the economic and social waste, putting it first, because it's respectable, it's measurable, and lately all sorts of people out there in the real world have been noticing that women haven't been pulling their weight. But long before this happened I used to think about the waste from the point of view of the individual women—not so much in terms of what they could do for society, but what a waste it is for *themselves* and how much they would gain by being participating members of society. If it were taken for granted that once a woman's children were grown and no longer needed her full time, she would find a specific place for herself (whether through a job, volunteer work, or in some other way), she would put to better use the little scraps of time available during her busiest years.

As it is now, the short stretches of time she can find for herself are usually frittered away. It's true that during the peak of her motherhood, before the children go to school, when all of them need her almost every hour of the night and day, she has neither time nor energy to spend. The hour here, the half-hour there are needed simply for "relief"—a stolen nap, a few snatched moments of window-shopping, a story read while wheeling a carriage or stirring a pot. I remember a friend who said it was a treat to go to the dentist because she got to sit down.

But this period passes. It passes so gradually, it's true, that there isn't a precise day when a woman can say she has free time to spend and ask herself how to spend it. And just as expenses rise imperceptibly to meet rising income (Parkinson's second law), so chores and errands and what Marion Sanders calls self-perpetuating puttering, what Veblen called ceremonial futility increase as women grow older and their home duties lighter. If a young mother knew, however, that at some future time she would be allowed, encouraged, and expected to use her time, training, and abilities for some purpose, she would have something specific to do with her scraps of time as soon as they started to become just a little bigger and more dependable. Having a goal, a realistic yet flexible goal, would also add zest to a woman's life while she is still young, with time only for a course here, a volunteered hour there, or an hour in the library now and then.

Of course, while she is completely tied down, it's hard for a girl to believe she'll ever have time on her hands, that her house and her days will be empty, and she herself will be unneeded. Reaching the age of forty is like having triplets or winning the Irish Sweepstakes, the unlikely kind of thing that happens only to other people. Yet word could get through to her, somehow, that this might just possibly happen to her.

Another thing that's likely to happen—and this is something that has not been generally recognized—is that a lot of girls who now foresee only marriage and motherhood for themselves will, at some period in their lives, be looking for jobs. The Women's Bureau estimates that of the girls now in high school 8 out of 10—whether because of widowhood, divorce, economic need, emotional need, or psychological need—will at some period be employed. If girls and women could accept this while young, they'd have motivation to keep their skills from rusting, their minds from shrinking, and their work habits from deteriorating.

Perhaps a representative of the Women's Bureau should be invited to confront girls in high school and in college (the majority of whom want and see only motherhood ahead) and say to them: "I have news for you! You will be looking for a job some day, so give it a thought now, so that you'll be qualified for the best, most interesting kind of work of which you are capable." If someone could say it so that the girls would really believe it, this would be helpful —just as it would have been helpful if someone had brought news to the academic and career-minded girls of my generation that, chances were, we would not be pleading at the bar, saving humanity, or running a corporation in ten or fifteen years; we'd be marketing and cooking meals, raising our children and cleaning our houses.

As it is now, even the brightest young girl takes any old job that has a salary attached because it is frankly a stopgap until her future husband comes along or (for the lucky, the truly "in" girls) until her present husband finishes college or professional school. After that, she thinks, she'll never have to see the inside of an office or store again.

Worse than that, it seems to me, is what happens to the women who have followed the prescribed course of devoting themselves fulltime to being wives, homemakers, and mothers and then find themselves—for one reason or another —looking for a job at the age of forty or fifty. They have to start at the bottom of the ladder. If they find themselves in the position of having to earn a living, it is wasteful and absurd, as well as unsatisfying, to plug away in a job far below one's capacities. If they don't have to earn money but are looking for worthwhile work, even volunteer organizations will use them in the lowliest assignments if their work habits and self-discipline have atrophied for lack of exercise. This is unsuitable for many and unbearable for some; and so, those who have any choice in the matter soon give up.

If girls could have the foresight to recognize at the beginning of their lives as women that this time will come—not only with hindsight, after a great deal of trial and error, disappointment, and heartbreak—they could try to look ahead, try to plan ahead, try to achieve some sort of balance between their work life and their personal life. My repeated use of the word "try" means I am well aware that one cannot see one's life stretching ahead, clearly and accurately. And as for planning, I realize that it is, in a sense, planning the unplannable. But if Herman Kahn and the Rand Corporation can think about the unthinkable, women should find that they have a lot to gain by planning the unplannable. If they had a general sort of goal, knowing perfectly well that it would be modified and that the road toward it would swerve and curve and, occasionally, backtrack, their journey would still be richer, more interesting, and more meaningful. If, further, they could accept such a life pattern, not as a makeshift, patched-up compromise, but as a complicated, intricate arrangement necessitated by the fact that they have the privilege and responsibility of being *both* mothers at home *and* women who have a place in the world outside the home, they could do the planning, the arranging (*and* the necessary *re*arranging) without resentment.

Last year in Belgium, while I was talking with some women about the problems connected with doing professional work while, at the same time, living a normal family life, one woman said something which I have thought of many times since then. This woman is a scientist, a *docent* at one of the universities, which is equal, approximately, to the rank of associate professor in America. She is the wife of a businessman, the mother of two sons—one at the university and one in medical school.

"When the boys were little," she told me, "my career, which was just beginning, could move along only very slowly since I was home a good deal then and couldn't spend as much time in the laboratory as my men colleagues. Even when my sons were older, but still young boys, and I had a chance to go to congresses and international meetings, for example—well, I just didn't go. I didn't really want to. Probably I didn't do as much research as I would have done had I been a man and concerned chiefly with my career. And so I didn't progress as much as if I'd been a man. I'm a *docent* now; I might perhaps have become a professor." She gave a shrug as if to say: "So what?" And then she spelled it out, quite beautifully I thought, by saying: "But that's all right for a woman because all the time you've had the pleasure of being a mother too."

And so, when I say that I'm content with second-string or second-level positions, I don't mean that women, because they are *women*, should be content with second best. I mean that if a woman is also going to run her home and be a wife to her husband and a mother to her children, it is a rare woman indeed who can hold down a full-time job which is on a par with her husband's, a rarer one still who can have a full-fledged career.

While I am wishing, I would like to get rid of the word "career" entirely. I've always been amused at the way the word "career" seems to go with the word "woman" whenever this general subject is being discussed. Most men (except for movie stars, boxers, and diplomats) have to be content with jobs. The reason the word "career" is so dangerous, I feel, when used freely, as it is, in connection with women is that many are left feeling that if they can't have a real "career," why bother at all?

Why bother? It isn't easy, I admit: this juggling of time, of energy, of one's very emotions. Sometimes you're frustrated in all your endeavors at once so that it's hard not to feel you've been left with the worst of both worlds. And yet I feel we have no choice. Maurice Chevalier is supposed to have confided to a friend: "Old age isn't so bad—not when you consider the alternative."

In much the same spirit, I seriously propose that the alternative to living a full, perhaps overfull life is being half-dead. And things being the way they are, women are more likely to become victims than men. As long ago as the turn of the century Justice Oliver Wendell Holmes' wife remarked that "Washington is full of interesting men; and the women they married when they were young." This remark was sad then, but it is sadder still today, for modern couples expect more of one another in the way of companionship. We do so for a host of reasons, but one of them has to do with sheer numbers. When you look at the picture on the cover of this conference announcement, a photograph of an old-fashioned family, it's hard to tell who's the mother, who's the father, who's the husband, who's the wife. Somewhere in that large and varied group, I can't help feeling, each man and each woman could surely find a congenial soul. Today, with families small and, furthermore, isolated from grandparents, in-laws, uncles, aunts, cousins, and grown brothers and sisters, an extra demand of understanding and companionship is asked of each husband and each wife—a shared growing and deepening far beyond "developing some interests so as not to bore Jim."

Husbands, particularly, are often asked to carry an extra burden when wives expect them to supply, through their work, not only the family's entire financial support but everything that makes life "interesting." Whether they mean friends, colleagues, prestige, or being in the know depends upon each woman and what is important to her, but there are a great many who live vicariously; there are a great many young ones, newly married, who plan and expect to live vicariously, to have their husband's contact with the world make up for the fact that they have none. This, I maintain, is too much to ask of a man. And so, for the sake of the marriage, if for no other reason, each woman should continue to grow with her husband, to enrich their shared life. Mostly, however, for her own sake should she live to the full and savor to the full her "long intense alliance with the world."

NOTES

[1] Agnes E. Meyer, "Women Aren't Men," *The Atlantic Monthly,* 186: 32–6, August, 1950. From *Out of These Roots* by Agnes E. Meyer, copyright 1950 by Agnes E. Meyer, reprinted by permission of Atlantic-Little, Brown and Company, publishers.

Identity and
Interpersonal Competence

Nelson N. Foote and
Leonard S. Cottrell

What makes the marriage partnership a continual experience of joy and discovery rather than becoming dismal routine? Why do some couples eagerly look forward to talking to each other, while others have little to say? Certainly, mere fulfillment of role expectations is not enough to keep the relationship attractive. Although doing one's duty (and having it done unto you) is to some extent gratifying, it is far from exciting. Foote suggests that husbands and wives must develop and maintain what he refers to as "interpersonal competence" so that they don't become inept and boring to each other as the years go by. Components of interpersonal competence are listed and discussed. The author claims that successful family interaction depends on the maintenance of these qualities.

Competence is a synonym for ability. It means a satisfactory degree of ability for performing certain implied kinds of tasks. Each of the abilities described below as components of interpersonal competence is found to some degree in any normal person, regardless of his previous experience. Nevertheless, as with virtually all human abilities, by practice and purposeful training wide differences result. In this sense, interpersonal competence although based upon inherited potentialities, and directly contributing to self-conceptions, may be compared to acquired skills. To conceive of interpersonal relations as governed by relative degrees of skill in controlling the outcome of episodes of interaction is to diverge greatly from some other explanations of characteristic differences in behavior.

From Nelson Foote and Leonard Cottrell, *Identity and Interpersonal Competence* (Chicago: University of Chicago Press, 1955), pp. 36–37, 40–41, 51–60. Reprinted by permission of the author and the University of Chicago Press.

The term "social skills" is now quite widely used. It might seem more advantageous and less awkward to employ it, rather than "interpersonal competence." Unfortunately, however, it has already accumulated a number of connotations which hinder its conveying what is intended here. Thus social skill often indicates correct etiquette or polish. At other times it means success in achieving popularity through display of coveted virtues.

Social skill is also used instead of a word such as rhetoric. In some of the numberless books on self-help and human relations readers are initiated into the various tricks and routines for persuading others—into the sort of skills that are necessary for salesmanship and supervision. While selling and supervision are legitimate activities, and success in these no doubt makes some use of interpersonal competence, skill in influencing others would be a very limited and limiting objective to impose upon family life.

Countless educational media—though ostensibly not commercially or manipulatively minded—likewise profess to furnish training for leadership, which is described in the language of social skill. Again, however, their emphasis tends to be on institutional ends, to the relative neglect of self-realization in day-to-day family living. But it is fairly often observed that a person can function quite successfully in his job or committee post, though his behavior as a husband or father is unsatisfactory to all concerned. Conversely, even the development of extraordinary competence in interpersonal relations—though it may help—cannot guarantee success in business or politics.

Despite these warnings against confusing interpersonal competence with the social skills of success literature, a word can be said in defense of the impulse which moves writers and readers of self-help books on human relations. Immense numbers of our fellow-citizens feel inept in their interpersonal relations; they sense narrow limits to their ability to influence or even to conciliate others. Their belief that something can be done about their ineptitude is hopeful and constructive. Were they to adopt the pessimistic alternative, and construe their fate as recalcitrant to all thought or effort, the result would undoubtedly be grave for them and the community at large.

Certainly no professional person in the field of family relations can lightly condemn the millions who read the endless stream of books, pamphlets, and columns upon marital and childrearing problems. Yet this too is a kind of self-help literature. The mounting demand for functional courses in marriage and parenthood may be interpreted in part as a response to the fact that knowledge and skill in these matters can no longer be simply absorbed through watching one's parents. The motives which inspire this demand are not merely intended to repair a deficit. More often the reader is confident that better practices are to be found than tradition affords; or he explicitly declares that he wants to do a better job than his parents did. In nearly all such expressions the assumption is evident that differing outcomes depend upon relative degrees of competence.

217

• • • •

The neutral or general value of interpersonal competence, considered as a prerequisite for the achievement of any other values of personality and family life, appeals to neo-Freudians as well as to pragmatists. Alfred Adler was perhaps the earliest to stress the incessant effort by the person from infancy onward to gain control of his world. And Adler also saw from the outset that the "power-seeker"—the neurotic individual who deliberately maneuvers to dominate others—is a person who, having been unsuccessful in winning their favorable response by normal means, strives to construct a situation in which he can extort involuntary deference.[1] Erich Fromm says the same of self-love and selfishness. Karen Horney, though denying the derivation of her thoughts from Adler, repeats almost the identical theme throughout her several works. Erik Erikson postulates the quest for mastery as a virtually universal motive. Yet none of these thinkers could be accused of advocating the domination or manipulation of others, not even of children by parents. All are advocates of some variant of self-realization. And all recognize the dependence of optimal development along self-chosen lines upon one's social relations with others.

At the level of common sense observation, people are seen to differ markedly in their aptitude or ineptitude for dealing satisfactorily with others. At the level of theoretical speculation, interpersonal competence as a general phenomenon appears to be based on what certain existentialist philosophers call transcendence.[2] This term summarizes the uniquely human processes of suspended action, memory, revery, foresight, reflection, and imagination, by means of which a person from birth onward escapes progressively from the control of his immediately given environment and begins to control it. It is by this freedom from the irresistible instincts and external stimuli, which chain the responses of lower animals, that the human being is enabled to modify his surroundings, to plan and create, to have a history and a future. His detachment from the present situation provides both the opportunity and the necessity for him to declare his own identity and values as an adult.

This capacity for transcending the immediately given and thus affecting and reconstructing it invites several levels of explanation, ranging from neurology to prehistory. The explanation most relevant here is the one based on man's ability to use symbols. Symbolization affords representation at will of that which is not present, and recombination of its elements—whether in language, dreams, art, or play. It is more than possible that inquiries into the abstract realms of symbolic processes will produce findings more potent in the development of interpersonal competence than the more proximate behavioral hypotheses ventured in the next chapter. It takes wings of greater breadth than the authors' however to fly in such thin air. We applaud those who will make the attempt while sticking closer to earth ourselves.

Instead of attempting, therefore, to further elaborate a general concept of the origins of interpersonal competence, our main strategy of definition will be analytical, to name its parts, as manifested in observable behavior. These we take to be (1) health, (2) intelligence, (3) empathy, (4) autonomy, (5) judgment, and (6) creativity. The final number and order of these components, as well as the names assigned to them, are the result of reflection, as well as extensive reference to previous literature and current discussion. Nonetheless they arose initially in quite different form through intensive pondering of what qualities distinguish inept from competent performance in interpersonal relations.

. . . .

The Components of Competence

Each of the component aspects of competence in interpersonal relations can be considerably elaborated and investigated. The decision as to how far to go in any particular instance depends on the particular project in mind and the amount of resources available. Here it is deemed suitable only to outline roughly a recognizable conceptual definition of each component, and not to attempt operational definition or the construction of any measures. We can then go on to consider some hypotheses about the purposeful development of each of the six components of competence.

1. *Health.*—In this component we include much more than mere absence of disease. Rather it signifies the progressive maximization—within organic limits—of the ability of the organism to exercise all of its physiological functions, and to achieve its maximum of sensory acuity, strength, energy, coordination, dexterity, endurance, recuperative power, and immunity. A popular synonym is "good physical condition." In some medical research circles, there is, in this positive sense, considerable discussion of the better operational criteria of health to take the place of such crude indices as, for example, gain in weight among children. Research in psychiatry and psychosomatic medicine has been finding not only that sexual competence and fertility depend on psychosocial development, but also physical health in general.[3] But the relationship runs in both directions.

Without good health, interpersonal episodes often diverge in outcome from wanted ends. Fatigue is a common example of this. While it can be and often is a symptom of complications in living, with certain other people it may also originate new difficulties. The overworked mother will lose her patience unless her reserve of energy, her ruggedness of physique, can carry her through the critical periods. The ailing person of either sex may find his dependence is not only a burden to others but means that he cannot complete the tasks that he formerly could. Endurance of strain makes physical demands, but the capacity to bear strain is not a constant; it can be cultivated in advance of its use. A striking example is the frequent recovery from despair and breakdown of interpersonal relations through vacation and rest, hygiene and recreation. On the positive, nontherapeutic side—in terms of optimal development—a benevolent spiral seems to extend from radiant health to a cheerful mien, from a cheerful mien to a friendly response, and back again to competence. The physiological substrates of interpersonal acts have been little studied within each social context; the body-mind dualism lingers on in the choice of research problems; by treating health as an element of competence, fresh possibilities arise, for the physiologist as well as the social psychologist.

Efficient criteria of health which are appropriate to the various developmental periods are needed, and so are economical devices for measuring these criteria. Also needed are hypotheses where the health component is regarded as a consequent as well as an antecedent, and finally there should be programs to test these hypotheses. Such hypotheses can of course range over the entire social, biological, and physical environment. For purposes of this report we limit our definition of the field to the relation of families or quasi-families to the development and maintenance of this component of competence.

2. *Intelligence.*—Since this component has been studied continuously and widely for over two generations, it would be presumptuous to elaborate upon it here. Scope of perception of relationships among events; the capacity to abstract and symbolize experience, to manipulate the symbols into meaningful generalizations, and to be articulate in communication; skill in mobilizing the resources of environment and experience in the services of a variety of goals; these are the kinds of capacities included in this category. It is significant that the construction of measures of intelligence is as controversial as ever, and that in any particular research project, the appropriateness and validity of the measure adopted is always a question of judgment.

The research implications of this component are toward appraisals of the findings of past research within the competence frame of reference and the design of research to fill the gaps in relevant knowledge. Of special interest will be the study of the interrelations of this component with the others we list.

In the planning-action context, the most promising line will be the appraisal of the effectiveness of present programs in creating the relevant antecedent conditions for maximizing the intelligence component, and the design of new sets of conditions which will strengthen or replace those currently operative. The conception of intelligence as a variable subject to planned development is exemplified in certain previous research studies[4] and a number of ambitious experimental programs of action, e.g., the X. G. project of the New York City public schools.

Health and intelligence have been far less often assumed to be variables subject to change through experimental programs than the remaining components of competence, yet they are no less psychosocial in their development. Research and action in respect to the following four components of competence may be less hampered by the weight of previous assumptions.

3. *Empathy.*—People appear to differ in their ability correctly to interpret the attitudes and intentions of others, in the accuracy with which they can perceive situations from others' standpoint, and thus anticipate and predict their behavior. This type of social sensitivity rests on what we call the empathic responses.[5] Empathic responses are basic to "taking the role of the

other" and hence to social interaction and the communicative processes upon which rests social integration. They are central in the development of the social self and the capacity for self-conscious behavior. No human association, and least of all democratic society, is possible without the processes indicated by this term. For this reason we must include empathic capacity as one of the essential components of interpersonal competence. The sign of its absence is misunderstanding; to measure its presence in the positive sense is a task now being attempted by a few investigators.

The kind of interaction experienced in the family as well as in other groups appears to depend heavily upon the degree to which empathic capacity develops, but experimental research on fluctuations in this element of competence has hardly begun. This lack in research is paralleled by a lack of explicit programs in action agencies aimed at the development of this type of skill. Yet it is so fundamental to social life of every kind that some social psychologists have come close to defining their field as the study of empathy.

4. *Autonomy.*—In the conception of the competent personality which we are defining in terms of its components, one essential element is perhaps best denoted by the word "autonomy," though the ordinary usage of the term does not include all the significance we shall assign to it here. Our present referents, expressed as aspects, are: the clarity of the individual's conception of self (identity); the extent to which he maintains a stable set of internal standards by which he acts; the degree to which he is self-directed and self-controlled in his actions; his confidence in and reliance upon himself; the degree of self-respect he maintains; and the capacity for recognizing real threats to self and of mobilizing realistic defenses when so threatened. That is, autonomy is taken to be genuine self-government, construed as an ability, not a state of affairs. A narrower definition, close to operational, is ease in giving and receiving evaluations of self and others.

Commencing with Piaget in the 1920's, the number of writers who have attempted to deal with autonomy has been growing steadily, but the process of making clearer what is meant by this term (or its near-equivalents like ego-strength and integrity) has as yet produced no satisfactory agreement upon its referents. Some writers treat it as a trait, some as a value, some as a set of rules for behavior, and some as a highly subjective, desired state of affairs.[6] We believe that progress in definition and measurement of this obviously very important though subtle complex will come most rapidly if definition is sought in terms of an acquired ability for handling those kinds of problematic interpersonal situations where self-esteem is threatened or challenged.

5. *Judgment.*—While critical judgment has long been understood to be acquired slowly with experience, more or less according to age, its operational definition and measurement is still a difficult task. Certain of the educational psychologists have perhaps gone furthest in differentiating this ability from intelligence, and in analyzing the conditions by which an educational or other agency may cultivate judgment among its pupils.[7]

Judgment refers here to the ability which develops slowly in human beings

221

to estimate and evaluate the meaning and consequences to one's self of alternative lines of conduct. It means the ability to adjudicate among values, or to make correct decisions; the index of lack of judgment (bad judgment) is mistakes, but these are the products of an antecedent process, in which skill is the important variable. Obviously neither small children nor incapacitated adults can make sound decisions in the sense indicated; and it is equally obvious that among normal adults there is wide variation in this ability. Some persons acquire reputations for unusually good judgment, and some others become conspicuous for the opposite. It is therefore highly proper to conceive of judgment as an acquired critical ability differing in degree among individuals.

Currently among several of the social sciences, though notably in economics, the study of decision-making and of value-choices is receiving much emphasis. Generally speaking, however, the various studies and seminars under way focus upon the outcome or the product of this process—upon ethics, logic, or some highly abstract calculus of contingencies and relative utilities; rarely do they focus upon the choosers, their identities, and the conditions under which their critical abilities develop. A thoroughly interpersonal concept of judgment, appropriate for studying its development, probably therefore must include the skill involved in getting others to be reasonable in discussion, and to handle criticism in a way that utilizes its value.

6. *Creativity.*—This component is perhaps the least amenable to precise definition and division into manageable variables which can be measured. It is ironical that the so-called tough-minded scientists and hard-headed practical people are inclined to look askance at this category as a proper object of scientific study, and yet all of these people demand appraisals of this quality in prospective associates on whom heavy responsibility for leadership and initiative will fall.

The idea of creativity is commonly associated with artistic and intellectual activities. We define it here as any demonstrated capacity for innovations in behavior or real reconstruction of any aspect of the social environment. It involves the ability to develop fresh perspectives from which to view all accepted routines and to make novel combinations of ideas and objects and so define new goals, endowing old ones with fresh meaning, and inventing means for their realization. In interpersonal relations, it is the ability to invent or improvise new roles or alternative lines of action in problematic situations, and to evoke such behavior in others. Among other things it seems to involve curiosity, self-confidence, something of the venturesomeness and risk-taking tendencies of the explorer, a flexible mind with the kind of freedom which permits the orientation of spontaneous play. While this is a none too satisfactory delineation of creativity, we can begin here and invite help in the search for a more satisfying one. In interpersonal relations the uncreative person is continually found in dilemmas and impasses—"at his wits' end"—but the valid indices of creativity are harder to discover. Rigidity obtrudes upon attention more than flexibility, for obvious reasons, but that is not to say it deserves more scientific attention.

Why Six Components of Competence?

This brief outline of our conception of the essential components of interpersonal competence is offered with no illusions as to its adequacy or finality. If we have succeeded in giving to the reader at least a rough working idea of the content and meaning the term has for us, and have stimulated critical thinking on its contemporary relevance or implications, our purpose for the moment has been served. Perhaps such reflection will result in the discovery of other skills and qualities which should be added to this list. For the present we are unable to offer additions or corrections, and have some reasons for assuming its completeness.

Readers of George Herbert Mead[8] will recall his distinction between the "me" and "I" phases of the self in personality development and social interaction. Looking at the elements of competence, three correspond roughly to the "me" phase and three to the "I" phase:

Me: Intelligence	I: Health
Empathy	Autonomy
Judgment	Creativity

The former refer to the vested and organized experience of the community as incorporated within personal conduct; the latter, to the active, assertive, and emergent features of human behavior, not reducible to standard roles in conventional situations. But while Mead, like Dewey, relied heavily upon biological explanation for the impulsive and unpredictable character of human development, it had nonetheless been his intention to show the emergence of novel identities within the process of interaction. The concepts of interpersonal autonomy and interpersonal creativity may help to complete his task. In any social act—any episode of interaction—all six capacities are and must be employed, though their prominence varies from phase to phase.

The cultural anthropologists have offered many attempts to classify the full range of human culture. These range from the classic division into technology, social organization, and ideology, through Lowie's "universal pattern of culture" and Malinowski's six-category analysis of institutions, to the extremely elaborate Yale cross-cultural index. It seems significant that the classical tripartite scheme can be detected underlying each of its more sophisticated successors. From quite a different angle, this old division seems to gain a vague additional warrant from Morris' division of the study of meaningful verbal relationships into semantics, syntactics, and pragmatics.[9] Considering the fondness of Western thinkers for indicating completeness by schemes of three elements and opposition by schemes of two, it is difficult to distinguish chicken from egg in trying to account for the recurrence of such schemes, i.e., do they describe reality, or is social reality not the precipitate of such linguistic constructions?

Probably neither metaphysics nor intellectual history has to be called on for defense of either the number or order of the elements of competence, however intriguing it is to speculate about their resemblance to previous schemes. Health and intelligence refer to the factual world of physical events and overt experience; both principally afford rational and efficient manipulation of the objects of the environment. Empathy and autonomy, by contrast, have to do with the relationships of selves and others, not as objects, but as human subjects with whom each person is engaged in the plots of the human drama. Judgment and creativity refer to the symbolized realm of not-present relationships, to the extent that these can be distinguished from the social and instrumental realms of immediate experience.

As mentioned at the outset of this chapter, the six elements of competence were arrived at principally through reflection upon previous research and upon the observable content of interpersonal behavior, and not from play with hyper-abstractions. If further abstraction, however, could demonstrate the completeness of a scheme that is made open-ended by the inclusion of creativity as its final element, then it would seem logical to suppose that our list of six would be lengthened by the addition only of subcategories, rather than by the addition of a seventh or eighth component.

With regard to order, the list is thought to proceed from the most given to the least given features of any interpersonal performance. Also, as will be seen in ensuing chapters, the order adopted is cognate with an order which appears not only empirically convenient in presenting types of family agencies and types of play, but also productive of further useful meditation about reciprocal implications. It would deprive the reader of some pleasant speculation to explore these exhaustively here; we prefer only to suggest the avenues which may be used to order and traverse the vast territory confronting us.

It appears to us that a community which organizes its activity so that it maximizes the number of healthy, intelligent, self-directing citizens, capable of viewing situations from perspectives other than their own, of weighing alternatives and making decisions, of defining new goals and inventing ways of achieving them, is in fact a democratic community and is producing members who can sustain it against all more pessimistic theories of human nature and the social order.

NOTES

[1] Alfred Adler, "The Family Constellation," *Understanding Human Nature* (Cleveland: The World Publishing Company, 1941).

[2] Ortega y Gasset, "The Self and the Other," *Partisan Review*, XIX, No. 4 (July-August, 1952). Simone de Beauvoir, *The Second Sex* (New York: Alfred A. Knopf, Inc., 1953). Robert Ulich, *The Human Career: A Philosophy of Self-transcendence* (New York: Harper and Brothers, 1955).

[3] Henry B. Richardson, *Patients Have Families* (New York: The Commonwealth Fund, 1948). Also, Metropolitan Life Insurance Company, *Statistical Bulletin,* XXXVI (New York: Metropolitan Life Insurance Company, 1955), published monthly. Innes H. Pearse, M.D., and Lucy H. Crocker, *The Peckham Experiment* (New Haven: Yale University Press, 1945).

4 Harold M. Skeels, Ruth Updegraff, Beth L. Wellman, and Harold M. Williams, "A Study of Environmental Stimulation: An Orphanage Preschool Project," *University of Iowa Studies in Child Welfare*, Vol. XV, No. 4, New Series, No. 363, December 1, 1938 (Iowa City: University of Iowa, 1938).

5 For a fuller treatment, see: Leonard S. Cottrell, Jr., and Rosalind F. Dymond, "The Empathic Processes," *Psychiatry*, XII, No. 4 (November, 1949), 355–59.

6 Andras Angyal, *Foundations for a Science of Personality* (New York: The Commonwealth Fund, 1941). Erik H. Erikson, *Childhood and Society* (New York: W. W. Norton and Co., 1950). Joanna Field (pseud.), *A Life of One's Own* (Harmondsworth: Penguin Books, 1952). Erich Fromm, *Man for Himself: An Inquiry into the Psychology of Ethics* (New York: Rinehart, 1947). Robert Lindner, *Prescription for Rebellion* (New York: Rinehart, 1952). Rollo May, *Man's Search for Himself* (New York: W. W. Norton, and Co., 1953). Henry A. Murray *et al., Explorations in Personality* (Cambridge: Harvard University Press, 1938). Jean Piaget, *The Moral Judgment of the Child* (Glencoe: The Free Press, 1948). David Riesman, *The Lonely Crowd* (New Haven: Yale University Press, 1950).

7 E.g., R. B. Raup, K. D. Benne, B. O. Smith, and G. E. Axtelle, *The Discipline of Practical Judgment in a Democratic Society*, 28th Yearbook of the National Society of College Teachers of Education (Chicago: University of Chicago Press, 1943). Also, Edward M. Glaser, *An Experiment in the Development of Critical Thinking* (New York: Bureau of Publications, Teachers College, Columbia University, 1941).

8 George H. Mead, *Mind, Self, and Society* (Chicago: The University of Chicago Press, 1934).

9 Charles Morris, *Signs, Language and Behavior* (New York: Prentice-Hall, Inc., 1946).

5

Children as Junior Partners

The arrival of children and their affect on the married couple is discussed here. Parenthood has been described as part of a grand plan to provide society with socialized beings. However, on a personal level the demands of parenthood are somewhat of a shock to new mothers and fathers in the United States. The guidelines for motherhood and the means of role socialization before the actual birth are few; the role of father is almost ignored. Even more difficult is the position of the lone parent—a frequent phenomenon in our society of high divorce and desertion rates.

Regardless of parental adjustment problems, children must be reared and it is likely that the socialization process will have a lasting effect on their personalities and *their* marital partnerships. In this area, the home atmosphere may be a greater force than all the various child rearing "techniques" and theories that vie for both academic and lay attention. Certainly, it has a potent effect on the viability of the parent-child partnership.

Not all goals that parents set for the socialization of their children are fulfilled. One in particular seems doomed by the pressure of outside social forces —the hope that children will think and act a great deal like their parents. A sociologist explains parent-youth conflict by showing its relationship to industrialization and illustrating why it is often beyond the power of the individual parent to prevent this generation gap.

Transition to Parenthood

Alice S. Rossi

Does parenthood just "come naturally" to the average wife and husband? Rossi thinks not and suggests, in fact, that in American society parenthood is more demanding and abrupt in transition than either marriage or occupation adjustment. Furthermore, less preparation is available for it than for other roles. Thus, parenthood is not an ordinary turn of events, but rather has many unique features that can trigger a crisis in the marriage.

THE PROBLEM

The central concern in this sociological analysis of parenthood will be with two closely related questions. (1) What is involved in the transition to parenthood: what must be learned and what readjustments of other role commitments must take place in order to move smoothly through the transition from a childless married state to parenthood? (2) What is the effect of parenthood on the adult: in what ways do parents, and in particular mothers, change as a result of their parental experiences?

To get a firmer conceptual handle on the problem, I shall first specify the stages in the development of the parental role and then explore several of the most salient features of the parental role by comparing it with the two other major social roles—the marital and work role. Throughout the discussion, special attention will be given to the social changes that have taken place

From Alice S. Rossi, "Transition to Parenthood," *Journal of Marriage and the Family*, February, 1968, pp. 26–39. Reprinted by permission of the author and The National Council on Family Relations. Paper presented to the American Orthopsychiatric Association, Washington, D.C., March 22, 1967. Grateful acknowledgment is made to the National Institutes of Health, sponsor of my work under a Research Career Development Award, and to my friend and former colleague Bernice Neugarten, at the University of Chicago, whose support and stimulation were critical in supplementing my sociological training with the human development perspective.

during the past few decades which facilitate or complicate the transition to and the experience of parenthood among young American adults.

From Child to Parent: An Example

What is unique about this perspective on parenthood is the focus on the adult parent rather than the child. Until quite recent years, concern in the behavioral sciences with the parent-child relationship has been confined almost exclusively to the child. Whether a psychological study such as Ferreira's on the influence of the pregnant woman's attitude to maternity upon postnatal behavior of the neonate,[1] Sears and Maccoby's survey of child-rearing practices,[2] or Brody's detailed observations of mothering,[3] the long tradition of studies of maternal deprivation[4] and more recently of maternal employment,[5] the child has been the center of attention. The design of such research has assumed that, if enough were known about what parents were like and what they in fact did in rearing their children, much of the variation among children could be accounted for.[6]

The very different order of questions which emerge when the parent replaces the child as the primary focus of analytic attention can best be shown with an illustration. Let us take, as our example, the point Benedek makes that the child's need for mothering is *absolute* while the need of an adult woman to mother is *relative*.[7] From a concern for the child, this discrepancy in need leads to an analysis of the impact on the child of separation from the mother or inadequacy of mothering. Family systems that provide numerous adults to care for the young child can make up for this discrepancy in need between mother and child, which may be why ethnographic accounts give little evidence of postpartum depression following childbirth in simpler societies. Yet our family system of isolated households, increasingly distant from kinswomen to assist in mothering, requires that new mothers shoulder total responsibility for the infant precisely for that stage of the child's life when his need for mothering is far in excess of the mother's need for the child.

From the perspective of the mother, the question has therefore become: what does maternity deprive her of? Are the intrinsic gratifications of maternity sufficient to compensate for shelving or reducing a woman's involvement in non-family interests and social roles? The literature on maternal deprivation cannot answer such questions, because the concept, even in the careful specification Yarrow has given it,[8] has never meant anything but the effect on the child of various kinds of insufficient mothering. Yet what has been seen as a failure or inadequacy of individual women may in fact be a failure of the society to provide institutionalized substitutes for the extended kin to assist in the care of infants and young children. It may be that the role requirements of maternity in the American family system extract too high a price of deprivation for young adult women reared with highly diversified interests and social expectations concerning adult life. Here, as at several points in the course of

229

this paper, familiar problems take on a new and suggestive research dimension when the focus is on the parent rather than the child.

BACKGROUND

Since it is a relatively recent development to focus on the parent side of the parent-child relationship, some preliminary attention to the emergence of this focus on parenthood is in order. Several developments in the behavioral sciences paved the way to this perspective. Of perhaps most importance have been the development of ego psychology and the problem of adaptation of Murray[9] and Hartmann,[10] the interpersonal focus of Sullivan's psychoanalytic theories,[11] and the life cycle approach to identity of Erikson.[12] These have been fundamental to the growth of the human development perspective: that personality is not a stable given but a constantly changing phenomenon, that the individual changes along the life line as he lives through critical life experiences. The transition to parenthood, or the impact of parenthood upon the adult, is part of the heightened contemporary interest in adult socialization.

A second and related development has been the growing concern of behavioral scientists with crossing levels of analysis to adequately comprehend social and individual phenomena and to build theories appropriate to a complex social system. In the past, social anthropologists focused as purely on the level of prescriptive normative variables as psychologists had concentrated on intrapsychic processes at the individual level or sociologists on social-structural and institutional variables. These are adequate, perhaps, when societies are in a stable state of equilibrium and the social sciences were at early stages of conceptual development, but they become inadequate when the societies we study are undergoing rapid social change and we have an increasing amount of individual and subgroup variance to account for.

Psychology and anthropology were the first to join theoretical forces in their concern for the connections between culture and personality. The question of how culture is transmitted across the generations and finds its manifestations in the personality structure and social roles of the individual has brought renewed research attention to the primary institutions of the family and the schools, which provide the intermediary contexts through which culture is transmitted and built into personality structure.

It is no longer possible for a psychologist or a therapist to neglect the social environment of the individual subject or patient, nor is the "family" they are concerned with any longer confined to the family of origin, for current theory and therapy view the adult individual in the context of his current family of procreation. So too it is no longer possible for the sociologist to focus exclusively on the current family relationships of the individual. The incorporation of psychoanalytic theory into the informal, if not the formal, training of the sociologist has led to an increasing concern for the quality of relationships in the family of origin as determinants of the adult attitudes, values, and behavior which the sociologist studies.

230

Quite another tradition of research has led to the formulation of "normal crises of parenthood." "Crisis" research began with the studies of individuals undergoing traumatic experiences, such as that by Tyhurst on natural catastrophes,[13] Caplan on parental responses to premature births,[14] Lindemann on grief and bereavement,[15] and Janis on surgery.[16] In these studies attention was on differential response to stress—how and why individuals vary in the ease with which they coped with the stressful experience and achieved some reintegration. Sociological interest has been piqued as these studies were built upon by Rhona and Robert Rapoport's research on the honeymoon and the engagement as normal crises in the role transitions to marriage and their theoretical attempt to build a conceptual bridge between family and occupational research from a "transition task" perspective.[17] LeMasters, Dyer, and Hobbs have each conducted studies of parenthood precisely as a crisis or disruptive event in family life.[18]

I think, however, that the time is now ripe to drop the concept of "normal crises" and to speak directly, instead, of the transition to and impact of parenthood. There is an uncomfortable incongruity in speaking of any crisis as normal. If the transition is achieved and if a successful reintegration of personality or social roles occurs, then crisis is a misnomer. To confine attention to "normal crises" suggests, even if it is not logically implied, successful outcome, thus excluding from our analysis the deviant instances in which failure occurs.

Sociologists have been just as prone as psychologists to dichotomize normality and pathology. We have had one set of theories to deal with deviance, social problems, and conflict and quite another set in theoretical analyses of a normal system—whether a family or a society. In the latter case our theories seldom include categories to cover deviance, strain, dysfunction, or failure. Thus, Parsons and Bales' systems find "task-leaders" oriented to problem solution, but not instrumental leaders attempting to undercut or destroy the goal of the group, and "sociometric stars" who play a positive integrative function in cementing ties among group members, but not negatively expressive persons with hostile aims of reducing or destroying such intragroup ties.[19]

Parsons' analysis of the experience of parenthood as a step in maturation and personality growth does not allow for negative outcome. In this view either parents show little or no positive impact upon themselves of their parental role experiences, or they show a new level of maturity. Yet many women, whose interests and values made a congenial combination of wifehood and work role, may find that the addition of maternal responsibilities has the consequence of a fundamental and undesired change in both their relationships to their husbands and their involvements outside the family. Still other women, who might have kept a precarious hold on adequate functioning as adults had they *not* become parents, suffer severe retrogression with pregnancy and childbearing, because the reactivation of older unresolved conflicts with their own mothers is not favorably resolved but in fact leads to personality deterioration[20] and the transmission of pathology to their children.[21]

Where cultural pressure is very great to assume a particular adult role, as it is for American women to bear and rear children, latent desire and psychological readiness for parenthood may often be at odds with manifest desire and actual ability to perform adequately as parents. Clinicians and therapists are aware, as perhaps many sociologists are not, that failure, hostility, and destructiveness are as much a part of the family system and the relationships among family members as success, love, and solidarity are.[22]

A conceptual system which can deal with both successful and unsuccessful role transitions, or positive and negative impact of parenthood upon adult men and women, is thus more powerful than one built to handle success but not failure or vice versa. For these reasons I have concluded that it is misleading and restrictive to perpetuate the use of the concept of "normal crisis." A more fruitful point of departure is to build upon the stage-task concepts of Erikson, viewing parenthood as a developmental stage, as Benedek[23] and Hill[24] have done, a perspective carried into the research of Raush, Goodrich, and Campbell[25] and of Rhona and Robert Rapoport[26] on adaptation to the early years of marriage and that of Cohen, Fearing et al.[27] on the adjustments involved in pregnancy.

ROLE CYCLE STAGES

A discussion of the impact of parenthood upon the parent will be assisted by two analytic devices. One is to follow a comparative approach, by asking in what basic structural ways the parental role differs from other primary adult roles. The marital and occupational roles will be used for this comparison. A second device is to specify the phases in the development of a social role. If the total life span may be said to have a cycle, each stage with its unique tasks, then by analogy a role may be said to have a cycle and each stage in that role cycle, to have its unique tasks and problems of adjustment. Four broad stages of a role cycle may be specified:

Anticipatory Stage

All major adult roles have a long history of anticipatory training for them, since parental and school socialization of children is dedicated precisely to this task of producing the kind of competent adult valued by the culture. For our present purposes, however, a narrower conception of the anticipatory stage is preferable: the engagement period in the case of the marital role, pregnancy in the case of the parental role, and the last stages of highly vocationally oriented schooling or on-the-job apprenticeship in the case of an occupational role.

Honeymoon Stage

This is the time period immediately following the full assumption of the adult role. The inception of this stage is more easily defined than its termination. In the case of the marital role, the honeymoon stage extends from the marriage ceremony itself through the literal honeymoon and on through an unspecified and individually varying period of time. Raush[28] has caught this stage of the marital role in his description of the "psychic honeymoon": that extended postmarital period when, through close intimacy and joint activity, the couple can explore each other's capacities and limitations. I shall arbitrarily consider the onset of pregnancy as marking the end of the honeymoon stage of the marital role. This stage of the parental role may involve an equivalent psychic honeymoon, that post-childbirth period during which, through intimacy and prolonged contact, an attachment between parent and child is laid down. There is a crucial difference, however, from the marital role in this stage. A woman knows her husband as a unique real person when she enters the honeymoon stage of marriage. A good deal of preparatory adjustment on a firm reality-base is possible during the engagement period which is not possible in the equivalent pregnancy period. Fantasy is not corrected by the reality of a specific individual child until the birth of the child. The "quickening" is psychologically of special significance to women precisely because it marks the first evidence of a real baby rather than a purely fantasized one. On this basis alone there is greater interpersonal adjustment and learning during the honeymoon stage of the parental role than of the marital role.

Plateau Stage

This is the protracted middle period of a role cycle during which the role is fully exercised. Depending on the specific problem under analysis, one would obviously subdivide this large plateau stage further. For my present purposes it is not necessary to do so, since my focus is on the earlier anticipatory and honeymoon stages of the parental role and the overall impact of parenthood on adults.

Disengagement -Termination Stage

This period immediately precedes and includes the actual termination of the role. Marriage ends with the death of the spouse or, just as definitively, with separation and divorce. A unique characteristic of parental role termination is the fact that it is not clearly marked by any specific act but is an attenuated process of termination with little cultural prescription about when the authority and obligations of a parent end. Many parents, however, experience the marriage of the child as a psychological termination of the active parental role.

UNIQUE FEATURES OF PARENTAL ROLE

With this role cycle suggestion as a broader framework, we can narrow our focus to what are the unique and most salient features of the parental role. In doing so, special attention will be given to two further questions: (1) the impact of social changes over the past few decades in facilitating or complicating the transition to and experience of parenthood and (2) the new interpretations or new research suggested by the focus on the parent rather than the child.

Cultural Pressure to Assume the Role

On the level of cultural values, men have no freedom of choice where work is concerned: They must work to secure their status as adult men. The equivalent for women has been maternity. There is considerable pressure upon the growing girl and young woman to consider maternity necessary for a woman's fulfillment as an individual and to secure her status as an adult.[29]

This is not to say there are no fluctuations over time in the intensity of the cultural pressure to parenthood. During the depression years of the 1930's, there was more widespread awareness of the economic hardships parenthood can entail, and many demographic experts believe there was a great increase in illegal abortions during those years. Bird has discussed the dread with which a suspected pregnancy was viewed by many American women in the 1930's.[30] Quite a different set of pressures were at work during the 1950's, when the general societal tendency was toward withdrawal from active engagement with the issues of the larger society and a turning in to the gratifications of the private sphere of home and family life. Important in the background were the general affluence of the period and the expanded room and ease of child rearing that go with suburban living. For the past five years, there has been a drop in the birth rate in general, fourth and high-order births in particular. During this same period there has been increased concern and debate about women's participation in politics and work, with more women now returning to work rather than conceiving the third or fourth child.[31]

Inception of the Parental Role

The decision to marry and the choice of a mate are voluntary acts of individuals in our family system. Engagements are therefore consciously considered, freely entered, and freely terminated if increased familiarity decreases, rather than increases, intimacy and commitment to the choice. The inception of a pregnancy, unlike the engagement, is not always a voluntary decision, for it may be the unintended consequence of a sexual act that was recreative in intent rather than procreative. Secondly, and again unlike the engagement, the termination of a pregnancy is not socially sanctioned, as shown by current resistance to abortion-law reform.

The implication of this difference is a much higher probability of unwanted pregnancies than of unwanted marriages in our family system. Coupled with the ample clinical evidence of parental rejection and sometimes cruelty to children, it is all the more surprising that there has not been more consistent research attention to the problem of *parental satisfaction*, as there has for long been on *marital satisfaction* or *work satisfaction*. Only the extreme iceberg tip of the parental satisfaction continuum is clearly demarcated and researched, as in the growing concern with "battered babies." Cultural and psychological resistance to the image of a non-nurturant woman may afflict social scientists as well as the American public.

The timing of a first pregnancy is critical to the manner in which parental responsibilities are joined to the marital relationship. The single most important change over the past few decades is extensive and efficient contraceptive usage, since this has meant, for a growing proportion of new marriages, the possibility of and increasing preference for some postponement of childbearing after marriage. When pregnancy was likely to follow shortly after marriage, the major transition point in a woman's life was marriage itself. *This transition point is increasingly the first pregnancy rather than marriage.* It is accepted and increasingly expected that women will work after marriage, while household furnishings are acquired and spouses complete their advanced training or gain a foothold in their work.[32] This provides an early marriage period in which the fact of a wife's employment presses for a greater egalitarian relationship between husband and wife in decision-making, commonality of experience, and sharing of household responsibilities.

The balance between individual autonomy and couple mutuality that develops during the honeymoon stage of such a marriage may be important in establishing a pattern that will later affect the quality of the parent-child relationship and the extent of sex-role segregation of duties between the parents. It is only in the context of a growing egalitarian base to the marital relationship that one could find, as Gavron has,[33] a tendency for parents to establish some barriers between themselves and their children, a marital defense against the institution of parenthood as she describes it. This may eventually replace the typical coalition in more traditional families of mother and children against husband-father. Parenthood will continue for some time to impose a degree of temporary segregation of primary responsibilities between husband and wife, but, when this takes place in the context of a previously established egalitarian relationship between the husband and wife, such role segregation may become blurred, with greater recognition of the wife's need for autonomy and the husband's role in the routines of home and child rearing.[34]

There is one further significant social change that has important implications for the changed relationship between husband and wife: the increasing departure from an old pattern of role-inception phasing in which the young person first completed his schooling, then established himself in the world of work, then married and began his family. Marriage and parenthood are increasingly taking place *before* the schooling of the husband, and often of the wife, has been completed.[35] An important reason for this trend lies in the fact that, during the same decades in which the average age of physical-sexual maturation has dropped, the average amount of education which young people obtain has been on the increase. Particularly for the college and graduate or professional school population, family roles are often assumed before the degrees needed to enter careers have been obtained.

Just how long it now takes young people to complete their higher education has been investigated only recently in several longitudinal studies of college-graduate cohorts.[36] College is far less uniformly a four-year period than high school is. A full third of the college freshmen in one study had been out of high school a year or more before entering college.[37] In a large sample of college graduates in 1961, one in five were over 25 years of age at graduation.[38] Thus, financial difficulties, military service, change of career plans, and marriage itself all tend to create interruptions in the college attendance of a significant proportion of college graduates. At the graduate and professional school level, this is even more marked: the mean age of men receiving the doctorate, for example, is 32, and of women, 36.[39] It is the exception rather than the rule for men and women who seek graduate degrees to go directly from college to graduate school and remain there until they secure their degrees.[40]

The major implication of this change is that more men and women are achieving full adult status in family roles while they are still less than fully adult in status terms in the occupational system. Graduate students are, increasingly, men and women with full family responsibilities. Within the family many more husbands and fathers are still students, often quite dependent on the earnings of their wives to see them through their advanced training.[41] No matter what the couple's desires and preferences are, this fact alone presses for more egalitarian relations between husband and wife, just as the adult family status of graduate students presses for more egalitarian relations between students and faculty.

Irrevocability

If marriages do not work out, there is now widespread acceptance of divorce and remarriage as a solution. The same point applies to the work world: we are free to leave an unsatisfactory job and seek another. But once a pregnancy occurs, there is little possibility of undoing the commitment to parenthood implicit in conception except in the rare instance of placing children for adoption. We can have ex-spouses and ex-jobs but not ex-children. This being so, it is scarcely surprising to find marked differences between the relationship of a parent and one child and the relationship of the same parent with another child. If the culture does not permit pregnancy termination, the equivalent to giving up a child is psychological withdrawal on the part of the parent.

This taps an important area in which a focus on the parent rather than the child may contribute a new interpretive dimension to an old problem: the long history of interest, in the social sciences, in differences among children associated with their sex-birth-order position in their sibling set. Research has largely been based on data gathered about and/or from the children, and interpretations make inferences back to the "probable" quality of the child's relation to a parent and how a parent might differ in relating to a first-born compared to a last-born child. The relevant research, directed at the parents (mothers in particular), remains to be done, but at least a few examples can be suggested of the different order of interpretation that flows from a focus on the parent.

Some birth-order research stresses the influence of sibs upon other sibs, as in Koch's finding that second-born boys with an older sister are more feminine than second-born boys with an older brother.[42] A similar sib-influence interpretation is offered in the major common finding of birth-order correlates, that sociability is greater among last-borns[43] and achievement among first-borns.[44] It has been suggested that last-borns use social skills to increase acceptance by their older sibs or are more peer-oriented because they receive less adult stimulation from parents. The tendency of first-borns to greater achievement has been interpreted in a corollary way, as a reflection of early assumption of responsibility for younger sibs, greater adult stimulation during the time the oldest was the only child in the family,[45] and the greater significance of the first-born for the larger kinship network of the family.[46]

Sociologists have shown increasing interest in structural family variables in recent years, a primary variable being family size. From Bossard's descriptive work on the large family[47] to more methodologically sophisticated work such as that by Rosen,[48] Elder and Bowerman,[49] Boocock,[50] and Nisbet,[51] the question posed is: what is the effect of growing up in a small family, compared with a large family, that is attributable to this group-size variable? Unfortunately, the theoretical point of departure for sociologists' expectations of the effect of the family-size variables is the Durkheim-Simmel tradition of the differential effect of group size or population density upon members or inhabitants.[52] In the case of the family, however, this overlooks the very important fact that family size is determined by the key figures *within* the group, i.e., the parents. To find that children in small families differ from children in large families is not simply due to the impact of group size upon individual members but to the very different involvement of the parents with the children and to relations between the parents themselves in small versus large families.

An important clue to a new interpretation can be gained by examining family size from the perspective of parental motivation toward having children. A small family is small for one of two primary reasons: either the parents wanted a small family and achieved their desired size or they wanted a large family but were not able to attain it. In either case, there is a low probability of unwanted children. Indeed, in the latter eventuality they may take particularly great interest in the children they do have. Small families are therefore most likely to contain parents with a strong and positive orientation to each of the children they have. A large family, by contrast, is large either because the parents achieved the size they desired or because they have more children than they in fact wanted. Large families therefore have a higher probability than small families of including unwanted and unloved children. Consistent with this are Nye's finding that adolescents in small families have better relations with their parents than those in large families[53] and Sears and Maccoby's finding that mothers of large families are more restrictive toward their children than mothers of small families.[54]

237

This also means that last-born children are more likely to be unwanted than first- or middle-born children, particularly in large families. This is consistent with what is known of abortion patterns among married women, who typically resort to abortion only when they have achieved the number of children they want or feel they can afford to have. Only a small proportion of women faced with such unwanted pregnancies actually resort to abortion. *This suggests the possibility that the last-born child's reliance on social skills may be his device for securing the attention and loving involvement of a parent less positively predisposed to him than to his older siblings.*

In developing this interpretation, rather extreme cases have been stressed. Closer to the normal range, of families in which even the last-born child was desired and planned for, there is still another element which may contribute to the greater sociability of the last-born child. Most parents are themselves aware of the greater ease with which they face the care of a third fragile newborn than the first; clearly, parental skills and confidence are greater with last-born children than with first-born children. But this does not mean that the attitude of the parent is more positive toward the care of the third child than the first. There is no necessary correlation between skills in an area and enjoyment of that area. Searls[55] found that older homemakers are *more* skillful in domestic tasks but experience *less* enjoyment of them than young homemakers, pointing to a declining euphoria for a particular role with the passage of time. In the same way, older people rate their marriages as "very happy" less often than younger people do.[56] It is perhaps culturally and psychologically more difficult to face the possibility that women may find less enjoyment of the maternal role with the passage of time, though women themselves know the difference between the romantic expectation concerning child care and the incorporation of the first baby into the household and the more realistic expectation and sharper assessment of their own abilities to do an adequate job of mothering as they face a third confinement. Last-born children may experience not only less verbal stimulation from their parents than first-born children but also less prompt and enthusiastic response to their demands—from feeding and diaper-change as infants to requests for stories read at three or a college education at eighteen—simply because the parents experience less intense gratification from the parent role with the third child than they did with the first. The child's response to this might well be to cultivate winning, pleasing manners in early childhood that blossom as charm and sociability in later life, showing both a greater need to be loved and greater pressure to seek approval.

One last point may be appropriately developed at this juncture. Mention was made earlier that for many women the personal outcome of experience in the parent role is not a higher level of maturation but the negative outcome of a depressed sense of self-worth, if not actual personality deterioration. There is considerable evidence that this is more prevalent than we recognize. On a qualitative level, a close reading of the portrait of the working-class wife in Rainwater,[57] Newsom,[58] Komarovsky,[59] Gavron,[60] or Zweig[61] gives little suggestion that maternity has provided these women with opportunities for personal growth and development. So too, Cohen[62] notes with some surprise that in her sample of middle-class educated couples, as in Pavenstadt's study of lower-income women in Boston, there were more emotional difficulty and lower levels of maturation among multiparous women than primiparous women. On a more extensive sample basis, in Gurin's survey of Americans viewing their mental health,[63] as in Bradburn's reports on happiness,[64] single men are less happy and less active than single women, but among the married respondents the women are unhappier, have more problems, feel inadequate as parents, have a more negative and passive outlook on life, and show a more negative self-image. All of these characteristics increase with age among married women but show no relationship to age among men. While it may be true, as Gurin argues, that women are more introspective and hence more attuned to the psychological facets of experience than men are, this point does not account for the fact that the things which the women report are all on the negative side; few are on the positive side, indicative of euphoric sensitivity and pleasure. The possibility must be faced, and at some point researched, that women lose ground in personal development and self-esteem during the early and middle years of adulthood, whereas men gain ground in these respects during the same years. The retention of a high level of self-esteem may depend upon the adequacy of earlier preparation for major adult roles: men's training adequately prepares them for their primary adult roles in the occupational system, as it does for those women who opt to participate significantly in the work world. Training in the qualities and skills needed for family roles in contemporary society may be inadequate for both sexes, but the lowering of self-esteem occurs only among women because their primary adult roles are within the family system.

Preparation for Parenthood

Four factors may be given special attention on the question of what preparation American couples bring to parenthood.

Paucity of preparation. Our educational system is dedicated to the cognitive development of the young, and our primary teaching approach is the pragmatic one of learning by doing. How much one knows and how well he can apply what he knows are the standards by which the child is judged in school, as the employee is judged at work. The child can learn by doing in such subjects as science, mathematics, art work, or shop, but not in the subjects most relevant to successful family life: sex, home maintenance, child care, interpersonal competence, and empathy. If the home is deficient in training in these areas, the child is left with no preparation for a major segment of his adult life. A doctor facing his first patient in private practice has treated numerous patients under close supervision during his interneship, but probably a majority of American mothers approach maternity with no previous child-care experience beyond sporadic baby-siting, perhaps a course in child psychology, or occasional care of younger siblings.

Limited learning during pregnancy. A second important point makes adjust-ment to parenthood potentially more stressful than marital adjustment. This is the lack of any realistic training for parenthood during the anticipatory stage of pregnancy. By contrast, during the engagement period preceding marriage, an individual has opportunities to develop the skills and make the adjustments which ease the transition to marriage. Through discussions of values and life goals, through sexual experimentation, shared social experi-ences as an engaged couple with friends and relatives, and planning and furnishing an apartment, the engaged couple can make considerable progress in developing mutuality in advance of the marriage itself.[65] No such head-start is possible in the case of pregnancy. What preparation exists is confined to reading, consultation with friends and parents, discussions between hus-band and wife, and a minor nesting phase in which a place and the equip-ment for a baby are prepared in the household.[66]

Abruptness of transition. Thirdly, the birth of a child is not followed by any gradual taking on of responsibility, as in the case of a professional work role. It is as if the woman shifted from a graduate student to a full professor with little intervening apprenticeship experience of slowly increasing respon-sibility. The new mother starts out immediately on 24-hour duty, with respon-sibility for a fragile and mysterious infant totally dependent on her care.

If marital adjustment is more difficult for very young brides than more mature ones,[67] adjustment to motherhood may be even more difficult. A woman can adapt a passive dependence on a husband and still have a suc-cessful marriage, but a young mother with strong dependency needs is in for difficulty in maternal adjustment, because the role precludes such dependency. This situation was well described in Cohen's study[68] in a case of a young wife with a background of co-ed popularity and a passive dependent relationship to her admired and admiring husband, who collapsed into restricted incapacity when faced with the responsibilities of maintaining a home and caring for a child.

Lack of guidelines to successful parenthood. If the central task of parent-hood is the rearing of children to become the kind of competent adults valued by the society, then an important question facing any parent is what he or she specifically can do to create such a competent adult. This is where the parent is left with few or no guidelines from the expert. Parents can readily inform themselves concerning the young infant's nutritional, clothing, and medical needs and follow the general prescription that a child needs loving physical contact and emotional support. Such advice may be sufficient to produce a healthy, happy, and well-adjusted preschooler, but adult com-petency is quite another matter.

In fact, the adults who do "succeed" in American society show a complex of characteristics as children that current experts in child-care would evalu-ate as "poor" to "bad." Biographies of leading authors and artists, as well as the more rigorous research inquiries of creativity among architects[69] or scien-tists,[70] do not portray childhoods with characteristics currently endorsed by mental health and child-care authorities. Indeed, there is often a predomi-

240

nance of tension in childhood family relations and traumatic loss rather than loving parental support, intense channeling of energy in one area of interest rather than an all-round profile of diverse interests, and social withdrawal and preference for loner activities rather than gregarious sociability. Thus, the stress in current child-rearing advice on a high level of loving support but a low level of discipline or restriction on the behavior of the child—the "developmental" family type as Duvall calls it[71]—is a profile consistent with the focus on mental health, sociability, and adjustment. Yet the combination of both high support and high authority on the part of parents is most strongly related to the child's sense of responsibility, leadership quality, and achievement level, as found in Bronfenbrenner's studies[72] and that of Mussen and Distler.[73]

Brim points out[74] that we are a long way from being able to say just what parent role prescriptions have what effect on the adult characteristics of the child. We know even less about how such parental prescriptions should be changed to adapt to changed conceptions of competency in adulthood. In such an ambiguous context, the great interest parents take in school reports on their children or the pediatrician's assessment of the child's developmental progress should be seen as among the few indices parents have of how well *they* are doing as parents.

NOTES

[1] Antonio J. Ferreira, "The Pregnant Woman's Emotional Attitude and its Reflection on the Newborn," *American Journal of Orthopsychiatry*, 30 (1960), pp. 553–561.

[2] Robert Sears, E. Maccoby, and H. Levin, *Patterns of Child-Rearing*, Evanston, Illinois: Row, Peterson, 1957.

[3] Sylvia Brody, *Patterns of Mothering: Maternal Influences During Infancy*, New York: International Universities Press, 1956.

[4] Leon J. Yarrow, "Maternal Deprivation: Toward an Empirical and Conceptual Re-evaluation," *Psychological Bulletin*, 58:6 (1961), pp. 459–490.

[5] F. Ivan Nye and L. W. Hoffman, *The Employed Mother in America*, Chicago: Rand McNally, 1963; Alice S. Rossi, "Equality Between the Sexes: An Immodest Proposal," *Daedalus*, 93:2 (1964), pp. 607–652.

[6] The younger the child, the more was this the accepted view. It is only in recent years that research has paid any attention to the initiating role of the infant in the development of his attachment to maternal and other adult figures, as in Ainsworth's research which showed that infants become attached to the mother, not solely because she is instrumental in satisfying their primary visceral drives, but through a chain of behavioral interchange between the infant and the mother, thus supporting Bowlby's rejection of the secondary drive theory of the infant's ties to his mother. Mary D. Ainsworth, "Patterns of Attachment Behavior Shown By the Infant in Interaction with His Mother," *Merrill-Palmer Quarterly*, 10:1 (1964), pp. 51–58; John Bowlby, "The Nature of the Child's Tie to His Mother," *International Journal of Psychoanalysis*, 39 (1958), pp. 1–34.

[7] Therese Benedek, "Parenthood as a Developmental Phase," *Journal of American Psychoanalytic Association*, 7:8 (1959), pp. 389–417.

[8] Yarrow, *op. cit.*

[9] Henry A. Murray, *Explorations in Personality*, New York: Oxford University Press, 1938.

[10] Heinz Hartmann, *Ego Psychology and the Problem of Adaptation*, New York: International Universities Press, Inc., 1958.

[11] Patrick Mullahy (ed.), *The Contributions of Harry Stack Sullivan*, New York: Hermitage House, 1952.

[12] E. Erikson, "Identity and the Life Cycle: Selected Papers," *Psychological Issues*, 1 (1959), pp. 1–171.

[13] J. Tyhurst, "Individual Reactions to Community Disaster," *American Journal of Psychiatry*, 107 (1951), pp. 764–769.

[14] G. Caplan, "Patterns of Parental Response to the Crisis of Premature Birth: A Preliminary Approach to Modifying the Mental Health Outcome," *Psychiatry*, 23 (1960), pp. 365–374.

[15] E. Lindemann, "Symptomatology and Management of Acute Grief," *American Journal of Psychiatry*, 101 (1944), pp. 141–148.

[16] Irving Janis, *Psychological Stress*, New York: John Wiley, 1958.

[17] Rhona Rapoport, "Normal Crises, Family Structure and Mental Health," *Family Process*, 2:1 (1963), pp. 68–80; Rhona Rapoport and Robert Rapoport, "New Light on the Honeymoon," *Human Relations*, 17:1 (1964), pp. 33–56; Rhona Rapoport, "The Transition from Engagement to Marriage," *Acta Sociologica*, 8, facs, 1–2 (1964), pp. 36–55; and Robert Rapoport and Rhona Rapoport, "Work and Family in Contemporary Society," *American Sociological Review*, 30:3 (1965), pp. 381–394.

[18] E. E. LeMasters, "Parenthood as Crisis," *Marriage and Family Living*, 19 (1957), pp. 352–355; Everett D. Dyer, "Parenthood as Crisis: A Re-Study," *Marriage and Family Living*, 25 (1963), pp. 196–201; and Daniel F. Hobbs, Jr., "Parenthood as Crisis: A Third Study," *Journal of Marriage and the Family*, 27:3 (1963), pp. 367–372. LeMasters and Dyer both report the first experience of parenthood involves extensive to severe crises in the lives of their young parent respondents. Hobbs' study does not show first parenthood to be a crisis experience, but this may be due to the fact that his couples have very young (seven-week-old) first babies and are therefore still experiencing the euphoric honeymoon stage of parenthood.

[19] Parsons' theoretical analysis of the family system builds directly on Bales' research on small groups. The latter are typically comprised of volunteers willing to attempt the single task put to the group. This positive orientation is most apt to yield the empirical discovery of "sociometric stars" and "task leaders," least apt to sensitize the researcher or theorist to the effect of hostile non-acceptance of the group task. Talcott Parsons and R. F. Bales, *Family, Socialization and Interaction Process*, New York: The Free Press, a division of the Macmillan Co., 1955.

 Yet the same limited definition of the key variables is found in the important attempts by Straus to develop the theory that every social system, as every personality, requires a circumplex model with two independent axes of authority and support. His discussion and examples indicate a variable definition with limited range: support is defined as High ($+$) or Low ($-$), but "low" covers both the absence of high support and the presence of negative support; there is love or neutrality in this system, but not hate. Applied to actual families, this groups destructive mothers with low-supportive mothers, much as the non-authoritarian pole on the Authoritarian Personality Scale includes both mere non-authoritarians and vigorously anti-authoritarian personalities. Murray A. Straus, "Power and Support Structure of the Family in Relation to Socialization," *Journal of Marriage and the Family*, 26:3 (1964), pp. 318–326.

20 Mabel Blake Cohen, "Personal Identity and Sexual Identity," *Psychiatry*, 29:1 (1966), pp. 1–14; Joseph C. Rheingold, *The Fear of Being a Woman: A Theory of Maternal Destructiveness*, New York: Grune and Stratton, 1964.

21 Theodore Lidz, S. Fleck, and A. Cornelison, *Schizophrenia and the Family*, New York: International Universities Press, Inc., 1965; Rheingold, *op. cit.*

22 Cf. the long review of studies Rheingold covers in his book on maternal destructiveness, *op. cit.*

23 Benedek, *op. cit.*

24 Reuben Hill and D. A. Hansen, "The Identification of a Conceptual Framework Utilized in Family Study," *Marriage and Family Living*, 22 (1960), pp. 299–311.

25 Harold L. Raush, W. Goodrich, and J. D. Campbell, "Adaptation to the First Years of Marriage," *Psychiatry*, 26:4 (1963), pp. 368–380.

26 Rapoport, *op. cit.*

27 Cohen, *op. cit.*

28 Raush *et al., op. cit.*

29 The greater the cultural pressure to assume a given adult social role, the greater will be the tendency for individual negative feelings toward that role to be expressed covertly. Men may complain about a given job but not about working per se, and hence their work dissatisfactions are often displaced to the non-work sphere, as psychosomatic complaints or irritation and dominance at home. An equivalent displacement for women of the ambivalence many may feel toward maternity is to dissatisfactions with the homemaker role.

30 Caroline Bird, *The Invisible Scar*, New York: David McKay Company, 1966.

31 When it is realized that a mean family size of 3.5 would double the population in 40 years, while a mean of 2.5 would yield a stable population in the same period, the social importance of withholding praise for procreative prowess is clear. At the same time, a drop in the birth rate may reduce the number of unwanted babies born, for such a drop would mean more efficient contraceptive usage and a closer correspondence between desired and attained family size.

32 James A. Davis, *Stipends and Spouses: The Finances of American Arts and Sciences Graduate Students*, Chicago: University of Chicago Press, 1962.

33 Hannah Gavron, *The Captive Wife*, London: Routledge & Kegan Paul, 1966.

34 The recent increase in natural childbirth, prenatal courses for expectant fathers, and greater participation of men during childbirth and postnatal care of the infant may therefore be a *consequence* of greater sharing between husband and wife when both work and jointly maintain their new households during the early months of marriage. Indeed, natural childbirth builds directly on this shifted base to the marital relationship. Goshen-Gottstein has found in an Israeli sample that women with a "traditional" orientation to marriage far exceed women with a "modern" orientation to marriage in menstrual difficulty, dislike of sexual intercourse, and pregnancy disorders and complaints such as vomiting. She argues that traditional women demand and expect little from their husbands and become demanding and narcissistic by means of their

children, as shown in pregnancy by an over-exaggeration of symptoms and attention-seeking. Esther R. Goshen-Gottstein, *Marriage and First Pregnancy: Cultural Influences on Attitudes of Israeli Women*, London: Tavistock Publications, 1966. A prolonged psychic honeymoon uncomplicated by an early pregnancy, and with the new acceptance of married women's employment, may help to cement the egalitarian relationship in the marriage and reduce both the tendency to pregnancy difficulties and the need for a narcissistic focus on the children. Such a background is fruitful ground for sympathy toward and acceptance of the natural childbirth ideology.

[35] James A. Davis, *Stipends and Spouses: The Finances of American Arts and Sciences Graduate Students, op. cit.;* James A. Davis, *Great Aspirations*, Chicago: Aldine Publishing Company, 1964; Eli Ginsberg, *Life Styles of Educated Women*, New York: Columbia University Press, 1966; Ginsberg, *Educated American Women: Self Portraits*, New York: Columbia University Press, 1967; National Science Foundation, *Two Years After the College Degree— Work and Further Study Patterns,* Washington, D.C.: Government Printing Office, NSF 63-26, 1963.

[36] Davis, *Great Aspirations, op. cit.;* Laure Sharp, "Graduate Study and Its Relation to Careers: The Experience of a Recent Cohort of College Graduates," *Journal of Human Resources*, 1:2 (1966), pp. 41–58.

[37] James D. Cowhig and C. Nam, "Educational Status, College Plans and Occupational Status of Farm and Nonfarm Youths," U.S. Bureau of the Census Series ERS (P-27), No. 30, 1961.

[38] Davis, *Great Aspirations, op. cit.*

[39] Lindsey R. Harmon, *Profiles of Ph.D.'s in the Sciences: Summary Report on Follow-up of Doctorate Cohorts, 1935–1960*, Washington, D.C.: National Research Council, Publication 1293, 1965.

[40] Sharp, *op. cit.*

[41] Davis, *Stipends and Spouses, The Finances of American Arts and Sciences Graduate Students, op. cit.*

[42] Orville G. Brim, "Family Structure and Sex-Role Learning by Children," *Sociometry*, 21 (1958), pp. 1–16; H. L. Koch, "Sissiness and Tomboyishness in Relation to Sibling Characteristics," *Journal of Genetic Psychology*, 88 (1956), pp. 231–244.

[43] Charles MacArthur, "Personalities of First and Second Children," *Psychiatry*, 19 (1956), pp. 47–54; S. Schachter, "Birth Order and Sociometric Choice," *Journal of Abnormal and Social Psychology*, 68 (1964), pp. 453–456.

[44] Irving Harris, *The Promised Seed*, New York: The Free Press, a division of the Macmillan Co., 1964; Bernard Rosen, "Family Structure and Achievement Motivation," *American Sociological Review*, 26 (1961), pp. 574–585; Alice S. Rossi, "Naming Children in Middle-Class Families," *American Sociological Review*, 30:4 (1965), pp. 499–513; Stanley Schachter, "Birth Order, Eminence and Higher Education," *American Sociological Review*, 28 (1963), pp. 757–768.

[45] Harris, *op. cit.*

[46] Rossi, "Naming Children in Middle-Class Families," *op cit.*

[47] James H. Bossard, *Parent and Child*, Philadelphia; University of Pennsylvania Press, 1953; James H. Bossard and E. Boll, *The Large Family System*, Philadelphia: University of Pennsylvania, 1956.

[48] Rosen, *op. cit.*

[49] Glen H. J. Elder and C. Bowerman, "Family Structure and Child Rearing Patterns: The Effect of Family Size and Sex Composition on Child-Rearing Practices," *American Sociological Review*, 28 (1963), pp. 891–905.

[50] Sarane S. Boocock, "Toward a Sociology of Learning: A Selective Review of Existing Research," *Sociology of Education*, 39:1 (1966), pp. 1–45.

[51] John Nisbet, "Family Environment and Intelligence," *in Education, Economy and Society*, ed. by Halsey *et al.*, New York: The Free Press, a division of the Macmillan Company, 1961.

[52] Thus Rosen writes: "Considering the sociologist's traditional and continuing concern with group size as an independent variable (from Simmel and Durkheim to the recent experimental studies of small groups), there have been surprisingly few studies of the influence of group size upon the nature of interaction in the family," *op. cit.*, p. 576.

[53] Ivan Nye, "Adolescent-Parent Adjustment: Age, Sex, Sibling, Number, Broken Homes, and Employed Mothers as Variables," *Marriage and Family Living*, 14 (1952), pp. 327–332.

[54] Sears *et al., op. cit.*

[55] Laura G. Searls, "Leisure Role Emphasis of College Graduate Homemakers," *Journal of Marriage and the Family*, 28:1 (1966), pp. 77–82.

[56] Norman Bradburn and D. Caplovitz, *Reports on Happiness*, Chicago: Aldine Publishing, 1965.

[57] Lee Rainwater, R. Coleman, and G. Handel, *Workingman's Wife*, New York: Oceana Publications, 1959.

[58] John Newsom and E. Newsom, *Infant Care in an Urban Community*, New York: International Universities Press, 1963.

[59] Mirra Komarovsky, *Blue Collar Marriage*, New York: Random House, 1962.

[60] Gavron, *op. cit.*

[61] Ferdinand Zweig, *Woman's Life and Labor*, London: Camelot Press, 1952.

[62] Cohen, *op. cit.*

[63] Gerald Gurin, J. Veroff, and S. Feld, *Americans View Their Mental Health*, New York: Basic Books, Monograph Series No. 4, Joint Commission on Mental Illness and Health, 1960.

[64] Bradburn and Caplovitz, *op. cit.*

[65] Rapoport, "The Transition from Engagement to Marriage," *op. cit.;* Raush *et al., op. cit.*

[66] During the period when marriage was the critical transition in the adult woman's life rather than pregnancy, a good deal of anticipatory "nesting" behavior took place from the time of conception. Now more women work through a considerable portion of the first pregnancy, and such nesting behavior as exists may be confined to a few shopping expeditions or baby showers, thus adding to the abruptness of the transition and the difficulty of adjustment following the birth of a first child.

[67] Lee G. Burchinal, "Adolescent Role Deprivation and High School Marriage," *Marriage and Family Living*, 21 (1959), pp. 378–384; Floyd M. Martinson, "Ego Deficiency as a Factor in Marriage," *American Sociological Review*, 22 (1955), pp. 161–164; J. Joel Moss and Ruby Gingles, "The Relationship of Personality to the Incidence of Early Marriage," *Marriage and Family Living*, 21 (1959), pp. 373–377.

[68] Cohen, *op. cit.*

[69] Donald W. MacKinnon, "Creativity and Images of the Self," in *The Study of Lives*, ed. by Robert W. White, New York: Atherton Press, 1963.

[70] Anne Roe, *A Psychological Study of Eminent Biologists, Psychological Monographs,* 65:14 (1951), 68 pages; Anne Roe, "A Psychological Study of Physical Scientists," *Genetic Psychology Monographs,* 43 (1951), pp. 121–239; Anne Roe, "Crucial Life Experiences in the Development of Scientists," in *Talent and Education*, ed. by E. P. Torrance, Minneapolis: University of Minnesota Press, 1960.

[71] Evelyn M. Duvall, "Conceptions of Parenthood," *American Journal of Sociology,* 52 (1946), pp. 193–203.

[72] Urie Bronfenbrenner, "Some Familial Antecedents of Responsibility and Leadership in Adolescents," in *Studies in Leadership*, ed. by L. Petrullo and B. Bass, New York: Holt, Rinehart, and Winston, 1960.

[73] Paul Mussen and L. Distler, "Masculinity, Identification and Father-Son Relationships," *Journal of Abnormal and Social Psychology,* 59 (1959), pp. 350–356.

[74] Orville G. Brim, "The Parent-Child Relation as a Social System: I. Parent and Child Roles," *Child Development,* 28:3 (1957), pp. 343–364.

The American Father

E. E. LeMasters

Much is known about the problems of the American mother, but what is really known about the problems of the American father? Next to nothing, says LeMasters, because sociologists, psychologists, and anthropologists ignore the father in their research efforts, considering him unimportant in their analyses of child rearing methods. The author describes the ambiguous role of fathers as it exists in society today and some of the problems of the average male in his married life, his work life, and other experiences as they affect his performance as a father.

THE NEGLECT OF THE AMERICAN FATHER IN FAMILY RESEARCH

There have been numerous best sellers written about American women,[1] but one has to look carefully to find the literature on the American male, especially in his role as husband and/or father.[2] It is true that novelists such as Ernest Hemingway, Norman Mailer, and others have written extensively about what it is to be a man (or to fail to be a man) but many of these works of literature focus on men in combat—not family combat but military combat.[3]

Most of the behavioral and social scientists have simply ignored husbands and fathers in their empirical studies, as we shall demonstrate later in this chapter. One outstanding exception was the work of the late Kinsey who scored his greatest publishing success with his first volume on the American male.[4] Another notable exception to this curtain of silence about males in the family can be found in the work of Pollak in his research on child guidance clinics and their treatment programs.[5]

This tendency to take the American male for granted is graphically illustrated in the work of Vincent on unmarried mothers: he found the ratio of studies on the girls as compared with the boys was 25 to 1.[6] In other words, there is considerable literature on unmarried mothers but hardly anything is known about unmarried fathers. This is understandable but hardly in the

From E. E. LeMasters, *Parents in Modern America* (Homewood, Ill: The Dorsey Press, 1970), pp. 138–156. Reprinted by permission of the Dorsey Press.

public interest. Unmarried mothers, after all, do not reproduce by budding; there has to be a partner to conceive (with perhaps one notable exception in Western history) and any well-organized attempt to control parenthood out of wedlock will have to take the unmarried father into account. As of now, however, practically nothing is known about him.

The writer has been amazed at the cavalier attitude researchers in the United States have taken toward the American husband-father. For example: in a famous study of 379 mothers a statement is made in the Foreword that the basic aim of the research was "to secure reliable information about the varieties of experience that many American children have had in their homes—with their parents—by the time they go to school."[7] Note the use of the word *parents* (not mothers), yet not a single father was interviewed in this elaborate research effort.

The subtitle of the report on this project is "A Report on Ways of Bringing Up Children," which might lead one to think that fathers had been consulted somewhere along the line. This is erroneous. The fathers' versions of child rearing were obtained through the mothers. As a father the writer would deny the validity of any attempt to get his version of parenthood from his wife, yet this has been standard practice in research on the American family.

In this same monograph this flat statement is made: "Since it was not feasible to interview the fathers, all the information we gained about their child-rearing attitudes and practices we obtained from the mothers."[8] One immediately thinks that it was simply too difficult to visit homes when fathers might be available for interviews but this seems not to have been the real reason for their exclusion. In the Foreword this statement is made: "We wish to express warm thanks to our interviewers. They carried heavy recording equipment through icy streets, made evening calls when the mothers' busy schedules did not permit daytime interviews, and entered with tact and sympathy into a mutual exploration with the mothers of matters that were not always easy to talk about."[9]

Such dedication to science is to be appreciated but one finds it hard to believe that such intrepid field interviewers would not also have brought back some data on what fathers think of child rearing if anybody had considered it important enough to include fathers in the sample. Offhand one might think that instead of using 379 mothers, perhaps a better approach would have been to split the sample into male and female groups. It is hard to escape the conclusion that these researchers were guilty of what Pollak says child guidance clinics have been guilty of: they don't think fathers are very important.[10] They will go to any lengths to talk with mothers but fathers are considered to be not accessible.

In the Sears study there is not even an elaborate defense of the exclusion of fathers from the sample, yet other features of the sample are discussed at some length. The writer can only say that in his opinion *any* study of parents that excludes half of the parents (the fathers) has a poor sample no matter how carefully the mothers in the study group were selected.

In another famous study of parents, probably the most elaborate published in recent years, there were 582 interviews with mothers but not one interview with a father.[11] The published report, however, is titled *The Changing American Parent*. And in the report itself the word *parent* seems to be equated with *mother* most of the time. These behavioral scientists, both well known and both well qualified, go to elaborate lengths to describe how mothers were selected for the sample, but no elaborate defense of the exclusion of fathers is deemed to be necessary.

In what is probably the best empirical study of divorce we have in the United States, Goode and his staff went to endless trouble to locate and interview a representative sample of 425 divorced mothers in Detroit, but not one divorced father was included in the sampling design.[12]

In three studies of American parents published since World War II, those by Sears and his associates, Miller and Swanson, and Goode, a total of 1,386 American mothers were studied in detail, but not one father was interviewed in any of these major research projects.[13] It appears that "the American father" has replaced "the American Indian" as the forgotten man.

At some point one has to ask the question: are fathers that easily disposed of in studying American parents? Freud certainly wrote at length about the father's role in child rearing, and child welfare agencies historically in our society have considered fathers so important that they have refused to place children for adoption with women who didn't have a husband, regardless of the ability of the women seeking to adopt a child.[14]

There is one study which supports those of us who do not think that parenthood can be studied properly without including fathers—that is the study of parents in a Toronto suburb published in a book called *Crestwood Heights*.[15] This piece of research included fathers in the research design and concluded that fathers and mothers in this upper middle-class suburb have some very different ideas about child rearing and parental roles. For one thing the mothers have been exposed to a great deal of human development material and psychiatric theory via the women's magazines, child study groups, PTA lectures, and so on. Not only have the fathers not been a full partner in this educational process but have often been opposed to it. Many of them apparently feel that their wives are too permissive with the children and are spoiling them. The fathers often feel that their sons in particular are not being readied for the competition and strife of upper middle-class life in the marketplace.[16]

It is clear that upper-class English men have always felt this way about the education of their sons and have packed them off at an early age to a Spartan boarding school run by men, thus taking the sons away from not only their mothers but *all* women during most of their developmental years.[17]

For those of us who have done family and/or marriage counseling it seems obvious that fathers and mothers very often disagree about ways of rearing children—in fact this may be more common than sex in marital disputes and conflicts.

249

It is still possible, of course, that one can accept the point of view that fathers are important in the child rearing process but that one can learn all one needs to know about them through their wives. We doubt this very much. So does Pollak. So do the people who did the research in Crestwood Heights. We are also convinced that fathers and mothers would very often have to be interviewed separately to obtain valid reports on their parental experience. It is easy to gloss over male and female differences in the glow of a joint interview with parents, but this often does not reveal the differences that lie beneath the surface of domestic tranquility.

Another reason why the writer believes that fathers need to be interviewed in studies of American parents lies in his conviction that there are substantial male and female subcultures in the American way of life and that these extend into the arena of child rearing.[18] It is known from empirical data that men and women differ in religious behavior in our society, in their sexual patterns, in their use of money, their use of alcohol, their political behavior, their willingness to desert children, and so forth.[19] On what basis can we assume that fathers and mothers do *not* differ on child rearing and parental roles?

Since mothers are much closer to children in our society than fathers are, it seems quite likely that they would view child rearing from a different point of view and that this could not always be obtained by interviewing the mother.

In a study of family life education which has become a classic, Brim found that the vast majority of such programs focused on mothers almost exclusively. He writes:

> The failure of almost all parent education programs to assess the social setting into which they introduce their educational materials, the failure to recognize that the mothers who are primarily involved in such programs have husbands, parents, and neighbors with whom they must deal, is lamentable, since it is recognized that in many instances the net result of introducing change on the part of one member into the family system is to produce friction, resentment, and hostility between husband and wife, which in turn is probably detrimental to the child.[20]

This is the view of Pollak also. And it is the belief of this writer that the approach to parents must not only be broadened at the point of family life education or treatment but also at the point of research design. For the most part this has not been the case in America in recent decades.

Role Analysis of the Father in Modern America

1. *The parental role is a peripheral role for the American male.* For the American mother the role of parent probably takes precedence over all other adult roles. For some women this may not be the case as they may choose to give priority to their role as wife or to an occupational role, but these women would seem to be in the minority in our child-centered society. Mrs. John F.

Kennedy has been quoted as saying: "If you fail with your children, then I don't think anything else matters very much."[21]

For the American father the situation is quite different. Two roles in particular—that of his job and that of military service—almost always have to be given priority over his role as parent. Since 1940 between 15 and 20 million men in our society have had to go to the corners of the earth to discharge their military obligations, and the fact that they might be fathers does not entitle them to automatic deferment.

Nobody knows how many millions of American fathers have had their family lives disrupted by the long arm of the job but the total must be astronomical. In an unpublished study of blue-collar construction workers the writer was impressed by the frequency with which these men had to work out of town to maintain steady employment.[22] Almost all of these men agreed that such jobs posed real problems for them and their families.

When a man is transferred in our society, he often moves to the new community months before his family is able to join him. During this period his wife has to assume some responsibility with the children that normally would belong to the husband. Then, when the family is reunited, roles have to be redistributed again and lines of authority reestablished. In one research project during World War II Hill discovered that it was not always easy to "pick up where they left off" when the father returned from the armed forces.[23]

It seems to us that this peripheral nature of the parental role is often overlooked by critics of the American father. They judge him as if children were the center of his life in the way they are for American mothers. In our judgment this is not only unfair to the fathers but also unrealistic.

2. *There is no biological base or imprinting for the father role at the human level as there is for the mother.* In a famous book Davis puts this point as follows: "The weak link in the family group is the father-child bond. There is no necessary association and no easy means of identification between these two as there is between mother and child."[24] He goes on to point out that almost all human societies have evolved complex social devices for binding the father to his children.

Mead is making this same point when she says that the role of father at the human level is a "social invention"—strictly speaking, he could be dispensed with once conception had taken place.[25] Most societies have chosen not to let the male escape so easily, but to tie him to the child has required elaborate cultural arrangements, whereas these are not usually necessary for the mother.

All of this means that fathers in our society (or any other society) are almost entirely dependent on proper socialization and positive induction into the role of parent if they are to perform this responsibility adequately. This sets up the possibility that the father-child bond will not be as dependable as the mother-child bond. This certainly seems to be the case in our society.

3. *The human father is a mammal.* Among other things man is a mammal— and in the entire mammalian series there are only two fathers who assume major responsibility for their offspring. Most male mammals are present for the fertilization and are seldom seen after that. The wolf, oddly enough, is one

of the exceptions, often helping to feed the young and baby-sitting with them while the mother is away from the den.[26]

Compared to other mammalian fathers the human father is a paragon of virtue. But he is still a mammal and some American fathers appear to function pretty much at that level. These are, however, only a small minority.

4. *The human father is also a primate.* In the literature on the monkeys and the great apes it appears that the father's role after procreation is to protect the female (or females) and their offspring, but with only one exception, already mentioned, does he ever assume any major responsibility for their daily care.[27] Here, again, the average human father makes the other primate fathers look bad.

5. *The father's parental role in the United States is peculiarly tied to the success or failure of the pair-bond between himself and his wife.* In a great many human societies a father can still be a good father even if his marriage leaves much to be desired: mistresses or women of some category other than wife are made available to him and he can still reside in his home and live with his wife and children.[28] This is usually not the case in our society. In modern America men are expected to be faithful to their wives or else leave the home and marry the other woman.

All of this means that if anything happens to the marriage of the American male he may find himself separated from his children and partially cut off from them—and this may happen in spite of his honest desires to be a good father. In other words it is difficult in our society to be a good father if you are not also a good husband. According to Lewis this has not been the case in societies such as Mexico.[29]

Other complications result if the marriage fails. Sooner or later the husband will find other feminine companionship, often with a woman who has children of her own, so that the man is now committed to two sets of children: his own offspring and those of his new love. In order to attract and hold a divorced woman or a widow with children, the male has to show a substantial interest in her children and their welfare—and in the process may neglect his own children.[30] Thus he may actually be doing a good job as a parent but with only one set of children, not necessarily his own.[31]

If we look at the figures on divorce, desertion and separation we can see that marital failure is probably one of the major roadblocks to the American father who sincerely wants to be a good parent.[32] This is not the case with the American mother who retains custody of the minor children in over 90 percent of the cases known to the courts.[33] As a matter of fact, marital failure may enhance the parental role of the mother: she now has the children more exclusively than before and probably extends the amount of time and effort she spends on them.[34]

The novelist Gold has a sketch in which a man is attempting to explain to a young daughter why he will not be living with her and her mother any more (they are getting a divorce). "I still love you," the father tries to explain, "but I no longer love your mother." He goes on to try to make it clear to the child that he still wants to be a *father* but not her mother's *husband*. This is too complex for the little girl and after a long silence she says: "I'm getting sick of big words like love."[35]

This dependence of the father role on the marital bond is often forgotten by critics of the American father. We think it needs to be kept in mind.[36]

6. *The idea that men and women are only superficially different.* In our society, since World War I, there has been a long-range tendency to regard men and women as equal—in itself a good thing in the opinion of this writer, but somewhere along the line equality became confused with *similarity*, which led to the idea that males and females at the human level are only superficially different. This is part of the togetherness approach to marriage in modern America.

It is the writer's belief that males and females at the human level are profoundly different—as Montagu argues[37]—and that this difference is most clearly seen in their diverse reactions to parenthood. The father may be delighted, indifferent, or annoyed at the idea of being a parent, and if he is not too enthralled there are often escape hatches through which he can keep his parental involvement to a minimum—longer hours of work, a second job to help with the increased expenses of rearing a family, or perhaps more time spent with his male peer group.

The mother may also be delighted, annoyed, or even appalled, but it is difficult for her to be indifferent. And it is also harder for her to escape. It is harder because of her inherent impulses as a female, and it is also harder because of society's attitude toward women who neglect their children.

This belief in male and female similarity results in criticism of the American father because he is not as close to his children as the mother. Parents, it is argued, as partners in the family enterprise, should share and share alike, and using this standard fathers are found wanting. Schaller makes it quite clear that no gorilla would ever get caught in such confusion: they know that mothers are different from fathers.[38] The male gorilla's job after procreation is to protect the group from attack. Anything else he does for his offspring represents a bonus that the group does not expect. We are not arguing that men are gorillas, although in many ways the behavior of gorillas is superior to that of man, but we are suggesting that the human male is not *entirely* different from the male gorilla and that their parental behavior reveals some similarities.

It seems to us that here again—the observers (and the critics) of fathers in our society have lost sight of man's organic nature: they overstress socialization and culture while minimizing evolution and man's place in the animal series.

Actually, judged by other mammalian and primate males, the human father is fantastically concerned about his young, but this does not mean that he is as close to them as their mother.

It might also be argued that compared to fathers in other human societies the American father is really a very conscientious parent: he provides for his children in the vast majority of cases, he plays with them, he baby-sits with them when their mother needs help, and in general he seems to like children.[39]

253

The main point in this section is that the father in our society is often judged by standards that should only be applied to mothers.

7. *The American father is poorly prepared for his parental role.* This was commented on to some extent earlier but a few words need to be added at this point. American boys simply do not receive the socialization that helps prepare girls to become mothers. Girls get dolls and baby buggies for Christmas when the boys get guns and footballs. Later on, in high school and college, courses in home economics and child development are elected primarily by girls. And even later, the women's magazines feature child rearing material while the men's magazines feature sports and girls in scanty outfits.

As a result of all this the average American male is quite unprepared to be a father—at least socially.[40] He enjoys the process of fertilization and may even look forward to being a father but he scarcely knows what he is getting into. To some extent, of course, this is also true of many American girls, but it seems to us that nature and our society prepare mothers for their parental role better than they do fathers.

SOME PROBLEMS OF THE AMERICAN FATHER

Many books have detailed the various problems of the woman in American society, including the reports of various government commissions established to assess the status of the female in our society.[41] We know of no similar effort to discover the status and the problems of the male in contemporary America. In fact, there are only a few books about him.[42]

In the pages following, a few of the major problems of the American male will be indicated. All of these, in the opinion of the writer, have relevance for an understanding of the American father.

1. *Economic problems.* Although he is relatively affluent the American father is under constant economic pressure to support his wife and children on an ever and ever higher plane.[43] This pressure can be verified by reviewing the huge increase in consumer credit in recent decades or by reading the personal bankruptcy notices in the evening paper. Some families have more or less solved this problem by having the mother take a job outside of the home. This undoubtedly takes some of the pressure off of the father but may place considerable stress on the mother. There might also be some loss of maternal supervision of the children, plus the possibility of some strain on the marriage.

The strategy of the mass media in our society is to keep several years ahead of the consumer. Just when you and I have decided that a certain type of home refrigerator is all we need the advertisers begin pushing a new and bigger model that we are supposed to aim for. This can be seen in the 1960's in the tremendous drive to outdate black and white television receivers and replace them with color sets. One father said to us: "Our black and white set works just fine but the wife and kids have been after me for six months to trade it in on a color set." He finally made the trade at Christmas time and found that his old set was worth only $50 on a trade. The new color set cost approximately $500. This man works in a factory and his take-home pay does not average over $400 a month. He says that he manages to get by only because his wife works also.

For the 20 or 30 percent of fathers on the bottom of the economic system the financial problems are more stark: they are faced with not being able to provide food, clothing, or housing for their families. They are also faced with the knowledge that in a society in which most people are reasonably well off, they are not. This is the meaning of "relative deprivation"—it isn't only what you don't have, it is also what the people around you *do* have.[44] In other words, it is quite different being hungry in India where millions are on the verge of starvation than it is being hungry in the United States where most people overeat.

The writer believes that *most* American fathers suffer from economic problems of one kind or another. We even interviewed a young physician earning $25,000 a year who said that his financial pressures were almost too much for him. Only those who have sweated out economic problems know how they can affect family life: the quality of the husband-wife relationship, the feeling of the children for their parents, and the attitude of the father and mother toward being parents. A man's self-image in our society is deeply affected by this ability to provide for his family. Many times the self-image is not too positive.

2. *Marital problems.* These have already been commented on in the previous section of this chapter and only need to be noted here. For the uninitiated, however, it needs to be emphasized that the divorce rate, which is what most Americans think of when they think about marital failure, does not tell the whole story by any means. We have not only divorce, but also separation, desertion, and a fourth type: "holy deadlock"—marriages which are never terminated but are essentially pathogenic for all involved.[45] It may well be that there are more holy deadlock marriages than there are divorces. We just don't know how many American marriages are of the "shell" or "facade" type.[46]

But no matter how one looks at it the failure of his marriage is a major problem for the American father.

3. *Sex life.* Kinsey and his research group found that the American male finds it difficult to confine his sexual interests to his wife.[47] Other studies have reported that the male does not think his wife is a good sexual partner.[48]

Part of the problem here is that the male adolescent peer group does not socialize for sexual monogamy: it stresses the fact that all women are legitimate sexual objects (except mothers and sisters) and that a man is a fool if he does not take advantage of any sexual opportunity. After living in this world for several years the man finds it difficult to think of his wife as the only legitimate sexual object. Girls at the office, wives of other men, divorced women—he finds many of these women sexually attractive and he often finds that they view him in the same light. In an urban society there are many opportunities for straying; the controls have to be internal because the external controls of the rural or village society are not present. A substantial number of married men find this situation somewhat more than they can manage.

In the Victorian world a married man would solve this problem by having an affair with a younger woman or a woman of a lower social class. If he was discreet, as Warren G. Harding was,[49] his wife would overlook the matter. And the man would be protected because marriage to this other woman was usually not possible.

Things are not so simple today. Men and women who become involved sexually in modern America are often from the same social class and marriage is always a possibility. Thus what starts out as an affair ends up in divorce and remarriage, with the father becoming separated from his children.

One can debate the morality of all of this endlessly. We are only interested in the father's sex life as it affects his marriage and hence his relationship with his children. It seems clear that (1) if his sex life with his wife is not satisfying, his tolerance of his marriage will be lowered, and (2) his tendency to look around for another sexual partner will be enhanced. In either event his role as father will suffer more or less.

4. *Drinking problem.* Our impression is that a substantial proportion of "bad" fathers in our society have a drinking problem. Trice reports that various estimates conclude that fathers are three to six times more likely to drink alcohol excessively in our society than are mothers.[50]

If a man drinks too much, there are at least four ways in which this affects his performance as a parent: (*a*) the drinking becomes a real strain on the family budget, and this is true at almost all economic levels except for the very wealthy; (*b*) the quality of the marriage suffers; (*c*) when the father is home he is not able to function normally—he is either too good to the children or he is abusive; (*d*) the attitude of the children toward him changes from positive to negative.[51]

For persons who have never known alcoholism at close range the events that take place between alcoholics and their families are unbelievable. Only recently we interviewed a young mother with two children who said that during a drinking bout her husband threatened to kill her and both children. When sober this sort of behavior was never apparent in this husband-father. The wife is now afraid of her husband and has obtained a separation.

This woman has reason to be afraid of her husband. The writer, using news reports, tallied 27 children and 7 wives who were murdered in Wisconsin during 1967 by husband-fathers who were reported by the authorities to have "been drinking."

It is true, of course, that excessive drinking by American mothers is becoming more and more frequent in our society, but in this analysis we are focusing on only the father.

This excessive drinking by the father is by no means confined to any one social class. It may be found at all socioeconomic levels in substantial numbers.

5. *The male peer group.* In his study of blue-collar workers in Boston, Gans found that the men liked to spend much of their spare time with other men,

away from their wives and children.[52] This sort of behavior was accepted in the particular ethnic group (Italian) and posed no great problems. But a great many American women these days view marriage and parenthood as a partnership and do not readily accept male-only activities. It is the writer's belief that a vast number of American men prefer to spend their spare time with other males and that this is one of the most difficult adjustments they have to make in modern marriage. A certain proportion of them refuse to make this concession to their wives and children and continue to spend most of their spare time with the boys.

At blue-collar levels there may be a certain amount of tolerance of "segregated sex roles" (as this behavior is called) but America is becoming increasingly a white-collar world and women seem to be less and less tolerant of staying home with the children.

To resolve this sort of strain the American male has to be domesticated more than he ever has in the past. To what extent this has been accomplished, or can be accomplished, we don't know. But some men are difficult to harness, as their wives have discovered. When this is the case it seems likely that the father's role is diminished or affected negatively in some way.

6. *Resentment of women.* In the last several decades, beginning with World War I, American women have been involved in a vast social revolution, the aim of which has been to give them equality with men.[53] This drastic upheaval has thrown the two sexes into more direct competition and has taken from men some of the special privileges they once had—the exclusive right to vote, control of most work opportunities, the double standard of sexual morality, and others. While most men may recognize that women are entitled to social equality, it is not always clear that they really like the position women have won for themselves. In talking with men informally the writer has been impressed with the underlying hostility that many American men seem to have toward the modern woman. In a recent election a prominent woman in our community was defeated for the school board—a position she was eminently qualified for. We asked a male friend of ours if he had voted for her. "No, I didn't," he said. "I think women are trying to take this town over. It's about time the men began to assert themselves."

This is the way many white persons now feel toward blacks: they are getting "too equal" and something will have to be done about it. It seems to us that the analogy here between the new position of women and the new position of blacks is very real: intelligent persons recognize the need for sexual equality and also for racial equality, but their emotions need more time to get used to the change.

One husband, in criticizing his wife, said to us: "She wanted to wear the pants, now let her take the consequences." In other words, if women want equality they should shoulder half of the load, whatever it is.

To the extent that modern American men do have hostility toward their wives, the role of father will be complicated by this feeling. In some men this is very evident, but we do not know how typical or atypical these men are.

257

Some General Observations on the American Father

1. *Today's father has more leisure.* It is fashionable in our society to romanticize the family system of an earlier historical period and to condemn the family of today. It is our belief that in some ways the contemporary American father is an improvement over his predecessors. A good example would be the amount of leisure time the modern father spends with his children. This will be illustrated with a case study.

We recently had a chance to interview at length a man almost 90 years old concerning his boyhood in rural Pennsylvania in the 1880's. This man's mind was quite alert and clear, even though his body was somewhat the worse for wear.

Growing up on a prosperous farm in eastern Pennsylvania in the latter part of the 19th century, Mr. D. could scarcely recall any "leisure" or "play" with his father. One reason was that leisure or recreation was considered to be bad in those days—character and salvation came from hard work.

This elderly man was quite sure that his father had never played baseball with his sons (there were five boys in this family), never went sledding or ice-skating with them in winter, never swam with them in the summer. He could remember doing all of these things, but never with either of his parents. Hunting was an exception: the father did hunt with his sons in the fall.

Mr. D. could recall his father and mother taking all of the children to the county fair in the fall; this was an annual event for the whole family and stood out in this elderly man's memory as the fun day of the year.

Vivid memories of *working* with his father on the farm were retained by this man—plowing and sowing seed in the fall and spring; harvesting the various crops; butchering in the fall; doing the endless daily chores.

Sunday was a day of rest, with only the essential work (feeding and watering the livestock) being done. Two church services were usually attended by the entire family.

In essence, this man from the 1880's has no memory of his father as a pal or companion.[54]

In contrast, fathers today go on camping trips with their children, play golf and other games with them, take annual family vacations as a group, go to drive-in movies in the family car, watch television together, and in general spend a lot of spare time with their wives and children.

In another case drawn from a later period (1900), there was a six-day week for the father—the five-day, 40-hour week had not yet become common in America.[55] Except for an occasional family picnic or a summer baseball game, the writer does not recall any recreation time spent with his father. And since this family lived in a small city instead of on a farm, there are also few memories of any experiences working beside the father.

In contrast to these two fathers from earlier periods in American history, we have spent literally thousands of hours in pure companionship with our two sons and in the process have seen other fathers doing the same thing.

It is not being proposed that today's father-child companionship pattern is necessarily superior to the father-child work relationship of the earlier rural America—our point is that the contemporary father *does* spend a lot of time with his children. One reason, of course, is that the time is available; he does not (as a rule) have the long work week that his father and grandfather had.

2. *Today's father is more domesticated.* There is some reason to believe that American men have changed drastically since World War II.[56] They are infinitely more domesticated than their male ancestors: they cook more meals, clean more homes, change more diapers, do more babysitting, remodel more rooms, and in general are more geared into family activities. Not everybody is entirely happy about this new American male—not even all of the men themselves—but like him or pity him, the current American male is a new breed.

In the last analysis only a "new man" can understand and live successfully with the contemporary American woman. It is simply not possible to produce a modern 20th century woman and expect her to settle for a 19th century man.

3. *The new male model is popular.* If today's American woman is unhappy with the American male she doesn't show it by refusing to marry; the marriage rate in our society is at an all-time high.[57] Even divorced men seem to be readily acceptable as marriage partners.[58] It may be that one of the factors producing the high marriage rate is the acceptability of the new male model.

It seems logical to assume that if women find the new American male acceptable as a husband they also find him acceptable as a father. The high birthrate following World War II would certainly seem to support this line of reasoning, but the birthrate as of 1968 has dropped, indicating that a number of variables are involved in our fluctuating birthrate.[59]

4. *Social class variations in father performance.* If data were available it might emerge that American fathers are least adequate at the top and bottom of the social class structure. Although no systematic studies of the upper-class father in our society have ever been made, it seems clear that their outside commitments force them to delegate much of their parental role to other persons, boarding school teachers, summer camp counselors, and the like.

At the bottom of the social class system there is considerable evidence that the lower-class father (the 20 or 30 percent at the poverty level) finds his parental responsibilities overwhelming.[60] Not only does he lack the money required to support his family, he also suffers from inadequate education, poor health (physical as well as mental), slum housing, high rates of marital instability, and a host of other problems.

It might be that the best American fathers are found at the stable blue-collar level and in the vast white-collar middle class.

5. *The effects of military service.* Some 15 to 20 million American men have served in the armed forces since World War II. Almost all of these men became fathers after returning to civilian life—if they were not already fathers at the time of induction.

We do not profess to know how military service affects a man's capacity to be a good father.[61] It might be that the experience helps men to mature, and maturity is certainly an asset in being a parent.

The great variety of humans encountered in the armed forces might also help future fathers understand some of the differences they will discover in their own children.

It is also possible that the destruction one sees in military service may be functional for fathers in helping them appreciate the preciousness of human life and motivate them not only to start families when they return home but also to nourish and protect them. This may actually have been a factor in the high birthrate that followed World War II in the United States.

It is difficult to identify the negative impact of military service on future fathers. There is an obvious "crudity factor" that all men in the armed forces are subjected to—crude and obscene language, crude bedroom stories, sexual promiscuity, excessive drinking, gambling—and it is difficult to see how this sort of life prepares a man to be a good husband or a good father.

The writer confesses that he does not know the net effect of military service on future fathers. It is only suggested that this experience be remembered when critics look at the current generation of American fathers.

6. *Differential impact of American culture.* If one looks at the social deviation rates, such as crime, alcoholism, drug addiction, and desertion,[62] it is possible to conclude that the destructive impact of American society is greater on males than females. One either has to believe this or accept Montagu's claim that women are the stronger sex.[63] It seems plausible that different cultures have a differential impact on the two sexes and that ours hits men harder than women. If this is true it would help to explain some of the paternal deficiencies noted in this chapter.

SUMMARY AND CONCLUSION

In this chapter we have noted the neglect of the American father in family research and have attempted to sketch in some of the basic facts that need to be kept in mind in thinking about fathers in our society.

In the previous chapter on the American mother it was hypothesized that the mother has become the Executive Director of the American family and that the father has been kicked upstairs to become Chairman of the Board.[64] If this is the case—and we recognize that this is only a hypothesis—then it makes a lot of difference whether the father supports the mother in her various efforts or undermines her administration. This is turn is likely to reflect the quality of the husband-wife relationship.

It is our personal belief that the American father does a better job than he is usually given credit for. But this judgment may be biased in that the writer is a father himself.

NOTES

[1] See E. E. LeMasters, *Parents in Modern America*, "The American Mother," pp. 118–137.

[2] In looking for books on the American male the writer came up with the following:

Elaine Kendall, *The Upper Hand* (Boston: Little, Brown & Co., 1965); Myron Brenton, *The American Male* (New York: Coward-McCann, 1966); Charles W. Ferguson, *The Male Attitude* (Boston: Little, Brown, & Co., 1966); and Margaret Mead, *Male and Female* (New York: William Morrow & Co., 1949). The Kendall book is basically satirical but very insightful; the Brenton Book is a survey of the current "male crisis"; the Ferguson book is scholarly but historical; the Mead study is cross-cultural. When this volume was nearly completed an excellent survey of the literature on fathers appeared: Leonard Benson, *Fatherhood: A Sociological Perspective* (New York: Random House, 1968).

[3] The most widely read novel about World War I and its impact on men was Ernest Hemingway's *A Farewell to Arms* (New York: Charles Scribner's Sons, 1929); one of the most powerful novels of World War II and its horrible toll of human lives and spirit was Norman Mailer's *The Naked and the Dead* (New York: Holt, Rinehart, and Winston, 1948).

[4] See Alfred Kinsey et al., *Sexual Behavior in the Human Male* (Philadelphia: W. B. Saunders Co., 1948). This large and technical work sold over 800,000 copies in the original edition.

[5] See Otto Pollak, *Integrating Sociological and Psychoanalytic Concepts* (New York: Russell Sage Foundation, 1956); also *Social Science and Psychotherapy for Children* (New York: Russell Sage Foundation, 1952). Pollak's point is that most of the child guidance clinic records examined by him more or less ignore the father of the child.

[6] Clark Vincent, *Unmarried Mothers* (New York: The Free Press, 1961), p. 3. In the writer's opinion this is the best study of unmarried mothers yet published.

[7] Robert R. Sears et al., *Patterns of Child Rearing* (Evanston, Ill.: Row, Peterson and Co., 1957), Foreword, p. vi.

It is interesting to note that in 1,140 pages, there are only five specific references to fathers in the *Handbook of Socialization Theory and Research* edited by David A. Goslin (Chicago: Rand McNally & Co., 1969).

[8] Sears, *op. cit.,* pp. 18–19.

[9] *Ibid.,* Foreword, p. vii.

[10] Pollak makes this point several times in the two studies cited previously.

[11] Daniel R. Miller and Guy E. Swanson, *The Changing American Parent* (New York: John Wiley & Sons, 1958), pp. 65–66.

[12] William J. Goode, *After Divorce* (New York: The Free Press, 1956). See chap. 2 for a description of the sample. While Goode's study was not focused primarily on the parent role, this was part of the research design (see chap. 21).

[13] Another study of American families and of the parental role interviewed 909 wife-mothers but no husband-fathers. See Robert O. Blood, Jr., and Donald M. Wolfe, *Husbands and Wives* (New York: The Free Press, 1960). If this study is added to the three above we find that 2,295 wife-mothers were interviewed and not one husband-father. The writer finds this approach to sampling unacceptable.

[14] See Alfred Kadushin, *Child Welfare Services* (New York: The Macmillan Co., 1967), chap. 10.

[15] John R. Seeley et al., *Crestwood Heights* (New York: Basic Books, 1956).

On the importance of interviewing husbands, see David Heer, "Measurement and Basis of Family Power: An Overview," *Marriage and Family Living,* 25 (1963), 133–139.

[16] See Seeley et al., *op. cit.*, pp. 193–194. "For such a man, the child-rearing theories which his wife espouses may seem arrant nonsense; and the male experts from whom she derives her information frequently appear to him, unless they are doctors, as inadequate men who have 'not been able to make the grade in the *really* masculine world.' "

[17] The news media in recent years have consistently reported the various Spartan schools to which the current Prince of Wales has been sent. See the study by Geoffrey Wakeford, *The Heir Apparent* (New York: A. S. Barnes & Co., 1967).

[18] For a good discussion of sexual subcultures see Jessie Bernard, *The Sex Game* (Englewood Cliffs, N.J.: Prentice-Hall, Inc., 1968); also E. E. LeMasters, *Modern Courtship and Marriage* (New York: The Macmillan Co., 1957), chaps. 22 and 23.

[19] These data are reviewed in LeMasters, *op. cit.* See also Ashley Montagu, *The Natural Superiority of Women* (New York: The Macmillan Co., 1968 ed.).

[20] Orville G. Brim, Jr., *Education for Child Rearing* (New York: Russell Sage Foundation, 1959), p. 70.

[21] See Theodore C. Sorensen, *Kennedy* (New York: Harper & Row, 1965), p. 381.

[22] This is an unpublished study of a tavern frequented by blue-collar construction workers.

[23] Reuben Hill, *Families Under Stress* (New York: Harper & Brothers, 1949).

[24] Kingsley Davis, *Human Society* (New York: The Macmillan Co., 1949), p. 400.

[25] Mead, *op. cit.*

[26] See Desmond Morris, *The Naked Ape* (New York: McGraw-Hill Book Co., 1967). On the wolf see Farley Mowat, *Never Cry Wolf* (Boston: Little, Brown & Co., 1963).

[27] See George B. Schaller, *The Mountain Gorilla* (Chicago: University of Chicago Press, 1963).

[28] George P. Murdock, *Social Structure* (New York: The Macmillan Co., 1949). In a survey of 250 human societies Murdock found that a majority of them permit a man to have more than one mate.

[29] See Oscar Lewis, *Five Families* (New York: Basic Books, 1959).

[30] In the tavern study referred to earlier the writer interviewed one man who was no longer close to his own children living in Indiana with their mother, but he was helping to care for three children who lived with the divorced woman he was then dating. Later on he married this second woman and for all practical purposes became the father of her children.

[31] For a good analysis of the millions of stepparents in our society see Anne W. Simon, *Stepchild in the Family* (New York: Odyssey Press, 1964).

[32] For a review of these data see Robert R. Bell, *Marriage and Family Interaction* (rev. ed.; Homewood, Ill.: The Dorsey Press, 1967), chap. 16.

[33] See Bell, *op. cit.*, p. 476.

[34] See E. E. LeMasters, "Holy Deadlock: A Study of Unsuccessful Marriages," *Sociological Quarterly*, 21 (1959), pp. 86–91; see also Morton M. Hunt, *The World of the Formerly Married* (New York: McGraw-Hill Book Co., 1966). When her marriage fails one of the common defense mechanisms of the American mother is her children.

[35] See Herbert Gold, *The Age of Happy Problems* (New York: Dial Press, 1962), pp. 27–33.

[36] This appears to be one of the findings of a study of 100 divorced men now in process at the School of Social Work, University of Wisconsin,. Madison, Wisc.

[37] Montagu, *op. cit.*

[38] Schaller, *op. cit.*

[39] The writer has over 20 newspaper clippings commenting on the interest the American armed forces men take in children all over the world.

[40] Benson, *op. cit.*, pp. 122–124, has a discussion of this.

[41] For the latest federal government study see Margaret Mead and Frances Kaplan, *American Women* (New York: Charles Scribner's Sons, 1965). This is the report of the President's Commission on the Status of Women. In the writer's state there is an active Governor's Commission on the Status of Women—as there are in many other states. The writer is entirely in favor of such commissions but would like to suggest that the American male could stand some study also.

[42] When Kendall, *op. cit.*, began to study the American male she discovered that for every book on men in the New York City Library there were literally hundreds of books on women. For some observations on the American father and his problems, see Brenton, *op. cit.*, chap. 5, "The Paradox of the Contemporary American Father." The recent volume by Benson, *op. cit.*, is the only scholarly work in recent decades to focus on the American father.

[43] For an interesting discussion of personal bankruptcy cases, see George Sullivan, *The Boom in Going Bust* (New York: The Macmillan Co., 1968).

[44] For an excellent analysis of poverty in our society, see the collection of essays, *Poverty: Views from the Left,* edited by Jeremy Larner and Irving Howe (New York: William Morrow & Co., 1968).

[45] In the paper "Holy Deadlock" cited earlier the writer pointed out that unsuccessful marriages that are never terminated legally are counted as successful marriages because they never show up in any other category.

[46] In their survey of upper middle-class married couples Cuber and Harroff concluded that perhaps two-thirds of these marriages had become "facade" marriages in the middle and later decades of life. See John Cuber and Peggy Harroff, *The Significant Americans* (New York: Appleton-Century, 1965). This study is marred by the fact that the authors do not bother to cite any of the previous studies of marriage in our society.

[47] Kinsey, *op. cit.*, p. 585, estimates that perhaps one half of U.S. husbands have committed adultery at least once.

[48] For a review of some of this data see Hunt, *op. cit.*

[49] President Harding apparently was married to a sexless woman who knew that he had at least two affairs with other women. See Francis Russell, *The Shadow of Blooming Grove: Warren G. Harding in His Times* (New York: McGraw-Hill Book Co., 1968).

[50] See Harrison M. Trice, *Alcoholism in America* (New York: McGraw-Hill Book Co., 1966), pp. 19–20.

[51] *Ibid.,* chap. 5.

[52] Herbert J. Gans, *The Urban Villagers* (New York: The Free Press, 1962).

[53] One of the best accounts of this era is in Frederick Lewis Allen, *Only Yesterday* (Harper & Row, 1957). This is an analysis of social change in our society since 1900. For an interesting analysis of the rise of women in our society, see Bren-

ton, *op cit.,* chap. 3, "Notes on the Femininization of Society." See also Benson, *op. cit.,* chap. 4, "The Passing of the Patriarch."

[54] Another case study of a farm father and his relationship with his children will be found in chap. 11.

[55] This case represents the writer's father.

[56] See Brenton, *op. cit.*

[57] These statistics are reviewed in Bell, *op. cit.,* pp. 138–139.

[58] *Ibid.,* pp. 496–501.

[59] For an analysis of these variables see Robert Winch, *The Modern Family* (New York: Holt, Rinehart and Winston, 1963 ed.), chap. 7.

[60] See E. E. LeMasters, *Parents In Modern America,* "Parents and Social Class," pp. 70–97.

[61] The following observations are based on three years' service during World War II. We doubt that it has changed much since then.

[62] For a review of this data see Marshall B. Clinard, *Sociology of Deviant Behavior* (New York: Rinehart & Co., 1968 ed.).

[63] Montagu, *op. cit.*

[64] Benson, *op. cit.,* pp. 99–100, writes: "A man wields power in the contemporary household only if he has the personal characteristics to pull it off or because of a unique pattern of domestic relationships, not because society backs him up with strong support."

Structural Problems
of the One-Parent Family

Paul Glasser and
Elizabeth Navarre

The attention of sociologists has been focused on the presumed isolation of the nuclear family (composed of mother, father and children, but no in-laws in the same household). However, little research effort has been expended on the more serious isolation and accompanying problems of the one-parent family. Such families are usually headed by women and have grave economic difficulties. The lone parent must handle all the tasks of running the family, even in a crisis. The demands are so great (when combined with making a living) that some tasks must be short-changed or ignored altogether. The areas of communications, family power structure, and affectional relationships are often the ones that become strained when one parent attempts to maintain the family alone.

INTRODUCTION

Recent concern about the problems of people who are poor has led to renewed interest in the source of such difficulties. While these are manifold and complexly related to each other, emphasis has been placed upon the opportunity structure and the socialization process found among lower socio-economic groups. Relatively little attention has been paid to family structure, which serves as an important intervening variable between these two con-

From Paul Glasser and Elizabeth Navarre, "Structural Problems of the One-Parent Family," *Journal of Social Issues,* January, 1965, pp. 98–109. Reprinted by permission of The Society for the Psychological Study of Social Issues. The conceptualization in this paper grew out of work on Project D-16, "Demonstration of Social Group Work With Parents," financed by a grant from the Children's Bureau, Welfare Administration, Department of Health, Education and Welfare. The authors are indebted to Professor Edwin Thomas for his suggestions.

siderations. This seems to be a significant omission in view of the major change in the structure of family life in the United States during this century, and the large number of one-parent families classified as poor. The consequences of the latter structural arrangements for family members, parents and children, and for society, is the focus of this paper.

One-parent families are far more apt to be poor than other families. This is true for one-fourth of those headed by a woman. Chilman and Sussman summarize that data in the following way:

> About ten percent of the children in the United States are living with only one parent, usually the mother. Nonwhite children are much more likely to live in such circumstances, with one-third of them living in one-parent families. Two-and-a-quarter million families in the United States today are composed of a mother and her children. They represent only one-twelfth of all families with children but make up more than a fourth of all that are classed as poor....
>
> Despite the resulting economic disadvantages, among both white and nonwhite families there is a growing number headed only by a mother. By 1960 the total was 7½ per cent of all families with own children rather than the 6 per cent of ten years earlier. By March 1962 the mother-child families represented 8½ per cent of all families with own children (4, p. 393).

When these demographic findings are seen in the context of the relative isolation of the nuclear family in the United States today, the structural consequences of the one-parent group take on added meaning. It may be seen as the culmination of the effective kin group.

> This "isolation" is manifested in the fact that members of the nuclear family, consisting of parents and their still dependent children, ordinarily occupy a separate dwelling not shared with members of the family of orientation.... It is, of course, not uncommon to find a (member of the family of orientation) residing with the family, but this is both statistically secondary, and it is clearly not felt to be the "normal arrangement" (9, p. 10).

While families maintain social contact with grown children and with siblings, lines of responsibility outside of the nuclear group are neither clear nor binding, and obligations among extended kin are often seen as limited and weak. Even when affectional ties among extended family members are strong, their spatial mobility in contemporary society isolates the nuclear group geographically, and increases the difficulty of giving aid in personal service among them (2, 6).

Associated with the weakening of the extended kinship structure has been the loss of some social functions of the family and the lessened import of others. Nonetheless, reproduction, physical maintenance, placement or status, and socialization are still considered significant social functions of the modern American family although they often have to be buttressed by other institutions in the community. At the same time, however, the personal functions of the family including affection, security, guidance and sexual gratification have been heightened and highlighted (3, 9). These functions are closely

266

and complexly related to each other but can serve as foci for analysis of the consequences of family structure. In the one-parent family neither reproduction nor sexual gratification can be carried out within the confines of the nuclear group itself. But more importantly, the other personal and social functions are drastically affected also, and it is to these that this paper will give its attention. A few of the implications for social policy and practice will be mentioned at the end.

While it is recognized that all individuals have some contact with others outside the nuclear group, for purposes of analytic clarity this paper will confine itself to a discussion of the relationships among nuclear family members primarily. Two factors will be the foci of much of the content. The age difference between parent and children is central to the analysis. Although it is understood that children vary with age in the degree of independence from their parents, the nature of their dependence will be emphasized throughout. The sex of the parent and the sex of the children is the second variable. Cultural definitions of appropriate behavior for men and women and for girls and boys vary from place to place and are in the process of change, but nonetheless this factor cannot be ignored. Since the largest majority of one-parent families are headed by a woman, greater attention will be given to the mother-son and mother-daughter relationships in the absence of the father.

STRUCTURAL CHARACTERISTICS OF ONE-PARENT FAMILIES AND THEIR CONSEQUENCES

Task Structure

The large majority of tasks for which a family is responsible devolve upon the parents. Providing for the physical, emotional, and social needs of all the family members is a full-time job for two adults. If these tasks are to be performed by the nuclear group during the absence or incapacity of one of its adult members, the crucial factor is the availability of another member with sufficient maturity, competence, and time to perform them. The two-parent family has sufficient flexibility to adapt to such a crisis. Although there is considerable specialization in the traditional sex roles concerning these tasks, there is little evidence that such specialization is inherent in the sex roles. It is, in fact, expected that one parent will substitute if the other parent is incapacitated and, in our essentially servantless society, such acquired tasks are given full social approval. However, in the one-parent family such flexibility is much less possible, and the permanent loss of the remaining parent generally dissolves the nuclear group.

Even if the remaining parent is able to function adequately, it is unlikely that one person can take over all parental tasks on a long-term basis. Financial support, child care, and household maintenance are concrete tasks involving temporal and spatial relationships, and in one form or another they account for a large proportion of the waking life of two adult family members. A

267

permanent adjustment then must involve a reduction in the tasks performed and/or a reduction in the adequacy of performance, or external assistance.

In addition to limitations on the time and energy available to the solitary parent for the performance of tasks, there are social limitations on the extent to which both the male and the female tasks may be fulfilled by a member of one sex. If the remaining parent be male, it is possible for him to continue to perform his major role as breadwinner and to hire a woman to keep house and, at least, to care for the children's physical needs. If, however, the solitary parent be a female, as is the more usual case, the woman must take on the male role of breadwinner, unless society or the absent husband provides financial support in the form of insurance, pensions, welfare payments, etc. This is a major reversal in cultural roles and, in addition, usually consumes the mother's time and energy away from the home for many hours during the day. There is little time or energy left to perform the tasks normally performed by the female in the household and she, too, must hire a female substitute at considerable cost. The effect of this reversal of the sex role model in the socialization of children has been a matter of some concern, but the emphasis has been upon the male child who lacked a male role model rather than upon the effect of the reversal of the female role model for children of both sexes. In both cases, the probability seems great that some tasks will be neglected, particularly those of the traditionally female specialization.

The wish to accomplish concrete household tasks in the most efficient manner in terms of time and energy expenditure may lead to less involvement of children in these tasks and the concomitant loss of peripheral benefits that are extremely important to the socialization process and/or to family cohesion. Some tasks may be almost completely avoided, especially those which are not immediately obvious to the local community, such as the provision of emotional support and attention to children. A third possibility is to overload children, particularly adolescents, with such tasks. These may be greater than the child is ready to assume, or tasks inappropriate for the child of a particular sex to perform regularly.

Females are often lacking in skills and experience in the economic world, and frequently receive less pay and lower status jobs than men with similar skills. The probability of lower income and lower occupational status for the female headed household are likely to lower the family's social position in a society, which bases social status primarily upon these variables. If the family perceives a great enough distance between its former level and that achieved by the single parent, it is possible that the family as a whole may become more or less anomic, with serious consequences in the socialization process of the children and in the remaining parent's perception of personal adequacy.

Communication Structure

Parents serve as the channels of communication with the adult world in two ways; first, as transmitters of the cultural value system which has previously been internalized by the parents; and secondly, as the child's contact with and representative in the adult world. Except for very young children, the parents are not the sole means of communication, but for a large part of the socialization process, the child sees the adult world through the eyes and by the experience of his parents, and even his own experiences are limited to those which can be provided for him within whatever social opportunities are open to his parents. More importantly, to the extent that the child's identity is integrated with that of the family, he is likely to see himself not only as his parents see him but also as the world sees his parents.

Since sex differences have been assumed in the ways men and women see the world and differences can be substantiated in the ways that the world sees men and women, the child can have a relatively undistorted channel of communication only if both parents are present. Therefore, whatever the interests, values, and opinions of the remaining parent, the loss of a parent of one sex produces a structural distortion in the communications between the child and the adult world and, since such communication is a factor in the development of the self-image, of social skills, and of an image of the total society, the totality of the child's possible development is also distorted.

The type and quality of experiences available even to adults tend to be regulated according to sex. In the two-parent family not only is the child provided with more varied experiences, but the parent of either sex has, through the spouse, some communication with the experiences typical of the opposite sex. Thus, the housewife is likely to have some idea of what is going on in the business or sports worlds even if she has no interest in them. The solitary parent is not likely to be apprised of such information and is handicapped to the extent that it may be necessary for decision making. The female who has taken on the breadwinner role may be cut off from the sources of information pertinent to the female role as she misses out on neighborhood gossip about the symptoms of the latest virus prevalent among the children, events being planned, the best places to shop, etc.

Finally, the solitary parent is likely to be limited in the social ties that are normal channels of communication. Most social occasions for adults tend to be planned for couples and the lone parent is often excluded or refuses because of the discomfort of being a fifth wheel. Her responsibilities to home and children tend to never be completed and provide additional reasons for refusing invitations. Lone women are particularly vulnerable to community sanctions and must be cautious in their social relationships lest their own standing and that of the family be lowered. Finally, the possible drop in social status previously discussed may isolate the family from its own peer group and place them among a group with which they can not or will not communicate freely.

Power Structure

Bales and Borgatta (1) have pointed out that the diad has unique properties and certainly a uniquely simple power structure. In terms of authority from which the children are more or less excluded by age and social norms, the one-parent family establishes a diadic relationship, between the parent and each child. Society places full responsibility in the parental role, and, therefore, the parent becomes the only power figure in the one-parent family. Consequently, the adult in any given situation is either for or against the child. Some experience of playing one adult against the other, as long as it is not carried to extremes, is probably valuable in developing social skills and in developing a view of authority as tolerable and even manipulable within reason, rather than absolute and possibly tyrannical. In the one-parent family the child is more likely to see authority as personal rather than consensual, and this in itself removes some of the legitimation of the power of parents as the representatives of society.

Even if benevolent, the absolutism of the power figure in the one-parent family, where there can be no experience of democratic decision making between equals in power, may increase the difficulty of the adolescent and the young adult in achieving independence from the family, and that of the parent in allowing and encouraging such development. Further, the adult, the power, the authority figure, is always of one sex, whether that sex be the same sex as the child or the opposite. However, in contemporary society where decision making is the responsibility of both sexes, the child who has identified authority too closely with either sex may have a difficult adjustment. The situation also has consequences for the parent, for when the supportive reinforcement or the balancing mediation which comes with the sharing of authority for decision making is absent, there may be a greater tendency to frequent changes in the decisions made, inconsistency, or rigidity.

Affectional Structure

The personal functions of the family in providing for the emotional needs of its members have been increasingly emphasized. There is ample evidence that children require love and security in order to develop in a healthy manner. Although there is nearly as much substantiation for the emotional needs of parents, these are less frequently emphasized. Adults must have love and security in order to maintain emotional stability under the stresses of life and in order to meet the emotional demands made upon them by their children. In addition to providing the positive emotional needs of its members, the family has the further function of providing a safe outlet for negative feelings as well. Buttressed by the underlying security of family affection, the dissatisfactions and frustrations of life may be expressed without the negative consequences attendant upon their expression in other contexts. Even within the family, however, the expressions of such basic emotions cannot go unchecked. The needs of one member or one sub-group may dominate to the point that the requirements of others are not fulfilled, or are not met in a manner acceptable to society. To some extent this danger exists in any group, but it is particularly strong in a group where emotional relationships are intensive. Traditionally, the danger is reduced by regulating the context, manner, and occasion of the expression of such needs.

Family structure is an important element both in the provision and the regulation of emotional needs. The increasing isolation of the nuclear family focuses these needs on the nuclear group by weakening ties with the larger kin group. Thus, both generations and both sexes are forced into a more intensive relationship; yet the marital relationship itself is increasingly unsupported by legal or social norms and is increasingly dependent upon affectional ties alone for its solidity. Such intense relationships are increased within the one-parent family, and possibly reach their culmination in the family consisting of one parent and one child.

In a two-person group the loss of one person destroys the group. The structure, therefore, creates pressure for greater attention to group maintenance through the expression of affection and the denial of negative feelings, and in turn may restrict problem-solving efforts. In a sense, the one-parent family is in this position even if there are several children because the loss of the remaining parent effectively breaks up the group. The children have neither the ability nor the social power to maintain the group's independence. Therefore, the one-parent family structure exerts at least some pressure in this direction.

However, where there is more than one child there is some mitigation of the pattern, though this in itself may have some disadvantages. In a group of three or more there are greater possibilities for emotional outlet for those not in an authority role. Unfortunately, there are also greater possibilities that one member may become the scapegoat as other members combine against him. In spite of the power relationships, it is even possible that the solitary parent will become the scapegoat if the children combine against her. This problem is greatest in the three-person family as three of the five possible

SUB-GROUP CHOICES AMONG GROUPS OF VARYING SIZES*

FIGURE 1: THE FOUR-PERSON GROUP

1. A, B, C, D	5. B, C, D	9. B, D
2. A, B, C	6. A, B	10. A, D
3. A, B, D	7. C, D	11. B, C
4. A, C, D	8. A, C	12. All persons independent; no sub-group

FIGURE 2: THE THREE-PERSON GROUP

1. A, B, C	3. A, B	5. All persons independent; no sub-group
2. B, C	4. A, C	

FIGURE 3: THE TWO-PERSON GROUP

1. A, B	2. Both persons independent; no sub-group

*Persons designated by letter.

sub-groups reject one member (Figure 2). The problem is also present in the four-person family, although the possible sub-groups in which the famil, combines against one member has dropped to four out of twelve (Figure 1). The relation of group structure to emotional constriction has been clearly expressed by Slater:

> The disadvantages of the smaller groups are not verbalized by members, but can only be inferred from their behavior. It appears that group members are too tense, passive, tactful, and constrained, to work together in a manner which is altogether satisfying to them. *Their fear of alienating one another seems to prevent them from expressing their ideas freely.* (Emphasis is ours.)
>
> These findings suggest that maximal group satisfaction is achieved when the group is large enough so that the members feel able to express positive and negative feelings freely, and to make aggressive efforts toward problem solving even at the risk of antagonizing each other, yet small enough so that some regard will be shown for the feelings and needs of others; large enough so that the loss of a member could be tolerated, but small enough so that such a loss could not be altogether ignored (11, p. 138).

Interpersonal relationships between parents and children in the area of emotional needs are not entirely reciprocal because of age and power differences in the family. Parents provide children with love, emotional support, and an outlet for negative feelings. However, while the love of a child is gratifying to the adult in some ways, it cannot be considered as supporting; rather it is demanding in the responsibilities it places upon the loved one. Support may be received only from one who is seen as equal or greater in power and discrimination. Nor can the child serve as a socially acceptable outlet for negative emotions to the extent that another adult can, for the child's emotional and physical dependency upon the adult makes him more vulnerable to possible damage from this source. The solitary parent in the one-parent family is structurally deprived of a significant element in the meeting of his own emotional needs. To this must be added the psychological and physical frustrations of the loss of the means for sexual gratification. In some situations involving divorce or desertion, the damage to the self-image of the remaining parent may intensify the very needs for support and reassurance which can no longer be met within the family structure.

The regulation of emotional demands of family members is similar in many ways to the regulation of the behavior of family members discussed under power structure. As there was the possibility that authority might be too closely identified with only one sex in the one-parent family, there is the similar danger that the source of love and affection may be seen as absolute and/or as vested in only one sex. Having only one source of love and security, both physical and emotional, is more likely to produce greater anxiety about its loss in the child, and may make the child's necessary withdrawal from the family with growing maturity more difficult for both parent and child. Again, as in the power structure, the identification of the source of love with only one sex is likely to cause a difficult adjustment to adult life, particularly if the original source of love was of the same sex as the child, for our society's expectations are that the source of love for an adult must lie with the opposite sex.

One of the most important regulatory devices for the emotional needs of the group is the presence and influence of members who serve to deter or limit demands which would be harmful to group members or to group cohesion, and to prevent the intensification of the influence of any one individual by balancing it with the influence of others. Parental figures will tend to have greater influence in acting as a deterrent or balance to the needs and demands of other family members because of their greater power and maturity. The loss of one parent removes a large portion of the structural balance and intensifies the influence of the remaining parent upon the children, while possibly limiting the ability of this parent to withstand demands made upon her by the children. There is also a tendency for any family member to transfer to one or more of the remaining members the demands formerly filled by the absent person (8). There would seem to be a danger in the one-parent family that:

1. The demands of the sole parent for the fulfillment of individual and emotional needs normally met within the marital relationship may prove intolerable and damaging to the children, who are unable to give emotional support or to absorb negative feelings from this source,

or:

2. The combined needs of the children may be intolerable to the emotionally unsupported solitary parent. Since the emotional requirements of children are very likely to take the form of demands for physical attention or personal service, the remaining parent may be subject to physical as well as emotional exhaustion from this source.

When emotional needs are not met within the family, there may be important consequences for the socialization of the children and for the personal adjustment of all family members. Further, fulfillment of such needs may be sought in the larger community by illegitimate means. The children may exhibit emotional problems in school or in their relations with their play group. A parent may be unable to control her own emotions and anxieties sufficiently to function adequately in society. When there are no means for the satisfaction of these demands they may well prove destructive, not only to the family group and its individual members, but to society as well.

The consequences of the problems discussed above may be minimized or magnified by the personal resources or inadequacies of the family members, and particularly the solitary parent in this situation. But, the problems are structural elements of the situation, and must be faced on this level if they are to be solved.

IMPLICATIONS FOR SOCIAL POLICY AND PRACTICE

The Introduction describes the growth of the number of one-parent families during the last generation. Chilman and Sussman go on to describe the financial plight of many of these families.

The public program of aid to families with dependent children (AFDC) that is most applicable to this group currently makes payments on behalf of children in nearly a million families. Three out of every four of these families have no father in the home. Less than half of the families that are estimated to be in need receive payments under the program and, "... with the low financial standards for aid to dependent children prevailing in many states, dependence on the program for support is in itself likely to put the family in low-income status.... The average monthly payment per family as reported in a study late in 1961 was only $112....

"The overall poverty of the recipient families is suggested by the fact that, according to the standards set up in their own states, half of them are still in financial need even with their assistance payment" (4, p. 394; 10).

There is increasing evidence that both the one-parent family structure and poverty are being transmitted from one generation to the next.

"A recently released study of cases assisted by aid to families with dependent children shows that, for a nationwide sample of such families whose cases were closed early in 1961" more than 40 per cent of the mothers and/or fathers were raised in homes where some form of assistance had been received at some time. "Nearly half of these cases had received aid to families with dependent children. This estimated proportion that received some type of aid is more than four times the almost 10 per cent estimated for the total United States population ..." (4, p. 395; 10).

If poverty and one-parent family structure tend to go together, providing increases in financial assistance alone may not be sufficient to help parents and children in the present and future generation to become financially independent of welfare funds. Under the 1962 Amendments to the Social Security Act states are now receiving additional funds to provide rehabilitation services to welfare families, and these programs have begun. Creative use of such funds to overcome some of the consequences of one-parent family structure is a possibility, but as yet the authors know of no services that have explicitly taken this direction.

A few suggestions may serve to illustrate how existing or new services might deal with the consequences of one-parent family structure:

1. Recognition of the need of the mother without a husband at home for emotional support and social outlets could lead to a variety of services. Recreation and problem-focused groups for women in this situation, which would provide some opportunities for socially sanctioned heterosexual relationships, might go a long way in helping these parents and their children.

2. Special efforts to provide male figures to which both girls and boys can relate may have utility. This can be done in day-care centers, settlement house agencies, schools, and through the inclusion of girls in programs like the Big Brothers. It would be particularly useful for children in one-parent families to see the ways in which adults of each sex deal with each other in these situations, and at an early age.

3. Subsidization of child care and housekeeping services for parents with children too young or unsuitable for day-care services would provide greater freedom for solitary mothers to work outside the home. Training persons as homemakers and making them responsible to an agency or a professional organization would reduce the anxiety of the working parent, and provide greater insurance to both the parent and society that this important job would be done well.

More fundamental to the prevention of poverty and the problems of one-parent family status may be programs aimed at averting family dissolution through divorce, separation and desertion, particularly among lower socio-economic groups. Few public programs have addressed themselves to this problem, and there is now a good deal of evidence that the private family agencies which provide counseling services have disenfranchised themselves from the poor (5). The need to involve other institutional components in the community, such as the educational, economic and political systems, is obvious but beyond the scope of discussion in this paper (7). Increasing the number of stable and enduring marriages in the community so as to prevent the consequences of one-parent family structure may be a first line of defense, and more closely related to treating the causes rather than the effects of poverty for a large number of people who are poor.

SUMMARY

One-parent families constitute more than a fourth of that group classified as poor, and are growing in number. Family structure is seen as a variable intervening between the opportunity system and the socialization process. The task, communication, power and affectional structure within the nuclear group are influenced by the absence of one parent, and the family's ability to fulfill its social and personal functions may be adversely affected. Some of the consequences of this deviant family structure seem related to both the evolvement of low socio-economic status and its continuation from one generation to the next. Solutions must take account of this social situational problem.

REFERENCES

1. Bales, R. F. and Borgatta, E. F. "Size of Group as a Factor in the Interaction Profile." In Hare, Borgatta and Bales (Eds.), *Small Groups*. New York: Knopf, 1955.
2. Bell, W. and Boat, M. D. Urban neighborhoods and informal social relations. *Amer. J. Soc.*, 1957, 43, 391–398.
3. Bernard, J. *American Family Behavior*. New York: Harper, 1942.
4. Chilman, C. and Sussman, M. Poverty in the United States. *J. Marriage and the Family*, 1964, 26, 391–395.

5. Cloward, R. A. and Epstein, I. Private social welfare's disengagement from the poor: the case of family adjustment agencies. Mimeographed, April 1964.

6. Litwak, E. Geographic mobility and extended family cohesion. *Amer. Soc. Rev.,* 1960, 25, 385–394.

7. Lutz, W. A. Marital incompatibility. In Cohen, N. E. (Ed.), *Social Work and Social Problems.* New York: National Association of Social Workers, 1964.

8. Mittleman, B. Analysis of reciprocal neurotic patterns in family relationships. In V. Eisenstein (Ed.), *Neurotic Interaction in Marriage.* New York: Basic Books, 1956.

9. Parsons, T. and Bales, R. F. *Family Socialization and Interaction Processes.* Glencoe, Illinois: The Free Press, 1954.

10. *Poverty in the United States.* Committee on Education and Labor, House of Representatives, 88th Congress, Second Session, April 1964. U.S. Government Printing Office, Washington, D. C.

11. Slater, P. E. Contrasting correlates of group size, *Sociometry,* 1958, 6, 129–139.

Personality Development—
The Special Task of the Family

Glenn R. Hawkes

Regardless of the original lack of commitment to, or training for, the roles of parenthood, male and female members of a marital partnership are responsible for the care and socialization of their children. What methods do families use to socialize their children and what effect do these methods have on the personality development of the child? Research has not yet established a clearcut cause-effect relationship between method and result. Hawkes attempts to look at the larger context of the home atmosphere and general parental attitude where some interesting guiding principles on child rearing emerge. The family's effectiveness in working with the child in the areas of internalization of discipline, development of life goals, dealing with aggression and competition, and sex role development is discussed from this broadened perspective.

American institutions are organized to give the basic role of personality development to the family. In our highly complex society some other social institutions may take on part of the job of supplementing the family in its critical task. In the examination of personality development in a dynamic society it is necessary that we look at the importance of the family in personality formation, examine where our knowledge has led us and attempt the development of theories which will aid us with further research.

Sigmund Freud's study of the neurotic personality threw light on the importance of infantile and childhood experiences in the shaping of adult behavior. His theoretical and methodological contributions represented a revolutionary appraisal of man's emotions and intellect which highlighted first

From Glenn R. Hawkes, "Personality Development—The Special Task of the Family," in *Family Mobility in Our Dynamic Society*, ed., Iowa State University Center for Agricultural Economic Development (Ames, Iowa: Iowa State University Press, 1965), pp. 114–30. Reprinted by permission of Iowa State University Press.

the developmental process and second the impact of early interactions on this process. It is to Freud and his disciples that we owe the impetus for the intensive study of parent-child relationships and the recognition that these relationships are central to the understanding of personality formation.

It is significant to note that the insights into early experiences arose out of therapeutic experiences with neurotic adults. The attempt to overcome these unfortunate early experiences gave rise to psychoanalysis as a mode of psychiatric treatment. The first insights, following the development of the Freudian theory, came through case studies. Case study is implicit in the psychoanalytical process; its aim is to learn everything relevant about one person's behavior and motivations as well as the origins of his motivations and his capacities for growth. The analyst must deal with the totality of a specific personality as it exists today with the historical context in which it grew and failed to blossom. The case study approach, fruitful in therapy, has never lent itself to the rigorous test of modern science. Conclusions drawn from one, two or a dozen cases do not provide the fodder for conclusive statistical tests.

Sociologists must have a word for the reactionary forces which led to the ascendency of John B. Watson following the temporary rejection of Freud and his followers. Watson's philosophy of the child in the family gave rise to this statement:

> There is a sensible way of treating children. Let your behavior always be objective and kindly, firm. Never hug and kiss them; never let them sit on your lap. If you must, kiss them once on the forehead when they say goodnight. Shake hands with them in the morning.[1]

Regardless of the allegiance of any one group, Freudian or behaviorist, the following statement from the Scope and Methods of the Family Service Agency expresses well the beliefs of either group:

> The quality of family relationships has profound effects, both positive and negative, on the emotional development and the social adjustment of all members of the family. Positive experiences within a family provide the foundation for satisfactory personality development from birth to maturity.[2]

Man in his attempts at new social orders has evolved groups other than the family for the socialization process. The Oneida Community (see page 345 of this book), the Hitler Youth and the Israeli Kibbutz (see page 358 of this book) are all examples of different and at least theoretically sound ways of rearing children. In each case, however, adaptations of the original have always swung back toward the basic primary family group. The future may hold a more appropriate group, but it seems not to have been found as yet. In spite of other changes taking place within the family this primary task of developing personality remains a critical charge to the family group.

This function consists of conditioning the young to the norms and patterns of the civilization in which the family is found. Moreover those groups— schools, churches, social agencies and so forth—which work with the young all state a part of their philosophy of programming as the strengthening of family life by "helping" families rather than superseding them.

Even though society takes many risks in allowing nearly all natural parents the right to rear their own children, this assurance runs through our laws and mores. Indeed one is on shaky ground in supporting this view as always the "best" way. There must be other basic reasons why society returns after each experimentation to the basic family group as the purveyor of culture to the young.

PARENTHOOD AS A VALUE

No doubt we view parenthood as a value. In spite of or because of religious belief in life after death, children can be viewed as a representation of immortality. They constitute a link between the parent and the future. Children are our "own flesh and blood" and they represent our reach into the future. In a very real sense children also help us retain our touch with the past. Seeing our own growth patterns repeated in them we are likely to recall nostalgically our days as youngsters. The paradox of this view is the realization that children may make us seem older because they symbolize our own aging process.

We become ego involved in the successes and failures of our children. They represent the products of our psychological recipes. Through their successes and failures we evaluate our ability to rear in a sound or unsound fashion. With rising technology there is less opportunity for the direct viewing of our accomplishments. The business deal has taken the place of the newly plowed field. A TV dinner substitutes for the home-cooked meal. A "number" painting replaces the original patchwork quilt as a mark of accomplishment. It is not surprising, therefore, to hear mothers and fathers compare the date of the first word, the Little League batting average and the report cards of their offspring. Children, more and more, become the symbols of status. They represent the concrete proof of our effectiveness.

Moreover, caring for and about children symbolizes, for many, the highest form of service to mankind. Here lies the opportunity to assist the less able, the smaller member of our society. To serve mankind is suggested as a mark of maturity. What better way to prove to ourselves and others that we are able to delay the satisfactions of our own needs and to help those who are less able to match their wits against the rigors of society and nature?

I wonder, furthermore, if one strong reason for the preservation of the primary family as the vehicle for the transmission of culture is the realization that children represent concrete or real property in our cultural eyes. Each child is the product of a pregnancy individually carried and born. Even though the psychiatrist George Preston[3] reminds us that successful parents lose their children and retain their property we still speak of children as "ours" or "mine." No matter how highly noble we may be, we do not give up our property without much suffering. In fact one reason for our mobility is the opportunity it seems to offer for the increase of property.

279

Granted, then, the role of the family as the primary external force in the personality development of the young, what are the effects of this parent-child relationship? How do certain parental practices contribute to or detract from healthy personality development? What is the nature of interaction which promises the greatest return for all of society? What types of attitudes and values should society encourage in order to be assured that manpower is conserved? What should be the nature of the educational process to insure increasing capability as the demands of the culture increase? In short, what has research told us is the most effective way to get the job done? And what can we expect from future research?

Specific Parental Practices

Much research energy over the past two or three decades has been expended in an effort to specify the effects of specific parental practices on the development of the child. Many of these practices have been scrutinized because of Freudian statements to the effect that they will lead to maldevelopment. Such practices as breast feeding, late weaning, severe toilet training, and spanking have been researched. The significance of these early parental practices has been repeatedly emphasized in the analytic literature and psychoanalytical clinical practice. Moreover, parent educators have been strongly influenced by "specific practice" theory. An examination of literature available to parents reflects the deep inroads such ideas have held.

Harold Orlansky[4] made an exhaustive analysis of the research literature up to 1946. He found that researchers had failed to produce a definitive answer to the question of the relation between specific practices with infants and character or personality development. His review provided also a critical look at the inadequate research that had been attempted up to that date. Any student of child development had to develop a more cautious attitude regarding some favorite assumptions about cause and effect and personality development.

Sewell, Mussen and Harris,[5] writing in the *American Sociological Review* in 1955, found that the intervening nine years had not changed the situation markedly. As a matter of fact some of their analyses showed that in some cases where a cause and effect was postulated, the effect was opposite to that postulated!

Such analyses would seem to leave us a choice of conclusions. We can conclude that there is no relationship between specific practices, or we can conclude that the dynamic interaction between child and parent is such that specific practices get lost in the total complex of relationships. Another choice open to us is to assume that a relationship does exist but that present theoretical and methodological problems are so complex we have not yet found a way to cut to the heart of the matter. Evidence from clinical practice seems to suggest that specific practices become overshadowed by their setting. Evidence is mounting that such an approach will help us find the answers we seek. The researcher, however, is left with a most difficult field of investigation.

Martin[6] has suggested that the problem is one of theory and method. Too long we have followed the scientific methods laid down by the physical scientists. He advances the notion that we need to re-think the development of theory. Cause and effect hypotheses, as they are traditionally formulated, might not be at all appropriate with such complex problems as personality formation and parent-child relationships. Again the researcher is left with a very small measure of comfort. His education and training have not equipped him with the skills needed for this grossly different approach.

Parenthood in the Larger Setting

Patterns of Child Rearing, the report of a study by Sears, Maccoby and Levin,[7] attempted to take a look at the larger scene. Their study involved much more than specific practice as related to specific effect. They got at the over-all feelings of mothers. With the extensive interview technique they discussed with their subjects motherhood, womanliness, wifehood and related subjects. Following the interviews the data were analyzed into seven key factors which seemed to cluster and organize. Of these key factors the "warmth" of the mother was found to be the most pervasive of influences. That is to say, severity of a specific practice such as toilet training was much less critical than the attitude of the mother toward body function and mess. If mothers rejected their role as woman and wife they also tended to reject their role as mother and nurturance provider. Attitudes tended to cluster and be pervasive, spilling over into relationships with the young. For that matter these attitudes cropped up in feeling about men and husbands also.

Viewing the over-all effects of punishment rather than a specific punishment as related to a specific mis-act on the part of the child led Sears, Maccoby and Levin to conclude:

> ... the amount and use of punishment that we measured was essentially a measure of a personality quality of the mothers. Punitiveness, in contrast with rewardingness, was a quite ineffectual quality for a mother to inject into her child training. The evidence for this conclusion is overwhelming. The unhappy effects of punishment have run like a dismal thread through our findings. Mothers who punished toilet accidents severely ended up with bed-wetting children. Mothers who punished dependency to get rid of it had more dependent children than mothers who did not punish. Mothers who punished aggressive behavior severely had more aggressive children than mothers who punished lightly. They also had more dependent children. Harsh physical punishment was associated with high childhood aggressiveness and with the development of feeding problems.
>
> Our evaluation of punishment is that it is ineffectual over the long term as a technique for eliminating the kind of behavior toward which it is directed.

The conclusions regarding permissiveness, when viewed in the larger context, were much less decisive. Permissive attitudes with aggression encourages the child to express himself in an aggressive fashion. On the other hand permissiveness was associated with a low frequency of feeding and toilet problems. More research needs to be done to unravel this complex attitude and its net effect upon the child being reared.

In a series of studies performed by Hattwick[8] in which the behavior of children was rated and related to factors in the home, confirmation was found of the associations between parent behavior and child personality patterns which were noted also in case studies of the children. Relationships were found between parental overattentiveness and infantile withdrawing behavior and dependency. Furthermore, inadequate parental attention led to aggressive behavior in children. When the home background was growth oriented, good social adjustment tended to result.

At Minnesota, Radke[9] investigated the relationships between parental discipline and authority and children's behavior and attitudes. She concluded that variations in the behavior of children are related to variations in home discipline and atmosphere. Even where these changes are slight she found a marked effect in her child subjects.

In attempting to find why certain children were well adjusted, Langdon and Stout[10] studied the home atmosphere of their subjects. No specific practice could be isolated with extensive analysis. As a matter of fact they found great variance in the practices in the homes. The pervading quality found, regardless of specific practice, was the acceptance of the child by his parents. He was viewed and then treated as a unique person with characteristics innately his. Again the larger look led to some conclusions that are useful in understanding the over-all effect of the parent-child relationship. It is also significant to note that socioeconomic class, occupation of parent, number of siblings and level of aspiration of parent were not found to be significant factors in the development of the well-adjusted child.

Nationwide attention has been focused on the study by the Gluecks.[11] They found in their study of 500 delinquent and 500 nondelinquent boys that five factors in the relationship of the boy to his parents which probably operated prior to school entrance could be evaluated and summated to produce a score that would be indicative of probable future delinquency. While our concern is not necessarily with delinquency we are concerned with parental attitudes and practices which seem to predispose to certain types of behavior on the part of offspring. The five factors found were: (1) discipline of the boy by the father, (2) supervision of the boy by the mother, (3) affection of the mother, (4) affection of the father and (5) cohesiveness of the family.

The potential for trouble was found in boys who were characteristically exposed to overstrict or erratic discipline by the father. (The term overstrict, I realize, is ambiguous. The Gluecks are not very helpful in this regard. One gets the picture of justice meted out in the letter of the law and not with the spirit. I can only presume that this is what overstrict means.) The boys were given "unsuitable" supervision by the mother. (One wonders about the meaning of unsuitable.) Indifference and/or hostility was shown on the part of both parents. There was much evidence that the collection of people called the family, in these cases, was not an integrated group. That is to say there were many signs that consensus of goals, values and ideas had not taken place.

The Gluecks used the "chance of becoming" approach. They found an element of predictability but it was not sufficient that one could postulate absolute cause and effect. Their work does constitute an important step in the direction of understanding the larger setting in which child growth takes place. Furthermore, the focus on parental attitudes as shapers of personality adds mounting evidence of the necessity of understanding such attitudes before we can understand more of the dynamics of personality adjustment as it proceeds within the family.

The Fels Research Institute[12] was an early leader in conducting research on the atmosphere of the home. Clusters of behavior were found to represent major dimensions of parental behavior. Warmth, for example, emerged in both clinical and statistical analyses. This cluster was found to be made up of acceptance, direction of criticism (approval-disapproval), affectionateness, rapport, child-centeredness, and intensity of contact.

Two other key clusters helped to define the general climate of the home—objectivity of the parents' attitudes toward the child and parental control. The summation of these clusters could help to give one a picture of the nature of the home and family as a child-rearing center. And yet, the clusters did not lend themselves to integration. Again, there is the logical conclusion that behavior must be seen in the larger setting in order to understand the dynamics of development. The job of the researcher is complicated.

Another complicating, but fascinating, pattern found by the Fels Research group related to the democratic home. Democracy was found to exist on a continuum from warm and spontaneous to cold and intellectual. Where democracy existed the child was given opportunity to explore, question and test reality. Children from such homes were found to be in favored positions in the peer groups although they were often aggressive and bossy. They were in favored positions because they made their aggressiveness and bossiness work. They also rated high on activities demanding intelligence, curiosity, originality and constructiveness. Democracy as a factor had impact on behavior of the offspring. But it had a varying effectiveness because, as pointed out earlier, democracy was found to be an attitudinal approach to living which could be warm and spontaneous or it could be cold, calculating and noninterfering. There is some evidence,[13] incidentally, that this latter type of democratic home may help to produce the scholar who can pursue an intellectual problem with the type of candid objectivity often needed.

The studies at Fels were some of the first attempts to study the complex family interrelationships related to personality development of the child. Their method of direct observation has been used more and more as investigators have come to grips with the sheer necessity of understanding personality development as a factor of the social context of the family. Ackerman,[14] Hawkes,[15] Pease and Hawkes[16] and Parsons and Bales[17] have all pointed out the necessity of direct observation as a method of understanding personality development. As Ackerman states:

> It is essential to view the dominant modes of behavior in the growing child as being shaped by the total psychosocial configuration of the family rather than by the child-parent relationship in isolation. What is implied here is the need to define parental role functioning and child-parent interaction in broader context of the psychosocial pattern of the family as a whole.

This direct observation of family interaction presents some very difficult problems to the researcher. He must find ways to minimize his effect on the interaction he wishes to observe. The complexity of the interaction is such that it is almost impossible to comprehend and analyze the total interaction process without destroying what it really means. Furthermore, he must find ways to control his perceptions so that his own attitudes, biases and mental sets do not delude him into observing only that which has relevance to him. Research in this type of methodology is moving forward. The very complexity of the method means that a breakthrough may be slow in coming.

Observation without a focus is not very meaningful. Theory of inter-relationships must keep pace with research in methodology. In fact, it is safe to say that the problems may be researched concurrently. In any event, the complex family setting in which personality development forges ahead must be studied along with the sheer dynamics of personality formation. More will be said concerning theory later in the chapter.

A perusal of journals, conferences and conventions concerning themselves with children and families leads one to the conclusion that there are fewer areas of greater concern than those related to personality formation of children within the modern mobile American family. Whether the mobility be vertical or horizontal these processes merit the attention of producers and consumers of research. Winch[18] describes them as follows: (1) internalization of discipline or development of conscience, (2) development of goals or the ego-ideal, (3) lasting effects of parental control or identification and possibly (4) sex-role development.

INTERNALIZATION OF DISCIPLINE

"Social man's most necessary nuisance"[19]—conscience—has its roots in the family. The newborn is ushered into the world with all kinds of needs which demand immediate gratification. When he is hungry, he demands food. When he needs to eliminate, he eliminates. When he wants freedom of movement or relief from pain his cries connote little patience with delay. The controls which ultimately come to govern his behavior are all controls from without. They differ from conscience controls in a major way: conscience controls come from within the individual. The process of socialization is to transform outer controls to inner controls. This process is called internalization.

Three things exemplify the internalization of controls: resistance to tempta-tion, feelings of guilt, and attaining of "good." Feelings of guilt occur when resistance to temptation has not been successful. In the more complete con-science, feelings of guilt occur when good has not been accomplished. The ultimate goal for maturity is to develop adequate conscience in children. Conscience can be too strong and it can be too weak. Early in the school years we often see manifestations of impossible ideals children have set up for them-selves and for other people. When these ideals are not attained we witness guilt feelings, often of a severe nature. Many of the most severe problems in therapy are produced by too much guilt.

There are, no doubt, gross cultural and class differences in conscience. Allison Davis[20] points out that the middle class contains vastly more future rewards for present self-denial than does the subculture of the lower class. It is consistent with these differences in rewards that middle-class morality should emphasize thrift, saving, prolonged professional and vocational training and mobility for opportunity rather than immediate gratification.

The subtle ways in which cultural standards and values are imparted within the family group poses real problems for families. A study by Harris[21] and associates typifies this process. Three thousand children between the ages of 10 and 16, from a variety of towns and cities, participated. The study aimed to link home duties with an attitude of responsibility. Results of the testing did not support the hypothesis that the number of home duties assumed by the child bore a substantial relation to his sense of responsibility. Nor was there any evidence that the relationship existed with older children who had more years of family training. There appeared to be a connection, however, between the sense of responsibility in children and the type of activities in which the parents participated. The subtle influence of action seemed to over-ride any verbal exhortations that were not backed by modeling in the adult members of the family.

In our modern mobile society with its complex problems of interaction and interrelatedness we are faced with some sobering societal deliberations. Can society tolerate the family as the cradle of conscience development? If we focus on problems of racial equality and race relations it becomes apparent that attitudes are deep-rooted and fostered early in the life of the child. Clinical evidence makes it abundantly clear that such attitudes are highly resistant to erosion. In many cases intensive therapy yields little in an attitudinal change. As we understand more about the process of internalization will it be necessary for society to develop some other institution to supplement the family in this area in order to foster the attitudes which society deems necessary to evolve?

One cannot assume that later experiences and peer associates do not have their impact. Yet the potency of the early experience is apparent. With an increasingly pluralistic society evolving primarily because of mobility, the problem takes on keener proportions.

If we take a look at the effect of religious institutions on moral and/or conscience standards we find that relatively few studies have been done. Those which have been done, however, point to the minimal effect of church attendance on honesty, cooperativeness and resistance to delinquency. With home attitude supplementation in this area society still has not found the way to re-enforce those conscience ideas which it deems vital.

Development of Goals

The development of goals or the inculcation in the child of an ego-ideal is an important part of parental function in personality development. Research by Havighurst, Robinson and Dorr[22] points out that the child, after suffering disenchantment with parents, moves to other adults in the surroundings for goal setting. In a strong kin family society this type of goal setting could occur with adult kin, and the larger families' "way of life" would be perpetuated. In a highly mobile society the absence of kin means a reaching out for other adults to furnish ideal images. This may lead to an enrichment by breeding diversity into a society, but it may also introduce discordant factors. In a recent book about adolescent society the Hechingers[23] point out the problems for adolescents who select as their ego-ideals other teen-agers. They maintain this reduces the urge to maturity in adolescent citizens. On the other hand, Moss and Gingles[24] and Burchinal[25] found that low parental aspirations was a factor related to the early marriage of adolescents. Possibly finding ego-ideals in other than their immediate family could have raised the level of aspiration of the adolescents. A higher level of aspiration might forestall many of the problems in adolescent marriages.

Differences between expectations of males and females, while undergoing radical change, still is a confusing element in the setting of goals. Komarovsky[26] and Wallin[27] report that girls and women suffer emotionally from uncertainty as to which goals and values are appropriate and expected of them. Miller and Swanson[28] report further confusion, not necessarily due to sex differences, but because of possible basic orientation shifts of the family from entrepreneurial to bureaucratic. It is to be anticipated that mobility may produce further changes in more families as technology and bureaucracy become factors in making families move both vertically and horizontally.

Mass communication may further complicate the problem of goal setting. Impressionable children exposed to a wide range of goals never before possible may be tempted or forced to select goals highly inappropriate to their primary family group.

Lasting Effects of Parental Control

One approach to understanding the lasting effects of parents or the socialization impact is to view it as a process in which the child learns what is expected of him because of his age, sex and social class. Related to this is the permanency of this learning. In American culture some of the most marked expectations concern the expression of aggression in competition and achievement. Middle-class parents instruct their small boys that it is not fitting to "pick" fights, particularly with someone smaller or with a girl. On the other hand, to fail to defend oneself or one's honor is to fail. The child must, therefore, learn the difference between these two situations.

In the lower class, there is little or no cultural pressure to avoid physical contact. It may, in fact, be encouraged. Both boys and girls are expected to protect themselves with strong action.

Competitive achievement may be defined as a close ally to aggression. In middle-class families this type of action is encouraged. As a matter of fact, middle-class families seem to seek out ways for their children to compete— Little League, Scouts, 4-H and so forth. Research by Douvan[29] contributes evidence that middle-class adolescents differ from lower-class adolescents in valuing achievement for its own sake. In this study subjects established a level of performance on being rewarded: middle-class subjects tended to carry on at a high level of performance when the reward was withdrawn; lower-class subjects did not.

The lasting effects of such teachings seem to show up in the different ways in which conflicts are resolved at the adult level. Labor union members protect their rights with strikes which sometimes lead to violence. Professional groups tend to resort to debate, influencing of public opinion and, in the main, avoid a show of physical force. In a fluid class society one would expect blending of these two diverse approaches. Recently teachers in Utah and New York threatened strikes, but the strikes did not materialize. The labor unions are accused of being less vigorous than formerly. Does this mean they are moving toward middle class? With vertical mobility the effects may be less lasting than in a rigid society. In this same vein of questioning one must look and be amazed at the ability of the southern Negro to persist in nonviolence when his early learnings must have prepared him for aggressive action. It is clear that there is some persistence, but it is equally clear that change is taking place. The more subtle impact of vertical mobility must tax the resources of families in knowing what approach to use in dealing with aggression.

SEX-ROLE DEVELOPMENT

In most cultures, sex-role development or sex-typing begins early in life. These differences extend far beyond anatomical characteristics but begin with them. Sex-role development refers to the identification the individual makes regarding his biological, sociological, and psychological self in the maleness-femaleness dimension. This identification comes about through his relationships with those of the same and the opposite sex.

In the family, boys find it natural and rewarding to pattern themselves after their fathers, and father is pleased to note this emulation of his qualities, attitudes and masculinity. The mother who loves the father finds such patterning acceptable in her son. Explorations, both conscious and unconscious, of being like mother convince the boy that this is not his proper or approved role. He goes back to his identification with his father. In the healthy family the same picture holds true for the girl.

Where there is parental disharmony the situation is different. When chronic antagonism exists between the parents, the boy finds that if he identifies with his father he loses his mother's love and approval. If he then tries to be like his mother, he incurs his father's anger besides risking the general disapproval connected with being a "sissy."

Many investigators have found that problems related to improper sex-role development precede the school-age period. They seem to have their roots in less than adequate functioning of one or both parents. With the confusion that exists today as to proper role, freedom of role decisions and other vital questions, it is readily apparent that some maladjustment should be present. In a society where vertical mobility may be assisted by the female assuming parts of the role traditionally held only by males we can expect children to be caught in the backwash. This will continue to occur until we have learned to institutionalize the changes that are taking place in our societal practice.

THEORY OF PERSONALITY DEVELOPMENT

Earlier in this chapter it was indicated that there would be a discussion of personality formation which seemed to lend itself to creative research and more particularly to the role of the family in this personality formation. Abraham H. Maslow, using well the theories of the past, has developed a concept or theory of motive hierarchy leading toward self-actualization which clearly defines many enlightened functions the family has and can play in personality formation.

According to Maslow[30] all an individual's capacities and energy are always mobilized in the interest of any strong motivational need. And although behavior is usually determined by multiple needs, only in its absence does a motivational need bcome an important determinant of behavior. Food, for example, would be a poor schoolwork incentive, because most children's hunger needs are taken care of by an almost automatic schedule of eating. Teacher approval is better, because the need for this boost to one's self-esteem is more constantly active. Further, according to Maslow, motives are hierarchically arranged; only as more basic motives are satisfied (at least minimally) do motives higher in the hierarchy become potent behavior determinants. But when motives lower in the hierarchy are satisfied, then automatically, because of the inherent nature of man, motives higher in the hierarchy motivate activity and effort. Motivational needs higher in the hierarchy keep man continuously striving as lower needs are satisfied. The hierarchical order is as follows:

1. Physiological needs, such as hunger, thirst, activity, rest.
2. Safety needs, security, and release from anxiety aroused by threats of various kinds.

3. Love needs, including love, affection, acceptance, and a feeling of belonging.
4. Esteem needs, including both self-esteem from mastery and confidence in one's worth, adequacy, and capacities, and esteem from social approval.
5. Need for self-actualization through creative self-expression in personal and social achievements; need to feel free to act, to satisfy one's curiosity, and to understand one's world.

The emergence of this fifth level of motivation, however, depends upon the prior satisfaction of the lower-order needs. A child who is hungry, insecure or unloved, whose confidence has been undermined, or who feels disapproved would not be expected to reach this fifth level. What better environment could be constructed than a family to provide for the first four needs? Within this *small* group with its adults he can be fed, clothed and sheltered, loved and encouraged to grow. Physical health and protection nearly always precede constructive and creative work. There is much reason to believe that if lower-level needs are met mobility can be handled by children with greater ease.

When all a child's lower-level needs are satisfied, he would not need to be pressed into constructive and creative study and work. In such activity for such a child, the opportunity for self-actualization in expression of talents and interests offers its intrinsic, high reward. According to Maslow's theory, a child is not driven or pressed to constructive effort; his energies for such effort from lower-order needs are released!

As Maslow states:

> From Freud we learned that the past exists now in the person. Now we must learn, from growth theory and self-actualization theory that the future also now exists in the person in the form of ideals, hopes, duties, tasks, plans, goals, unrealized potentials, mission, fate, destiny, etc. One for whom no future exists is reduced to the concrete, to hopelessness, to emptiness. For him, time must be endlessly "filled." Striving, the usual organizer of most activity, when lost, leaves the person unorganized and unintegrated. Mobility and striving seem to be very much related.
>
> Of course, being in a state of Being needs no future, because it is already *there.* Then Becoming ceases for the moment and its promissory notes are cashed in the form of the ultimate rewards, i.e., the peak experiences, in which time disappears and hopes are fulfilled.[31]

Adaptation of research efforts to this theory gives us a framework of insights into how the family succeeds or fails in its task of developing personality in the child. For adequate parenting some measure of self-actualizing must have occurred for parents. If we view children as *becoming* we would assess their development in the hierarchical order. Possibly one task is to assure ourselves that investigators are operating at the self-actualizing level. If not, we can hardly expect creativity from their efforts.

Undoubtedly the future will give us further refinement of Maslow's theory, or it may be even supplanted. In any event our task is to lend all of our creative resources to the task of determining how best we can grow the "best" children in a dynamic and mobile society.

NOTES

[1] John B. Watson, *Psychological Care of Infants and Children*, W. W. Norton, New York, 1928, pp. 81–82.

[2] Family Service Association of America, "Scope and Methods of the Family Service Agency," New York, 1953.

[3] George Preston, *The Substance of Mental Health*, Rinehart and Co., New York, 1946.

[4] Harold Orlansky, "Infant Care and Personality," *Psychological Bulletin*, 46:1–48, 1949.

[5] W. H. Sewell, P. H. Mussen and C. W. Harris. "Relationships Among Child Training Practices," *Amer. Soc. Rev.*, 20:137–48, 1955.

[6] W. E. Martin, "Rediscovering the Mind of the Child: A Significant Trend in Research in Child Development," *Merrill-Palmer Quarterly*, 6:67–76, 1959–60.

[7] R. S. Sears, E. E. Maccoby and H. Levin. *Patterns of Child Rearing*, Row, Peterson and Co., Evanston, Ill., 1947, p. 484.

[8] B. W. Hattwick, "Interrelations Between the Preschool Child's Behavior and Certain Factors in the Home," *Child Development*, 7:200–26, 1936.

B. W. Hattwick and M. Stowell, "The Relation of Parental Over-Attentiveness to Children's Work Habits and Social Adjustments in Kindergarten and the First Six Grades of School," *Jour. of Educational Research*, 30:169–76, 1936–37.

[9] M. J. Radke, "The Relation of Parental Authority to Children's Behavior and Attitudes," University of Minnesota Institute of Child Welfare Monograph Series, No. 22, 1946.

[10] G. Langdon and I. W. Stout, *The Discipline of Well-Adjusted Children*, John Day, New York, 1952.

[11] S. Glueck and E. Glueck, *Unraveling Juvenile Delinquency*, Harvard University Press, Cambridge, Mass., 1950.

[12] A. L. Baldwin, J. Kalhorn and F. H. Breese, "The Appraisal of Parent Behavior," Psych. Monographs, Vol. 63, No. 4, 1949.

[13] Frank Barron, *Creativity and Psychological Health*, D. Van Nostrand Co., Princeton, N.J., 1963.

[14] N. W. Ackerman, "An Orientation to Psychiatric Research on the Family," *Marriage and Family Living*, 19:68–74, 1957.

[15] G. R. Hawkes, "The Child in the Family," *Marriage and Family Living*, 19:46–51, 1957.

[16] D. Pease and G. R. Hawkes, "Direct Study of Child-Parent Interactions," *Journal of Orthopsychiatry*, Vol. 30, No. 3, July, 1960.

[17] T. Parsons and R. F. Bales, *Family Socialization and Interaction Process*, Free Press, Glencoe, Ill., 1955.

[18] Robert F. Winch, *The Modern Family*, revised ed., Holt, Rinehart and Winston, New York, 1963.

[19] R. R. Sears, "The Growth of Conscience," in I. Iscoe and H. W. Stevenson, eds., *Personality Development in Children*, University of Texas Press, Austin, 1960.

[20] Allison Davis, "American Status System and the Socialization of the Child," *Amer. Soc. Rev.,* 6:345–54, 1941.

[21] D. G. Harris, K. G. Clark, A. M. Rose and F. Valasek, "The Relationship of Children's Home Duties to an Attitude of Responsibility," *Child Development,* 25:21–28, 1954.

[22] R. J. Havighurst, Myra Robinson and Mildred Dorr, "The Development of the Ideal Self in Childhood and Adolescence," *Jour. of Educational Research,* 40:241–57, 1946.

[23] Grace Hechinger and Fred Hechinger, "Teen-Age Tyranny," William Morrow and Co., New York, 1963.

[24] J. J. Moss and R. J. Gingles, "The Relationship of Personality to the Incidence of Early Marriage," *Marriage and Family Living,* 21:373–77, 1959.

[25] L. G. Burchinal, "Adolescent Role Deprivation and High School Age Marriage," *Marriage and Family Living,* 21:378–84, 1959.

[26] M. Komarovsky, "Cultural Contradictions and Sex Roles," *Amer. Jour. of Sociology,* 52:189, 1946.

[27] Paul Wallin, "Cutural Contradictions and Sex Roles: A Repeat Study," *Amer. Soc. Rev.,* 15:288–93, 1950.

[28] D. R. Miller and G. E. Swanson, *The Changing American Parent,* John Wiley & Sons, New York, 1958.

[29] Elizabeth Douvan, "Social Status and Success Strivings," *Jour. of Abnormal and Social Psychology,* 52:219–23, 1956.

[30] A. H. Maslow, "A Theory of Human Motivation," *Psychological Review,* 50:370–96, 1943.

A. H. Maslow, *Toward a Psychology of Being,* D. Van Nostrand Co., Princeton, N.J., 1962.

[31] *Ibid.,* pp. 199–200.

The Sociology of
Parent-Youth Conflict

Kingsley Davis

The generation gap is one of the most dismaying of parental experiences. After intensely socializing their children to think like they do, parents find that their children are often actively opposed to their way of life. Davis analyzes the phenomenon of parent-youth conflict within a societal framework. He explains how rapid social change, the length of time between generations, physiological differences between adolescents and their middle-aged parents, the decline in parental authority in Western industrial countries, and the economic and sexual competition of the different generations contribute to different belief and action systems. From his analysis, we can see that perhaps the only way to avoid the generation gap is to return to primitive tribal living.

It is in sociological terms that this paper attempts to frame and solve the sole question with which it deals, namely: Why does contemporary western civilization manifest an extraordinary amount of parent-adolescent conflict?[1] In other cultures, the outstanding fact is generally not the rebelliousness of youth, but its docility. There is practically no custom, no matter how tedious or painful, to which youth in primitive tribes or archaic civilizations will not willingly submit.[2] What, then, are the peculiar features of our society which give us one of the extremest examples of endemic filial friction in human history?

Our answer to this question makes use of constants and variables, the constants being the universal factors in the parent-youth relation, the variables being the factors which differ from one society to another. Though one's attention, in explaining the parent-youth relations of a given milieu, is focused on the variables, one cannot comprehend the action of the variables without

From Kingsley Davis, "The Sociology of Parent-Youth Conflict," *American Sociological Review,* August, 1940, pp. 523–35. Reprinted by permission of the author and The American Sociological Association.

292

also understanding the constants, for the latter constitute the structural and functional basis of the family as a part of society.

THE RATE OF SOCIAL CHANGE

The first important variable is the rate of social change. Extremely rapid change in modern civilization, in contrast to most societies, tends to increase parent-youth conflict, for within a fast-changing social order the time interval between generations, ordinarily but a mere moment in the life of a social system, becomes historically significant, thereby creating a hiatus between one generation and the next. Inevitably, under such a condition, youth is reared in a milieu different from that of the parents; hence the parents become old-fashioned, youth rebellious, and clashes occur which, in the closely confined circle of the immediate family, generate sharp emotion.

That rapidity of change is a significant variable can be demonstrated by three lines of evidence: a comparison of stable and nonstable societies;[3] a consideration of immigrant families; and an analysis of revolutionary epochs. If, for example, the conflict is sharper in the immigrant household, this can be due to one thing only, that the immigrant family generally undergoes the most rapid social change of any type of family in a given society. Similarly, a revolution (an abrupt form of societal alteration), by concentrating great change in a short span, catapults the younger generation into power—a generation which has absorbed and pushed the new ideas, acquired the habit of force, and which, accordingly, dominates those hangovers from the old regime, its parents.[4]

THE BIRTH-CYCLE, DECELERATING SOCIALIZATION, AND PARENT-CHILD DIFFERENCES

Note, however, that rapid social change would have no power to produce conflict were it not for two universal factors: first, the family's duration; and second, the decelerating rate of socialization in the development of personality. "A family" is not a static entity but a process in time, a process ordinarily so brief compared with historical time that it is unimportant, but which, when history is "full" (i.e., marked by rapid social change), strongly influences the mutual adjustment of the generations. This "span" is basically the birth-cycle —the length of time between the birth of one person and his procreation of another. It is biological and inescapable. It would, however, have no effect in producing parent-youth conflict, even with social change, if it were not for the additional fact, intimately related and equally universal, that the sequential development of personality involves a constantly decelerating rate of socialization. This deceleration is due both to organic factors (age—which ties it to the birth-cycle) and to social factors (the cumulative character of social experience). Its effect is to make the birth-cycle interval, which is the period of youth, the time of major socialization, subsequent periods of socialization being subsidiary.

Given these constant features, rapid social change creates conflict because to the intrinsic (universal, inescapable) differences between parents and children it adds an extrinsic (variable) difference derived from the acquisition, at the same stage of life, of differential cultural content by each successive generation. Not only are parent and child, at any given moment, in different stages of development, but the content which the parent acquired at the stage where the child now is, was a different content from that which the child is now acquiring. Since the parent is supposed to socialize the child, he tends to apply the erstwhile but now inappropriate content (see Diagram). He makes this mistake, and cannot remedy it, because, due to the logic of personality growth, his basic orientation was formed by the experiences of his own childhood. He cannot "modernize" his point of view, because he is the product of those experiences. He can change in superficial ways, such as learning a new tune, but he cannot change (or *want* to change) the initial modes of thinking upon which his subsequent social experience has been built. To change the basic conceptions by which he has learned to judge the rightness and reality of all specific situations would be to render subsequent experience meaningless, to make an empty caricature of what had been his life.

Although, in the birth-cycle gap between parent and offspring, astronomical time constitutes the basic point of disparity, the actual sequences, and hence the actual differences significant for us, are physiological, psychosocial, and sociological—each with an acceleration of its own within, but to some degree independent of, sidereal time, and each containing a divergence between parent and child which must be taken into account in explaining parent-youth conflict.

PHYSIOLOGICAL DIFFERENCES

Though the disparity in chronological age remains constant through life, the precise physiological differences between parent and offspring vary radically from one period to another. The organic contrasts between parent and *infant,* for example, are far different from those between parent and adolescent. Yet whatever the period, the organic differences produce contrasts (as between young and old) in those desires which, at least in part, are organically determined. Thus, at the time of adolescence the contrast is between an organism which is just reaching its full powers and one which is just losing them. The physiological need of the latter is for security and conservation, because as the superabundance of energy diminishes, the organism seems to hoard what remains.

Such differences, often alleged (under the heading of "disturbing physiological changes accompanying adolescence") as the primary cause of parent-

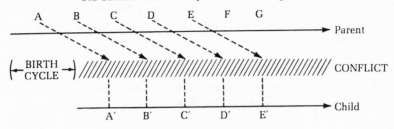

Old Cultural Content Acquired at Each Stage of Life

New Cultural Content at Each Stage

*Because the birth-cycle interval persists throughout their conjoint life, parent and child are always at a different stage of development and their relations are always therefore potentially subject to conflict. E.g., when the parent is at stage D, the child is at stage B. But social change adds another source of conflict, for it means that the parent, when at the stage where the child now is, acquired a different cultural content from that which the child must now acquire at that stage. This places the parent in the predicament of trying to transmit old content no longer suited to the offspring's needs in a changed world. In a stable society, B and B' would have the same cultural content. In a changing society, they do not, yet the parent tries to apply the content of $A, B, C,$ etc., to the corresponding stages in the child's development, $A', B', C',$ etc., which supposedly and actually have a different content. Thus, a constant (the birth-cycle) and a variable (social change) combine to produce parent-youth conflict.

Though the birth-cycle remains absolutely the same, it does not remain relatively the same, because it occupies, as time goes on, a successively smaller percentage of the total time lived. Furthermore, because of the decelerating rate of socialization, the difference in the total amount of cultural content as between parent and child becomes less pronounced. After the period of adolescence, for example, the margin is reduced to a minimum, which explains why a minimum of conflict is achieved after that stage.

adolescent strife, are undoubtedly a factor in such conflict, but, like other universal differences to be discussed, they form a constant factor present in every community, and therefore cannot in themselves explain the peculiar heightening of parent-youth conflict in our culture.

The fact is that most societies avoid the potential clash of old and young by using sociological position as a neutralizing agent. They assign definite and separate positions to persons of different ages, thereby eliminating competition between them for the same position and avoiding the competitive emotions of jealousy and envy. Also, since the expected behavior of old and young is thus made complementary rather than identical, the performance of cooperative functions is accomplished by different but mutually related activities suited to the disparate organic needs of each, with no coercion to behave in a manner unsuited to one's organic age. In our culture, where most positions are *theoretically* based on accomplishment rather than age, interage competition arises, superior organic propensities lead to a high evaluation of youth (the so-called "accent on youth"), a disproportionate lack of opportunity for youth manifests itself, and consequently, arrogance and frustration appear in the young, fear and envy, in the old.

PSYCOSOCIAL DIFFERENCES: ADULT REALISM VERSUS YOUTHFUL IDEALISM

The decelerating rate of socialization (an outgrowth both of the human being's organic development, from infant plasticity to senile rigidity, and of his cumulative cultural and social development), when taken with rapid social change and other conditions of our society, tends to produce certain differences of orientation between parent and youth. Though lack of space makes it impossible to discuss all of these ramifications, we shall attempt to delineate at least one sector of difference in terms of the conflict between adult realism (or pragmatism) and youthful idealism.

Though both youth and age claim to see the truth, the old are more conservatively realistic than the young, because on the one hand they take Utopian ideals less seriously and on the other hand take what may be called operating ideals, if not more seriously, at least more for granted. Thus, middle-aged people notoriously forget the poetic ideals of a new social order which they cherished when young. In their place, they put simply the working ideals current in the society. There is, in short, a persistent tendency for the ideology of a person as he grows older to gravitate more and more toward the status quo ideology, unless other facts (such as a social crisis or hypnotic suggestion) intervene.[5] With advancing age, he becomes less and less bothered by inconsistencies in ideals. He tends to judge ideals according to whether they are widespread and hence effective in thinking about practical life, not according to whether they are logically consistent. Furthermore, he gradually ceases to bother about the *untruth* of his ideals, in the sense of their failure to correspond to reality. He assumes through long habit that, though they do not correspond perfectly, the discrepancy is not significant. The reality of an ideal is defined for him in terms of how many people accept it rather than how completely it is mirrored in actual behavior.[6] Thus, we call him, as he approaches middle age, a realist.

The young, however, are idealists, partly because they take working ideals literally and partly because they acquire ideals not fully operative in the social organization. Those in authority over children are obligated as a requirement of their status to inculcate ideals as a part of the official culture given the new generation.[7] The children are receptive because they have little social experience—experience being systematically kept from them (by such means as censorship, for example, a large part of which is to "protect" children). Consequently, young people possess little ballast for their acquired ideals, which therefore soar to the sky, whereas the middle-aged, by contrast, have plenty of ballast.

This relatively unchecked idealism in youth is eventually complicated by the fact that young people possess keen reasoning ability. The mind, simply as a logical machine, works as well at sixteen as at thirty-six.[8] Such logical capacity, combined with high ideals and an initial lack of experience, means that youth soon discovers with increasing age that the ideals it has been taught are true and consistent are not so in fact. Mental conflict thereupon ensues, for the young person has not learned that ideals may be useful without being true and consistent. As a solution, youth is likely to take action designed to remove inconsistencies or force actual conduct into line with ideals, such action assuming one of several typical adolescent forms—from religious withdrawal to the militant support of some Utopian scheme—but in any case consisting essentially in serious allegiance to one or more of the ideal moral systems present in the culture.[9]

A different, usually later reaction to disillusionment is the cynical or sophomoric attitude; for, if the ideals one has imbibed cannot be reconciled and do not fit reality, then why not dismiss them as worthless? Cynicism has the advantage of giving justification for behavior that young organisms crave anyway. It might be mistaken for genuine realism if it were not for two things. The first is the emotional strain behind the "don't care" attitude. The cynic, in his judgment that the world is bad because of inconsistency and untruth of ideals, clearly implies that he still values the ideals. The true realist sees the inconsistency and untruth, but without emotion; he uses either ideals or reality whenever it suits his purpose. The second is the early disappearance of the cynical attitude. Increased experience usually teaches the adolescent that overt cynicism is unpopular and unworkable, that to deny and deride all beliefs which fail to cohere or to correspond to facts, and to act in opposition to them, is to alienate oneself from any group,[10] because these beliefs, however unreal, are precisely what makes group unity possible. Soon, therefore, the youthful cynic finds himself bound up with some group having a system of working ideals, and becomes merely another conformist, cynical only about the beliefs of other groups.[11]

While the germ of this contrast between youthful idealism and adult realism may spring from the universal logic of personality development, it receives in our culture a peculiar exaggeration. Social change, complexity, and specialization (by compartmentalizing different aspects of life) segregate ideals from fact and throw together incompatible ideologies while at the same time providing the intellectual tools for discerning logical inconsistencies and empirical errors. Our highly elaborated burden of culture, correlated with a variegated system of achieved vertical mobility, necessitates long years of formal education which separate youth from adulthood, theory from practice, school from life. Insofar, then, as youth's reformist zeal or cynical negativism produces conflict with parents, the peculiar conditions of our culture are responsible.

297

Since social status and office are everywhere partly distributed on the basis of age, personality development is intimately linked with the network of social positions successively occupied during life. Western society, in spite of an unusual amount of interage competition, maintains differences of social position between parent and child, the developmental gap between them being too clearcut, the symbiotic needs too fundamental, to escape being made a basis of social organization. Hence, parent and child, in a variety of ways, find themselves enmeshed in different social contexts and possessed of different outlooks. The much publicized critical attitude of youth toward established ways, for example, is partly a matter of being on the outside looking in. The "established ways" under criticism are usually institutions (such as property, marriage, profession) which the adolescent has not yet entered. He looks at them from the point of view of the outsider (especially since they affect him in a restrictive manner), either failing to imagine himself finding satisfaction in such patterns or else feeling resentful that the old have in them a vested interest from which he is excluded.

Not only is there differential position, but also *mutually* differential position, status being in many ways specific for and reciprocal between parent and child. Some of these differences, relating to the birth-cycle and constituting part of the family structure, are universal. This is particularly true of the super- and subordination summed up in the term *parental authority*.

Since sociological differences between parent and child are inherent in family organization, they constitute a universal factor potentially capable of producing conflict. Like the biological differences, however, they do not in themselves produce such conflict. In fact, they may help to avoid it. To understand how our society brings to expression the potentiality for conflict, indeed to deal realistically with the relation between the generations, we must do so not in generalized terms but in terms of the specific "power situation." Therefore, the remainder of our discussion will center upon the nature of parental authority and its vicissitudes in our society.

Because of his strategic position with reference to the new-born child (at least in the familial type of reproductive institution), the parent is given considerable authority. Charged by his social group with the responsibility of controlling and training the child in conformity with the mores and thereby insuring the maintenance of the cultural structure, the parent, to fulfill his duties, must have the privileges as well as the obligations of authority, and the surrounding community ordinarily guarantees both.

The first thing to note about parental authority, in addition to its function in socialization, is that it is a case of authority within a primary group. Simmel has pointed out that authority is bearable for the subordinate because it touches only one aspect of life. Impersonal and objective, it permits all other aspects to be free from its particularistic dominance. This escape, however, is lacking in parental authority, for since the family includes most aspects of life, its authority is not limited, specific, or impersonal. What, then, can make this authority bearable? Three factors associated with the familial primary group help to give the answer: (1) the child is socialized within the family, and therefore knowing nothing else and being utterly dependent, the authority is internalized, accepted; (2) the family, like other primary groups, implies identification, in such sense that one person understands and responds emphatically to the sentiments of the other, so that the harshness of authority is ameliorated;[12] (3) in the intimate interaction of the primary group control can never be purely one-sided; there are too many ways in which the subordinated can exert the pressure of his will. When, therefore, the family system is a going concern, parental authority, however inclusive, is not felt as despotic.

A second thing to note about parental authority is that while its duration is variable (lasting in some societies a few years and in others a lifetime), it inevitably involves a change, a progressive readjustment, in the respective positions of parent and child—in some cases an almost complete reversal of roles, in others at least a cumulative allowance for the fact of maturity in the subordinated offspring. Age is a unique basis for social stratification. Unlike birth, sex, wealth, or occupation, it implies that the stratification is temporary, that the person, if he lives a full life, will eventually traverse all of the strata having it as a basis. Therefore, there is a peculiar ambivalence attached to this kind of differentiation, as well as a constant directional movement. On the one hand, the young person, in the stage of maximum socialization, is, so to speak, *moving into* the social organization. His social personality is expanding, i.e., acquiring an increased amount of the cultural heritage, filling more powerful and numerous positions. His future is before him, in what the older person is leaving behind. The latter, on the other hand, has a future before him only in the sense that the offspring represents it. Therefore, there is a disparity of interest, the young person placing his thoughts upon a future which, once the first stages of dependence are passed, does not include the parent, the old person placing his hopes vicariously upon the young. This situation, representing a *tendency* in every society, is avoided in many places by a system of respect for the aged and an imaginary projection of life beyond the grave. In the absence of such a religio-ancestral system, the role of the aged is a tragic one.[13]

Let us now take up, point by point, the manner in which western civilization has affected this *gemeinschaftliche* and processual form of authority.

1. Conflicting Norms. To begin with, rapid change has, as we saw, given old and young a different social content, so that they possess conflicting norms. There is a loss of mutual identification, and the parent will not "catch up" with the child's point of view, because he is supposed to dominate rather than follow. More than this, social complexity has confused the standards *within* the generations. Faced with conflicting goals, parents become inconsistent and confused in their own minds in rearing their children. The children, for example, acquire an argument against discipline by being able to point to some family wherein discipline is less severe, while the parent can retaliate by pointing to still other families wherein it is firmer. The acceptance of parental attitudes is less complete than formerly.

2. *Competing Authorities.* We took it for granted, when discussing rapid social change, that youth acquires new ideas, but we did not ask how. The truth is that, in a specialized and complex culture, they learn from competing authorities. Today, for example, education is largely in the hands of professional specialists, some of whom, as college professors, resemble the sophists of ancient Athens by virtue of their work of accumulating and purveying knowledge, and who consequently have ideas in advance of the populace at large (i.e., the parents). By giving the younger generation these advanced ideas, they (and many other extrafamilial agencies, including youth's contemporaries) widen the intellectual gap between parent and child.[14]

3. *Little Explicit Institutionalization of Steps in Parental Authority.* Our society provides little explicit institutionalization of the progressive readjustments of authority as between parent and child. We are intermediate between the extreme of virtually permanent parental authority and the extreme of very early emancipation, because we encourage release in late adolescence. Unfortunately, this is a time of enhanced sexual desire, so that the problem of sex and the problem of emancipation occur simultaneously and complicate each other. Yet even this would doubtless be satisfactory if it were not for the fact that among us the exact time when authority is relinquished, the exact amount, and the proper ceremonial behavior are not clearly defined. Not only do different groups and families have conflicting patterns, and new situations arise to which old definitions will not apply, but the different spheres of life (legal, economic, religious, intellectual) do not synchronize, maturity in one sphere and immaturity in another often coexisting. The readjustment of authority between individuals is always a ticklish process, and when it is a matter of such close authority as that between parent and child it is apt to be still more ticklish. The failure of our culture to institutionalize this readjustment by a series of well-defined, well-publicized steps is undoubtedly a cause of much parent-youth dissension. The adolescent's sociological exit from his family, via education, work, marriage, and change of residence, is fraught with potential conflicts of interest which only a definite system of institutional controls can neutralize. The parents have a vital stake in what the offspring will do. Because his acquisition of independence will free the parents of many obligations, they are willing to relinquish their authority; yet, precisely because their own status is socially identified with that of their offspring, they wish to insure satisfactory conduct on the latter's part and are tempted to prolong their authority by making the decisions themselves. In the absence of institutional prescriptions, the conflict of interest may lead to a struggle for power, the parents fighting to keep control in matters of importance to themselves, the son or daughter clinging to personally indispensable family services while seeking to evade the concomitant control.

4. *Concentration within the Small Family.* Our family system is peculiar in that it manifests a paradoxical combination of concentration and dispersion. On the one hand, the unusual smallness of the family unit makes for a strange intensity of family feeling, while on the other, the fact that most pursuits take place outside the home makes for a dispersion of activities. Though apparently

300

contradictory, the two phenomena are really interrelated and traceable ultimately to the same factors in our social structure. Since the first refers to that type of affection and antagonism found between relatives, and the second to activities, it can be seen that the second (dispersion) isolates and increases the intensity of the affectional element by sheering away common activities and the extended kin. Whereas ordinarily the sentiments of kinship are organically related to a number of common activities and spread over a wide circle of relatives, in our mobile society they are associated with only a few common activities and concentrated within only the immediate family. This makes them at once more instable (because ungrounded) and more intense. With the diminishing birth rate, our family is the world's smallest kinship unit, a tiny closed circle. Consequently, a great deal of family sentiment is directed toward a few individuals, who are so important to the emotional life that complexes easily develop. This emotional intensity and situational instability increase both the probability and severity of conflict.

In a familistic society, where there are several adult male and female relatives within the effective kinship group to whom the child turns for affection and aid, and many members of the younger generation in whom the parents have a paternal interest, there appears to be less intensity of emotion for any particular kinsman and consequently less chance for severe conflict.[15] Also, if conflict between any two relatives does arise, it may be handled by shifting mutual rights and obligations to another relative.[16]

5. *Open Competition for Socioeconomic Position.* Our emphasis upon individual initiative and vertical mobility, in contrast to rural-stable regimes, means that one's future occupation and destiny are determined more at adolescence than at birth, the adolescent himself (as well as the parents) having some part in the decision. Before him spread a panorama of possible occupations and avenues of advancement, all of them fraught with the uncertainties of competitive vicissitude. The youth is ignorant of most of the facts. So is the parent, but less so. Both attempt to collaborate on the future, but because of previously mentioned sources of friction, the collaboration is frequently stormy. They evaluate future possibilities differently, and since the decision is uncertain yet important, a clash of wills results. The necessity of choice at adolescence extends beyond the occupational field to practically every phase of life, the parents having an interest in each decision. A culture in which more of the choices of life were settled beforehand by ascription, where the possibilities were fewer and the responsibilities of choice less urgent, would have much less parent-youth conflict.[17]

6. *Sex Tension.* If until now we have ignored sex taboos, the omission has represented a deliberate atempt to place them in their proper context with other factors, rather than in the unduly prominent place usually given them.[18] Undoubtedly, because of a constellation of cultural conditions, sex looms as an important bone of parent-youth contention. Our morality, for instance, demands both premarital chastity and postponement of marriage, thus creating a long period of desperate eagerness when young persons practically at the peak of their sexual capacity are forbidden to enjoy it. Naturally, tensions

arise—tensions which adolescents try to relieve, and adults hope they will relieve, in some socially acceptable form. Such tensions not only make the adolescent intractable and capricious, but create a genuine conflict of interest between the two generations. The parent, with respect to the child's behavior, represents morality, while the offspring reflects morality *plus* his organic cravings. The stage is thereby set for conflict, evasion, and deceit. For the mass of parents, toleration is never possible. For the mass of adolescents, sublimation is never sufficient. Given our system of morality, conflict seems well nigh inevitable.

Yet it is not sex itself but the way it is handled that causes conflict. If sex patterns were carefully, definitely, and uniformly geared with nonsexual patterns in the social structure, there would be no parent-youth conflict over sex. As it is, rapid change has opposed the sex standards of different groups and generations, leaving impulse only chaotically controlled.

The extraordinary preoccupation of modern parents with the sex life of their adolescent offspring is easily understandable. First, our morality is sex-centered. The strength of the impulse which it seeks to control, the consequent stringency of its rules, and the importance of reproductive institutions for society, make sex so morally important that being moral and being sexually discreet are synonymous. Small wonder, then, that parents, charged with responsibility for their children and fearful of their own status in the eyes of the moral community, are preoccupied with what their offspring will do in this matter. Moreover, sex is intrinsically involved in the family structure and is therefore of unusual significance to family members *qua* family members. Offspring and parent are not simply two persons who happen to live together; they are two persons who happen to live together because of past sex relations between the parents. Also, between parent and child there stand strong incest taboos, and doubtless the unvoiced possibility of violating these unconsciously intensifies the interest of each in the other's sexual conduct. In addition, since sexual behavior is connected with the offspring's formation of a new family of his own, it is naturally of concern to the parent. Finally, these factors taken in combination with the delicacy of the authoritarian relation, the emotional intensity within the small family, and the confusion of sex standards, make it easy to explain the parental interest in adolescent sexuality. Yet because sex is a tabooed topic between parent and child,[19] parental control must be indirect and devious, which creates additional possibilities of conflict.

SUMMARY AND CONCLUSION

Our parent-youth conflict thus results from the interaction of certain universals of the parent-child relation and certain variables the values of which are peculiar to modern culture. The universals are (1) the basic age or birth-cycle differential between parent and child, (2) the decelerating rate of socialization with advancing age, and (3) the resulting intrinsic differences between old and young on the physiological, psychosocial, and sociological planes.

Though these universal factors *tend* to produce conflict between parent and child, whether or not they do so depends upon the variables. We have seen that the distinctive general features of our society are responsible for our excessive parent-adolescent friction. Indeed, they are the same features which are affecting *all* family relations. The delineation of these variables has not been systematic, because the scientific classification of whole societies has not yet been accomplished; and it has been difficult, in view of the inter-related character of societal traits, to seize upon certain features and ignore others. Yet certainly the following four complex variables are important: (1) the rate of social change; (2) the extent of complexity in the social structure; (3) the degree of integration in the culture; and (4) the velocity of movement (e.g., vertical mobility) within the structure and its relation to the cultural values.

Our rapid social change, for example, has crowded historical meaning into the family time-span, has thereby given the offspring a different social content from that which the parent acquired, and consequently has added to the already existent intrinsic differences between parent and youth, a set of extrinsic ones which double the chance of alienation. Moreover, our great societal complexity, our evident cultural conflict, and our emphasis upon open competition for socioeconomic status have all added to this initial effect. We have seen, for instance, that they have disorganized the important relation of parental authority by confusing the goals of child control, setting up competing authorities, creating a small family system, making necessary certain significant choices at the time of adolescence, and leading to an absence of definite institutional mechanisms to symbolize and enforce the progressively changing stages of parental power.

If ours were a simple rural-stable society, mainly familistic, the emancipation from parental authority being gradual and marked by definite institutionalized steps, with no great postponement of marriage, sex taboo, or open competition for status, parents and youth would not be in conflict. Hence, the presence of parent-youth conflict in our civilization is one more specific manifestation of the incompatibility between an urban-industrial-mobile social system and the familial type of reproductive institutions.[20]

NOTES

[1] In the absence of statistical evidence, exaggeration of the conflict is easily possible, and two able students have warned against it. E. B. Reuter, "The Sociology of Adolescence," and Jessie R. Runner, "Social Distance in Adolescent Relationships," both in *Amer. J. Sociol.,* November 1937, 43:415–16, 437. Yet sufficient nonquantitative evidence lies at hand in the form of personal experience, the outpour of literature on adolescent problems, and the historical and anthropological accounts of contrasting societies to justify the conclusion that in

comparison with other cultures ours exhibits an exceptional amount of such conflict. If this paper seems to stress conflict, it is simply because we are concerned with this problem rather than with parent-youth harmony.

[2] Cf. Nathan Miller, *The Child in Primitive Society*, New York, 1928; Miriam Van Waters, "The Adolescent Girl Among Primitive Peoples," *J. Relig. Psychol.*, 1913, 6:375–421 (1913) and 7:75–120 (1914); Margaret Mead, *Coming of Age in Samoa*, New York, 1928, and "Adolescence in Primitive and Modern Society," 169–88, in *The New Generation* (ed. by V. F. Calverton and S. Schmalhausen, New York, 1930; A. M. Bacon, *Japanese Girls and Women*, New York and Boston, 1891 and 1902.

[3] Partially done by Mead and Van Waters in the works cited above.

[4] Soviet Russia and Nazi Germany are examples. See Sigmund Neumann, "The Conflict of Generations in Contemporary Europe from Versailles to Munich," *Vital Speeches of the Day*, August 1, 1939, 5:623–28. Parents in these countries are to be obeyed only so long as they profess the "correct" (i.e., youthful, revolutionary) ideas.

[5] See Footnote 11 for necessary qualifications.

[6] When discussing a youthful ideal, however, the older person is quick to take a dialectical advantage by pointing out not only that this ideal affronts the aspirations of the multitude, but that it also fails to correspond to human behavior either now or (by the lessons of history) probably in the future.

[7] See amusing but accurate article, "Fathers Are Liars," *Scribner's Magazine*, March, 1934.

[8] Evidence from mental growth data point to a leveling off of the growth curve at about age 16. For charts and brief explanations, together with references, see F. K. Shuttleworth, *The Adolescent Period*, Monographs of the Society for Research in Child Development, III, Serial No. 16 (Washington, D.C., 1938), Figs. 16, 230, 232, 276, 285, 308.

Maturity of judgment is of course another matter. We are speaking only of logical capacity. Judgment is based on experience as well as capacity; hence, adolescents are apt to lack it.

[9] An illustration of youthful reformism was afforded by the Laval University students who decided to "do something about" prostitution in the city of Quebec. They broke into eight houses in succession one night, "whacked naked inmates upon the buttocks, upset beds and otherwise proved their collegiate virtue...." They ended by "shoving the few remaining girls out of doors into the cold autumn night." *Time*, October 19, 1936.

[10] This holds only for expressed cynicism, but so close is the relation of thought to action that the possibility of an entirely covert cynic seems remote.

[11] This tentative analysis holds only insofar as the logic of personality development in a complex culture is the sole factor. Because of other factors, concrete situations may be quite different. When, for example, a person is specifically trained in certain rigid, other-worldly, or impractical ideals, he may grow increasingly fanatical with the years rather than realistic, while his offspring, because of association with less fanatical persons, may be more pragmatic than he. The variation in group norms within a society produces persons who, whatever their orientation inside the group, remain more idealistic than the average outsider, while their children may, with outside contacts, become more pragmatic. Even within a group, however, a person's situation may be such as to drive him beyond the everyday realities of that group, while his

children remain undisturbed. Such situations largely explain the personal crises that may alter one's orientation. The analysis, overly brief and mainly illustrative, therefore represents a certain degree of abstraction. The reader should realize, moreover, that the terms "realistic" and "idealistic" are chosen merely for convenience in trying to convey the idea, not for any evaluative judgments which they may happen to connote. The terms are not used in any technical epistemological sense, but simply in the way made plain by the context. Above all, it is not implied that ideals are "unreal." The ways in which they are "real" and "unreal" to observer and actor are complex indeed. See T. Parsons, *The Structure of Social Action,* 396, New York, 1937, and V. Pareto, *The Mind and Society,* III: 1300–04, New York, 1935.

[12] House slaves, for example, are generally treated much better than field slaves. Authority over the former is of a personal type, while that over the latter (often in the form of a foreman-gang organization) is of a more impersonal or economic type.

[13] Sometimes compensated for by an interest in the grandchildren, which permits them partially to recover the role of the vigorous parent.

[14] The essential point is not that there are other authorities—in every society there are extrafamilial influences in socialization—but that, because of specialization and individualistic enterprise, they are *competing* authorities. Because they make a living by their work and are specialists in socialization, some authorites have a competitive advantage over parents who are amateurs or at best merely general practitioners.

[15] Margaret Mead, *Social Organization of Manua,* 84, Honolulu, Bernice P. Bishop Museum Bulletin 76, 1930. Large heterogeneous households early accustom the child to expect emotional rewards from many different persons. D. M. Spencer, "The Composition of the Family as a Factor in the Behavior of Children in Fijian Society," *Sociometry* (1939), 2:47–55.

[16] The principle of substitution is widespread in familism, as shown by the wide distribution of adoption, levirate, sororate, and classificatory kinship nomenclature.

[17] M. Mead, *Coming of Age in Samoa,* 200 ff.

[18] Cf., e.g., L. K. Frank, "The Management of Tensions," *Amer. J. Sociol.,* March 1928, 33:706–22; M. Mead, *op. cit.,* 216–17, 222–23.

[19] "Even among the essentially 'unrepressed' Trobrianders the parent is never the confidant in matters of sex." Bronislaw Malinowski, *Sex and Reproduction in Savage Society,* 36 (note), London, 1927, p. 36n. Cf. the interesting article, "Intrusive Parents," *The Commentator,* September 1938, which opposes frank sex discussion between parents and children.

[20] For further evidence of this incompatibility, see the writer's "Reproductive Institutions and the Pressure for Population," *(Brit.) Sociol. Rev.,* July 1937, 29: 289–306.

6

Family Partnerships as Mini-Cultures

As family decisions and practices evolve into shared expectations and routine ways of doing things, it is not surprising that the family itself develops a culture that is as distinctive as the exotic cultures studied by anthropologists. This culture sets the atmosphere of family living and is crucial to the enjoyment or disenchantment of family members.

Unlike isolated primitive tribes, the family culture is affected by, and affects, the outer society. To comprehend components of family climates, the social structure of which they are a part must be understood. The marked contrast in life styles between black families with grave monetary problems and white families with a comfortable standard of living is a dramatic case in point. Yet it is not merely a simple lesson in the unhappiness that can be wrought by economic hardship; economic plenty can create its own difficulties, as is seen in the discussion here of suburban families. Furthermore, economic strain can be handled more effectively by some ideologies of family role responsibilities than others—as the description of the Black Muslim family structure illustrates.

Disenchantment with the cultural possibilities of family styles, or with society as it affects the family and the individual, has been present throughout history. Coupled with such discontent have been attempts to construct a new family form, as discussed in the opening article. But utopia through family restructuring is not always easy to achieve. This is illustrated by descriptions of the Oneida Community, the kibbutz, and some present-day hippie communes. Nevertheless, such attempts are instructive because they highlight some of the problems inherent in family, or group, living.

307

Family Ritual as an Instrument in Culture Transmission

James H. Bossard and
Eleanor S. Boll

Families are important for the transmission of the general culture to its members. However, as Bossard and Boll point out, there are alternative ways of doing things that have a socializing effect, which are specific to an individual family. These activities become the rituals and repeated behaviors that make up the unique mini-culture of each family. In a review of families of an earlier day, the authors illustrate how these customs and behavior patterns shape a life style within a family.

At the present time, it is believed that one of the most important remaining functions of the family is the transmission of the culture to successive generations. In a civilization as complex as ours this function must be highly selective in its performance. It has become, then, most important to discover exactly how culture is transmitted in the family and upon what bases selectivity rests. Ralph Linton has classified the content of culture into three categories: Universals, Specialties, and Alternatives. This last class of culture content has special significance in its transference in the modern family. For, though Universals are common to all "sane, adult members of one culture group,"

> There are in every culture a considerable number of traits (Alternatives) which are shared by certain individuals but which are not common to all members of the society ... the elements ... varying from the special and quite atypical ideas and habits of a particular family to such things as different schools of painting or sculpture. Aside from the nature of the participation in them, all these Alternatives have this in common: they represent different reactions to the same situations or different techniques for achieving the same ends. The cultures of

From James H. Bossard and Eleanor S. Boll, *Ritual In Family Living* (Philadelphia: University of Pennsylvania Press, 1950), pp. 39–49. Reprinted by permission of University of Pennsylvania Press.

small societies living under primitive conditions usually include only a moderate number of such Alternatives, while in such a culture as our own they are very plentiful. . . . Certain elements are transmitted in family lines. The members of one family may be taught to say a particular form of grace at meals . . . while other families transmit a grace of a different sort. . . . Most of the descriptions of cultures which are now extant are heavily weighted on the side of Universals and Specialties. This is due partly to the difficulty of obtaining information about the Alternatives, partly to a quite natural desire to make the description as coherent as possible. The only Alternatives which will be noted will usually be those which have large numbers of adherents. As a result, the participation of the average individual in the culture of his society is made to appear much more complete than it actually is, and the differences between different groups of individuals are minimized. Any one who has come to know a "primitive society" well can testify that its members do not show the dead level of cultural conformity which these reports suggest.[1]

If this be true, how much more misleading are reports of contemporary civilized groups if the Alternatives which are so much more numerous here are not thoroughly considered. Family rituals, as found in autobiographies, seem to be a fruitful field for investigating some of these Alternatives as they are selected and passed on to children. Four different aspects of such transmission are discussed in the following paragraphs: (1) A ritual was a family's specific conclusion, from its own experience, of the best way to meet a certain situation. Thus there was passed on to children, through ritual, a selected way of doing a thing—an overt behavior pattern. (2) The behavior pattern of a ritual was an expression of certain attitudes, largely parental attitudes. The behavior, then, became a concrete means of attitude communication between parents and children. (3) A ritual was a behavior pattern with a *purpose*. The whole ritual scheme of a family, therefore, objectified into behavior, and was one means of transmitting the family direction, or goals. (4) The material content of rituals, family-selected, became cultural tools for social participation of the children who inherited them. Though these four aspects are not wholly disparate, they will be treated separately here and, at the sacrifice of "the quite natural desire to make the description as coherent as possible," as many differences as material and space permit will be presented.

1. The autobiographers clearly showed rituals as selective transmitters of behavior patterns on the basis of race, creed, social class, economic status, educational level, urban or rural life, and other individual differences. Traditional Jewish rituals in the home, for instance, were mentioned by three authors. In one home they were preserved faithfully and passed down as an honorable heritage. In a second home, they were abandoned for the family, but taught to the children so that they might observe certain forms in the presence of respected orthodox Jewish guests. The third author was deprived of all knowledge of such ritual at home, and was repelled by it in his grandparents' home, since it was so different from his family's adopted Anglo-Saxon rites. Walter Damrosch and his wife preserved the old-country traditional Christmas ritual with a determination to pass it on intact to their children.

Many of the different forms surrounding Christmas rites varied according to traditional ethnic practices. The opening of gifts on Christmas Eve, as one example, was a procedure in many families of German descent, while Christmas-morning present-opening was more characteristic of English-descended families. Lest this seem insignificant, the reader may undeceive himself by discussing this difference with acquaintances. If he is one who does the opening on Christmas Eve, he may be surprised at the ferocity with which he is accused of "cheating" by a confirmed Christmas-morning opener. The whole family behavior on Sunday differed markedly on the basis of the sect, or individual family creed. Other, more intimate, rituals transmitted as obligatory patterns of life maintain:

> that small children do not eat at table with parents; that they are not only present at the table but help with serving; that the whole family is waited upon by servants; that the servant sits at table with the family except when company comes; that meals are strictly utilitarian until Sunday guests make dinner an elaborate and proper social occasion; that children participate in guest situations only as silent, well-behaved onlookers; that children always entertain guests by showing off their talents.[2]

Ritualistic behavior passed on to children the practices:

> that money is earned by the father, owned by him, and doled out at his pleasure to wife and children, who have no real rights as concerns family income; that it is earned by father who hands it over to mother to keep the household running; that money is to be enjoyed and spent freely by the whole family when it is obtainable, and is unimportant when it is scarce; that the whole family participates in paying financial obligations to others first, and then lives carefully on what is left; that one never makes a purchase without first comparing all advertisements to buy at the lowest price; that one buys only during bargain sales.

Through rituals, authors came to know:

> that the bathroom is a place where one considerately takes turns, and calls out frankly in cases of emergency; that it is a place into which one sneaks surreptitiously and from which it is a profound shame to be seen emerging.

Rituals defined that:

> family recreation means games, reading aloud, plays or concerts at home; or necessitates "going out": visits to friends, theatres, circuses or musicals.

They set as the one right pattern of life for some children:

> that a family must go away from home for a summer vacation each year; that Saturdays are "fun" days; that certain holidays are celebrated and others ignored; that one takes a bath and changes underclothes at certain set intervals, daily, weekly; that one has a "best" suit of clothing reserved for special occasions; that one "dresses" for dinner each night; that a particular hour of the day is proper for rising, eating, retiring.

This is by no means an exhaustive list of the elements of obligatory family behavior passed on to the autobiographers through ritual, or of the differences from family to family. But these few examples may be sufficient to imply the importance of ritual in such a process.

2. Every ritual found in the case material conveyed to the reader some transferable parental attitude. The variety cannot even be intimated here. But a few of the most common were these:

(a) Writers commented on their own attitudes toward illness in terms of the procedures which surrounded such occasions in their homes. Frazier Hunt writes:

> It was always a joy to be just a little sick when Auntie [who was "Mother" to him] was around to take care of you. Not that I particularly liked to soak my feet in a mustard bath or to have my throat rubbed with goose grease and wrapped in a red flannel rag, but I did like the outpouring of affection and concern. Toward evening Auntie'd come into the bedroom with a pan of warm water, a washcloth, and a towel, and ever so gently she'd bathe my face and hands and comb my hair. Then she'd disappear and in a few minutes return with a tray and a white napkin over it, and there'd be a poached egg, milk toast, and a cup of sassafras tea.[3]

Corra Harris concludes a description of her family's rites during illness by saying: "I always felt blessed and happy at such times."[4] In contrast to these cheerful and philosophical attitudes toward indisposition, Hugh Faussett describes his father's "morbid" ritual. Hugh's mother had died, and the child himself was of weak constitution. His father:

> ... could indulge his anxiety only by insisting that I should be swaddled in flannel, should be surfeited with milk, and never be exposed without a thick coat to the dangers of a cold wind. This fear of the elements was to become more and more pronounced ... until he shrank from every draught as the sure precursor of a chill and refused, even in mild weather, to have any windows open in the room in which he sat. With characteristic thoroughness he would have rooms "aired" at regular intervals when no one was occupying them, and then once again seal them against the cold currents which he feared.[5]

(b) Living as they did at a time when much of an early formal education was received at home, nine autobiographers described rituals surrounding it. Two authors whose parents made them learn their lessons while standing, and who stood beside them while they studied, mentioned their great awe of "learning," but felt oppressed by the responsibility. Others considered the education process as a grand and challenging game. These people were accustomed, when children, to having a whole large family gather around a table together each evening for a certain period, and engage in a kind of family-learning competition.

(c) Discipline, through regularity of practices, became a reasonable, constructive technique, such as a lecture from Father to explain the costs of vice;

an amusing distraction from sin, such as the forcing of battling brothers to laugh together and so forget wrath; and a vengeful device, such as the hanging up of children by a roller towel, leaving them uncomfortable and helpless, with feet dangling.

(d) Through Sunday observances and family religious rites, the religion they symbolized came to be regarded as humane, valuable, and otherworldly; and also as fearful, repressive, and inescapable.

(e) Interesting examples of the communication of contrasting attitudes toward nudity and intimate functions of the body appeared in the rituals. The Milnes, at one time, had a bathroom with two tubs in it, and the rite was for Ken and Alan to "toss" for the larger tub, then play a game of "catch" with the soap, while keeping a sponge in place between the tub and the backs of their necks. A second author, however, describes his daily visits to the bathroom as a fearsome and secret rite between him and his nurse alone. So obligatory were the selected personnel and the furtiveness that when once another servant offered to substitute, the boy resisted to the point of humiliating accident.

(f) Even attitudes toward how one should greet a new day—eagerly, cheerfully, energetically; or morosely and reluctantly with as much procrastinating as possible—were communicated to the autobiographers by the habitual ways in which their parents awakened them, and the procedures surrounding their daily rising.

Small though this sample of attitudes be, even this list is significant in terms of individual differences. A psychiatrist could perhaps draw a fairly lifelike sketch solely on the basis of how a man feels about health, education, discipline, religion, the body and its functions, and how he behaves when he gets up in the morning.

3. One of the analytic steps in this study was to take the entire ritual structure of each family out of its context, strip if of any qualitative or attitudinal comments from the author, and let it stand alone as an individual-family framework of customary behavior in many recurring situations. This step proved to be very rewarding in that these stark frameworks let in light upon the directioning of family life with undoubtedly more clarity and veracity than the writers (beset by incomplete memory, inhibitions, and exhibitionism) could attain were they asked specifically to describe their family's goals and purposes.[6] As an example, a comparison of two of these excerpts will have to suffice. These two were selected on the basis of differences in ritual structure. But it is of interest to note that both families were religious, well-to-do, and well educated.

(a) The Carter family[7] enjoyed these rituals:

> (1) daily—a cold bath; a breakfast for which every member of the family *had* to be on time; grace before the meal; family prayers after breakfast with the servants present and a very set routine; every-evening family gatherings with Father or Mother telling stories or reading aloud, a musical program by the children or games played with the whole family; bedtime for the children at nine o'clock, with individual and simple prayers before bed.

(2) Sunday—church; family prayers postponed till evening; a day of not doing things they did on weekdays; a chafing-dish supper, often with friends, prepared by Mother since servants were dismissed early; family prayers without the servants.

(3) holidays—"gave up" something for Lent; "gorged" on Thanksgiving; had tree, presents, filled stockings, and carols on Christmas; fireworks on Fourth of July, which was a day restricted to family alone, on other holidays guests were invited.

(4) vacation—visit away from home inevitable for at least a month each summer, though their home town was a summer resort.

(5) medical—phosphate which it was a deadly sin not to drink before it stopped fizzing; castor oil with orange juice; "the basin"; "the croup kettle"; one trip to Boston to the hospital to see each new baby in the family; trips to Boston at regular intervals to visit dentist.

(6) discipline—recitation by quarreling brothers of a Bible verse which always made them laugh and make up; mouthwashing with soap; a lecture in Father's study; confinement for meditation and memorization of hymns.

(7) play—children teased Mother by calling her "Allie"; Mother teased Father by tickling; Father drove children out of his and Mother's bedroom at night by starting to take off his trousers.

(b) In contrast to the Carter family, the Hare family had these rituals.[8]

(1) daily—breakfast at 8 with Mother in dining room with doors open on to garden terrace; lessons with Mother or other relative after breakfast, a time of screaming, crying, and hearty bangs over the knuckles; at 12 a walk with Mother which was always in the nature of a lesson in botany, or a walk to a girls' school where Mother sat in the courtyard overhung with laburnums and taught the children; at 1, dinner, always roast mutton and rice pudding until, before the child was 6, the practice was instituted of elaborating on the delicious puddings to follow, only to have them snatched away just as the child was prepared to eat his, and he was then told to take them to some poor person in the village; after lunch the child read aloud, Josephus and Froissart's *Chronicles;* at 3 a drive in the carriage with Mother to visit distant cottages, often ending at the Rectory; at 5 a half hour for the child to "amuse himself," during which he usually "heard the cat's lessons"; at 5:30 tea with his nurse in the servants' hall; evenings, Mother read aloud to old parents, at which time, if books were beyond child's comprehension, he was permitted to play with some ivory fish.

(2) religious—fasting on Wednesdays and Fridays, on which day there was no butter or pudding.

(3) holiday—Christmas: inappropriate presents from family with necessary show of gratitude from child; usual pastimes cleared away; required to sit for hours reading Foxe's *Book of Martyrs;* two 8-mile walks to church; evening visit to the Rectory.

(4) allowance—no regular time or amount set, but a periodic rapid calculation by Mother as to what child needed and an allotment of just that much and no more.

These total ritual structures in their comparison speak amply for themselves of the ways in which family selective culture of the most subjective sort can insinuate itself into the lives of children through rituals. Seen also in the ritual

313

structures of families studied were, among others, these prime motives: the guiding of a talented member into a chosen career; social climbing; social respectability; worldly sophistication; and scrupulous unconventionality.

4. The material content of family rites varied 100 per cent in the autobiographers' case histories. But certain generalized similarities and differences were discernible, from family to family, in the tools which these rites offered to children.

(a) In the case of the many rituals which involved reading aloud, some families used only religious books; others only the classics, or histories; some, light novels of an admittedly "trashy" kind. Several families read all types of literature and also current newspapers and periodicals. In the case of an isolated farm family, reading was strictly of the last-mentioned kind, as being the family's only contact with the living outside world. Some authors mentioned no reading rites at all. Some wrote their own family literature.

(b) Music formed a large part of the content of rituals. For some families music meant family concerts; to others it was a program at a concert hall; and to still others, snatches of songs upon rising and retiring. Families specialized in learning one instrument, or in having each member play a different one. The kinds of composition made familiar through ritual varied from the ponderous classics and opera, through sentimental melodies and folk songs, to collections of bawdy sea ballads.

(c) Family games offered to children a significantly selected list of accomplishments. There were, for instance, in different families a noticeable emphasis upon: "gentlemen's" sports; Bible bees; card games; the displaying of individual artistic talents. Several families tended strictly to out-of-door games of a simple nature, the walk being the thing. One family played a game of languages; they spoke Roumanian one day, German the next, and Greek the third day. A few families played dinner-table question-and-answer games with rewards for correctness; one restricting questions to the subject of opera; the others including a wide range of cultural subjects and current events.

(d) The actual roles which children took in rituals became tools for useful action. For many children—and most of these were farm-living and/or from modest-income families—these consisted of knowing how to work, in the house or on the farm. In a second group of families, the children learned how to conform and how to study. These were usually small but ambitious families. And in a third group, children learned how to express themselves individually, while at the same time participating socially. Children given these tools were ordinarily from larger families, but with comfortable incomes and social standing.

(e) Finally, the range of social tools found in the ritual of any one family must be considered. For comparison's sake, two extremes are presented. Gertrude Lawrence, the incomparable actress, described four childhood rituals: two were concerned with how to be respectable, though devastatingly poor; and the other two were leisure-time rituals which featured the child as an infant phenomenon of an actress. To read her later life, surprisingly enough, is to read almost exactly what one might guess as a snap judgment solely on

314

the basis of her having early acquired such tools.[9] As a contrast, John Carter, whose whole family ritual structure was briefed a few pages earlier, writes this:

> If anything, our home was too happy and too comfortable. Its outlook was frankly romantic—or perhaps truly realistic—for it really preferred good food, comfortable beds, good literature, good conversation and good music to the demands of the dusty world. . . . It was hard to leave such a sanctuary for the $30-a-week jobs and the hall bedrooms of city boarding houses, and the bitter struggle for riches and existence in the 1920's. We were, if anything, the heirs of an imperial tradition and were admirably equipped to serve as government officials or colonial administrators or something Kiplingesque and comfortably self-sacrificing, rather than to go out in a competitive industrial society to earn a living.[10]

NOTES

[1] Ralph Linton, *The Study of Man,* New York, D. Appleton-Century Company, 1936, pp. 273–79.

[2] For a discussion of the role of the family dinner table in culture transmission, see James H. S. Bossard, *The Sociology of Child Development,* New York, Harper & Brothers, 1948, chapter VIII.

[3] Frazier Hunt, *One American,* New York, Simon and Schuster, Inc., 1938, p. 17.

[4] Corra Harris, *My Book and Heart,* Houghton Mifflin Co., 1924, pp. 7–8.

[5] Hugh I'Anson Faussett, *A Modern Prelude,* London, Jonathan Cape, 1936, pp. 35–36.

[6] The authors suggest that students collecting personal-history documents by the method of presenting topical outlines to the subjects would find it profitable to include the topic of family rituals whenever part of their research is family goals, values, ambitions, etc. For here some of them will show up in terms of customary behavior and may be a helpful and enlightening supplement to what the subject *thinks* are his family goals, etc.

[7] John Franklin Carter, *The Rectory Family,* New York, Coward-McCann, Inc., 1937.

[8] Hare, *op. cit.*

[9] Gertrude Lawrence, *A Star Danced,* New York, Doubleday, Doran and Company, Inc., 1945.

[10] Carter, *op. cit.,* pp. 5–6.

Husbands and Wives

Elliot Liebow

Poverty and job discrimination can take a terrible toll on the male-female partnership, as this selection from Liebow's study of a Black ghetto, Tally's Corner, illustrates. Perhaps the loss of pride and self-worth (ingredients possibly essential to being responsible to and supportive of another) suffer most of all. The result is a home culture in which interactions can, at best, be described as chaotic and where disappointments in the marital partnership are deemed so inevitable that many will not risk such a formal commitment.

A few of the streetcorner men expect to get married sooner or later. A few are married. Most of the men have tried marriage and found it wanting.

To be married is to be formally, legally married, to have a marriage certificate, to "have papers." The rights and duties conferred by marriage are clear-cut, unambiguous; they are those rights and duties set forth in the marriage vows and by the courts. Individuals may fail to exercise their rights or neglect their duties but they do not deny them.

Men and women are careful to distinguish between marriage on the one hand and "common law," "shacking up," "living with" and other consensual unions on the other. There is, of course, a large overlap. The rights and duties which attach to consensual unions are patterned after those which attach to marriage and, in practice, some consensual unions are publicly indistinguishable from marriage. There are two principal differences. First, the rights and duties of consensual unions generally have less public force behind them. The result is that an act which violates both the marital and consensual union invokes a stronger sanction in the case of marriage. A second difference is that, in consensual unions, rights and duties are less clearly defined, especially at the edges. The result is that while everyone would agree that a given act stands in violation of the marital relationship, there could be—and frequently

From Elliot Liebow, *Tally's Corner* (Boston: Little, Brown and Company, 1967), pp. 103, 104, 106–07, 108–10, 116–21, 121–24, 126–31. Reprinted by permission of Little, Brown and Company.

is—widespread disagreement as to whether the same act stands in violation of a consensual union.

. . . .

A partner to a consensual union may explicitly point out the distinction between their own relationship and marriage in order to challenge the other's right or as justification for his own behavior. Thus, one woman walked away in a huff from a man who was trying to get her to accompany him with the reminder that *"I'm your girl friend, not your wife."* And Leroy, at a time when he had been living with Charlene for several months, conceded that his rights were compromised by the fact that they were not formally, legally married. They had had an argument which brought their relationship almost to the breaking point. Later the same day Leroy left a note for Charlene which concluded: "I have decided to let you think it over until 6 p.m. Sunday. Until then, you can go where you want to, do what you want to, because like you said, I don't have any papers on you yet." [1]

The distinction between marriage and consensual union is also carefully drawn in the labels one applies to the incumbents in the two relationships. The terms husband and wife, for example, are almost always reserved for formally married persons. Thus, Sea Cat explains that "Priscilla is my old lady. My wife lives over in Northeast."

. . . .

Thus marriage, as compared with consensual union, is clearly the superior relationship. Marriage has higher status than consensual union and greater respectability. Not only are its rights and duties better defined and supported with greater public force but only through marriage can a man and woman lay legitimate claim to being husband and wife.

But as the man on the streetcorner looks at the reality of marriage as it is experienced day in and day out by husbands and wives, his universe tells him that marriage does not work. He knows that it did not for his own mother and father and for the parents of most of his contemporaries. He knows that Lonny strangled his wife and almost paid with his own life as well. He sees Clarence trying to keep his wife from getting at the woman she has found him with while two of their four children look on in frightened silence. He knows that Tom Tom, whose busboy job did not pay enough to support his wife and children, moved away from his family so they would become eligible for ADC. He sees Leroy and Charlene circling slowly on the sidewalk, with Charlene holding a broken Coke bottle thrust in front of her and Leroy pawing at her with his right arm wrapped in his jacket. He sees Tonk standing on the corner where his wife works as a waitress, afraid himself to take a job because the word is going around that she is "cutting out" on him. He sees Shirley bury her face in her hands and shudder, partly perhaps because

317

the Christmas wind has again ripped away the blanket nailed across the window but mainly because she and Richard are trying to decide whether to send the children to Junior Village[2] or take them to the waiting room at Union Station for the night. And at two in the morning, he sees Leroy and Charlene, with Leroy holding their year-old son in his arms, anxiously looking for someone, anyone, to take them to Children's Hospital because their sleeping baby had just been bitten on the cheek by a rat.

These are the things he sees and hears and knows of streetcorner marriage: the disenchantment, sometimes bitter, of those who were or still are married; the public and private fights between husband and wife and the sexual jealousy that rages around them; husbands who cannot feed, clothe and house their wives and children and husbands who have lost their will to do so; the terror of husband and wife who suddenly find themselves unable to ward off attacks on the health and safety of their children. Nor is there—to redeem all this even in part—*a single marriage among the streetcorner men and their women which they themselves recognize as a "good" marriage.*

· · · ·

WHY MARRIAGE DOES NOT WORK

The Theory of Manly Flaws

As the men look back on their broken marriages, they tend to explain the failure in terms of their personal inability or unwillingness to adjust to the built-in demands of the marriage relationship. Sea Cat, for example, admits to a group of men on the corner that his marriage broke up because he simply *could not bring himself to subordinate his independence to the demands of a joint undertaking.*

> I was married once and once was enough. I can't live that way, having someone tell me when to get up, when to eat, "go here," "go there." Man, I've got to be master. I've got to be kingpin.[3]

Stoopy blamed the failure of his marriage on his weakness for whiskey and would tell how angry his wife used to become when he got drunk and spent or gambled away the rent money. She put up with him longer than he had a right to expect her to, he said. Even now, when she comes on Saturday mornings to pick up money for the children, she says she is willing to try again if he will promise never to get drunk, but he knows he could not stick to such a promise, even though he loves her and the children and would like them to get back together.

Stoopy, like Sea Cat, showed no rancor when his wife took him to court for nonsupport. Stoopy and Sea Cat had let their wives down; they were the ones who had violated the marital agreement and their wives were doing what they had a perfect right to do.

318

Tally felt much the same way. When he was living with his wife, his drinking and "bad language" rightly disturbed her. Also, he couldn't stay away from other women. But he still loved her and if she would give him another chance, he would "put down" all those things which come so easily to a man but which a wife is justified in refusing to accept in a husband.

> ... I love my wife. When I go to bed at night [it's as if] she's with me, and my kids are, too. Deep down in my heart, I believe she's coming back to me. I really believe it. And if she do, I'm going to throw out all these other women. I'm going to change my whole life.

On close inspection, it is difficult to accept these self-analyses of marital failure at full face value. Quite apart from the fact that it seems to be the men who leave their wives, rather than the other way around, these public assumptions of blame express a modesty that is too self-serving to be above suspicion. In each instance, the man is always careful to attribute his inadequacies as a husband to his inability to slough off one or another attribute of manliness, such as independence of spirit, a liking for whiskey, or an appetite for a variety of women. They trace their failures as husbands directly to their weaknesses as men, to their manly flaws.[4]

Simple and self-serving, this theory of manly flaws to account for the failure of marriage has a strong appeal for the men on the streetcorner.[5] But the theory is too pat, too simple; one senses that it violates the principle of sufficient cause. The relational complexities of marriage and its breakdown want answers which touch on these complexities. A more detailed examination of sexual infidelity—the largest and most common manly flaw—suggests that these flaws are not too damaging in themselves but that each is rooted in a host of antecedents and consequences which reach into the very stuff of marriage.

Sexual Infidelity as a Manly Flaw

Tally's contention that he would "throw out all those women" if his wife would only return to him was acceptable as a declaration of good intentions, but none of the men on the streetcorner would accept it as a description of what would happen in fact. One of the most widespread and strongly supported views the men have of themselves and others in that men are, by nature, not monogamous; that no man can be satisfied with only one woman at a time.[6] This view holds that, quite apart from his desire to exploit women, the man seeks them out because it is his nature to do so. This "nature" that shapes his sex life, however, is not human nature but rather an animality which the human overlay cannot quite cover. The man who has a wife or other woman continues to seek out others because *he has too much "dog" in him.*

> Men are just dogs! We shouldn't call ourselves human, we're just dogs, dogs, dogs! They call me a dog, 'cause that's what I am, but so is everybody else— hopping around from woman to woman, just like a dog.

"It don't matter how much a man loves his wife and kids," said Clarence, "he's gonna keep on chasing other women. . . . A man's got too much dog in him." The others agreed with Clarence and remained in complete agreement throughout the discussion which followed.[7]

The dog in man which impels him to seek out an ever-expanding universe of sex is a push-pull affair. A "new" woman is, by common consent, more stimulating and satisfying sexually than one's own wife or girl friend. The man also sees himself performing better with "new meat" or "fresh meat" than with someone familiar to him sexually. Men in their late twenties or older pooh-pooh the suggestion that they are not as good sexually as they were in their late teens or early twenties, maintaining that their performance in any given sex encounter depends less on age or any other personal factor than on the woman they happen to be with. Variety is not only the spice of sex life, it is an aphrodisiac which elevates the man's sexual performance. The point is perhaps best made by a standard joke which frequently appeared when the subject of sexual competence came up. It was told more as a fact of life than as a subject of humor.

> An old man and his wife were sitting on their porch, rocking slowly and watching a rooster mount one hen, then another. When the rooster had repeated this performance several times, the old woman turned to her husband and said, "Why can't you be like that rooster?"
> "If you look close," the old man said, "you'll see that that rooster ain't knockin' off the same hen each time. If he had to stick with the same one, he wouldn't do no better than me."

In attempting to sustain simultaneous relationships with one's wife and one or more other women, it frequently happens that one such relationship compromises the other. The marriage relationship, in particular, may suffer sexual damage. The man who admits this is not thereby diminished. He does not have to—nor does he—boast of the frequency with which he can engage in sex nor of the number of times he can achieve an orgasm in any given encounter. In special circumstances, he can even admit to not being able to engage in sex and, in doing so, enhance his image as a man who is successful with women. This is the case, for example, when the men talk about coming home from an engagement with another woman and being unable or unwilling to meet the sexual demands of their wives or women they are living with.

This predicament is freely admitted to in an almost boastful manner. On the streetcorner, it is a source of great merriment, with each man claiming to have a characteristic way of dealing with it. Sea Cat claims that he usually feigns sleep or illness; Clarence insists on staying up to watch the late show on TV, waiting for his wife to give up and go to sleep; Richard manufactures an argument and sleeps anywhere but in bed with Shirley; others feign drunkenness, job exhaustion, or simply stay away from home until their wives are asleep or until morning when the household is up and beginning another day.

. . . .

Another Point of View

Not all the men hold to the theory of manly flaws in accounting for the failure of their marriage. Sometimes, even those who do may give alternate explanations. In general, those who do not blame themselves for the failure of their marriage blame their wives, rather than family, friends, marriage itself, or the world at large.

. . . .

To pay the rent, buy the groceries, and provide for the other necessary goods and services is the sine qua non of a good husband. There are, of course, several possible alternate sources of financial support—the wife herself, friends or relatives, or public or private agencies—but it remains peculiarly the (good) husband's responsibility, not anyone else's.[8]

The primacy ascribed to financial support derives from two analytically separable sources of value: the simple use value, in and of itself, of supporting and maintaining the lives of one's wife and children; and the expressive or symbolic value associated with providing this support.[9] Men and women both agree that providing financial support has a weightiness that goes beyond its simple use value. One of the men was talking to several others, derogating someone he didn't particularly care for. "But one thing you got to say," he conceded, "when he was living with her, he stone[10] took care of her and the children."

By itself, the plain fact of supporting one's wife and children defines the principal obligation of a husband. But the expressive value carried by the providing of this support elevates the husband to manliness. He who provides for his wife and children has gone a long way toward meeting his obligations to his family as he sees them. Drinking, gambling, or seeing other women may detract from but cannot, by themselves, nullify his performance. Both as husband and father, he has gone a long way toward proving himself a man.

Few married men, however, do in fact support their families over sustained periods of time. Money is chronically in short supply and chronically a source of dissension in the home. Financial support for herself and her children remains one of the principal unmet expectations of the wife. Moreover, although providing such support would be, so far as the husband is concerned, necessary and sufficient, the wife—who seldom gets even this much—wants more, much more.

She wants him to be a man in her terms, a husband and father according to her lights. It is not enough that he simply give money for her and the children's support, then step away until the next time he shares his pay day with them. She wants him to join them as a full-time member of the family, to participate in their affairs, to take an active interest in her and the children, in their activities, in their development as individuals. She wants his ultimate

321

loyalty to be to her and the children, and she wants this loyalty to be public knowledge. She wants the family to present a united front to the outside world.

Most important of all, perhaps, she wants him to be *head of the family,* not only to take an interest and demonstrate concern but to take responsibility and to make decisions. She wants him to take charge, to "wear the pants," to lay down the rules of their day-to-day life and enforce them. She wants him to take over, to be someone she can lean on. Alas, she ends up standing alone or, even worse perhaps, having to hold him up as well.

Wryly, and with a bitterness born of experience, Shirley smiles to herself and says,

> I used to lean on Richard. Like when I was having the baby, I leaned on him but he wasn't there and I fell down.... Now, I don't lean on him anymore. I pretend I lean, but I'm not leaning.

Shirley had not always surrendered with quiet resignation. Like Lorena and other women, she too had tried to cajole, tease, shame, encourage, threaten or otherwise attempt to make her man a man. Lorena said that in the beginning of her marriage, she used to pray to God, "Make John a good husband and father." Then she realized that "that's not God's job, that's my job," and she changed her prayers accordingly: "Lord, this is Lorena Patterson. You know all about me. You know what I need."

So Lorena took on herself the job of making John a good husband and father, but it didn't work. She blames herself for the failure of her marriage but she blames John, too. John was a boy, she said, not a man. He wasn't the "master."

> I want the man to wear the pants but John made me wear the pants, too. His pants had a crease in them, mine had a ruffle, but I was wearing the pants, too.

NOTES

[1] The time of this episode (October 1962) is especially significant. Charlene was then in her ninth month with Leroy's child but even the imminence of parenthood could not elevate their respective rights and duties to those of husband and wife.

[2] Washington, D.C.'s home for neglected and dependent children.

[3] Women, too, want the man to be "master," but the word means one thing to husbands, another to wives.

[4] "... people do not simply want to excel; they want to excel as a man or as a woman, that is to say, in those respects which, in their culture, are symbolic of their respective sex roles.... Even when they adopt behavior which is considered disreputable by conventional standards, *the tendency is to be disreputable in ways that are characteristically masculine and feminine.*" (Emphasis added.) Albert K. Cohen, *Delinquent Boys,* p. 138.

[5] In an imaginative discussion of adaptations to failure in the evolution of delinquent subcultures, Cloward and Ohlin hypothesize that "collective adaptations are likely to emerge where failure is attributed to the inadequacy of existing institutional arrangements; conversely, when failure is attributed to personal de-

322

ficiencies, solitary adaptations are more likely." Richard A. Cloward and Lloyd E. Ohlin, *Delinquency and Opportunity: A Theory of Delinquent Gangs,* p. 125. The "theory of manly flaws," when seen as an adaptation to failure in marriage, does not appear to fit this hypothesis, or at least suggests another possibility: a collective adaptation in which the participants agree to attribute failure to themselves as individuals.

[6] "In lower social levels there is a somewhat bitter acceptance of the idea that the male is basically promiscuous and that he is going to have extramarital intercourse, whether or not his wife or society objects." Alfred C. Kinsey, Wardell B. Pomeroy, and Clyde E. Martin, "Social Level and Sexual Outlet," p. 307.

[7] But a few minutes later, when the question arose as to whether women have as much dog in them as men, the men were less sure of their answers and disagreed among themselves. One said that women have as much dog in them as men but that a good woman also has a lot of pride and that's what keeps her from acting the same way men do. Another said that women have less dog in them, hence their more conservative sexual behavior. A third opinion held that women had more dog than men but that this was obscured by the double standard which inhibited women's freedom of action. And still another held that some women have less dog than men, some more, and that this accounted for the division of women into "good" and "bad."

[8] Providing financial support is so intimately associated with the husband that, on one curious occasion, financial support was argued to be one of two paramount considerations in defining sex and kinship roles. Charlene was pregnant but she and Leroy were not yet married when Leroy got into a heated argument with Beverly, the bull-dagger (Lesbian) who was living with Charlene's mother, Malvina. They cursed one another and Leroy took out his knife. Beverly was indignant, and pointed out that Leroy should be more respectful because she, Beverly, was his stepfather-in-law! Her argument rested on the twin assertions that she was sleeping with Malvina and supporting her.

Beverly should have left well enough alone. Leroy was willing to acknowledge some merit in her argument but when Beverly claimed she was even more of a man than Leroy, this was too much. Laughing about it the next day, Leroy recalls what followed: "I said, 'If you're more of a man than I am, pull your meat out and lay it on this rail.' I put mine on the rail and she said, 'I'm not that common. I don't do my lovin' that way.'"

[9] Studies of a variety of lower-class populations emphasize that, for the man, self-respect, status, self-esteem, etc., is intimately bound up with the ability to support one's family: "The man's role is financial and his status in the household depends rather stringently on his ability as a breadwinner: his self-respect is closely tied to his financial independence." Josephine Klein, *Samples from English Cultures,* Vol. I, p. 164; "A man who . . . is unable to carry out his breadwinning role . . . falls a great distance in the estimation of himself, his wife and children, and his fellows." J. H. Robb, *Working-Class Anti-Semite,* quoted in *Samples from English Cultures,* Vol. I, p. 164; "The Negro man . . . cannot provide the economic support that is a *principal male function* in American society. As a result, the woman becomes the head of the family, and the man a marginal appendage who deserts or is rejected by his wife . . ." Herbert J. Gans, "The Negro Family: Reflections on the Moynihan Report," p. 48.

[10] An intensive, in this case meaning "really took care . . ."

Black Muslim and
Negro Christian
Family Relationships

Harry Edwards

As indicated in the first article in this chapter, family cultures consist of many acts, often repeated and ritualized and so taken for granted that they almost have a separate vitality. Where do these habitual ways of acting come from? Edwards contrasts Christian and Muslim blacks to illustrate how their varying family behavior patterns—the roles of the husband and wife in the family, child-rearing practices, relationships with in-laws, and general outlook on family life—can be traced to the values and belief systems of each religion.

The notion that the Nation of Islam has possibly exerted positive as well as negative influences upon its members became the originating idea out of which the major questions for this study emerged. Specifically, the study focused upon a comparison between Muslim and lower-class Negro Christian families.

Due largely to the work of Frazier, many Americans became aware of the chaos and instability extant within many lower-class American Negro families. Frazier portrays the lower-class Negro family as matriarchal in structure, often common-law in nature, and characterized by an adult male figure functioning almost solely in a procreative capacity.[1]

From Harry Edwards, "Black Muslim and Negro Christian Family Relationships," *Journal of Marriage and the Family*, November, 1968, pp. 604–11. Reprinted by permission of the author and The National Council on Family Relations. The study reported here is a revised presentation of the author's Master's Thesis, "The Black Muslim Family: A Comparative Study." The research for the thesis was partially supported by the Departmental research funds and was conducted January, 1965, through January, 1966, inclusive. Appreciation is expressed to Alvin Rudoff, Ph.D., Director of the Center for Interdisciplinary Studies, San Jose State College, for his aid in the preparation of this paper.

Although there have been many studies that have enlarged upon some of the specific aspects of Frazier's work, in the nearly two decades since its publication, there has been no study done on the lower-class American Negro of comparable scope or sociological import. Since the surprisingly rapid expansion of an isolated incident aboard a bus in Montgomery, Alabama, into what has become known as the "Negro Revolt" and the occurrence of other significant events, it is doubtful that the nature and structure of the lower-class Negro family, as described by Frazier, have remained unchanged. Indeed there is some recent evidence, albeit controversial, that tends to substantiate the oft-voiced speculation that the Negro family is in the process of still further deterioration.[2] Many students of the race problem in America are becoming more aware of the role the instability of the lower-class Negro family plays in hindering the implementation of some practical solutions to the problems involved.

Although the civil rights movement has, for the most part, had as a goal integration of the black American into the existing social fabric, it has also given rise to an abundance of what have been termed "black Nationalist" organizations. These organizations have not stressed the need for a racially integrated society but have advocated the development of a racially and socially plural society—as in the case of several so-called Afro-American organizations—or they have pushed for complete racial separatism—physical and social—as is the case with the Nation of Islam. Most of these black Nationalist organizations have developed special programs of study and training to prepare themselves to assume roles in their unique version of the "great society." One aspect of this training and preparation has been the attempt to alter the pattern of family relationships characterizing the lower-class Negro family. There are increasing signs, particularly in large urban centers, that these attempts have been at least partially successful.

METHODOLOGY

The basic design for the study involved the comparison of matched pairs of families—one group of families affiliated with the Nation of Islam, the other group affiliated with lower-class Negro Christian churches. The major technique employed was the focused interview supplemented by a great deal of participant observation and the occasional use of informants. The interviews focused on four specific areas of family relations: husband-wife, extended kinships, parent-child, and family-community.

The sample consisted of 14 families from each group. They were matched for mean spouse educational attainment, mean spouse income, race, and the factor of having a minimum mean time of four years in active affiliation with their respective religious organizations. The highest level of educational attainment for the families was 12 and one-half years. Most were considerably lower. The bulk of the spouses were educated in southern public schools. The yearly family income ranged from about $2,000 to a high of $5,500. All members of the sample lived in the same geographical area and were phenotypically Negroid.[3] Each family had at least a minimum mean time in active affiliation with its church or mosque of four years; however, the Muslims as a group averaged five and one-half years while the Christians' average was 11 years. The lesser mean active affiliation time among families of the former group may be due to a number of factors, among which are the traditional religious posture of the American Negro and the more recent proselytizing success of the Nation of Islam.

Although detailed information of all of the families involved in this study is not presently readily available, there are sufficient data to substantiate the following brief statements regarding the general occupational and family profiles of the Muslim and Christian groups.

On the whole, Muslim families were wage-earning families in contrast to Christian families which tended to be non-wage earners. The types of jobs held by Muslims ranged from low-income jobs—selling papers and manual part-time labor—to relatively high-income jobs—steady factory work and fork-lift operations. Those Muslims holding low-income or part-time jobs usually held more than one job. For instance, it was not unusual to find a Muslim selling papers during morning work hours and busing dishes during the afternoon work hours.

In the Christian families, by contrast, the modal condition was one of unemployment. The female spouses typically earned what steady wage income came into these families. The jobs held were low-income ones; part-time jobs were held also. These were usually jobs of a service nature—waitress, domestic, and hair-straightener. In the cases of both Muslim and Christian families, the higher paying jobs were held by persons with relatively high rank in the two religious organizations (e.g., incomes over $4,000 were earned by assistant ministers and student ministers in the Christian and Muslim groups, respectively).

The Christian spouses were, on the average, older than the Muslim spouses. They also had a greater number of children than did the Muslims. However, the Muslim families were characterized by a stair-step succession of births, whereas the Christian families were less intensively prolific. There is evidence to support the contention that the discrepancy between these two contrasting birth patterns may have been due to differing attitudes toward birth control. Also, the fact that working female spouses would have been considerably inconvenienced by a continuous succession of nine-month gestation periods was probably a factor of some impact in determining this discrepancy.

All of the families involved in this study lived in the same geographical area—an area characterized by dilapidated housing, rats, and high unemployment rate, as well as other conditions typical of the black ghettos across the United States.

326

Results

The results will be reported for each of the four areas of family relations. In each instance, the responses of the Muslim group will be compared to those of the Christian group.

Husband-Wife Relationships

The questions in the area of husband-wife relationships were directed toward ascertaining those role functions of each spouse that involved work, money authority, decision making, and the use of leisure time. The literature is replete with references to the characteristic tendency toward the use of physical expression, often in the form of violence, among lower-class Negroes. This violence is often also present in husband-wife relationships, particularly as these relationships revolve around such fiscal problems as the procurement and allocation of money.

For the Christian families, the state of one spouse's financial and material affluence as perceived by the other played a greater role in determining the degree of stability of their relationship than did the same situation among the Muslims. All but one Christian case responded with at least a qualified "yes" to the question of whether they thought the female spouse should work. They indicated a "balance of authority" between themselves and their spouses. Through contributing a portion of money to the family income equal to or greater than that of their husbands, the Christian females felt themselves to be more justified and secure in expressing or seeking the realization of their own individual desires, opinions, and decisions in the marriage situation. Though not all of the Christian females worked, the majority did bring money into the family. This was primarily due to welfare and child support payments from previous relationships. In light of this, it would appear that the welfare system is indirectly perpetuating the matriarchal family structure among these lower-class Negroes by making welfare aid and child support payments payable directly to the female spouse in the household.

The Muslims' opinions regarding the desirability of married females working were the exact opposite of those expressed by the Christian groups. In fact, the Muslims were against any female holding an income-producing job, whether married or not. They felt that a woman's place was in the home and the task of earning a living was the sole responsibility of the adult male. This conviction was expressed adamantly by both male and female spouses. The majority of these Muslim women seemed to believe that their main task in life was to be good wives and mothers ("good" being synonymous with Muslim). Most, if not all, authority was vested in the role of the male. Consonant with this authority, the Muslims reported that all major decisions affecting the family were made by the male. In the majority of cases, such decisions as where to live and what purchases to make, as well as when to make them, were made by the Muslim male. This is in contrast to the Christian families wherein the females made these decisions. The responses of the Christian families relative to decision making and authority, both of which were anchored in the female's role because of income production, tended to lend substantial validity to the notion that the lower-class Christian families functioned within a matriarchal structure. The Muslim families, by contrast, through family role definition prescribed by Black Muslim dogma, have established for themselves a more patriarchal family system. This role clarity appeared to reduce intrafamily conflict considerably for the Muslim families.

For the most part, Muslim respondents regarded intrafamily conflict of any type as totally unnecessary and avoidable. By contrast, the Christian respondents thought such conflict to be unavoidable and some physical violence inevitable "if two people lived together long enough." The Muslim mechanism for avoiding trouble involved a use of the fundamental teachings of their religion in the face of impending conflict. Statements were often made to the effect that, when conflict threatened, the spouses concerned merely "got on the side of Islam" and the wrong fell of its own weight. No such responses came from the Christian, nor was there any evidence of their gravitating toward religious fundamentals in time of impending conflict between spouses.

The duties of each Muslim spouse in the marriage situation were outlined in astonishingly minute detail and taught in training sessions held specifically for this purpose. The female was trained to fulfill her principal duties—those of mother and housewife. She was taught, among other things, how to cook, what to cook, how often to cook, how to sew, and how to keep house. She was trained in home economy and maintenance. The male spouse likewise was taught his responsibilities and how to fulfill them. These predetermined responsibilities and the activities that they generate were so calculated as to avoid a conflict. They further placed the Muslim male spouse in the position of the productive, contributing breadwinner and protector of his family. By contrast, the typical Christian response to questions as to who held what responsibilities was: "It depends."

Another contrast between the two types of families was in the extent of "idling" activity. The Christian male spouses participated in this "idling" or "killing time" far more than did the Muslims. Not once did the author find a Muslim male in any of the local "hangouts" or in an idling situation. First of all, most of the idling places were also places where drinking and smoking were common pastimes. Muslim ideology forbids the use of either alcohol or tobacco. There were two other factors which contributed to this lack of an idling custom among Muslims. First, due to the Muslims' overt enthusiasm for their religion, they were often unwelcome at idling places. Their constant tendency to emphasize the decadent and useless behavior of the "regulars" of such places made them unwelcome, even on the occasional "fishing expeditions" to hangouts frequented by the "dead." Secondly, the Muslims did not have free time to participate in idling. After fulfilling a predetermined schedule of activities, the Muslim males would spend a great preportion of their leisure time on "fishing expeditions." These expeditions were considered part of their duties as Muslims. They believed that the final hour for North America was near. They, likewise, believed it to be their duty to save as many black men as possible.[4] Not to make an attempt to do so was considered behavior unworthy of a Muslim.

Family—Extended Kin Relationships

A number of situations determined the break between the Muslim spouses and their relatives. In those cases where the parents and in-laws of the Muslim spouses lived within the area, "uniting with" the Nation of Islam was contrary to their wishes of these relations. This assumes added significance since the majority of these parents and in-laws belonged to Christian churches. Also of significance in the break between Muslim spouses and their parents was the inflexibility of the Muslim spouses in their adherence to the behavioral codes of the Nation of Islam. It was found that conscientious Muslims did not smoke, drink, or curse, nor did they tolerate these prohibited indulgences within their homes. Since many of the Muslims' relatives did in fact indulge in these habits, a situation of mutual intolerance and estrangement soon followed. Of relevance here also were the reactions of the parents and in-laws to the Muslims, particularly as these reactions focused upon the behavior and activities of the Muslim female spouse. Muslim females never straightened their hair or wore make-up of any kind. The resulting appearance of the female was often a point of criticism and mockery from relatives, particularly it seemed from the female spouse's mother. This situation, too, was intolerable. No Muslim tolerated criticism or mockery of moral directives emanating from the Honorable Elijah Muhammed—especially not in his own home, which is next to the mosque in its sanctity.

The Christians, by contrast, maintained continual, if not stable, relationships with their relatives. Generational ties were particularly characteristic of the Christian female spouses and their mothers. In only a few cases did the mothers of the female spouses actually live in the same homes with them. However, even though the physical propinquity was not there, psychosocial closeness was very much in evidence. The telephone was the major medium for contact. The majority of Christian females indicated that their primary confidants, creditors, and advisers were their mothers. Several Christian female spouses noted that their mothers were the first to learn of their pregnancies, plans to work, and other such important occurrences.

Among the Muslims, no such relationships existed. In discussions with the female spouses at the mosque, it was made abundantly clear that the primary, and often the only, confidants for these women were their husbands. There were apparently never any occasions for these Muslim females to borrow goods or money from anyone, since such decisions were typically made by the male spouse. And for the female to do so "over the head" of the male spouse would have been in direct opposition to Muslim directives regarding her proper role in the family.

Parent-Child Relationships

The responses of the Christian spouses show that they conformed more closely to the generally held lower-class Negro subcultural attitudes and practices with regard to children and child rearing than did the Muslim spouses. The differences between the two groups' relationships with their children did not begin with the actual socializing effects of home life on the child, but with the parents' attitudes towards birth control.

The Muslim subjects expressed indignation and disgust at the queries on birth control methods. Not a single Muslim respondent reported that any methods of birth control, "natural" or otherwise, had been used by either spouse since they became serious adherents to the ideology of the Nation of Islam. The Christian respondents, on the other hand, not only stated that they had used or were using various birth control devices, but several subjects also reported that they regretted not having practiced birth control more often and more consistently. While the Christians had more children than did the Muslims, the spacing of the children in the latter group was characterized by a stair-step succession of births, whereas child births in the former group were erratically spaced. Apparently the desire for children also helped determine to a large extent parents' interaction with the child. By removing any question of the desirability of children, regardless of circumstance, the Muslims also removed one potential source from which a child's emotional and social maladjustment might arise. In doing so, they quite possibly may have opened the door to other problems, such as poverty-stricken families and lack of adequate living space, which could have equally as damaging effects on the child as the lack of proper parent-child emotional relationship. However, the Muslims felt that poverty and "overpopulation" were merely manifestations of what they considered to be the white man's intrinsically evil nature and his criminal use of the world's resources. As such, these afflictions would pass away with him. The act of practicing birth control because one does not desire children was, on the other hand, viewed as an act against the Nation of Islam and, therefore, against Allah.

Given the birth of a child, the Muslim and Christian groups also exhibited differing attitudes with regard to child-rearing practices. These differences involved the acceptability and effectiveness of various disciplinary practices as well as the manner in which these practices should be carried out. The Christians had few reservations concerning the use of physical punishment. Generally they held the opinion that, after the age when a child knows that what he is doing is wrong, other forms of punishment are only minimally effective.

The Muslims generally indicated that they held the use of physical punishment in close reserve, to be used only at those times when all other forms of chastisement failed. The reasons were very similar to those given for not advocating the use of physically coercive measures between spouses. They also indicated that there was seldom any need for physical punishment because of

330

the effectiveness of Muslim child-rearing methods and the example of proper behavior provided by the parents.

Of significance in the area of disciplinary practices were the subjects' responses to questions pertaining to youths who get into trouble. Their differing points of view began with their ideas concerning the concept of "trouble" itself. The Christians' responses tended to indicate that they considered a child to be in trouble when (and if) he was caught in a compromising situation. The Muslims, on the other hand, considered any individual to be in trouble when a transgression was conceived, regardless of whether he actually committed the act, much less whether he was caught. They reasoned that such an idea was indicative of a more deep-seated anomaly which at best could give rise to more un-Muslimlike behavior. In short, the Christians considered the onset of trouble to be the point at which relevant authority figures become aware of the act and the person responsible for it, whereas the Muslims considered the commencement of trouble to be that point at which the idea for the act was consciously conceived. Consistent with their varying conceptions of trouble were the two groups' opinions as to what types of trouble young people "inevitably" get into. The Christians felt that it was inevitable that youth would get into trouble because of a spirit of curiosity and the need to experiment. Among these acts were included sexual offenses and thefts of varying degrees of seriousness. The Muslims, on the other hand, considered only one type of trouble as inevitable—that which a black man might encounter as a Muslim in a white man's society. They saw sexual offenses, thefts, and other law violations as inexcusable and, hence, intolerable. They argued that such behavior was only the consequence of the black man's attempt to imitate the white man.

While the Christian respondents did not endorse premarital sexual relations, neither did they express violent opposition to it. Instead, their responses indicated that their main effort was directed towards the preparation of their offspring to "protect themselves because you sure can't stop them." The Christians also permitted their offspring to begin the use of cosmetics and other such accoutrements at an earlier age than the general society would consider as appropriate. The Muslims abhorred the use of any cosmetics at any time and any age.

Although the Christian subjects, as a group, had greater educational aspirations for their children than did the Muslims, the latter group took more positive steps toward the fulfillment of their more limited aspirations. The Muslims expressed an intense determination that their children should finish school. This determination originated primarily from the Muslims' belief that knowledge, from whatever source, is "the key to all things." They felt that knowledge acquired within the walls of the white man's schools had value when interpreted within the context of Muslim ideology. Their respect for the law and their determination to adhere to its dictates were also chief factors underlying their efforts to keep their children in school. However, they were extremely hostile towards higher education and its more specialized knowl-

331

edge. While adamantly insisting on an absence of truancy and on rigorous study habits for their offspring through high school, they felt just as strongly against their children continuing in the existing system of higher education. Among the reasons for these anti-college feelings were criticisms of the curriculum in history and science. It was felt that these subject areas did not acknowledge the works of Allah and the original black man before the dawn of the white man's recorded history. It was also thought that the white man has left out of his history and science books those contributions and achievements made by black individuals and nations and, in some cases, that he had even claimed these achievements and contributions as his own. Finally, the Muslims reported that the black youth who was away from his own people while attending these institutions would find it difficult not to believe "the white man's lies," primarily because he would have no one to explain to him how and why these lies were being propagated.

The Christians by comparison, who were much less strict about the school attendance and study habits of their children, placed a high value on college for their offspring. However, they apparently had little notion of the sacrifices necessary if these aspirations were to be realized.

Though the Muslims' educational aspirations for their children were more limited than those of the Christians, the Muslims' aspirations were, nevertheless, more realistic with respect to their prevailing economic and social situations. The probability of their attaining these limited goals would appear to be much higher than the Christian group's chances of realizing the educational goals to which they aspire for their offspring. In general, then, the Christians advocated the use of the severest form of punishment for their offspring, but were very lenient and permissive with regard to their children's engaging in the illicit forms of behavior which, at the very least, might prompt such punishment. Their only justification for this inconsistency would appear to be that the punishment is not administered for the commitment of the act, but for being caught. They also held high educational goals for their offspring but did little to attain them.

Family-Community Relationships

An analysis of responses pertaining to family-community relations revealed that the Muslim families had almost no contact with any institution other than that to which they maintained religious ties. The Christians, by comparison, reported an array of extra-religious institutional contacts and commitments. Overwhelmingly the most common contact was that reported to have taken place with various welfare institutions. Of the Christian families, 93 percent had applied for and received some type of public aid within a three-year period as opposed to 21 percent of the Muslim families. Likewise, 64 percent of the Christian families reported that they had had contact with some branch of the local law enforcement system as opposed to 21 percent of the Muslim group.

Considering the Christian families' reports as to their attitudes towards "trouble"—especially that most characteristic of juveniles—and these families' economic situations and work habits, their reports of institutional contact with respect to welfare and law enforcement agencies were strikingly consistent. Likewise, the Muslims' institutional contacts of the sort discussed above followed more or less consistently from their expressed views on trouble and their values on industriousness and the economic independence of the family.

The two groups were diametrically opposed to one another on the question of the desirability of social clubs for either adults or youths. While the Christians thought that such clubs were highly beneficial, the Muslims viewed any type of social club with intense suspicion and distrust. Not all of the Christians belonged to social clubs, only a little over one-half. However, even among those Christians not belonging to clubs, such membership was not considered undesirable. While no Muslims belonged to any social club, neither was there any consistent answer given as to why such was the case. This suggests that the Muslims possibly had no direct policy against such affiliation but may have discouraged it through more indirect means. Among these means might have been the prohibition against the consumption of liquor, the preparation of relatively rigid activity schedules for members, and the declaration that time should not be used wastefully ("wasted time" being defined as all of that time not used in Muslim goal attainment).

The Muslims were also concerned with economic and social "welfare." There were two facets to the Nation of Islam's approach to changing the economic and social situation of the black man in the ghetto. First of all, there was no need for the potential Muslim to apply separately for material aid and then for aid in adjusting socially and psychologically to his responsibilities. When a person applied to and was accepted by the Nation of Islam, as a Muslim, regardless of what the precipitating factor behind his decision to apply was (be it economic hardship or the need for spiritual security), he is exposed to the entire program. That is, efforts were immediately initiated by the Muslims to ascertain and at least partially satisfy his economic needs; efforts were made to secure work for him that he was qualified to do or to train him for the types of jobs that were available; and he was resocialized to the Muslim orientation to life. Secondly an attempt was made by the Muslims to show the convert that his social and psychological orientations to life were inextricably interconnected with his poverty-stricken or socially deteriorating situation and that to change the latter would inevitably change the former. This task was made easier by the fact that the same individuals who gave him aid and found him a job were also the people who attempted to resocialize him —his "Muslim brothers." Material aid and resocialization were both administered by the same people, under the same roof, and at the same time. It is perhaps through this technique that the Muslim convert may have come to see economic betterment and security as part and parcel of religious, social, and psychological change.

DISCUSSION

In the family relationships of the two groups, there is evidence of two differing foundations for authority. The first of these foundations is manifest in the relationships observed among Muslim families. It derives its legitimization from a basis of respect on the part of the female spouse for the role and position of her husband and the acceptance of her role as a supporting one. This female role is not, however, without its relative advantages. Since, traditionally, the lower-class Negro family has not been organized on a foundation of primary authority, it would appear that the Nation of Islam has had some success in narrowing the gap between the family structure and interactional patterns of its members and those of American middle-class society.

The Christians' family relationships may be characterized as deriving from a second basis of authority. These relationships appear to have been grounded in the spouses' desires for physical comfort, economic security, and a subtle type of respect that emerges from conflict situations. As the economic situation changed, there apparently also occurred commensurate changes in the balance of authority and the overall status of the marriage relationship.

The Muslims approximated the dominant group's values concerning family relationships to a far greater extent than did the Christians. The same general statement holds for the Muslims' relationships with their children. It seems that the Muslims anchored the appropriate role characteristics with the appropriate sexes as prescribed within the context of traditional American values. The Muslim male earned a living, protected his family, and was chief representative of his family in outside social dealings, while the Muslim female concentrated her efforts primarily in the area of child rearing and housekeeping. This is in contrast to the typical lower-class American Negro family life style, where, because of the social heritage and the disadvantaged position of Negroes in American society, there developed a matriarchal family type which has become extremely unstable. If we are in fact moving more and more toward an urban, neolocal, nuclear family type, the Muslims would appear to be less deviant than the lower-class Negro Christians. Also in the area of family-community relationships, the Muslims typified the wage-earning, noncriminal, middle-class ideal to a greater extent than did the Christians.

On the basis of these findings, there would appear to be some questions as to the accuracy of the popular notion concerning the degree of social and psychological nonconformity extant within the Nation of Islam. From the perspective of the uninformed public, the Muslims are seen as in a state of rebellion—as totally rejecting the values and goals of this society and replacing them with their own values and goals. Because of their separatist ideology and their refusal to participate in various institutions of the society, persons who are fairly well informed might view the Muslims as an organized group of either rebels or retreatists. However, the results of this study tend to portray the Muslims as, again in Merton's terminology, primarily ritualists who have

334

adopted and "black-washed" a version of American middle-class values and goals while simultaneously rejecting the institutionalized means to their attainment.

Although the Muslims are shown to be lower class in terms of income, education, and general environment, they are very middle class in many other respects—especially with regard to such issues as sex practices, the value put upon education (with some qualifications), personal hygiene and grooming, the high value placed upon work and industriousness, and their intense interest in developing and maintaining a high degree of mental and physical alertness. These are clearly not the characteristics typically found to exist throughout the lower-class Negro subculture.

In conclusion it seems clear that the Muslims were not only more conforming than the Christians in their adherence to what appear to be traditional American values regarding intrafamily behavior, but also that there exists a narrower gap between the Muslims' ideational values and their normative behavior.

Although a severe access problem exists with regard to researching the Nation of Islam and its membership, it is hoped that much research will be forthcoming, particularly since it is only through this means that accurate social and psychological portraits of this significant group can be obtained.

NOTES

[1] E. F. Frazier, *The Negro Family in the United States,* New York: Citadel Press, 1948.

[2] Evans and Novak column entitled "The Moynihan Report," *New York Herald Tribune,* August 18, 1965; Benjamin F. Payton, "The President, the Social Experts, and the Ghetto: An Analysis of an Emerging Strategy in Civil Rights," unpublished paper, pp. 1–9; Peter Goldman, "The Splintering Negro Family—A Confidential Report," *Newsweek* (August 9, 1965).

[3] Both the Muslim and Christian religious bodies, however, numbered among their memberships persons of other racial extraction.

[4] The Muslims ignore completely the traditional grouping of homo sapiens by race. Hence, any nonwhite by Muslim definition is a "black brother" (these racial brothers include such racially diversified people as Chinese, Filipinos, Mexicans, Indians [Eastern], North American Indians, Arabs, Negroes, Africans, Japanese, Eskimos, etc.).

Suburbia U.S.A.

Time Magazine

The search for a better way of life than the city can offer has led millions of young families to move to the suburbs. There they find a mini-culture based on endless activities and organizational participation as well as lawn care and backyard barbeques. While suburbanites do not have the monetary problems of slum dwellers, they find that relative economic security is no guarantee of happiness, for they are confronted with stifling conformity in the community and boredom in the marriage.

The wreath that rings every U.S. metropolis is a green garland of place names and people collectively called Suburbia. It weaves through the hills beyond the cities, marches across flatlands that once were farms and pastures, dips into gullies and woodlands, straddles the rocky hillocks and surrounds the lonesome crossroads. Oftener than not it has a lilting polyphony that sings of trees (Streamwood, Elmwood, Lakewood, Kirkwood), the rolling country (Cedar Hill, Cockrell Hill, Forest Hills), or the primeval timberlands (Forest Grove, Park Forest, Oak Park, Deer Park). But it has its roots in such venerable names as Salem, Greenwich, Chester, Berkeley, Evanston, Sewickley and Rye.

In those towns and hills and groves last week the spendor of a new summer seemed, as always, to give a new lilt to life. The hills and fields triumphed with fresh green grass. In the old towns, the giant oaks and elms threw rich new shade across the white colonial mansions and the square, peaked-roofed clapboard houses. In fresh-minted subdivisions, sycamore striplings strained at their stakes to promise token cover for the bare houses of glass, steel, stone and shingle that have sprouted (19 million since 1940) as from a bottomless nest of Chinese boxes. School buses headed toward the season's last mile; power mowers and outboard motors pulsed the season's first promise. Fragrance of honeysuckle and roses overlay the smell of charcoal and seared beef. The thud of baseball against mitt, the abrasive grind of roller skate against con-

From "Americana: The Roots of Home," *Time,* June 20, 1960, pp. 14–18.

crete, the jarring harmony of the Good Humor bell tolled the day; the clink of ice, the distant laugh, the surge of hi-fi through the open window came with the night.

A MARCH FOR CAUSES

For better or for worse, Suburbia in the 1960s is the U.S.'s grass-roots. In Suburbia live one-third of the nation, roughly 60 million people who represent every patch of democracy's hand-stitched quilt, every economic layer, every laboring and professional pursuit in the country. Suburbia is the nation's broadening young middle class, staking out its claim across the landscape, prospecting on a trial-and-error basis for the good way of life for itself and for the children that it produces with such rapidity. It is, as Social Scientist Max Lerner (*America as a Civilization*) has put it, "the focus of most of the forces that are remaking American life today."

If Suburbia's avid social honeybees buzz from address to address in search of sweet status, Suburbia is at the same time the home of the talented and distinguished Americans who write the nation's books, paint its paintings, run its corporations and set the patterns. If its legions sometimes march into frantic activity with rigorous unison, they march for such causes as better schools, churches and charities, which are the building blocks of a nation's character. If Suburbia's ardent pursuit of life at backyard barbecues, block parties and committee meetings offends pious city-bred sociologists, its self-conscious strivings to find a better way for men, women and children to live together must impress the same observers.

Suburbia is a particular kind of American phenomenon, and its roots lie in a particular kind of American heritage. In a casual, ill-planned way it is the meeting ground between the growing, thriving city and the authentic U.S. legend of small-town life. Says Sociologist Alvin Scaff, who lives in Los Angeles' suburban Claremont: "If you live in the city, you may be a good citizen and interest yourself in a school-board election, but it is seldom meaningful in human terms. In a suburb, the chances are you know the man who is running for the school board, and you vote for or against him with more understanding." Says Don C. Peters, president of Pittsburgh's Mellon-Stuart Co. (construction) and chairman of the board of supervisors of suburban Pine Township: "The American suburb is the last outpost of democracy, the only level left on which the individual citizen can make his wishes felt, directly and immediately. I think there's something idealistic about the search for a home in the suburbs. Call it a return to the soil. It's something that calls most people some time in their lives." When France's Charles de Gaulle saw San Francisco's suburban Palo Alto on his trip to the U.S. six weeks ago, he hailed Suburbia as *"magnifique."*

Man has been moving to the suburbs ever since he invented the urbs. *"Rus mihi dulce sub urbe est,"* sang the Roman epigrammatist Martial in the 1st century A.D. "To me, the country on the outskirts of the city is sweet." And small wonder, for the towns and walled cities of Europe, from ancient times through the Middle Ages and beyond, were airless, fetid places choking with humanity. The big crisis of the cities came with the Industrial Revolution. In England lonely voices cried out against the grime and stench of the cities. "Hell is a city much like London," wrote Shelley, "a populous and smoky city."

By the early 20th century, middle-class Suburbia was a reality in England, and Social Historian C.F.G. Masterman was perhaps the first of a legion of urban critics to draw a bead on it. Each little red house, he wrote in 1909, "boasts its pleasant drawing room, its bow window, its little front garden... The women, with their single domestic servants, now so difficult to get, and so exacting when found, find time hangs rather heavy on their hands. But there are excursions to shopping centers in the West End and pious sociabilities, occasional theater visits and the interests of home."

Flowering Green

Long before England's Masterman had his say, Philadelphians and Bostonians were moving to the outskirts of town. Ben Franklin packed up, left Philadelphia's High Street and unpacked again at the corner of Second and Sassafras, grumbling that "the din of the Market increases upon me; and that with frequent interruptions has, I find, made me say some things twice over." And after all, as one proud New Englander says, "When Paul Revere needed help for the city of Boston, where did he go? The suburbs!"

At first the countryside communities leafed and budded with the homes of the well to do, who could afford to come and go by the seasons. By the turn of the century, U.S. Suburbia was flowering with permanent residents. Freed from the city by the trolley and rapid-transit services, and then by the automobile, hoisted gradually by a strengthening economy, the new middle-income families swept beyond the gates to buy homes of their own, from which they could commute to their jobs. When World War II ended, the sweep to the suburbs turned into a stampede. The veterans came home, the legion of war workers burst out of crowded city quarters, and in battalions they set out to find homes, where the land was greener and cheaper. New settlements spread across acre upon acre; small, sleepy old towns were inundated by newcomers, and the suburban way of life became the visible substance of what a hardworking nation was working so hard for. "Eventually," observes Humorist-Exurbanite James Thurber (Cornwall, Conn.) of the steady spread of Suburbia, "this country will be called the United Cities of America. One suburb will pile into another until in New York State there'll only be Albany and New

York City; and they can really fight it out in the streets. If they start shoveling in San Diego, buildings will tumble in Bangor."

THE WOMEN

The key figure in all Suburbia, the thread that weaves between family and community—the keeper of the suburban dream—is the suburban housewife. In the absence of her commuting, city-working husband, she is first of all the manager of home and brood, and beyond that a sort of aproned activist with a penchant for keeping the neighborhood and community kettle whistling. With children on her mind and under her foot, she is breakfast getter ("You can't have ice cream for breakfast because I say you can't"), laundress, house cleaner, dishwasher, shopper, gardener, encyclopedia, arbitrator of children's disputes, policeman ("Tommy, didn't your mother ever tell you that it's not nice to go into people's houses and open their refrigerators?").

If she is not pregnant, she wonders if she is. She takes her peanut-butter sandwich lunch while standing, thinks she looks a fright, watches her weight (periodically), jabbers over the short-distance telephone with the next-door neighbor. She runs a worn track to the front door, buys more Girl Scout cookies and raffle tickets than she thinks she should, cringes from the suburban locust— the door-to-door salesman who peddles everything from storm windows to potato chips, fire-alarm systems to vacuum cleaners, diaper service to magazine subscriptions. She keeps the checkbook, frets for the day that her husband's next raise will top the flood of monthly bills (it never will)—a tide that never seems to rise as high in the city as it does in the suburbs.

She wonders if her husband will send her flowers (on no special occasion), shoos the children next door to play at the neighbor's house for a change, paints her face for her husband's return before she wrestles with dinner. Spotted through her day are blessed moments of relief or dark thoughts of escape.

AUTO NATION

In Suburbia's pedocracy huge emphasis is placed on activities for the young (Washington's suburban Montgomery County, Md.—pop. 358,000—spends about $34 million a year on youth programs). The suburban housewife might well be a can-opener cook, but she must have an appointment book and a driver's license and must be able to steer a menagerie of leggy youngsters through the streets with the coolness of a driver at the Sebring trials; the suburban sprawl and the near absence of public transportation generally mean that any destination is just beyond sensible walking distance. Most children gauge walking distance at two blocks. If the theory of evolution is still working, it may well one day transform the suburban housewife's right foot into a flared paddle, groved for easy traction on the gas pedal and brake.

As her children grow less dependent on her, Suburbia's housewife fills her newfound time with a dizzying assortment of extra-curricular projects that thrust her full steam into community life. Beyond the home-centered dinner parties, Kaffee-klatsches and card parties, there is a directory-sized world of organizations devised for husbands as well as for wives (but it is the wife who keeps things organized). In New Jersey's Levittown, a projected 16,000-unit replica of the Long Island original, energetic suburbanites can sign up for at least 35 different organizations from the Volunteer Fire Department to the Great Books Club, and the Lords and Ladies Dance Club, not to mention the proliferating list of adult-education courses that keep the public school lights glowing into the night. "We have a wonderful adult-education program," says Suburbanite (Levittown, L.I.) Muriel Kane (two children), "where women can learn how to fix their own plumbing and everything."

FIGHTING IN THE THICKETS

Since Suburbia was conceived for children (and vice versa), the Suburban housewife is the chief jungle fighter for school expansion and reform. Beyond that the path leads easily to the thickets of local politics. Only recently, after the Montgomery County manager whacked $11 million from the 1961 school budget, the county council was invaded by an indignant posse of 1,000 P.T.A. members. The council scrambled to retreat, not only restored the cuts, but added a few projects of its own for good measure. The tax rate jumped 5¢ per $100 valuation as a result but there was scarcely a whimper.

To the north, in New York's suburban Scarsdale, the women's sense of responsibility has the same ring. Says Housewife Rhea Hertel (Woman's Club, Neighborhood Association, P.T.A., League of Women Voters): "If you're receiving benefits and not contributing, what kind of person are you?" Adds Scarsdale's Grace Fitzwater (Hitchcock Presbyterian Church, Woman's Club, P.T.A.): "When we lived in New York City, I roared with laughter at this sort of thing. I never knew anyone in the city who was civic; out here I don't know anybody who isn't." Says Florence Willett, 44, who is the new mayor of Detroit's suburban Birmingham: "Women feel a greater need for taking their share of the work. With husbands away at work and hampered by long commuting, women can share and contribute more. Don't ever say we run the suburbs, though."

TALENT

With a little prodding from his wife, the suburban husband develops a big yen to mix in Government affairs at the local level. How can the head of the house, father of the brood, refuse to campaign for school bonds or stand for

340

the board of education—particularly when his firm urges him to be civic-minded? The result is that Suburbia often shines with the kind of topnotch talent that makes troubled big-city fathers wince with envy. In Kansas City's suburban Prairie Village, for example, the $1-a-year mayor is a lawyer with a growing practice, the president of the city council is a Procter & Gamble Co. division manager and the head of the village planning commission is assistant to the president of a manufacturing firm. In Philadelphia's suburban Swarthmore, the town council includes a Philadelphia banker, a Du Pont engineer, the president of a pipeline company and a retired executive of Swarthmore College.

Biggest of the problems that such people face is Suburbia's growing morass of overlapping services and functions, especially in counties that have experienced a big building rush. In the 17 towns that comprise Denver's four-county suburban area, for example, there are 27 school districts, 35 water districts, 59 sanitation districts. The Suburbia of Portland, Ore. embraces three counties, 178 special service districts, 60 school districts, twelve city governments. And the granddaddy of them all is the megalopolis of Los Angeles which is fish-netted with 72 separate governments and an uncounted array of districts, authorities, and floating unincorporated communities.

But suburbanites, more than their urban or rural brethren, tend to want to get things fixed. Lakewood, Calif., 22 miles south of downtown Los Angeles, was just another boondock of 5,000 people ten years ago when the boom thundered. A development group poured $200 million into 17,000 homes ($8,000-$11,000) and a big shopping center. As residents took hold, the sense of frustration that came from long-distance county rule and the absence of local administered services flashed into a new, self-starting energy. Lakewood, with a present population of 75,000, incorporated itself in 1954, sank its own home-nurtured political roots and fashioned an identity of its own. Then, while running its own affairs, it devised a method of contracting for police, road maintenance and building maintenance to the county government. The "Lakewood Plan" was later copied by many other California communities. So ably has Lakewood fashioned its living pattern to suit itself that many Lakewood families who might have moved on to more expensive, status-setting locales, have decided to stay where they are.

"Anybody Home?"

The suburbanite has been prodded, poked, gouged, sniffed and tweaked by armies of sociologists and swarms of cityside cynics, but in reality he is his own best critic. Organized suburban living is a relatively new invention, and already some of its victims are wondering if it has too much organization and too little living. The pressure of activity and participation in the model suburb of Lakewood, for example, can be harrowing. The town's recreation league boasts 110 boys' baseball teams (2,000 players), 36 men's softball teams, ten housewives' softball teams. In season, the leagues play 75 boys' and 30 men's basketball teams, 77 football teams, all coached by volunteers, while other activities range through drama, dance and charm classes, bowling, dog-training classes, "Slim 'n' Trim" groups, roller skating, photography, wood-craft, and lessons in how to ice a cake. Says Joy Hudson, 35, mother of three children: "There is a problem of getting too busy. Some weeks my husband is home only two nights a week. My little boy often says, 'Anybody going to be home tonight?' " Suburbia, echoed Exurbanite Adlai Stevenson (Libertyville, Ill.) recently, is producing "a strange half-life of divided families and Sunday fathers."

The parental press to keep the youngsters busy has created an image of an Organization Child, or Boy in the Grey Flannel Sneakers. The thriving Cub Scout movement is a wondrous machine of 1,822,062 beanie-capped boys who visit fire stations, make kites and tie knots, all *en masse*, and the Little League has more than a million little sports who are cheered on by an equal number of overexuberant daddies. "Some kids," says Long Island School Psychologist Justin Koss, "need the Little League. But some need to dig in their own back-yards, too. The trouble is that plenty of parents think that if their kid isn't in Little League, there's something abnormal about him." Declares Shirley Vandenberg, 33 (three children), of Portland, Ore.'s suburban Oak Grove: "We don't need Blue Birds and Boy Scouts out here. This is not the slums. The kids out here have the great outdoors. I think people are so bored, they organize the children, and then try to hook everyone else on it. And then the poor kids have no time left to just lie on their beds and daydream." Says Jean Chenoweth (two teen-age children), who moved to a Denver house from the suburbs: "Parents do nine-tenths of the work. I had a Blue Bird Group for three years, and we never accomplished a cotton-picking thing— they just came for the refreshments as far as I could see." Making her choice, Mrs. Chenoweth devotes her spare time to fund raising for a school for handi-capped children and making recordings for the blind.

In those suburbs where families, income, education and interest are homog-enized, suburbanites sometimes wonder whether their children are cocooned from the rest of the world. "A child out here sees virtually no sign of wealth and no sign of poverty," says Suburbanite Alan Rosenthal (Washington's Rock Creek Palisades). "It gives him a tendency to think that everyone else lives just the way he does." Suburbanite-Author Robert Paul *("Where Did You Go?" "Out." "What Did You Do?" "Nothing.")* Smith (New York City's Scarsdale), complains that Scarsdale is "just like a Deanna Durbin movie: all clean and unreal. Hell, I went to school in Mount Vernon, N.Y., with the furnace man's son—you don't get that here."

DEN OF CONFORMITY

And what of the grownups themselves? For some, the suburban euphoria often translates itself into the suburban caricature. The neighborhood race for bigger and better plastic swimming pools, cars and power mowers is still being run in some suburbs, and in still others, the chief warm-weather occupation is neighbor watching (Does she hang her laundry outside to dry? Does he leave his trash barrels on the curb after they have been emptied?). In Long Island's staid, old Garden City, observes Hofstra Assistant Sociology Professor William Dobriner, "they don't care whether you believe in God, but you'd better cut your grass." In close-by Levittown, a poll of householders some time ago showed that the No. 1 topic on people's minds was the complaint that too many dogs were running unleashed on the lawns. Topic No. 2 was the threat of world Communism.

The all-weather activities often center on frenzied weekend parties in the "den," attended by neighbors, who each in his turn will throw a potato-chip and cheese-dip party on succeeding weekends. Cries a Chicago suburban woman: "I'm so sick and tired of seeing those same faces every Friday and Saturday night, I could scream." In Kansas City's suburban Overland Park, three jaded couples formed an "Anti-Conformity League" to fight group-think, disbanded it soon afterward because, explains ex-Schoolteacher Ginger Powers (two children), "it was getting just too organized to be anti-conformist."

Though suburban wife-swapping stories are the delight of the urban cocktail party, immorality in the suburbs is no more or less prevalent than it is in the cities. But an adventuresome male commuter does have one advantage: he can pursue a clandestine affair easily in the city merely by notifying his suburban wife that he is being kept at the office. One sign of the times is that Private Detective Milton Thompson of suburban Kansas City is also a marriage counselor, has handled 300 marital cases in the past three years. The usual story: "The husband plays on the Missouri side of the river before he gets out here. Maybe it's just a few extra-dry martinis with the gang from his office. Maybe not. Anyway, Mama has a little more money than average. She has a maid. That gives her a heck of a lot of time to sit around and think. If hubby is late—boy, does she think."

Suburbia's clergymen tend to be most keenly aware of Suburbia's disappointments and Suburbia's promise. "Many people," complains Kansas City Rabbi Samuel Mayerberg, "mistake activity for usefulness." Says Dr. Donald S. Ewing, minister of Wayland's Trinitarian Congregational Church near Boston: "Suburbia is gossipy. So many of the people are on approximately the same level economically and socially. They're scrambling for success. They tend to be new in the community and they're unstable and insecure. When they see someone else fail, in work or in a family relationship, they themselves feel a rung higher, and this is a great reason for gossip. I think socially we're flying apart—we don't meet heart to heart any more, we meet at cocktail parties in a superficial way. We value smartness rather than depth, shine rather than spirit. But I think people are sick of it; they want to get out of it."

In Chicago's suburban Elk Grove Village, busy Lutheran Minister Martin E. Marty, who writes for the *Christian Century,* and who devotes much of his time to patching up corroding marriages, sighs wearily: "We've all learned that Hell is portable. I think we're seeing a documentable rebellion going on against the postwar idea of mere belongingness and sociability. We all agree that Suburbia means America. It's not different, but it's typical. Solve Suburbia's problems and you solve America's problems."

Buddhas & Babies

The fact surrounding all the criticism and self-searching is that most suburbanites are having too good a time to realize that they ought to be unhappy with their condition.

At week's end, as they nursed their power mowers down the lawn, Suburbia's men paused here and there to enjoy a spell of nothing more salacious than wife-watching. Tanned, brief-clad women sprawled in their chaises and chatted about babies, Khrushchev, Japan and the P.T.A. In the patios, the amateur chefs prepared juicy sacrifices on the suburban Buddhas—the charcoal grills. Mint-flavored iced tea or tart martinis chilled thirsty throats, and from across hedgerows and fences came the cries of exultant youngsters and the yells and laughter of men and women engaged in a rough-and-tumble game of croquet or volleyball. (In Springfield Township, near Philadelphia, nine couples recently pounded through a rousing volleyball match; five of the women were pregnant, but no emergency deliveries were made that day.)

Thus the suburban counterpoint leaps forward in optimistic measure, creating a new framework for the American theme. True, as in every place, every suburban husband wishes he earned more money, every mother with young children wishes she had more help, small boys wish there were fewer days of school, small girls wish there were fewer small boys, and babies all wish there was no such thing as strained spinach. Nevertheless, there is scarcely a man or woman living in all those hills and groves beyond the cities who does not sing with Martial: *Rus mihi dulce sub urbe est.*

Experimental Family Organization: An Historico-Cultural Report on The Oneida Community

William M. Kephart

The commune form of marriage espoused by hippies and flower children is not a new phenomenon. From time to time through history, men and women have become disenchanted with the nuclear family and have attempted to set up utopian communities where some form of group cooperation—economic, child rearing, and even sexual—replaced individual control of these activities. The Oneida community was such an enterprise. As testimony to its success, it survived over 30 years. The practices that held it together, and the climate of family living that this commune was able to generate, are described here.

Not long ago the writer had the interesting experience of talking with a woman whose father had been born in the George Washington-Thomas Jefferson period. The woman is a daughter of John Humphrey Noyes, founder of the Oneida Community. Although a number of non-monogamous forms of family organization have appeared on the American scene—e.g., polygyny (the Mormons), celibacy (the Shakers, the Father Divine Movement)—the most radical form remains the group marriage experiment of the Oneida Community.

Subsequent to some correspondence, the President of Oneida, Ltd., invited the writer to spend some time at the site of the Old Community. During the visit, there was opportunity to interview a number of people, including officers of the company, local historians, and persons whose parents had been members

From William M. Kephart, "Experimental Family Organization: An Historic-Cultural Report on the Oneida Community," *Marriage and Family Living*, August, 1963, pp. 261–68. Reprinted by permission of the author and The National Council on Family Relations. Expanded version of paper read at the August, 1962, meeting of the National Council on Family Relations, Storrs, Connecticut. The study was facilitated by a grant from the University of Pennsylvania Committee on the Advancement of Research. Although not included herein, an extensive list of bibliographical materials is available. Interested persons may write the author.

of the Oneida group. In addition, the Mansion House Library was opened, which made it possible to examine the unique collection of newspapers, journals, and books formerly published by John Humphrey Noyes and his followers.

Finally, it was the writer's privilege to interview several of the *surviving members* of the Oneida Community. As of the time of the interviews, thirteen members were still living, and while they are all in their 80's and 90's, their minds are sharp, their memories remarkably clear. And when it is remembered that their former leader, Noyes, was living during the time when John Adams, Paul Revere, Thomas Jefferson, and other Revolutionary figures were alive, one cannot help but feel the vital continuum of American history. At any rate, the writer was not only graciously received but was able to compile some significant material, the bulk of which has not heretofore appeared in the literature.

By way of background, it should be mentioned that the Community was founded in 1848 on the old Indian lands along the Oneida Creek in central New York State. John Humphrey Noyes, founder and long-time leader of the group, was a graduate of Yale Theological Seminary, although his theological views and Perfectionist philosophy had proved too heretical for the people of Putney, Vermont, where he had been preaching. Noyes' theology revolved around spiritual equality which, as he interpreted it, included both the economic and sexual spheres. In the Kingdom of God, all persons were to love and to share equally—a so-called Bible communism. Noyes gained some adherents, and in Putney the little group of Perfectionists actually started to practice what they preached. Predictably, however, there was little future for the group in an area that had been close to the heart of Puritanism, and Noyes and his followers were eventually run out of town.

Reassembling at Oneida, New York, they constructed a large Community Mansion House, and by expanding their efforts were able to increase the size of the group to several hundred members. And for many decades the Oneida Community sustained one of the most unusual social experiments the world has ever seen. Economic communism, group marriage, scientific breeding, sexual equality—it couldn't happen here, but it did! Indeed, the Community flourished until around 1880, after which a business enterprise (Oneida, Ltd.) was set up and the stock apportioned among the members. It is hoped that the following remarks will shed some light on this very remarkable historico-cultural episode, one which—for some reason—has been neglected by both historians and sociologists.

SOCIAL ORGANIZATION AND FAMILY FUNCTIONS

What was there, in the elements of social organization, which successfully held the Community together in the face of both internal problems and external pressures? To begin with, much of the communality of action derived from the fact that the entire membership was housed under one roof. The original

346

communal home was built in 1849, but because of the increase in members it was replaced in 1862 by a spacious brick building known as the Mansion House. In subsequent years, wings were added as needed. The building still stands, in its entirety; in fact, during my visit to Oneida, I stayed at the Mansion House and can attest to the fact that it is a striking architectural form, internally as well as externally. Noyes helped both in the planning and in the actual construction, and while sociologists might question the extent to which physical structure influences social organization, the Mansion House would seem to be a case in point.

Although each adult had a small room of his own, the building was designed to encourage a feeling of togetherness, hence the inclusion of a communal dining hall, recreation rooms, library, concert hall, outdoor picnic area, etc. It was in the Big Hall of the Mansion House that John Humphrey Noyes gave most of his widely-quoted home talks. It was here that musical concerts, dramas, readings, dances, and other forms of socializing were held. Community members were interested in the arts, and were able to organize such activities as symphony concerts, glee club recitals, and Shakespearian plays, even though practically all the talent was home grown. Occasionally, outside artists were invited, but on a day-to-day basis the Community was more or less a closed group, with members seldom straying very far from home base. What might be called their reference behavior related entirely to the group. The outside community was, figuratively and literally, "outside," and was always referred to as The World. It was this system of *integral closure,* sustained over several decades, which served as a primary solidifying force.

Standard reference works make much of economic and sexual communism as being the definitive features of the Oneida Community. As adduced from both interview and documentary materials, however, it would seem that the *communality of action* and the utilization of integral closure were, from a sociological view, paramount. And, of course, it was the Mansion House itself which served as the structural base for practically all Community activity. Insofar as the Perfectionists were concerned, the totality of their existence lay within the walls of the Mansion House. The building was designed to encompass and facilitate this totality pattern, and from all accounts it served its purpose well.

Most of those interviewed were unable to separate the Old Community from the Mansion House. In their minds the two had become one, a fusion of the social and the structural, which, again, underscores the pervasiveness of the physical setting. Even today the building serves as a kind of community center. Most of the surviving members live there, and a good many of the direct descendants live within a block or two; in fact, as the descendants themselves age, they are likely to move into the Mansion House to spend their remaining years. In the words of one of the informants:

> We all love the old place. Many of our folks lived there, and most of us played there as kids. We know the building down to the last brick and board. It's odd, so many of the people who move away seem to come back when they get older

and live in the Mansion House. It's because they had such good times and such happy memories.

It should not be thought that life in the old Community was a continual round of entertainment. The Oneidans built their own home, raised their own food, made all their own clothes (including shoes!), did their own laundry, ran their own school, and performed countless other collective tasks. The performance of these necessary communal chores apparently served as a basic part of the congelation process. To be more specific, one of the interviewees stated that:

> As children we loved to visit the various departments they used to have: the laundry, the kitchen, the fruit cellar, the bakery, the dairy, the dining room, the ice house, the tailor shop—they even had a Turkish Bath in the basement. The thing is that small groups of people worked side by side in most of these places, and they were able to talk with each other as they worked. Many of the jobs—in the kitchen and bakery, for example—were rotated. It's hard to explain, but my mother used to tell me that no matter how menial the job was, they were so busy talking to each other that the time always flew. It was this sort of thing, year after year, that gave rise to a kindred spirit.

Again, from a "family" perspective, it was this *functional partitioning*—the execution of economic tasks through primary group involvement—which helped to explain the success of the Oneida Community. Virtually all of their activities were designed to accentuate the *we*, rather than the *I*, and the economic sphere was no exception. Special abilities were recognized; indeed, wherever possible, occupational assignments were made on the basis of individual aptitudes. But at one time or another most of the work had to be rotated or shared, and so it was with Community life in general. The roles of the members were made crystal clear, and whether the activity in question was social, economic, sexual, or spiritual, the Oneida Perfectionists invariably turned against the *culte du moi* in favor of what to them was a selfless collectivism.

Human nature being what it is, of course, there were inevitable lapses on the part of certain members. Role conflicts sometimes did occur, and it was to counteract any tendency toward selfishness or ego-involvement that the much-publicized system of Mutual Criticism was inaugurated. Although details varied over the years, the general system involved a member who evidenced signs of personal aggrandizement being brought before a committee of peers who, frankly and objectively, attempted to pinpoint his social malfeasance. None of the persons talked with had undergone Mutual Criticism inasmuch as they were too young at the time. (Children were not included in this part of the Oneida program.) From all reports, however, the system of Mutual Criticism was well received. None of those interviewed could recall hearing of any adverse comments; in fact, it appears that as the membership increased, the system came to be applied not only to deviants but to any one who was seriously desirous of self-improvement. The following three comments[1] appeared during 1871-1872 in the *Oneida Circular,* the Community's weekly newspaper:

> I feel as though I had been washed; felt clean through the advice and criticism given. I would call the truth the soap; the critics the scrubbers; Christ's spirit the water.
> Criticism is administered in faithfulness and love without respect to persons. I look upon the criticisms I have received since I came here as the greatest blessings that have been conferred upon me.
> However painful, we have seen it yielding the peaceable fruits of righteousness to them who have been exercised thereby—I am confident, moreover, that instead of producing enmity and grudging, the criticisms that have been performed have increased the love and confidence of the members toward each other.

Although children were not subjected to Mutual Criticism, the meaning of group primacy was impressed upon them in a variety of ways. For instance, an episode was reported as occurring around 1850 involving all the girl children. Prior to this time there had been several large dolls which, like all material things in the Community, were shared. Some kind soul thought it would be helpful if each of the girls had a doll of her own, and this policy was put into effect. However, it developed that the youngsters began to spend too much time with their dolls, and not enough on household chores, Bible reading, and Community matters in general. Accordingly, on a specified occasion, all the girls joined hands in a circle around the stove, and one by one were persuaded to throw their dolls into the fire. For the rest of the Community's existence, dolls were never allowed in the nursery.

Adults, too, were subject to self-imposed deprivations whenever they felt the group welfare threatened, and by present-day standards "group welfare" was given a most liberal interpretation. Several of the informants, for example, mentioned dietary and other restrictions that were adopted over the years. Although the Perfectionists ate well, meat was served sparingly, pork not at all. Lard was not used for shortening. Alcoholic beverages were prohibited, as were tea and coffee. Smoking also came to be taboo. The reasoning behind these prohibitions is not always clear, but presumably the Oneidans were dead set against *informal distractions* of an "anti-family" nature. Thus, dancing and card playing were permitted, since they were regarded as social activities, while coffee-drinking and smoking were condemned on the ground that they were individualistic and appetitive in nature. One of the interviewees made the following points:

> I imagine the prohibitions were pretty well thought out. They didn't just spring up, but developed gradually. I know there were some differences of opinion, but the main thing was that certain practices were felt to be bad for group living. They believed that coffee-drinking was habit-forming, and that people looked forward to it too much—and this would somehow weaken Community ties. Remember, they were trying to create a spiritual and social brotherhood, and they spent much more time in the art of developing relationships

than we do. They had to. After all, hundreds of them were living together as a family, and they worked at it day after day. They were successful, too, for they held together for almost two generations without a major quarrel.

The followers of John Humphrey Noyes were hard-working, well-behaved citizens, among whom crime and delinquency were virtually unknown. Because of this, they were generally respected by the surrounding community and by most everyone else who came into actual contact with them. Nevertheless, the Oneidans were different. They knew it and The World knew it: in fact, this *secular differentiation* reinforced what I have called their system of integral closure and thereby served as another binding factor in the interest of group solidarity. By way of illustration, the Oneida women wore a very distinctive attire: in a period of floor-length skirts the Perfectionist ladies wore short ones (knee length) with loose trousers or "pantalettes" down to the shoes. I was shown some of the original dresses, and my impression was that they would create quite a stir even today. How must they have been viewed by outsiders 100 years ago! Moreover, all the Oneida women bobbed their hair, a custom which the Community instituted in 1848—and which was not introduced into The World until 1922 (by dancer Irene Castle). At any rate, it is easy to see why secular differentiation of this kind strengthened group identity. The following comment is illustrative:

> Your asking of sociological questions about what held the Community together reminds me of something my aunt used to tell. The old Oneidans kept pretty much to themselves, but during the summer months they would sometimes permit visitors. Some Sunday afternoons whole trainloads of visitors would come. They were served picnic-style on the lawn of the Mansion House. I think they were charged $1.00 for the whole thing. Of course, the visitors couldn't get over the way the Oneida women dressed, and they kept staring. My aunt always felt that the way outsiders always looked at them and talked about them had a great deal to do with their feelings of closeness.

Another measure which apparently helped to integrate Community membership was their widely-publicized system of economic communism. Personal ownership of wealth and private property of any kind were taboo, down to and including children's toys. Several of the informants mentioned the fact that in the early days of the Community the Oneidans had rough going; in fact, around 1850 their agricultural economy was in such poor shape that it was necessary for them to sell their watches in order to make ends meet. Fortunately, one of their members developed a steel trap, the manufacture of which involved a secret process of spring tempering. Demand for the traps proved great, and before long it was commonplace for the entire Community to turn out in order to meet the deadline for a large order.

From 1855 on, the Oneidans were without financial worry; in fact, when they broke up around 1880, the treasury showed a balance of some $600,000, no small sum for the period in question. (It was this money which was used to form a joint stock company, which organization today is known as Oneida, Ltd., Silversmiths.) But whether the Community was struggling for survival, as it was during the early period, or whether it was able to reap a financial harvest, as it was during later years, available evidence suggests that collectivistic endeavors, coupled as they were with the other measures described herein, tended to strengthen intra-community bonds.

A final force which served to unite the Perfectionists was their religion and their spiritual devoutness; indeed, it would not be far from the mark to say that the Oneida Community was basically a religious organization. Their social, economic, and sexual beliefs all stemmed from the conviction that they were following God's word as expounded by John Humphrey Noyes. Following the so-called preterist position, Noyes preached that Christ had already returned to earth and that redemption or liberation from sin was an accomplished fact. It followed, therefore, that the spiritual world was autonomous, free, and quite independent of the temporal order. From this perspective, it is easy to see why Noyes was often antagonistic to temporal or "external" law. The essence of his religious teachings, incidentally, can be found in *The Berean,* a lengthy volume which has been called the Bible of the Oneida Community. Contents of *The Berean* range from the semi-mystical to the philosophically profound, but in many areas the teachings are heretical, especially when seen in the light of mid-nineteenth-century religionism.

Because of heresy, Noyes' license to preach had been revoked earlier in Vermont, but following revocation the scope and dogmatic intensity of his preachings increased. Nevertheless, his Oneida followers continued to believe passionately in his religious pronouncements, and any attempt to understand the conjoint nature of the group must take this factor into account. One informant, who had been born into the Community, put it in these words:

> Their religion was different and they were well aware of it. They were also a very devout group. The combination of difference and devoutness made them feel close to one another. Today, you go to church on Sunday, but it doesn't make you feel any closer to the rest of the congregation. Things were different in the Community. Religion brought them together. It wasn't just on Sunday, either—it was part of their everyday living. As a result, the atmosphere was much more spiritual than anything you'd find today, outside of the religious orders.

What was the net result of all of the above measures? From what was said, it appears that the Oneidans were able to maintain a remarkably cohesive form of family and social organization. Conformity was maintained through a patterned series of social controls which, contrary to the usual system of imposure, actually emanated from *within* the membership. As a result, normative interaction was stable enough, over the years, to debar the cliquishness and factionalism which seem to characterize so many of the smaller religious bodies. Those interviewed were nearly unanimous in their belief that the old Oneida Community was an effectively organized, well integrated, and happy group. The following three comments speak for themselves:

> I was a child in the old Community, and I can tell you that they were a happy group. They used to meet nightly in the Big Hall to socialize, discuss problems,

etc. The outside world had their get-togethers on Saturday night. We had ours every night, and it was something to look forward to. Of course, I was only a child at the time—they disbanded before I was 10—and children like to glorify their childhood. Still, when anybody asks me about the old days, my dominant memory is one of contentment and happiness.

I was too young to remember much. But as I grew older and asked my relatives about the Community days, their faces would light up. My own folks were "come outers"; that is, they thought the thing had gone on long enough and weren't too sorry when the group broke up. But even they loved to talk about the "old days" and how much they missed them. They were wonderful people and they had wonderful times.

I was not born in the old Community, although many of my relatives were. But from the way they all talked about life in the Mansion House, they were living life to the fullest. They were able to combine the spiritual, the economic, and the social, and make it really work. At the very end there was some bitterness—about who should take over the leadership—but that's another part of the story.

Sexual Practices

Although their family and social organization were unique, it was the Community's bizarre sexual system which attracted national and international attention. Just as Mormonism is invariably linked with polygyny, so the Oneida Community seems destined to be associated with group marriage. John Humphrey Noyes believed neither in romantic love nor in monogamous marriage, such manifestations being considered selfish and smacking of possessiveness. He taught that all men should love all women and that all women should love all men, and while no attempt was made to impose this reciprocality on The World, group marriage (or "Complex Marriage," as it was called) continued throughout the whole of the Community's existence.

Sex relations within the group were reportedly easy to arrange inasmuch as the men and women all lived in the Mansion House. If a man desired sexual intercourse with a particular woman, he was supposed to make his wish known to a Central Committee, who would convey his desire to the woman in question. If the latter consented, the man would go to her room at bedtime and spend an hour or so with her before returning to his own room. No woman was forced to submit to a sexual relationship which was distasteful to her, and the committee system presumably afforded her a tactful method for turning down unwelcome suitors. It was understood by all concerned that their sexual latitude did not carry with it the rights of parenthood. Only the select were permitted to have children, a point which will be discussed later.

The above facts relating to the sex practices of the Oneidans are those generally contained in texts and encyclopedic references. Many of the really significant sexual questions, however, have never been raised, let alone answered. To what extent did the women refuse sexual requests? Did men and women tend to form more-or-less permanent pairs or was there, in fact, a system of group marriage? Did women initiate sexual requests or, as in The World, was it the men who invariably took the initiative? Was the committee system really used by the Oneida males, or was this merely a formality which was easily by-passed? Did not the women of the Community have difficulty in adjusting, sexually, to a large number of different partners? Was not the factor of male jealousy a problem? And so on. In brief, group marriage is such a rare phenomenon on this earth that ethnographers have sometimes questioned its very existence. Apparently this system of matrimony has too many inherent disadvantages to prevail as a dominant societal form. Contravening a wealth of historical and cross-cultural evidence, therefore, how were the Oneidans able to adjust to group marriage so successfully over a relatively long period? Or were there problems that simply never came to light? One of those interviewed made the following remarks:

> I grant the questions are of interest to family scholars, but look at it from our view. If somebody came to you and asked questions concerning the sex life of your parents and grandparents, you'd have a tough time answering. The same with us. When the old Community broke up, there was a natural reluctance to discuss sex. Former members didn't discuss their own sex lives, and naturally their children and grandchildren didn't pry. I often wish the old people had had a regular system of marriage. Then we wouldn't have had such bad publicity— most of it incorrect or misleading. If it weren't for the sex part, the Oneida Community might have been forgotten long ago.

One of the company officers supplied the following interesting, if sad, information. During the decades of the Community's existence, many of the Oneidans were in the habit of keeping diaries. (Diary-keeping was evidently much more common in the 19th century than it is today.) Some of the Perfectionists also accumulated bundles of personal letters. After the Community broke up, and as the members died over the years, the question arose as to what to do with all these documents. Since so much of the material was of a personal and sexual nature, since names were named, and inasmuch as the children and the grandchildren of these "names" were still living, it was decided to store all the old diaries, letters, and other personal documents in the vaults of Oneida, Ltd. A few years ago a company officer—who happened to be one of the informants—received permission to examine the material in order to see what should be done with it:

> I went through some of the stuff—old diaries and things—and a lot of it was awfully personal. Names and specific happenings were mentioned—that kind of thing. Anyway, I reported these facts to the company, and it was decided that in view of the nature of the material, it should all be destroyed. So one morning we got a truck—and believe me, there was so much stuff we needed a truck—loaded all the material on and took it out to the dump and burned it. We felt that divulging the contents wouldn't have done ourselves or anybody else any good.

Thus went a veritable gold mine of pertinent information! There can be no doubt that the burned material would have shed much light on the sexual patterns of the Oneida Perfectionists. As it is, to reconstruct the operative functionings of group marriage would be a most formidable task; indeed, substantive answers to many of the sex questions may never be found. From the company's viewpoint, of course, the destruction of the above-mentioned documents was understandable. Oneida, Ltd. is not in business to further the cause of socio-historical research, and irrespective of how much the material may have benefited sociologists, there was always the possibility that the contents might have proved embarrassing to the company or to some of the direct descendants.

This diary-burning episode has been mentioned in some detail not only to bring the historico-cultural picture up to date but to point out why it is that for all the uniqueness of their system, next to nothing is known of the actual sex practices of the Perfectionists. The present study may shed a little light on the subject, but it should be kept in mind that like most other Americans of the period, the old Oneidans did not openly discuss sexual matters, so that the children and grandchildren interviewed were probably less informed on this subject than on any of the others that were discussed.

One of the qustions asked was whether the factor of male jealousy did not make itself felt. The answer appears to be in the negative. As one of the interviewees put it:

> I don't think it was much of a problem. Certainly the old folks, when they talked about the Community, never made any issue of it. Their religious teachings emphasized spiritual equality, and their whole way of life was aimed at stamping out feelings of envy and jealousy. Also, with so many women to choose from, why would a man experience feelings of jealousy? Once in a while a man and woman would be suspected of falling in love—"special love" they called it— but it happened infrequently. When it did, the couple were separated. One would be sent to Wallingford, Connecticut—we had a small Community branch there for a while.

Although respondents were agreed that the men readily adjusted to a plurality of women partners, they were generally silent on the question of how the Oneida females adjusted to a variety of male partners. It is unfortunate that so little information was available on this point, for this issue—in my opinion, at least—is a crucial one. In effect, the Oneida women were encouraged to have sex relations with a variety of men, but were not supposed to become emotionally involved with any of the men with whom they were having these relations! The American woman of today tends to emotionalize and romanticize her sexual experience, and it would be hard for her to have any empathetic understanding of the Oneida system, wherein neither romance nor monogamous love were supposed to play any part in the sex act. As for the Oneida women, themselves, one can but conjecture. If they were indeed gratified by sexual variety, all human experience would be in for a contradiction. And yet—given the prevailing social system and their religious orientation —who is to say just what feminine feelings really were. In the absence of the

354

diary material, it is problematical whether this question will ever be fully answered.

One thin clue was the belief by four of the interviewees that at least in terms of overt behavior the female refusal rate was not high. The company officer who had examined a small portion of the material-to-be-burned reported that there was nothing therein to indicate that female refusal was a problem. Another male respondent stated that he had been informed by an old Community member that the latter "had never been refused." Two female interviewees had been told by an older woman member that the refusal rate was probably low. Most of the informants, however, had no specific information to offer, and evidence on this point seems likely to remain fragmentary.

The question whether the Oneida women ever took the initiative in requesting sexual relations drew a generally negative response. Several interviewees reported that they knew of some coquetry on the part of certain women, but that they had never heard of anything more direct. Two of the older female respondents stated that there was one known case where a woman went to a man and asked to have a child by him. In this instance, however, the implication is not clear, inasmuch as the Perfectionists differentiated sharply between sex for procreation and sex for recreation. All reports considered, it seems doubtful whether Oneida females were any more disposed to assume the role of active partner than were females in society at large.

That the Perfectionists institutionalized sexual freedom is a matter of record; in fact, the term "free love" appears to have been coined by the Oneidans around 1850. At the same time, certain sexual rules—some written, some unwritten—were developed, and consensus was strong enough to effect optimal conformity. Oneidans were enjoined to act like ladies and gentlemen at all times. Coarse behavior, vulgar or suggestive language, overt displays of sexuality—such behaviorisms were not tolerated. As a matter of fact, the evidence available suggests that sexual activity was not openly discussed within the Community, and it is doubtful whether the subject of "Who was having relations with whom?" ever became common knowledge. It was said, for instance, that one male member who became too inquisitive on this score was literally thrown out of the Community, an act which represented the only expulsion in the group's history.

The extent to which the committee system was utilized is not clear. Officially, male members were supposed to get permission from the Central Committee, or at least from the Chairman of the Committee (usually an older woman), before having sexual relations with a given female, but several of the persons interviewed had reservations on this point. The most pointed response was the following:

> Well, I've thought about the committee business, and I've talked with some of the old folks about it. I'm inclined to think it was kind of a formality that declined with the passage of time. Perhaps in the beginning it was adhered to. Also, it may have been that the first time a man and a woman had relations a go-between was consulted, but I doubt whether further relations called for any

formal permission. Of course, in order to have children, committee approval was needed, but from the strictly sexual view I think it was considered pretty much private business.

The Eugenics Program. A vital component of the Oneida sexual system was the eugenics program, usually referred to as Stirpiculture. Noyes had been impressed with the writings of Darwin and Galton, and from the very beginning had decided that the Community should follow the principles of scientific propagation. Accordingly, he requested the Perfectionists to refrain from having children until such time as adequate financial resources were built up, and published accounts make much of the fact that during the 20 years it took to achieve economic self-sufficiency the Oneidans were successful in their efforts at fertility control. The type of birth control used was *coitus reservatus,* sexual intercourse up to but not including ejaculation. Male orgasm was permissible only with women who had passed menopause; in fact, it was with this group of females that the younger men were supposed to learn the necessary ejaculatory control. After the twenty-year period, 53 women and 38 men were chosen to be parents, or stirps, and the eugenics program was officially inaugurated. During the ensuing ten years, 58 children were born into the Community, after which period the Perfectionists disbanded.

So much for the published accounts. From the information which could be pieced together, these accounts are somewhat inaccurate. To begin with, some children *were* born into the Community prior to 1869, the year the eugenics program was started. The technique of *coitus reservatus,* therefore, was not 100 per cent effective, though in view of its rather bizarre nature it seems to have worked reasonably well.[2]

It should also be pointed out that several children were born after the eugenics program had started who were *not* the offspring of stirps. Understandably, a number of the women who had failed to be chosen as prospective parents were still desirous of having babies, and a few reportedly did their utmost to achieve motherhood. Mentioned, for instance, was a passage in one of the burned diaries in which a man, referring to his sexual activities with a particular woman, made the remark, "She tried to make me lose control." In spite of some marked exceptions, however, those who were not chosen as stirps seem to have accepted their lot without question.

The actual criteria and methods for selecting the stirps have never been revealed. It is known that committees were set up to make the selection, but what standards they used is something of a mystery. Noyes served on the committees, and it would seem that it was he who largely decided which of the Perfectionists were qualified for parenthood. It was said that Noyes, himself, fathered a dozen children, so that evidently he was not adverse to self-selection.

Whatever the criteria used, and whatever the relative contributions of heredity and environment, the Stirpiculture program was apparently a success. As a group, the children born of selected parents led a healthy and vigorous life. Their death rate was reportedly lower than that of the surrounding community;[3] in fact, as mentioned earlier, thirteen of the Stirpiculture children are still living, a figure substantially greater than actuarial expectancy. Interviews revealed that a number of the children had achieved eminence in the business and professional world, several had written books, and nearly all had in turn borne children who were a credit to the community.

It might be well at this point to clear up a misconception relative to the child-rearing program of the Community. It is true that the children were not raised by their parents. Infants were under the care of their mothers up to the age of 15 months, but thereafter were moved to the children's section of the Mansion House. And while the youngsters were treated with kindness by their parents, the Community made a conscious effort to play down feelings of sentimentality between parents and offspring, the feeling being that Perfectionists should treat all children as their own, and vice versa.

It is not true, however, that the child-rearing system was one of impersonality. Children were shown ample affection and kindness, and they apparently enjoyed the zest of group living; at least, all those interviewed felt certain that childhood in the Old Community was a happy and exhilarating experience. As one of the "children" put it:

> Well, I remember one little girl always wanted her mother. She'd stand outside her window and call to her, even though the mother wasn't supposed to answer. Other than that particular case, all the children seemed happy enough. Everybody was good to us. You knew you were loved because it was like a big family. Also, there were so many activities for the youngsters, so many things to do, well—believe me—we were happy children. Everybody around here will give you the same answer on that!

NOTES

[1] Harriet M. Worden, *Old Mansion House Memories,* Kenwood, Oneida, N.Y.: privately printed, 1950, pp. 15–16.

[2] It should be mentioned that in the minds of the Perfectionists the system was by no means bizarre. *Coitus reservatus* was looked upon not only as an effective method of birth control but as a means of *emotionally elevating* sexual pleasure. Interestingly enough, in Aldous Huxley's recent best-selling *Island* (N.Y., Harper, 1962), *coitus reservatus* is the method used by the Utopian society of Pala: "Did you ever hear of the Oneida Community?" Ranga now asked. "Basically, *maithuna* is the same as what the Oneida people called *coitus reservatus.* . . . But birth control is only the beginning of the story. Maithuna is something else. Something even more important. Remember," he went on earnestly, "the point that Freud was always harping on . . . the point about the sexuality of children. What we're born with, what we experience all through infancy and childhood, is a sexuality that isn't concentrated on the genitals; it's a sexuality diffused throughout the whole organism. That's the paradise we inherit. But the paradise gets lost as the child grows up. Maithuna is the organized attempt to regain that paradise." (pp. 86–87)

[3] H. H. and G. W. Noyes, "The Oneida Community Experiment in Stirpiculture," *Eugenics, Genetics and the Family,* 1 (1932), pp. 374–386.

The Kibbutz as a
Communal Society

Melford E. Spiro

The formation of the kibbutz in Israel reflected certain dissatisfactions of Jews with the marriage system in Europe. Their aim was to create a communal life style that abolished the authority of the male over wife and children and that encouraged a group spirit rather than loyalty to one person (as in the Oneida Community). Spiro discusses how kibbutz members attempted to meet these aims and some of the difficulties they encountered both with young couples and in socialization of the children. He also discusses a gradual shift in the next generation toward a more traditional form of love and marriage.

It is difficult to decide whether the family or even marriage, in their conventional forms, exist in Kiryat Yedidim.* From its very inception, Kiryat Yedidim has stressed two polar entities—the individual and the community—and it has attempted to minimize, if not to eliminate, any intermediate groups between the two. In its conventional sense, not even the "nuclear" family exists in the kibbutz, except in a highly attenuated form. In a broader sense, however, one might say that the whole kibbutz is a family—a large extended family. In either case, it is premature to evaluate the kibbutz family, for Kiryat Yedidim is in a state of transition, and it is difficult to predict what structures might yet emerge. It is apparent, for example, from an examination of the history of Kiryat Yedidim, and from conversations with the vattikim.** that it had originally expected to destroy both marriage and the family in their conven-

From Melford E. Spiro, *Kibbutz: Venture in Utopia* (Cambridge: Harvard University Press, 1956), pp. 110–18, 120–22, 123–26. Reprinted by permission of the author and Harvard University Press.

*"Kiryat Yedidim" is Hebrew for "City of Friends" and is the name of a kibbutz in Israel.

**The founding residents of the kibbutz.

tional meanings. The changing attitudes of the vattikim, however, as well as the attitudes of the sabras* toward marriage and the family, and the changing social conditions in the kibbutz—brought about by the existence of children and grandchildren—have served to create a structural fluidity in these kibbutz groupings.

It will be remembered that the vattikim, when members of the Youth Movement, were in rebellion against the Jewish culture of the shtetl, as well as against the bourgeois culture of the European city. And among the many aspects of these cultures that they wished to change were the "false" sexual morality of the city, the "patriarchal" authority of the male, the "dependence" of the child on his father, and the "subjection" of women. Their rebellion against the first two traditions led them to a radical revision of the marriage relationship; their opposition to the latter two led to a serious modification of the traditional family.

We shall first consider the marriage relationship. The Youth Movement had a strong "puritanical" tinge, and its general emphasis on "purity" in living extended to its attitude toward sexual relations. Love, for the sixteen-year-olds in the movement, was a serious matter, not to be taken lightly, as it was by the "decadent" *bourgeoisie*. "We were serious; we were too serious," said one vattika, critically. They were opposed to even mild flirtations; and one vattika recalls, as an historic curiosity, a weekend trip they had taken to the mountains in Europe, in which there was "not even a kiss." "We thought," she commented, "that we were supermen. In this sense, the young sabras are healthier than we were; we were confused."

When these people, in their late teens and early twenties, arrived in Palestine, they were confronted with the problem of establishing their own sexual morality, and this task was not easy. "It was difficult," commented this vattika, "from an erotic point of view." The sex ratio was 2:1—sixty males and thirty females—which was difficult enough. In addition, they were supposed to live together in one community, but not as couples. "It is little wonder that we were all," as she put it, "concerned with sex." This was the period in their history when Freud was studied seriously, not so much for intellectual stimulation, as for practical guidance. But Freud "only created greater confusion."

After some initial soul-searching, the pioneers attempted to arrive at a satisfactory relationship between the sexes by trial-and-error. They were convinced that it was possible to create a relationship between the sexes on a sounder and more natural foundation than that which characterized "bourgeois" marriage, and they experimented with many substitutes including informal polygyny and polyandry. They attempted to break down the traditional attitude of sexual shame in which they had been reared by instituting a mixed shower, but that experiment was soon abandoned—"Our previous training was too strong." As for marriage, they believed—and still believe—that a union between a man and a woman was their own affair, to be entered

*Native-born kibbutz residents.

359

into on the basis of love and to be broken at the termination of love; neither the union nor the separation were to require the permission or the sanction of the community. Today, for example, if a couple wishes to marry, the partners merely ask for a joint room; if they wish a divorce, they return to separate rooms. It should be added, however, that since the kibbutz is not an autonomous society, it must take account of the laws of the land, according to which illegitimate children have no civil rights. Hence, when a woman becomes pregnant, the couple becomes legally married.

It is in this same spirit that kibbutz children have received their sexual education. Children are discouraged from engaging in sexual experimentation, but they are taught in school about sexual matters in an objective way. The high school youth are also discouraged from engaging in sexual experiences, as well as from forming romantic attachments, not for reasons of sexual morality, but because it is felt that such experiences divert their energies and interests from their intellectual and social activities. On the other hand, the sexes share common rooms in the dormitories from infancy through high school graduation and they share a common shower until they enter high school. In the not too distant past, showers were shared in the high school as well, but this practice was abandoned by the children themselves.

Upon entering the kibbutz as full-fledged members, the recent high school graduates may enter into sexual relationships with impunity. Sexual affairs are viewed as the exclusive concern of the couples involved until they fall in love and decide to get married. When that occurs they apply to the housing committee for a common room, and the granting of this request constitutes the official community recognition and sanction of the marriage.

From the very beginning the terms, "marriage," "husband," "wife," were abandoned because of their invidious connotations. A man and woman do not get "married"; they become a "pair" (*zug*). A woman does not acquire a "husband," she acquires a "young man" (*bachur*) or a "companion" (*chaver*). By the same token, a man acquires not a "wife," but a "young woman" (*bachura*) or a "companion" (*chavera*). Divorces were frequent in the past, but they created few hardships, since there were no legal problems involved, and few of the couples had as yet had children. For there seemed to have been a common understanding when they were still living in work camps, that they would delay having children until a permanent settlement had been acquired. Even after they settled in Kiryat Yedidim, however, the chaverim felt that they should not raise children until the geographic and economic conditions of the *kibbutz* were improved. (They were living in swampland, and suffered a serious shortage of food.)

In the past when two persons fell in love and became united as a "couple," they attempted to deny their relationship, as it were, by seldom being seen together in public, or by acting casually towards each other if they were to meet in a public place. Partners were even "ashamed" to enter the dining room together; they would enter separately and eat at different tables. One chavera tells how embarrassed she was when her husband not only insisted on entering the dining room with her, but went so far as to put his arm around her in

360

public. During our stay in Kiryat Yedidim, a number of chaverim went on a trip which marked an important occasion in their history, because it was the first times that mates accompanied each other on a trip. In the past, this was unheard of; each would go his separate way and, returning, would greet everyone in the kibbutz except his mate.

The reason for this public "denial" of a strong bond between partners seems to have been twofold. In the first place, to have acted otherwise would have been "bourgeois," and the kibbutz viewed bourgeois behavior as a stigma. Secondly, Kiryat Yedidim, it will be recalled, emphasized group living as an end in itself, so that the individual's strongest tie was supposed to be with the entire community. It was, therefore, important for a person who had acquired a "companion" to emphasize the fact that he had not divorced himself from the group life, and that he was not creating a private life or developing private interests that would sever his ties with the group.[1]

But the opposition of the kibbutz to bourgeois marriage rested not only on its antagonism to the "false" and "hypocritical" sexual morality of this marriage; it was based also on the strong feminist philosophy of the Youth Movement. The bourgeois woman, as viewed by the chaverim, is little better than a chattel servant. She has few legal rights or political privileges, and she is economically and socially dependent upon her husband. Her "place" is in the home, and her main task is to serve her husband and her children. In their new society, women were to be the equals of men in all matters—their subjection to men in bourgeois society being a result of the social system rather than of natural inferiority. But if the traditional marriage arrangements were to be perpetuated, women could not become men's equals. They would again be legally dependent upon their husbands, since their legal status would be that of Mrs. So-and-so. They would be socially dependent upon their husbands, since their social status would depend upon the latter's social status. And they would be economically dependent upon their husbands, for they would again be relegated to housework, while their husbands remained the providers. If this "patriarchal authority" of the husband was to be destroyed, it was necessary to change the legal, social, and economic status of women. This, the kibbutz feels, has been achieved.

The abolition of the marriage ceremony, the chaverim assert, has abolished the woman's legal subjection to the man. She does not assume his name, and her legal status in the community is not that of his wife, but that of a chavera of the kibbutz. Hence, both are chaverim of the kibbutz, equal in all respects. Though living in the same room, they remain legally distinct as far as the kibbutz is concerned. Nor is the woman's social status dependent upon that of her husband. A woman's prestige is not enhanced by the fact that her husband is recognized as a leader, as a skilled worker, or as a person of great knowledge; nor is it lowered because he is stupid, irresponsible, or highly inefficient. Moreover, the absence of private ownership in property and of differential wealth makes it impossible for a woman to enjoy prestige because of her husband's economic fortunes. Finally, her economic dependence upon her husband has been destroyed by making men and women co-equals in the economic life of the kibbutz. Since the woman, like the man, works in the kibbutz economy rather than in her own home, she earns her own living and is not dependent upon her husband for her support. A woman satisfies her economic needs, therefore, not as a dependent of her husband whose labor provides for her, but as an independent worker in her own right whose contribution to the economic welfare of the community equals that of her husband. Should she desire to divorce him, she need have no fear of losing her source of economic support. Moreover, woman's inferior position in the economy was abolished, it is believed, by destroying the traditional division of labor based on sex. In the early days of the kibbutz, sexual division of labor was minimal. Both men and women shared the work in the kitchen and other traditional "female" occupations, and they both shared the work on the roads, on the tractors, and in other traditional "male" occupations. Today, this is no longer the case although some women still work in the fields, and men take their turn at kitchen work. When the "problem of the women" is examined it will be observed that much of the original feminist philosophy, and even more of its practice, has undergone a considerable change. Nevertheless, the basic structure of the marriage relationship remains today as it was in the past, with but two changes. Divorce, which was relatively frequent in the past, has become infrequent. This increase in marriage stability probably is due to the fact that the vattikim are no longer the hot-blooded young rebels they were in their youth, and that their married children seem to be opposed to divorce on principle. Actually, the entire attitude of the kibbutz towards sex seems to have undergone a great change. Sexual promiscuity is viewed with suspicion, and extramarital affairs, although not censured, are no longer approved. The one extramarital affair which occurred during the writer's stay (of which he was aware, that is) was viewed by many chaverim as "adultery," though the word was never used.

The second important change has been the public recognition and the admission of a "couple" relationship. Spouses go on trips together, take their vacations together, and eat their evening meals together, as a matter of course, without shame and embarrassment. Moreover, one occasionally hears a woman referring to her mate as "my husband" (baali), an idiom that would have been taboo in the past. When the author chided one of the women for using this term, she remarked, "What's the difference? In the past, these things meant a lot to us; but now that we're older, they don't mean very much."

Some sabras go so far as to have a public celebration when they become a "couple," something that would have been shocking in their parents' generation. But an even greater deviation on the part of the sabras, and one which some viewed as a serious breach of kibbutz morality, occurred during our stay. Two sabras, who had been a "couple" for two years, decided to become legally married in order to preclude the criticism they would encounter in Jerusalem, where they were to study. The night of the ceremony, the bride's father arranged for a festive celebration of the Chatuna (religious marriage) of his daughter. The criticism of this by kibbutz members was on two counts—the reference to the marriage in religious terms, and the celebration of the occasion as if the marriage ceremony really marked the beginning of their marriage, when, from the point of view of the kibbutz, they had been officially married two years earlier.

. . . .

The kibbutz "family" includes two adults of opposite sex who "maintain a socially approved sexual relationship" and their "own or adopted" children. As we have already observed, however, it does not include economic cooperation, nor does it include common residence, since the children live in separate children's dormitories. This "family," moreover, does not have the function of education and socialization, since this function is fulfilled by the "nurses" and teachers in the communal dormitories as part of the system of "collective education," a system which arose as a function of the kibbutz protest against the "patriarchal" father and the "subjection" of women.

One way in which the "dependence" of the child upon the "patriarchal" father could be eliminated was to remove the child physically from the father, and to entrust him to the care of some other person. This was done by instituting children's dormitories, in which specialized "nurses" and teachers, rather than the father (and/or the mother) raise the children. As the education journal of The Federation puts it,

> The changes in the family, whose economic foundations have been uprooted, have brought about a change in the status of the man and woman in the kibbutz society, and with that a change of the status of the father and mother in the family. This is most pronounced with respect to the function of the father, for all his ruling privileges, the source of his formal authority, are destroyed.

The father not only does not rear the child, but he also has no specific responsibility for him. The child is provided for by the kibbutz as a whole; he receives his food in the dormitory dining room, his clothes from the dormitory storeroom, his medical care from the dispensary, and his housing in the dormitories. This is a deliberate policy, the aim of which is to prevent the child from feeling economically dependent upon the father which, according to kibbutz analysis, is the greatest source of the father's authority in bourgeois society. The official book on education, published by The Federation, puts it clearly: one of the results of the system of collective education has been that:

> . . .the child is emancipated from the rule of the father of the family. . . . In the patriarchal family the child is dependent economically and legally on the father as provider, on the "master of the household," which is not true in the kibbutz. The child is not dependent, in any objective sense, except on the kibbutz as a whole.

Again, we read that:

> . . . related to the economic structure of the family in the kibbutz (is the fact that) the kibbutz has put an end to the patriarchate. . . . The father does not

enjoy the superior position that was the privilege of the "economic provider" in the ordinary society.

. . . .

In sum, the kibbutz has succeeded in eliminating most of the characteristics and functions of the traditional family. The parents have little responsibility for the physical care or for the socialization of their children; the relationship between mates does not include economic cooperation; and parents and children do not share a common residence. Taking these facts, alone, into consideration it may be concluded that the family, as characterized by Murdock, does not exist in the kibbutz. On the other hand, though the family does not exist in a structural-functional sense, it does exist in a psychological sense. Although parents and children do not share a common residence, they are deeply attached to each other and comprise a distinct and recognizable social group. Moreover, the chaverim themselves refer to this group as a *mishpacha,* or family.[2]

The one characteristic of all kibbutzim, on which all observers are in unanimous agreement, is the attachment of parents for their children. Kiryat Yedidim, like other kibbutzim, is a child-centered society, par excellence. Children are prized above all else. In observing the kibbutz and from interviewing parents one receives the distinct impression that no sacrifice is too great to make for the children. Adults are willing to live in sub-standard housing as long as children may live in stuccoed brick dormitories. Adults share two shower rooms—one for males and one for females—and two toilets, but each children's dormitory has its own shower and toilets. Adults are content to eat dairy meals and few desserts, so that the children may enjoy meat and desserts at almost every meal. Adults work long hours in the fields with brief annual vacations, while their children receive a high school education, including many extracurricular activities, so that they work—even when high school seniors— only a few hours a day, and enjoy a three-month summer vacation. Finally, so that parents may devote the late afternoon to their children, the kibbutz works during the heat of the day even in the summer, instead of taking a long afternoon siesta and beginning the afternoon work after the hottest part of the day has passed.

This general attitude of Kiryat Yedidim toward all its children is a reflection, of course, of the attitude parents have toward their own children. These parents, to be sure, do not have the many responsibilities that parents in other societies have for their children. But, instead of weakening the parental tie, the kibbutz system of "collective education" has strengthened it. For most parents, the entire day is a prelude to the brief period in the late afternoon when they are joined by their children. Upon return from work—4:30 in winter and 5:30 in summer—the parents shower, change their clothes, and hasten to the children's dormitories to greet their children, if the latter have not already arrived at the parental rooms. The next two hours are sacred;

they are to be devoted exclusively to the children, and nothing is allowed to interfere. During this "children's hour" all activities in the kibbutz come to a standstill; one wit has observed that if the bordering Arab state were to attack the kibbutz at that time, it would win a handy victory, since the chaverim could not be induced to leave their children. In summer, parents and children spend their time romping on the grass, playing games, visiting the animals, strolling through the fields. In winter, they are confined to their rooms, and activities consist of playing, reading, listening to music, and talking. When it is time for the children to return to their dormitories, they are usually accompanied by their parents, and the final departure is sometimes difficult for both. Parents and children are together not only every afternoon, but on Saturdays and holidays as well.

The eagerness of parents to see their children is equalled only by the eagerness of the children to see their parents. This is not surprising. In the dormitories the children must not only share their nurse's love with many other children, but they are subjected to her discipline as well. Furthermore, they must conform to the regimen and routine which dormitory life demands. In their parental room, on the other hand, they can monopolize their parents— most children have no more than a couple of siblings—they are seldom disciplined, and they are indulged to the point where the chaverim say they are "spoiled." Hence it is, that children generally mean their parental room when they refer to "my room," and they brag about the abilities and accomplishments (real or imagined) of their parents, much as children in our own society.

NOTES

[1] On another "level," the denial of sexual relationships may be viewed as part of the sexual puritanism that characterized the philosophy of the youth movement. This puritanism is still an integral part of kibbutz life. One seldom, if ever, hears sexual references in a mixed group, and even in an all-male work detail, for example, the conversation seldom includes sexual jokes or references. The author encountered not a single incident of the above.

[2] For an extended discussion and attempted resolution of this entire problem, see Spiro, "Is the Family Universal?"

Getting Back to the
Communal Garden

Sara Davidson

Two hippie communes, as described by Davidson, seem far more unorganized than their Oneida and kibbutz counterparts. The emphasis on individualism, drugs, and primitive living for its own sake, and the absence of overriding religious traditions, also differentiate the new group arrangements from earlier attempts. Davidson describes some of the dissensions that have beset these communes in the areas of cooperative living and child rearing, and reports on how members try to solve these problems.

When Bill (Wheeler) bought the ranch in 1963, looking for a place to paint and live quietly, he built the studio for his family. Four years later, when he opened the land to anyone who wanted to settle there, the county condemned his studio as living quarters because it lacked the required amount of concrete under one side. Bill moved into a tent and used the studio for his painting and for community meetings.

Bill is a tall, lean man of thirty with an aristocratic forehead, straight nose, deep-set blue eyes, and a full beard and flowing hair streaked yellow by the sun. His voice is gentle with a constant hint of mirth, yet it projects, like his clear gaze, a strength, which is understood in this community as divine grace. Quiet, unhurried, he progresses with steady confidence toward a goal or solution of a problem. He is also a voluptuary who takes Rabelaisian delight in the community's lack of sexual inhibitions and in the sight of young girls walking nude through the grass. He lives at the center of the ranch with his third wife, Gay, twenty-two, and their infant daughter, Raspberry. His humor and self-assurance make it easy for those around him to submit to the hippie credo that "God will provide," because they know that what God does not, Bill Wheeler will.

. . . .

On a bluff behind Wheeler's garden, the steam bath is set to go. Red-hot rocks are taken from the fire into a plastic tent that can be sealed on all sides. Shifts of eight or nine people undress and sit on the mud floor, letting out whoops, chanting and singing. Gallon wine jugs filled with water are poured

From Sara Davidson, "Open Land: Getting Back to the Communal Garden," *Harper's Magazine,* June, 1970, pp. 92–102. Reprinted by permission of Curtis Brown, Ltd.

on the rocks, and the tent fills up with steam so hot and thick that the children start coughing and no one can see anyone else. After a few minutes, they step out, covered with sweat, and wash off in a cold shower. The women shampoo their hair and soap up the children. The men dig out ticks from under the skin. Much gaiety and good-natured ogling, and then, as the last shift is coming out, a teen-age visitor carrying the underground *Berkeley Tribe* wanders in and stops, dumbfounded, staring with holy-fool eyes, his mouth open and drooling, at all that flesh and hair and sweat.

The garden, like a jigsaw puzzle whose pieces have floated together, presents the image of a nineteenth century tableau: women in long skirts and shawls, men in lace-up boots, coveralls, and patched jeans tied with pieces of rope, sitting on the grass playing banjos, guitars, lyres, wood flutes, dulcimers, and an accordion. In a field to the right are the community animals—chickens, cows, goats, donkeys, and horses. As far as the eye can see, there are no houses, no traffic, nothing but verdant hills, a stream, and the ocean with whitecaps rising in the distance. Nine-year-old Michelle is prancing about in a pink shawl and a floppy hat warbling, "It's time for the feast!" Nancy says, "The pickin's are sort of spare, because tomorrow is welfare day and everybody's broke." She carries from the outdoor wood stove pots of brown rice—plain, she says, "for the purists who are on Georges Ohsawa's ten-day brown-rice diet"—and rice with fruit and nuts for everyone else; beans, red and white; oranges and apples; yogurt; hash; pot; acid; mescaline. A girl says there are worms in the green apples. Another, with a studious voice and glasses, says, "That's cool, it means they were organically grown. I'd rather eat a worm than a chemical any day." They eat with their fingers from paper plates, and when the plates are gone, directly from the pot. A man in his forties with red-spotted cheeks asks me if I have any pills. "I'll take anything. I'm on acid now." I offer him aspirin. He swallows eight.

Everyone who lives at Wheeler's ranch is a vegetarian. By some strange inversion, they feel that by eating meat they are hastening their own death. Vegetarianism is, ironically, the aspect of their life-style that aggravates even the most liberal parents. ("What? You won't eat meat? That's ridiculous!") Bill Wheeler says that diet is "very very central to the revolution. It's a freeing process which people go through, from living on processed foods and eating gluttonous portions of meat and potatoes, to natural foods and a simple diet that is kinder to your body. A lot has to do with economics. It's much cheaper to live on grains and vegetables you can grow in your garden. When Gay and I moved here, we had to decide whether to raise animals to slaughter. Gay said she couldn't do it. Every Thanksgiving, there's a movement to raise money to buy turkeys, because some people think the holiday isn't complete without them. But an amazing thing happens when carrion is consumed. People are really greedy, and it's messy. The stench and the grease stay with us for days."

. . . .

Bill Wheeler refers to his ranch as "the land," and talks about people who live on the land, babies that are born on the land, music played on the land.

367

He "opened the land," as he phrases it, in the winter of 1967, after Sonoma County officials tried to close Morning Star by bulldozing trees and all the buildings except Gottlieb's house. Some Morning Star people moved to Wheeler's, but others traveled to New Mexico, where they founded Morning Star East on a mesa near Taos owned by another wealthy hippie. The Southwest, particularly northern New Mexico and Colorado, has more communes on open land than any other region. The communes there are all crowded, and Taos is becoming a Haight-Ashbury in the desert. More land continues to be opened in New Mexico, as well as in California, Oregon, and Washington. Gottlieb plans to buy land and deed it to God in Holland, Sweden, Mexico, and Spain. "We're fighting against the territorial imperative," he says. "The hippies should get the Nobel Prize for creating this simple idea. Why did no one think of it before the hippies? Because hippies don't work, so they have time to dream up truly creative ideas."

It was surprising to hear people refer to themselves as "hippies"; I thought the term had been rendered meaningless by overuse. Our culture has absorbed so much of the style of hip—clothes, hair, language, drugs, music—that it has obscured the substance of the movement with which people at Morning Star and Wheeler's still strongly identify. Being a hippie, to them, means dropping out completely, and finding another way to live, to support oneself physically and spiritually. It does not mean being a company freak, working nine to five in a straight job and roaming the East Village on weekends. It means saying no to competition, no to the work ethic, no to consumption of technology's products, no to political systems and games. Lou Gottlieb, who was once a Communist party member, says, "The entire Left is a dead end." The hippie alternative is to turn inward and reach backward for roots, simplicity, and the tribal experience. In the first bloom of the movement, people flowed into slums where housing would be cheap and many things could be obtained free—food scraps from restaurants, second-hand clothes, free clinics and services. But the slums proved inhospitable. The hippies did nothing to improve the dilapidated neighborhoods, and they were preyed upon by criminals, pushers, and the desperate. In late 1967, they began trekking to rural land where there would be few people and life would be hard. They took up what Ramon Sender calls "voluntary primitivism," building houses out of mud and trees, planting and harvesting crops by hand, rolling loose tobacco into cigarettes, grinding their own wheat, baking bread, canning vegetables, delivering their own babies, and educating their own children. They gave up electricity, the telephone, running water, gas stoves, even rock music, which, of all things, is supposed to be the cornerstone of hip culture. They started to sing and play their own music— folky and quiet.

Getting close to the earth meant conditioning their bodies to cold, discomfort, and strenuous exercise. At Wheeler's, people walk twenty miles a day, carrying water and wood, gardening, and visiting each other. Only four-wheel-drive vehicles can cross the ranch, and ultimately Bill wants all cars banned. "We would rather live without machines. And the fact that we have no good roads protects us from tourists. People are car-bound, even police. They would never come in here without their vehicles." Although it rains a good part of the year, most of the huts do not have stoves and are not waterproof. "Houses shouldn't be designed to keep out the weather," Bill says. "We want to get in touch with it." He installed six chemical toilets on the ranch to comply with county sanitation requirements, but, he says, "I wouldn't go in one of those toilets if you paid me. It's very important for us to be able to use the ground, because we are completing a cycle, returning to Mother Earth what she's given us." Garbage is also returned to the ground. Food scraps are buried in a compost pile of sawdust and hay until they decompose and mix with the soil. Paper is burned, and metal buried. But not everyone is conscientious; there are piles of trash on various parts of the ranch.

Because of the haphazard sanitation system, the water at Wheeler's is contaminated, and until people adjust to it, they suffer dysentery, just as tourists do who drink the water in Mexico. There are periodic waves of hepatitis, clap, crabs, scabies, and streptococcic throat infections. No one brushes his teeth more than once a week, and then they often use "organic toothpaste," made from eggplant cooked in tinfoil. They are experimenting with herbs and Indian healing remedies to become free of manufactured medicinal drugs, but see no contradiction in continuing to swallow any mind-altering chemical they are offered. The delivery of babies on the land has become an important ritual. With friends, children, and animals keeping watch, chanting, and getting collectively stoned, women have given birth to babies they have named Morning Star, Psyche Joy, Covelo Vishnu God, Rainbow Canyon King, and Raspberry Sundown Hummingbird Wheeler.

The childbirth ritual and the weekly feasts are conscious attempts at what is called "retribalization." But Wheeler's Ranch, like many hippie settlements, has rejected communal living in favor of a loose community of individuals. People live alone or in monogamous units, cook for themselves, and build their own houses and sometimes gardens. "There should not be a main lodge, because you get too many people trying to live under one roof and it doesn't work," Bill says. As a result, there are cliques who eat together, share resources, and rarely mix with others on the ranch. There was one group marriage between two teen-age girls, a forty-year-old man, and two married couples, which ended when one of the husbands saw his wife with another man in the group, pulled a knife, and dragged her off, yelling, "Forget this shit. She belongs to me."

With couples, the double standard is an unwritten rule: the men can roam but the women must be faithful. There are many more men than women, and when a new girl arrives, she is pounced upon, claimed, and made the subject of wide gossip. Mary Cordelia Stevens, or Corky, a handsome eighteen-year-old from a Chicago suburb, hiked into the ranch one afternoon last October and sat down by the front gate to eat a can of Spam. The first young man who came by invited her to a party where everyone took TCP, a tranquilizer for horses. It was a strange trip—people rolling around the floor of the tipi, moaning, retching, laughing, hallucinating. Corky went home with one guy and stayed with him for three weeks, during which time she was almost constantly stoned. "You sort of have to be stoned to get through the first days here," she says. "Then you know the trip." Corky is a strapping, well-proportioned, large-boned girl with a milkmaid's face and long blond hair. She talks softly, with many giggles: "I love to go around naked. There's so much sexual energy here, it's great. Everybody's turned on to each other's bodies." Corky left the ranch to go home for Christmas and to officially drop out of Antioch College; she hitchhiked back, built her own house and chicken coop, learned to plant, do laundry in a tin tub with a washboard, and milk the cows. "I love dealing with things that are simple and direct."

Bill Wheeler admires Corky for making it on her own, which few of the women do. Bill is torn between his desire to be the benefactor-protector and his intolerance of people who aren't self-reliant. "I'm contemptuous of people who can't pull their own weight," he says. Yet he constantly worries about the welfare of others. He also feels conflict between wanting a tribe, indeed wanting to be chieftain, and wanting privacy. "Open land requires a leap of faith," he says, "but it's worth it, because it guarantees there will always be change, and stagnation is death." Because of the fluidity of the community, it is almost impossible for it to become economically self-sufficient. None of the communes have been able to live entirely off the land. Most are unwilling to go into cash crops or light industry because in an open community with no rules, there are not enough people who can be counted on to work regularly. The women with children receive welfare, some of the men collect unemployment and food stamps, and others get money from home. They spend very little—perhaps $600 a year per person. "We're not up here to make money," Bill says, "or to live like country squires."

When darkness falls, the ranch becomes eerily quiet and mobility stops. No one uses flashlights. Those who have lived there some time can feel their way along the paths by memory. Others stay in their huts, have dinner, go to sleep, and get up with the sun. Around 7:00 P.M., people gather at the barn with bottles for the late milking. During the week, the night milking is the main social event. Corky says, "It's the only time you know you're going to see people. Otherwise you could wander around for days and not see anyone." A girl from Holland and two boys have gathered mussels at a nearby beach during the day, and invite everyone to the tipi to eat them. We sit for some time in silence, watching the mussels steam open in a pot over the grate. A boy with glassy blue eyes whose lids seem weighted down starts to pick out the orange flesh with his dirt-caked hands and drops them in a pan greased with Spry. A mangy cat snaps every third mussel out of the pan. No one stops it. . . .

Nancy, in her shack about a mile from the tipi, is fixing a green stew of onions, cabbage, kale, leeks, and potatoes; she calls to three people who live nearby to come share it. Nancy has a seventeen-year-old, all-American-girl face—straight blond hair and pink cheeks—on a plump, saggy-stomached mother's body. She has been married twice, gone to graduate school, worked as a social worker and a prostitute, joined the Sexual Freedom League, and taken many overdoses of drugs. Her children have been on more acid trips than most adults at the ranch. "They get very quiet on acid," she says. "The experience is less staggering for kids than for adults, because acid returns you to the consciousness of childhood." Nancy says the children have not been sick since they moved to Wheeler's two years ago. "I can see divine guidance leading us here. This place has been touched by God." She had a vision of planting trees on the land, and ordered fifty of exotic variety, like strawberry guava, camellia, and loquat. Stirring the green stew, she smiles vacuously. "I feel anticipant of a very happy future."

. . . .

Roads across the upper Northwest are flat and ruler-straight, snowbound for long months, turning arid and dusty in the summer. At an empty crossing in a poor, wheat-growing county, the road suddenly dips and winds down to a valley filled with tall pines and primitive log cabins. The community hidden in this natural canyon is Freedom Farm, founded in 1963. It is one of the oldest communes to be started on open land. The residents—about twenty-four adults and almost as many children—are serious, straightforward people who, with calculated bluntness, say they are dropouts, social misfits, unable or unwilling to cope with the world "outside." The community has no rules, except that no one can be asked to leave. Because it predates the hippie movement, there is an absence of mystical claptrap and jargon like "far out." Only a few are vegetarians. Members do not want the location of the farm published for fear of being inundated with "psychedelic beggars."

The farm is divided into two parts—80 acres at the north end of the canyon and 120 acres at the south. The families live separately, as they do at Wheeler's, but their homes are more elaborate and solidly built. The first house in the north end is a hexagonal log cabin built by Huw Williams, who started the farm when he was nineteen. Huw is slight, soft-spoken, with a wispy blond beard. His face and voice are expressionless, but when he speaks, he is likely to say something startling, humorous, or indicative of deep feeling. When I arrived, he was cutting out pieces of leather, wearing a green-and-brown lumberman's shirt and a knife strapped to his waist. His wife, Sylvia, was nursing their youngest son, while their two-year-old, Sennett, wearing nothing but a T-shirt, was playing on the floor with a half-breed Norwegian elkhound. The cabin was snugly warm, but smelled faintly of urine from Sennett peeing repeatedly on the rug. There was a cast-iron stove, tables and benches built from logs, a crib, an old-fashioned cradle, and a large bed raised off the floor for warmth and storage space. On the wall there was a calendar opened to January, although it was March.

I asked Huw how the community had stayed together for seven years. He said, deadpan, "The secret is not to try. We've got a lot of rugged individualists here, and everyone is into a different thing. In reflection, it feels good that we survived. A lot of us were from wealthy backgrounds, and the idea of giving it all up and living off the land was a challenge." Huw grew up on a ranch 40 miles from the canyon. "I had everything. When I was fourteen, I had my own car, a half-dozen cows, and $600 in the bank." When he was fifteen, his house

371

burned down and he saw his elaborate collections—stamps, models, books—disappear. He vowed not to become attached to possessions after that, and took to sleeping outdoors. He remembers being terrified of violence, and idolized Gandhi, Christ, and Tolstoy. At seventeen, he became a conscientious objector and began to work in draft resistance. While on a peace walk from New Hampshire to Washington, D.C., he decided to drop out of the University of Washington and start a nonviolent training center, a community where people could live by sharing rather than competing. He persuaded his mother to give him 80 acres in the canyon for the project, rented a house, called the Hart House, and advertised in peace papers for people to come and share it with him.

The first summer, more than fifty came and went and they all lived in the Hart House. One of the visitors was Sylvia, a fair-skinned girl with long chestnut hair and warm wistful eyes that hint of sadness. They were married, and Huw stopped talking about a peace center and started studying intentional communities. He decided he wanted a community that would be open to anyone, flexible, with no prescribed rules to live by. Work would get done, Huw felt, because people would want to do it to achieve certain ends. "It's a Western idea. You inspire people by giving them a goal, making it seem important; then they'll do anything to get there." If people did not want to work, Huw felt, forcing them would not be the answer.

The results were chaotic. "Emotional crises, fights over everything. A constant battle to get things done. A typical scene would be for one guy to spend two hours fixing a meal. He had to make three separate dishes—one for vegetarians, one for nonvegetarians, and one for people who wouldn't eat government-surplus food. He would put them on the table, everybody would grab, and if you stood back you got nothing. When people live that close together, they become less sensitive, and manners go right out the window. It was educational, but we knew it wasn't suitable for raising children." The group pooled resources and bought another 120 acres two miles away. Huw and Sylvia built their own cabin and moved out of the Hart House; another couple followed. Then around 1966, the drug scene exploded and the farm was swamped with speed freaks, runaways, addicts, and crazies. A schism grew between the permanent people and the transients. The transients thought the permanents were uptight and stingy. The permanents said the transients were abusing the land. When most of the permanents had built their own cabins, they began talking about burning down the Hart House. I heard many versions of the incident. Some say a man, whom I shall call George, burned it. Some say everyone did it. Some said they watched and were against it but felt they should not stop it. Afterwards, most of the transients left, and the farm settled into its present pattern of individual families tending their own gardens, buying their own supplies, and raising their own animals. Each family has at least two vehicles—a car and a tractor, or a motorcycle or truck. Huw says, "We do our share of polluting."

The majority at Freedom live on welfare, unemployment compensation, and food stamps. A few take part-time jobs picking apples or wheat, one does free-lance writing, and some do crafts. Huw makes about $50 a month on his leather work, Ken Meister makes wall hangings, Rico and Pat sell jewelry to psychedelic shops, and Steve raises rabbits. Huw believes the farm could support itself by growing organic grains and selling them by mail order, but he hasn't been able to get enough cooperation to do this. "It's impossible to have both a commune, where everyone lives and works collectively, and free land, where anyone can settle," he says. "Some day we might have a commune on the land, but not everyone who lived on the land would have to join it."

The only communal rituals are Thanksgiving at the schoolhouse and the corn dance, held on the first full moon of May. Huw devised the corn dance from a Hopi Indian ceremony, and each year it gets wilder. Huw builds a drum, and at sundown everyone gathers on a hillside with food, wine, the children in costumes, animals, and musical instruments. They take turns beating the drum but must keep it beating until dawn. They roast potatoes, and sometimes a kid, a pig, or a turkey, get stoned, dance, howl, and drop to sleep. "But that's only once a year," one of the men says. "We could have one every month, and it would hold the community together." Not everyone wants this solidarity, however. Some are like hermits and have staked out corners of the canyon where they want to be left alone. The families who live nearby get together for dinners, chores, and baby-sitting. At the north end, the Williamses, the Swansons, and the Goldens pop in and out constantly. On the day I arrive, they are having a garden meeting at the Swansons' to decide what to order for spring planting.

The Swansons, who have three young children, moved into the canyon this year after buying, for $1,000, the two-story house a man called Steve had built for his own family. Steve had had a falling out with Huw and wanted to move to the south acres. The Swansons needed a place they could move into right away. The house has the best equipment at the farm, with a flush toilet (sectioned off by a blanket hung from the ceiling), running water, and electricity that drives a stove, refrigerator, and freezer. Jack Swanson, an outgoing, ruddy-faced man of thirty-five, with short hair and a moustache, works on a newspaper 150 miles away and commutes to the farm for weekends. His wife, Barbara, twenty-four, is the image of a Midwestern college girl: jeans cut off to Bermuda length, blouses with Peter Pan collars, and a daisy-printed scarf around her short brown hair. But it is quickly apparent that she is a strong-willed nonconformist. "I've always been a black sheep," she says. "I hate supermarkets—everything's been chemically preserved. You might as well be in a morgue." Barbara is gifted at baking, pickling, and canning, and wants to raise sheep to weave and dye the wool herself. She and Jack tried living in various cities, then a suburb, then a farm in Idaho, where they found they lacked the skills to make it work. "We were so ill-equipped by society to live off the earth," Jack says. "We thought about moving to Freedom Farm for three or four years, but when times were good, we put it off." Last year their third child was born with a lung disease which required months of hospitalization and left them deep in debt. Moving to the farm seemed a way out. "If we had stayed in the suburbs, we found we were spending everything we made, with rent and car payments, and could never pay off the debts. I had to make more and more just to stay even. The price was too high for what we wanted in life," Jack says. "Here, because I don't pay rent and because we can raise food ourselves, I don't have to make as much money. We get help in farming, and have good company. In two or three months, this house is all mine—no interest, no taxes. Outside it would cost me $20,000 and 8 per cent interest."

A rainstorm hits at midnight and by morning the snow has washed off the canyon walls, the stream has flooded over, and the roads are slushy mud ruts. Sylvia saddles two horses and we ride down to the south 120. There are seven cabins on the valley floor, and three hidden by trees on the cliff. Outside one of the houses, Steve is feeding his rabbits; the mute, wiggling animals are clustering around the cage doors. Steve breeds the rabbits to sell to a processor and hopes to earn $100 a month from the business. He also kills them to eat. "It's tough to do," he says, "but if people are going to eat meat, they should be willing to kill the animal." While Steve is building his new house, he has moved with his wife and four children into the cabin of a couple I shall call George and Liz Snow. George is a hefty, porcine man of thirty-nine, a drifter who earned a doctorate in statistics, headed an advertising agency, ran guns to Cuba, worked as a civil servant, a mason, a dishwasher, and rode the freights. He can calculate the angles of a geodesic dome and quote Boccaccio and Shakespeare. He has had three wives, and does not want his name known because "there are a lot of people I don't want to find me."

Steve, a hard-lived thirty-four, has a past that rivals George's for tumult: nine years as an Army engineer, AWOL, running a coffee house in El Paso, six months in a Mexican jail on a marijuana charge, working nine-to-five as chief engineer in a fire-alarm factory in New Haven, Connecticut, then cross-country to Spokane. Steve has great dynamism and charm that are both appealing and abrasive. His assertiveness inevitably led to friction in every situation, until, tired of bucking the system, he moved to the farm. "I liked the structure of this community," he says. "Up there, I can't get along with one out of a thousand people. Here I make it with one out of two." He adds, "We're in the business of survival while the world goes crazy. It's good to know how to build a fire, or a waterwheel, because if the world ends, you're there now."

Everyone at Freedom seems to share this sense of imminent doomsday. Huw says, "When the country is wiped out, electricity will stop coming through the wires, so you might as well do without it now. I don't believe you should use any machine you can't fix yourself." Steve says, "Technology can't feed all the world's people." Stash, a young man who lives alone at the farm, asks, "Am I going to start starving in twenty years?"

Steve: "Not if you have a plot to garden."

Stash: "What if the ravaging hordes come through?"

Steve: "Be prepared for the end, or get yourself a gun."

There is an impulse to dismiss this talk as a projection of people's sense of their own private doom, except for the fact that the fear is widespread. Stewart Brand writes in the *Whole Earth Catalog*: "One barometer of people's social-

374

confidence level is the sales of books on survival. I can report that sales on *The Survival Book* are booming; it's one of our fastest moving items."

Several times a week, Steve, Stash, and Steve's daughter Laura, fourteen, drive to the small town nearby to buy groceries, visit a friend, and, if the hot water holds out, take showers. They stop at Joe's Bar for beer and hamburgers —40 cents "with all the trimmings." Laura, a graceful, quiet girl, walks across the deserted street to buy *Mad* magazine and look at rock record albums. There are three teen-agers at the farm—all girls—and all have tried running away to the city. One was arrested for shoplifting, another was picked up in a crash pad with seven men. Steve says, "We have just as much trouble with our kids as straight, middle-class parents do. I'd like to talk to people in other communities and find out how they handle their teen-agers. Maybe we could send ours there." Stash says, "Or bring teen-age boys here." The women at the farm have started to joke uneasily that their sons will become uptight businessmen and their daughters will be suburban housewives. The history of utopian communities in this country has been that the second generation leaves. It is easy to imagine commune-raised children having their first haute-cuisine meal, or sleeping in silk pajamas in a luxury hotel, or taking a jet plane. Are they not bound to be dazzled? Sylvia says, "Our way of life is an over-reaction to something, and our kids will probably overreact to us. It's absurd. Kids run away from this, and all the runaways from the city come here."

In theory, the farm is an expanded family, and children can move around and live with different people or build houses of their own. In the summer, they take blankets and sleeping bags up in the cliffs to sleep in a noisy, laughing bunch. When I visited, all the children except one were staying in their parents' houses. Low-key tension seemed to be running through the community, with Steve and Huw Williams at opposite poles. Steve's wife, Ann, told me, "We don't go along with Huw's philosophy of anarchy. We don't think it works. You need some authority and discipline in any social situation." Huw says, "The thing about anarchy is that I'm willing to do a job myself, if I have to, rather than start imposing rules on others. Steve and George want things to be done efficiently with someone giving orders, like the Army."

At dinner when the sun goes down, Steve's and George's house throbs with good will and festivity. The cabin, like most at the farm, is not divided into separate rooms. All nine people—Steve, Ann, and their four children, the Snows and their baby—sleep on the upstairs level, while the downstairs serves as kitchen, dining and living room. "The teen-agers wish there were more privacy," Steve says, "but for us and the younger children, it feels really close." Most couples at the farm are untroubled about making love in front of the children. "We don't make a point of it," one man says, "but if they happen to see it, and it's done in love and with good vibrations, they won't be afraid or embarrassed."

While Ann and Liz cook hasenpfeffer, Steve's daughters, Laura and Karen, ten, improvise making gingerbread with vinegar and brown sugar as a substitute for molasses. A blue jay chatters in a cage hung from the ceiling. Geese honk outside, and five dogs chase each other around the room. Steve plays the guitar and sings. The hasenpfeffer is superb. The rabbits have been pickled for two days, cooked in red wine, herbs, and sour cream. There are large bowls of beets, potatoes, jello, and the gingerbread, which tastes perfect, with home-made apple sauce. Afterwards, we all get toothpicks. Liz, an uninhibited, roly-poly girl of twenty-three, is describing how she hitchhiked to the farm, met George, stayed, and got married. "I like it here," she says, pursing her lips, "because I can stand nude on my front porch and yell, fuck! Also, I think I like it here because I'm fat, and there aren't many mirrors around. Clothes don't matter, and people don't judge you by your appearance like they do out there." She adds, "I've always been different from others. I think most of the people here are misfits—they have problems in communicating, relating to one another." Ann says, "Communication is ridiculous. We've begun to feel gossip is much better. It gradually gets around to the person it's about, and that's okay. Most people here can't say things to each other's face."

. . . .

It becomes clear why, in a community like this, the sex roles are so well-defined and satisfying. When men actually do heavy physical labor like chopping trees, baling hay, and digging irrigation ditches, it feels very fulfilling for the woman to tend the cabin, grind wheat, put up fruit, and sew or knit. Each depends on the other for basic needs—shelter, warmth, food. With no intermediaries, such as supermarkets and banks, there is a direct relationship between work and survival. It is thus possible, according to Huw, for even the most repetitive jobs such as washing dishes or sawing wood to be spiritually rewarding. "Sawing puts my head in a good place," he says. "It's like a yogic exercise."

In addition to his farming and leather work, Huw has assumed the job of teacher for the four children of school age. Huw believes school should be a free, anarchic experience, and that the students should set their own learning programs. Suddenly given this freedom, the children, who were accustomed to public school, said they wanted to play and ride the horses. Huw finally told them they must be at the school house every day for at least one hour. They float in and out, and Huw stays half the day. He walks home for lunch and passes Karen and another girl on the road. Karen taunts him, "Did you see the mess we made at the school?"

"Yes," Huw says.

"Did you see our note?"

Huw walks on, staring at the ground. "It makes me feel you don't have much respect for the tools or the school."

She laughs. "Course we don't have any respect!"

"Well, it's your school," Huw says softly.

Karen shouts, "You said it was your school the other day. You're an Indian giver."

Huw: "I never said it was my school. Your parents said that." Aside to me, he says, "They're getting better at arguing every day. Still not very good, though." I tell Huw they seem to enjoy tormenting him. "I know. I'm the only adult around here they can do that to without getting clobbered. It gives them a sense of power. It's ironic, because I keep saying they're mature and responsible, and their parents say they need strict authority and discipline. So who do they rebel against? Me. I'm going to call a school meeting tonight. Maybe we can talk some of this out."

. . . .

In the evening, ten parents and five children show up at the school, a one-room house built with eighteen sides, so that a geodesic dome can be constructed on top. The room has a furnace, bookshelves and work tables, rugs and cushions on the floor. Sylvia is sitting on a stool in the center nursing her son. Two boys in yellow pajamas are running in circles, squealing, "Ba-ba-ba!" Karen is drawing on the blackboard—of all things, a city skyscape. Rico is doing a yoga headstand. Steve and Huw begin arguing about whether the children should have to come to the school every day. Steve says, in a booming voice, "I think the whole canyon should be a learning community, a total educational environment. The kids can learn something from everyone. If you want to teach them, why don't you come to our house?" Huw, standing with a clipboard against his hip, says, "They have to come here to satisfy the county school superintendent. But it seems futile when they come in and say I'm not qualified to teach them. Where do they get that?"

Steve says, "From me. I don't think you're qualified." Huw: "Well, I'm prepared to quit and give you the option of doing something else, or sending them to public school."

Steve says, "Don't quit. I know your motives are pure as the driven snow...."

Huw says, "I'm doing it for myself as well, to prove I can do it. But it all fits together."

They reach an understanding without speaking further.

Steve then says, "I'd like to propose that we go door-to-door in this community and get everyone enthused about the school as a center for adult learning and cultural activity first, and for the kiddies second. Because when you turn on the adults, the kids will follow. The school building needs finishing—the dome should be built this summer. Unless there's more enthusiasm in this community, I'm not going to contribute a thing. But if we get everybody to boost this, by God I'll be the first one out to dig."

Huw says, "You don't think the people who took the time to come tonight is enough interest? I may be cynical, but I think the only way to get some of the others here would be to have pot and dope."

Steve: "Get them interested in the idea of guest speakers, musicians, from India, all over. We can build bunk dorms to accommodate them."

Huw: "Okay. I think we should get together every Sunday night to discuss ideas, hash things over. In the meantime, why don't we buy materials to finish the building?"

On the morning I leave, sunlight washes down the valley from a cloudless sky. Huw, in his green lumberman's shirt, rides with me to the top road. "My dream is to see this canyon filled with families who live here all the time, with lots of children." He continues in a lulling rhythm: "We could export some kind of food or product. The school is very important—it should be integrated in the whole community. Children from all over could come to work, learn, and live with different families. I'd like to have doctors here and a clinic where people could be healed naturally. Eventually there should be a ham radio system set up between all the communities in the country, and a blimp, so we could make field trips back and forth. I don't think one community is enough to met our needs. We need a world culture."

Huw stands, with hands on hips, the weight set back on his heels—a small figure against the umber field. "Some day I'm going to inherit six hundred more acres down there, and it'll all be free. Land should be available for anybody to use like it was with the Indians." He smiles with the right corner of his mouth. "The Indians could no more understand owning land than they could owning the sky."

7

Marital Crises – Threats to the Partnership

"... in sickness and in health, for better or for worse, for richer or for poorer, 'til death do you part" neatly summarizes many of the crises a marriage partnership is expected to weather. The advent of physical or mental illness should bring forth family reinforcement and aid, not recrimination and denial of support and companionship. Yet, when the incapacity is alcoholism, other attitudes may prevail. Fluctuation in family economic status should not drive partners apart, but divorce and desertion statistics by social class suggest that it does create discord and division. Faithfulness to one's spouse is often a very complicated issue. And when death terminates the marriage, it leaves one partner in a peculiar social situation for which the marriage vows offer no guidance.

This chapter examines the details of how the marital mandates work out in real life. What sorts of problems do marriage partners face and how do these problems and attempts at solutions affect all partners—both senior and junior? Obviously, with the high divorce rate in this country, married couples cannot be said to be an unqualified success in handling crises, despite the promises so often lightly given in their marriage vows.

The general and unique characteristics of people who get a divorce, as well as the diversity of reactions to it, are also discussed. Divorce or connubial happiness are not the only alternatives, however. Some marriages continue in a state of "holy deadlock," neither offering enough comfort or companionship to be pleasurable nor enough dissension to force a break-up.

The problems of the lone survivor of a marriage deserve additional sociological attention. Widowhood can be a dismal and lonesome period. The same is doubtless true for divorcees. Is it any wonder that those who can actively seek a new partnership?

379

Alcoholism and the Family

Joan K. Jackson

For many families in the United States, alcoholism is an agonizing personal concern involving the relationships of all immediate family members. As Jackson points out, an alcoholic father or mother strains the very existence of family ties because there are no prescribed ways for a family to react to this deviance as there is in the case of other disabilities. The situation for young children is, quite logically, particularly puzzling—especially if they have the opportunity to compare their alcoholic parent with the parents of their friends. The way in which family members become aware of and handle this crisis to some extent determines its outcome—not only for the drinker himself, but for the way in which role expectations in the family are established and maintained in the future.

U ntil recently it was possible to think of alcoholism as if it involved the alcoholic only. Most of the alcoholics studied were inmates of publicly supported institutions: jails, mental hospitals, and public general hospitals. These ill people appeared to be homeless and tieless. As the public became more aware of the extent and nature of alcoholism and that treatment possibilities existed, alcoholics who were still integral parts of the community appeared at clinics. The definition of "the problems of alcoholism" has had to be broadened to include all those with whom the alcoholic is or has been in close and continuing contact.

At present we do not know how many nonalcoholics are affected directly by alcoholism. However, an estimate can be derived from the available statistics

From Joan K. Jackson, "Alcoholism and the Family," *Annals of the American Academy of Political and Social Science,* January, 1958, pp. 90–98. Reprinted by permission of the author and The American Academy of Political and Social Science. Joan K. Jackson, Ph.D., Seattle, Washington, Research Instructor, Department of Psychiatry, University of Washington School of Medicine and Consultant, Firland Sanatorium, Seattle, was formerly a Research Assistant, Department of Sociology, McGill University. This study was supported in part by the National Institute of Mental Health, U. S. Public Health Service.

on the marital histories of alcoholics. The recurrently arrested alcoholic seems to affect the fewest nonalcoholics. Reports range from 19 per cent to 51 per cent who have never married[1]—that is, from slightly more than the expected number of single men to three to four times the expected rate. The vast majority who had married are now separated from their families. Alcoholics who voluntarily seek treatment at clinics affect the lives of more people than jailed alcoholics. While the number of broken marriages is still excessive, approximately the expected number of voluntary patients have been married.[2] Any estimate of nonalcoholics affected must take into consideration not only the present marital status of alcoholics, but also the past marital history. About one-third of the alcoholics have been married more than once. Jailed alcoholics had multiple marriages less frequently than clinic alcoholics.

There has been no enumeration of the children and other relatives influenced by alcoholism. From the author's studies it can be estimated that for each alcoholic there are at least two people in the immediate family who are affected. Approximately two-thirds of the married alcoholics have children, thus averaging two apiece. Family studies indicate that a minimum of one other relative is also directly involved. The importance of understanding the problems faced by the families of alcoholics is obvious from these figures. To date, little is known about the nature of the effects of living with or having lived with an alcoholic. However, there is considerable evidence that it has disturbing effects on the personalities of family members.

Once attention had been focused on the families of alcoholics, it became obvious that the relationship between the alcoholic and his family is not a one-way relationship. The family also affects the alcoholic and his illness. The very existence of family ties appears to be related to recovery from alcoholism. Some families are successful in helping their alcoholic member to recognize his need for help and are supportive of treatment efforts. Yet other types of families may discourage the patient from seeking treatment and may actually encourage the persistence of alcoholism. It is now believed that the most successful treatment of alcoholism involves helping both the alcoholic and those members of his family who are directly involved in his drinking behavior.[3]

THE ALCOHOLIC AND HIS CHILDREN

The children are affected by living with an alcoholic more than any other family member. Personalities are formed in a social milieu which is markedly unstable, torn with dissension, culturally deviant, and socially disapproved. The children must model themselves on adults who play their roles in a distorted fashion. The alcoholic shows little adequate adult behavior. The nonalcoholic parent attempts to play the roles of both father and mother, often failing to do either well.

The child of an alcoholic is bound to have problems in learning who he is, what is expected of him, and what he can expect from others. Almost inevitably his parents behave inconsistently towards him. His self-conception evolves in a situation in which the way others act towards him has more to do with the current events in the family than with the child's nature. His alcoholic parent feels one way about him when he is sober, another when drunk, and yet another during the hangover stage.

What the child can expect from his parents will also depend on the phase of the drinking cycle as well as on where he stands in relation to each parent at any given time. Only too frequently he is used in the battle between them. The wives of alcoholics find themselves disliking, punishing, or depriving the children preferred by the father and those who resemble him. Similarly, the child who is preferred by, or resembles, the mother is often hurt by the father. If the child tries to stay close to both parents he is caught in an impossible situation. Each parent resents the affection the other receives while demanding that the child show affection to both.

The children do not understand what is happening. The very young ones do not know that their families are different from other families. When they become aware of the differences, the children are torn between their own loyalty and the views of their parents that others hold. When neighbors ostracize them, the children are bewildered about what *they* did to bring about this result. Even those who are not ostracized become isolated. They hesitate to bring their friends to a home where their parent is likely to be drunk.

The behavior of the alcoholic parent is unpredictable and unintelligible to the child. The tendency of the child to look for the reasons in his own behavior very often is reinforced inadvertently by his mother. When father is leading up to a drinking episode, the children are put on their best behavior. When the drinking episode occurs, it is not surprising that the children feel that they have somehow done something to precipitate it.

Newell[4] states that the children of alcoholics are placed in a situation very similar to that of the experimental animals who are tempted towards rewards and then continually frustrated, whose environment changes constantly in a manner over which they have no control. Under such circumstances experimental animals have convulsions or "nervous breakdowns." Unfortunately, we still know very little about what happens to the children or about the duration of the effects.

Yet some of the children appear undisturbed. The personality damage appears to be least when the nonalcoholic parent is aware of the problems they face, gives them emotional support, keeps from using them against the alcoholic, tries to be consistent, and has insight into her own problems with the alcoholic. It also appears to mitigate some of the child's confusion if alcoholism is explained to him by a parent who accepts alcoholism as an illness.

THE ALCOHOLIC AND HIS WIFE

The wives of alcoholics have received considerably more attention than the children. The focus tends to be on how they affect the alcoholic and his alcoholism, rather than on how alcoholism and the alcoholic affect them. Most writers seem to feel that the wives of alcoholics are drawn from the ranks of emotionally disturbed women who seek out spouses who are not threatening to them, spouses who can be manipulated to meet their own personality needs. According to this theory, the wife has a vested interest in the persistence of the alcoholism of her spouse. Her own emotional stability depends upon it. Should the husband become sober, the wives are in danger of decompensating and showing marked neurotic disturbances.[5]

A complementary theory suggests that pre-alcoholic or alcoholic males tend to select certain types of women as wives. The most commonly reported type is a dominating, maternal woman who uses her maternal role as a defense against inadequate femininity.

Any attempt to assess the general applicability of this theory to *all* the wives of alcoholics runs into difficulties. First, the only wives who can be studied by researchers are those who have stayed with their husbands until alcoholism was well under way. The high divorce rate among alcoholics suggests that these wives are the exception rather than the rule. The majority of women who find themselves married to alcoholics appear to divorce them. Second, if a high rate of emotional disturbance is found among women still living with alcoholics, it is difficult to determine whether the personality difficulties antedated or postdated the alcoholism, whether they were partly causal or whether they emerged during the recurrent crises and the cumulative stresses of living with an alcoholic. Third, the wives who were studied were women who were actively blocking the treatment of their husbands, who had entered mental hospitals after their husbands' sobriety, who were themselves seeking psychiatric care, or who were in the process of manipulating social agencies to provide services. It is of interest that neither of the studies which deal with women who were taking an active part in their husbands' recovery process comment upon any similarities in the personality structures of the wives.[6]

It is likely that the final test of the hypotheses about the role of the wives' personalities in their husbands' alcoholism will have to await the accumulation of considerably more information. No alcoholic personality type has been found on psychological tests; no tests have been given to the wives of alcoholics. Until we know more about the etiology of alcoholism and its remedy, the role of the wives' personalities in its onset, in its persistence, and in its alleviation will remain in the realm of speculation.

No one denies that the wives of active alcholics are emotionally disturbed. In nonthreatening situations, the wives are the first to admit their own concerns about "their sanity." Of over one hundred women who attended a discussion group at one time or another during the past six years, there was not one who failed to talk about her concerns about her own emotional health. All of the women worry about the part which their attitudes and behavior play in the persistence of the drinking and in their families' disturbances. Although no uniform personality types are discernible, they do share feelings of confusion and anxiety. Most feel ambivalent about their husbands. However, this group is composed of women who are oriented towards changing themselves and the situation rather than escaping from it.

The Impact of Alcoholism on the Family

When two or more persons live together over a period of time, patterns of relating to one another evolve. In a family, a division of functions occurs and roles interlock. For the family to function smoothly, each person must play his roles in a predictable manner and according to the expectations of others in the family. When the family as a whole is functioning smoothly, individual members of the family also tend to function well. Everyone is aware of where he fits, what he is expected to do, and what he can expect from others in the family. When this organization is disrupted, repercussions are felt by each family member. A crisis is under way.

Family crises tend to follow a similar pattern, regardless of the nature of the precipitant. Usually there is an initial denial that a problem exists. The family tries to continue in its usual behavior patterns until it is obvious that these patterns are no longer effective. At this point there is a downward slump in organization. Roles are played with less enthusiasm and there is an increase in tensions and strained relationships. Finally an improvement occurs as some adjustive technique is successful. Family organization becomes stabilized at a new level. At each stage of the crisis there is a reshuffling of roles among family members, changes in status and prestige, changes in "self" and "other" images, shifts in family solidarity and self-sufficiency and in the visibility of the crisis to outsiders. In the process of the crisis, considerable mental conflict is engendered in all family members, and personality distortion occurs.[7] These are the elements which are uniform regardless of the type of family crisis. The phases vary in length and intensity depending on the nature of the crisis and the nature of the individuals involved in it.

When one of the adults in a family becomes an alcoholic, the over-all pattern of the crisis takes a form similar to that of other family crises. However, there are usually recurrent subsidiary crises which complicate the over-all situation and the attempts at its resolution. Shame, unemployment, impoverishment, desertion and return, nonsupport, infidelity, imprisonment, illness and progressive dissension also occur. For other types of family crises, there are cultural prescriptions for socially appropriate behavior and for procedures which will terminate the crisis. But this is not so in the case of alcoholism. The cultural view is that alcoholism is shameful and should not occur. Thus, when facing alcoholism, the family is in a socially unstructured situation and must find the techniques for handling the crisis through trial and error behavior and without social support. In many respects, there are marked similarities between the type of crisis precipitated by alcoholism and those precipitated by mental illness.

384

Attempts to Deny the Problem

Alcoholism rarely emerges full-blown overnight. It is usually heralded by widely spaced incidents of excessive drinking, each of which sets off a small family crisis. Both spouses try to account for the episode and then to avoid the family situations which appear to have caused the drinking. In their search for explanations, they try to define the situation as controllable, understandable, and "perfectly normal." Between drinking episodes, both feel guilty about their behavior and about their impact on each other. Each tries to be an "ideal spouse" to the other. Gradually not only the drinking problem, but also the other problems in the marriage, are denied or sidestepped.

It takes some time before the wife realizes that the drinking is neither normal nor controllable behavior. It takes the alcoholic considerably longer to come to the same conclusion. The cultural view that alcoholics are Skid Row bums who are constantly inebriated also serves to keep the situation clouded. Friends compound the confusion. If the wife compares her husband with them, some show parallels to his behavior and others are in marked contrast. She wavers between defining his behavior as "normal" and "not normal." If she consults friends, they tend to discount her concern, thus facilitating her tendency to deny that a problem exists and adding to her guilt about thinking disloyal thoughts about her husband.

During this stage the family is very concerned about the social visibility of the drinking behavior. They feel that they would surely be ostracized if the extent of the drinking were known. To protect themselves against discovery, the family begins to cut down on their social activities and to withdraw into the home.

Attempts to Eliminate the Problem

The second stage begins when the family defines the alcoholic's drinking behavior as "not normal." At this point frantic efforts are made to eliminate the problem. Lacking clear-cut cultural prescriptions for what to do in a situation like this, the efforts are of the trial and error variety. In rapid succession, the wife threatens to leave the husband, babies him during hangovers, drinks with him, hides or empties his bottles, curtails money, tries to understand his problem, keeps his liquor handy for him, and nags at him. However, all efforts to change the situation fail. Gradually the family becomes so preoccupied with the problem of discovering how to keep father sober that all long-term family goals recede into the background.

At the same time isolation of the family reaches its peak intensity. The extreme isolation magnifies the importance of all intrafamily interactions and events. Almost all thought becomes drinking-centered. Drinking comes to symbolize all conflicts between the spouses, and even mother-child conflicts are regarded as indirect derivatives of the drinking behavior. Attempts to keep the social visibility of the behavior at the lowest possible level increase.

The husband-wife alienation also accelerates. Each feels resentful of the other. Each feels misunderstood and unable to understand. Both search frantically for the reasons for the drinking, believing that if the reason could be discovered, all family members could gear their behavior in a way to make the drinking unnecessary.

The wife feels increasingly inadequate as a wife, mother, woman, and person. She feels she has failed to make a happy and united home for her husband and children. Her husband's frequent comments to the effect that her behavior causes his drinking and her own concerns that this may be true intensify the proces of self-devaluation.

DISORGANIZATION

This is a stage which could also be entitled "What's the use?" Nothing seems effective in stabilizing the alcoholic. Efforts to change the situation become, at best, sporadic. Behavior is geared to relieve tensions rather than to achieve goals. The family gives up trying to understand the alcoholic. They do not care if the neighbors know about the drinking. The children are told that their father is a drunk. They are no longer required to show him affection or respect. The myth that father still has an important status in the family is dropped when he no longer supports them, is imprisoned, caught in infidelity, or disappears for long periods of time. The family ceases to care about its self-sufficiency and begins to resort to public agencies for help, thereby losing self-respect.

The wife becomes very concerned about her sanity. She finds herself engaging in tension-relieving behavior which she knows is goalless. She is aware that she feels tense, anxious, and hostile. She regards her pre-crisis self as "the real me" and becomes very frightened at how she has changed.

ATTEMPTS TO REORGANIZE IN SPITE OF THE PROBLEM

When some major or minor subsidiary crisis occurs, the family is forced to take survival action. At this point many wives leave their husbands.

The major characteristic of this stage is that the wife takes over. The alcoholic is ignored or is assigned the status of the most recalcitrant child. When the wife's obligations to her husband conflict with those to her children, she decides in favor of the children. Family ranks are closed progressively and the father excluded.

As a result of the changed family organization, father's behavior constitutes less of a problem. Hostility towards him diminishes as the family no longer expects him to change. Feelings of pity, exasperation, and protectiveness arise.

The reorganization has a stabilizing effect on the children. They find their environment and their mother more consistent. Their relationship to their father is more clearly defined. Guilt and anxiety diminish as they come to accept their mother's view that drinking is not caused by any behavior of family members.

Long-term family goals and planning begin again. Help from public agencies is accepted as necessary and no longer impairs family self-respect. With the taking over of family control, the wife gradually regains her sense of worth. Her concerns about her emotional health decrease.

Despite the greater stabilization, subsidiary crises multiply. The alcoholic is violent or withdraws more often; income becomes more uncertain; imprisonments and hospitalizations occur more frequently. Each crisis is temporarily disruptive to the new family organization. The symbolization of these events as being caused by alcoholism, however, prevents the complete disruption of the family.

The most disruptive type of crisis occurs if the husband recognizes that he has a drinking problem and makes an effort to get help. Hope is mobilized. The family attempts to open its ranks again in order to give him the maximum chance for recovery. Roles are partially reshuffled and attempts at attitude change are made, only to be disrupted again if treatment is unsuccessful.

Efforts to Escape the Problem

The problems involved in separating from the alcoholic are similar to the problems involved in separation for any other reason. However, some of the problems are more intense. The wife, who could count on some support from her husband in earlier stages, even though it was a manipulative move on his part, can no longer be sure of any support. The mental conflict about deserting a sick man must be resolved as well as the wife's feelings of responsibility for his alcoholism. The family which has experienced violence from the alcoholic is concerned that separation may intensify the violence. When the decision is made to separate because of the drinking, the alcoholic often gives up drinking for a while, thereby removing what is apparently the major reason for the separation.

Some other events, however, have made separation possible. The wife has learned that the family can run smoothly without her husband. Taking over control has bolstered her self-confidence. Her orientation has shifted from inaction to action. The wife also has familiarity with public agencies which can provide help, and she has overcome her shame about using them.

Reorganization of the Family

Without the father, the family tends to reorganize rather smoothly. They have already closed ranks against him and now they feel free of the minor disruptions he still created in the family. Reorganization is impeded if the alcoholic continues to attempt reconciliation or feels he must "get even" with the family for deserting him.

The whole family becomes united when the husband achieves sobriety, whether or not separation has preceded. For the wife and husband facing a sober marriage after many years of an alcoholic marriage, the expectations for marriage without alcoholism are unrealistic and idealistic.

Many problems arise. The wife has managed the family for years. Now her husband wishes to be reinstated as head of the house. Usually the first role he re-establishes is that of breadwinner. With the resumption of this role, he feels that the family should reinstate him immediately in all his former roles. Difficulties inevitably follow. For example, the children are often unable to accept his resumption of the father role. Their mother has been mother and father to them for so long that it takes time to get used to consulting their father. Often the father tries to manage this change overnight, and the very pressure he puts on the children towards this end defeats him.

The wife, who finds it difficult to believe that her husband is sober permanently, is often unwilling to relinquish her control of family affairs even though she knows that this is necessary to her husband's sobriety. She remembers when his failures to handle responsibility were catastrophic to the family. Used to avoiding any issues which might upset him, the wife often has difficulty discussing problems openly. If she permits him to resume his father role, she often feels resentful of his intrusion into territory she has come to regard as her own. If he makes any decisions which are detrimental to the family, her former feelings of superiority may be mobilized and affect her relationship with him.

Gradually the difficulties related to alcoholism recede into the past and family adjustment at some level is achieved. The drinking problem shows up only sporadically—when the time comes for a decision about permitting the children to drink or when pressure is put on the husband to drink at a party.

Personality Disturbances in Family Members

Each stage in the crisis of alcoholism has distinctive characteristics. The types of problems faced, the extent to which the situation is structured, the amount of emotional support received by individual family members, and the rewards vary as to the stage of the crisis. Some stages "fit" the personalities of the individuals involved better than others.

Although each stage of the crisis appears to give rise to some similar patterns of response, there is considerable variation from family to family. The wife whose original personality fits comfortably into denying the existence of the problem will probably take longer to get past this phase of the crisis than the wife who finds dominating more congenial. The latter will probably prolong the stage of attempting to eliminate the problem. Some families make an adjustment at one level of the crisis and never seem to go on to the next phase.

With the transition from one stage to another, there is the danger of marked personality disturbance in family members. Some become their most disturbed when drinking first becomes a problem; others become most disturbed when the alcoholic becomes sober. In the experience of the author, there has been little uniformity within families or between families in this respect. However, after two or three years of sobriety, the alcoholics' family members appear to resemble a cross section of people anywhere. Any uniformities which were obvious earlier seem to have disappeared.

THERAPY AND THE FAMILY

The major goal of the families of most alcoholics is to find some way of bringing about a change in father's drinking. When the alcoholic seeks treatment, the family members usually have very mixed feelings towards the treatment agency. Hope that father may recover is remobilized and if sobriety ensues for any length of time, they are grateful. At the same time, they often feel resentment that an outside agency can accomplish what they have tried to do for years. They may also resent the emotional support which the alcoholic receives from the treatment agency, while they are left to cope with still another change in their relationship to him without support.

Most families have little awareness of what treatment involves and are forced to rely on the alcoholic patient for their information. The patient frequently passes on a distorted picture in order to manipulate the family situation for his own ends. What information is given is perceived by the family against a background of their attitudes towards the alcoholic at that point in time. The actions they take are also influenced by their estimate of the probability that treatment will be successful. The result is often a family which works at cross purposes with therapy.

Recently there has been a growing recognition that the family of the alcoholic also requires help if the alcoholic is to be treated successfully. An experiment was tried at the Henry Phipps Psychiatric Clinic of Johns Hopkins Hospital. Alcoholics and their wives were treated in concurrent group therapy sessions. The Al-Anon Family Groups provide the same type of situation for the families of AA members and have the additional asset of helping the families of alcoholics who are still not interested in receiving help for themselves. Joint treatment of alcoholics and the members of their family aims at getting a better understanding of the underlying emotional disturbance, of the relationship between the alcoholic and the person who is most frequently the object and stimulus of the drinking behavior, and of the treatment process.[8]

Joint treatment of the alcoholic and his family has other assets, as Gliedman and his co-workers point out.[9] Joint therapy emphasizes the marriage. In addition, with both spouses coming for help, there is less likelihood that undertaking treatment will be construed as an admission of guilt or that therapy will be used as a weapon by one against the other. The wife's entrance into therapy is a tacit admission of her need to change too. It represents a hopeful attitude on the part of both the alcoholic and his wife that recovery is possible and creates an orientation towards working things out together as a family unit.

The members of an Al-Anon group with which the author is familiar receive understanding of their problems and their feelings from one another, emotional support which facilitates change in attitudes and behavior, basic information about solutions to common problems, and information about the treatment process and about the nature of alcoholism as an illness. Shame is alleviated and hope engendered. The nonalcoholic spouses gain perspective on what has happened to their families and on the possibilities of changing towards greater stability. Anxiety diminishes in an almost visible fashion. As they gain perspective on the situation, behavior tends to become more realistic and rewarding. By no means the least important effect derived from membership in the group is a structuring of what has seemed to be a completely unstructured situation and the feelings of security which this engenders.

NOTES

[1] J. K. Jackson, "The Problem of the Alcoholic Tuberculous Patient," in P. J. Sparer (Ed.), *Personality, Stress and Tuberculosis* (New York: International Universities Press, 1956), pp. 504–38; R. Straus and S. D. Bacon, "Alcoholism and Social Stability: A Study of Occupational Integration in 2,023 Male Clinic Patients," *Quarterly Journal of Studies on Alcohol,* Vol. 12, June 1951, pp. 231–60.

[2] *Ibid.*; E. P. Walcott and R. Straus, "Use of a Hospital Facility in Conjunction with Outpatient Treatment of Alcoholics," *Quarterly Journal of Studies on Alcohol,* Vol. 13, March 1952, pp. 60–77; F. E. Feeny, D. F. Mindlen, V. H. Minear, E. E. Short, "The Challenge of the Skid Row Alcoholic: A Social, Psychological and Psychiatric Comparison of Chronically Jailed Alcoholics and Cooperative Clinic Patients," *Quarterly Journal of Studies on Alcohol,* Vol. 16, December 1955, pp. 645–67.

[3] D. J. Myerson, "An Active Therapeutic Method of Interrupting the Dependency Relationship of Certain Male Alcoholics," *Quarterly Journal of Studies on Alcohol,* Vol. 14, September 1953, pp. 419–26; L. H. Gliedman, D. Rosenthal, J. Frank, H. T. Nash, "Group Therapy of Alcoholics with Concurrent Group Meetings of Their Wives," *Quarterly Journal of Studies on Alcohol,* Vol. 17, December 1956, pp. 655–70.

[4] N. Newell, "Alcoholism and the Father Image," *Quarterly Journal of Studies on Alcohol,* Vol. 11, March 1950, pp. 92–96.

[5] D. E. MacDonald, "Mental Disorders in Wives of Alcoholics," *Quarterly Journal of Studies on Alcohol,* Vol. 17, June 1956, pp. 282–87; M. Wellman, "Toward an Etiology of Alcoholism: Why Young Men Drink Too Much," *Canadian Medical Association Journal,* Vol. 73, November 1, 1955, pp. 717–25; S. Futterman, "Personality Trends in Wives of Alcoholics," *Journal of Psychiatric Social Work,* Vol. 23, 1953, pp. 37–41.

[6] J. K. Jackson, "The Adjustment of the Family to the Crisis of Alcoholism," *Quarterly Journal of Studies on Alcohol*, Vol. 15, December 1954, pp. 562–86; Gliedman, Rosenthal, Frank, and Nash, *op. cit.* (note 3 *supra*).

[7] W. Waller (revised by Reuben Hill), *The Family: A Dynamic Interpretation* (New York: Dryden Press, 1951), pp. 453–61.

[8] Gliedman, Rosenthal, Frank, and Nash, *op. cit.* (note 3 *supra*).

[9] *Ibid.*

Unemployment—Crisis of the Common Man

Ruth Shonle Cavan

Since the 1929 depression rocked the foundations of the family as well as the economy, there was a paucity of research concern with the problem of unemployment as it affects the family. A renewed interest in poverty alleviation has resulted in growing awareness that many families (especially those of minority status) must cope with chronic long-term or intermittent unemployment. Additionally, the American economy fluctuates in such a way as to leave the middle-class man stranded without a job from time to time. Thus Cavan's article, written in 1950, has current application to an important source of family crises of a large portion of our population. She reviews the research findings available on family interactions and role changes and adjustments during times of unemployment of the husband, and delineates the types of families that do or do not weather financial setbacks. Various types of unemployment and the diversity of their effects are also discussed.

Any period of widespread, prolonged unemployment raises the specter of possible family disorganization and even disintegration. The Great Depression of the 1930's led to a number of studies of family reactions to unemployment and lowered income. These studies can lay the foundation for current studies and even for current methods of alleviation, with some consideration for the differences between the 1930's and the late 1950's.

In order to sharpen our view of the impact of unemployment on family life, this review of the depression studies is organized according to social class, so far as such a classification is possible in studies made before the concept of social class was well defined.[1]

From "Unemployment—Crisis of the Common Man," *Marriage and Family Living*, May, 1959, pp. 139–46. Reprinted by permission of the author and the National Council on Family Relations.

The social classes discussed here are as follows:

1. The lower-lower class family:
   a. with long-term or permanent unemployment,
   b. with regular repetitive unemployment,
   c. usually employed, except in time of personal or economic emergency;
2. The family of the "common man," that is, upper-lower and lower-middle class, regularly employed except in time of great economic emergency;
3. The upper-middle class.

The family of the common man is discussed first, since the traumatic impact of unemployment seems most acute in this social class.

THE COMMON MAN, UPPER-LOWER AND LOWER-MIDDLE CLASSES

The conditions imposed by unemployment and lowered income are most significant when seen against a backdrop of what the common man wants, expects, and has partially achieved. One of the chief values of the common man is to be self-supporting at all times, with a backlog of moderate savings. Often the family prides itself on "getting ahead," with a goal of upward mobility, if not for the parents, at least for their children. Wives may work regularly or intermittently and older children work, but the husband is the chief and most steady worker and makes the largest contribution to the family budget. Typically, his status is recognized as the highest in the family. The effort toward upward mobility is chiefly in the acquisition of rather expensive equipment, not always paid for, or in moving into a better neighborhood than the one in which the family originally lived. Culturally and socially, the family may not have established itself in the next higher class. Hence, considerable emphasis is placed on visible material possessions which are symbols of status.

Four depression studies that concentrated on the common man are:[2] Cavan and Ranck, whose study of one hundred Chicago families included sixty-eight of common-man status; Komarovsky, who concentrated on fifty-nine cases; Bakke, *The Unemployed Worker*, based on a number of studies made between 1932 and 1939; and *Citizens Without Work*, by the same author, an eight-year study of twenty-four families suffering prolonged unemployment.

Reaction to Unemployment

A loss of or reduction in employment and hence in income among these families poses a many-sided threat: loss of the symbols of social class status; eventual probable application for relief; disorganized personal reactions; disorganization and rearrangement of roles within the family; downward social mobility.

393

First came the financial adjustment. At least at the beginning of the depression, there was disbelief that the situation was anything except a normal short lay-off. Men therefore were inclined to speak of deserving a short vacation. When no recall came, they sought employment first in their special skill, then in a less specialized and lower paid type of work, finally in any work, and eventually at odd jobs. [Cavan and Ranck, Bakke]. This devaluation of job status was a long-drawn out procedure. For as long as six months, skilled workers held out for the old wages, but by the end of twelve months, 85 percent were willing, although often resentful, to take any kind of job. [Bakke ch. 8]

If other members of the family found work, their employment eased the financial strain, but often produced interpersonal strains.

As unemployment was prolonged, resources (symbols of status) were used with the following order of frequency: credit, small savings, loans, selling or pawning goods, and cashing of insurance policies. [Bakke, ch. 8; Cavan and Ranck, p. 84] Expenses were reduced by having the telephone removed, not taking summer vacations, dropping club memberships, and the like. Some families moved to less expensive living quarters; others moved in with relatives. As long as possible, invisible reductions were made; but eventually it was not possible to conceal the financial condition from neighbors. The final and most difficult financial adjustment was in applying for relief. For these self-supporting and often upwardly mobile families, relief was regarded as a personal disgrace. It was also the end of their hopes for upward mobility and often was preceded by definite downward mobility, partly because personal resources had to be reduced to a very low point before the family would be accepted by most relief agencies.

During this period of declining employment and exhaustion of resources, three types of reaction occurred.

1. Emotional reactions of husband and wife. The period preceding application for relief was a harrowing one as the family resisted the change in self-conception that relief made necessary. Worry, discouragement, and despondency were common emotional reactions. When forced to apply for relief, husband and wife cried at the agency. Definitely neurotic symptoms occurred in a minority of cases, as extreme insomnia, hysterical laughter, burning spots on the body, and suicide threats. However, out of the total of one hundred Chicago cases there were only two suicides, neither attributable solely to the depression. Husband and wife often shared equally in the emotional tension. In some families, one member, often the husband, became more disturbed than the others. A few drank heavily and several had "nervous breakdowns." [Cavan and Ranck, pp. 55–66; Komarovsky, pp. 36 ff., 66 ff.]

2. Changes in roles within the family. Although the husband is the chief earner in the family of the common man, it is accepted that the wife works when necessary, and that older children have an obligation to work part or full time as soon as they reach the legal age for employment. It was less true in the early 1930's than now that the wife works as a matter of choice and not simply from necessity. But even in the 1930's the employment of the

394

wife was not taken as a threat to the husband's superior status, so long as it was conceded that the wife's employment was temporary.

The unemployment of the husband affected roles in three ways. First, when the husband could not find any work, his role suffered in the eyes of other members of the family. Wives sometimes lost their respect or accused their husbands of not trying to find work. Unless the husband could work out some role in the household (difficult to do), he really had no role to play. [Cavan and Ranck, Komarovsky, various items]

Second, when some members of the family usurped the role of the husband as chief wage earner, interpersonal relationships became strained. Apparently actual reduction in dollars earned was less devastating than change in roles; or, dire poverty was easier to bear than the husband's loss of status to some previously subordinate member. It seems to make little difference what members worked or how much or how little each earned, provided that the husband remained the largest contributor to the family purse. Tension was increased by the custom of children contributing their money to the family through the mother, who then often became the bursar for the family. [Cavan, Komarovsky, Bakke]

Third, when the family finally applied for relief and was accepted as a client, further rearrangement of roles became necessary. The relief worker assumed a role superior to that of the husband. Since the relief worker was usually a woman, and dealt primarily with the wife, the husband now found himself subordinate both to his wife and to the woman relief worker. [Bakke]

3. Change in social class status. In the hierarchy of social class levels, families on relief are relegated to lower-lower class status. Especially for upward mobile families, their descent to lower-lower class was embittering. When these families were forced to move, the search for lower rent sometimes brought many relief families into the same neighborhood. Baake speaks of entire neighborhoods of relief families.

As the depression progressed, certain cushions were devised. One of these was the Works Progress Administration (WPA), established in 1935, which provided work relief. At first, WPA workers were contrasted with persons still on relief; their self-respect increased and their social status was slightly improved. But in time, WPA workers were identified with relief cases and contrasted with persons privately employed. Their status and self-respect then again declined. [Bakke, ch. 12]

Another cushion was unemployment compensation, established in 1938, and by now a customary way to tide over short periods of unemployment. The implications of unemployment compensation are discussed later in this paper.

Readjustment of Family

Emotional disturbance usually continued until the family reached a level, however low, of stability. As soon as the family accepted this level as probably permanent, reorganization began as the family adjusted itself to its new level.

As the depression decreased and various members of the family found work, upward mobility sometimes began again; however, older members of the family often were unable to regain their former personal status, so that the family status might be organized around the older children as the chief earners.

Bakke divides the readjustment process into experimental and permanent. He says that few families remained disorganized for a very long period of time. In experimental readjustment, the husband accepted his lowered status and a new hierarchy of statuses began to develop, with the wife granted the authority to manage finances and each child assigned a status relative to earning capacity. New interests and new plans for children developed, appropriate to the new social class status. The family drew together again with new roles that fitted together into an integrated pattern. Permanent readjustment came when the family stopped comparing the meager present with the more comfortable past, accepted rationalizations for the lowered status, and renewed a full round of family activities although of a different type than formerly.

In other families, the disarrangement of roles and lowering of statuses were less severe and consequently readjustment came more quickly. When the family did not have to make a residential move, loss of social status was less noticeable. Avoidance of relief through reduced expenses or help from relatives saved the family from the greatest humiliation. Activities and goals could be modified without great disorganization. [Cavan and Ranck, ch. 7]

Pre-unemployment Factors

Two studies, Cavan and Ranck, and Komarovsky, emphasized the previous family organization as a factor in the way in which families of the common man reacted to the depression.

Cavan and Ranck used the concept of well organized family, defined as a family with a high degree of unity and reciprocal functioning. Although well and poorly organized familes varied in their reactions to unemployment, in general well organized families fared better than the poorly organized. They suffered emotionally as they approached the relief status, but also attempted to adjust realistically. The family group remained intact and as the lower status was accepted, family goals of a new type evolved. The family group worked together to overcome their problems.

Families disorganized prior to the depression tended to become more disorganized. Previous latent tensions between husband and wife or between parents and children came into the open under the increased tension of unemployment and low income. In a few cases the parents separated, adolescent children ran away from home, or the family broke into several small units. In some of these families, stability increased with the entrance of a relief agency whose worker helped to hold the family together by permitting the members to become dependent upon her. [Cavan and Ranck, ch. 7]

Komarovsky limited her research to a study of the relation between the husband's role as the economic provider of the family and his authority in the family. In forty-five out of fifty-nine cases, all on relief one or more years, the husband did not lose his authority in the family. In these families the authority of the husband was based either on love and respect, or on the traditional semi-patriarchal organization of the common-man family. Unemployment was not interpreted as a reflection on the husband.

When the authority of the husband was based on fear of the husband or was maintained for utilitarian purposes, his unemployment was followed by loss of respect and loss of authority. In some of these families, the wife did not respect her husband prior to the unemployment. When unemployment freed her from economic dependence upon him, the thin veneer of submission cracked. The husbands attempted to force respect from wife and children, psychologically or physically, or selected a few areas of dominance about which they would not yield; some sought compensation in alcohol or religion.

Summary of the Common Man and Unemployment

In general the upper-lower and lower-middle class families suffered greatly from prolonged unemployment which violated deeply revered values of the common man: relief substituted for self-support; transfer of the highest family status from the husband to some previously subordinate member of the family; and downward social mobility. The lengthy period of downgrading to relief status was the most difficult and was marked by severe emotional reactions. Readjustment came with acceptance of the condition of poverty and reorganization of the family in harmony with the reality of the situation. The well organized family with unity of purpose and reciprocal functioning of members in which the husband held his status on the basis of love and respect or tradition weathered the adjustment better than poorly organized families or those in which fear and utilitarian motives were at the basis of the hierarchy of statuses.

THE UPPER-MIDDLE CLASS

The upper-middle class was less affected by the depression than the common man, and very few persons became relief clients.[3] Most upper-middle workers remained in their accustomed positions, sometimes at higher incomes than prior to the depression. The few whose businesses failed or who became unemployed tended to re-establish themselves by their own efforts.

However, one study concentrated on families, primarily upper-middle class, which had suffered a decrease of at least 25 per cent in their income, often accompanied by total or partial unemployment.[4] The reaction of these families was severe but was related chiefly to changes of personal status within the family. With a few exceptions, the families were able to remain in their homes and thus were saved one of the drastic steps in downward social mobility. They also managed to get along without applying for relief.

Angell's main focus was on the effect of reduced income on interpersonal relationships among family members. The two elements of family life found most significant in type of adjustment were integration and adaptability. Angell applied these concepts to the way in which families accepted changes in relative status of family members, especially to lowered status of the husband. The most severe test came when the husband yielded his dominant status to someone else, for example, to the wife who became the chief wage earner. When the husband was able to retain his previous status or modified it only slightly, adjustment was easier. Successful adjustment to modified or markedly changed status called for a change of roles and acceptance of the change by all concerned.

Readjustment of roles without personal or familial disorganization was accomplished most readily by integrated, adaptable families. Unadaptable families, regardless of the degree of integration, experienced personal and/or family disorganization. Unintegrated families with a low degree of adaptability made unpredictable responses.

It was also found that adaptability increased with a non-materialistic philosophy of life, freedom from traditionalism, and responsibleness of the parents.

One may summarize Angell's study of upper-middle class families by saying that adaptability is more important than integration in adjusting to lowered income, but that the unstructured, unintegrated, and unadaptable family tends to increase in disintegration.

The Lower-Lower Class Family

Although lower-lower class families experience more unemployment than any other class, they are least affected by it. They may earlier have suffered from it, but in time they tend to accept unemployment as a normal way of life. These families contrast sharply with the unemployment families in the common man class and the upper-middle class.

Long Term or Permanent Unemployment

Permanently unemployed families are relief clients year in and year out, in prosperity as well as in depression; or they have found some unrespectable way to live without working. By the time unemployment is reached, there are usually physical and personality deficiencies, such as disease, vagrancy, petty thievery, alcoholism, unstable emotional reactions, or inability to work with others or to accept authority. Which of these conditions are causes and which effects of unemployment, it seems impossible to say. These deficiencies become a permanent part of the situation and often are used to manipulate relief agencies or the public into giving aid. They become assets rather than disintegrating elements in the family.

These families tend to accept their impoverished status and to stabilize family life at a dependency level. Some members may have been reared in similar families and thus have been socialized into this type of family from birth. Others, however, have slipped downward. With time, some kind of adjustment is made and the family develops rationalizations or a philosophy of life, appropriate family roles, and relationships with the outside world that enable it to function.

In his study, *The Beggar*, Gilmore describes a family in which begging set the mode of life through sixty years and five generations.[5] Beggars not reared in begging families sometimes reach this status after intermittent periods on relief. When all private resources have been exhausted and relief is unavailable or inadequate, these families turn to begging. Soon they have developed a philosophy that they cannot or should not work in ordinary occupations; they refer to begging as work. Even though all members of the family may not beg, the whole family shares the begging philosophy, since the social status of the family is determined by even one begging member. Society places the beggar at one of the lowest social levels, but the beggar himself is protected from feeling debased by his philosophy.

Begging is a family project, which helps to unify the family. Whichever members of the family can make the greatest appeal for sympathy go out to beg, with the family as a whole sharing the proceeds. Parents who thus provide well for their children have family roles of authority and respect.

Studies of families permanently on relief also show how unemployment is accepted as a normal status. The function of the relief agency is important. The longitudinal study of one hundred Chicago families made in 1934-35 by Cavan and Ranck yielded twelve families that had been wholly or partially on relief prior to the depression. In time of high employment, they nevertheless lived in the social world of the permanently unemployed. Many of these families included at least one disorganized person, often the husband, whose disabilities gave justification for the relief status in the eyes of the family. The families held together, having adjusted family roles to the personalities of their members, sometimes in unorthodox ways. Important in the family organization was the relief agency, which often assumed functions typical of a husband. The agency supplied money, sometimes managed the budgeting, helped the family plan, and in general gave stability and security in many areas other than financial.

A third report throws light on mobile unemployed families.[6] When the Atomic Energy Commission established a plant in southern Ohio, many mobile families were drawn into the area for employment. Social services were approached by six mobile families who were not seeking employment, but whose histories showed that their mode of life was constant migration back and forth across the country in battered automobiles, their means of support whatever they could get from relief agencies. The husbands as a rule were very infantile and dependent in personality type; the wives were docile. They wanted to be cared for by the agency. The family units were closely organized and void of conflict. The men maintained their family status through the skill with which they could manipulate the relief workers or community sentiment in their favor. Although the means were unconventional, the husband still held high status as the good provider. As with public begging, the technique of appeal was well developed. The man made the appeal for sympathy, playing up the needs of his family, and ingratiating himself with the relief worker or others in the community who might help him. As a rule, the men were at first successful in arousing interest and securing aid. As soon as efforts were made to provide employment, the family quietly disappeared, to turn up later in some other city. As with the dependent families in the Chicago study, already cited, the relief agency tended to assume many of the functions normally held by the husband.

It seems to be possible to conclude from studies of permanently unemployed people that permanent unemployment is not a traumatic, disorganizing experience. It is accepted as the customary way of life. The family devises ways to support itself without work and builds up a supporting philosophy and integrated family roles.

Regular, Repetitive Unemployment

The seasonal worker who follows a yearly routine of alternating periods of employment and unemployment typifies the above category. According to Hathaway's 1934 study of the migratory family, and other fragmentary sources, these families often are not rooted in any community and the standard of living tends to be low.[7] The families are not, however, disorganized. They have accepted the mobile life and the rotation of employment and unemployment as normal for themselves. Often a regular route is followed year after year and the family knows in advance where it is likely to be throughout the working season. The off-season often finds each family in the same city every year. If the family has not been able to save sufficient money for the off-season, relief is sought. The whole yearly pattern can be foreseen. There is therefore no shock, no crisis, when seasonal unemployment comes; and there is a technique for handling the lack of funds.

The families are organized with the father as head. He makes the arrangements for work for the family as a unit. He therefore has authority and respect. Once the family has accepted migrancy as a way of life, the husband fulfills his role if he makes good contacts for work during the working seasons; he is not considered a failure if the family must apply for relief in the off season.

The seasonal working family, like the permanently dependent family, illustrates adjustment to unemployment, the maintenance of roles within the family, and as a consequence little personal or family disorganization as a result of unemployment. Since both types of family tend to be at a bare subsistence level with or without relief, there is no question of downward social mobility. These two types of unemployment are cited to illustrate that unemployment is not necessarily disorganizing, when it is part of the customary way of life, when roles are integrated, and when the family has developed techniques acceptable to itself for securing maintenance when there is no earned income.

One or More Members Usually Employed

These families are marginal between self-support and dependence on relief agencies—between the common man and the permanently unemployed.

They are usually able to meet their own expenses, but any emergency that either throws the chief wage earner out of work or increases expenses leads the family to some source of temporary help. These temporary lapses from financial self-sufficiency are recognized as emergencies beyond personal control. They do not cause the family to change its conception of itself as self-supporting, nor do family roles change, although one member of the family may temporarily carry out the functions of another member.

A few such families appeared among the one hundred Chicago families studied by Cavan and Ranck. The long-continued unemployment of the depression came as a crisis with which the families could not cope. They could not understand the cause of the depression unemployment, as they had been able to understand previous short periods of distress. They were forced to apply for relief for an indefinite period of time. They were also compelled to change their conception of themselves as self-supporting, and to adjust roles and sometimes class status to conform to their relief status. The reactions of these families were similar to the reactions of common man families who had never been on relief prior to the depression.

CONCLUSIONS

Briefly, one may conclude that the following reactions to prolonged unemployment may be expected:

1. The common man struggles to maintain personal status, family integration, and social class status.

2. The upper-middle class family (when affected at all) struggles to maintain personal roles, especially of the father, within the family.

3. The permanently or seasonally unemployed accept their position as normal, adjust personal statuses and roles, and integrate relief agencies or public donors into the family.

4. Even when family disorganization is marked, the family tends to reorganize once the downward decline in personal and class status reaches a stable point.

5. Characteristics facilitating good adjustment are a well organized family prior to unemployment, adaptability, responsibleness, and a non-materialistic and non-traditional philosophy of life.

Applicability of the 1930 Research to the 1950 Family

A higher percentage of married women work now than in the early 1930's, a situation that gives more economic security. We assume that the family is more equalitarian in its functioning. Do these two facts, taken together, mean that the unemployed husband could yield the dominant role (which he still retains) more gracefully to his wife than he could in the early 1930's? If so, his emotional disturbance should be less.

The great number of cars, summer homes, electrical household equipment, suburban homes, and college educations that have been bought since World War II suggest increased upward mobility, or at least the collection of material symbols of upward mobility. Many of these are being bought on the installment plan and therefore are insecurely owned. Would prolonged unemployment bring a great downward movement in social class status? Such a movement would increase bitterness and disappointment.

Do families of the common man category have the same aversion to relief that they had in the 1930's? To anything called "relief," probably they have. But the nation-wide forms of relief instituted by the federal government in the 1930's operate under sugar-coated names such as pension, aid, insurance, and compensation. The fact that employees pay into Old Age and Survivor's Insurance has created a widespread idea that they also pay into other forms of aid, such as Old Age Assistance or Pensions and Unemployment Compensation. Actually, they have not done so, but their belief that they have makes it easier for them to apply. The eligibility rules for public assistance programs have been widely publicized and people are urged to apply when eligible; they are not urged to be strong, independent, and self-sufficient. Nor does the public agency probe into family relationships or violate the feeling of privacy of the family. When eligibility rules have been met, the applicant receives a check which he may spend as he chooses. It seems probable, therefore, that the unemployed person today accepts Unemployment Compensation as his due and not as charity.

Unemployment Compensation is designed to tide a family or worker over a short period of unemployment. It is much less than the person's wages and it runs for only a few months. If the person becomes re-employed soon, he does not lose social class status and probably family roles are not disturbed. However, if he has no other income, he must reduce expenses and if he has private resources he must dip into them. With long term unemployment, the Unemployment Compensation runs out along with the private resources. At this point, the person is in the same position that the 1930 unemployed person was when he had exhausted his resources; Unemployment Compensation has simply postponed or prolonged the decline to relief status.

It seems probable that the socio-psychological trends and adjustments of the 1930's would be found in the 1950's, but that the conditions under which these trends and adjustments would work themselves out have changed.

NOTES

[1] Family life according to social class is discussed in Ruth Shonle Cavan, *The American Family,* New York: Thomas Y. Crowell Company, 1953, Part II.

[2] Ruth Shonle Cavan and Katherine Howland Ranck, *The Family and the Depression,* Chicago: University of Chicago Press, 1938; Mirra Komarovsky, *The Unemployed Man and His Family,* New York: Dryden Press, 1940; E. Wight Bakke, *The Unemployed Worker, A Study of the Task of Making a Living without a Job,* New Haven: Yale University Press, 1940, No. 1; and Bakke, *Citizens without Work,* New Haven: Yale University Press, 1940, No. 2. No. 1 and No. 2 are used in the text to distinguish Bakke's two books.

[3] W. Lloyd Warner and Paul S. Lunt, *Social Life of a Modern Community,* New Haven: Yale University Press, 1941, pp. 277–279; Winona L. Morgan, *The Family Meets the Depression,* Minneapolis: University of Minnesota Press, 1939.

[4] Robert Cooley Angell, *The Family Encounters the Depression,* New York: Charles Scribner's Sons, 1936.

[5] Harlan W. Gilmore, *The Beggar,* Chapel Hill: University of North Carolina Press, 1940, pp. 168–182; Chapter 5 on "Urban Beggardom" also is pertinent to family reactions.

[6] Martha Bushfield Van Valen, "An Approach to Mobile Dependent Families," *Social Casework,* 37 (April, 1956), pp. 180–186.

[7] Studies of migrant workers usually are focused on conditions of work, health problems, and lack of education for the children. Few give very much information on family organization, roles, or reaction to unemployment. Some insight can be gleaned from Marion Hathaway, *The Migratory Worker and Family Life,* Chicago: University of Chicago Press, 1934. *The American Child,* published bi-monthly, November to May, by the National Child Labor Committee, contains numerous articles regarding the handicaps of migratory life for children.

Healthy and Disturbed
Reasons for Having
Extramarital Relations

Albert Ellis

Considering the extent of extramarital activity in the United States, it is astounding that researchers in marriage and family have done so little in this area. Thus, we must turn to a social psychologist's essay on adultery. In his discussion of the various reasons for having extra-marital sex, Ellis suggests that the desire for sexual variety and the enjoyment of sexual adventures outside of marriage is perfectly normal. However, he feels that the proper handling of such an affair is important so as not to upset the marriage. This view, of course, gives little thought to the feelings of the non-married partner to an adulterous affair or the left-out spouse.

P sychologists and sociologists, as Whitehurst points out, tend to look upon extramarital relations as an unusual or deviant form of behavior and to seek for disturbed motivations on the part of husbands and wives who engage in adulterous affairs. Although there is considerable clinical evidence that would seem to confirm this view, there are also studies—such as those of Kinsey and his associates (11, 12) and of Cuber and Harroff (1)—which throw considerable doubt on it. In my own observations of quite unusual adulterers—unusual in the sense that both partners to the marriage agreed upon and carried out extramarital affairs and in many instances actually engaged in wife-swapping—I have found that there are usually both good and bad, healthy and unhealthy reasons for this type of highly unconventional behavior (4); and if this is true in these extreme cases, it is almost certainly equally true or truer about the usual kind of secret adulterous affairs that are much more common in this country.

From Albert Ellis, "Healthy and Disturbed Reasons for Having Extramarital Relations," in *Extra-Marital Relations,* ed., Neubech and Gerhard (Englewood Cliffs, N. J.: Prentice-Hall, 1969), pp. 153–61. Reprinted by permission of Prentice-Hall.

Let me now briefly review what I consider to be some of the main healthy and disturbed reasons for extramarital unions. My material for the following analysis comes from two main sources: (1) clinical interviews with individuals with whom I have had psychotherapy and marriage and family counseling sessions; (2) unofficial talks with scores of non-patients and non-counselees whom I have encountered in many parts of this country and who are presumably a fairly random sample of well-educated middle-class adults, most of whom have been married for five years or more. Although the first group of my interviewees included a high percentage of individuals whose marriages were far from ideal and were in many cases quite rocky, the second group consisted largely of individuals who had average or above-average marriages and who were, at the time I spoke to them, in no danger of separation or divorce.

From my talks with these individuals—some of which were relatively brief and some of which took, over a series of time, scores of hours—I am inclined to hypothesize the following healthy reasons for husbands and wives, even when they are happily married and want to continue their marital relationships, strongly wanting and doing their best to discreetly carry on extramarital affairs:

Sexual varietism. Almost the entire history of mankind demonstrates that man is not, biologically, a truly monogamous animal; that he tends to be more monogynous than monogamic, desiring one woman at a time rather than a single woman for a lifetime, and that even when he acts monogynously he craves strongly occasional adulterous affairs in addition to his regular marital sex. The female of the human species seems to be less strongly motivated toward plural sexuality than is the male; but she, too, when she can have varietistic outlets with social impunity, quite frequently takes advantage of them (5).

A healthy married individual in our society is usually able to enjoy steady sex relations with his spouse; but he frequently tends to have *less* marital satisfaction after several years than he had for the first months or years after his wedding. He lusts after innumerable women besides his wife, particularly those who are younger and prettier than she is; he quite often enhances his marital sex enjoyment by thinking about these other women when copulating with his spouse; he enjoys mild or heavy petting with other females at office parties, social gatherings, and other suitable occasions; and he actually engages in adulterous affairs from time to time, especially when he and his wife are temporarily parted or when he can otherwise discreetly have a little fling with impunity, knowing that his spouse is not likely to discover what he is doing and that his extramarital affair will not seriously interfere with his marriage and family life. The man who resides in a large urban area and who never once, during thirty or more years of married life, is sorely tempted to engage in adultery for purposes of sexual variety is to be suspected of being indeed biologically and/or psychologically abnormal; and he who frequently has such desires and who occasionally and unobtrusively carries them into practice is well within the normal healthy range.

Love enhancement. Healthy human beings are generally capable of loving pluralistically, on both a serial and a simultaneous basis. Although conjugal or familial love tends to remain alive, and even to deepen, over a long period of years, romantic love generally wanes in from three to five years—particularly when the lovers live under the same roof and share numerous unromantic exigencies of life. Because romantic love, in spite of its palpable disadvantages, is a uniquely exciting and enlivening feeling and has many splendid repercussions on one's whole life, a great number of sensible and stable married individuals fall in love with someone other than their spouses and find, on some level, a mutual expression of their amative feelings with these others. To be incapable of further romantic attachments is in some respects to be dead; and both in imagination and in practice hordes of healthy husbands and wives, including those who continue to have a real fondness for their mates, become involved in romantic extramarital affairs. Although some of these affairs do not lead to any real sexual actualization, many of them do. The result is a great number of divorces and remarriages; but, in all probability, the result is an even greater number of adulterous love affairs that, for one reason or another, do not lead to legal separation from the original mate but which are carried on simultaneously with the marriage.

Experiential drives. Loving, courting, going to bed with, and maintaining an ongoing relationship with a member of the other sex are all interesting and gratifying experiences, not only because of the elements of sex and love that are involved in these happenings but also because the sex-love partners learn a great many things about themselves and their chosen ones, and because they experience thoughts, feelings, and interchanges that would otherwise probably never come their way. To live, to a large degree, is to relate: and in our society intimate relationships usually reach their acme in sex-love affairs. The healthy, experience-hungry married individual, therefore, will be quite motivated, at least at times during his conjugal life, to add to the experience which he is likely to obtain through marriage itself, and often to return to some of the high levels of relating with members of the other sex which he may have known before he met his spouse. His desires to experiment or to re-experience in these respects may easily prejudice him in favor of adultery—especially with the kinds of members of the other sex who are quite different from his mate, and with whom he is not too likely to become closely related outside of his having an extramarital liaison.

Adventure seeking. Most people today lead routinized, fairly dull, unadventurous lives; and their chances of fighting the Indians, hunting big game in Africa, or even trying a new job after working in the same one for a decade or more are reasonably slim. One of the few remaining areas in which they can frequently find real excitement and novelty of a general as well as a specifically sexual nature is in the area of sex-love affairs. Once this area is temporarily closed by marriage, child-rearing, and the fairly scheduled pursuits that tend to accompany domestic life, the healthy and still adventure-seeking person frequently looks longingly for some other outlets; and he or she is likely to find such outlets in extramarital relationships. This does not mean that all life-loving mates must eventually try to jazz up their humdrum existences with adulterous affairs; but it does mean that a certain percentage of creative, adventure-seeking individuals will and that they will do so for reasonably sensible motives.

Sexual curiosity. Although an increasing number of people today have premarital sex experiences and a good number also have sex affairs between the time their first marriage ends by death or divorce and their next marriage begins, there are still many Americans, especially females, who reach the age of forty or fifty and have had a total of only one or two sex partners in their entire lives. Such individuals, even when they have had fairly satisfactory sex relations with their spouses, are often quite curious about what it would be like to try one or more other partners; and eventually a good number of them do experiment in this regard. Other individuals, including many who are happily married, are driven by their sex curiosity to try extramarital affairs because they would like to bring back new techniques to their own marriage bed, because they want to have at least one orgiastic experience before they die, or because some other aspect of their healthy information-seeking in sexual areas cannot very well be satisfied if they continue to have purely monogamous relations.

Social and cultural inducements. Literally millions of average Americans occasionally or frequently engage in adultery because it is the approved social thing to do at various times and in certain settings which are a regular part of their lives. Thus, normally monogamous males will think nothing of resorting to prostitutes or to easily available non-prostitutes at business parties, at men's club meetings, or at conventions. And very sedate women will take off their girdles and either pet to orgasm or have extramarital intercourse at wild drinking parties, on yacht or boat cruises, at vacation resorts, and at various other kinds of social affairs where adulterous behavior is not only permitted but is even expected. Although Americans rarely engage in the regular or periodic kinds of sex orgies which many primitive peoples permit themselves in the course of their married lives, they do fairly frequently engage in occasional orgiastic-like parties where extramarital affairs are encouraged and sometimes become the rule. This may not be the healthiest kind of adulterous behavior but it is well within the range of social normality and it often does seem to satisfy, in a socially approved way, some of the underlying sensible desires for sexual experience, adventure, and varietism that might otherwise be very difficult to fulfill in our society.

Sexual deprivation. Many husbands and wives are acutely sexually deprived, either on a temporary or permanent basis. They may be separated from each other for reasons beyond their control—as when the husband goes off on a long business trip, is inducted into the armed forces, or is in poor physical health. Or they may live together and be theoretically sexually available to each other, but one of them may have a much lower sex drive than the other, may be sexually incompetent, or may otherwise be an unsatisfying bed partner even though he or she is perfectly adequate in the other aspects of marital life. Under such circumstances, the deprived mate can very healthfully long for and from time to time seek out extramarital affairs; and in many such instances this mate's marriage may actually be benefited by the having of such affairs, since otherwise acute and chronic sexual deprivation in the marriage may encourage hostilities that could easily disrupt the relationship.

The foregoing reasons for engaging in extramarital affairs would all seem to be reasonably healthy, though of course they can be mixed in with various neurotic reasons, too. Nor do these reasons exhaust the list of sane motivations that would induce many or most married individuals to strongly desire, and at times actually to have, adulterous liaisons. On the other side of the fence, however, there are several self-defeating or emotionally disturbed impulses behind adultery. These include the following:

Low frustration tolerance. While almost every healthy married person at times desires extramarital affairs, he does not truly need to have them, and he can usually tolerate (if not thoroughly enjoy) life very well without them, especially if his marriage is relatively good. The neurotic individual, however, frequently convinces himself that he needs what he wants and that his preferences are necessities. Consequently, he makes himself so desperately unhappy when he is sexually monogamous that he literally drives himself into extramarital affairs. Being a demander rather than a preferrer, he then usually finds something intolerable about his adulterous involvements, too; and he often winds up by becoming still more frustrated, unhappier, and even downright miserable and depressed. It is not mariage and its inevitable frustrations that "bug" him; it is his unreasonable expectation that marriage should not be frustrating.

Hostility to one's spouse. Low frustration tolerance or unrealistic demandingness leads innumerable spouses to dislike their partner's behavior and to insist that the partner therefore ought not be the way he or she is. This childish insistence results in hostility; and once a married person becomes hostile, he frequently refuses to face the fact that he is making himself angry. He vindictively wants to punish his mate, he shies away from having sex with her (or encourages her to shy away from having sex with anyone who is as angry at her as he is), and he finds it much easier to have satisfactory social-sexual relations with another woman than his wife. He usually "solves" his problem only temporarily by this method, since as long as he remains anger-prone, the chances are that he will later become hostile toward his adulterous inamorata, and that the same kind of vicious circle will occur with his relations with her.

Self-deprecation. A great number of spouses are so perfectionistic in their demands on themselves, and so self-castigating when they do not live up to these demands, that they cannot bear to keep facing their mates (who are in the best positions to see their inadequacies). Because they condemn themselves for not being excellent economic providers, housekeepers, parents, sex partners, etc., they look for outside affairs in which fewer demands will be made on them or where they will not expect themselves to act so perfectly; and they feel more "comfortable," at least temporarily, while having such affairs, even though the much more logical solution to their problem would often be to work things out in their marriages while learning not to be so self-flagellating.

Ego-bolstering. Many married men feel that they are not really men and many married women feel that they are not really women unless they are continually proving that they are by winning the approval of members of the other sex. Some of them also feel that unless they can be seen in public with a particularly desirable sex partner, no one will really respect them. Consequently, they continually seek for conquests and have adulterous affairs to bolter their own low self-esteem rather than for sexual or companionship purposes.

Escapism. Most married individuals have serious enough problems to face in life, either at home, in their work, in their social affairs, or in their attitudes toward themselves. Rather than face and probably work through these problems, a number of these spouses find it much easier to run to some diverting affairs, such as those that adultery may offer. Wives who are poor mothers or who are in continual squabbles with their parents or their in-laws can find many distracting times in motel rooms or in some bachelor's apartment. Husbands who won't face their problems with their partners or with their employees can forget themselves, at least for an afternoon or an evening, in some mistress's more than willing arms. Both husbands and wives who have no vital absorbing interests in life, and who refuse to work at finding for themselves some major goal which would give more meaning to their days, can immerse themselves in adulterous involvements of a promiscuous or long-term nature and can almost forget about the aimlessness of their existences. Naturally, extramarital affairs that are started for these reasons themselves tend to be meaningless and are not vitally absorbing. But surely they are more interesting than mahjongg and television!

Marital escapism. Most marriages in many respects leave much to be desired; and some are obviously completely "blah" and sterile and would better be brought to an end. Rather than face their marital and family problems, however, and rather than courageously arrange for a separation or a divorce, many couples prefer to avoid such difficult issues and to occupy themselves, instead, in extramarital liaisons, which at least sometimes render their marriages slightly more tolerable.

Sexual disturbances. Sexual disturbances are rather widespread in our society—particularly in the form of impotence or frigidity of husbands and wives. Instead of trying to understand the philosophic core of such disturbances, and changing the irrational and self-defeating value systems that usually cause them (2, 3, 6, 7, 8, 9, 10), many husbands and wives follow the line of least resistance, decide to live with their sexual neuroses, and consequently seek out nonmarital partners with whom they can more comfortably retain these aberrations. Thus, frigid wives, instead of working out their sexual incompatibilities with their husbands, sometimes pick a lover or a series of lovers with whom they are somewhat less frigid or who can more easily tolerate their sexual inadequacies. Impotent husbands or those who are fixated on some form of sex deviation, rather than getting to the source of their difficulties and overcoming them in their relations with their wives, find prostitutes, mistresses, or homosexual partners with whom they can remain "comfortably" deviant. In many instances, in fact, the spouse of the sexually disturbed individual is severely blamed for his or her anomaly, when little or no attempt has been made to correct this anomaly by working sexually with this spouse.

Excitement needs. Where the healthy married person, as shown previously in this paper, has a distinct desire for adventure, novelty, and some degree of excitement in life and may therefore be motivated to have some extramarital affairs, the disturbed individual frequently has an inordinate need for excitation. He makes himself, for various reasons, so jaded with almost every aspect of his life that he can only temporarily enjoy himself by some form of thrill-seeking such as wild parties, bouts of drunkenness, compulsive moving around from place to place or job to job, or drug-taking. One of the modes of excitement-seeking which this kind of a disturbed person may take is that of incessantly searching for extramarital affairs. This will not cure his basic jadedness, but will give him surcease from pain for at least a period of time—as do, too, the alcohol and drugs that such individuals are prone to use.

If the thesis of this paper is correct, and there are both healthy and unhealthy reasons for an individual's engaging in extramarital sex relations, how can any given person's motives for adultery be objectively assessed? If Mrs. X, a housewife and mother of two children, or Mr. Y, a businessman and father of a teenage son, get together with other single or married individuals and carry on adulterously, how are we to say if one is or both are driven by sane or senseless motives? The answer is that we would have to judge each case individually on the basis of much psychological and sociological information, to determine what the person's true impulses are and how neurotic or psychotic they seem to be. To make such judgments, however, some kind of criteria have to be drawn up; and although this is difficult to do at present, partly because of our still limited knowledge of healthy individuals and social norms, I shall take a flyer and hazard an educated guess as to what these criteria might possibly be. Judging from my own personal, clinical, and research experience, I would say that the following standards of healthy adulterous behavior might be fairly valid:

1. The healthy adulterer is non-demanding and non-compulsive. He prefers but he does not need extramarital affairs. He believes that he can live better with than without them, and therefore he tries to arrange to have them from time to time. But he is also able to have a happy general and marital life if no such affairs are practicable.

2. The undisturbed adulterer usually manages to carry on his extramarital affairs without unduly disturbing his marriage and family relationships nor his general existence. He is sufficiently discreet about his adultery, on the one hand, and appropriately frank and honest about it with his close associates, on the other hand, so that most people he intimately knows are able to tolerate his affairs and not get too upset about them.

410

3. He fully accepts his own extramarital desires and acts and never condemns himself or punishes himself because of them, even though he may sometimes decide that they are unwise and may make specific attempts to bring them to a halt.

4. He faces his specific problems with his wife and family as well as his general life difficulties and does not use his adulterous relationships as a means of avoiding any of his serious problems.

5. He is usually tolerant of himself when he acts poorly or makes errors; he is minimally hostile when his wife and family members behave in a less than desirable manner; and he fully accepts the fact that the world is rough and life is often grim, but that there is no reason why it *must* be otherwise and that he can live happily even when conditions around him are not great. Consequently, he does not drive himself to adultery because of self-deprecation, self-pity, or hostility to others.

6. He is sexually adequate with his spouse as well as with others and therefore has extramarital affairs out of sex interest rather than for sex therapy.

Although the adulterer who lives up to these criteria may have still other emotional disturbances and may be having extramarital affairs for various neurotic reasons other than those outlined in this paper, there is also a good chance that this is not true. The good Judeo-Christian moralists may never believe it, but it would appear that healthy adultery, even in our supposedly monogynous society, *is* possible. Just how often our millions of adulterers practice extramarital relations for good and how often for bad reasons is an interesting question. It is hoped that future research in this area may be somewhat helped by some of the considerations pointed out in the present paper.

REFERENCES

1. Cuber, John S., and Harroff, Peggy B. *The Significant Americans.* New York: Appleton-Century-Crofts, Inc., 1965.
2. Ellis, Albert. *Reason and Emotion in Psychotherapy.* New York: Lyle Stuart, 1962.
3. Ellis, Albert. *The Art and Science of Love.* New York: Lyle Stuart and Bantam Books, 1969.
4. Ellis, Albert. *Suppressed: Seven Key Essays Publishers Dared Not Print.* Chicago: New Classic House, 1965 (especially Chap. 4).
5. Ellis, Albert. *The Case for Sexual Liberty.* Tucson: Seymour Press, 1965.
6. Ellis, Albert. *Sex Without Guilt.* New York: Lyle Stuart and Grove Press, 1966.
7. Ellis, Albert. *The Search for Sexual Enjoyment.* New York: Macfadden-Bartell, 1966.
8. Ellis, Albert. *If This Be Sexual Heresy.* New York: Lyle Stuart and Tower Publications, 1966.
9. Ellis, Albert, and Harper, Robert A. *Creative Marriage.* New York: Lyle Stuart and Tower Publications, 1966.

10. Ellis, Albert, and Harper, Robert A. *A Guide to Rational Living*. Englewood Cliffs, N.J.: Prentice-Hall, Inc., 1967, and Hollywood: Wilshire Books, 1967.
11. Kinsey, Alfred C., *et al. Sexual Behavior in the Human Male*. Philadelphia: W. B. Saunders, 1948.
12. Kinsey, Alfred C., *et al. Sexual Behavior in the Human Female*. Philadelphia: W. B. Saunders, 1953.

Marital Problems, Help-Seeking, and Emotional Orientation as Revealed in Help-Request Letters

James E. DeBurger

For what kinds of marital problems do people seek professional help? Who is more likely to seek such help—the husband or the wife? What differences can be discerned in the types of problems that concern the husband and wife and in their emotional orientation to them? DeBurger attempts to answer some of these questions by analyzing the letters people write to marriage counselors. Again, it will not surprise readers of this volume that the major complaints were to be found in the areas of affectional and sexual relations. Personality problems were also mentioned quite frequently. However, husbands and wives differed as to the details of the same general problem, as well as in their emotional reaction to it. (For the beginning student, the technical details of this article may be ignored. It is the general *content that is important.)*

A student perusing the literature on marital problems may find some recent research based on clinical, mass-communications, and survey data which delineates the characteristics of persons engaged in the process of seeking help for such problems.[1] However, sparse indeed are published reports based on systematic analysis of "natural" data voluntarily provided by persons in the initial phases of dealing with their marital problems.[2] The question, "Who seeks marriage counseling?" probably cannot be answered adequately from records kept by clinics or counselors. For, as marriage counselors well know, there is a phenomenal rate of attrition in the referral process. It would seem

From James DeBurger, "Marital Problems, Help-Seeking, and Emotional Orientation as Revealed in Help-Request Letters," *Journal of Marriage and the Family,* November, 1967, pp. 712–21. Reprinted by permission of the author and The National Council on Family Relations.

that more empirically derived knowledge is needed about persons in the very first stages of "help-seeking"; information of this kind might be useful in comparing those who are actually counseled with the much larger population of those who have indicated "need" for counseling or for purposes of validating generalizations about marital problems based on client populations. Such knowledge might also contribute to the less practical but basic task of testing hypotheses about relations between familial social structure and family problems, sex differences in potential for marital conflict, etc.

This article briefly summarizes selected findings of a study which focused on verbal materials produced by persons who were in the first stages of seeking professional help for their marital problems. In one recent ten-year period (1950-1959), the national office of the American Association of Marriage Counselors received 15,430 letters. Of this number, 93 percent (14,323) were "help-request" letters wherein the correspondent sought referral and/or other guidance in connection with his marital troubles. The research discussed here concentrated on these help-request letters. At least two previously published studies dealt with letters received by "lovelorn" or advice columnists.[3] The writer is not aware, however, of any systematic, large-scale study of help-request letters which included correspondents of both sexes and in which all correspondents were explicitly seeking help for marital problems.

METHOD AND PROCEDURES

As might be expected, there was much variation in the content of the 14,323 help-request letters; some were sparse on details while others were relatively profuse. The documents ranged in length from one to 15 pages, each represented one marriage, and each contained a request for referral and/or other help. From this overall collection, 1,412 letters were selected for intensive analysis. To qualify for inclusion in this subgroup, each document had to contain (1) a specification of the problem for which help was sought, (2) basic information regarding geographic source and residence, and (3) information pertaining to at least two aspects of the reported marital problem (e.g. duration of the problem, number of persons involved, etc.). Letters in this subgroup were therefore of greater length and comparatively richer in detail than the other documents. The summary of findings presented here is based on data from the subgroup of 1,412 letters. For all items in which comparisons between the overall collection (14,323) and subgroup (1,412) were possible, no statistically significant differences were found. For example, the proportion of males to females in the subgroup (18 percent males, 82 percent females) was almost identical to the proportions observed in the overall collection of letters. For fuller discussion of the larger project on which this article is based, the reader is referred to the original work.[4]

The content analysis of the letters was formulated so that optimum information might be derived in regard to: (1) the demographic characteristics of the correspondents, (2) the kinds of problems they revealed, (3) their patterns of help-seeking, and (4) their emotional orientation regarding their problems and the related help-seeking. Empirical questions suggested by prior research were formulated so that the coding procedure would yield the four kinds of data enumerated above. For each case, a total of 75 content items was recorded on a code sheet from which an IBM card record was then prepared. The reliability of coding was checked by two measures applied to a ten-percent sample of the documents. The first of these consisted of a "test-retest" measure of the investigator's consistency in coding; for this, the percentage of agreement in coding of all data on two separate occasions was 91 percent. The second check involved a measure of inter-analyst agreement, using two trained coders; for this, the percentages of agreement ranged from 75 to 93 percent for independent codings on the same set of documents.[5]

Prior research bearing on sex differences in marital problems suggested the feasibility of comparing husbands and wives on each set of findings produced by the content analysis.[6] In comparing husbands and wives as groups, a frequency criterion was used (e.g., proportionate differences in the appearance of a particular theme in the letters). The basic methodological assumption was that the writing of a help-request letter represented a verbal opportunity for the correspondent to relate various aspects of his marital trouble. Variations in occurrence of particular content items might therefore be explainable under theoretically based expectations of sex differentials. The Chi-square statistic was used for testing the significance of group differences in the proportions indicating various content items; a probability level of .05 was used for determining significance.

Summary of Findings

Description of the Correspondents

Results of preliminary sorting for the content analysis showed that 82 percent (1,160) of the help-request letters were written by wives. A similar predominance of females in voluntary problem-disclosure and initial help-seeking has been observed in other research.[7] Each case was categorized as either "blue-collar" or "white-collar" social class. In 676 cases, this classification was based on occupational information revealed by the correspondent; for the remainder, the social class situation of the correspondent was estimated by a technique based upon the verbal quality of the communication, stationery quality, and the mode of writing. This technique has been previously employed in several content analyses.[8] White-collar classification was assigned to 61 percent of the cases, and 39 percent were categorized as blue-collar social class.[9]

Various other descriptive characteristics may be summarized.

(1) *Residence.* All correspondents were United States residents. Using Census Bureau listings of urbanized areas and urban place,[10] 97 percent of the correspondents were classified as urban and 3 percent as rural. There was a

rank-order correlation coefficient of .95 between the proportion of letters from each region and the number of married couples in each region as reported by the United States Census. Differences in sex representation by regions were not statistically significant.

(2) *Race and religion.* Information regarding their race was seldom explicitly revealed by the correspondents; only four non-white cases were identified in the preliminary coding, and these were not included in the subgroup of 1,412. It was assumed that all marriages represented by the help-requests were white. On the basis of information from 14 percent of the correspondents, 90 percent were Protestant.

(3) *Age.* Information regarding age was revealed by 979 of the correspondents. Most correspondents (60 percent of the wives, 70 percent of the husbands) were under 40 years of age. Mean age was 39 for husbands and 36 for wives.

(4) *Parental status.* This datum was reported by 90 percent of the wives and 86 percent of the husbands. Two-thirds of those reporting parental status had no more than three children; the mean number of children was 2.7 for all correspondents who reported this item.

(5) *Length of marriage.* In 1,098 cases, the help-request letter provided information on the length of marriage. In 758 cases, the correspondent explicitly stated how long he had been married. In the remaining 340 cases, estimates of this datum were based on relevant information in the help-request letter. Relevant information included time reference points, indirect references to length of marriage, and other similar information. Approximately 56 percent of the correspondents had been married for less than ten years. The mean length of marriage for both husbands and wives was approximately 12 years.

Revealed Problems

On the basis of a preliminary analysis of the documents, eight categories were developed which subsumed specific problems or "themes" (statements identifying the nature of the problem) expressed in the documents.[11] The revealed problems were then classified as "major" or as "secondary." A major problem was one seemingly regarded by the correspondent as central—the chief cause of the marital unhappiness; each document was coded to reflect but one major problem. Secondary problem themes included any complaints or problems that were disclosed in the letter, apart from the one coded as the major problem. A given document might thus disclose several secondary problems or none. The content analysis developed a total of 30 problem-themes which were grouped in eight categories. Table 1 shows these eight categories of major problems along with the themes which they subsume.[12]

It is apparent from Table 1 that major problems tend to cluster in the two areas of interaction represented by affectional and sexual relations, with problems involving personality relations coming next in order of prominence.[13] Thus, among those persons who perceived themselves as seriously needing

TABLE 1.

Major Problems Revealed by Husbands and Wives in 1,412 Help-Request Letters

CATEGORY AND RELATED THEMES	HUSBAND	WIFE	TOTAL
Affectional Relations	11.5%	31.0%	27.6%
1. Spouse cold, unaffectionate			
2. Spouse is in love with another			
3. Have no love feelings for spouse			
4. Spouse is not in love with me			
5. Spouse attracted to others, flirts			
6. Excessive, "insane" jealousy			
Sexual Relations	42.1	20.6	24.4
1. Sexual relations "unsatisfactory"			
2. Orgasm inability; frigidity, impotence			
3. Sex deprivation; insufficient coitus			
4. Spouse wants "unnatural" sex relations			
Role Tasks-Responsibilities	0.0	6.0	4.9
1. Disagreement over 'who should do what'			
2. Spouse's failure to meet material needs			
Parental-Role Relations	0.0	1.7	1.4
1. Conflict on child discipline			
2. Parent-child conflict			
Intercultural Relations	11.5	11.4	11.4
1. In-law relations troublesome			
2. Religion and religious behavior			
Situational Conditions	4.0	3.4	3.5
1. Financial difficulties, income lack			
2. Physical illness, spouse or self			
Deviant Behavior	7.5	8.7	8.5
1. Heavy drinking, alcoholism of mate			
2. Own heavy drinking or alcoholism			
3. Spouse's "loose" sex behavior			
4. Own illicit sex behavior			
5. Compulsive gambling			
Personality Relations	23.4	17.2	18.3
1. Spouse domineering, selfish			
2. Own "poor" personality, instability			
3. Clash of personalities; incompatible			
4. Spouse's violent temper tantrums			
5. Spouse withdrawn, moody, "neurotic"			
6. Spouse quarrelsome, bickering, nagging			
7. Spouse irresponsible, undependable			
Total	100.0% n = 252	100.0% n = 1160	100.0% N = 1412

Chi-square = 91.80; P < .001 (8 categories × husband-wife status).

professional help, major marital problems connected with the intimate patterns of interaction between mates far outweighed other types. Speculation suggests that these findings reflect a pervasive cultural emphasis on marriage as an emotionally gratifying pair-relationship. Thus, revealed marital problems may increasingly tend to reflect difficulties associated with the attainment of happiness in *interspouse relations* (rather than the attainment of harmony with the socio-cultural context, such as kin, community, religion, etc.). In connection with this speculation on the matter of interspouse happiness, it is interesting to note that problems associated with parental roles ranked lowest in the major problems revealed by the correspondents. Although more than four-fifths of the correspondents reported parental status, less than two percent of the 1,412 revealed major marital problems reflecting this area of interaction. In other research using families not characterized by overt marital problems and help-seeking,[14] parental-role problems were much more frequently revealed.

Sex differences in major problems. A central question in this research concerned possible sex differences in revealed problems; prior research suggested the strong likelihood that such differences would be found in our data. Students of marital interaction have quite commonly assumed that various differences in the subcultural backgrounds of males and females may account in part for differences in the kinds of conflicts and problems typically experienced by husbands and wives. In the present research it was assumed not only that husbands and wives may differ in problem-experiencing, but also that these differential problems would be expressed by persons in the process of seeking help. Presumably, each correspondent was free to impart whatever knowledge he desired about himself and his problems. An implicit question in this research concerned the similarity of sex differentials found in this data to sex differentials revealed by studies using relatively structured questionnaire and interview data. The bulk of our current knowledge about marital relations is derived from data of the latter type.

As Table 1 shows, husbands and wives differ significantly in regard to the kinds of major marital problems revealed in their help-request letters. A salient finding was that husbands and wives differ significantly in their revelation of problems which involve sexual and affectional relations. A significantly larger proportion of husbands than wives revealed problems associated with sexual relations, whereas many more wives than husbands revealed problems associated with affectional relations. This finding converges strongly with theory and empirical evidence on sex differentials stemming from early research by Terman and later studies by Burgess and Wallin.

Table 1 also shows that more wives than husbands revealed major problems associated with role-tasks-responsibilities. This finding seems consistent with the hypothesis that wives may be more prone than husbands to perceive problems associated with the cultural conflict and ambiguity surrounding the female's marital roles.[15] Although there was little reason to expect a particular sex differential in revealed problems involving personality relations, the data show a significantly larger proportion of husbands than wives revealing this type of problem.

Sex differences on specific themes. In addition to comparing husbands and wives on categories of problems (as in Table 1), checks were also made of sex differentials in the revelation of some specific problem-*themes* which seemed likely in view of prior research.[16] A significantly larger proportion of wives than husbands disclosed these themes: (1) "mate's excessive jealousy," (2) "mate is in love with another," (3) "mate wants sex relations too often," (4) "disgust with sexual relations per se," (5) "disagreement over division of labor in the family," (6) "mate's heavy drinking," and (7) "mate's extramarital sex relations." A significantly larger proportion of husbands than wives, as was expected, revealed themes expressing: (1) "unsatisfactory sexual rela-

418

tions with the mate," (2) "sex deprivation or insufficient frequency of marital coitus," and (3) "moodiness or neurotic behavior of the mate." In each of these comparisons, the group differences were significant at a probability level of .05 or below.

Contrary to expectations, husbands and wives as groups did not differ significantly in the proportions revealing the following themes: (1) "mate is cold or too seldom displays affection," (2) "in-law relations are troublesome," (3) "nagging by the mate," and (4) "mate is irresponsible."

Sex differences by social class. Husband-wife differences in the disclosure of four categories of major problems were checked for possible variation by social class of the correspondents. As the data in Table 2 indicate, the direction of husband-wife differences seen earlier (Table 1) persists when the cases are grouped by social class. It is apparent, however, that the sex differentials are more pronounced in cases identified as blue-collar social class. While more than one-fifth of the white-collar husbands disclosed major problems in the affectional relations category, none of the blue-collar husbands indicated this problem type. On the other hand, major problems involving intramarital sexual relations were much more frequently revealed by blue-collar husbands than by their white-collar counterparts. The proportions of white-collar husbands and wives reporting problems which involved personality relations were appreciably larger than for blue-collar husbands and wives. It may also be noted that, in the white-collar class, sex differences in revelation of personality problems are much more pronounced than in the blue-collar cases.

Variation by length of marriage. Analysis of those letters in which the duration of the marriage had been explicitly reported by the correspondent (758) revealed some association between length of marriage and disclosure of problems associated with affectional, sexual, and personality relations. Attention was confined to these categories of problems because of their relatively greater

TABLE 2.
MAJOR PROBLEMS REVEALED BY HUSBANDS AND WIVES, ARRANGED BY CATEGORY OF PROBLEM AND SOCIAL CLASS

MAJOR PROBLEM CATEGORY	SOCIAL CLASS			
	WHITE-COLLAR*		BLUE-COLLAR†	
	Husband	*Wife*	*Husband*	*Wife*
Affectional Relations	23.4%	32.4%	0.0%	28.6%
Sexual Relations	22.7	18.9	61.8	23.8
Role Tasks-Responsibility	0.0	4.0	0.0	9.5
Personality Relations	30.7	20.3	15.4	11.9
Other Major Problems	23.2	24.4	22.8	26.2
Total	100.0%	100.0%	100.0%	100.0%
	(n = 124)	(n = 740)	(n = 128)	(n = 420)

*Chi-square (husband-wife status × problem categories) = 13.79; P < .01.
†Chi-square (husband-wife status × problem categories) = 93.26; P < .001.

frequency in the documents. The tabulation for this arrangement included each case where either a major or a secondary problem was coded for the categories shown in Table 3. Since the number of cases is rather small and since most of our data pertain to marriages of less than ten years' duration, the findings on this point are quite tentative. However, in terms of an analogous "trend," as shown in Table 3, the analysis has certain implications: (1) For both husband and wife groups, the proportions revealing problems connected with affectional relations tend to increase as length of marriage increases. (2) Revealed problems associated with intramarital sexual relations show considerable decrease over time for husbands; for wives, however, the proportions revealing sexual relations problems are appreciably less than for husbands, but tend to persist in the later years of marriage. (3) For both husbands and wives, problems involving personality relations are revealed by relatively small proportions in the earliest period, but tend to increase with the duration of marriage. This evidence somewhat converges with other research showing changes in critical areas of marital interaction over the duration of marriage.[17] Multiple revelation of problems is also suggested by Table 3. Analysis showed that for both husbands and wives, reports of more than one of these three problems were least frequent in the earliest period and most frequent in marriages of 20 or more years' duration.

TABLE 3.

PROPORTION OF HUSBAND AND WIFE GROUPS REVEALING
AFFECTIONAL, SEXUAL, AND PERSONALITY RELATIONS
PROBLEMS, BY LENGTH OF MARRIAGE

	LENGTH OF MARRIAGE			
PROBLEM CATEGORY	LESS THAN 1 YEAR	1-9 YEARS	10-19 YEARS	20+ YEARS
Affectional Relations*				
Husband	41.7% (5/12)	60.6% (40/66)	61.1% (22/36)	61.9% (13/21)
Wife	36.4% (16/44)	50.2% (152/303)	40.6% (65/160)	48.3% (56/116)
Sexual Relations†				
Husband	50.0% (6/12)	31.8% (21/66)	36.1% (13/36)	14.3% (3/21)
Wife	34.1% (15/44)	28.7% (87/303)	23.1% (37/160)	25.9% (30/116)
Personality Relations‡				
Husband	25.0% (3/12)	48.5% (32/66)	44.4% (16/36)	76.2% (16/21)
Wife	31.8% (14/44)	48.5% (147/303)	50.0% (80/160)	61.2% (71/116)

* Husband: $X^2 = 5.98$, P < .30; Wife: $X^2 = 9.04$, P < .10.
† Husband: $X^2 = 22.22$, P < .001; Wife: $X^2 = 132.63$, P < .001.
‡ Husband: $X^2 = 9.20$, P < .10; Wife: $X^2 = 11.90$, P < .02.
Note: Chi-square values above are for combined tests of proportions indicating the given problems in each of the time segments; degrees of freedom = 4 for each Chi-square.

420

Revealed Help-Seeking Behavior

In the analysis of the help-request letters, items illustrative of the correspondent's search for help were recorded. Each letter was, in itself, a component in the help-seeking process; in coding, therefore, certain aspects of each letter were examined (e.g., length, descriptiveness, indications of "urgency," etc.). In addition, each letter was coded for information provided by the correspondent in regard to his relations with sources of help prior to writing the help-request letter. A review of the literature on this topic provided some questions to guide coding and suggested some likely sex differences in help-seeking behavior.[18]

A brief comment seems appropriate in regard to the approximate five-to-one ratio of females to males among the correspondents. Other studies of persons utilizing professional help-sources have shown a similar disproportionate representation of females; the proportion of females to males seems especially high in the initial phases of help-seeking.[19] This sex differential may imply support for the hypothesis that wives are relatively more involved in and committed to their marital roles than are husbands; hence, wives may be more highly motivated than husbands to seek professional help as a means of preserving marriage.

Letter-writing as a first step. Analysis showed that the help-request letter represented, for most correspondents, a first step toward contact with a formal helping agency. Only 303 of the correspondents reported that they had sought out some source of help prior to writing a help-request letter. Husbands and wives did not differ significantly in this respect. A related question concerns the prior sources of help which had been explored by these 303 correspondents. Four major sources of help were reported in the following proportions: physicians, 41 percent; clergymen, 19.5 percent; psychiatrists or psychologists, 18.8 percent; and attorneys, 12.2 percent. Help had been sought from miscellaneous others (relatives, friends, astrologists, etc.) by the remaining 8.5 percent. There were no statistically significant differences between husbands and wives in regard to these reported sources of help. A significant social class difference was found in only one instance: proportionately more white-collar than blue-collar correspondents consulted psychiatrists or psychologists.

Sources of information about marriage counseling. In 936 letters, correspondents reported their sources of information concerning the role of AAMC as a referral agency for professional marriage counseling. For both husbands and wives, magazines were by far the most frequently reported source of information about help for a troubled marriage. Approximately 92 percent of each group reported magazines as their source of information. Only two percent of each group had learned of the referral role of AAMC directly from professionals (physicians, clergymen, etc.) in their local community. Other reported sources of information included newspaper articles, lectures, friends, radio or TV programs, and books. Husbands and wives did not differ significantly in their reported sources of information about professional marriage counseling. Neither were any significant differences found when the data were grouped by correspondent's social class.

One implication of this data is that some forms of the mass media may serve significant functions in linking problems and troubled marriages with suitable sources of help. In this connection, most of the prominent women's and family-oriented magazines have, in recent years, carried "case record" articles which deal with marital problems. Such articles are often accompanied by an offer to refer troubled persons to competent counselors. Articles dealing with marital problems (especially "case histories") conceivably afford a means by which a troubled marriage or a specific problem may be identified. "Models" of appropriate help-seeking and problem-solving behavior may also be provided in such materials.[20]

The preceding speculation raises a broad but pertinent question which is not adequately treated in the literature of family research: namely, the impact of culture on the patterns and dynamics of the help-seeking process. The question of how Americans actually do try to solve their marital problems cannot be separated from the related question of how they "ought" to solve them in the light of relevant cultural norms. The role of mass media is probably crucial in the transmission of socially approved models of help-seeking and in providing channels of communication between troubled persons and professional sources of help.

Characteristics of letter content. Since these letters were presumably components in the correspondent's process of help-seeking, content items were coded which seemed illustrative of various aspects of this process. One such item, *urgency*, was coded on the basis of the correspondent's requests for expediency in a reply to his letter. A total of 214 or 15 percent of the correspondents expressed urgency. Husbands and wives were not significantly differentiated on this item, nor were group differences significant when the cases were grouped by social class.

Another relevant content item was *mutuality* or joint appeals for help appearing in the letters. When a correspondent indicated that his spouse was also desirous of pursuing a solution for the marital problem or when the letter was apparently written and/or signed by both spouses, the help-request was classified as *mutual*. Analysis showed relatively little mutuality for either the husbands (14.3 percent) or the wives (14.8 percent), and the husband-wife differences are obviously not significant. An arrangement of the data by social class of the correspondents showed no significant differences by class.

The coding process also provided tabulations on the *length* and *descriptiveness* of the documents. The length of the average help-request letter was 255 words. Our expectation that letters from wives would be somewhat lengthier than those from husbands was not supported by the analysis. An overall Chi-square test (husband-wife status $\times$ letter-length group) did not show group differences significant at the .05 level of probability. A ten-percent sample of the letters was coded to check for possible group differences in verbal descriptiveness. The descriptiveness of each document was ascertained by counting all phrases using adjectives, adverbs, or symbolisms descriptive of self, spouse,

422

or problem. Contrary to expectations, sex differences in verbal descriptiveness were not statistically significant when the descriptive words in each letter were viewed as proportions of the total words in each letter.

Disclosures by the correspondent reflecting an *awareness of economic aspects* of the help-seeking process were also tabulated. With regard to proportions revealing general concern with economic aspects of help-seeking (queries about counseling fees, etc.), there was little difference between husbands and wives (husbands, 13 percent; wives, 16 percent). The data do show, however, that significantly more wives (11.5 percent) than husbands (6.7 percent) stressed a need for economy in the help-seeking or counseling process. A rearrangement of the data by social class of the correspondents showed no differences in these patterns.

Seasonal variation. The analysis revealed some interesting seasonal variation in the writing of help-request letters. A significantly larger proportion of the husbands wrote during relatively colder seasons; 31.4 percent of the husbands' letters were written during January, February, or March. On the other hand, a significantly larger proportion of the wives wrote during relatively warmer seasons; 35 percent of the wives' letters were written during July, August, or September. In passing it may be noted that the question of seasonal and cyclical variation has received attention in various studies.[21]

Information requested. By far the most frequent request from correspondents was for the title of a book or manual which could be read for purposes of solving the marital problem at hand. This kind of request, reflective perhaps of the "do-it-yourself" tendency in American culture, came from 97 percent of the husbands and 98 percent of the wives. There are implications here, perhaps, of a "cook-book" approach to marital problems which embodies the notion of ready-made formulas for the achievement of happiness and the solution of problems. Again the salience of this request may imply a strong tendency toward "self-help" in marital problem-solving, comparable to the phenomena of self-diagnosis and self-treatment in physical illness.

Four other kinds of information, all bearing on intimate aspects of marriage, were requested by the correspondents in the following proportions: (1) information on the control of procreation, 3.6 percent of the husbands and 1.9 percent of the wives; (2) information on techniques of sexual relations, 8.7 percent of the husbands and 2.6 percent of the wives; (3) information on aphrodisia, 13.1 percent of the husbands and 9.0 percent of the wives; (4) information on physiological aspects of marriage, such as sex anatomy, impotence, etc., 17.5 percent of the husbands and 8.9 percent of the wives. In items 2 through 4, the proportion of husbands was significantly larger than of wives; a rearrangement by social class made no difference in these patterns. A few scattered requests for other kinds of specific information were also found in the letters (e.g., legal aid, employment services, etc.).

Revealed Emotional Orientation

Some brief comments on emotional orientation will complete this summary of findings. Emotional orientation was defined in terms of (1) revealed feelings or emotional states which presumably were related to the correspondent's marital problems and (2) reported feelings or anticipations regarding the outcome of help-seeking.

In view of certain sex-role differentials existing in the family system, it was expected that husbands and wives would differ appreciably in revealed emotional orientation.[22] Survey data collected by Gurin show, in this connection, that women report more problems and greater stress in marriage than do husbands. Gurin also found that women to a greater extent than men consciously experience tension and dwell on their problems and that more wives than husbands feel inadequate in their familial roles.[23] Table 4 summarizes the emotional-orientation themes which were developed by the content analysis.

Sex differences in reported negative feelings. A larger proportion of wives than husbands reported feeling that they were degraded by the spouse. Also, wives more often than husbands revealed their feelings of anger and resentment toward the mate. The data further show that many more wives than husbands reported felt experiences of depression, nervous exhaustion, and

TABLE 4.

EMOTIONAL ORIENTATION AND EXPERIENCE INDICATED BY
HUSBANDS AND WIVES, SHOWN BY SOCIAL CLASS

| | SOCIAL CLASS | | | | | |
| | White-Collar | | | Blue-Collar | | |
THEME	Husband $n=124$	Wife $n=740$	(2×2) X^2	Husband $n=128$	Wife $n=420$	(2×2) X^2
1. "I am tired, nervous, depressed because of our trouble."	12.1%	29.2%	15.8*	12.5%	37.6%	28.5*
2. "Life not worth living . . . feel like killing myself."	1.6	2.4	.3	2.3	3.3	.3
3. "I feel degraded. I am treated like dirt."	8.9	15.4	3.7	6.2	24.7	20.7*
4. Angry, resentful toward spouse	6.4	31.1	32.1*	3.9	34.3	45.7*
5. Disillusioned, "disappointed . . . in married life."	8.9	35.1	34.0*	7.0	15.4	6.0*
6. Self-blame for problem	21.8	15.7	2.9	21.9	13.3	5.5*
7. Spouse blamed for problem	25.0	44.8	17.2*	29.7	56.4	28.1*
8. Appeal for reinforcement	4.0	3.6	.04	3.1	4.0	.2
9. Optimism, "believe our problem can be straightened out."	40.3	33.0	2.6	35.9	25.0	5.9*
10. Despairing, "afraid there's no hope."	11.3	16.2	2.0	8.6	21.2	10.4*

* Chi-square significant at .05 level or below.

disillusionment with their marriage. Suicidal feelings were reported by only about two percent of each group. Grouping the correspondents by social class had little effect on the magnitude or direction of differences between husbands and wives with regard to these items. However, in the white-collar class, the husband-wife differential in regard to reports of felt degradation (Item 3, Table 4) was not statistically significant at the .05 level.

Attribution of blame. In 638, or 45 percent of the cases, the correspondent revealed his feelings as to who should be blamed for the marital trouble. The data also show that husbands and wives differ appreciably in their attributions of blame. A much larger proportion of wives than husbands blamed their mate for the marital trouble; also, more husbands than wives attributed blame to themselves. However, it may be noted that the sex difference in self-blaming was not significant for correspondents in the white-collar class. These findings generally seem consistent with prior theory and research.[24] Prominence in self-blame by husbands may be related to the male's greater initiative in certain forms of behavior which are strongly associated with revealed marital problems. Again, assuming a persisting tendency in this culture to portray marital failure in terms of wrongdoer and wronged, it may be that blame would more likely be attached to the relatively more initiatory, aggressive role of the husband than to the relatively passive role of the wife.

Anticipated outcome of help-seeking. The data show an appreciable difference between husbands and wives in regard to their disclosure of two items which reflect emotional orientation to help-seeking. Husbands more often than wives indicated *optimism* and less often indicated pessimism regarding possibilities for successful solution of their marital problems. Although the overall comparison of proportions of husbands and wives disclosing these two items showed significant group differences, the arrangement by social class shows that most of this difference is traceable to correspondents in the blue-collar social class.

One could speculate that these differences in emotional orientation in regard to problems and the possible outcome of help-seeking stem from integral sex-role differences in marriage. Thus, the centrality of the wife's role probably ensures that she will have more immediate and persisting contact with the everyday dynamics and content of a troubled marriage. These conditions may account, in part, for the sex differential in revealed feelings of despair, depression, degradation, and disappointment.

Appeals for reinforcement. Research on letters to advice columnists has shown that correspondents frequently appeal for validation or reinforcement of their position regarding the nature of their problem and the best solution for it.[25] In the present study, no more than four percent of the correspondents sought this effect in their help-request letters. Also, the difference in proportions of husbands and wives revealing this item was not significant when the cases were grouped by social class. Writing a help-request letter may have served partially to put troublesome factors in a proper perspective and thereby decreased the correspondent's tendency to seek reinforcement.

CONCLUDING COMMENTS

Data presented in this summary of selected findings from a content analysis of help-request letters show that husbands and wives differ significantly in their revelations of marital problems, help-seeking behavior, and emotional orientation. These differential patterns persisted generally when the cases were also arranged by social class of the correspondent. This persistence is perhaps reflective of rather widespread and common patterns of expectation in regard to happiness in marital relations and in regard to acceptable modes of help-seeking. One hypothesis which the present data suggest is that, among seriously troubled spouses, marital unhappiness is mainly defined in terms of unsatisfactory patterns of intimate relations between mates and that these relations are largely affectional and sexual in character. The quality of intimate relations between mates may become increasingly relevant to definitions of marital happiness or unhappiness as the familial group in this society becomes primary in character and less dependent on extended kinship relations.[26]

In regard to sex differentials found in this content analysis, there may be methodological significance in the observation that findings in this study converge remarkably well with evidence developed in prior research using structured data and different methods. In view of the difficulties ordinarily associated with collection of data from seriously troubled marriages, content analysis of verbal materials produced by persons in the process of help-seeking may have considerable potential for contributing to our knowledge of marital problems and conflicts. Also, data of this nature, used in conjunction with evidence developed through a more structured method, may be able to semantically reveal aspects of experience which might not be uncovered by other techniques. Much "natural" data may be available in the form of letters, diaries, legal transcripts, etc., for the student of familial experience who wishes to develop fuller knowledge about the meaning of problems to those who experience them.

NOTES

[1] For example, Bernadette F. Turner, "Common Characteristics Among Persons Seeking Professional Marriage Counseling," *Marriage and Family Living,* 16 (May, 1954), pp. 143–144; Dorothy F. Beck, *Patterns in Use of Family Agency Service,* New York: Family Service Association of America, 1962; Walter Gieber, "The Lovelorn Columnist and Her Social Role," *Journalism Quarterly,* 37 (November, 1960), pp. 499–514; Christine A. Hillman, "An Advice Column's Challenge for Family-Life Education," *Marriage and Family Living,* 16 (February, 1954), pp. 51–54; Gerald Gurin *et al., Americans View Their Mental Health,* New York: Basic Books, 1960, Part II, "Solving Problems of Adjustment."

[2] By "natural" materials we mean such as are produced under the self-motivation of the subject, or voluntary rather than researcher-elicited data. Relevant to use

426

of such material, see Gordon W. Allport, *The Use of Personal Documents in Psychological Science,* New York: Social Science Research Council, 1942.

[3] Gieber, *op. cit.;* and Hillman, *op. cit.;* cf. also Wardell B. Pomeroy, "An Analysis of Questions on Sex," *Psychological Record,* 10 (July, 1960), pp. 191–201.

[4] James E. DeBurger, *Husband-Wife Differences in the Revelation of Marital Problems: A Content Analysis,* unpublished Ph.D. thesis, Indiana University, 1966.

[5] The check on coding reliability followed procedures suggested in Eric F. Gardner and George G. Thompson, *Social Relations and Morale in Small Groups,* New York: Appleton-Century-Crofts, 1956, pp. 194–196.

[6] Ernest W. Burgess and Paul Wallin, *Engagement and Marriage,* Philadelphia: J. B. Lippincott, 1953; Harvey J. Locke, *Predicting Adjustment in Marriage,* New York: Henry Holt and Co., 1951; Lewis M. Terman *et al., Psychological Factors in Marital Happiness,* New York: McGraw-Hill, 1938; Gerald Gurin *et al., op. cit.* Also see Orville Brim *et al.,* "Relations Between Family Problems," *Marriage and Family Living,* 23:3 (1961), pp. 219–226.

[7] Cf. Gieber, *op. cit.,* p. 503; Gurin, *op. cit.,* pp. 303–344; and Turner, *op. cit.,* p. 144.

[8] Modifications were made of a method used by Gieber, *op. cit.;* also see Rowena Wyant and Herta Herzog, "Voting via the Senate Mailbag," *Public Opinion Quarterly,* 5 (Fall, 1941), pp. 359–382.

[9] Gieber, *op. cit.,* p. 503, described 68 percent of his cases as "low" socioeconomic class and 21 percent as "middle" class. Hillman's cases, *op. cit.,* p. 52, were mainly blue-collar status.

[10] U.S. Census Bureau, *Census of Population: 1950,* Vol. 1, Washington, D.C.: U.S. Government Printing Office, pp. 48–65; and same title for 1960, Vol. 1, p. 263.

[11] Bernard Berelson, *Content Analysis,* New York: The Free Press, a division of the Macmillan Co., 1952, pp. 138–140.

[12] A set of detailed tables covering the material summarized in this article and materials not discussed here may be obtained without cost from the author.

[13] In this classification scheme, it was assumed that revealed marital problems tend to reflect unhappiness in basic areas of interaction within marriage. Cf. William J. Goode, "Family Disorganization," in *Contemporary Social Problems,* ed. by Robert K. Merton and Robert A. Nisbet, New York: Harcourt, Brace and World, 1961, p. 431.

[14] Brim, *op. cit.*

[15] Cf. Robert F. Winch, *The Modern Family,* New York: Holt, Rinehart, and Winston, 1963, pp. 412–423.

[16] Cf. Burgess and Wallin, *op. cit.;* Locke, *op. cit.;* Terman *et al., op. cit.*

[17] Some works which focus on or include material bearing on this matter would include: Robert O. Blood and Donald Wolfe, *Husbands and Wives,* New York: The Free Press, a division of the Macmillan Co., 1960; Beck, *op. cit.;* Charles W. Hobart, "Disillusionment in Marriage and Romanticism," *Marriage and Family Living,* 20 (1958), pp. 156–162; James H. S. Bossard and Eleanor Boll, "Marital Unhappiness in the Life Cycle," *Marriage and Family Living,* 17 (1955), pp. 10–14; Peter C. Pineo, "Disenchantment in the Later Years of Marriage," *Marriage and Family Living,* 23 (1961), pp. 3–11; and Vincent D. Mathews and Clement S. Mihanovich, "New Orientations on Marital Maladjustment," *Marriage and Family Living,* 25 (1963), pp. 300–304.

[18] Cf. Gurin, *op. cit.,* pp. 326, 332–370; Turner, *op. cit.*

[19] Gieber, *op. cit.;* Gurin, *op. cit.;* Turner, *op. cit.*

[20] The author is currently engaged in research in this area. Cf. Gieber, *op. cit.*

[21] Cf. Clifford Kirkpatrick and Eugene Kanin, "Male Sex Aggression on a University Campus," *American Sociological Review*, 22 (February, 1957), pp. 52–58. Seasonal variation has received attention in areas of sociological study other than the family. Regarding deviant behavior, see the summary of relevant research in Elmer H. Johnson, *Crime, Correction, and Society*, Homewood, Ill.: Dorsey Press, 1964, pp. 64–69.

[22] Winch, *op. cit.*, pp. 411–417.

[23] Gurin, *op. cit.*, p. xvi.

[24] Gurin, *op. cit.*, p. 131; also cf. E. E. LeMasters, *Modern Courtship and Marriage*, New York: Macmillan Co., 1957, pp. 363–367, regarding subcultural background factors which may be important in differential sex patterns.

[25] Gieber, *op. cit.*

[26] Clifford Kirkpatrick, *The Family: As Process and Institution*, New York, Ronald Press Co., 1963, p. 137.

What Is a Typical FM?

Morton M. Hunt

For one marriage in four, unresolved problems eventually trigger divorce. What is the typical divorced person like? How does the divorce affect him or her? What sort of a life does a divorced person lead? In his popular study of FM's (formerly marrieds), Hunt indicates that while divorce statistics do reveal some general social patterns, personal reactions to this experience may vary tremendously. This is because a divorced person enters a new world where the type of problems confronting him are quite different from what he has experienced in the past.

Who are the members of the hidden society of the Formerly Married, and what are typical FMs like? Are there an archetypal man and woman, formerly married, as universally relevant to that condition as, say, Cressida is to all faithless mistresses, Don Juan to all heartless seducers, Pierrot to pale and wan fond lovers, Kate to shrews? No; not if one is honest about it. The typical FM man or woman, like the typical American, German, or Italian, is a statistical abstraction. FMs, as a category, tend to share certain kinds of experience and certain mores and values, but they arrive at this consensus by many different routes, and use the common culture in very different fashions.

Let us look in momentarily upon a handful of FMs to see what this means:

—Manhattan, the fashionable East Side, late one morning in January. Bright sun, street noises; behind the darkened window of an apartment, however, all is still dim and quiet. Then the alarm rings, the woman stirs and wakes: ah, yes, time to get up—lunch with Doris at the Modern Museum, an auction at Parke-Bernet, cocktails with the New Man, dinner with the children (a bore, but the right thing to do). How were they this morning?—all right, no doubt; the maid always gets them off to school on time so Mother can sleep; she *needs* her sleep after getting in at four A.M. from an evening of the dis-

From Morton M. Hunt, *The World of the Formerly Married* (New York: McGraw-Hill Book Company, 1966), pp. 14–24. Reprinted by permission of McGraw-Hill Book Company.

cothèques. What a life—better than the one she knew at college or as a single working girl; and sweeter, too, for having been wrung, after a long battle, from that impossible dolt of a husband. Thank god, at least he's well-off—the only good thing about him; alimony keeps everything going, though a bit on the thin edge now and then. A self-indulgent, selfish life?—yes, but why not?—one lives only once, and she's not hurting anyone by it, is she? At thirty-eight, she has years of a boring marriage to make up for. *Carpe diem;* Old Time is still a-flying, and all that. What a joy *not* to be saddled with one man, and still to be attractive enough (but some days only after much effort) to be propositioned by nearly every man she goes out with. And she knows the secret now: ask nothing of them—no emotion, no commitment—be gay, playful, seductive, give in when you wish, but *ask nothing*—and you will be popular, and busy, and happy; perhaps it can't last indefinitely, but the end is not in sight and meanwhile her ex-husband has to pay for it all, and it serves him right.

—Suburb of Hartford; sleet is driving down, and winter night has fallen, although it is only six P.M. A car pulls into a driveway, and out steps a weary-looking slender woman of thirty-two, home from a dull day in the insurance office, carrying a heavy briefcase full of business papers. She enters, and is leaped upon by two exuberant little boys; the teen-aged baby-sitter, meanwhile, puts on her coat and leaves. Now to start dinner (while keeping up a running conversation with both boys), then serve, clean up, help the boys with homework, get them bathed and bedded; then rinse out some things, wash her hair, pick up a dozen toys, make sandwiches for their school lunches; then an hour or so with her business papers; then a phone call from a male friend who wants her to come with him for a weekend at an inn near Danbury (she'd love to, though she's too tired to feel the Urge, but how could she leave the boys for a whole weekend?) ; and setting the clock for seven A.M., into bed after midnight, when suddenly and unexpectedly, after turning out the light, she succumbs to a fit of tears and convulsive sobbing.

—The cocktail lounge of the Mayflower Hotel in Washington. A trim, tanned man of thirty-four, handsome though prematurely bald, is explaining with a disarming grin and twinkling eye to the Young Thing with him why he is a dedicated run-around, twice-divorced and separated now from his third wife. "I think it's something about my endocrine system," he says (and she cannot tell if he is teasing her or means it), "because after a year or so, no matter how jolly the lady I'm living with or married to, I find myself unable to resist the temptation of some new girl—you, this time, but just because we're a terrific thing already, don't figure it's forever. I'm hopeless—but charming. Besides, you seemed to *like* my endocrine system. . . ." She blushes and looks nervously about, thinking back upon the afternoon. But she feels in her heart that he is teasing her only to hide his deeper feelings, so she smiles at him and studies him with shining eyes.

—A run-down, lower-middle-class neighborhood in Cleveland; a somewhat shabby home converted into a rooming house. On the third floor (musty smell of rotting carpet, feeble bulb overhead leaking yellow light), behind a closed

430

door, a paunchy grey-haired man (but only forty-one), pallid and waxy-looking, lies on the bed in wrinkled clothes and stares at the TV set. For over two years, since the break-up of his marriage, he has gone directly from the drafting room at five-thirty P.M. to a short-order joint for the $1.75 blue-plate special (the counterman sings out the order to the kitchen as he comes in, without even asking him); from there he either goes to a movie, walks the streets for hours and stares in shop windows, sits in some bar, drinking very slowly and never talking to anyone, or comes home to watch TV. He is not looking for company; he has turned down invitations from old friends until they have stopped asking him, and has even carefully managed not to open his door at the same time as the man across the hall for these two years. He luxuriates in his suffering and wears the hairshirt of loneliness against his quivering skin to atone for some unnamed failure to have loved well enough. Once a month or so he picks up a prostitute at one of the nearby bars when he is drunk, but he can never quite remember in the morning whether it was any good or not.

—A cocktail lounge in a hotel in St. Louis. A small woman in her forties, chubby but pretty, is sitting alone and toying with a Brandy Alexander. The house detective passes through, spots her, and shakes his head; he cannot figure it out. This is the fifth day; each day he has seen this woman—who looks to him like a suburban housewife (he is right), well-bred, demure, and rather prissy—hanging around near the bar, accepting drinks, and leaving for dinner with different men. She is surely not a hooker, but what is she? He could not guess the truth: she is a desperate, panicky divorcée on a one-week binge of seduction after a year of chastity and a lifetime of propriety; this week is the first and only she will ever spend in this fashion. Having been cast off by her husband for another woman, after twenty-some years of marriage, she has wept, fasted, shrieked out loud at night until the room rang, haunted the doctor's office, and at last flung herself into this desperate effort to prove something that can never be permanently proved. Each day she allows herself to be picked up ("But it's so easy!" she says to herself, shocked), taken to dinner, escorted to a room and stripped and possessed (she pretends passion, but feels anesthetized); then, feeling victorious but befouled, she goes to her own room, drinks herself to sleep, awakens full of horror and shame—and by late afternoon, the passion for revenge returning, starts out all over again.

—A pleasantly furnished small apartment overlooking the lake, in downtown Chicago; a man of fifty, strong-featured and well-built, is unpacking his bags, having just arrived back from one of his many sales trips. He thumbs through a date book—nothing on for tonight—then through an address book, and makes three calls until he finds one of his female friends who is free and will come over, later on, to talk to him, make dinner for him, and sleep with him. She knows what he is—a divorced man who has lived this way for ten years, dislikes it but is hopelessly embittered about marriage, and has nothing to offer her but light camaraderie and sex (the moment any woman hints at deeper feelings, or begins to arouse them in him, he suddenly becomes completely busy, or rude, or hypercritical, until the danger is eliminated). He is pessimistic and self-critical, calls his own behavior promiscuous, selfish, and unreliable; but he also says he thinks this is the way it has to be, since he could succeed neither in marriage nor in any of the three deep relationships he tried right after divorce. When an old friend asked him about loneliness, he said that he was never troubled by it. "I have lots of friends," he explained, "money enough to go out whenever I want, and there are always plenty of women available to give me whatever relief I need. I tell every woman I meet just what I am, but she always hopes for the best—and while she's finding out the truth, at least we're temporarily keeping each other from feeling the emptiness of our lives."

Which of these could we call typical, which the master design, the universal pattern? All and none. And we might have seen many more, all varied. We might have looked in on beatniks, surfers, or ski bums, young, tanned, bored, casual, often promiscuous, rarely involved—many of them the debris and detritus of wrecked marriages. But they are no more representative of all FMs than are the thickwaisted, greying men and women in discussion groups of Parents Without Partners chapters throughout the country, earnestly exploring under the guidance of psychologists the reasons for marital failure and the problems involved in remarriage.

There are young ones, the new breed, who marry and divorce while still childless, too soon to have had any deep emotional ties to sever; one cannot tell them from never-married people by word or deed (it is always a surprise to learn that they have been married and divorced), and some of them, if they ever talk about it, say that they broke up not because they quarrelled, but because they were bored, or fell out of love, or simply drifted into separate ways without noticing what was happening. In their late twenties, they can hardly recall anything—sometimes not even the looks—of the mates they once slept with. Typical?—yes, of themselves; but infinitely remote from those others, married half a lifetime, who, when the children are grown, are amazed to discover that they can no longer endure the confinement of a frustrating union and start out late—terribly late—to try to remake their lives. Writes a cultured woman professor, passively married for twenty-five years to an uncouth, overpowering man, "In middle age I couldn't keep up the front. It is in middle age that one gives up hope that things will change, and the situation, which before was only distasteful, becomes unbearable. One can't live without hope." But even with late-won hope, such a person will for the rest of her life be bound to him: nearly all her memories, her adult experiences, are engraved upon her brain in the form of "*we* visited," "*we* saw," and "*we* used to have...."

FMs, in short, inhabit a territory of their own, but enter it by many a road and make many different kinds of adjustment to it. Rather than a single archetype, there are numerous archetypes; we will keep an eye on them all, and try to identify the several main groups or patterns into which they fit, the major kinds of experience they have, and the principal ways in which they handle the situations that confront them.

SOME VITAL—AND FREQUENTLY SURPRISING—STATISTICS

If we cannot symbolize the FM population through one or two typical specimens, we can at least get some fairly clear idea of who and what the FMs are by examining a handful of statistics. And despite the depressing sound of that word, we will find some of them interesting, for the bright light shed by exact numbers shows up many a popular misconception.

First, however, there is one common notion that the statistics do *not* disprove—namely, that the chance of divorce is about one in four. In 1962, the latest year for which detailed and accurate analyses are available, there were 413,000 divorces and 1,557,000 marriages in the United States—about a one-to-four ratio. Some statisticians say this does not indicate the risk, since it compares current marriages to divorces of marriages made in earlier years, when the number of marriages per year was appreciably less. But when statistician Paul Jacobson made an exceedingly subtle analysis of the year-by-year fall-out rate of marriages made earlier, and extrapolated his findings to the present day, he found that marriages now being made do, in fact, have about a one-in-four chance of ending in divorce. He points out, however, that this is the risk for all marriages, including remarriages (whose risk is higher than normal); if one considers only *first* marriages, the risk of divorce is about one in five.

And who were the 826,000 or so people who got divorced in 1962? The risk of divorce is one in four, but not for every segment of society. Any given couple's chances will vary greatly from that figure according to such factors as where they live, what the husband does for a living, or the color of their skin. Census data show, for instance, that the divorce rate among farm laborers and farm foremen is over twice as high as that among professional and technical men; that eight percent of all actors, but only one third of one percent of all clergymen, are currently divorced; and that the divorce rate is nearly four times as great in the West as in the Northeast. San Mateo County, California, may take the prize for the highest rate; a recent state legislative report indicated a ratio of seventy divorces per hundred marriages in that county. (Among other surprises, it is worth pointing out in passing that the American divorce rate, though currently the world's highest, is far from the highest known in history; in recent times, Japan, Algeria, Israel, Russia, and Egypt have all topped it.)

Neither the risk-of-divorce figures nor the annual crop of divorces gives us any true picture of the size of the World of the Formerly Married. In 1962, data from the Census Bureau showed a total of 5,498,000 separated or divorced persons—but even this huge number is probably lower than reality, since some deserted women and deserting men are either ashamed or afraid to tell the truth.

One very widespread misconception is that within this population of formerly married persons there are several times as many left-over and discarded women as men; it is often said, in fact, that a divorced woman can hardly find any suitable divorced men. In actual fact, the ratio—though unfavorable to

433

women—is only about three-to-two, both among the divorced and separated. The misconception arises from the far greater ease with which men can hunt out female companions. Because it is so much more permissible for men to make the advances, they have far less need to use neutral meeting-grounds such as clubs, parties, resorts, and cruises—and it is therefore at just such places that one often sees five or ten times as many unattached women as men, senses the female desperation in the face of the odds, and gets an exaggerated notion of the sex ratio in the FM world.

Another erroneous notion is that divorce is the chosen pattern of the upper classes, and desertion or domestic-relations court the pattern of the lower ones. All the popular media—television, movies, tabloids, novels, plays—reinforce the impression that it is the chic, the well-off, the college-educated professionals and businessmen, who are most prone to divorce. Yet for at least fifteen years, every analysis by statisticians and sociologists has shown that the divorce rate is higher among those of low socio-economic status than among the middle and upper-middle classes. According to the computations of various researchers, for instance, unskilled or semi-skilled laborers are about three times as likely to get divorced as professional people and proprietors; low-income families are about twice as prone to divorce as those of average or above-average income; and non-whites, whose average socio-economic status is markedly lower than that of whites, have been more divorce-prone than whites in every census year but one since 1890.

A great deal of the writing and comment about divorce in recent years has correctly emphasized the risk of divorce among those who marry too young: teen-age husbands have a divorce rate more than three times, and teen-age wives almost four times, as high as that for the total population: one out of four men and two out of five women getting divorced are under twenty-nine. But figures like these tend to make us forget that people get divorced at all ages, even though the rate declines with age: half of all divorcing men are over 34.5 and a half of all divorcing women are over 31. Moreover, the youngest divorced people remarry rapidly and disappear from the ranks, while older ones take their time, or are less desirable and so tend to linger a while. As a result, the World of the Formerly Married is not a world of very young adults; half of all divorced persons, and nearly half of all separated persons, are between their mid-thirties and their mid-fifties, as appears in the following summary of census figures for 1962. (I have combined the figures for men and women; the distribution of each sex is generally similar, though women are not quite so concentrated in the 45-to-54-year bracket as men.)

Another exaggerated belief that the figures belie is that the great bulk of divorces occurs very early in marriage. It is undeniable that more break-ups occur during the first year or two than later, and that divorces resulting from these early breakups reach a maximum rate three years after marriage; but this is only the peak of the curve, and not the bulk of the cases. In actual fact, the divorce rate diminishes only gradually, year by year, after that peak; nearly forty percent of all broken marriages last ten or more years before being dissolved, and thirteen percent last more than twenty years. For the United

Age	Separated	Divorced
14 to 24	265,000	155,000
25 to 34	558,000	611,000
35 to 44	621,000	714,000
45 to 54	510,000	813,000
55 to 64	282,000	516,000
65 and up	201,000	252,000
	2,437,000	3,061,000

States as a whole, the median duration of marriage at the time of divorce is 7.3 years. ("Median" means that as many marriages ending in divorce lasted more than 7.3 years as lasted less.)

And while it is true in general that the longer a marriage lasts, the smaller is the risk of divorce, there are certain groups of marriages which show increased risks after many years. People who married in 1933, for instance, had a higher divorce rate between the tenth and fifteenth years of marriage than in either of the previous five-year periods; perhaps economic difficulties in the Depression delayed marital break-up until they could afford to make one household into two. Some students of American divorce think that if a census were taken of recent middle-class divorces—none now exists, since the published government data make no class distinctions—one would find a definite secondary peak of late marital break-up around the fifteenth year—a time when children are beyond the critical nursery and grade school years, and the forces binding man and wife together have begun to diminish. My own modest survey hints at this, showing eighteen percent of separations as coming in four or less years, twenty-nine percent between the fifth and ninth years, thirty-one percent between the tenth and fourteenth years, and twenty-two percent in or beyond the fifteenth year. One might guess that this is due to the slower achievement of maximum career potential among such people, or to their greater concern about the psychological impact of divorce on children. But possibly even more pertinent is a finding of the Kansas City Study of Adult Life, made by a team of social scientists from the University of Chicago several years ago: by age forty or so, lower-status people have more or less given up on life, and no longer see the future in terms of expansion and fulfillment but in terms of decline towards death; middle-class people of that age are generally only just reaching the pinnacle of their powers and see themselves as still young, healthy, and vital. It may well be that middle-class persons are willing to take a chance on divorce and remarriage long after lower-class persons have abandoned hope of improving their lives.

According to a treasured folk belief, children hold marriages together; the inevitable deduction would be that most FMs are childless. But statistics show the notion to be inaccurate; in fact, the more acceptable divorce becomes to Americans as a solution to marital difficulties, the less force children exert in keeping marriages intact. People used to feel that they should endure their miseries and stay together for the sake of the children; today they are giving ever greater weight to their own right to happiness, or perhaps coming to think that it is no favor to children to maintain an unhappy marriage for their benefit. The change is taking place rapidly: in 1948 only forty-two percent of divorcing people had children under eighteen, but by 1955 the figure was up to forty-seven percent, and by 1962 had leaped to sixty percent, involving 537,000 children that year. For some reason, the trend is most marked in the Northeast, where sixty-nine percent of divorcing people now have minor children.

If the belief about children's effect on marriage seems to be rebutted by the statistics, the one about "the family that prays together stays together" seems to be upheld, as advertised; devout churchgoers, whatever their brand of belief, are less likely to join the ranks of the Formerly Married than non-churchgoers or people of weak belief. But this does not prove that the devout have happier or more successful marriages; it proves only that strong religious ties tend to inhibit the urge to divorce. Even this, however, is changing. Catholics are the largest religious denomination in which divorce has been all but forbidden, but the divorce rate among them is steadily increasing.

Another popular impression only superficially validated by statistics is that divorce is a product of the sinful big city: the data indicate that divorce is about fifty per cent more common among urban people than among farm families. But this does not constitute proof that the city corrupts people; it may merely allow them more latitude to carry out wishes that they and their country cousins alike harbor in their souls.

The Formerly Married are not the only inhabitants of their special world; several other kinds of people drift in and out of it, the most numerous being the widowed and the never-married. Widows and widowers outnumber FMs two to one, although fewer of them are evident in the World of the Formerly Married than this might lead one to expect; the reason is that most of them are considerably older than most FMs and four-fifths of them are women for whom it is socially unacceptable—and not often possible, to begin with—to date or have relationships with much younger partners. Moreover, at any age widows and widowers do not interact easily even with FMs of their own age; although both face many of the same problems of loneliness, disruption of habits, and practical difficulties in running their home, the psychological make-up of the widowed and their feeling about what has happened to them are profoundly different from those of the Formerly Married, and each finds in the other much that is suspect, unsympathetic, or even antagonistic.

Never-married people—"single" people, in popular terminology—also inter-act with FMs, particularly at the younger age levels, where the very briefly married are almost indistinguishable from those who have never tried; indeed, the former are as apt to seek out the society of single people as that of the Formerly Married. At somewhat older age levels, a certain number of chronic bachelors and unmarried women mix with FMs, but mutual suspicion of each other, lack of common experience, and difference in outlook are even more effective as deterrents to choosing each other than in the case of the Formerly Married and the widowed.

436

Such is the polymorphous World of the Formerly Married: more lower-than middle-class (though we shall henceforth concentrate on the latter), more parental than non-parental, more nearly middle-aged than young; a world not of frivolous, hedonistic, footloose youths but of earnest, conscientious, somewhat harassed but hopeful adult Americans.

The Trauma of Children When Parents Divorce

Judson T. Landis

When parents decide that their marriage partnership has failed, they have more than just their own happiness and well-being to consider. How will their children feel when they are told about the impending divorce? Is a child's attitude toward his parents changed by their break-up? How will the child's future attitude toward marriage be affected? Are all children equally affected? These and other questions are discussed by Landis, who indicates that the past social context of the family, plus the manner in which the divorce is handled, are crucial to the effect on the children.

The present research was undertaken in an effort to gain further insights and to answer some questions arising out of two previous studies of children of divorced parents.[1] The sample was composed of 295 University students, all children of divorced parents.[2] Each student was asked to complete an eight-page anonymous questionnaire covering certain items of his family background, his evaluation of the home before he learned of the prospect of his parents' divorce, his reactions to the divorce, a postmarital history of the parents, including remarriages, and the adjustment of the child to the parents' divorce and remarriage. Half of the students were registered in the family sociology course. The others were university students not presently registered in the family sociology course. No attempt was made to get a random sample of children of divorced parents, since such a small proportion of university students are from divorced families. (Data from student information files collected by the author from 1950–1959 shows that approximately 10 percent of the family sociology students are from divorced or separated homes.) One-third of the student respondents were men and two-thirds were women. Thirty-two percent were from one-child families; 48 percent were from two-

From Judson T. Landis, "The Trauma of Children When Parents Divorce," *Marriage and Family Living*, February, 1960, pp. 7–13. Reprinted by permission of the author and The National Council on Family Relations.

child families; and the remaining 20 percent were from families of three or more children. Fifty-three percent of the fathers were in a profession or in business and 52 percent had some education beyond high school; one-third had a college or graduate degree. One-third of the mothers had some education beyond high school and 23 percent had a college or graduate degree. The parents had been married an average of thirteen years before divorce. The average age of the 295 children had been 9.4 years when the parents divorced.

In analyzing the data it became clear that children of divorce cannot be treated as a homogeneous group. Divorce of parents affects children in various ways, depending upon such factors as the age of the child at the time of the divorce and how the child viewed the home situation before he learned of the possible divorce.

There are certain potentially traumatic situations existing for the child of divorcing parents. First, there is the necessity to adjust to the knowledge that divorce will probably take place; (2) there is the necessity to adjust to the fact of divorce; (3) there is the possibility that in the predivorce or postdivorce years one or both parents may "use" the child as a weapon against the other, with traumatic effects upon the child; (4) there is the necessity for a redefining of relationships with parents; (5) the new status of being the child of divorced parents may necessitate new adjustments with the peer group; (6) some trauma may result for children who recognize the implications of their parents' failure in marriage; and (7) there may be problems of adjustment for the child if the parents remarry. Our data will be considered in terms of these seven potentially traumatic situations for the child of divorcing parents.

Preliminary analyses of the data on the 295 children indicated that it was necessary to separate the sample into two groups—those who remembered the time preceding their parents' divorce and those who did not. Thirty-eight percent of the children (112) were too young at the time of the divorce to remember the circumstances in the home before the divorce took place. This does not mean that there was no trauma for this group of children, only that they were too young at the time of the occurrences to be able to furnish information later. However, many of these children could give information on their adjustment following the divorce.

The remaining 183 children were divided into three groups, according to how the child viewed the home situation before he learned of the possible divorce. A surprisingly large percentage of the children considered their homes happy or very happy before they learned that their parents would separate or divorce. Data from this group led us to hypothesize that parental divorce itself might be traumatic for some children, but for others the parents' divorce might mean relief from tension and the beginning of the child's emotional recovery: if the child had considered his home to be happy, the prospect and the fact of divorce might be traumatic; but if there had been continued hostility and conflict in the home, the divorce might mean relief from tension for the child.

Each respondent was asked to rate his home on a four-point scale as he remembered it before he learned of the possible separation or divorce. The rating was in terms of his sense of family unity, his feeling of security or insecurity, and his evaluation of the general happiness or unhappiness in the home. The three variables probably all measured one thing—the general happiness of the home from the child's point of view before he sensed there would be separation or divorce. The top third of the sample felt there was family unity, believed that it was a happy family, and felt secure in the family. The children in the lowest third felt there was little or no family unity, believed the home to be unhappy or very unhappy, and had little or no security. In our analysis we shall report upon differences between the responses of the top third and the lowest third concerning their experiences in the seven potentially traumatic experiences of the child whose parents are divorcing (See Table 1).

TABLE 1.
THE DESCRIPTION OF THE HOME BY 183 CHILDREN OF DIVORCED PARENTS AS REMEMBERED BEFORE THEY LEARNED OF A POSSIBLE SEPARATION OR DIVORCE

DESCRIPTION OF HOME AND SELF	⅓ HAPPIEST N = 61	⅓ UNHAPPIEST N = 61	TOTAL* N = 183
In terms of family unity:			
Closely united family	54.1	—	18.6
Moderate unity in family	44.3	11.5	39.3
Little family unity	1.6	55.7	31.1
No family unity	—	32.8	10.9
	$X^2 = 96.00$		df = 3 P < .001
Your feelings of security:			
Very secure	78.7	—	30.1
Secure	21.3	24.6	41.0
Little security	—	62.3	24.6
No security	—	13.1	4.4
	$X^2 = 94.28$		df = 2 P < .001
In terms of general happiness or unhappiness in the home:			
Very happy family	32.8	—	10.9
Happy family	65.6	9.8	50.8
Unhappy family	1.6	67.2	30.6
Very unhappy family	—	23.0	7.6
	$X^2 = 97.24$		df = 3 P < .001
In terms of your personal happiness or unhappiness as a child:			
Very happy	67.2	3.3	29.7
Happy	31.1	46.7	52.7
Unhappy	1.6	40.0	14.3
Very unhappy	—	10.0	3.3
	$X^2 = 65.95$		df = 2 P < .001
		(N = 61, 60, 182)	
The relationship between your father and mother:			
Constant open conflict	1.7	46.7	22.0
Moderate open conflict	13.8	41.7	30.5
Little open conflict	17.2	8.3	15.8
No open conflict	53.4	1.7	24.3
No open conflict, but I sensed their unhappiness	13.8	1.7	7.3
	$X^2 = 68.84$		df = 3 P < .001
		(N = 58, 60, 177)	

*Total represents two-thirds shown, plus one-third of sample not shown.

FINDINGS OF THE STUDY

It is often assumed that divorce is almost always preceded by great unhappiness and open conflict, but our findings bring out rather clearly that from the viewpoint of the child the pre-divorce home may be quite satisfactory. Of the 183 children who could remember their homes before they learned of a possible divorce, 19 percent considered the family closely united; 30 percent reported that they felt very secure; 11 percent rated the home as very happy; 30 percent reported their childhood as very happy and 24 percent reported no open conflict in their family. A minority, 22 percent, reported constant open conflict between parents.

Table 2 summarizes the most common reactions of the children when they learned of the possible divorce. The first potentially traumatic experience is this first awareness of the prospect of a parental divorce. In this sample it was the mother, in more than half the cases, who told the child of the impending divorce. It will be observed that a significantly larger percentage of the children who thought the home unhappy reacted by thinking the divorce was the best for all concerned, and the third who thought the home was happy found it hard to believe that divorce could happen in their family. In general the first knowledge of divorce seemed to be a traumatic experience for those who believed theirs to be a happy home. Those who believed their homes to be happy were caught by surprise and were unprepared to accept divorce; whereas open conflict and unhappiness in the other type of home seems to have prepared the child for the possibility of divorce.

TABLE 2.
THE IMMEDIATE REACTION REPORTED BY 183 CHILDREN OF DIVORCED PARENTS WHEN LEARNING THEIR PARENTS WOULD PROBABLY SEPARATE OR DIVORCE

REACTION	$\frac{1}{3}$ HAPPIEST N = 61	$\frac{1}{3}$ UNHAPPIEST N = 61	TOTAL N = 183
Thought it was best for all concerned[1]	19.7	54.1	34.4
Couldn't believe that it had happened to us[2]	42.6	16.4	33.3
Fought against it and tried to prevent it	13.1	11.5	14.2
I was happy	1.6	14.8	6.0
I was unhappy and upset	52.5	57.4	51.9
I was worried and anxious about my future	14.8	27.9	20.2
Hated father[3]	4.9	19.7	8.7
Hated mother	1.6	8.2	3.3
Did not understand	18.0	8.2	12.0
Indifferent	6.6	3.3	4.9
Miscellaneous reactions	19.7	11.5	15.3

[1] $X^2 = 8.89$ df = 1 P < .01.
[2] $X^2 = 6.23$ df = 1 P < .02.
[3] $X^2 = 4.26$ df = 1 P < .05.

441

The second adjustment for the child comes with the actual occurrence of divorce. Approximately one-third of the sample indicated one of the following reactions: "upset, worried, confused"; "acceptance, best solution for all"; "relief that it was over with and settled." Again, the children who considered their homes happy had the greatest difficulty adjusting to the fact of divorce, None of those who considered their homes happy, but one-fifth of those who considered their homes unhappy, reported that they were glad when the divorce was a fact. Those from unhappy homes reported greater relief that it was settled and greater acceptance of a view that the divorce was the best for all concerned.

Table 3 summarizes how these respondents felt the divorce had affected their feelings of security and personal happiness. It will be observed that for the entire group the effect of the divorce was to make the children feel less secure and less happy than was true before the divorce. When we study the two groups of children according to how they viewed the homes before knowledge of divorce, we see that those from apparently happy homes indicate either no change in feelings of security and personal happiness or they shift to feeling less secure or less happy. On the other hand, those who saw the homes as unhappy report greater security and happiness after the divorce. Again, the greater trauma occurred among children who thought their homes were happy before they learned of the divorce.

When the respondents were asked concerning any changes in their attitude toward the divorce with the passing of time, 28 percent of those who had thought they had a happy home and 64 percent of those who had considered

TABLE 3.
PERCENTAGE DISTRIBUTION OF FEELINGS OF SECURITY AND
PERSONAL HAPPINESS OR UNHAPPINESS FOLLOWING
PARENTS' DIVORCE AS REPORTED BY 183
CHILDREN OF DIVORCED PARENTS

DESCRIPTION OF FEELINGS	$\frac{1}{3}$ HAPPIEST N = 61	$\frac{1}{3}$ UNHAPPIEST N = 61	TOTAL N = 183
Your feelings of security:			
Much more secure	—	14.5	1.9
Somewhat more secure	—	27.3	14.3
No change in feelings of security	45.0	21.8	34.3
Less secure	36.7	20.0	30.9
Much less secure	18.3	16.4	14.9
	$X^2 = 32.57$		df $= 3$ P $< .001$
		(N $= 60, 55, 175$)	
In terms of your personal happiness or unhappiness:			
Much happier than before	3.3	11.9	6.7
Somewhat happier	5.0	37.3	21.9
No change in happiness	46.7	23.7	36.0
Less happy	30.0	18.6	25.3
Much less happy	15.0	8.5	10.1
	$X^2 = 24.24$		df $= 3$ P $< .001$
		(N $= 60, 59, 178$)	

the homes unhappy reported that they now believed that the marriage was a mistake in the first place. Of those who saw the home as happy 16 percent now felt the divorce was a mistake, while only 3 percent of those who saw the home as unhappy thought the divorce was a mistake.

The third potential trauma for the child comes if he is "used" by one or both parents in the pre-or postdivorce period. Forty-four percent of all of the 295 respondents reported that they felt they had been "used" by one or both parents. This included children who were too young to remember the home before the divorce but old enough to remember experiences following the divorce. Table 4 summarizes how these 295 respondents felt they had been "used" by their parents. It will be observed that on all items children who were from homes considered unhappy before the divorce were more likely to report being "used" during and after the divorce. The trauma associated with being "used" by parents appears to be more severe among those children who saw the home as unhappy before the divorce.

The fourth potentially traumatic experience is the necessity for redefining feelings and attitudes toward one or both parents. The children in this study

TABLE 4.

PERCENTAGE DISTRIBUTION OF SPECIFIC WAYS IN WHICH 295 CHILDREN OF DIVORCED PARENTS REPORTED THEY WERE "USED" BY ONE PARENT AGAINST THE OTHER BEFORE, DURING, OR AFTER THE DIVORCE

WAY IN WHICH PARENT "USED" CHILD	$\frac{1}{3}$ HAPPIEST N = 61	$\frac{1}{3}$ UNHAPPIEST N = 61	TOTAL* N = 295
One tried to get information from me about the other	21.3	41.0	21.0
Asked to testify against one parent in court[1]	4.9	21.3	7.8
Asked to back up arguments of other in family quarrels[2]	1.6	31.1	9.8
Not permitted to talk to one parent	—	3.3	1.0
Not permitted to see one parent	3.3	8.2	4.1
One told untrue things about the other[3]	18.0	42.6	17.6
One gave messages to me to give to the other	9.8	11.5	7.1
I was used as a go-between in quarrels	—	13.1	3.7
One or both played on my sympathy[4]	14.8	52.5	25.8
Neither ever used me[5]	60.7	24.6	44.4
Miscellaneous responses and too young to remember	4.9	9.8	20.0

* Total represents two-thirds shown, plus one-third not shown, plus 112 respondents who were too young to remember family before divorce but old enough to remember postdivorce years.

[1] $X^2 = 6.25$ df $= 1$ P $< .02$.
[2] $X^2 = 16.20$ df $= 1$ P $< .001$.
[3] $X^2 = 6.08$ df $= 1$ P $< .02$.
[4] $X^2 = 23.00$ df $= 1$ P $< .001$.
[5] $X^2 = 12.10$ df $= 1$ P $< .001$.

felt closer to their mothers than to their fathers. The effect of divorce seemed to be to increase the emotional distance between children and their fathers. Table 5 summarizes how close respondents felt toward mothers and fathers before and after the divorce.

For a child to have to shift from a close to a distant relationship with one or both parents may be a traumatic experience. There may also be considerable disillusionment if the child accepts what one parent says about the other. The child may come to believe that the one he has felt close to and has looked up to is in reality one he cannot trust and respect. The shift away from the father is explained in part by the child's coming to accept the views of the mother about the father. Of the 295 children in this study 74 percent went to live with the mother and only 9 percent went to live with the father. One would expect

TABLE 5.
PERCENTAGE DISTRIBUTION OF RELATIONSHIPS WITH MOTHER AND FATHER BEFORE LEARNING OF POSSIBLE DIVORCE AND AFTER DIVORCE WAS A FACT AS REPORTED BY 183 CHILDREN OF DIVORCED PARENTS

RELATIONSHIP BEFORE DIVORCE	$\frac{1}{3}$ HAPPIEST N = 61	$\frac{1}{3}$ UNHAPPIEST N = 61	TOTAL N = 183
Your relationship with your mother:			
Very close	55.7	28.3	40.9
Close	37.7	36.7	40.3
Not close	6.6	26.7	15.5
Distant	—	8.3	3.3
	$X^2 = 17.34$		df = 2 P < .001
		(N = 61, 60, 181)	
Your relationship with your father:			
Very close	36.1	10.0	17.7
Close	50.8	31.7	43.6
Not close	9.8	40.0	29.8
Distant	3.3	18.3	8.8
	$X^2 = 29.17$		df = 3 P < .001
		(N = 61, 60, 181)	
RELATIONSHIP AFTER DIVORCE AS COMPARED TO BEFORE DIVORCE			
Your relationship with your mother:			
Much closer to mother	36.7	23.0	27.6
Somewhat more close	21.7	32.8	32.6
No change in closeness	23.3	27.9	24.9
Less close	13.3	9.8	11.0
Much less close	5.0	6.6	3.9
	$X^2 = 2.56$		df = 3 P < .50
		(N = 60, 61, 181)	
Your relationship with your father:			
Much closer to father	11.7	3.3	8.8
Somewhat more close	10.0	11.5	10.4
No change in closeness	18.3	31.1	25.3
Less close	31.7	13.1	23.1
Much less close	28.3	41.0	32.4
	$X^2 = 7.09$		df = 3 P < .10
		(N = 60, 61, 182)	

the closer relationship with the mother as the father drops out of the home and the mother and children reunite.

The children who thought their homes happy before the divorce were much closer to their mothers and fathers than were those children who thought their homes unhappy. However, after the divorce both groups were drawn closer to their mothers and both groups became less close to their fathers.

The fifth potentially traumatic situation comes in reconciling the divorced status of one's parents with peer group associations. Two-thirds of the respondents reported that the parents' divorce did not affect their confidence in associating with friends. Among the third who did feel self-confidence was affected, some reported that confidence was increased while others reported it was decreased. It was those children from homes considered happy who reported greater trauma. Seven percent of these reported greater confidence while 22 percent reported less confidence in associating with friends. On the other hand, of those children who reported their homes unhappy, 25 percent reported feeling more confident and 17 percent reported feeling less confident in associating with friends after the divorce. This may mean that with the conflict past some children feel they can associate more freely and invite friends to their homes, while others would be reluctant to invite friends home and ill at ease with peers because of the changed parental status.

Each respondent was asked to report on how he felt his parents' marital status had affected his social acceptability and whether he had used "face-saving" techniques after the divorce. A summary of this information is given in Table 6. All 295 respondents are included, since children very young at the time of divorce seem, later, to have about the same reactions in associating with friends as do children older at the time of the divorce. Differences are not significant on this point between the third of the respondents who thought their homes happy and the third who thought their homes unhappy.

It might seem that if a child is very young when the parents divorce, and if both parents remarry quickly, the child might not feel a loss of face. Yet the data show that such a child may feel as different from other children as the child who has only one parent, because he has to explain two sets of parents and possibly four sets of grandparents as well as step-brothers and sisters. The child with one parent can say that the other parent is dead but the child with two sets of parents may find it difficult to explain his extra family members.

Some trauma may result for children who recognize the implications of parental failure in marriage. Table 7 gives a summary of how the respondents believed their feelings and attitudes toward their own future marriage had been affected. Responses here did not differ significantly among the different groups. The responses to the items in Table 7 show that it was those from the unhappiest homes who indicated that their attitudes toward marriage had been affected most by their parents' divorce. They expressed caution about marriage, determination to make a better choice, and so on throughout most of the items.

Since it is not generally known among young people that there is a high relationship between the failure of parents in marriage and the failure of

TABLE 6.

PERCENTAGE DISTRIBUTION OF ADJUSTMENTS REPORTED
WITH FRIENDS AND ASSOCIATES BY 295 CHILDREN
OF DIVORCED PARENTS

DESCRIPTION OF ADJUSTMENT	⅓ HAPPIEST N = 61	⅓ UNHAPPIEST N = 61	TOTAL N = 295
Did you feel that your parents' marital status had any effect upon your social acceptability with friends and associates?			
I felt different from other children	23.0	29.5	22.7
I felt inferior to other children	13.1	23.0	16.3
Embarrassed to face friends	11.5	11.5	10.2
Was ashamed that parents were divorced	29.5	23.0	21.4
It was a blow to my pride	8.2	8.2	6.8
Had no effect at all upon me	49.2	41.0	42.4
We moved and new friends did not know[1]	3.3	19.7	10.2
Envious of those with happy homes	1.6	4.9	5.4
Friends from divorced homes, so accepted	6.6	6.6	3.4
Did not tell friends or talk about it	1.6	—	2.0
Miscellaneous responses	4.9	1.6	13.6
Did you feel the need of "face-saving" techniques when discussing or having to give information on the marital status of your parents?			
Sometimes lied about where one parent was	11.5	8.2	9.5
Said one parent was dead	4.9	8.2	3.7
Said one parent was on a trip, at sea, or would be with us later	4.9	1.6	4.4
Talked as though parents were not divorced	19.7	16.4	15.3
Associated largely with other children who were from separated or divorced homes	3.3	3.3	3.7
Did not mention divorce except to those who came from broken homes	3.3	4.9	6.8
Never felt need to "save face"— just told the truth	72.1	75.4	70.5
Avoided subject, but truthful if asked	16.4	11.5	14.9
Never had to give information	—	1.6	1.4
Miscellaneous responses	—	—	.7

[1] $X^2 = 5.74$ df $= 1$ P $< .02$.

children in marriage, it would seem that this potentially traumatic phase of adjustment to divorce might not be traumatic for many children of divorce. However, other research shows that children of divorced parents have much less confidence in their ability to have successful marriages than do children from happy homes.[3]

Our final analysis was to relate the reported feelings and reactions of the children to the postdivorce status of the parents. The data seem to show that

TABLE 7.
PERCENTAGE DISTRIBUTION OF WAYS IN WHICH PARENTS' DIVORCE HAS AFFECTED CHILDREN'S ATTITUDES TOWARD MARRIAGE AS REPORTED BY 295 CHILDREN OF DIVORCED PARENTS

ATTITUDE TOWARD MARRIAGE	⅓ HAPPIEST N = 61	⅓ UNHAPPIEST N = 61	TOTAL N = 295
It has made me more cautious about marriage	72.1	77.0	67.5
I am bitter about marriage	—	3.3	1.7
Determined to make a better choice	47.5	72.1	60.0
It has made me more aware of the problems of marriage	80.3	82.0	76.9
I have a more realistic picture of marriage	50.8	63.9	53.9
I never want to get married	—	1.6	1.0
It has made me more willing to compromise in getting along with others	47.5	67.2	53.9
It has given me more determination to work at making a success of my marriage	75.4	80.3	76.6
I will wait until I am older to marry	13.1	19.7	14.9
I have little confidence in making a success of my marriage	1.6	4.9	2.7
Aware of the consequences of failure	11.5	—	3.7
No effect	1.6	1.6	1.7

marriages which the children viewed as unhappy before they knew of the divorce are also the cases in which neither parent or only the mother remarries. Marriages which the children viewed as happy before they knew of a possible divorce are cases in which the father or both mother and father are more likely to remarry. If neither parent remarried, or if only the mother remarried, a larger percentage of the children reacted to the knowledge that divorce would probably take place by thinking it was for the best of all concerned, and fewer were unhappy and upset. A larger percentage of these children felt more secure after the divorce and fewer felt less secure after the divorce; also, they reported being "used" much more extensively in the ways parents "use" children in marital discord than did children from cases in which only the father or both parents remarried. Sixty-one percent of those from cases in which neither parent remarried reported being "used"; 50 percent, if only the mother remarried; 43 percent, if the father remarried; and only 36 percent, if both parents remarried. If neither parent remarried the children generally reported a greater variety of ways in which their parents "used" them.

SIBLING ORDER AND THE TRAUMA OF DIVORCE

We hypothesized that sibling order and number of siblings would have some effect upon the extent to which the experience of parental divorce was trau-

447

matic. Responses were analyzed by whether those responding were oldest, youngest, in-between, or onlies. There were no significant differences in how the four different groups described the homes before divorce and the divorce experience as it affected them.

AGE OF CHILD AND THE TRAUMA OF DIVORCE

The respondents were next divided into three groups, by age at the time of the parental divorce: 5-8 (81), 9-12 (63), and 13-16 (59), and then considered by their description of the home before they knew of the possible divorce and their description of the trauma of divorce. This analysis revealed some significant differences between the age groupings. In general the 5-8 age group tended to feel more secure, to rate themselves happier, and to have been less aware of the conflict between their mothers and fathers before they knew of the divorce. Fewer indicated they were unhappy and upset by the divorce and more indicated they did not understand what was going on. More of the 5-8 age group indicated there was no change in their feelings of security, and fewer indicated that their parents tried to "use" them in the divorce and postdivorce years. This group also expressed fewer feelings of inferiority in associating with friends than did those in the groups older at the time of the divorce. There were no significant differences in how the three age groups felt the experience of going through divorce had affected their attitudes toward their own future marriages.

SUMMARY OF FINDINGS

1. This study of 295 young people, all of whom were from divorced homes, brings out rather clearly the unsoundness of grouping together and discussing all children of divorced homes as if they were a homogeneous group affected in the same ways by the divorces of their parents. In this group of 295 children of divorced parents, 38 percent were too young to remember the home before and at the time of the divorce.

2. Of children old enough to remember the home before the divorce there are several situations and relationships which seem to be traumatic for the child as he "goes through" divorce with his parents. How traumatic the specific situations are for the child seems to be closely related to how the child viewed the home before the divorce. For those who saw their homes as happy the divorce and adjustment to divorce was more traumatic than it was for those children who found themselves in unhappy homes characterized by open conflict between parents.

3. Children too young to remember the home before the divorce, as well as those who remember the divorce, may feel different from other children and thus resort to "face-saving devices" in the postdivorce years.

4. It appears that the worst predivorce situations from the viewpoint of the child are the cases in which the parents are less likely to remarry.

5. Sibling order analyses did not reveal significant differences in how the children viewed the divorce and their adjustment to divorce.

6. Younger children who were old enough at the time of divorce so that they remembered events tended to be less aware of the traumatic effects of divorce than older children.

NOTES

[1] Judson T. Landis, "The Pattern of Divorce in Three Generations," *Social Forces,* XXXIV (March, 1956), 213–216; and "A Comparison of Children of Divorced and Children of Happy or Unhappy Non-Divorced Parents on Parent-Child Relationships, Dating Maturation, and Sex and Marriage Attitudes," paper read before the Annual Meeting of the National Council on Family Relations, Minneapolis, August 27, 1955.

[2] Cases of separation or of remarriage of the same spouse after divorce were eliminated from the study.

[3] Landis, *op. cit.*

Holy Deadlock: A Study of Unsuccessful Marriages

E. E. LeMasters

Divorce is not the only outcome of marriages that flounder on various crises or are riddled with dissension. Some bad marriages continue intact in a state of armed truce. LeMasters refers to these marriages with the rather poetic title of "holy deadlock." His research interest includes the questions of whether couples with a history of maladjustment ever make peace with each other, what toll their state of holy deadlock took on them and their children, and what held the couples together in the face of such an extensive absence of mutual affection and interests. An interesting finding is that men seem to suffer more personal disorganization in a bad marriage than do women.

Not all cases of marital maladjustment arise from major crises and not all end in divorce. This article traces the history of thirty-six couples, caught in a chain of conflict situations that had extended over at least ten years' time. The study covers such items as degree of personal disorganization, effect on children, and reasons that held the couple together.

INTRODUCTION

Some years ago Waller demonstrated that divorced persons in our society suffer personal disorganization as the price of marital failure.[1] More recently, in a careful study of divorced women, Goode has shown again that divorce is no bed of roses, sociologically speaking.[2]

In the present study a somewhat different problem has been posed: what happens to married couples whose marriages have failed but who *don't* sepa-

From "Holy Deadlock: A Study of Unsuccessful Marriages," *The Midwest Sociologist,* July, 1959, pp. 86–91. Reprinted by permission of The Midwest Sociological Society.

rate or divorce? More specifically, the study attempts to answer the following questions: (1) Do the couples who don't separate or divorce escape personal disorganization, as measured by such indices as alcoholism, mental illness, etc.? (2) Do couples with a long history of marital conflict (ten years minimum in this study) ever "solve" their marital problems? (3) What are the effects of such marriages on the children?

In an attempt to discover some tentative answers to these questions, 36 marriages characterized by chronic husband-wife conflict were analyzed. To be included in the sample, the cases had to meet three requirements: (1) both spouses had to regard the marriage as unsuccessful; (2) this condition must have persisted for at least ten years; and (3) the marriage had to be intact— that is, they were still living together. No case which met these requirements was excluded.

The couples were located through friends, attorneys, physicians, ministers, and marriage counselors. An average of three hours was spent interviewing each couple. With four exceptions, both spouses were seen.

The sample is basically white, urban, Protestant, and middle-class, with scattered cases falling into diverse socio-economic categories. No claim is made for the representativeness of the sample. In view of the limited nature of the study, the findings are presented as being suggestive rather than conclusive.

THE FINDINGS

Data bearing on the three questions posed for the study will be presented first. Other material which might be of interest to research persons and practitioners in this field will be discussed later.

1. *Do the couples who don't separate or divorce escape personal disorganization?* The evidence from these cases is that they don't. Of the 36 married couples, objective evidence of personal disorganization could be demonstrated for one or both spouses in 27 cases (75%).[3] The most frequent types of disorganization were alcoholism, chronic psychosomatic illness, neurotic or psychotic behavior, occupational disorganization, extramarital affairs, and a syndrome of patterns best described by Schulberg's term, "disenchantment."[4] The table below summarizes the distribution of these types of personal disorganization.

TYPES OF PERSONAL DISORGANIZATION IN 36 UNSUCCESSFUL MARRIAGES

TYPE	HUSBANDS	WIVES
Alcoholism	14	6
Psychosomatic illness	5	12
Neurotic-psychotic behavior	8	10
Occupational disorganization	17	0
Extramarital affairs	12	6
Disenchantment	18	22

It is not known, of course, what these persons would have been like had they married someone else (or not married at all). Nor is it possible to know what their adjustment would have been had they separated or divorced. Keeping these limitations in mind, it still seems well established that these couples did not escape the destructive impact of marital failure by avoiding separation or divorce.

2. *Do couples with a long history of marital conflict ever "solve" their marital problems?* A recent follow-up of these couples revealed that of the 29 still living together, not one couple had been able to work out what seemed to them to be a satisfactory marriage. The implications of this finding will be presented later.

3. *What are the effects of such marriages on the children?* One would assume a high incidence of disorganization in the children of these couples. The data, however, do not seem to support such an assumption. Of the 76 children in these marriages, only 7 have ever been referred to a child guidance clinic or school psychologist for diagnosis or therapy for emotional or behavioral problems. And only 3 children in the sample have ever been booked for a juvenile offense. Furthermore, of the male children who have served in the armed forces (17), none has been rejected or discharged for psychiatric reasons or behavioral problems.

It is recognized that the above "tests" are very crude and that a psychiatric screening might prove these children to have been damaged emotionally in various ways. Most certainly they have not had an optimum opportunity to develop their capacities as human beings. But using such crude measuring devices as school and community adjustment, plus performance in the armed forces, these children appear to be a relatively "normal" group.

This finding does not agree with that of Despert,[5] who concludes that chronic marital conflict is often more damaging to children than separation or divorce. It is also not entirely in line with the findings of Goode, whose divorced women felt their children to be better adjusted after the divorce.[6]

If other studies should support our findings in this point, how could one explain the ability of these children to be well organized in spite of their negative home environment? The writer suggests several possible interpretations: (1) the conclusion of Orlansky that children are tougher emotionally than has generally been thought;[7] (2) the possibility that children are not as aware of parental conflict as child psychiatrists have supposed—for example, the findings of Burchinal and his co-workers that the relationship between parental acceptance of children and the adjustment of the children was negligible;[8] (3) that modern society permits the child enough contacts with other human beings that the parents are custodians of personality rather than its shapers;[9] (4) that genetic factors are crucial in personality disorganization and that these operate independently of parental conflict—for example, the findings of Kallmann on schizophrenia.[10] The work of Sewell in which infant care techniques did not correlate significantly with later school adjustment might also be fitted into this analysis.[11]

Regardless of the interpretation of this finding, it could be maintained with some logic that the results of this study support the argument that parents should continue their marriage "for the benefit of the children."

OTHER OBSERVATIONS ON THE CASES

Differential Reaction Patterns of Husbands and Wives

The husbands and wives in this sample utilized quite different substitute satisfaction patterns to soften the blow of marital failure. The men tended to turn to (a) their job, (b) liquor, (c) other women. With the wives, however, the major substitute satisfactions were (a) their children, (b) a job, (c) religion, and (d) community service.

As Kinsey would have predicted, extramarital affairs were reported for twice as many husbands as wives.[12] It is interesting to note that the extramarital affairs tended to follow rather than precede the marital failure, thus raising the question whether this so-called "cause" of marital difficulty may be an effect instead.

Of the two sets of substitute satisfactions, it appears that those of the husbands are potentially more destructive. The writer has the distinct impression from these cases that husbands are more likely to be severely damaged by chronic marital failure than are the wives. This is contrary to the old saying that "the woman pays," but it may be true nevertheless. Unfortunately, the best study available on divorced persons, that cited by Goode, did not cover the post-divorce adjustment of the husbands, hence gives us no comparable data.

If it is true that men do suffer more damage than women from marital failure, the interpretation would seem to be that the substitute satisfactions of the women are more in line with the basic values of the society—increased interest in their children, greater participation in church affairs, etc.

The Process of Disenchantment

Given the romantic approach to marriage in American society, it would seem logical to expect some degree of trauma in these couples. Of the 72 husbands and wives in the sample, 40 (56 percent) exhibited what we have chosen to call "disenchantment." These persons have lost their faith in romance and are cynical (if not bitter). In the most severe cases they refer to love as "a joke"; some perceive themselves as "suckers." They also use the expression "kid stuff" in referring to the romantic complex.

Careful study of these 40 persons reveals a process of disenchantment; (a) the feeling of concern that the marriage has not gone as they had expected; (b) a stage of determined effort to be brave and to solve their problems; (c)

453

this is followed by a stage of hostility toward the partner for not "cooperating" in the effort to save the marriage; (d) and then resignation and perhaps bitterness.

It is worthwhile to note that these couples do not exhibit a stage (e) described by Waller and Goode—namely, the therapeutic excitement of a new love affair and the possibility of another marriage. If it is true that the best treatment for a broken love affair is a new one, as the above studies seem to indicate, then one of the prices paid by these couples for not terminating their marriage is their inability to form new meaningful love relationships. With a very few exceptions, the extramarital affairs reported by the couples failed to be deep enough to heal the wounds from the marital failure.

Counseling Efforts with These Couples

Marriage counselors, ministers, and psychotherapists consulted by this sample (14 had consulted at least one of the above) seem in general to have been committed to keeping these couples together. In view of the fact that not one of the couples eventually succeeded in building what they regarded as an adequate marriage, one wonders why more effort was not directed at helping the couples dissolve what was for most of them essentially a destructive relationship. It would seem that professional practitioners working with such couples may be reflecting a cultural bias in their counseling efforts—that the function of the counselor is to keep the marriage intact no matter what the cost.

It is undoubtedly true that the counselor who suggests separation or divorce is open to the charge of "undermining" marriage and of not being able to "save marriages." It is also true, however, that the counselor who fails to consider separation or divorce for marriages such as these must face the fact that some of these couples will deteriorate seriously if the relationship is continued for any length of time. Actually, not even the Catholic moral code demands that destructive marriages be continued. And as Gold says, divorce (with or without remarriage) can be therapeutic for some persons.[13]

How Did Some of the Couples Escape Disorganization?

It will be remembered that of the 36 couples, disorganization could not be demonstrated for nine (25 percent) of the couples. If marriage is so crucial in our society in meeting basic needs, how is one to explain the fact that one-fourth of these husbands and wives apparently succeeded in living constructive lives in spite of what might have been a disastrous marital relationship?

It is suggested that the following interpretations may be helpful in understanding these cases: (1) Differential ability to tolerate frustration. It is well recognized in psychiatry that humans vary widely in their ability to absorb physical or psychic punishment. World War II supplied ample evidence of this for the men in the armed forces. Sociologists who specialize in crime, alcoholism, and the entire field of deviation are well aware of the fact that what drives one man to murder (or drink) will scarcely upset another man (or woman). (2) Displacement of hostility and other forms of negative emotion. Some persons express their hostility directly onto the marriage partner, others turn the emotion back on themselves, whereas still others displace the feeling onto the outside world—employees working under them, employers, minority groups, the economic system, etc. Whatever the device, the emotion which might damage the married partners is not released within the primary group, thus minimizing the destructive effects within the family itself. It could be maintained that these nine marriages did produce damage but that it was to persons outside the intimate circle. As one wife said of her husband: "He doesn't get ulcers—he gives them to *other* people." (3) The development of separate worlds for the husband and wife. Difficult as it may be to believe, it is possible in modern society to live as man and wife and hardly interact with each other. One man, for example, seeing that his marriage was unsuccessful, arranged to be assigned a wide territory which kept him away from home six weeks at a time. Another case was more ingenious: the man would arise about five A.M., prepare his own breakfast and leave for work. He lunched downtown (although he could easily have come home for lunch), had an early dinner in the evening and went to bed about seven. His wife, on the other hand, always stayed in bed until her husband had gone to work, and she usually stayed up until two or so in the morning. As this pattern developed, it became possible for them to live together while spending only about two hours together in the evening (from 5 to 7). They each slept with one of the children, so that part of the day or night did not involve interaction either. In a very pragmatic way, this couple worked out a style of life which held to the barest minimum their opportunity to express hostility.

A more common pattern involving separate worlds finds the husband becoming increasingly absorbed in his career, while the wife immerses herself in the children, community service, the church, etc. This sort of behavior represents what has been called "sublimation" in the redirection of sexual drives—the energy which might normally go into husband-wife interaction is expressed through other channels which meet with society's approval. Thus these couples minimize the potential destructiveness of the marriage and are actually industrial and community leaders in many cases. Sloan Wilson describes such a marriage in *Man in the Gray Flannel Suit*.[14] Oddly enough, society and the community often do benefit from such marriages—in these cases there was one children's hospital and one low cost housing project which owe their existence to a poor marriage.

In view of the above, it appears that there are various ultimate reactions to an unsuccessful marriage, some of which are more socially desirable than others.

Why Did They Stay Together?

In a few cases only psychiatric theory would appear to explain why some of these couples continued living together. In perhaps the "worst" case, the

455

man and wife seemed to hate each other, yet were unable to separate. They had no children, nor did their religious beliefs prevent separation. Yet they lived on together for over twenty years. One might say that they were locked together in a deadly struggle to see which one would break first. The man finally became an invalid, at which point the wife seemed to feel that she had "won." In such cases there seems to be a desire to "get even" with the partner. The reasoning (if such it can be called) seems to be like this: you have ruined my life by marrying me, and the only way I can pay you back is by living with you and ruining your life too. Separation, it seems, is too good for the partner: he or she must be made to pay. Oddly enough, such marriages are recorded statistically in our society as being "successful," since no separation, desertion, or divorce is ever recorded. It should be said that only a small number of cases (three) exhibited such psychopathic characteristics.

A more typical reason for continuing the relationship was the desire to give the children a normal home life. And in these cases, there seems to have been some reality content in this desire. This reason for living together was mentioned by 24 of the couples (66%).

There was also the hope, at least in the early years of discord, that matters would improve. Then by the time it became clear that the problems were not being solved, there were children to think of, community position to consider, financial complications, etc.

How Did They Choose Each Other?

Although it is beyond the scope of this paper to attempt to answer this question, two observations can be made: (1) lengthy dating and courtship in themselves do not necessarily prevent unsuccessful marriages in our society— 14 of these couples (39%) had gone together for over three years before marrying. This supports Goode's finding that the divorces in his sample could not be explained by this variable. It appears that we need some way to measure the depth and intensity of courtship rather than just its duration in time. (2) Winch's theory of the unconscious nature of psychodynamic attraction between future marital partners merits further attention.[15] Some of the most incompatible couples in this sample seemed to be pulled toward each other by forces of which they had no real understanding.

CONCLUSION

The sample and the research design in this study are not adequate to support any definitive generalizations. But as suggestions for further research two findings seem of special interest: (1) that marital failure not terminated by separation or divorce has a differential impact on the two sexes, with the male suffering the more severe damage. (It is unfortunate that the best study we have of divorce, that by Goode, focused on wives exclusively, thus providing no comparable data on this finding.) (2) That the adjustment of the children in these marriages did not seem to reflect that of the parents. Although the indices of adjustment used in this study are admittedly very crude, their direction is so impressive that the matter merits systematic study. Furthermore, they are not entirely unsupported by more carefully designed research published in recent years.[16]

It is hoped that these two findings in particular will be subjected to further analysis by other sociologists.

NOTES

[1] Willard Waller, *The Old Love and the New,* New York: Liveright, 1930.

[2] William J. Goode, *After Divorce,* Glencoe: The Free Press, 1956.

[3] For a discussion of the concept of personal disorganization, see Marshall B. Clinard, *Sociology of Deviant Behavior,* New York: Rinehart and Company, 1957.

[4] Budd Schulberg, *The Disenchanted,* New York: Random House, 1950.

[5] J. Louise Despert, *Children of Divorce,* New York: Doubleday, 1953.

[6] See Goode, *op. cit.,* ch. 21.

[7] Harold Orlansky, "Infant Care and Personality," *Psychological Bulletin,* 46 (1949), 1–48.

[8] Lee G. Burchinal, Glenn R. Hawkes, and Bruce Gardner, "The Relationship Between Parental Acceptance and Adjustment of Children," *Child Development,* 28 (March, 1957), 65–77.

[9] This is partly implied in Cohen's analysis of the impact of the peer group on gang behavior. See Albert K. Cohen, *Delinquent Boys, The Culture of the Gang,* Glencoe: The Free Press, 1955.

[10] Franz J. Kallmann, "The Genetic Theory of Schizophrenia," in *Personality in Nature, Society, and Culture,* edited by Clyde Kluckhohn and Henry A. Murray, New York: Alfred A. Knopf, 1949.

[11] William H. Sewell, "Infant Training and the Personality of the Child," *American Journal of Sociology,* 58 (1952), 150–159.

[12] Alfred C. Kinsey *et al., Sexual Behavior in the Human Male,* Philadelphia: W. B. Saunders, 1948.

[13] Herbert Gold, "Divorce as a Moral Act," *The Atlantic Monthly,* November, 1957.

[14] Sloan Wilson, *Man in the Gray Flannel Suit,* New York: Simon and Schuster, 1955.

[15] Robert Winch, *Mate-Selection,* New York: Harper and Brothers, 1958.

[16] See references 7, 8, 9, 10, and 11.

Widowhood Status in the United States: Perspective on a Neglected Aspect of the Family Life-Cycle

Felix M. Berardo

The death of one marriage partner (usually the man), before the other in this country is one crisis in marriage that cannot be "coped with" in the usual meaning of the word. Rather, it must be adjusted to. As Berardo points out, however, little research has been done on what life is like for the survivor, usually an elderly widow. The average age of widows, their economic circumstances, their employment possibilities, and their social life are important clues, available through demographic data, to the mini-culture in which they find themselves. Even from this limited picture, it can be seen that more attention should be paid the social state in which a woman (or man) finds herself when death strikes down her partner.

Widowhood is rapidly becoming a major phenomenon of American society. National census data indicate that there are close to 11 million widowed persons among our population today, the large majority of whom are women.[1] Over the past several decades the widowed female has, in fact, been outdistancing her male counterpart by a continually widening margin. Whereas the number of widowers has remained relatively constant from 1930 to the present, female survivors have shown a substantial rise during this period. Thus, in 1940 there were twice as many widows as there were widowers. During the following decade widows increased by more than 22 percent while the number of widowers rose by only 7 percent. By 1960 the ratio of widows to widowers had risen to more than 3½ to 1, and throughout the decade has continued to climb to a present ratio of more than 4 to 1. Currently, there are well over

From Felix Berardo, "Widowhood Status in the United States," *Family Coordinator*, July, 1968, pp. 191–202. Reprinted by permission of the author and The National Council on Family Relations.

eight and three-quarter million widows in the nation, and their total is expected to continue expanding.[2] Widowhood then is emerging as an important area for sociological inquiry because of the growing and extensive population involved. (Unless specified otherwise, the term widowhood as used in this paper will have reference to female survivors and their families only.)

For a variety of reasons, however, widowhood as a topic of study has not engaged the specific interests of sociological investigators to any appreciable extent, although there has been occasional recognition of the need for empirical data regarding their patterns of accommodation. Over a decade ago, for example, Kutner and his associates pointed out that "the effects and sequelae of widowhood have received little attention in empirical research. Widows are coming to represent a sizeable group in American life and there is a growing need for information regarding their pattern of adjustment" (Kutner, *et al.*, 1956, p. 19). In the more recent *Handbook of Social Gerontology* one reviewer particularly notes the lack of references to widowhood in the various publications of that specialized field and related areas, remarking: "It is striking that this inevitable and universal phase of life would be so patently neglected as an area of serious study" (Williams, 1961). In 1965, a sociologist employed with the federal government made a similar observation, stating:

"While much is made of the shock of retirement in gerontological literature, little is made of the shock of bereavement. Both are the common expectation of mankind and each should be studied. But in our society there is a strange silence about death and fear of death that is present with older people" (Kent, 1965, p. 14).

Finally, an informal survey of textbooks currently utilized in marriage and family courses reveals that in many instances the topic of widowhood is given only cursory attention and in still others the subject is not even raised. Such apparent disregard and lack of research concerning this special phase of the family life-cycle appears somewhat anomalous, indeed, in light of the fact that three out of every four wives in the United States survive their husbands.

This paper seeks to call specific attention to this neglected aspect of the family life-cycle. It will attempt to accomplish this goal primarily in two ways: (a) by highlighting the acute and problematic aspects of widowhood status through a concentration on significant sociodemographic indicators which characterize the contemporary condition of the widow and her family, and (b) by critically assessing the interdisciplinary scientific efforts concerning the study of widowhood, with particular emphasis on the sociological research orientation. In the latter connection, this paper represents an argument for a more extensive and systematic development of sociological knowledge concerning the phenomenon of widowhood in the United States and by emphasizing some needed areas of research on the social correlates of widowhood status.

Socio-Demographic Profile on American Widowhood

Widowhood has long been known to entail a variety of social problems at the local level, being related to adult and child dependency, poverty, unemployment, illness, and the more significant facts of family disorganization and of women's insecure industrial status (Phelps, 1938). In order to more fully portray the magnitude of the problem in contemporary society it is necessary to present a concise but somewhat abbreviated demographic profile on American widowhood. In addition to serving as a point of information regarding certain baseline data, the picture to be presented hopefully will also provide proper amplification of the current social conditions surrounding female survivors and will set the stage for exploring the sociological dimensions of their status for both the family and society.

It should be noted at the outset that from a statistical standpoint widowhood is largely a problem of the aged woman. As a result of the impact of advances in medical technology, pervasive health programs, etc., on decreasing mortality prior to midlife, widowhood for the most part has been postponed to the latter stages of the family life-cycle. Around the turn of the twentieth century about 1 in 25 persons was 65 years old or older, as compared to 1 in 11 in the present decade. Since the gains in longevity have been more rapid for females than for males, the growing proportion of elderly women in our population is accentuating the problem of widowhood. Thus, currently more than three-fifths of the widows in the United States are 65 years of age or over (almost another fourth are between 55-64) and "unless the trends in male and female mortality are sharply reversed, the excess of women over men at the upper ages will increase, and our older population will contain a larger proportion of widows" (Sheldon, 1958, p. 93).

Widowhood and Income

Because the majority of widows are aged, their economic circumstances are usually below average. A special survey of widows 55 years of age or older, for example, revealed that almost two-thirds of the husbands left a sum total of assets (including cash, savings, life insurance, property value of the home, and other assets) of less than $10,000 to their families; 44 percent left assets of less than $5,000. Equally significant, the median income of the wives in the year preceding the survey was less than $2,000 (Institute for Life Insurance, 1964). These figures are comparable to some extent with census data on the aged which shows the median income of the widowed as a group to be less than $1,200 per year, in comparison to almost $3,000 for the aged married. The census data also indicate that widows have substantially lower assets than nonwidows in all age groups (Epstein and Murray, 1967).

One thing is clear—the available evidence on income levels lends little support to the occasional stereotype of "the wealthy widow," as a statistically prevalent type among our aged population. In this connection, it is frequently stated that women, as a consequence of outliving their husbands, control a great deal of the inherited wealth in the United States. It is said, for example, that they are beneficiaries of 80 percent of all life insurance policies (National Consumer Finance Association, 1963). It is true that as beneficiaries, women

460

in the United States received more than two-thirds of the nearly $5 billion paid in 1965 following the death of a policyholder. Such gross figures, however, can be misleading. In the study cited earlier, for example, almost three-fourths of the husbands owned less than $5,000 in life insurance at the time of their death, and an additional 20 percent owned less than $10,000. Moreover, many of these women have to use what small amounts of insurance their husbands did carry to pay for funeral expenses, medical bills, taxes, mortgages, and so on, leaving them with only small savings on which to survive.

There is no doubt that life insurance has become a principal defense against the insecurity and risk of widowhood in our urban, industrial society with its attendant nuclear family system. It is a concrete form of security which in some instances may help the bereaved family to avoid an embarrassing and reluctant dependence on relatives and/or the state in the case of untimely death. Nevertheless, it has been the experience of investment bankers and the like that few female suvivors are capable of handling the economic responsibilities brought about by the husband's death, inasmuch as they know very little about matters of real estate, titles, mortgage, contracts, stocks, bonds, and matters of property[3] (Schwabacher, 1963).

Widowhood and Employment

Because they frequently encounter serious economic problems soon after their husbands have passed away, many wives find it necessary to seek employment. This is particularly the case where dependent children are involved; approximately 900,000 female survivors carried this responsibility in 1960. Moreover, at that time over half of all widows under age 35 were either employed or else seeking work. At ages 35-54, this proportion rises to nearly two-thirds (Metropolitan Life, 1966).

While women entering widowhood at the older ages are not as likely to have dependent children in the home, they are nevertheless often faced with a similar problem of self-support, since Social Security benefits provide for the minimum necessities only. Moreover, the obstacles to securing employment at this stage of the life-cycle are often rather difficult to overcome. Typically, these women have been absent from the labor market for several years and are, therefore, at a disadvantage with respect to the educational and occupational demands of current employment. In addition, they are frequently confronted with a subtle but pervasive discrimination on the part of the employers who are not in favor of hiring older persons, let alone older women. Since the majority of all widows, but in particular the aged widows, are unemployed, they are unable to support themselves and consequently are partly or wholly dependent on the assistance of children or relatives, and on public or private funds. While the 1965 amendments to the Social Security Act broadened and substantially increased benefits available to widows and their dependent children, their economic circumstances still remain far from satisfactory (Palmore, *et al.*, 1966).

461

Female survivors who have obtained employment are heavily concentrated in the low-paying jobs. Over one-third are private household or other service workers; one-fifth are clerical and kindred workers, and one-seventh are operatives and kindred workers. Less than one-tenth of all widows are engaged in professional or technical occupations. In any event, research indicates that playing a role in the productive economy is predictive of favorable adaptation to widowhood. Kutner, *et al.*, for example, found that an employed widow in later life tends to be better adjusted, that is, to have higher morale, than both a housewife who has never worked and a retired widow (Kutner, *et al.*, 1956). The acts of preparing for work, carrying out one's tasks, and returning home are viewed as being intimately connected to feelings of personal worth, self-esteem, and significance in life. This has led to the suggestion that:

"For widowed women, there is a need for a service that will provide occasional jobs, such as babysitting, service as companions for bedridden persons, and occasional light housekeeping tasks. Many widows have never been in the labor force and have never acquired skills in any other line. These kinds of jobs frequently coincide with their experience as homemakers"[4] (Kutner, *et al.*, 1956, p. 254).

. . . .

Widowhood Mortality and Mental Health

That widowhood presents serious problems of personal adjustment and mental health is rather well established. Empirical research has consistently demonstrated that the widowed typically have higher death rates, a greater incidence of mental disorders, and a higher suicide rate than their married counterparts. More specifically:

The Widowed Die Sooner. Analyses of National Vital Statistics and Census data for the United States reveal that the widowed have a significantly higher mortality rate than married persons of the same age, and that among young widowed people there is a particularly high excess of mortality (Kraus and Lilienfeld, 1959). Additional investigations in this country and abroad have supported these findings. Moreover, recent research by Rees and Lutkins (1967) has provided rather dramatic statistical confirmation of the long-standing hypothesis that a death in the family produces an increased post-bereavement mortality rate among close relatives, with the greatest increase in mortality risk occurring among surviving spouses. At present, little is known of the primary causative agents underlying this association between bereavement and mortality. Homogamy, common affection, point to an unfavorable environment, and loss of care have all been suggested as possible influences. Moreover:

"Personality factors, social isolation, age (old people withstand bereavement better than young), and the nature and magnitude of the loss itself all seem to be important factors. When the bereaved person is supported by a united and affectionate family, when there is something left to live for, when the person has been adequately prepared for the loss, and when it can be fitted into a secure religious or philosophical attitude to life and death there will seldom be much need for professional help. When, however, the bereaved person is left alone in a world which is seen as hostile and insecure, when the future is black and the loss has not been prepared for, help may be needed" (Rees and Lutkins, 1967, p. 3).

Widowhood and Suicide. Durkheim is generally recognized as the first well known sociologist to stress the connection between widowhood and suicide:

"The suicides, occurring at the crisis of widowhood ... are really due to domestic anomie resulting from the death of husband or wife. A family catastrophe occurs which affects the survivor. He is not adapted to the new situation in which he finds himself and accordingly offers less resistance to suicide" (Durkheim, 1951, p. 259).

Numerous investigations have since demonstrated that within a given age group, the suicide rates of the widowed are consistently higher than the married. A review of these studies indicates that suicide—whether attempted or actual—frequently tends to be preceded by the disruption of significant social interaction and reciprocal role relationships through the loss of a mate (Rushing, 1968). Moreover, these studies further reveal that the death of one or both parents in childhood is common among attempted and actual suicide victims; that the incidence of suicide among such persons when they attain adulthood is much greater than that for comparable groups in the general population.

Widowhood, Social Isolation, and Mental Health. That a high correlation exists between marital status and mental illness has been repeatedly noted in the scientific literature. While considerable professional controversy prevails over identification of the exact sequence of the antecedent-consequent conditions which predispose individuals toward various forms of organic and psychogenic disorders, there is little disagreement with the general hypothesis that "the emotional security and social stability afforded by married life makes for low incidence of mental illness" (Adler, 1953, p. 185). Again, the evidence is quite consistent that the widowed experience a substantially higher rate of mental disorders than the still married, particularly among the older populations.

The association between marital status and mental disorders has been shown to be a function of several intervening factors, including age, socio-economic status, physical condition, and the degree as well as duration of social isolation (Bellin and Hardt, 1958; Lowenthal, 1964, 1965). Problems of social isolation, often accompanied by distressing loneliness, are especially germane to the personal adjustment of aged female survivors, a very high proportion of whom are residing alone as occupants of one-person households. Fried and Stern (1948), for example, found that almost two-thirds of the widowed in their study were dissatisfied with the single state and were lonesome even after 10 years of widowhood. The loss of a husband not only creates many practical problems of living alone, but also produces a social vacuum in the life of the aged widow which is difficult to fill. She may find herself "marooned" in an environment which generally requires paired relationships as a prerequisite to social participation.[5] Consequently, various researchers have found that, compared to married women, widows are more apt to feel economically insecure, unhappy, to suffer from fears of being alone and from loss of self-esteem as women, to exhibit undue anxiety and emotional tensions, and to lack self-confidence. In the case of widows who are still mothers:

"There are the objective problems of limited income and the need to find the time and energy for a job to augment it and still be the kind of mother children need in the circumstances—a mother who can maintain a home, discipline and educate young people, and insure their positive emotional growth. Then there are the countless problems of guilt, fear, frustration and loneliness, ever-present and always threatening" (Ilgenfritz, 1961, p. 41).

To summarize at this point, it can be seen that a rather dismal picture of widowhood status emerges from the brief socio-demographic profile presented in the preceding pages. Clearly, the majority of women survivors generally have had to face a multiplicity of personal and familial adjustment problems while at the same time attempting to establish a satisfactory adaptation to a new and relatively undefined social role. Their economic position is likely to be insecure; more often than not they will need to seek employment, especially if young children are still in the home, and we only have touched on the various difficulties associated with these conditions. Moreover, in comparison to the still married, the widow faces the possibility of an early mortality, and there is a more than average probability that she will develop some mental disorder or even commit suicide.

•   •   •   •

In this paper we have concentrated on the widow in American society. The same type of inquiry, however, needs to be undertaken with respect to the widower, about whom scientific information is even less adequate. Currently, there are well over 2 million widowers in our population, and it can be assumed that the structuring of their adaptation would be different from that of their female counterparts (Berardo, 1967). Unless or until extensive and systematic investigations of widowhood and widowerhood are undertaken and completed, the sociology of isolation will exhibit an unnecessary lag in its development.

NOTES

[1] The national data, of course, reflect the marital status of individuals at the time of the census enumeration only. It should be noted that people in the status of widowhood today may not be in this status tomorrow. Moreover, many currently married persons were once in the widowhood status (U.S. Bureau of the Census, 1967, p. 33).

[2] Three major factors are generally cited to account for the growing excess of widows in the United States, namely: (a) mortality among women is lower than among men and, therefore, larger numbers of women survive to advanced years; (b) wives are typically younger than their husbands and, consequently, even without the sex differences in mortality have a greater probability of out-living their husbands; (c) among the widowed, remarriage rates are considerably lower for women than men. Other major factors which also have an impact on widowhood status are the effects of war casualties, depressions, and disease pandemics (Jacobson, 1959, pp. 24–27).

[3] Actually, the economic dilemma in which widows often find themselves is frequently brought about as a direct result of the failure of husbands to plan their estates and advise their wives. "The truth is that most men leave their affairs in a jumble. This is not because their lives are unduly complicated, but simply because they can't seem to get around to the task of setting up a program for their families that would automatically go into operation upon their death. Death is unpleasant to think about and always seems remote. The tendency is to put the problem off and plan 'to get to it one of these days' " (*Changing Times*, 1961, pp. 9–14). Moreover, many husbands themselves are incapable of making sensible financial decisions and preparations.

[4] A federally sponsored program which dovetails rather nicely with the employment needs of older widows who lack specialized technical skills is the recently initiated Foster Grandparent Project developed by the Office of Economic Opportunity. Under this project, the federal government awards grants of money to the states to be used to employ older people as "foster grandparents" to work with and serve as companions for the mentally retarded, physically handicapped, delinquent, emotionally disturbed, and dependent and neglected children in institutions, day care centers, and homes (*Look*, 1966, pp. 67–71).

[5] Blau has demonstrated that the degree of social isolation among older widows is partially conditioned by the prevalence of similar age-sex peer groupings in the social structure (Blau, 1961).

REFERENCES

Adler, Leta M., "The Relationship of Marital Status to Incidence and Recovery from Mental Illness," *Social Forces*, XXXII (1953), 185–194.

Bellin, Seymour S., and Robert H. Hardt, "Marital Status and Mental Disorders among the Aged," *American Sociological Review*, XXIII (1958), 155–162.

Blau, Zena S., "Structural Constraints on Friendships in Old Age," *American Sociological Review*, XXVI (1961), 429–439.

Durkheim, Emile, *Suicide: A Study in Sociology* (Glencoe: The Free Press, 1951).

Epstein, Lenore A., and Janet H. Murray, *The Aged Population of the United States*, U.S. Department of Health, Education, and Welfare, Social Security Administration, Office of Research and Statistics, Research Report No. 19, U.S. Government Printing Office, Washington, D.C., 1967.

Fried, Edrita G., and Karl Stern, "The Situation of the Aged within the Family," *American Journal of Orthopsychiatry*, XVIII (1948), 31–54.

"How to Help Your Widow," *Changing Times* (November 1961), pp. 9–14.

Ilgenfritz, Marjorie P., "Mothers on Their Own—Widows and Divorcées," *Marriage and Family Living,* XXIII (1961), 38–41.

Institute for Life Insurance, *Some Data on Life Insurance Ownership and Related Characteristics of the Older Population,* 1964 (mimeographed).

Kent, Donald P., *Aging—Fact and Fancy,* U.S. Department of Health, Education, and Welfare, Welfare Administration, Office of Aging, OA No. 224 (Washington, D.C.: U.S. Government Printing Office, 1965).

Kraus, Arthur S., and Abraham M. Lilienfeld, "The Widowed Die Sooner," *Journal of Chronic Diseases,* X (1959), 207.

Kutner, Bernard, D. Fanshel, A. M. Togo, and T. S. Langner, *Five-Hundred over Sixty* (New York: Russell Sage Foundation, 1956).

Lowenthal, Marjorie F., "Social Isolation and Mental Illness in Old Age," *American Sociological Review,* XXIX (1964), 54–70.

Lowenthal, Marjorie F., "Antecedents of Isolation and Mental Illness in Old Age," *Archives of General Psychiatry,* XII (1965), 245–254.

Metropolitan Life Insurance Company, "Widows and Widowhood," *Statistical Bulletin,* XLVII (1966), 3–6.

National Consumer Finance Association, *Finance Facts,* Educational Service Division, Washington, D.C., January, 1963.

Palmore, Erdman, Gertrude L. Stanley, and Robert H. Cormier, *Widows with Children under Social Security,* The 1963 National Survey of Widows with Children under OASDHI. U.S. Department of Health, Education, and Welfare, Social Security Administration, Office of Research and Statistics, Research Report No. 16 (Washington, D.C.: U.S. Government Printing Office, 1966).

Phelps, Harold A., *Contemporary Social Problems* (rev. ed.; New York: Prentice-Hall, 1938), Ch. XV, pp. 516–540.

Rees, W. Dewi, and Sylvia G. Lutkins, "Mortality of Bereavement," *British Medical Journal,* IV (1967), 13–16.

Rushing, William A., "Individual Behavior and Suicide," in Jack P. Gibbs, ed., *Suicide* (New York: Harper and Row, 1968), Ch. 4.

Schwabacher, Albert E., Jr., "The Repository of Wealth," in Seymour M. Farber and Roger H. L. Wilson, eds., *The Potential of Women* (New York: McGraw-Hill, 1963), pp. 241–254.

Sheldon, Henry D., *The Older Population of the United States* (New York: John Wiley and Sons, 1958).

U.S. Bureau of the Census, *Statistical Abstract of the United States: 1967* (88th Edition), Washington, D.C., 1967, p. 33, Table 32, Marital Status of the Population, by Sex: 1890–1966.

Williams, Richard W., "Changing Status, Roles, and Relationships," in Clark Tibbitts, ed., *Handbook of Social Gerontology* (Chicago: University of Chicago Press, 1961), pp. 261–297.

8

Emerging
Conceptualizations
of Strong
Family Partnerships

Early scholars studying the family attempted to discover the reasons for "marital happiness" without ever questioning whether there was such a well-defined emotion or judgment. This chapter illustrates that happiness in marriage is very complex and is composed of many things. In addition, marital satisfaction is apparently highly variable over time and between spouses.

Despite the current emphasis on individualism, young men and women still seek the security of a marital partnership and are still having children and forming permanent families. Some ingredients that would make for strong bonds of love among family members, as well as satisfaction with the family atmosphere, are suggested here. It is further suggested that this family climate would be improved by a looser structure, in keeping with the individualism of the times, where each family member would *earn* the other's company by being a worthwhile person to spend time with. Certainly this is one of the primary reasons marital partnerships are formed in the first place.

Satisfaction with Various Aspects of Marriage over the Life Cycle: A Random Middle Class Sample

Wesley R. Burr

A "happy marriage" is not all of one piece. Couples can be pleased with some areas of their partnership, disappointed with others. Husbands and wives do not necessarily parallel each other's judgment in a given area and their feelings may wax and wane through the years. Realizing this, Burr has undertaken to investigate satisfaction (not happiness) with certain aspects of marriage— financial, social, task performance, marriage, sex, and children—as they fluctuate through the life cycle of couples. The author contrasts his findings with those of previous studies on this subject and suggests that rather than a gradual decline in marital satisfaction as the years go by, there are many fluctuations, both sharp and gradual, depending on the area of interaction being investigated. Thus, the answer to the question, "Did they live happily ever after?" is very complex indeed.

There has been an increase in recent years in the use of the family life cycle as an explanatory variable, and it has been used to explain such varied phenomena as consumer buying patterns (Foote, 1961), marital power (Blood and Wolfe, 1960), life satisfaction (Rose, 1955), mental health (Rose, 1954), marital success or adjustment (Bossard and Boll, 1955), etc. The research reported in this paper is a further addition to this type of research in that it is an attempt to add, in what is hoped is a cumulative manner, to the earlier studies on how marital satisfaction varies systematically in different stages of the family life cycle.

From "Satisfaction with Various Aspects of Marriage over the Life Cycle," *Journal of Marriage and the Family,* February, 1970, pp. 29–37. Reprinted by permission of the author and The National Council on Family Relations.

Since the goal of this project is to explain variance in marital satisfaction, it is imperative that this concept of "satisfaction" be clearly identified. It is even more important that it be carefully defined in this project since it has been used in earlier research as a synonym for such other terms as marital success, happiness, adjustment, etc., and the phenomenon that is denoted in most of the previous work is so conceptually unclear.[1] In the present research the term "satisfaction" is defined as a subjective condition in which an individual experiences a certain degree of attainment of a goal or desire.

There are, of course, many different goals that are sought in marriage, and because of this, it is fairly clear, but not conceptually very precise, to refer to marital satisfaction. It is conceptually much more precise to identify specific goals in the marital experience, and to be concerned with the degree to which people are satisfied with the attainment of these particular goals. This type of conceptual precision is especially valuable when satisfaction with some aspects of marriage varies independently with satisfaction in other areas. To help attain this conceptual precision, an attempt is made in this study to distinguish conceptually between satisfaction with six different aspects of the marital relationship, and then to operationalize each of them separately. The areas selected are: (1) the way finances are handled, (2) the couple's social activities, (3) the way the spouse performs his or her household tasks, (4) the companionship in the marriage, (5) the sexual interaction, and (6) the relationships with the children.

This particular method of conceptualizing the dependent variable overcomes several limitations in the methods that have been used in most of the earlier research. The most frequently used conceptualization of the marital "success" type variable was initially introduced by Burgess and Cottrell (1939). In this method several conceptually distinct phenomena such as consensus, permanence, happiness, and specific behavior patterns such as who gives in to whom, are grouped together into one rather omnibus concept. In addition, the nature of the successful marital state is predefined by the criteria that are selected *by the researcher* to measure it. In regard to this latter point, in social groups where these particular criteria are not applicable the concept is not only meaningless, it is misleading. The method used in the present research, of being concerned only with the phenomena of subjective satisfaction, overcomes both of these limitations in the earlier technique. It provides a concept that has considerably greater clarity, is much closer to being unidimensional, and does not have the bias that occurs when the criteria of success are predefined.

However, the system of conceptualizing which is being used in the present research also has its limitations, and these should be kept in mind. It deals only with the attainment of one particular type of marital outcome variable, satisfaction, and this may or may not co-vary with variation in such other aspects of marriage as personal development, effective socialization, stability, functionality, etc. Also, the present system provides no assessment of overall or general marital success. In addition, it deals with subjective satisfaction only in regard to six specific aspects of marriage, and there are other areas where measuring satisfaction may be equally or more important. The present conceptualization thus denotes a very narrow area of concern, and in doing this, it ignores many other phenomena.

Previous Research

There are several earlier studies which have data relevant to understanding how these types of variables change over the life cycle. The earlier studies differ considerably in the ways they conceptualize and operationalize their dependent variables, but they nonetheless provide some basis for hypothesizing about the relationships that are being studied in the present project.

The first of these earlier studies was carried out over 30 years ago at the University of Chicago (Lang, 1932). In this project the investigators obtained ratings of marital "happiness" in a sample of couples who had been married up to 16 years. They divided the sample according to length of time married and found a slight, gradual decline in the mean happiness score over the 16-year period.

This initial finding of a gradual decrease in "happiness" was later refined by Pineo (1961) in his analysis of the 20-year follow-up in the longitudinal study begun by Burgess and Wallin (1953). These couples were studied first during engagement, again after four or five years of marriage, and then a third time after 20 years of marriage. Pineo's (1961:3) data indicated that there was a "general drop in marital 'satisfaction and adjustment'" which he conceptualized as a process of disenchantment. It should be noted, however, that the term "satisfaction" was not used in the same way it is defined in the present research. It was rather a general term including such phenomena as love, permanence, consensus, etc. His analysis of the data, however, also demonstrated that there was a decrease between the time periods in his study in each of the areas that were components of marital satisfaction.

Pineo's study is uniquely valuable in that a large number of different aspects of marriage were studied, but it is limited by the fact that all stages of the life cycle were not included in the sample. This is the case because the married couples were contacted only twice and the data gave no insight into changes during the intervening stages and those that occur after 20 years of marriage.

The other major attempt to measure life-cycle variations in this type of variable was by Blood and Wolfe (1960). They interviewed over 900 wives in an area probability sample of Detroit, and part of their data is concerned with the way the wife's marital satisfaction varies over the life cycle. They used the term "marital satisfaction," but it was somewhat different from the definition in the present study. Their measure of satisfaction was made by weighing "reported satisfaction with standard of living, companionship, understanding, and love and affection (plus the congruity of her expected and desired number of children), by the comparative importance she attached to each of the five aspects of marriage" (Blood and Wolfe, 1960:102). Their use of the term "satisfaction" is closer to the way it is used in the present study than in any of the other previous studies; but they used it as a general overall measure and the congruence dimension is slightly different.

Blood and Wolfe found gradual decreases in satisfaction until the children were launched, and then a slight rise followed by a decline in the retired group. They analyzed only the general variable of satisfaction with marriage as a whole, and did not take into account any of the more specific dimensions of marital satisfaction.

There have been two cross-cultural replications of the Blood and Wolfe study. One was undertaken by Hill (1967) in Belgium, but the data have not yet been published. The other was by Blood (1967) in Japan. In this replication, the researchers interviewed a sample drawn from the Tokyo metropolitan area, and they used the same measures as in the earlier study. They again found that later periods in the life cycle were characterized by decreases in satisfaction.

There have also been several smaller studies that have relevant data. In Bossard and Boll's (1955) study of large families, they analyzed the ratings made by their subjects of the marital happiness of 440 of their siblings. They then divided these couples into age groups and compared the proportions that were rated either happy or medium-to-unhappy. They found significant variations for the women, with the age group of 20-29 being relatively happier than the older ages. They also summarize their case history data in the following manner:

> Our case material, then, suggests the late forties and early fifties as a crisis period for many women: their children no longer retain their earlier dependence, their husbands are inadequate as sexual mates, and the menopause casts its passing shadows. . . . The material on the marital lives of brothers who were rated contains many references to the decade of the fifties as a similar crisis period in the lives of married men. Here, however, the frustrations and unhappiness tend to center around occupational rather than sexual matters (Bossard and Boll, 1955:14).

Deutscher (1959) published a study of 49 middle class couples in the post-parental stages of their life cycle. His findings are useful in understanding life cycle variations as he contrasts the couples' feelings about several aspects of their life with the way they were in previous stages. On the basis of earlier literature that speculated about the difficulties of the post-parental stages of life, he seemed to expect the post-parental stage to be more problematic—especially for the women. When the data were actually analyzed, however, it was found that most of the couples defined their present condition as better than the period that just preceded it, of having grown children in the home.

Luckey (1966) has also published a study that provides some valuable data on life cycle variations. In her sample the average length of marriage was about seven years, and she found that most of the changes in the way a person describes his spouse on the Leary Interpersonal Checklist were in a less favorable direction.

Thus, considerable data have been gathered on how marital satisfaction varies in different stages of the life cycle. There are, however, several major deficiencies in this earlier research that need to be corrected. There is only one study that combines (1) an analysis of satisfaction with (2) all of the stages of the family life cycle, and (3) investigates both sexes. This is Blood's Japanese replication, and the analysis of these data is so brief that it only concludes there were decreases over the years of marriage. The results indicate that it is not presently known with any degree of surety how different types of satisfaction vary over the life cycle. In addition, the sampling procedures are a crucial factor in studying this problem, and, with the exception of the Blood and Wolfe study, all of the above-mentioned studies used accidental rather than random samples. This limits the generalizability of the findings, and makes it more necessary that each of the findings obtained in the earlier research be tested with new samples that have an identifiable universe.

THE HYPOTHESES

There are several trends in this earlier research that seem sufficiently clear to serve as a basis for making hypotheses in the present study. First, there tends to be a pattern of decreasing satisfaction over the life cycle in most of the earlier research. Thus, the first hypothesis is:

> There is a decrease in satisfaction from the early stages of the family life cycle to the later stages.

There is no evidence that most of this decrease occurs at any particular time in the life cycle, and several of the studies found a gradual decline. Pineo (1961:10) stated that a marked decline occurred in the early years in his sample, and that this occurred slightly earlier for the men than the women, but he published no data in support of this conclusion. A second hypothesis is:

> The rate of decrease is gradual and occurs over a long period rather than being substantial at any one stage.

The earlier studies also seem to suggest that the period in the life cycle having the least satisfaction is just prior to the launching of children. For example, Bossard and Boll's interview data suggest that the late forties and early fifties are most problematic. Also, Deutscher found the launching years usually slightly more pleasant than the previous period, and Blood and Wolfe found the lowest scores on both love and marital satisfaction occurred in the stages having unlaunched but grown children. This results in a third hypothesis that:

> The lowest satisfaction scores occur just prior to the launching of children.

It would be possible to make other hypotheses about how satisfaction varies, but it was decided that the scarcity of either theoretical ideas or empirical data suggesting other relationships provided little basis for making them. Rather, it seemed defensible to use this study to test the above-stated hypotheses and help provide other data upon which subsequent theoretical formulations can then be based. It should be noted that the earlier research provides no basis for hypothesizing about how satisfaction with any of the six more specific aspects of marriage differ in their patterns of variation. The most defensible method of analysis thus seems to be one of comparing the variation in each area of satisfaction with these hypotheses to see if and how they vary.

THE DATA

The data were gathered as part of a larger study of marital interaction. The sample used was a random sample of 147 intact couples in a group of census tracts that had been selected to eliminate lower socioeconomic strata. The subjects were randomly selected from residential addresses on the streets of the selected census tracts. Useable data were gathered from 116 of these couples, and it is the data from this group that is reported in this study. The remaining 21 percent of the original sample either refused (11 percent), could not be contacted (3 percent), or provided insufficient data (7 percent). All of the age groups and stages of the family life cycle were represented in the sample. The mean age of the husbands was 47.5 and of the wives, 45.6. The sample tended to be well educated, having a mean of 13.5 years of education for the men and 12.7 for the women. About 85 percent grew up in the Midwest and about half had migrated from either small towns or rural areas to the city. They were slightly more Catholic and Lutheran in their religious affiliation than the general U.S. population, and probably as a result of this, they had slightly more children (2.58) than the general population.

The data were gathered by means of a pre-arranged session in the subjcts' homes during which time each subject completed a rather lengthy questionnaire and was interviewed by trained researchers. The husband and wife were interviewed separately, and the data that were used to divide the sample into life cycle categories were obtained while interviewing the wife. The ages of the children and whether or not they were in the home were the major criteria for determining which stage of the life cycle each couple was presently in. It was originally intended that the life cycle categories developed by Duvall (1957) would be used, but when the sample was actually divided according to her system, it was noted that several categories were very small. Because of this, it was decided to alter her system by collapsing the childbearing with the pre-school stage. The criteria for dividing the sample into stages to make the cross-sectional analysis, and the number of couples in each stage, are identified in Table 1.

The degree of satisfaction with each of the areas of marriage was operationalized by having the subjects respond to three questions in regard to each of the six areas of marital interaction. The questions for the wives in the area of handling family finances were:

473

1. How often do I get mad or angry at something in regard to the way money is handled in our family?
   (1) very frequently.
   (2) frequently.
   (3) occasionally.
   (4) seldom.
   (5) very seldom.
   (6) never.
2. How much improvement could there be in the way money is handled in the family?
   (1) none.
   (2) very little.
   (3) some.
   (4) quite a bit.
   (5) a great deal.
3. How satisfied am I with the way money is handled?
   (1) perfectly satisfied.
   (2) quite satisfied.
   (3) satisfied.
   (4) a little dissatisfied.
   (5) very dissatisfied.

The responses were scored according to the numbers in parentheses, and the sums hence could range from 3 to 16 for each area.

TABLE 1.
FAMILY LIFE CYCLE CATEGORIES

STAGE NO.	TITLE	NUMBER OF COUPLES	CRITERIA FOR INCLUSION IN SAMPLE
1	Pre-child	12	Never have had children, and married less than 7 years.
2	Young children	14	Oldest child under 6 years of age.
3	School age	15	Oldest child between 6–12.
4	Teen-age	30	Oldest child between 13–20.
5	Launching	24	Oldest child over 20 and still at home, or even if no children are 20 but one has left home.
6	Post-parental	11	All children launched.
7	Retired	10	Husband retired.

THE FINDINGS

The data on how the various types of satisfaction vary over the life cycle are presented in Figures 1 through 6 [See pp. 475–477.] On the basis of Hypothesis One, it was expected that a discernible decrease would occur in satisfaction in the later stages of the life cycle, but it is interesting to note that

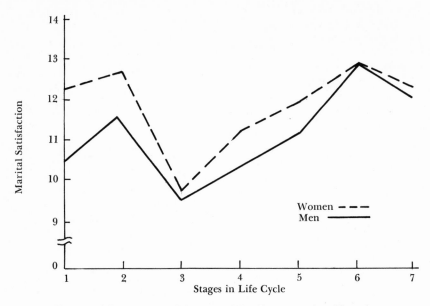

FIGURE 1. SATISFACTION WITH THE WAY FINANCES ARE HANDLED
OVER THE LIFE CYCLE

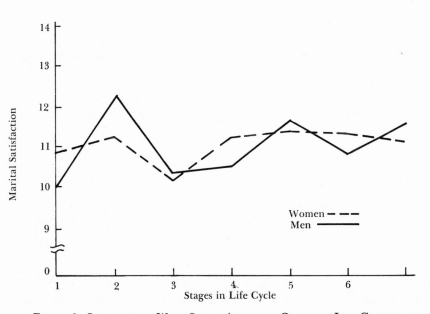

FIGURE 2. SATISFACTION WITH SOCIAL ACTIVITIES OVER THE LIFE CYCLE

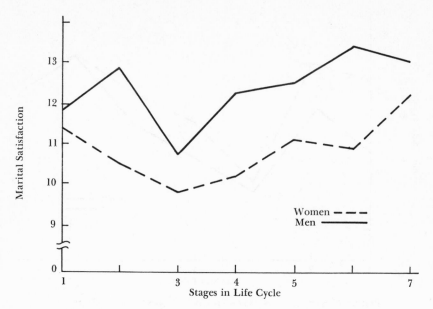

FIGURE 3. SATISFACTION WITH TASKS OVER THE LIFE CYCLE

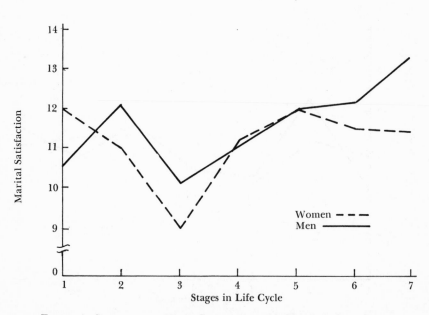

FIGURE 4. SATISFACTION WITH COMPANIONSHIP OVER THE LIFE CYCLE

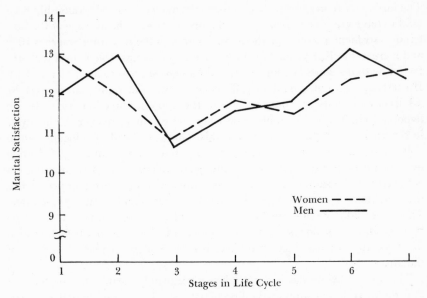

FIGURE 5. SATISFACTION WITH SEX OVER THE LIFE CYCLE

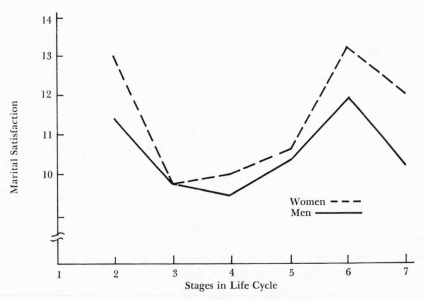

FIGURE 6. SATISFACTION WITH CHILDREN OVER THE LIFE CYCLE

there are no major trends of decreasing scores in any of the six areas of satisfaction and several of them actually tend to rise over most of the life cycle. The husbands' scores for finances, task performance, and companionship each tend to have gradual increases after the initial stages. The average of the husbands' satisfaction scores for the financial area in the first three stages is 10.5, and increases to 12.1 in the last three stages. The comparable figures for satisfaction with tasks are 11.9 and 13.1, and for companionship are 10.9 and 12.4. If t-tests are computed on these differences, they are all significant beyond the .01 level of confidence, and they are in the opposite direction from the one hypothesized. The women only experience this gradual rise over the life cycle in the area of task performance, and this is not statistically significant, but in none of the six areas is there any general pattern of a decline in satisfaction over the life cycle. One of the most limiting conditions of this particular project is the size of the sample, but when these life-cycle stages are grouped in this manner, there is an N of 41 in the first three stages and 45 in the last three. Thus, the data provide evidence that in this sample, contrary to the first hypothesis, there is no systematic decline over the life cycle in satisfaction with these six areas of marriage, and there is even a slight increase in several of the areas.

The second hypothesis is not rendered completely meaningless by the fact that the data do not support the first hypothesis. The second hypothesis deals with the issue of gradual changes vs. abrupt changes in satisfaction over the life cycle, and even though there are no overall decrements over the life cycle, there is some indication of variation between stages, and the gradualness of these changes is an important concern.

The data seem to indicate that rather than having any type of gradual trend in satisfaction, there are several relatively abupt variations in some types of satisfaction and virtually no variation in others. The most abrupt overall change seems to be from the pre-school stage to the school stage when there is a discernible drop for both the husbands and wives in satisfaction in most of the areas. The closest thing to a gradual trend in satisfaction over a long period of time is in the tendency to have a gradual increase in several areas after the school-age stage. This continues up to the retirement stage for the husband in the area of companionship, and until the post-parental stage in finances, task performance, sex, and relations with children. For the wives it continues to retirement in task performance and sex, and to the post-parental stage in finances and relationships with the children. This gradual trend does not seem to occur in regard to social activities, where there seems to be the least life cycle variation.

The third hypothesis deals with the stage of the life cycle that seems to be the most difficult. Earlier research has indicated that this probably is the pre-launching stage, but in this sample, the school-age stage is fraught with greater difficulty. This stage has the lowest score for both husbands and wives in finances, task performance, companionship, sex, and relationships with children. In addition, in most of these areas there is a major drop from the pre-school stage, and an increase after this stage. In fact, the only areas where the satisfaction is lower in another stage is in the husbands' relations with the children in the teenage stage, and their social activities in the pre-child stage. The adolescent stage, as would be expected by the earlier research, is persistently more problematic.

The analyses of the data that are possible with the second and third hypotheses do not lend themselves very well to testing for statistical significance. If specific contrasts had been hypothesized before the data were gathered, it would have been possible to identify some alpha limits, but there was little basis for this. There is some precedent in the literature for using a t-test, or a one-way analysis of variance test, for testing the significance of this type of changes. When the t-test is used in this manner, however, it has little more than intuitive value. The significance of the tests made with it are impaired when it is used for more than one randomly selected contrast. The F-ratio only gives a test of the significance of the variation over all of the stages, and is thus addressed to a very different question than the variations from one particular stage to another. Because of these limitations, no attempts are being made to assess the statistical significance of these inter-stage variations.

There are several other aspects of these data that deserve comment in addition to the relevance of the data for testing the hypotheses. One aspect deals with the differences between the six areas in their overall variation. Some of the areas have major variations over the life cycle in satisfaction while others have substantially less variation. The least variation occurs for both sexes, but especially for the husbands, in the area of social activities. The most abrupt variation seems to occur for both sexes in regard to relationships with the children, and next in regard to finances and companionship. There also seems to be a sex difference in the satisfaction with the task performance, with the wives being less satisfied than the husbands. The sexes are the most similar in the variation in satisfaction in regard to relationships with their children. Another finding in these data which could hardly be anticipated from earlier research, and which is difficult to explain, is that on every measure the husbands are less happy in the pre-child stage than the stage where there are pre-school children in the home.

SUMMARY

The data from a random sample of middle-class couples indicate that the school-age stage of the family may be plagued with difficulties that have not been appreciated in the family sociology literature. The sample is sufficiently small that additional research will need to be undertaken to further test these findings, but conclusions that satisfaction with various aspects of marriage gradually decreases over the life cycle, and that the pre-launching stage is the most difficult, should be viewed with less certainty.

479

NOTES

[1] I have elsewhere criticized the rather gross lack of conceptual clarity in the literature in conceptualizing this type of marital outcome variable. See Wesley R. Burr, "Marital Satisfaction: A Conceptual Reformulation, Theory and Partial Test of the Theory," unpublished Ph.D. Dissertation, 1967, University of Minnesota, Ch. 1.

REFERENCES

Blood, Robert O. and Donald M. Wolfe, *Husbands and Wives: The Dynamics of Married Living*. Glencoe, Illinois: The Free Press, 1960.

Blood, Robert O., *Love Match and Arranged Marriage*. New York: The Free Press, 1967.

Bossard, James H. and Eleanor Stoker Boll, "Marital unhappiness in the life cycle." *Marriage and Family Living, 17* (February, 1955): 10–14.

Burgess, Ernest W. and Leonard S. Cottrell, *Predicting Success or Failure in Marriage*. New York: Prentice-Hall, 1939.

Burgess, Ernest W. and Paul Wallin, *Engagement and Marriage*. Philadelphia: Lippincott, 1953.

Deutscher, Irwin, *Married Life in the Middle Years*. Kansas City, Missouri: Community Studies, 1959.

Duvall, Evelyn, *Family Development*. New York: Lippincott, 1957.

Foote, N. (ed.), *Consumer Behavior,* Vol. 5, *Models of Household Decision Making*. New York: New York University Press, 1961.

Hill, Reuben, personal communication, 1967.

Lang, Richard O., "A study of the degree of happiness or unhappiness in marriage." Unpublished Master's Thesis, University of Chicago, 1932.

Locke, Harvey J. and Karl M. Wallace, "Short marital adjustment and prediction tests: Their reliability and validity." *Marriage and Family Living, 21* (August, 1959): 251–55.

Luckey, E. B., "Number of years married as related to personality perception and marital satisfaction." *Journal of Marriage and the Family, 28* (February, 1966): 44–48.

Pineo, Peter C., "Disenchantment in the later years of marriage." *Marriage and Family Living, 23* (February, 1961): 3–11.

Rose, Arnold M., *Theory and Method in the Social Sciences*. Minneopolis: The University of Minnesota Press, 1954. "Factors associated with the life satisfaction of middle class, middle-aged persons." *Marriage and Family Living, 17* (February, 1955): 15–19.

480

What Is a Strong Family?

Herbert A. Otto

The term, "a strong family" is often bandied about but is almost as difficult to pin down as "marital happiness" or "satisfaction." Here Otto attempts to indicate, via empirical research, just what types of personal interactions family members themselves see as contributing to the strength of their own family. As always, there is much to learn by breaking down over-arching concepts such as "family strength" into interactional components. That these components are abstract qualities such as "emotional support," "ability to communicate," "encourages other," and "encourages growth of family members" will come as no surprise, for they are echoed in various forms in other chapters throughout the book.

Very often, teachers, social workers and members of other helping professions, as well as lay persons, describe a family as being a "good" family—or a "strong" family. Their comments might lead to the assumption that they had some specific "good" qualities or "strengths" in mind. A closer examination, however, reveals considerable confusion and lack of clarity about the meaning of family strengths. Not only is there considerable confusion on this point on the part of those observing families, but it has been found that most families are not too clear about what may be their own strengths.

Currently in a series of research projects at the Graduate School of Social Work, University of Utah, we have been exploring this area. These projects are entitled "The Family Resource Development Project" and "The Personal Resource Development Project." The purpose of this research is to seek some answers to the following questions:

1. What are individual and family strengths?
2. How do we help individuals and families recognize and utilize their strengths and resources more fully?
3. How do we work with strengths?

From Herbert A. Otto, "What is a Strong Family," *Marriage and Family Living*, February, 1962, pp. 77–80. Reprinted by permission of the author and The National Council on Family Relations.

In this article we will confine our discussion to the first of these questions.

As a part of these research projects, a pilot study was conducted to find what families considered their strengths to be. A total of twenty-seven families filled in the Family Strength Questionnaire which asked them to respond to this open-ended item, "The following are what we consider to be major strengths in our family: ⸻." The blank lines were to be filled in. The questionnaire was filled in by both husband and wife in consultation with each other.

The following list indicates what the families considered to be their strengths and the number of times these strengths were mentioned:

a.	Shared faith, religious and moral values	22
b.	Love, consideration and understanding	17
c.	Common interests, goals and purpose	15
d.	Love and happiness of children	13
e.	Working and playing together	10
f.	Sharing specific recreational activities	10
g.	Being in accord on discipline	5
h.	Respect for individuality of family members	5
i.	Shared sense of humor	4
j.	Enjoying companionship	4
k.	Good health	4
l.	Desire for learning and education	4
m.	Miscellaneous	34
	TOTAL	147

The twenty-seven families listed a total of only one hundred forty-seven strengths with an average of only five strengths for each family. The large number of families (twenty-two) listing "Shared faith, religious and moral values" as a strength is not surprising, as all families were church affiliated. The large number of "Miscellaneous" strengths indicates that families vary considerably as to what they consider strengths. Such items as "home-making," "intelligence," "financial solvency," "acceptance of each other's limitations," and "trying new things" were some of the "Miscellaneous" strengths. Other "Miscellaneous" strengths were "agreement on expenditures," "trusting each other," "shared family traditions," and "liking people."

An outgrowth of the pilot study was the development of a framework of family strengths. It is presented in the hope that it will contribute toward a clarification of the concept of family strengths.

The dictionary defines strength as the "quality or state of being strong; ability to do or bear; solidity or toughness; that quality which tends to secure results."

The assumption can be made that "the quality of strength" is the end result of certain interacting components or factors which produce this quality. Family strength is, therefore, seen as the end product of a series of ever-changing factors or components. These components must be seen as fluid, interacting and related. They are not independent but interrelated, and variations in these abilities, capacities, or strengths occur throughout the life cycle of the family. The components are defined as "strengths" but with the recognition that, as an aggregate, they result in "Family Strength."

What, then, were the components as indicated by these twenty-seven families? Eleven different ones were distinguished. Each will be noted and some brief comments made about it. Family strength may be composed of:

1. *The ability to provide for the physical, emotional, and spiritual needs of a family.*

Ability to provide for the family's physical needs implies not merely provision of food and shelter. There is the matter of management as well. For example, from the humblest home to the mansion, the way the physical space is used may be constructive and creative, or restrictive. The living room parlor or the out-of-bounds dining room for children comes to mind immediately.

Similarly, qualitative differences are distinguished in a family's preparation and use of food. Some families purchase, plan, and prepare meals together and make this "fun" as well as educational. These seemingly mundane functions can represent both a strength and a strengthening process. Finally, as a part of providing for the family's physical needs, health is included as a strength, and it is recognized that providing for family health is a strengthening process.

Providing for the emotional needs of the family includes the giving of affection or love, understanding, and trust. This is seen as a two-way process, with parents providing for the emotional needs of the children and the children also giving to the parents.

The ability to provide for the spiritual needs of the family includes the sharing of basic beliefs, and spiritual or religious values, as well as sharing the doubts and concerns about religious beliefs. Providing an environment of honesty and integrity is a family strength.

2. *The ability to be sensitive to the needs of the family members.*

This includes sensitivity of the husband to the wife's needs. The children's sensitivity to the needs of the parents is also seen as a strength.

Wives often seem to be more sensitive to the needs of husbands, than husbands are to the needs of their wives. Frequently we hear wives make remarks such as this—"Darling, you have worked too hard lately. What you need is some quiet time—why not go fishing?"

More rarely husbands will comment—"I know this daily grind with children and housework is getting you down. What you need is more adult company. Let's do something about it."

3. *The ability to communicate.*

The ability to communicate in depth with each other—express both a wide range of emotions and feelings, as well as to communicate ideas, concepts, beliefs, and values, is a family strength. Communication is seen as including verbal expression as well as sensitive listening.

483

For example, if a family can communicate and share the depth of feeling and thought occasioned by a beautiful sunrise or sunset, this is a strength as well as a strengthening process. Also, children try out their "intellectual muscles" by communicating newly acquired ideas and beliefs to the family. Some parents will respond negatively. "Where did you pick up these *strange* ideas? That's a lot of nonsense!" Other parents will encourage their children to communicate and think independently by saying, "Isn't this an interesting idea! Now let's follow through and see where it will lead us."

4. *The ability to provide support, security and encouragement.*

Giving family members a feeling of security, the sense that the family is "behind them" with moral and other support, providing them with encouragement in their various endeavors, is a source of family strength. Especially important is encouragement to seek new areas of growth, to develop creativity, imagination, and independent thinking.

One family held periodic "creativity sessions" during which family members were urged to think up new and better ways to improve family living. New ideas on furniture arrangement, interior decorations and food preparation were encouraged, and family problems were "brainstormed."

5. *The ability to establish and maintain growth-producing relationships within and without the family.*

The ability of family members to relate to each other and other persons so as to produce maximum growth and maturation is considered a family strength. Implicit is the concept that interpersonal relationships are the major media of personality growth, and that the apex of creativity in interpersonal relations is to stimulate and encourage other persons to grow and to make fuller use of their potential.

Examples of growth producing relationships can be found at all age levels. One six-year-old, for instance, told her mother, "Mommie, I talked and talked to Ruthie and told her animals hurt like we do, and she said she would stop hitting and hurting animals. Then we went and gave her dollie a good spanking."

6. *The capacity to maintain and create constructive and responsible community relationships in the neighborhood and in the school, town, local and state governments.*

It is a family strength to assume responsibility and leadership in relation to local, social, cultural, and political organizations and activities. This implies involvement, membership, or active participation and interest, on a selective basis, in relation to these areas.

7. *The ability to grow with and through children.*

When parents can actively utilize their relationships with their children as a means of growth and maturation, this can be called a strength. For example, one mother, member of a P.T.A. study group, said, "My child has taught me more about telling the truth and how we really feel, than anything ever has. She will come right out and tell you things that no adult would tell you. This is the type of honesty we need."

8. *An ability for self-help, and the ability to accept help when appropriate.*

Strength lies not only in the family's ability to help itself, but also in the capacity to accept and seek help when needed. Such help might be proffered or sought from agencies, organizations, individuals, or professional sources.

9. *An ability to perform family roles flexibly.*

It is a strength when family members can "fill in" and assume each other's roles as needed. For example, a father can function as a "mother" and children can temporarily be "parents" to their father and mother.

10. *Mutual respect for the individuality of family members.*

When family members are recognized, respected and treated as individuals, rather than as stereotypes or categories, this is a strength. Parents are not only "daddies" and "mommies" or seen as providers and "doers for children," but are recognized as individuals and persons in their own right who need to be treated as such. Similarly children are not only "the baby" or "the oldest." They have their own distinct individuality which, unfortunately, is often obscured by such categorization. One father illustrated this by saying, "We kept calling our youngest 'the baby' when he wasn't a baby any more. This kept him back. When we stopped this he really bloomed."

11. *A concern for family unity, loyalty, and interfamily cooperation.*

Although these qualities can be considered as outcomes of family strengths, the presence of these factors is also seen as a family strength.

In understanding a family, more than the total range of family strengths should be taken into consideration. It should be recognized that strength factors can, in certain situations and circumstances, become an impediment or detract from the effective functioning of the family. For example, a family which sees self-help as a major strength may, rather than call on outside help, wrestle with a problem for a long period of time with a consequent stultifying and discouraging effect on family members. This even though using such outside help would have led to a much more productive solution to the problem both in terms of effort, time, and overall effect on the family. Lack of flexibility in the use of a strength has, therefore, resulted in an impediment.

Finally, family strengths are not isolated variables, but form clusters or constellations which are dynamic, fluid, interrelated, and interacting. Current and past literature, with a few exceptions, reflects much emphasis and study of the pathology of the family and pathological processes within the family. However, by extending our understanding and knowledge of what we mean by family strengths and resources, we are in a better position to help families in the development of their strengths, resources, and potentialities.

Commitment, Value Conflict and the Future of the American Family

Charles W. Hobart

Having begun this book with readings that focused on the importance of seeing the family in society, it is fitting that we return to the societal level when postulating the future of the American family. Hobart discusses those functions lost by the family and the important functions it still retains, as well as the general weakening over the years of the community control that holds marriages together. Yet in a social world that is increasingly unstable and changeable, the family still offers security through close relationships. The family can be the locus of all those human values and sentiments not found elsewhere in our urbanized, mechanized existence—loving and caring for someone because of who they are, not because of what they can do. If a family can offer these important intangibles to its members, plus a culture where family members experience enjoyment and exhilaration in interaction, then in a society full of meaninglessness· and contradictions the family represents values that give life meaning.

T here are many attempts to characterize the nature of modern society: the affluent society, the other-directed society, the managerial society, the mass society, the expert society, the pluralistic society, the achieving society, the insane society. Most of these characterizations share at least one underlying assumption, that as a society we tread where man has never trod before, that there are qualitative differences between our society and earlier ones which make extrapolation on the basis of earlier societal experience unreliable at best, and often completely invalid.

One consequence is that the continued utility of many features fundamental

From Charles W. Hobart, "Commitment, Value Conflict. and the Future of the American Family," *Marriage and Family Living*, August, 1963, pp. 405–12. Reprinted by permission of the author and The National Council on Family Relations.

to earlier societies becomes problematic. Examples include the segregation of sex roles, homogeneity of culture, widespread status ascription. It is both important and difficult to speculate about what further structural modifications may be in the offing. So long as an institution provides functions prerequisite to the survival of any human social system we must think in terms not of the disappearance of the institution but of the evolution of functional alternatives.

It is in this context that the following discussion of the future of the family is set. This paper deals first with the argument that the family as we know it is becoming obsolete, and with some recent changes in social structure which are contributing to this apparent obsolescence. Second there is a discussion of value conflicts and of future societal development given continued pre-eminence of materialistic values. Finally there is consideration of bases for anticipating a value revolution which would facilitate renewed commitment to family relationships.

There is no need to cite the varied evidence which seems to suggest the progressive obsolescence of the family as we know it. Some maintain that the family, no longer an economic necessity, is an inefficient, artificial, arbitrary, outmoded structuring of relationships. Barrington Moore, in his provocative "Thoughts of the Future of the Family" protests such "obsolete and barbaric features" as "the obligation to give affection as a duty to a particular set of persons on account of the accident of birth," "the exploitation of socially sanctioned demands for gratitude, when the existing social situation no longer generates any genuine feeling of warmth."[1] Moore concludes that "one fine day human society may realize that the part-time family, already a prominent part of our social landscape, has undergone a qualitative transformation into a system of mechanized and bureaucratized child rearing" since "an institutional environment can be . . . warmer than a family torn by obligations its members resent."[2]

In contradiction to this position, it is the thesis of this paper that though the family is from some value perspectives an outdated structural unit, defined in terms of responsibility and commitment it remains a necessary condition for the development and expression of humanity. Furthermore, if it in fact is such a necessary condition, concern for its effective survival should help to shape the course of the future development of society.

It must be admitted that the family is undergoing changes, both within itself and in relation to the rest of society, which tend significantly to weaken its solidarity. At least four of these changes may be mentioned: 1) loss of functions; 2) increased personal mobility within society; 3) the decline of status ascription and the increase in status achievement; and 4) the ascendency of materialistic values.

1. In regard to loss of family functions, note that not only has the emergence of separate and distinct institutions accomplished the functional depletion of the once omnifunctional family, but active family membership has become optional in our day. Social status placement is primarily based on occupational achievement, rather than family ascription. There are now no imperious deterrents to a solitary family-alienated existence; all necessary services are avail-

able commercially. In fact, family responsibilities today distract and detract from single-minded pursuit of highly prized personal success in most occupations—scholarly, commercial, or professional.

Americans *are* getting married with greater frequency than ever before, a reflection, perhaps, of the increasing significance of companionship and emotional security within the family for people today. But if they marry for companionship and security, the high level of divorce rates[3] suggests that Americans seek divorce when they fail to attain these goals.

2. The rate of spatial mobility of Americans today is remarkable: in the last decade one half of all families in the States have moved every five years. Some consequences of this unprecedented movement have been: 1) increase in the number and variety of readjustments which a family must make; 2) radical loss of support of the family by neighborhood, friendship, and kinship primary groups; and 3) weakened discouragement of separation and divorce by these groups. Thus increased mobility may be seen as 1) precipitating more crises and adjustment difficulties within the family, 2) stripping the family of external supports at the very time of heightened stress, and 3) weakening the opposition to traditionally disapproved means of resolving difficulties, such as divorce.

Since mobility involves physical removal from the informal controls exercised by primary groups, Howard S. Becker's conceptualization of commitment becomes relevant to this discussion. Becker conceives of commitment as an act, consciously or unconsciously accomplished, whereby a person involves additional interests of his ("side bets") directly in action he is engaged in, which were originally extraneous to this action. Becker emphasizes that the process is relative to the values or valuables of the person.[4] I am emphasizing its relativity to the importance of the reference groups in whose eyes he stands to gain or lose on his "side bets."

In Becker's terms, then, commitment in marriage was once strengthened by making side bets involving staking one's reputation on one's trustworthiness, loyalty, fidelity in marriage. These bets were secured by the scrutiny of unchanging reference groups: close neighbors, fellow parishioners, occupational associates. The increasing speed of physical mobility as well as the growth of value confusion and of heterogeneous sub-cultures have tended to sharply depreciate the coin with which side bets to marital commitment were once made. This devaluation further weakens the stability of marriage.

3. Another trend in American society which appears to have a powerful potential for further weakening the family is suggested by the phrase "proliferation of associations," "personality market," "individuation." These suggest a growing contrast with the recent past when most close relationships of people were traditionally defined ascribed relationships with mate and children, with other kin, with neighbors, with fellow parishioners. Today, more and more relationships are achieved. They are "cultivated" in school, at work, in voluntary associations; they are promoted through friends and professional or business contacts.

The significant point is that rather than being ascribed, and thus traditionally defined and delimited, relationships are now more often achieved and thus more idiosyncratic and potentially boundless. Herein lies their threat to the family, for they, like many other aspects of contemporary life, may readily infringe upon family claims, may alienate members from the family. Note that at one time only men, as sole breadwinners of the family, were vulnerable to these possibilities, in work and voluntary association situations. Their colleagues in these situations were other men, thus posing no threat to devotion to the wife at home. But with the spectacular increase in the employment of married as well as unmarried women, both sexes are vulnerable, and increasingly their work and voluntary association relationships *may* endanger the marriage bond. With this bond under greater stress, the decline of the primary group discouragements to divorce becomes increasingly consequential.

The proliferation of achieved, and thus potentially unlimited, relationships for both men and women is by no means exclusively dysfunctional. Restriction of "close" relationships to a small circle of sharply limited ascribed relationships tends to be delimiting as far as growth of the person is concerned. Mead and others have demonstrated that the personality is a social product, and personality growth can occur only in relationships. Hence a small circle of ascribed relationships tends to be stultifying in at least three ways. In the first place, since the limits of an ascribed relationship are traditionally defined in terms of convention and appropriateness, the personality potential in an ascribed relationship is far more limited than in the more open, uncircumscribed achieved relationship. Second, since the circle of ascribed relationships is more homogeneous than the range of possible achieved relationships, the latter may awaken a broader range of latent potentialities within the person. Third, the circle of ascribed relationships may soon be rather thoroughly explored and exhausted, especially given geographical immobility, early in life. By contrast, the opportunities for new achieved relationships may last until death and may be limited only by the activity and involvement of the person. Thus it seems that the increase in proportion of achieved relationships is a necessary condition for acualization of more human potential in society.

I noted above that any achieved relationship, particularly a cross sex one, may jeopardize the marriage bond and perhaps parental responsibilities. Yet, given extensive and rapid spatial and vertical mobility, almost all relationships tend to be shifting sand, lacking in dependability and security, providing no basis on which to build a life. The very impermanence of these manifold relationships heightens the need for *some* relationships which are dependable; which can be, invariably, counted on; which will not be weakened or destroyed by the incessant moving about of people. Such secure relationships can only be found, given the structural peculiarities for our society today, within the family. Actualization of this security within the family depends upon commitment, a commitment symbolized in the phrase "in sickness and in health, for better or for worse, for richer or for poorer, till death do you part."

4. A final source of instability within the family is the value confusion which appears to be one of the hallmarks of our age. The crucial significance of values depends upon the fact that man is a being who must *live* his life since

it is not lived for him by imperious drives or instincts, as Fromm says.[5] Man, thus emancipated from the security of nature's control, needs human community to humanize him and to structure his choice between the alternatives which confront him. The basis for choice is a set of values, generated in society, in terms of which choice priorities may be assigned.

One linkage between values and the family lies in the fact that the original unit of human community and the universal humanizing unit of all societies is the family. It is in the family that many of the most important values, bases for choice, are learned. The family not only transmits values; it is predicated on, and in fact symbolizes, some of the distinctively "human" values: tenderness, love, concern, loyalty.

Man's capacity for consistent and responsible action depends on his being able to orient himself and to act on the basis of commitment to values; thus a certain level of value consistency is important. But a prominent feature of American society today is a pervasive value conflict. The family depends upon and symbolizes "inefficient values" of being, knowing, caring, loving, unconditionally committing oneself. These values are incompatible with the urban industrial values of production, achievement, exchange, quantification, efficiency, success. Simultaneous unlimited commitment to people—in love and concern—and to achievement, success, prosperity, is impossible. The resultant tension in a society which pays uncritical lip-service to both sets of values is disruptive and potentially incapacitating. It tends toward resolution in favor of the "inhuman" urban values. Fromm has noted that as a society we tend to *love things*, and *use people*, rather than the reverse. And Whyte has remarked that the "organization men" he interviewed seemed to prefer to sacrifice success in marriage to career success, if forced to choose between them.

This value confusion is, of course, a source of instability within the American family. A family presumes unlimited commitment between family members: "till death do you part" between husband and wife, "all we can do for the kids" on the part of parents toward children. But the priority of these love and concern values is directly challenged by success and achievement values which may imply that status symbols are more important than babies; that what a child *achieves* is more important than what he *is*; that what we *own* is more important that what we *are*. Thus the stage is set for conflict between a success oriented husband and a child-people welfare oriented wife, or for a rather inhuman family which values things over people, and which may raise children who have difficulty living down this experience of worthlessness.

The question may be raised whether what one does versus what one is are polar characteristics, or is not what one does a part of what one is? Purely logically the latter is of course true. But social-psychologically speaking, there are significant differences in the way these two value emphases influence the process and consequences of parent-child interaction. Briefly, parents who emphasize *doing* respond to their children in terms of conditional love, and the child comes to feel that he is unacceptable unless he conforms, and also unless he meets certain "production quotas." By contrast, parents who emphasize *being* respond to their children in terms of unconditional love,

490

and their children come to feel that they are intrinsically acceptable and love-worthy. Successful performance is thus a matter of much more anxious pre-occupation for the former than for the latter ideal type of child.

This review of some changes in family and society—loss of functions, increased mobility, increased status achievement, and ascendancy of materialistic values—has pointed out that some of these changes have functional as well as dysfunctional consequences. What are the likely prospects for the future? Which way will the value conflict be resolved? What are the preconditions, the prospects, and the probable consequences of more explicit self-conscious commitment to the family?

Let us look first at some further consequences of the value predicament in our society today. Consider the emerging character type in America. Torn from family commitments by the demands of urban living—dedication to efficiency, success, etc.—modern man is often alienated from himself and from others.[6] To escape the anxious awareness of his inability to express his humanity and to relate to others through his role as a functionary in a bureaucratic system, he is tempted to identify with the system, becoming, in Mills' terms, a "cheerful robot."[7] In Riesman's terms he is the "other-directed,"[8] forever adapting to the demands of the situation, of the people at hand; in Fromm's terms he is the "personality package," an exchangeable commodity to be sold for success.[9]

The ecology of the American city likewise reflects this value pattern and has important consequences for the family. Most cities can be characterized as central places for the merchandizing of goods and credits. They are the center of great webs of communication and transportation through which our economy of exchange functions. The natural areas of the city are determined by land values: the allocation of people and facilities is in accord with who can pay. Thus it is not for the family that the city functions, and it is not in accord with the values foundational to the family that people and facilities are located. Because the city is not a livable habitat for family units, families have fled to the suburbs. Here children can play, but here too, mothers are often stranded, driven to distraction by childish babbling from which there is no escape, and fathers are missing, early and late, commuting.

From an institutional perspective the family is weakening, and again our value confusion is involved. No longer a necessary economic unit, the family continues to provide for the socialization of children and for companionship. Yet even in these two remaining areas the family is losing significance. Children have more and more been turned over to schools, and, in some instances, nursery schools and Sunday schools, for a major portion of their socialization, as parents occupy themselves with other activities. More significant than the time turned over to such institutional socialization of children is the responsibility that parents more than willingly relinquish or do not recognize as theirs. There appears to be little concern in America today that the shaping of a human life, a human personality, a future of happiness or hell, which is best accomplished in a primary group, is turned over ever earlier and for longer periods to secondary, impersonal, social, agencies. In these agencies children can only be "handled" and manipulated in groups, rather than cared for as individuals.

Leisure time is used by some to cultivate companionship with wife and children. But for many it appears that what time is spent together is seldom spent primarily in *being* together, but rather in *doing* simultaneously: watching T.V., going someplace, being entertained. Leisure is thus often an escape from the tension of urban life which pulls people in different directions, a distraction from "the great emptiness."[10]

The family persists because people want and need the family. The problem is that, having often lost the family in its meaningful sense as a primary commitment, people want a fantasy; they compulsively seek security. They get disillusionment.[11] Pulled apart by the value conflict of our society they want both personal loving involvement and social efficient achievement, and often they can commit themselves to neither. Thus straddling both ways of life, they can only distract themselves from their predicament.

This admittedly pessimistic overview forces us to confront a further question. What kind of a *future* is in store for our society? Will time tolerate the tension of values, will it tolerate the embarrassing persistence of the family? Some current trends suggest the resolution of the tension in favor of materialistic urban values which place a premium on man, the efficient doer.

To be more explicit, the character type of the future, according to some, will be the true functionary, the "cheerful robot." "Human engineering" seems determined to insuring that man is socialized into this mold, his human anxieties conditioned out. The power structure of the society will be even more centralized than the current structure. The city will rid itself of remaining small shops and other lingering evidences of human sentiment, so that where there is now variety and diversity, there will be functional monotony. With the rapid increase in urban population there is the prospect that the inefficiency of suburban living will be eliminated and people will be housed in compact apartments or even in some collective arrangement.

The family as we know it will be eliminated from this society, Moore has suggested,[12] and Skinner, in *Walden II*,[13] agrees.[14] Children, housed separately, will not endanger the efficiency of adult activity. They will not be left to the haphazard care of their accidental parents but will be socialized by behavioral conditioning experts. Couples will have no use for life-long commitments and will often tend to go their separate ways. Each man for himself by himself will escape into the mass of interchangeable associates. Such is the vision of the future that some foresee.

But it seems undeniable that such a future would, in one sense, mean the end of human society. Human society is not an automatic process as are subhuman spheres of life. There is reason to believe that man, *as we know him,* has to care enough to carry on,[15] and to care enough he has to have a reason; life has to have some meaning. Without at least the illusion, the vision, of human ends that today's contradiction of values yet provides man, what would keep him going? Thus it seems impossible to conceive of the future of man in the above terms. Something more or less than man might emerge to carry on something more or less than human society, but such speculation is best left to science fiction writers.

But while the inhuman potential in current trends is not only sobering but frightening, the *human* possibilities are also unparalleled. An alternative future depends upon a value revolution in American society—not just the emergence of an unambiguous value hierarchy, but a displacement of the now pre-eminent success, efficiency, productivity, prosperity values by the more human oriented being, knowing, caring, loving values. This revolution is in fact over-due; it is prerequisite to our continued societal survival. It is heralded by Win-ston White's provocative discussion *Beyond Conformity* which maintains that we are even now undergoing "a shift from emphasis on the development of economic resources to the development of human resources—particularly the capacities of personalities." [16] A society of scarcity must encourage productivity and efficiency upon pain of greater scarcity, poverty and starvation. But in an affluent society, plagued not by *underproduction* but by *underconsumption,* production-increasing values *are in fact dysfunctional,* aggravating the chronic overproduction problem. In the affluent society, the implementation of "hu-man" values is not only possible as it is not in a society of scarcity, it is also functional in the sense of diverting initiative and energy from the productive sphere, where they threaten to aggravate existing over-production, to other areas where they may serve to free people to be more themselves.

A key to this value change lies in renewed commitment to the family and in thus re-establishing the centrality of the commitment to inefficient, human values which the family relationship symbolizes. There are some who would try to solve the problems of our heterogeneous society in terms of restructuring (Fromm's work communities for example), of eliminating structurally some of the diversity and complexity of our society. But this is the kind of short-sightedness that tries to move forward by moving backward. To look wistfully at the beauty and relative simplicity of the rigidly structured life in a primitive society without at the same time realizing that our human potentialities are greater than would be realized in such a society is the kind of irresponsibility that evades the task at hand. This is the most significant point made in *Beyond Conformity.* White sees human personality as emancipated from ascriptive ties in contemporary society. Since man is no longer *determined* automatically by family, church, or occupation, greater individuality of personality is possible. In the absence of automatic structural determinants, man is "indeed, forced to be free," to become more individualistic.[17]

It follows from this that the family of the future must not be defined in terms of more structure, but in terms of less explicit structure. It must at once be flexible enough for increasingly individuated people, yet a stable basic unit for human life. The family as a commitment implies freedom in the definition of the marital relationship in order to meet the demands of the particular way of life of the two people involved. For its members, family relationships should be a part of a larger pattern of meaningful, involving relationships. Only thus, individually defined and not exclusive, can the family tie avoid being a trapping, arbitrarily binding, stultifying commitment for its members.

493

Defined in this way, the family would be a sustaining, liberating, and humanizing influence since it would invest life in modern society with context, continuity, and direction. As a commitment, a limiting choice, an orienting value complex, it would permit a decisive stance in the urban sea of alternatives, not an artificial reduction of the alternatives.

Are there any alternative side bet possibilities in our day to shore up the marriage commitment, which have not suffered the erosion of effectiveness noted earlier in contemporary society? I think that the answer is yes. It is an answer which is not only compatible with, but dependent on, the fact that, since *doing* is inescapably becoming less important in contemporary society than *being*, husbands and wives are increasingly chosen because of the persons that they *are*, rather than what they can *do*. Increasingly mates may be known deeply and loved for what they are. To know and love the person in this way is to feel for and care for the person. Love in this sense, then, involves the inadvertent side bet of deeply feeling with and for caring about this person. A risking of the marriage vows involves immediate apprehension of the pain this causes my mate, as my own pain. My empathy with and ego involvement with my mate guarantees a "side bet penalty" which is likely to be heavier than the attractiveness of what I stand to gain from my breach of commitment.

Here is a basis for a new, deeper commitment to the family, in so far as couple members dare to invest themselves to this extent, in each other. And in this deeper commitment, more of meaning in life would be discovered in the experience of human values, the intrinsic values of being, becoming, knowing and being known, caring and being cared for, in contrast to the values of doing and achieving. And out of this profound experiencing of human values might come the basis for the slow revolution in values which would further facilitate deeper commitment to the family, and in time the reorientation of contemporary society.

The implications of such a changed significance of the family and such a value revolution for future society are many. The character type which could emerge in this kind of family setting would be neither the chameleon-like other-directed nor the rigid, artificially dogmatic inner-directed, to use Riesman's terms. Instead there could emerge the autonomous individual who is able to see and consciously choose between the alternatives; who knows himself and can express himself in decisive, directed action; who retains his sense of identity discovered *beyond* role, in the various roles he must play. Not merely functioning, having sold his soul "true believer" fashion, not living oblivious of alternatives, he could consciously exercise the greatest sense of freedom and responsibility that man has ever known; he could live Winston White's vision.[18]

With renewed emphasis on *being* rather than on *doing*, the family and the concern with human relationships which it symbolizes could once again be an organizing principle in society. With less emphasis on over-efficiency our society could significantly cut down the length of the working day. Such a work schedule would make possible an enriched home life. While older children were in school both men and women could work, if they chose, and thus

494

perhaps develop specialized interests. The specialization of their work could be balanced by the vocations of homemaking and greater involvement in parenthood for both men and women, and by the opportunity to develop other interests in their leisure time. A shorter work day would mean that children could once again be socialized more within the family primary group. The school could accomplish its distinctive function of transmitting knowledge in half a day, leaving the humanization responsibility to the home. Here the inefficient process of growing up could take place in a context where there is time for each child, and where each child is valued and known as an individual. In the home children need not be collectively handled, regimented and manipulated as they must be at school, but might be better freed to become, to find themselves, to develop their unique potentials.

In addition to assuming the responsibility for socializing children, such a family could provide meaningful and sustaining relationships which are a prerequisite to open, undefended, loving relationships with others. As I noted above, it is inevitable that most relationships in an urban society will be time-bound, that the demands of complex and highly mobile living will pull people apart, but the family can offer the element of permanence which other relationships cannot. And thus safeguarded by their family-centered security against being left unbearably alone when the hour of separation came, people could dare to invest themselves in a number of invaluable but often short term relationships whose dissolution would otherwise be unbearable. Increased leisure time would enable individuals to develop these relationships both within and without the family.

The question arises, could people really bear to spend more time with their families than they now do? To this a number of things can be said. In the first place, people presumably would not have the same need that they do today to escape the emptiness of shallow family-togetherness by constantly doing or being with different people. Time spent together could be on a more meaningful level than it can now be. Secondly, time would also be spent in other meaningful, involving relationships with non-family members which would mean that the family would not seem a trap and would not degenerate into a stagnating aggregate of individuals. The family would lose the compulsive exclusive security which makes it dull for those who spend most of their leisure time with their family and dare not do otherwise. Assuming a commitment of family members to each other more profound than any based merely on exclusion or external structure, family members could tolerate an element of genuine insecurity in their relationships which would not have to be evaded and would keep the relationship from being static and dull.

Finally young people, no longer stranded, disoriented, alienated from parents—as they often are now when neither adolescents nor parents know each other—would not have to escape compulsively, haphazardly into marriage. They could postpone marriage until they knew what they wanted, what they needed and what they were entering into.

There are a few shreds of evidence that the American family may in fact be evolving in the direction advocated in this paper. Hilsdale, in a rather sensitive interviewing study, sought to discover whether subjects entered marriage with an absolute commitment to marriage, or merely a commitment to trial of marriage. He found that 80% entered with an absolute commitment. This commitment was, significantly, associated with an "almost total absence of starry-eyed Hollywood-type 'romantic love.' " [19] Another finding of this study was the preoccupation of his subjects with communication: they felt that their marriage would last "because we can talk to each other, because we can discuss our problems together." [20] Hilsdale terms this faith "magical," but it can also be seen as a reaction to the fact that in an increasingly impersonal society, people cannot talk with each other. In this light it appears as both awareness by people of their need to really communicate with another, and a commitment to safeguard this highly valued and important aspect of the marriage relationship. Moreover, there is evidence that communication is related to marital adjustment. [21]

In this paper I have argued that if an affluent society is to survive, it must undergo a value revolution which will make what we have called human values pre-eminent over production values. Such a society-wide evaluation would eliminate a major source of the compromised commitment, of the value conflict between and within the family members, and of the inadequate and distorting socialization of children, which exist in the American family today. There seems to be reason for hoping that such a value revolution may come out of the changing pattern of husband-wife relationship. If this should continue such that the family were restructured along the lines suggested by these values, people could find the security and sustenance which they need, but often cannot find, in today's world. The nature of contemporary urban society makes this increasingly necessary for a number of reasons. Earlier alternative bases of family solidarity are disappearing, and thus commitment is an increasingly crucial bond. Increasingly, the family is the only security base available to man today. Where a commitment-based family security is dependably available to man, he will have a basis for relating fearlessly to the greater varieties of people available to him in a society organized in terms of achieved statuses, deepening and enriching himself and others in the process.

NOTES

[1] Barrington Moore, "Thoughts on the Future of the Family," in Maurice R. Stein, Arthur J. Vidich and David M. White, *Identity and Anxiety,* Glencoe, Ill.: The Free Press, 1960, pp. 393–94.

[2] *Ibid.,* p. 401.

[3] See, for example, U.S. Bureau of the Census, *Statistical Abstract of the United States,* Washington, D.C., 1961, p. 48.

[4] Howard S. Becker, "Notes on the Concept of Commitment," *American Journal of Sociology,* 66 (July, 1960), p. 35.

[5] Erich Fromm, *The Same Society,* New York: Holt, Rinehart, and Winston, 1960, p. 24.

[6] A few recent titles in the growing literature on alienation in modern man include: *American Journal of Psychoanalysis,* A Symposium on Alienation and the Search for Identity, Vol. 21, no. 2, 1961; Eric and Mary Josephson, *Man Alone, Alienation in Modern Society,* New York: Dell Publishing Co., 1962; Robert Nisbet, *The Quest for Community,* New York: Oxford University Press, 1953; Fritz Pappenheim, *The Alienation of Modern Man,* New York: Monthly Review Press, 1959; Maurice Stein, *The Eclipse of Community,* Princeton: Princeton University Press, 1960; Maurice Stein, Arthur Vidich and David White, Eds., *Identity and Anxiety;* Survival of the Person in Mass Society, Glencoe, Ill.: Free Press, 1960; Allen Wheelis, *The Quest for Identity,* New York: W. W. Norton, 1958.

[7] C. Wright Mills, *The Sociological Imagination,* New York: Oxford University Press, 1959, p. 171.

[8] David Riesman, Nathan Glazer, Reuel Denny, *The Lonely Crowd,* New York: Doubleday Anchor Books, 1956.

[9] Erich Fromm, *The Art of Loving,* New York: Harper and Bros., 1956, p. 3.

[10] Robert MacIver, "The Great Emptiness," in Eric Larrabee and Rolf Meyersohn, Eds., *Mass Leisure,* Glencoe, Illinois: The Free Press, 1958, pp. 118–122.

[11] Charles W. Hobart, "Disillusionment in Marriage and Romanticism," *Marriage and Family Living,* Vol. 20 (May, 1958), pp. 156–162.

[12] Barrington Moore, *op. cit.*

[13] B. F. Skinner, *Walden Two,* New York: The Macmillan Co., 1948.

[14] But note that the evolution of child handling procedures in the Jewish communal kibbutzim is in the direction of granting parents more access to their children and permitting children to spend more time in their parents' apartments. John Bowlby, *Maternal Care and Mental Health,* Geneva: World Health Organization, 1952, pp. 42–43.

[15] William H. R. Rivers, "The Psychological Factor," in W. H. R. Rivers, ed., *Essays on the Depopulation of Melanesia,* Cambridge, England: The University Press, 1922.

[16] Winston White, *Beyond Conformity,* New York: The Free Press of Glencoe, Ill., 1961, p. 162.

[17] *Ibid.,* p. 164.

[18] Winston White, *op. cit.*

[19] Paul Hilsdale, "Marriage as a Personal Existential Commitment," *Marriage and Family Living,* 24 (May, 1962), p. 142.

[20] *Ibid.,* p. 143.

[21] Charles W. Hobart and William J. Kausner, "Some Social Interactional Correlates of Marital Role Disagreement and Marital Adjustment," *Marriage and Family Living,* 21 (Aug., 1959), p. 263.

71 72 73 74   9 8 7 6 5 4 3 2 1